SECOND EDITION

# MARKETING
# An Introduction

## Philip Kotler
Northwestern University

## Gary Armstrong
University of North Carolina

*Library of Congress Cataloging-in-Publication Data*

KOTLER, PHILIP.
    Marketing : an introduction / Philip Kotler, Gary Armstrong. --
2nd ed.
        p.    cm.
    ISBN 0-13-556408-5
    1. Marketing.   2. Marketing--Management.   I. Armstrong, Gary.
II. Title.
HF5415.K625 1990                                    89-22881
658.8--dc20                                         CIP

Editorial/production supervision: ESTHER S. KOEHN
Development editor: RON LIBRACH
Interior design: LINDA CONWAY, MAUREEN EIDE, JANET SCHMID
Cover Design: BRUCE KENSELAAR
Manufacturing buyer: LAURA CROSSLAND
Photo research: CHRISTINE PULLO
Photo editor: LORI MORRIS-NANTZ

© 1990, 1987 by Prentice-Hall, Inc.
A Division of Simon & Schuster
Englewood Cliffs, New Jersey 07632

**MARKETING: AN INTRODUCTION, Second Edition**
**Philip Kotler/Gary Armstrong**

Printed in the United States of America

10  9  8  7  6  5  4  3  2  1

ISBN 0-13-556408-5

Prentice-Hall International [UK] Limited, *London*
Prentice-Hall of Australia Pty. Limited, *Sydney*
Prentice-Hall Canada Inc., *Toronto*
Prentice-Hall Hispanoamericana, S.A., *Mexico*
Prentice-Hall of India Private Limited, *New Delhi*
Prentice-Hall of Japan, Inc., *Tokyo*
Prentice-Hall of Southeast Asia Pte. Ltd., *Singapore*
Editora Prentice-Hall do Brasil, Ltda., *Rio de Janeiro*

To Nancy, Amy, Melissa, and Jessica;
Kathy, Casey, and Mandy

# About the Authors

As a team, Philip Kotler and Gary Armstrong provide a blend of skills uniquely suited to writing an introductory marketing text. Professor Kotler is one of the world's leading authorities on marketing. Professor Armstrong is an award-winning teacher of undergraduate business students. Together they make the complex world of marketing practical, approachable, and enjoyable.

Philip Kotler is S. C. Johnson & Son Distinguished Professor of International Marketing at the Kellogg Graduate School of Management, Northwestern University. He received his master's degree at the University of Chicago and his Ph.D. at M.I.T., both in economics. Dr. Kotler is author of *Marketing Management: Analysis, Planning, Implementation, and Control* (Prentice Hall), now in its sixth edition and the most widely used marketing textbook in graduate schools of business. He has authored several other successful books, and he has written over eighty articles for leading journals. Dr. Kotler's numerous honors include the *Paul D. Converse Award* given by the American Marketing Association to honor "outstanding contributions to science in marketing" and the *Stuart Henderson Britt Award* as Marketer of the Year. In 1985, he was named the first recipient of two major awards: the *Distinguished Marketing Educator of the Year Award* given by the American Marketing Association and the *Philip Kotler Award for Excellence in Health Care Marketing* presented by the Academy for Health Care Services Marketing. Dr. Kotler has served as chairman of the College on Marketing of the Institute of Management Sciences (TIMS) and as director of the American Marketing Association. He has consulted with many major American companies on marketing strategy.

Gary Armstrong is Professor and Chairman of Marketing in the Graduate School of Business Administration at the University of North Carolina at Chapel Hill. He holds undergraduate and masters degrees in business from Wayne State University in Detroit, and he received his Ph.D. in marketing from Northwestern University. Dr. Armstrong has contributed numerous articles to leading business journals, and his doctoral dissertation received the American Marketing Association's first-place award. As a consultant and researcher, he has worked with many companies on marketing research, sales management, and marketing strategy. But Professor Armstrong's first love is teaching. He is currently very active in the teaching and administration of North Carolina's undergraduate business program. His recent administrative posts include Associate Director of the Undergraduate Business Program and Director of the Business Honors Program, among others. He works closely with business-student groups and has received several campus-wide and School of Business teaching awards. He is the only two-time recipient of the school's Award for Excellence in Undergraduate Teaching.

# Contents

# 2

# Strategic Planning and Marketing's Role in the Organization   24

# 3

# Planning, Implementing, and Controlling Marketing Programs   50

# 4

## Marketing Research and Information Systems  78

# 5

## The Marketing Environment  106

# 6

## Consumer Markets and Consumer Buyer Behavior  140

# 7

# Organizational Markets and Organizational Buyer Behavior 174

# 8

# Market Segmentation, Targeting, and Positioning  200

---

## PART 4
## DEVELOPING THE MARKETING MIX

# 9

# Designing Products: Products, Brands, Packaging, and Services  224

# 13

# Placing Products: Distribution Channels and Physical Distribution   322

# 16

## Promoting Products: Advertising, Sales Promotion, and Public Relations 404

# 17

## Promoting Products: Personal Selling and Sales Management 436

# 20

# Marketing and Society   508

# Preface

*Marketing: An Introduction* is designed to help students learn about the basic concepts and practices of modern marketing in an enjoyable and practical way. Although marketing is all around us and we all need to know something about it, most students are surprised to find out that marketing is so widely used. Marketing is used not only by manufacturing companies, wholesalers, and retailers but by all kinds of individuals and organizations. Lawyers, accountants, and doctors use marketing to manage demand for their services. So do hospitals, museums, and performing-arts groups. No politician can get the needed votes and no resort the needed tourists without developing and implementing marketing plans.

People at all levels of these organizations need to know how to define and segment a market and to develop need-satisfying products and services for chosen target markets. They must know how to price their offerings to make them attractive and affordable and how to choose middlemen to make their products available to customers. And they need to know how to advertise and promote products so that customers will know about and want them. Clearly, marketers need a broad range of skills in order to sense, serve, and satisfy consumer needs.

Students also need to know about marketing in their roles as consumers and citizens. Because someone is always trying to sell us something, we need to recognize the methods they use. And when students enter the job market, they must conduct "marketing research" to find the best opportunities and develop the best ways to "market" themselves to prospective employers. Many students will start their careers with marketing jobs in salesforces, in retailing, in advertising, in research, or in one of a dozen other marketing areas.

# APPROACH AND OBJECTIVES

Several factors guided the development of *Marketing: An Introduction*. Most students learning marketing want a broad picture of its basics, but they don't want to drown in a sea of details. They want to know not only about important marketing principles and concepts, but also about how these concepts are applied in actual marketing-management practice. And they want a text that presents the complex and fascinating world of marketing in an easy-to-grasp, lively, and enjoyable way.

*Marketing: An Introduction* serves all of these important needs of beginning marketing students. We have tried to make the book as complete as possible, covering all of the main topics that marketers and consumers need to study. Yet we have kept length moderate to make it manageable for beginning marketing students to cover during a single quarter or semester.

*Marketing: An Introduction* covers important marketing principles and concepts that are supported by research and evidence from economics, the behavioral sciences, and modern management theory. Yet it takes a practical, marketing-management approach. Concepts are applied through countless examples of situations in which both well-known and little-known companies assess and solve their marketing problems. Color illustrations, "Marketing Highlight" exhibits, and longer cases present further applications.

Finally, *Marketing: An Introduction* makes learning marketing easy and enjoyable. Its writing style and level are well-suited to the beginning marketing student. The book tells the stories that reveal the drama of modern marketing. Kellogg's abrupt repositioning to meet changing baby-boomer lifestyles; why Greyhound no longer operates a bus line; the abrupt rise and fall of New Coke, the Edsel of the 1980s; how little-known Oshkosh found a niche with "designer trucks"; Beecham's stunning marketing malpractice suit against its own research firm; 3M's legendary emphasis on new product development; tiny Vernor ginger ale's shining success in the shadows of such giants as Coke and Pepsi; how Revlon sells not just products but hopes and dreams; Caterpillar's bitter price war with Komatsu; Kodak's attack on Fuji Film on the Japanese manufacturer's home turf; Century City Hospital's innovative use of marketing to capture demand in key market segments; Gerber's difficult social-responsibility decisions following a product-tampering scare. These and dozens of other examples and illustrations throughout each chapter reinforce key concepts and bring marketing to life for the student.

Thus, *Marketing: An Introduction* gives the beginning marketing student a complete yet manageable, conceptual yet applied and managerial, introduction to the basics of marketing. Its style, level, and extensive use of examples and illustrations make the book easy to grasp and enjoyable to read.

# CHANGES IN THE SECOND EDITION

The Second Edition of *Marketing: An Introduction* offers many improvements in content, style, and presentation that make the text even more effective and enjoyable than the First. Dozens of new color photos and illustrations have been added to illuminate key points and make the text more visually appealing. Throughout, tables, figures, examples, and references have been thoroughly updated; hundreds of new examples have been added within the text material.

This edition also includes more than 40 "Marketing Highlights" and chapter-opening examples to dramatize concepts and illustrate them with actual business applications. With the help of Michele Bunn of the State University of New York at Buffalo, all of the cases in the Second Edition have been either replaced or substantially revised. Cases are now placed at the end of each chapter, with each case carefully crafted to help students apply the principles and concepts discussed in that chapter. An additional comprehensive case has been added at the end of the text.

The Second Edition of *Marketing: An Introduction* also includes substantial new or improved material on a wide range of topics: responding to the marketing environment, important new consumer markets, regionalized marketing strategies, segmenting industrial markets, product quality and design, speeding up new-product development, test marketing, direct marketing (nonstore retailing), off-price retailing, the increased use of "push" promotional strategies, public relations, consumer- and trade-promotion tools, inside selling and telemarketing, marketing strategies for service firms, marketing ethics and social responsibility, finding competitive advantages, and global marketing strategies.

# LEARNING AIDS

Many aids provided within this book also help students to learn about marketing. The main features are:

- □ *Chapter Objectives.* Each chapter begins with objectives that prepare the student for the chapter material and point out learning goals.
- □ *Opening Examples.* Each chapter starts with a dramatic marketing story that introduces the chapter material and arouses student interest.
- □ *Full-Color Figures, Photographs, and Illustrations.* Throughout each chapter, key concepts and applications are illustrated with vivid full-color visual materials.
- □ *Marketing Highlights.* Additional examples and important information are highlighted in special exhibits throughout the text.
- □ *Summaries.* Each chapter ends with a summary that wraps up its main points and concepts.
- □ *Review Questions.* Each chapter concludes with a set of review questions covering main chapter points.
- □ *Key Terms.* Key terms are highlighted and clearly defined on the page on which they appear.
- □ *Case Studies.* Cases for class or written discussion are provided at the end of each chapter. A final, comprehensive case appears after the last chapter. These 21 cases challenge students to apply marketing principles to real companies in real situations.
- □ *Appendixes.* Two appendixes, "Marketing Arithmetic" and "Careers in Marketing," provide additional, practical information for students.
- □ *Glossary.* At the end of the book, an extensive glossary provides quick reference to the key terms found in the text.
- □ *Indexes.* A subject index, a name index, and an index of companies and products—new to this edition—help students quickly find information and examples in the book.

# SUPPLEMENTS

A successful marketing course requires more than a well-written book: It requires a dedicated teacher and a complete set of supplemental learning and teaching aids. The following aids support the Second Edition of *Marketing: An Introduction:*

□ *Annotated Instructor's Edition.* Prepared by George Franke of Virginia Polytechnic and State University, the AIE is an innovative new teaching resource that combines the student text with a comprehensive set of teaching materials. Compiled especially for the instructor, it contains suggestions for organizing and teaching the introductory marketing course, chapter summaries, answers to chapter discussion questions, teaching tips, case commentaries, and much more. Page-by-page annotations provide reference to color transparencies, discussion ideas, and hundreds of recent examples and anecdotes for use in class. The AIE is also available in a binder format with chapter folders containing the AIE, Test Item File, Study Guide, and Color Transparencies for each chapter.

□ *Lecture Outlines on Disk.* Available in a variety of word-processing programs, lecture outlines on disk enable instructors to customize instructional materials for class preparation. Following the *Annotated Instructor's Edition*, these outlines include all chapter titles, all headings, all key terms, all annotations, and all learning objectives. These outlines are available for IBM and Macintosh computers.

□ *Test Item File.* The Test Item File contains about 3,000 multiple-choice, true-false, and essay questions. The questions are available in the Test Item File booklet, on computer tape, or through the Prentice Hall Computerized Testing Service. The Diploma test-generating and gradebook system is also available for preparing and editing tests containing test-bank or teacher-designed questions and administering grades on IBM, Apple II, and Macintosh personal computers.

□ *Study Guide.* An important learning tool, this improved guide provides review questions for each chapter, along with carefully designed application exercises.

□ *Full-Color Transparencies.* The Transparencies Package includes over 130 full-color transparencies—about half with important figures and illustrations from the book and half with advertisements and illustrations not found in the book.

□ *Videos.* The Prentice Hall Video Series offers 24 segments keyed to the chapters in *Marketing: An Introduction.* A comprehensive Video Guide is also available and includes the following: video running times, illustrated primary and secondary concepts, video summaries, discussion questions and answers, and multiple-choice, true-false, and essay questions with answers. In addition, two complete reels of advertisements are available to adopters of the Second Edition of *Marketing: An Introduction.*

□ *Computer Applications: The Mart: Computer Applications in Introductory Marketing.* Thoroughly class-tested, this new book-disk package enables students to make marketing decisions through interactive computer exercises. *Mart* is available shrinkwrapped to the Second Edition of *Marketing: An Introduction.*

□ *Wall Street Journal Applications.* Immediately following the glossary, we have included several pages of recent marketing examples carefully selected from *The Wall Street Journal.* These can be used to enhance textbook coverage and classroom discussions. Adopters of *Marketing: An Introduction* are also entitled to a complimentary 15-week subscription to *The Wall Street Journal* so that they can continue to update examples from the text through current articles of interest. Students are entitled to a reduced-rate subscription to *The Wall Street Journal*.

□ *Additional Supplements.* Additional supplements include *Readings in Marketing* (by Cox and Blair) and "Product Manager," a practical marketing simulation game that operates on microcomputers.

# ACKNOWLEDGMENTS

No book is the work only of its authors. We owe much to the pioneers of marketing who first identified its major issues and developed its concepts and techniques. Our thanks also go to our colleagues at the J. L. Kellogg Graduate School of Management, Northwestern University, and at the Graduate School of Business Administration, University of North Carolina at Chapel Hill, for ideas and suggestions. We owe special thanks to George Franke, who prepared the *Annotated Instructor's Edition* and coordinated many of the book's supplements, and to Michele Bunn for her work on timely, lively, and practical cases for the text. We also thank Richard Clewett and Charles Lamb for their work on previous editions. In addition, we acknowledge the contributions of Thomas Paczkowski and Ronald Weir in preparing the *Study Guide* and *Test Item File*, respectively.

Many reviewers at other colleges provided valuable comments and suggestions. We are indebted to the following colleagues:

Gemmy Allen
Mountain View College

Arvid Anderson
University of North Carolina,
  Wilmington

Ronald Coulter
Southwest Missouri State
  University

John de Young
Cumberland County College

Lee Dickson
Florida International University

Mike Dotson
Appalachian State University

Jack Forrest
Belmont College

John Gauthier
Gateway Technical Institute

Eugene Gilbert
California State University,
  Sacramento

Esther Headley
The Wichita State University

Sandra Heusinkveld
Normandale Community College

James Kennedy
Navarro College

Eric Kulp
Middlesex County College

Gregory Lincoln
Westchester Community College

John Lloyd
Monroe Community College

Dorothy Maass
Delaware County Community
  College

James McAlexander
Iowa State University

Donald McBane
Texas Tech University

Veronica Miller
Fashion Institute of Design &
  Merchandising

William Morgenroth
University of South Carolina,
  Columbia

Sandra Moulton
Technical College of Alamance

Lee Neumann
Bucks County Community College

Dave Olsen
North Hennepin Community
    College

Thomas Paczkowski
Cayuga Community College

Robert L. Powell
Gloucester County College

Robert Ross
The Wichita State University

André San Augustine
The University of Arizona

Eberhard Scheuing
St. John's University

Pamela Schindler
Wittenberg University

Raymond Schwartz
Montclair State College

Jack Sheeks
Broward Community College

Ira Teich
Long Island University

Andrea Weeks
Fashion Institute of Design &
    Merchandising

Sumner White
Massachusetts Bay Community
    College

Burl Worley
Allan Hancock College

We also owe a great deal to the people at Prentice Hall who helped to develop this book. Our editor, Whitney Blake, provided determination, strong encouragement, and fresh insights. Esther Koehn, production editor, did her usual fine job of guiding the book smoothly through each stage of production. Ron Librach, development editor, provided valuable assistance throughout the course of the project. Additional thanks go to Lori Morris-Nantz and Christine Pullo for their help with photos, and to Linda Conway, Maureen Eide, and Janet Schmid for development of the design for the cover and the interior of the book.

Finally, we owe many thanks to our families—Nancy, Amy, Melissa, and Jessica Kotler, and Kathy, Casey, and Mandy Armstrong—for their constant support and encouragement. To them, we dedicate this book.

PHILIP KOTLER
GARY ARMSTRONG

# MARKETING
## An Introduction

# 1

# Social Foundations of Marketing: Meeting Human Needs

## CHAPTER OBJECTIVES

After reading this chapter, you should be able to

1. Define *marketing* and discuss its role in the economy
2. Compare the five marketing management philosophies
3. Identify the goals of the marketing system
4. Explain how marketing can be used by different kinds of business and nonbusiness organizations

Marketing touches all of us every day of our lives. We wake up to a Sears radio alarm clock playing an American Airlines commercial advertising a Bahamas vacation. We then enter the bathroom, brush our teeth with Crest Tartar Control, shave with Gillette Foamy, gargle with Scope, and use other toiletries and appliances produced by manufacturers around the world. Then we put on our Levi's jeans and Nike shoes and head for the kitchen, where we drink Minute Maid orange juice and pour Borden milk over a bowl of Kellogg's Rice Krispies. Later, we drink a cup of Maxwell House coffee with two teaspoons of Domino sugar while munching on a slice of Sara Lee coffee cake.

We consume oranges grown in California and coffee imported from Brazil, read a newspaper made of Canadian wood pulp, and tune in to radio news coming from as far away as Australia. We fetch our mail to find a Metropolitan Museum of Art catalog, a letter from a Prudential insurance salesperson offering services, and coupons saving us money on our favorite brands. We step out the door and drive our car to the Northbrook Court Shopping Center with its Neiman-Marcus, Lord & Taylor, Sears, and hundreds of other stores filled with goods from floor to ceiling. Later, we exercise at a Nautilus Fitness Center, have our hair trimmed at Super Cuts, grab a McDLT at McDonald's, and plan a trip to Disney World at a Thomas Cook travel agency.

The *marketing system* has made all this possible with little effort on our part. It has given us a standard of living that our ancestors could not have imagined.

The marketing system that delivers our high standard of living consists of many large and small companies, all seeking success. Two business researchers, Tom Peters and Robert Waterman, studied many successful companies—companies like Hewlett-Packard, Frito-Lay (PepsiCo), Procter & Gamble, 3M, McDonald's, and Marriott—to find out what made them tick. They reported the results in what became the best-selling business book of all time, *In Search of Excellence.*[1] They found that these companies shared a set of basic marketing principles: Each boasted a keen understanding of its customers, strongly defined markets, and the ability to motivate its employees to produce high quality and value for its customers.

In a second book, Peters and Nancy Austin offer more stories about companies doing smart and wonderful things to improve their customers' satisfaction.[2] They describe how IBM collects customer ratings of its sales and service people and gives awards to employees who best satisfy customers. They explain how The Limited studies women's clothing needs and creates the right store systems for different market segments (The Limited, Limited Express, Victoria's Secret, Sizes Unlimited). And they tell of Stew Leonard's supermarket in Norwalk, Connecticut, where Stew sits down with eight customers for a few hours each Saturday to talk about how he can improve customer service.

Marketing has become a key factor in business success. And the term *marketing* must be understood not in the old sense of making a sale—"selling"—but rather in the new sense of *satisfying customer needs.* Today's companies face increasingly stiff competition, and the rewards will go to those who can best read customer wants and deliver the greatest value to their target consumers. In the marketplace, marketing skills will separate the amateurs from the professionals.

In this chapter, we will define marketing and its core concepts, describe the major philosophies of marketing thinking and practice, discuss the goals of the marketing system, and explain how marketing is used by different kinds of organizations.

## WHAT IS MARKETING?

What does the term *marketing* mean? Many people mistakenly think of marketing only as selling and promotion. And no wonder—every day, Americans are bombarded with television commercials, newspaper ads, direct mail, and sales calls. Someone is always trying to sell us something. It seems that we cannot escape death, taxes, or selling.

Therefore, many students are surprised to learn that selling is only the tip of the marketing iceberg: It is but one of several marketing functions—and often not the most important one. If the marketer does a good job of identifying consumer needs, developing good products, and pricing, distributing, and promoting them effectively, these goods will sell very easily.

Everyone knows something about "hot" products to which consumers have flocked in droves. When Polaroid designed its Spectra camera, when Coleco first sold Cabbage Patch Dolls, and when Ford introduced its Taurus model, these manufacturers were swamped with orders. They had designed the "right" products—not "me-too" products, but ones offering new benefits. Peter Drucker, a leading management thinker, has put it this way: "The aim of marketing is to make selling superfluous. The aim is to know and understand the customer so well that the product or service fits him and sells itself."[3]

This does not mean that selling and promotion are unimportant, but rather that they are part of a larger "marketing mix"—a set of marketing tools that

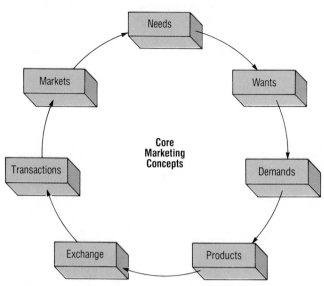

FIGURE 1–1   Core Marketing Concepts

**marketing** A social and managerial process by which individuals and groups obtain what they need and want through creating and exchanging products and value with others.

**human need** A state of felt deprivation.

work together to affect the marketplace. We will define **marketing** as a social and managerial process by which individuals and groups obtain what they need and want through creating and exchanging products and value with others.[4] To explain this definition, we will look at the following key terms: *needs, wants, demands, products, exchange, transactions,* and *markets.* These concepts are shown in Figure 1–1 and discussed below. As the figure shows, the core marketing concepts are linked, with each concept building on the one before it.

## Needs

The most basic concept underlying marketing is that of human needs. A **human need** is a state of felt deprivation. Human beings have many complex needs. They include basic *physical* needs for food, clothing, warmth, and safety; *social* needs for belonging and affection; and *individual* needs for knowledge and self-expression. These needs are not invented on Madison Avenue: They are a basic part of the human makeup.

*Kaiser Sand & Gravel Company's marketing mission is to "find a need and fill it."*

**human want** The form taken by a human need as it is shaped by culture and individual personality.

**demands** Human wants that are backed by buying power.

**product** Anything that can be offered to a market for attention, acquisition, use, or consumption and might satisfy a need or want; it includes physical objects, services, persons, places, organizations, and ideas.

When a need is not satisfied, a person will do one of two things—look for an object that will satisfy it or try to reduce the need. People in industrial societies may try to find or develop objects that will satisfy their desires. People in less-developed societies may try to reduce their desires and satisfy them with what is available.

## Wants

A second basic concept in marketing is that of **human wants**—the form taken by human needs as they are shaped by culture and individual personality. A hungry person in Bali may want mangoes, suckling pig, and beans. A hungry person in the United States may want a hamburger, French fries, and a Coke. Wants are described in terms of objects that will satisfy needs. As a society evolves, the wants of its members expand. As people are exposed to more objects that arouse their interest and desire, producers try to provide more want-satisfying products and services.

Many sellers confuse wants and needs. A manufacturer of drill bits may think that the customer needs a drill bit, but what the customer really needs is a hole. These sellers may suffer from "marketing myopia."[5] They are so taken with their products that they focus only on existing wants and lose sight of underlying customer needs. They forget that a physical product is only a tool to solve a consumer problem. These sellers have trouble if a new product comes along that serves the need better or cheaper. The customer with the same *need* will *want* the new product.

## Demands

People have almost unlimited wants but limited resources. Thus, they want to choose products that provide the most satisfaction for their money. When backed by buying power, wants become **demands.**

It is easy to list the demands in a society at a given time. In a single year, 240 million Americans might purchase 67 billion eggs, 2 billion chickens, 5 million hair dryers, 133 billion domestic air-passenger miles, and over 20 million lectures by college English professors. These and other consumer goods and services lead in turn to a demand for more than 150 million tons of steel, 4 billion tons of cotton, and many other industrial goods. These are but a few of the demands in a $3.5 trillion economy.

Consumers view products as bundles of benefits and choose products that give them the best bundle for their money. Thus, a Ford Festiva means basic transportation, a low price, and fuel economy. A Mercedes means comfort, luxury, and status. Given their wants and resources, people choose the product whose benefits add up to the most satisfaction.

## Products

Human needs, wants, and demands suggest that there are products available to satisfy them. A **product** is anything that can be offered to a market for attention, acquisition, use, or consumption and might satisfy a need or want.

Suppose a person feels the need to be more attractive. We will call all the products that can satisfy this need the *product choice set*. This set may include new clothes, hair-styling services, a Caribbean suntan, exercise classes, and many other items or services. These products are not all equally desirable. Those that are more available and less expensive, such as clothing and a new haircut, are likely to be purchased first. Moreover, the closer the products come to matching consumers' wants, the more successful they will be. Thus,

*Products do not have to be physical objects. Here the "product" is a trip to the zoo.*

producers must know what consumers want and must provide products that come as close as possible to satisfying those wants.

The concept of *product* is not limited to physical objects. Anything capable of satisfying a need can be called a product. In addition to goods and services, products include *persons, places, organizations, activities,* and *ideas.* A consumer decides which entertainers to watch on television, which places to go on a vacation, which organizations to contribute to, and which ideas to support. To the consumer, these are all products. If at times the term *product* does not seem to fit, we could substitute such terms as *satisfier, resource,* or *offer.* All describe something of value to someone.

## Exchange

Marketing occurs when people decide to satisfy needs and wants through exchange. **Exchange** is the act of obtaining a desired object from someone by offering something in return. Exchange is only one of many ways people can obtain a desired object. For example, hungry people could find food by hunting, fishing, or fruit gathering. They could beg for food or take food from someone else. Finally, they could offer money, another good, or a service in return for food.

As a means of satisfying needs, exchange has much in its favor. People do not have to prey on others or depend on donations. Nor must they possess the skills to produce every necessity for themselves. They could concentrate on making things they are good at making and trade them for needed items made by others. Thus, the society ends up producing much more than under any other alternative.

Exchange is the core concept of marketing.[6] For an exchange to take place, several conditions must be satisfied. Of course, there must be at least two parties, and each must have something of value to the other. Each party must also want to deal with the other party; each must be free to accept or reject the other's offer. Finally, each party must be able to communicate and deliver.

These conditions simply make exchange *possible.* Whether exchange actually *takes place* depends on the parties' coming to an agreement. If they agree, we must conclude that the act of exchange has left both of them better off (or at least not worse off): After all, each was free to reject or accept the offer. In this sense, just as production creates value, exchange creates value. It gives people more consumption possibilities.

## Transactions

**transaction** A trade between two parties that involves at least two things of value, agreed-upon conditions, a time of agreement, and a place of agreement.

**monetary transaction** A marketing transaction in which goods or services are exchanged for money.

**barter transaction** A marketing transaction in which goods or services are traded for other goods or services.

**market** The set of actual and potential buyers of a product.

Whereas exchange is the core concept of marketing, a transaction is marketing's unit of measurement. A **transaction** consists of a trade of values between two parties. In a transaction, we must be able to say that A gives *X* to B and gets *Y* in return. For example, you pay Sears $400 for a television set. This is a classic **monetary transaction.** But not all transactions involve money. In a **barter transaction,** you might trade your old refrigerator in return for a neighbor's secondhand television set. A barter transaction can also involve services as well as goods—for example, when a lawyer writes a will for a doctor in return for a medical exam (see Marketing Highlight 1–1). A transaction involves at least two things of value, conditions that are agreed upon, a time of agreement, and a place of agreement.

In the broadest sense, the marketer tries to bring about a response to some offer. And the response may be more than simply "buying" or "trading" goods and services in the narrow sense. A political candidate, for instance, wants a response called "votes," a church wants "membership," a social-action group wants "idea acceptance." Marketing consists of actions taken to obtain a desired response from a target audience toward some product, service, idea, or other object.

## Markets

The concept of transactions leads to the concept of a market. A **market** is the set of actual and potential buyers of a product. To understand the nature of a market, imagine a primitive economy consisting of only four people: a fisherman, a hunter, a potter, and a farmer. Figure 1–2 shows the three different ways in which these traders could meet their needs. In the first case, *self-sufficiency,*

# Marketing Highlight 1–1

## GOING BACK TO BARTER

With today's high prices, many companies are returning to the primitive but time-honored practice of barter—trading goods and services that they make for other goods and services that they need. Currently, companies barter over $275 billion worth of goods and services a year worldwide, and the practice is growing rapidly.

Companies use barter to increase sales, unload extra goods, and save cash. For example, when Climaco Corporation was overstocked with bubble bath, it swapped the excess for $300,000 worth of advertising space for one of its other products. McDonnell Douglas traded planes to Yugoslavia for hams and tools,

and Pierre Cardin served as a consultant to China in exchange for silks and cashmeres. The cash-poor U.S. Olympics Committee bartered the promotional use of its Olympic logo for products and services needed by its staff and athletes. It obtained free transportation from United Airlines, 500 cars from Buick, clothing from Levi Strauss, and shoes from Nike. It even traded the logo for a swimming pool built by McDonald's.

As a result of this increase in barter activity, many kinds of specialty companies have appeared to help other companies with their bartering. Retail-trade exchanges and trade clubs arrange barter for small retailers. Larger

corporations use trade consultants and brokerage firms. Media brokerage houses provide advertising in exchange for products, and international barter is often handled by countertrade organizations. One trading company, Barter Systems, Inc., operates 62 trading centers around the United States. A letter that it recently sent to some of its 25,000 clients stated: "Wanted: $300,000 worth of dried milk or cornflakes in exchange for an airplane of equal value."

Sources: See Linda A. Dickerson, "Barter to Gain a Competitive Edge in a Cash-Poor Economy, *Marketing News,* March 16, 1984, pp. 1-2; and Arthur Bragg, "Bartering Comes of Age," *Sales & Marketing Management,* January 1988, pp. 61-63.

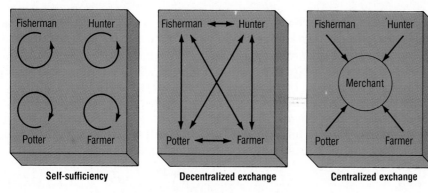

FIGURE 1-2   Evolution toward Centralized Exchange

they gather the needed goods for themselves. Thus, the hunter spends most of the time hunting but also takes time to fish, make pottery, and farm to obtain the other goods. The hunter is less efficient at hunting, and the same is true of the other traders.

In the second case, *decentralized exchange,* each person sees the other three as potential "buyers" who make up a market. Thus, the hunter may make separate trips to trade meat for the goods of the fisherman, the potter, and the farmer.

In the third case, *centralized exchange,* a new person called a *merchant* appears and locates in a central area called a *marketplace.* Each trader brings goods to the merchant and trades for other needed goods. Thus, rather than transacting with the other providers, the hunter transacts with one "market" to obtain all needed goods. Merchants and central marketplaces greatly reduce the total number of transactions needed to accomplish a given volume of exchange.[7]

As the number of persons and transactions increases in a society, the number of merchants and marketplaces also increases. In advanced societies, markets need not be physical locations where buyers and sellers interact. With modern communications and transportation, a merchant can easily advertise a product on late evening television, take orders from hundreds of customers over the phone, and mail the goods to buyers on the following day without having had any physical contact with them.

A market can grow up around a product, a service, or anything else of value. For example, a *labor market* consists of people who are willing to offer their work in return for wages or products. In fact, various institutions, such as employment agencies and job-counseling firms, will grow up around a labor market to help it function better. The *money market* is another important market that emerges to meet the needs of people so that they can borrow, lend, save, and protect money. The *donor market* has emerged to meet the financial needs of nonprofit organizations.

## Marketing

The concept of markets finally brings us full circle to the concept of marketing. Marketing means working with markets to bring about exchanges for the purpose of satisfying human needs and wants. Thus, we return to our definition of marketing as a process by which individuals and groups obtain what they need and want by creating and exchanging products and value with others.

Exchange processes involve work. Sellers must search for buyers, identify their needs, design good products, promote them, store and deliver them, and set prices for them. Such activities as product development, research, communication, distribution, pricing, and service are core marketing activities.

Although we normally think of marketing as being performed by sellers, buyers also perform marketing activities. Consumers do "marketing" when

**demarketing** Marketing in which the task is to reduce demand either temporarily or permanently.

**marketing management** The analysis, planning, implementation, and control of programs designed to create, build, and maintain beneficial exchanges with target buyers for the purpose of achieving organizational objectives.

**production concept** The philosophy that consumers will favor products that are available and highly affordable and that management should therefore focus on improving production and distribution efficiency.

they search for the goods they need at prices they can afford. Company purchasing agents do "marketing" when they track down sellers and bargain for good terms. A *seller's market* is one in which sellers have more power and buyers must be the more active "marketers." In a *buyer's market*, buyers have more power and sellers have to be more active "marketers."

In the early 1950s, the supply of goods began to grow faster than the demand. Most markets became buyer's markets, and marketing became identified with sellers trying to find buyers. This book will take this point of view and examine the marketing problems of sellers in a buyer's market.

# MARKETING MANAGEMENT

Most people think of a marketing manager as someone who finds enough customers for the company's current output. But this view is too limited. Every organization has a desired level of demand for its products. At any point in time, there may be no demand, adequate demand, irregular demand, or too much demand. Marketing managers, therefore, can be concerned not only with finding and *increasing* demand but also with *changing* or even *reducing* it.

For example, the Golden Gate Bridge sometimes carries more traffic than experts think safe, and Yellowstone Park is usually overcrowded in the summertime. In these and other cases of too much demand, the needed marketing task, called **demarketing,** is to find ways to reduce demand temporarily or permanently. Demarketing may involve actions such as raising prices and reducing service. It does not aim to destroy demand, but only to reduce it.[8] Thus, marketing management seeks to affect the level, timing, and nature of demand in a way that will help the organization achieve its objectives. Simply put, marketing management is *demand management*.

We define **marketing management** as the analysis, planning, implementation, and control of programs designed to create, build, and maintain beneficial exchanges with target buyers for the purpose of achieving organizational objectives. Marketing managers include sales managers and salespeople, advertising executives, sales-promotion people, marketing researchers, product managers, pricing specialists, and others. We will say more about these marketing jobs in Chapters 2 and 3 and in Appendix B, "Careers in Marketing."

# MARKETING MANAGEMENT PHILOSOPHIES

We have described marketing management as carrying out tasks to achieve desired exchanges with target markets. What *philosophy* should guide these marketing efforts? What weight should be given to the interests of the organization, customers, and society? Very often these interests conflict.

There are five alternative concepts under which organizations conduct their marketing activities: the *production, product, selling, marketing,* and *societal marketing* concepts.

## *The Production Concept*

The **production concept** holds that consumers will favor products that are available and highly affordable and that management should therefore focus on improving production and distribution efficiency. This concept is one of the oldest philosophies guiding sellers.

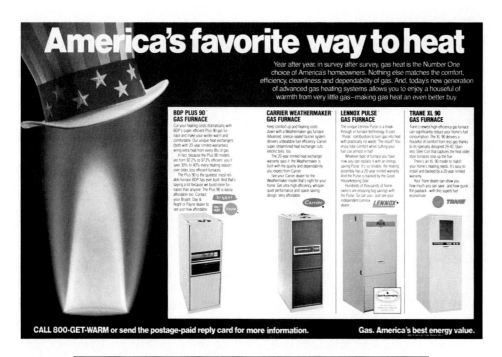

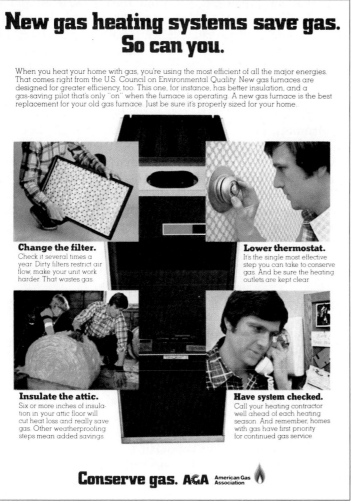

*Managing demand: During the gas shortages of the 1970s, the American Gas Association demarketed natural gas by telling people how to conserve. Then when gas supplies grew in the 1980s, the AGA ran ads to stimulate sales while continuing to emphasize energy efficiency.*

**product concept** The idea that consumers will favor products that offer the most quality, performance, and features and that the organization should therefore devote its energy to making continuous product improvements.

**selling concept** The idea that consumers will not buy enough of the organization's products unless the organization undertakes a large-scale selling and promotion effort.

The production concept is a useful philosophy in two types of situations. The first occurs when the demand for a product exceeds the supply. Here, management should look for ways to increase production. The second situation occurs when the product's cost is too high and improved productivity is needed to bring it down. For example, Henry Ford's whole philosophy was to perfect the production of the Model T so that its cost could be reduced and more people could afford it. He joked about offering people a car of any color as long as it was black. Today, Texas Instruments (TI) follows this philosophy of increased production and lower costs in order to bring down prices. It won a major share of the American hand-calculator market with this philosophy. But when TI used the same strategy in the digital watch market, it failed. Although they were priced low, customers did not find TI's watches very attractive. In its drive to bring down prices, TI lost sight of something else that its customers wanted—namely, *attractive*, affordable digital watches.

## The Product Concept

Another major concept guiding sellers, the **product concept**, holds that consumers will favor products that offer the most quality, performance, and features, and that an organization should thus devote energy to making continuous product improvements. Some manufacturers believe that if they can build a better mousetrap, the world will beat a path to their door.[9] But they are often rudely shocked. Buyers may well be looking for a solution to a mouse problem, but not necessarily for a better mousetrap. The solution might be a chemical spray, an exterminating service, or something that works better than a mousetrap. Furthermore, a better mousetrap will not sell unless the manufacturer designs, packages, and prices it attractively, places it in convenient distribution channels, brings it to the attention of people who need it, and convinces them that it is a better product.

The product concept can also lead to "marketing myopia." For instance, railroad management once thought that users wanted *trains* rather than *transportation* and overlooked the growing challenge of airlines, buses, trucks, and automobiles. Many colleges have assumed that high school graduates want a liberal arts education and have thus overlooked the increasing challenge of vocational schools.

## The Selling Concept

Many organizations follow the **selling concept,** which holds that consumers will not buy enough of the organization's products unless it undertakes a large selling and promotion effort. The concept is typically practiced with *unsought goods*—those that buyers do not normally think of buying (say, encyclopedias and funeral plots). These industries must be good at tracking down prospects and selling them on product benefits.

The selling concept is also practiced in the nonprofit area. A political party, for example, will vigorously sell its candidate to voters as a fantastic person for the job. The candidate works in voting precincts from dawn to dusk, shaking hands, kissing babies, meeting donors, making speeches. Much money is spent on radio and television advertising, posters, and mailings. Candidate flaws are hidden from the public because the aim is to get the sale, not worry about consumer satisfaction afterward.

*The marketing concept: GE promises consumer satisfaction.*

**marketing concept** The marketing management philosophy that holds that achieving organizational goals depends on determining the needs and wants of target markets and delivering the desired satisfactions more effectively and efficiently than competitors.

## The Marketing Concept

The **marketing concept** holds that achieving organizational goals depends on determining the needs and wants of target markets and delivering the desired satisfactions more effectively and efficiently than competitors. Surprisingly, this concept is a relatively recent business philosophy. The marketing concept has been stated in such colorful ways as "Find a need and fill it" (Kaiser Sand & Gravel); "We do it like you'd do it" (Burger King); and "We're not satisfied until you are" (GE). J. C. Penney's motto also summarizes the marketing concept: "To do all in our power to pack the customer's dollar full of value, quality, and satisfaction."

The selling concept and the marketing concept are frequently confused. Figure 1–3 compares the two concepts. The selling concept takes an *inside-out* perspective. It starts with the factory, focuses on the company's existing products, and calls for heavy selling and promotion to obtain profitable sales. By contrast, the marketing concept takes an *outside-in* perspective. It starts with a well-defined market, focuses on customer needs, coordinates all the marketing activities affecting customers, and makes profits by creating customer satisfaction. Under the marketing concept, companies produce what consumers want, thereby satisfying consumers and making profits.

Many successful and well-known companies have adopted the marketing concept. Procter & Gamble, IBM, and McDonald's follow it faithfully (see

**societal marketing concept** The idea that the organization should determine the needs, wants, and interests of target markets and deliver the desired satisfactions more effectively and efficiently than competitors in a way that maintains or improves the consumer's and society's well-being.

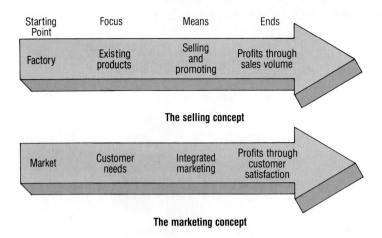

FIGURE 1–3    The Selling and Marketing Concepts Contrasted

Marketing Highlight 1–2). We also know that the marketing concept is practiced more among consumer-goods companies than industrial-goods companies and more among large companies than small companies. On the other hand, many companies claim to practice the marketing concept but do not. They have the *forms* of marketing—such as a marketing vice-president, product managers, marketing plans, marketing research—but not the *substance*. Several years of hard work are needed to turn a sales-oriented company into a marketing-oriented company.[10]

## The Societal Marketing Concept

The **societal marketing concept** holds that the organization should determine the needs, wants, and interests of target markets. It should then deliver the desired satisfactions more effectively and efficiently than competitors in a way that maintains or improves the consumer's *and the society's* well-being. The societal marketing concept is the newest of the five marketing management philosophies.

The societal marketing concept questions whether the pure marketing concept is adequate in an age of environmental problems, resource shortages, rapid population growth, worldwide inflation, and neglected social services. It asks if the firm that senses, serves, and satisfies individual wants is always doing what is best for consumers and society in the long run. According to the societal marketing concept, the pure marketing concept overlooks possible conflicts between short-run consumer *wants* and long-run consumer *welfare*.

Consider the Coca-Cola Company. Most people see it as a highly responsible corporation producing fine soft drinks that satisfy consumer tastes. Yet, certain consumer and environmental groups have voiced concerns that Coke has little nutritional value, can harm people's teeth, contains caffeine, and adds to the litter problem with disposable bottles and cans.

Such concerns and conflicts led to the societal marketing concept. The societal marketing concept calls upon marketers to balance three considerations in setting their marketing policies: company profits, consumer wants, and society's interests. Originally, most companies based their marketing decisions largely on short-run company profit. Eventually, they began to recognize the long-run importance of satisfying consumer wants, and the marketing concept emerged. Now many companies are beginning to think of society's interests when making their marketing decisions. Many of them have made large sales and profit gains by practicing the societal marketing concept.

## MCDONALD'S APPLIES THE MARKETING CONCEPT

McDonald's Corporation, the fast-food hamburger retailer, is a master marketer. With over 10,000 outlets in 50 countries and over $14.3 billion in annual sales, McDonald's doubles the sales of its nearest rival, Burger King, and triples those of third-place Wendy's. Nineteen million customers pass through the famous golden arches every day, and an astounding 96 percent of all Americans ate at McDonald's at least once last year. McDonald's now serves 145 hamburgers per second. Credit for this performance belongs to a strong marketing orientation: McDonald's knows how to serve people and adapt to changing consumer wants.

Before McDonald's appeared, Americans could get hamburgers in restaurants or diners. But consumers often encountered poor hamburgers, slow and unfriendly service, unattractive décor, unclean conditions, and a noisy atmosphere. In 1955, Ray Kroc, a 52-year-old salesman of milkshake-mixing machines, became excited about a string of seven restaurants owned by Richard and Maurice McDonald. Kroc liked their fast-food restaurant concept and bought the chain for $2.7 million. He decided to expand the chain by selling franchises, and the number of restaurants grew rapidly. As times changed, so did McDonald's. It expanded its sit-down sections, improved the décor, launched a breakfast menu, added new food items, and opened new outlets in high-traffic areas.

Kroc's marketing philosophy is captured in McDonald's motto of "Q.S.C. & V.," which stands for *q*uality, *s*ervice, *c*leanliness, and *v*alue. Customers enter a spotlessly clean restaurant, walk up to a friendly counterperson, quickly receive a good-tasting hamburger, and eat it there or take it out. There are no jukeboxes or telephones to create a teen-age hangout. Nor are there any cigarette machines or newspaper racks—McDonald's is a family affair, appealing strongly to children.

McDonald's has mastered the art of serving consumers, and it carefully teaches the basics to its franchisees and employees, all of whom take training courses at McDonald's "Hamburger University" in Elk Grove Village, Illinois. They emerge with a degree in "Hamburgerology" and a minor in French fries. McDonald's monitors product and service quality through continuous customer surveys and puts great energy into improving hamburger production methods in order to simplify operations, bring down costs, speed up service, and bring greater value to customers. Beyond these efforts, each McDonald's restaurant works to become a part of its neighborhood through community-involvement and service projects.

The McDonald's focus on consumers has made it the world's largest food-service organization. The company's huge success has been reflected in the increased value of its stock over the years: 250 shares of McDonald's stock purchased for less than $6,000 in 1965 would be worth over a million dollars today!

Sources: See Kathleen Deveny, "Meet Mike Quinlan, Big Mac's Attack CEO," *Business Week*, May 9, 1988, pp. 92–97; and Penny Moser, "The McDonald's Mystique," *Fortune*, July 4, 1988.

*McDonald's motto is "quality, service, cleanliness, and value."*

# THE GOALS OF THE MARKETING SYSTEM

Marketing affects everyone in our society. Marketing affects so many people in so many ways that it often stirs controversy. Some people intensely dislike modern marketing activity, charging it with ruining the environment, bombarding the public with senseless ads, creating unnecessary wants, teaching greed to youngsters, and committing several other sins. Consider the following:

> For the past 6,000 years the field of marketing has been thought of as made up of fast-buck artists, con-men, wheeler-dealers, and shoddy-goods distributors. Too many of us have been "taken" by the touts or con-men; and all of us at times have been prodded into buying all sorts of "things" we really did not need, and which we found later on we did not even want.[11]

Others vigorously defend marketing:

> Aggressive marketing policies and practices have been largely responsible for the high material standard of living in America. Today through mass, low-cost marketing we enjoy products which once were considered luxuries, and which still are so classified in many foreign countries.[12]

What should a society seek from its marketing system? Four alternative goals have been suggested: maximize *consumption*, maximize *consumer satisfaction*, maximize *choice*, and maximize *quality of life*.

## *Maximize Consumption*

Many business executives believe that marketing's job should be to stimulate maximum consumption, which will in turn create maximum production, employment, and wealth. This view is echoed in such headlines as "IBM Woos Home Computer Buyers with New Generation Models," "New Pepsi Ads and Promotions Hype Sales," and "Circuit City Moves West, Serves New Markets." The assumption is that the more people buy and consume, the happier they are. "More is better" is the war cry. Yet some people doubt that increased material goods mean more happiness. They see too many affluent people leading unhappy lives. Their philosophy is "less is more" and "small is beautiful."

## *Maximize Consumer Satisfaction*

Another view holds that the goal of the marketing system is to maximize consumer satisfaction, not simply the quantity of consumption. Buying a new car or owning more clothes counts only if this adds to the buyer's satisfaction.

Unfortunately, consumer satisfaction is difficult to measure. First, nobody has figured out how to measure the total satisfaction created by a particular product or marketing activity. Second, the satisfaction that some individual consumers get from the "goods" of a product or service must be offset by the "bads," such as pollution and environmental damage. Third, the satisfaction that some people get from consuming certain goods, such as status goods, depends on the fact that few other people have these goods. Thus, it is hard to evaluate the marketing system in terms of how much satisfaction it delivers.

## *Maximize Choice*

Some marketers believe that the goal of a marketing system should be to maximize product variety and consumer choice. The system would enable consumers to find goods that exactly satisfy their tastes. Consumers would be able to fully realize life-style goals and, therefore, maximize their overall satisfaction.

Unfortunately, maximizing consumer choice comes at a cost. First, goods and services will be more expensive because producing great variety increases production and inventory costs. In turn, higher prices reduce consumers' real income and consumption. Second, the increase in product variety will require greater consumer search and effort. Consumers will have to spend more time learning about and evaluating different products. Third, more products will not necessarily increase the consumer's real choice: There may be hundreds of brands of beer in the United States, but most of them taste the same. Thus, when a product category contains many brands with few differences, consumers face a choice that is really no choice at all. Finally, not all consumers welcome great product variety. For some consumers, too much choice leads to confusion and frustration.

## Maximize Life Quality

Many people believe that the goal of a marketing system should be to improve the *quality of life*. This includes not only the quality, quantity, availability, and cost of goods but also the quality of the physical and cultural environments. Advocates of this view would judge marketing systems not just by the amount of direct consumer satisfaction but also by the impact of marketing on the quality of the environment. Most people would agree that quality of life is a worthwhile goal for the marketing system. But they would also agree that "quality" is hard to measure and that it means different things to different people.

# THE RAPID ADOPTION OF MARKETING ■

Most people think that only large companies operating in capitalistic countries use marketing, but marketing actually occurs both inside and outside the business sector and in all kinds of countries.

## In the Business Sector

In the business sector, different companies become interested in marketing at different times. General Electric, General Motors, Sears, Procter & Gamble, and Coca-Cola saw marketing's potential almost immediately. Marketing spread most rapidly in consumer packaged-goods companies, consumer durables companies, and industrial equipment companies—roughly in that order. Producers of such commodities as steel, chemicals, and paper adopted marketing later, and many still have a long way to go.

Within the past decade, consumer service firms, especially airlines and banks, have adopted modern marketing practices. Marketing has also attracted the interest of insurance and financial services companies. The latest business groups to take an interest in marketing are professionals such as lawyers, accountants, physicians, and architects. Until recently, professional associations have not allowed their members to engage in price competition, client solicitation, and advertising. But the U.S. antitrust division has ruled that such restraints are illegal. Accountants, lawyers, and other professional people moved quickly to advertise and to price aggressively.

### In the International Sector

Marketing is practiced not only in the United States but in the rest of the world. In fact, several European and Japanese multinationals—companies like Nestlé, Siemens, Toyota, and Sony—often outperform their U.S. competitors. Multinationals have spread modern marketing practices throughout the world. As a result, management in smaller countries is beginning to ask: Just what is marketing? How does it differ from plain selling? How can we introduce marketing into our firm? How will it make a difference and how much?

In socialist countries, marketing has traditionally had a bad name. However, such marketing functions as marketing research, branding, advertising, and sales promotion are now spreading rapidly in these countries. The USSR now has over 100 state-operated advertising agencies and marketing-research firms. It is encouraging joint ventures with Western advertising agencies and has established a professorship of marketing at its Moscow Institute of Management. Many companies in Poland and Hungary have marketing departments, and most socialist universities now teach marketing.[13]

### In the Nonprofit Sector

Marketing is also currently attracting the interest of *nonprofit* organizations such as colleges, hospitals, museums, symphonies, and even police departments. Consider the following developments:

> Facing low enrollments and rising costs, many private colleges are using marketing to attract students and funds. St. Joseph's College in Rensselaer, Indiana, obtained a 40 percent increase in freshman enrollments by advertising in *Seventeen* and on several rock radio stations.

> As hospital costs and room rates soar, many hospitals face underutilization, especially in their maternity and pediatrics sections. Many are taking steps toward marketing. A Philadelphia hospital, competing for maternity patients, offers a steak and champagne dinner with candlelight for new parents. St. Mary's Medical Center in Evanston, Indiana, uses innovative billboards to promote its emergency care service. Other hospitals, in an effort to attract physicians, have installed services such as saunas, chauffeurs, and private tennis courts.[14]

These organizations have marketing problems. Their administrators are struggling to keep them alive in the face of changing consumer attitudes and smaller financial resources. Many such institutions have turned to marketing as a possible answer to their problems.

In addition, U.S. government agencies are showing an increased interest in marketing. For example, the U.S. Postal Service and Amtrak have marketing plans for their operations. The U.S. Army has a marketing plan to attract recruits and is in fact one of the top advertising spenders in the country. Other government agencies are now marketing energy conservation, nonsmoking, and other public causes.

## ■ PLAN OF THE BOOK

The following chapters will expand on the marketing topics introduced in this chapter. Table 1–1 outlines the plan of the book. Part 1, "Understanding Marketing and the Marketing Management Process," provides a general intro-

Are you still collecting the same old stuff?

Well there's a lot of enjoyment in stamp collecting, too.

Particularly now with our new American Wildlife Stamp Set. A single sheet of 50 beautifully detailed animal, bird, reptile, and insect stamps. Each featuring a creature that roams, crawls, or flies across the United States.

This special commemorative issue is a great introduction to the joys of stamp collecting. A hobby that kids of all ages can find both educational and fascinating.

Head to your post office today for this special issue commemorating America's natural wildlife heritage. Then you, too, can enjoy something new. With the fun of collecting U.S. commemorative stamps.

Available nationwide June 13.

Start something new with stamps.

U.S. Postal Service

*Marketing in the nonprofit sector: the United States government is now one of the country's largest advertisers.*

TABLE 1–1   Plan of the Book

---

*Part One—Understanding Marketing and the Marketing Management Process*

Social foundations of marketing: meeting human needs (Chapter 1)
Strategic planning and marketing's role in the organization (Chapter 2)
Planning, implementing, and controlling marketing programs (Chapter 3)

*Part Two—Analyzing Marketing Opportunities*

Marketing research and information systems (Chapter 4)
The marketing environment (Chapter 5)

*Part Three—Selecting Target Markets*

Consumer markets and consumer buying behavior (Chapter 6)
Organizational markets and organizational buyer behavior (Chapter 7)
Market segmentation, targeting, and positioning (Chapter 8)

*Part Four—Developing the Marketing Mix*

Designing products (Chapters 9 and 10)
Pricing products (Chapters 11 and 12)
Placing products (Chapters 13 and 14)
Promoting products (Chapters 15, 16, and 17)

*Part Five—Extending Marketing*

International marketing (Chapter 18)
Services marketing and nonprofit marketing (Chapter 19)
Marketing and society (Chapter 20)

marketing. Chapter 2 discusses the marketing management process and marketing's role in the organization's overall strategic plan. Chapter 3 looks at how marketing strategies and programs are planned, implemented, and controlled by people in the organization's marketing department.

Part 2, "Analyzing Market Opportunities," looks at the ways marketers seek attractive opportunities in the marketing environment. In Chapter 4, we discuss the importance of marketing research and information both in preparing marketing plans and in analyzing the marketing environment. Chapter 5 describes the actors and forces in the rapidly changing marketing environment.

Part 3, "Selecting Target Markets," examines the key characteristics of the company's markets. Chapter 6 examines consumer markets; Chapter 7 looks at organizational markets. Chapter 8 describes the art of selecting appropriate markets. The marketer first segments the market, then selects target segments and positions the company's products in chosen segments.

Part 4, "Developing the Marketing Mix," looks at the major marketing activities of the firm—designing, pricing, placing, and promoting products and services. In Chapters 9 through 17, we will look at the various concepts that guide marketing managers and at the techniques they use to develop attractive offers and market them successfully.

Part 5, "Extending Marketing," looks at topics of current interest. Chapter 18 discusses international marketing; Chapter 19 discusses services and nonprofit marketing. The last chapter, "Marketing and Society," returns us to the basic question of marketing's role and purpose in society—both its contributions and its shortcomings.

The book ends with two appendixes. The first presents the marketing arithmetic used by marketing managers when making a variety of decisions. The second discusses marketing careers and shows how students can apply marketing principles in their search for desirable jobs.

## ◾ SUMMARY

*Marketing* touches everyone's life. It is the means by which a standard of living is developed and delivered to a people. Many people confuse marketing with *selling*, but in fact marketing occurs both before and after the selling event. Marketing actually combines many activities—marketing research, product development, distribution, pricing, advertising, personal selling, and others—designed to sense, serve, and satisfy consumer needs while meeting the organization's goals.

Marketing is human activity directed at satisfying needs and wants through *exchange processes*. The core concepts of marketing are *needs*, *wants*, *demands*, *products*, *exchange*, *transactions*, and *markets*.

*Marketing management* is the analysis, planning, implementation, and control of programs designed to create, build, and maintain beneficial exchanges with target markets for the purpose of achieving organizational objectives. Marketers must be good at managing the level, timing, and composition of demand, since actual demand can be different from what the organization wants.

Marketing management can be guided by five different philosophies. The *production concept* holds that consumers will favor products that are available at low cost and that management's task is to improve production efficiency and bring down prices. The *product concept* holds that consumers favor quality products and that little promotional effort is thus required. The *selling concept* holds that consumers will not buy enough of the company's products unless they are stimulated through heavy selling and promotion. The *marketing concept* holds that a company should research the needs and wants of a well-defined target market and deliver the desired satisfactions. The *societal marketing concept* holds that the company should generate customer satisfaction and long-run societal well-being as the key to achieving both its goals and its responsibilities.

Marketing practices have a major impact on people in our society. Different goals have been proposed for a marketing system, such as maximizing *consumption, consumer satisfaction, consumer choice,* or *quality of life*. Interest in marketing is growing as more organizations in the business, international, and nonprofit sectors recognize the ways in which marketing can improve performance.

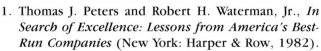

1. Why should *you* study marketing?

2. *In Search of Excellence* describes the marketing principles of many top companies. How can you apply these principles to market yourself and improve your chances of landing the job you want after graduation?

3. Economist John Kenneth Galbraith argues that the desires stimulated by marketing activities are not "genuine": "A man who is hungry need never be told of his need for food." Do you agree with this criticism? Why or why not?

4. Describe how the notions of products, exchanges, and transactions apply when you buy a soft drink from a vending machine. Do they also apply when you vote for a political candidate?

5. Many people dislike or fear some products and would not "demand" them at any price. For example, how might a health-care marketer manage the *negative* demand for such products as mammograms?

6. Identify organizations in your town that practice the production concept, the product concept, and the selling concept. How could these organizations become more marketing-oriented?

7. The headline for a Merrill Lynch ad says, "The reason we're a leader in so many areas isn't how much we talk but how attentively we listen." In what ways can companies "listen" to consumers? How does this help them practice the marketing concept?

8. According to economist Milton Friedman, "Few trends could so thoroughly undermine the very foundations of our free society as the acceptance by corporate officials of a social responsibility other than to make as much money for their stockholders as possible." Do you agree or disagree? What are some drawbacks of the societal marketing concept?

9. Many proposals have been made to ban all cigarette advertising in the United States. Would such a ban conflict with the goals of our marketing system? Does your answer depend on which goal you think appropriate for our society?

10. Why have many nonprofit organizations adopted marketing techniques in recent years? For example, how does your school market itself to attract new students?

# REFERENCES

1. Thomas J. Peters and Robert H. Waterman, Jr., *In Search of Excellence: Lessons from America's Best-Run Companies* (New York: Harper & Row, 1982).

2. Thomas J. Peters and Nancy Austin, *A Passion for Excellence: The Leadership Difference* (New York: Random House, 1985).

3. Peter F. Drucker, *Management: Tasks, Responsibilities, Practices* (New York: Harper & Row, 1973), pp. 64–65.

4. Here are some other definitions: "Marketing is the performance of business activities that direct the flow of goods and services from producer to consumer or user." "Marketing is getting the right goods and services to the right people at the right place at the right time at the right price with the right communication and promotion." "Marketing is the creation and delivery of a standard of living." In 1985, the American Marketing Association approved this definition: "Marketing is the process of planning and executing the conception, pricing, promotion, and distribution of ideas, goods, and services to create exchanges that satisfy individual and organizational objectives."

5. See Theodore Levitt's classic article, "Marketing Myopia," *Harvard Business Review,* July-August 1960, pp. 45–56.

6. For more discussion on marketing as an exchange process, see Franklin S. Houston and Jule B. Gassenheimer, "Marketing and Exchange," *Journal of Marketing,* October 1987, pp. 3–18.

7. The number of transactions in a decentralized exchange system is given by $N(N-1)/2$. With four persons, this means $4(4-1)/2=6$ transactions. In a centralized exchange system, the number of transactions is given by $N$, here 4. Thus, a centralized exchange system reduces the number of transactions needed for exchange.

8. For more discussion on demand states, see Philip Kotler, *Marketing Management: Analysis, Planning, Implementation, and Control,* 6th ed. (Englewood Cliffs, NJ: Prentice Hall, 1988), pp. 12–13.

9. Ralph Waldo Emerson offered this advice: "If a

man . . . makes a better mousetrap . . . the world will beat a path to his door.'' Several companies, however, have built better mousetraps yet failed. One was a laser mousetrap costing $1,500. Contrary to popular assumptions, people do not automatically learn about new products, believe product claims, or willingly pay higher prices.

10. For more on the marketing concept, see Theodore Levitt, ''Marketing and Its Discontents,'' *Across the Board,* February 1984, pp. 42–48; and Franklin S. Houston, ''The Marketing Concept: What It Is and What It Is Not,'' *Journal of Marketing,* April 1986, pp. 81–87.

11. Richard N. Farmer, ''Would You Want Your Daughter to Marry a Marketing Man?'' *Journal of Marketing,* January 1967, p. 1.

12. William J. Stanton and Charles Futrell, *Fundamentals of Marketing,* 8th ed. (New York: McGraw-Hill, 1987), p. 7.

13. See Elisa Tinsley, ''The Soviet Promise of Expanded Markets: Consumer Demand Growing,'' *Advertising Age,* January 6, 1986, p. 38; and Wolfgang J. Koschnick, ''Russian Bear Bullish on Marketing,'' *Marketing News,* November 21, 1988, pp. 1, 18.

14. For other examples, and for a good review of non-profit marketing, see Philip Kotler and Alan R. Andreasen, *Strategic Marketing for Nonprofit Organizations* (Englewood Cliffs, NJ: Prentice Hall, 1987).

# Case 1

## THE ELECTRIC FEATHER PIROGUE: GOING WITH THE MARKETING FLOW

The Fin and Feather Products Company of Marshall, Texas, produces a line of small, versatile, lightweight boats called the Electric Feather Pirogue (pronounced *pē rō*). The term ''feather'' was chosen to emphasize the light weight of the boat and ''electric'' because it is propelled by an electric trolling motor. The name *Pirogue* refers to the historic small riverboats used on the Louisiana bayous. The kayak-shaped boat is 12 feet long, 38 inches wide, and 12 inches deep. It comes complete with motor and has a load capacity of about 540 pounds. Power is provided by a standard 12-volt automotive-type storage battery. The built-in Shakespeare motor is available with 18-pound or 24-pound thrust. The hull is handcrafted fiberglass, sturdily constructed by a hand-layup process.

The stable, flat-bottomed Pirogue can operate in very shallow water, so it is ideally suited for fishing, duck hunting, bird watching, or just leisure stream cruising. The propeller is protected from submerged objects by specially engineered motor guards on each side of the exposed drive unit. A 1½-inch sheet of polyurethane foam is built into the bottom to provide flotation. The boat is extremely simple to operate. A panel just below the wraparound gunwale contains two control switches—a forward-off-reverse switch and a low-medium-high speed switch. A horizontal lever just above the panel provides steering control. There is only one moving part in the entire control system. The 3-speed, 18-pound thrust motor has a maximum speed of 10 miles an hour, and the 4-speed, 24-pound thrust motor can attain a speed of 14 miles an hour. The company furnishes a one-year unlimited warranty on the boat, and the Shakespeare Company provides a similar warranty on the motor.

The company produced only one basic model of the boat but offered optional equipment that provided some variation within the product line. Retail prices ranged from approximately $490 to $650, depending on motor size and optional equipment. Although designed to accommodate two people, the standard model has only one molded plastic seat. The second seat, deluxe swivel seats, marine carpeting, and tonneau cover are the major optional items. No trailer is required because the boat fits nicely on the roof of even the smallest car or in the back of a station wagon or pickup truck. Without battery, the Pirogue weighs only about 80 pounds and can easily be handled by one person.

In Year 1 (the base year), Mr. Bill Wadlington purchased controlling interest in, and assumed managerial control of, the seven-year-old Fin and Feather Products Company. One of Mr. Wadlington's first moves was to adopt a strict cash-and-carry policy: Supplies and equipment were paid for at the time of purchase, and all sales were for cash prior to shipment whether shipment was to a dealer or directly to a customer. All shipments were F.O.B. the factory in Marshall, Texas. As a result of this policy, the firm has no accounts receivable and virtually no accounts payable. Mr. Wadlington anticipated sales of between 800 and 1000 units in Year 1. This volume would approach plant capacity and produce a wholesale dollar volume of approximately $350,000 to $400,000. After only six months of operation, Mr. Wadlington would not predict an exact annual net-profit figure, but he was very optimistic about the first year's profit prospect. It was also difficult to predict exactly what future volume would be, but sales had shown a steady increase throughout the first half of the year. The flow of inquiries from around the United States and from several foreign countries made the future look bright.

The company hired no outside salespeople, and Mr. Wadlington was the only in-house salesman. There were 15 independent dealers around the country who bought at wholesale and assumed a standard markup. There was no formal agreement or contract between the company and the dealers, but to qualify as a dealer, an individual or firm's initial order had to be for at least five boats. Subsequent orders could be for any quantity desired. Dealers' orders had to be accompanied by a check for the entire amount of the purchase.

In addition to the dealers, the company had 20 agents who were authorized to take orders in areas outside dealer territories. These agents accepted orders for direct shipment to customers and were paid a commission for the boats they sold. Agents were not assigned a specific territory but could not sell in areas assigned to dealers. As with all sales, agent orders had to be prepaid. Direct orders from individuals were accepted at the factory when the customer lived outside a dealer territory. Most direct sales were the result of the company's advertisements in such magazines as *Ducks Unlimited, Outdoor Life, Argosy, Field and Stream,* and *Better Homes and Gardens.*

Mr. Wadlington had not established a systematic promotional program. The services of an out-of-state advertising agency were used to develop and place ads and to help with brochures and other promotional materials. Almost all negotiations with the agency were handled by phone or mail. The amount of advertising done at any time depended on existing sales volume. As sales declined, advertising was increased; when orders approached plant capacity, advertising was curtailed. Magazines were the primary advertising medium. The dealers and agents were provided with attractive, professionally prepared brochures. The company had exhibited, or had plans to exhibit, at boat shows in Texas, Ohio, and Illinois. Arrangements had been completed for Pirogues to be used as prizes on one of the more popular network game shows.

A detailed analysis of sales, in terms of who was buying the boats and for what purpose, had not been made. However, Mr. Wadlington did know that one of the most successful ads was in *Better Homes and Gardens.* An examination of orders produced by the ad indicated that they were primarily from women who were buying the boat for family use. There had been reports of the boats being used as utility boats for large houseboats and yachts, but the extent of such use was unknown. Although orders had been coming in from all parts of the country, the best sales areas had been in the eastern and southeastern parts of the United States. Mr. Wadlington attributed this, at least in part, to the fact that the company's past sales efforts had been concentrated almost exclusively in the southern and southwestern areas of the country. After the company began using national media, totally new markets were tapped. The Pirogue had virtually no direct competition, particularly outside the Texas-Louisiana area.

*Questions*

1. Is Mr. Wadlington practicing the marketing concept? If not, which of the marketing philosophies does he follow?

2. What are the characteristics of the people who make up the market for the Electric Feather Pirogue? Describe the needs and wants that are satisfied by the product.

3. Mr. Wadlington seems to be opposed to changing his present marketing system. Apparently, he believes that his current plan is working because sales are strong and profits are satisfactory, and he would ask, "Why not stick with a winner?" How would you respond to Mr. Wadlington's assumptions?

4. What recommendations would you make to Mr. Wadlington if he wanted to adopt the marketing concept?

*Source:* This case was prepared by Robert H. Solomon and Janelle C. Ashley of Stephen F. Austin State University as a basis for class discussion. Used with permission.

# 2

# Strategic Planning and Marketing's Role in the Organization

## CHAPTER OBJECTIVES

**After reading this chapter you should be able to:**

1. Explain company-wide strategic planning and its four steps
2. Describe how companies develop mission statements and objectives
3. Explain how companies evaluate and develop their "business portfolios"
4. Explain marketing's role in strategic planning
5. Describe the marketing management process and the forces that influence it

**M**ost people think they know a lot about the Greyhound Corporation. Over the decades, Greyhound has become an American institution, with its buses cruising the nation's highways and connecting our cities and towns with convenient, inexpensive transportation. Surveys show that the venerable Greyhound name finishes second only to Coca-Cola in consumer-recognition tests. In fact, however, consumers know very little about Greyhound Corporation. For example, most people would be startled to learn that this company no longer operates buses in the U.S. In 1987, facing industry deregulation, a deteriorating market, rising costs, stiff airline competition, and severe labor problems, the company made a profound and wrenching decision: It sold Greyhound Lines, the business upon which its history and culture had been built. The bus line still operates under the "Greyhound" name, but the Greyhound Corporation no longer owns it.

What then, you may ask, *does* Greyhound Corporation do? The answer—lots of things, some familiar, some not. The sale of the bus line was just part of a sweeping program to restructure a struggling

Greyhound Corporation. In the early 1980s, following 20 years of poorly planned diversification, Greyhound management set out to turn its scattered collection of businesses into a leaner, more sharply focused, more profitable company. It sold off dozens of businesses which had poor growth potential or which no longer fit its growth strategy, ultimately shedding companies totaling $3 billion dollars in annual sales. Gone, among others, are its meatpacking operation, mortgage insurance unit, computer leasing company, knitting supplies business, and, of course, the bus line. At the same time, Greyhound adopted a strategy of "growth by design." Building on its trimmer, more clearly focused base, it expanded its remaining businesses through internal growth and careful acquisition.

Today, the Greyhound Corporation operates four major business groups—*consumer products, services, transportation manufacturing,* and *financial services.* Its *consumer products* group (contributing about 35 percent of total company revenues) markets many familiar brands, but few consumers would connect them with Greyhound. The best known include Dial, Tone, and Pure&Natural hand soaps, Armour Star canned meats, Lunch Bucket microwave meals, Purex laundry products, StaPuf fabric softener, Sno Bol toilet bowl cleaner, and Brillo scouring pads.

Greyhound's greatest recent growth has been in its *services* group, which now contributes about 45 percent of company revenues. It consists of such diverse businesses as Traveler's Express, the nation's largest issuer of money orders, Premier Cruise Lines, the "official cruise line of Walt Disney World," and Greyhound Food Management, which operates restaurants (including 38 Burger King franchises) and factory cafeterias. However, almost half of Greyhound's services revenues derive from businesses that serve airlines and air travelers. Greyhound Airport Services provides baggage handling, fueling, and other ground services to airlines; the recently acquired Dobbs food services prepares some 200,000 in-flight meals daily for more than 60 airlines and also operates restaurants, lounges, gift shops, newsstands, and duty-free shops at major airports and hotels.

Two other business groups provide Greyhound with smaller but still substantial revenues. Its *transportation manufacturing* group (about 11 percent of sales) is the country's largest bus producer and bus parts supplier. Greyhound recently expanded this group by purchasing General Motors' bus building and parts business. By contrast, Greyhound has recently scaled down and redirected its *financial services* business (about 9 percent of company revenues), selling off its computer leasing and mortgage insurance units and focusing on special market niches, mostly providing commercial and real estate financing for mid-size companies.

Thus, Greyhound isn't Greyhound buses anymore. Instead, it has been transformed into a modern, vigorous consumer products and services company. During the past several years, through a series of dramatic strategic planning actions, management has forged a new streamlined Greyhound Corporation—one better matched to its changing market opportunities. In fact, the company is even considering changing its name to better reflect its new direction and focus.

Although it has yet to fully meet its financial goals, most analysts believe that Greyhound is on the right track. But continuing to keep this large and diversified portfolio of businesses on track will be no easy task. Strategic planning is a never-ending process, and Greyhound management will continue to face many difficult questions. What new businesses should be added to the company and which old ones should be dropped? Which current businesses should receive more emphasis and which should be scaled back? How can management best position the company for success in its fast-changing environment? According to Greyhound Chairman John Teets, "No company can wholly [shape] the environment in which it will operate, but it *can* exploit circumstances, wringing from them the best alternatives and opportunities . . . The job of management always has been to see the company not as it is, but as it can grow to be. Change is inevitable, and management must guide the forces of change to create value for shareholders. At Greyhound, we believe in renewing the company day-by-day."[1]

All companies must look ahead and develop long-term strategies to meet the changing conditions in their industries. No one strategy is best for all companies. Each company must find the game plan that makes the most sense given its situation, opportunities, objectives, and resources. The hard task of selecting an overall company strategy for long-run survival and growth is called *strategic planning.*

Marketing plays an important role in strategic planning. It provides information and other inputs to help prepare the strategic plan. In turn, strategic planning defines marketing's role in the organization. Guided by the strategic plan, marketing works with other departments in the organization to achieve overall strategic objectives.

In this chapter, we will look first at the organization's overall strategic planning. Next, we will discuss marketing's role in the organization as it is defined by the overall strategic plan. Finally, we will look at the marketing management process—the process that marketers undertake to carry out their role in the organization.

# OVERVIEW OF PLANNING

## Benefits of Planning

Many companies operate without formal plans. In new companies, managers are so busy they often have no time for planning. In mature companies, many managers argue that they have done well without formal planning and that it therefore cannot be too important. They may resist taking the time to prepare a written plan. They may argue that the marketplace changes too fast for a plan to be useful—that it would end up collecting dust.

Yet, formal planning can yield many benefits. It encourages management to think ahead systematically and improves interactions between company executives. It forces the company to sharpen its objectives and policies, leads to better coordination of company efforts, and provides clearer performance standards for control. And the argument that planning is less useful in a fast-changing environment makes little sense. In fact, the opposite is true: Sound planning helps the company to anticipate and respond quickly to environmental changes and to better prepare for sudden developments.

## Kinds of Plans

Companies usually prepare annual plans, long-range plans, and strategic plans. The **annual plan** describes the current marketing situation, company objectives, the marketing strategy for the year, the action program, budgets, and controls. Top management approves this plan and uses it to coordinate marketing activities with production, finance, and other areas of the company.

The **long-range plan** describes the major factors and forces affecting the organization over the next several years. It includes long-term objectives, the major marketing strategies that will be used to attain them, and the resources required. This long-range plan is reviewed and updated each year so that the company always has a current long-range plan. For example, American Hospital Supply has a "rolling" five-year plan. Its annual plan is a detailed version of the first year of the long-range plan. Managers prepare a five-year plan for each product early in the year and an annual plan later in the year. The five-year plan is revised each year because the environment changes and planning assumptions need to be reviewed.

The company's annual and long-range plans deal with current businesses and how to keep them going. Management must also plan which businesses the company should stay in or drop and which new ones it should pursue. The environment is full of surprises, and management must design the company to withstand shocks. *Strategic planning* involves adapting the firm to take advantage of opportunities in its constantly changing environment.

**annual plan** A short-range marketing plan that describes company objectives, the current marketing situation, the marketing strategy for the year, the action program, budgets, and controls.

**long-range plan** A marketing plan that describes the major factors and forces affecting the organization over the next several years and outlines long-term objectives, major marketing strategies, and resources required.

**strategic planning** The process of developing and maintaining a strategic fit between the organization's goals and capabilities and its changing marketing opportunities.

# STRATEGIC PLANNING

Strategic planning sets the stage for the rest of the planning in the firm. We define **strategic planning** as the process of developing and maintaining a strategic fit between the organization's goals and capabilities and its changing marketing opportunities. It relies on developing a clear company mission, supporting objectives, a sound business portfolio, and coordinated functional strategies.

**mission statement** A statement of the organization's purpose—of what it wants to accomplish in the larger environment.

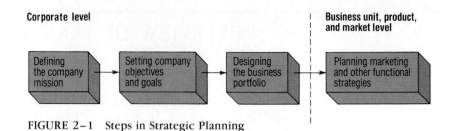

FIGURE 2-1   Steps in Strategic Planning

The steps in the strategic planning process are shown in Figure 2–1. At the corporate level, the company first defines its overall purpose and mission. This mission is then turned into detailed supporting objectives that guide the whole company. Next, headquarters decides what portfolio of businesses and products is best for the company and how much support to give each one. Each business and product unit must in turn develop detailed marketing and other departmental plans that support the company-wide plan. Thus, marketing planning occurs at the business-unit, product, and market levels. It supports company strategic planning with more detailed planning for specific marketing opportunities. We discuss each of the strategic planning steps in more detail below.

## Defining the Company Mission

An organization exists to accomplish something. At first, it has a clear purpose or mission, but over time its mission may become unclear as the organization grows and adds new products and markets. Or the mission may remain clear, but some managers may no longer be committed to it. Or the mission may remain clear but may no longer be the best choice given new conditions in the environment.

When management senses that the organization is drifting, it must renew its search for purpose. It is time to ask: What is our business? Who is the customer? What do consumers value? What will our business be? What should our business be? These simple-sounding questions are among the most difficult the company will ever have to answer. Successful companies continuously raise these questions and answer them carefully and completely.

Many organizations develop formal mission statements that answer these questions. A **mission statement** is a statement of the organization's purpose—what it wants to accomplish in the larger environment. A clear mission statement acts as an "invisible hand" that guides people in the organization so that they can work independently and yet collectively toward overall organizational goals.

Companies traditionally defined their business in product terms, such as "We manufacture furniture," or in technological terms, such as "We are a chemical-processing firm." But market definitions of a business are better than product or technological definitions. Products and technologies eventually become out-of-date, but basic market needs may last forever. A market-oriented mission statement defines the business in terms of satisfying basic customer needs. Thus, AT&T is in the communications business, not the telephone business. Visa defines its business not as credit cards, but as allowing customers to exchange value—to exchange such assets as cash on deposit or equity in a home for virtually anything, anywhere in the world. And Sears's mission is not to run department stores but to provide a wide range of products and services that deliver value to middle-class, home-owning American families.

Management should avoid making its mission too narrow or too broad. A lead pencil manufacturer that says it is in the communication equipment business is stating its mission too broadly. Mission statements should be specific

*Company mission: Visa defines its mission not as credit cards, but as allowing customers to exchange their assets for virtually anything, anywhere in the world.*

and realistic. Many mission statements are written for public relations purposes and lack specific, workable guidelines. The statement "We want to become the leading company in this industry by producing the highest-quality products with the best service at the lowest prices" sounds good but is full of generalities and contradictions. It will not help the company make tough decisions.[2]

## Setting Company Objectives and Goals

The company's mission needs to be turned into detailed supporting objectives for each level of management. Each manager should have objectives and be responsible for reaching them.

As an illustration, the International Minerals and Chemical Corporation is in many businesses, including the fertilizer business. The fertilizer division does not say that its mission is to produce fertilizer. Instead, it says that its mission is to "increase agricultural productivity." This mission leads to a hierarchy of objectives: business objectives, marketing objectives, and, finally, a marketing strategy (see Figure 2–2). The mission of increasing agricultural productivity leads to the company's business objective of researching new fertilizers that promise higher yields. But research is expensive and requires improved profits to plow back into research programs. So another major objective becomes "to improve profits." Profits can be improved by increasing sales or reducing costs. Sales can be increased by increasing the company's share of the U.S. market, by entering new foreign markets, or both. These goals become the company's current marketing objectives.

**business portfolio** The collection of businesses and products that make up the company.

**portfolio analysis** A tool by which management identifies and evaluates the various businesses that make up the company.

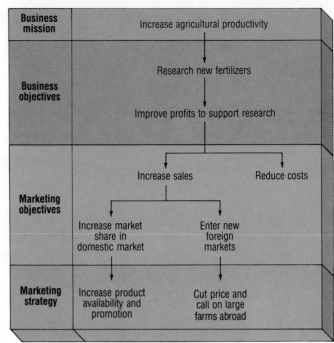

FIGURE 2–2
Hierarchy of Objectives for the International Minerals and Chemical Corporation, Fertilizer Division

Marketing strategies must be developed to support these marketing objectives. To increase its U.S. market share, the company may increase its product's availability and promotion. To enter new foreign markets, the company may cut prices and target large farms abroad. These are its broad marketing strategies.

Each marketing strategy will then have to be spelled out in greater detail. For example, increasing the product's promotion will call for more salespeople and more advertising, both of which will have to be spelled out. In this way, the firm's mission is translated into a set of objectives for the current period. The objectives should be as specific as possible. The objective to "increase our market share" is not as useful as the objective to "increase our market share to 15 percent by the end of the second year."

## Designing the Business Portfolio

Guided by the company's mission statement and objectives, management must now plan its business portfolio. A company's **business portfolio** is the collection of businesses and products that make up the company. The best business portfolio is the one that best fits the company's strengths and weaknesses to opportunities in the environment. The company must (1) analyze its *current* business portfolio and decide which businesses should receive more, less, or no investment, and (2) develop growth strategies for adding *new* products or businesses to the portfolio.

### Analyzing the Current Business Portfolio

The major tool in strategic planning is business **portfolio analysis,** whereby management evaluates the businesses making up the company. The company will want to put strong resources into its more profitable businesses and phase down or drop its weaker businesses. It can keep its portfolio of businesses up-to-date by withdrawing from declining businesses and strengthening or adding growing businesses. For example, in recent years, Kraft has strengthened its portfolio by selling off many less-attractive nonfood businesses while adding such promising ones as Lender's Bagel Bakery, Früsen Glädjé and

Charl's ice creams, Tombstone frozen pizza, and All-American Gourmet frozen foods.

Management's first step is to identify the key businesses making up the company. These can be called its strategic business units. A **strategic business unit (SBU)** is a unit of the company that has a separate mission and objectives and can be planned independently from other company businesses. An SBU can be a company division, a product line within a division, or sometimes a single product or brand.

Identifying SBUs can be difficult. In a large corporation, should SBUs be defined at the level of companies, divisions, product lines, or brands? At Greyhound, is the Consumer Products Division an SBU or is the Dial brand an SBU? Thus, defining basic business units for portfolio analysis is often a complex task.

The next step in business portfolio analysis calls for management to assess the attractiveness of its various SBUs and decide how much support each deserves. In some companies, this is done informally. Management looks at the company's collection of businesses or products and uses judgment to decide how much each SBU should contribute and receive. Other companies use formal portfolio-planning methods.

The purpose of strategic planning is to find ways in which the company can best use its strengths to take advantage of attractive opportunities in the environment. So most standard portfolio-analysis methods evaluate SBUs on two important dimensions—the attractiveness of the SBU's market or industry and the strength of the SBU's position in that market or industry. The best-known of these portfolio-planning methods was developed by the Boston Consulting Group, a leading management consulting firm.[3]

Using the Boston Consulting Group (BCG) approach, a company classifies all its SBUs in the **growth-share matrix** shown in Figure 2–3. On the vertical axis, *market-growth rate* provides a measure of market attractiveness. On the horizontal axis, *market share* serves as a measure of company strength in the market. By dividing the growth-share matrix in the way indicated, four types of SBUs can be distinguished:

- **Stars.** Stars are high-growth, high-share businesses or products. They often need heavy investment to finance their rapid growth. Eventually, their growth will slow down, and they will turn into cash cows.

**strategic business unit (SBU)** A unit of the company that has a separate mission and objectives and can be planned independently of other company businesses.

**growth-share matrix** A tool used in strategic planning to classify a company's strategic business units according to market-growth rate and market share.

**stars** High-growth, high-share businesses or products; they often require heavy investment to finance their rapid growth.

FIGURE 2–3   The BCG Growth-Share Matrix

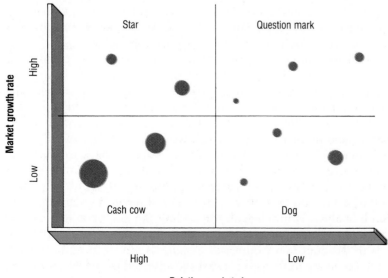

□ **Cash cows.** Cash cows are low-growth, high-share businesses or products. These established and successful SBUs need less investment to hold their market share. Thus, they produce a lot of cash that the company uses to pay its bills and support other SBUs that need investment.

□ **Question marks.** Question marks are low-share business units in high-growth markets. They require a lot of cash to hold their share, let alone increase it. Management has to think hard about which question marks it should try to build into stars and which should be phased out.

□ **Dogs.** Dogs are low-growth, low-share businesses and products. They may generate enough cash to maintain themselves but do not promise to be a large source of cash.

The ten circles in the growth-share matrix represent a company's ten current SBUs. The company has two stars, two cash cows, three question marks, and three dogs. The areas of each circle are proportional to the SBU's dollar sales. This company is in fair shape, although not in good shape. Fortunately, it has two good-sized cash cows whose income helps finance the company's question marks, stars, and dogs. The company should take some decisive action concerning its dogs and its question marks. The picture would be worse if the company had no stars, too many dogs, or only one weak cash cow.

Once it has classified its SBUs, the company must determine what role each will play in the future. One of four strategies can be pursued for each SBU. The company can invest more in the business unit in order to *build* its share. Or it can invest just enough to *hold* the SBU's share at the current level. Or it can *harvest* the SBU, increasing its short-term cash flow by investing little or nothing in it regardless of the long-term effect. Finally, the company can *divest* the SBU by selling it or phasing it out and using the resources elsewhere.

As time passes, SBUs change their position in the growth-share matrix. Each SBU evolves. Many SBUs start out as question marks and move into the star category if they succeed. They later become cash cows as market growth falls, then finally turn into dogs toward the end of their life cycles. The company needs to add new products and units continuously so that some of them will become stars and eventually cash cows to help finance its other SBUs.

The BCG and other formal methods developed in the 1970s revolutionized strategic planning. But such approaches have limitations. They can be difficult, time-consuming, and costly to implement. Management may find it difficult to define SBUs and measure market share and growth. In addition, these approaches focus on classifying *current* businesses but provide little advice for *future* planning. Management must still rely on its own judgment to set the business objectives for each SBU, to decide what resources each will be given, and to figure out which new businesses should be added.

Formal approaches can also lead the company to place too much emphasis on market-share growth or growth through entry into attractive new markets. Using these approaches, many companies plunged into unrelated and new high-growth businesses that they did not know how to manage—with very bad results. At the same time, they were often too quick to abandon, sell, or milk to death their healthy mature businesses. Despite these and other problems, and although many companies have dropped formal matrix methods in favor of more-customized approaches better suited to their situations, most companies remain firmly committed to strategic planning. Roughly 75 percent of the *Fortune* 500 companies practice some form of portfolio planning.[4]

Such analysis is no cure-all for finding the best strategy. But it can help management to understand the company's overall situation, to see how each business or product contributes, to assign resources to its businesses, and to orient the company for future success. When used properly, strategic planning is just one important aspect of overall strategic management, a way of thinking about how to manage a business.[5]

## Developing Growth Strategies

Beyond evaluating current businesses, designing the business portfolio involves finding future businesses and products the company should consider. One useful device for identifying growth opportunities is the *product/market expansion grid*.[6] This grid is shown in Figure 2–4. Below, we apply it to Kraft.

*Market Penetration* ▪ First, Kraft management might consider whether the company's major brands can achieve deeper **market penetration**—making more sales to present customers without changing products in any way. For example, to increase its dairycase sales, Kraft might cut prices, increase advertising, get its products into more stores, or obtain better shelf positions for them. Basically, Kraft management would like to increase usage by current customers and attract customers of other brands to Kraft.

*Market Development* ▪ Second, Kraft management might consider possibilities for **market development**—identifying and developing new markets for current products. For example, managers at Kraft could review *demographic markets*—infants, preschoolers, teen-agers, young adults, senior citizens—to see if any of these groups could be encouraged to buy or buy more Kraft products. The managers could also look at *institutional markets*—restaurants, food services, hospitals—to see if sales to these buyers could be increased. And managers could review *geographical markets*—France, Thailand, India—to see if these markets could be developed. All these are market-development strategies.

*Product Development* ▪ Third, management could consider **product development**—offering modified or new products to current markets. Kraft products could be offered in new sizes, with new ingredients, or in new packaging—all representing possible product modifications. Kraft could also launch new brands to appeal to different users, or it could launch other food products that its current customers might buy. All of these are product-development strategies.

*Diversification* ▪ Fourth, Kraft might consider **diversification**. It could start up or buy businesses entirely outside of its current products and markets. For example, the company's recent moves into such "hot" industries as fitness equipment, health foods, and frozen foods represent diversification. Some companies try to identify the most attractive emerging industries. They feel that half the secret of success is to enter attractive industries instead of trying to be efficient in an unattractive industry. But many companies that diversified too

**market development** A strategy for company growth by identifying and developing new market segments for current company products.

**market penetration** A strategy for company growth by increasing sales of current products to current market segments without changing the product in any way.

**product development** A strategy for company growth by offering modified or new products to current market segments.

**diversification** A strategy for company growth by starting up or acquiring businesses outside the company's current products and markets.

FIGURE 2–4  Market Opportunity Identification through the Product/Market Expansion Grid

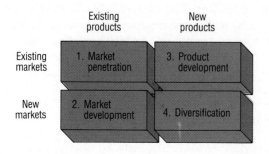

*Market penetration and market development: Arm & Hammer increases market penetration by suggesting new uses; Jockey develops a new market—women.*

broadly in the 1960s and 1970s are now narrowing their market focus and getting back to the basics of serving one or a few industries that they know best (see Marketing Highlight 2–1).

## Planning Functional Strategies

The company's strategic plan establishes what kinds of businesses the company will be in and its objectives for each. Then, more detailed planning must take place within each business unit. Each functional department—marketing, finance, accounting, purchasing, manufacturing, personnel, and others—plays an important role in the strategic-planning process. First, each department provides information for strategic planning. Then, management in each business unit prepares a plan that states the role that each department will play. The plan shows how all the functional areas will work together to accomplish strategic objectives.

Each functional department deals with different publics to obtain inputs the business needs—inputs such as cash, labor, raw materials, research ideas, and manufacturing processes. For example, marketing brings in revenues by negotiating exchanges with consumers. Finance arranges exchanges with lenders and stockholders to obtain cash. Thus, the marketing and finance departments must work together to obtain needed funds for the business. Similarly, the personnel department supplies labor, and purchasing obtains materials needed for operations and manufacturing.

### Marketing's Role in Strategic Planning

There is much overlap between overall company strategy and marketing strategy. Marketing looks at consumer needs and the company's ability to satisfy

## Marketing Highlight 2–1

## AMERICAN BUSINESS GETS BACK TO THE BASICS

During the 1960s and 1970s, strategic planners in many American companies got expansion fever. It seemed that everyone wanted to get bigger and grow faster by broadening their business portfolios. Companies milked their stodgy but profitable core businesses to get the cash needed to acquire glamorous, faster-growing businesses in more attractive industries. It didn't seem to matter that many of the acquired businesses fit poorly with old ones, or that they operated in markets unfamiliar to company management.

Thus, many firms exploded into huge conglomerates, sometimes containing hundreds of unrelated products and businesses operating in a dozen diverse industries. Managing these "smorgasbord" portfolios often proved difficult. Conglomerate managers soon learned that it was tough to run businesses in industries they knew little about. Many newly acquired businesses bogged down under added layers of corporate management and increased administrative costs. Meanwhile, the profitable core businesses that had financed the acquisitions withered from lack of investment and management attention.

By the mid-1980s, as attempt after attempt at scatter-gun diversification foundered, acquisition fever gave way to a new philosophy—getting back to the basics. The new trend has many names—"narrowing the focus," "sticking to your knitting," "the contraction craze," "the urge to purge." They all mean narrowing the company's market focus and getting the firm back to the basics of serving one or a few core industries that it knows best. The company sheds businesses that don't fit its narrowed focus and rebuilds by concentrating resources on other businesses that do. The result is a smaller but more-focused company, a more muscular firm serving fewer markets but serving them much better.

Today, companies in all industries are getting back in focus and shedding unrelated operations. According to one survey, 56 percent of all *Fortune* 500 companies have begun the slimming-down process during the last five years. Some companies have taken drastic steps. For example, during the 1970s huge Gulf & Western acquired businesses in dozens of diverse industries ranging from auto products and industrial equipment to apparel and furniture, from cement and cigars to racetracks and video games. But since 1983, it has focused on entertainment, information, and financial services, purging the company of over 50 operations that made up nearly half its sales. Similarly, ITT, after diversifying wildly during the 1960s and 1970s, is divesting $1.7 billion worth of businesses that don't fit its new focus.

Several food companies have also made strong moves back to the bread-and-butter basics. Quaker Oats sold off its specialty retailing businesses—Jos. A. Banks (clothing), Brookstone (tools), and Eyelab (optical)—and will probably sell its profitable Fisher-Price toy operation. It used the proceeds to strengthen current food brands and to acquire the Golden Grain Macaroni Company (Rice-a-Roni and Noodle-a-Roni) and Gaines Foods (pet foods), whose products strongly complement Quaker's. General Mills ended 20 years of diversification by lopping off most of its nonfood businesses and moving back to the kitchen. It sold such companies as Izod (fashions), Monet (jewelry), Parker Brothers (games), Kenner (toys), and Eddie Bauer and Talbots (specialty retailers) while increasing investment in its basic consumer food brands (Wheaties and other cereals, Betty Crocker cake mixes, Gorton's seafoods, Gold Medal flour) and restaurants (Red Lobster, Darryl's).

These and other companies have concluded that bigger is not always better and that fast-growing businesses in attractive industries are not good investments if they spread the company's resources too thin or if the company's managers can't run them properly. They have learned that a company without market focus—one that tries to serve too many diverse markets—might end up serving few markets well.

Sources: See Thomas Moore, "Old-Line Industry Shapes Up," *Fortune*, April 27, 1987, pp. 23–32; David Lieberman and Joe Weber, "Gulf & Western: From Grab Bag to Lean, Mean, Marketing Machine," *Business Week*, September 14, 1987, pp. 152–56; and Walter Kiechel III, "Corporate Strategy for the 1990s," *Fortune*, February 29, 1988, pp. 34–42.

them; these same factors guide the company mission and objectives. Most company strategy planning deals with marketing variables—market share, market development, growth—and it is sometimes hard to separate strategic planning from marketing planning. In fact, in some companies, strategic planning is called "strategic marketing planning."

Marketing plays a key role in the company's strategic planning in several ways. First, marketing provides a guiding *philosophy*—company strategy should revolve around serving the needs of important consumer groups. Second, marketing provides *inputs* to strategic planners by helping to identify attractive market opportunities and to assess the firm's potential for taking advantage of them. Finally, within individual business units marketing designs *strategies* for reaching the unit's objectives.[7]

Within each business unit, marketing management must figure out the best way it can help to achieve strategic objectives. Some marketing managers will find that their objective is not necessarily to build sales. It may be to hold existing sales with a smaller marketing budget, or it may actually be to reduce demand. Thus, marketing management must manage demand to the level decided upon by the strategic planning prepared at headquarters. Marketing helps to assess each business unit's potential, but once the unit's objective is set, marketing's task is to carry it out profitably.

### Marketing and the Other Business Functions

There is much confusion about marketing's importance in the firm. In some firms, it is just another function—all functions count in the company and none takes leadership. This view is illustrated in Figure 2–5A. If the company faces slow growth or a sales decline, marketing may temporarily become more important (Figure 2–5B).

Some marketers claim that marketing is the major function of the firm. They quote Drucker's statement: "The aim of the business is to create customers." They say it is marketing's job to define the company's mission, products, and markets and to direct the other functions in the task of serving customers (Figure 2–5C).

More-enlightened marketers prefer to put the customer at the center of the company. They argue that all functions should work together to sense, serve, and satisfy the customer (Figure 2–5D).

Finally, some marketers say that marketing still needs to be in a central position to be certain that customers' needs are understood and satisfied (Figure 2–5E). These marketers argue that the firm cannot succeed without customers, so the key task is to attract and hold customers. Customers are attracted by promises and held through satisfaction, and marketing defines the promise and

FIGURE 2–5   Alternative Views of Marketing's Role in the Company

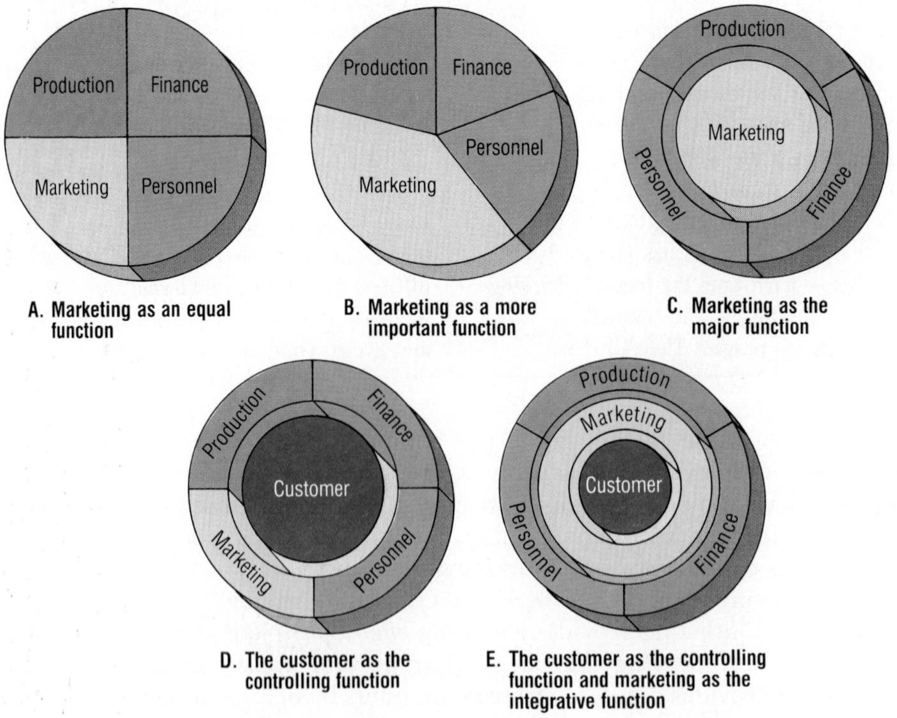

A. Marketing as an equal
   function

B. Marketing as a more
   important function

C. Marketing as the
   major function

D. The customer as the
   controlling function

E. The customer as the controlling
   function and marketing as the
   integrative function

ensures its delivery. But because actual consumer satisfaction is affected by the performance of other departments, marketing must play an integrative role to help ensure that all departments work together toward consumer satisfaction.

## Conflict between Departments

Each business function has a different view of which publics and activities are most important. Manufacturing focuses on suppliers and production; finance is concerned with stockholders and sound investment; marketing emphasizes consumers and products, pricing, promotion, and distribution. Ideally, all the functions should blend to reach the firm's overall objectives. But in practice, departmental relations are full of conflicts and misunderstandings. Some conflict results from differences of opinion as to what is in the best interest of the firm. Some results from real trade-offs between departmental well-being and company well-being. And some conflict results from unfortunate departmental stereotypes and biases.

Under the marketing concept, the company wants to blend all the different functions toward consumer satisfaction. The marketing department takes the consumer's point of view. But other departments stress the importance of their own tasks, and they may resist bending their efforts to the will of the marketing department. Because departments tend to define company problems and goals from their own points of view, conflicts are inevitable. Table 2–1 shows the main point-of-view differences between marketing and other departments.

TABLE 2–1   Point-of-View Differences between Marketing and Other Departments

| Department | Emphasis | Marketing Emphasis |
|---|---|---|
| R&D | Basic research | Applied research |
| | Intrinsic quality | Perceived quality |
| | Functional features | Sales features |
| Engineering | Long design lead time | Short design lead time |
| | Few models | Many models |
| | Standard components | Custom components |
| Purchasing | Narrow product line | Broad product line |
| | Standard parts | Nonstandard parts |
| | Price of material | Quality of material |
| | Economical lot sizes | Large lot sizes to avoid stockouts |
| | Purchasing at infrequent intervals | Immediate purchasing for customer needs |
| Manufacturing | Long production lead time | Short production lead time |
| | Long runs with few models | Short runs with many models |
| | No model changes | Frequent model changes |
| | Standard orders | Custom orders |
| | Ease of fabrication | Appearance |
| | Average quality control | Tight quality control |
| Inventory | Fast-moving items, narrow product line | Broad product line |
| | Economical level of stock | High level of stock |
| Finance | Strict rationales for spending | Intuitive arguments for spending |
| | Hard-and-fast budgets | Flexible budgets to meet changing needs |
| | Pricing to cover costs | Pricing to further market development |
| Accounting | Standard transactions | Special terms and discounts |
| | Few reports | Many reports |
| Credit | Full financial disclosures by customers | Minimum credit examination of customers |
| | Low credit risks | Medium credit risks |
| | Tough credit terms | Easy credit terms |
| | Tough collection procedures | Easy collection procedures |

This is the promise
no other major hotel chain makes.
A promise of hospitality
from the people of Holiday Inn.
We promise that
throughout your entire stay,
we will meet the high standards
you expect from Holiday Inn hotels.
And if ever anything isn't right, tell us.

We promise to make it right.
Because we won't make you pay
for unsatisfactory service.
The Holiday Inn Hospitality Promise.
It's a promise we keep.
For one simple reason.

**We want you back.**

*Holiday Inns recognizes that all of the company's people must work to sense, serve, and satisfy customer needs.*

When marketing tries to develop customer satisfaction, it often causes other departments to do a poorer job *in their terms*. Marketing department actions can increase purchasing costs, disrupt production schedules, increase inventories, and create budget headaches. Yet marketers must get all departments to "think consumer," to look through the customer's eyes, and to put the consumer at the center of company activity.

Marketing management can best gain support for its goal of consumer satisfaction by working to understand the company's other departments. Marketing managers must work closely with managers of other functions to develop a system of functional plans under which the different departments can work together to accomplish the company's overall strategic objectives.[8]

# THE MARKETING MANAGEMENT PROCESS

The strategic plan defines the company's overall mission and objectives. Within each business unit, marketing plays a role in helping to accomplish overall strategic objectives. Marketing's role and activities in the organization are shown in Figure 2–6, which summarizes the entire *marketing management process* and the forces influencing company marketing strategy.

Target consumers stand in the center. The company identifies the total market, divides it into smaller segments, selects the most-promising segments, and focuses on serving and satisfying these segments. It designs a marketing mix made up of factors under its control—product, price, place, and promotion. To find the best marketing mix and put it into action, the company engages in marketing analysis, planning, implementation, and control. Through these activities, the company watches and adapts to the marketing environment. We will now look briefly at each factor in the marketing management process. In later chapters, we will discuss each factor in more depth.

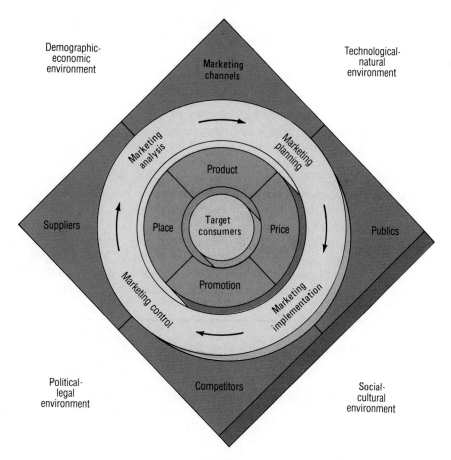

**FIGURE 2–6** Factors Influencing Company Marketing Strategy

## Target Consumers

Sound marketing requires a careful analysis of consumers. Suppose a company is looking at possible markets for a potential new product. The company first needs to make a careful estimate of the current and future size of the market and its various segments. To estimate current market size, the company would identify all competing products, estimate their current sales, and determine whether the market is large enough.

Equally important is future market growth. Companies want to enter markets that show strong growth prospects. Growth potential may depend on the growth rate of certain age, income, and nationality groups that use the product more than others. Growth may also be related to larger developments in the environment, such as economic conditions, advances in technology, and life-style changes. For example, the future market for quality children's toys and clothing is strongly related to current birthrates, trends in consumer affluence, and projected family life styles. **Forecasting**—predicting what consumers are likely to do under a given set of conditions—is difficult, but it must be performed in order to make a decision about the market. The company's marketing information specialists will probably use complex techniques to measure and forecast demand.

Suppose the forecast looks good. The company now has to decide *how* to enter the market. Companies know that they cannot satisfy all consumers in a given market—at least not all consumers in the same way. There are too many different kinds of consumers with too many different kinds of needs. And some companies are in a better position to serve certain segments of the market. Thus, each company must divide up the total market, choose the best segments,

**market segmentation** The process of classifying customers into groups with different needs, characteristics, or behaviors.

**market segment** A group of consumers who respond in a similar way to a given set of marketing stimuli.

and design strategies for profitably serving chosen segments better than its competitors. This process involves three steps: *market segmentation, market targeting,* and *market positioning.*

### Market Segmentation

The market consists of many types of customers, products, and needs, and the marketer has to determine which segments offer the best chance in which to achieve company objectives. Consumers can be grouped in various ways based on geographic factors (regions, cities), demographic factors (sex, age, income, education), psychographic factors (social classes, life styles), and behavioral factors (purchase occasions, benefits sought, usage rates). The process of classifying customers into groups with different needs, characteristics, or behaviors is called **market segmentation.**

Every market is made up of market segments, but not all ways of segmenting the market are equally useful. For example, Tylenol would gain little by distinguishing between male and female users of pain relievers if both respond the same way to marketing stimuli. A **market segment** consists of

# Marketing Highlight 2-2

## MARKET SEGMENTATION AND TARGETING: "DESIGNER TRUCKS" BY OSHKOSH

Have you ever heard of the Oshkosh Truck Corporation? Perhaps not. But chances are good that you've seen some Oshkosh trucks around without realizing it. Oshkosh is the world's largest producer of crash, fire, and rescue trucks for airports. It also makes those "forward placement" concrete carriers—the ones that pour conveniently from the front but look as though they were put together backwards. In an environment where large, diversified truck manufacturers are having trouble, the smaller and more-focused Oshkosh is thriving. The reason: smart market

segmentation and targeting.

Oshkosh produces specialized heavy-duty trucks for customers who need unique, innovative designs for specific uses in adverse operating conditions. "Oshkosh is to trucks what Armani is to clothes. It builds designer trucks: heavy-duty, off-road, all-wheel drive, frequently custom-designed vehicles that sell for anywhere from $36,000 to $750,000." Until the early 1980s, Oshkosh focused on special municipal and commercial segments with its unique concrete carriers and crash, fire, and

rescue vehicles. But then, in 1981, it added a new target—the U.S. military. It began with a contract for 2,450 Heavy Expanded Mobility Tactical Trucks (HEMTT). The $120,000 HEMTT, an eight-wheel drive, all-terrain vehicle that carries up to 11 tons, quickly won the respect of military users and buyers. Since 1982, Oshkosh's defense business has soared, with contracts totaling more than $1.5 billion. Military orders now account for 84 percent of total Oshkosh sales.

Oshkosh's focused segmentation and targeting strategy has produced

*Oshkosh Trucking specializes in "designer trucks" for use in adverse operating conditions.*

consumers who respond in a similar way to a given set of marketing stimuli. In the car market, for example, consumers who choose the biggest, most comfortable car regardless of price make up one market segment. Another market segment would be customers who care mainly about price and operating economy. It would be difficult to make one model of car that was the first choice of every consumer. Companies are wise to focus their efforts on meeting the distinct needs of one or more market segments. They should study the geographic, demographic, behavioral, and other characteristics of each market segment to evaluate its attractiveness as a marketing opportunity.

**market targeting** The process of evaluating each market segment's attractiveness and selecting one or more segments to enter.

## Market Targeting

After a company has defined market segments, it can enter one or many segments of a given market. **Market targeting** involves evaluating each market segment's attractiveness and selecting one or more segments to enter. A company with limited resources might decide to serve only one or a few special segments. This strategy limits sales but can be very profitable (see Marketing Highlight 2–2). Or a company might choose to serve several related segments—

spectacular sales and profit results. The company's sales jumped from $72 million in 1981 to over $400 million by 1987. Over the last five years, profits have grown an average 64 percent per year; return on equity last year reached 38 percent. In fact, Oshkosh has been so successful that numerous competitors have begun to invade its snug specialty truck niche, hoping to share in the sumptuous returns.

With competition increasing rapidly in current segments, Oshkosh is developing new ones. For example, it's targeting municipal markets with new crash, fire, and rescue vehicles modified for emergency snow removal. And Oshkosh is working to establish itself in international specialty truck segments. "It built a set of powerful low-gear trucks to haul a 3,000-ton Saudi desalinization plant from the sea to the sands miles inland. For a Brazilian job, it created another set of monsters to carry 18 massive turbine generators, each weighing in at over six million pounds, at three miles an hour for 90 days"—a feat that won Oshkosh a mention in *The Guiness Book of World Records*. Such projects testify to the company's versatility in meeting the needs of the special segments it serves. Says one Oshkosh executive, "We can build [a vehicle] in volumes of as low as one and as high as a thousand and still make money on it."

Thus, Oshkosh has built a strong position in a number of small, highly specialized market segments. Compared with truck industry giants such as General Motors, Ford, and Navistar, Oshkosh is a fairly small operator. But it is faster-growing and more profitable than its larger, less-focused competitors. And in its designer-truck segments, Oshkosh is the major player. Through smart market segmentation and targeting, Oshkosh has proved that small can be beautiful.

Sources: See Stuart Gannes, "The Riches in Market Niches," *Fortune*, April 27, 1987, p. 228. Extracts from Jagannath Dubashi, "Designer Trucks," *Financial World*, May 19, 1987, pp. 35-36.

**market positioning** Arranging for a product to occupy a clear, distinctive, and desirable place relative to competing products in the minds of target consumers.

perhaps those that have different kinds of customers but with the same basic wants. Or a large company might decide to offer a complete range of products to serve all market segments.

Most companies enter a new market by serving a single segment, and if this proves successful, they add segments. Large companies eventually seek full market coverage. They want to be the "General Motors" of their industry. GM says that it makes a car for every "person, purse, and personality." The leading company normally has different products designed to meet the special needs of each segment.

### Market Positioning

Once a company has decided which market segments to enter, it must decide what "positions" it wants to occupy in those segments. A product's *position* is the place the product occupies in consumers' minds relative to competitors. If a product is perceived to be exactly like another product on the market, consumers will have no reason to buy it.

**Market positioning** is arranging for a product to occupy a clear, distinctive, and desirable place relative to competing products in the minds of target consumers. Thus, marketers plan positions that distinguish their products from competing products and give them the greatest strategic advantage in their target markets. For example, the Hyundai automobile is positioned on low price as "the car that makes sense." Chrysler offers "the best-built, best-backed American cars"; Pontiac says "we build excitement"; and at Ford, "quality is job one." Jaguar is positioned as "a blending of art and machine," while Saab is "the most intelligent car ever built." Mercedes is "engineered like no other car in the world"; the luxurious Bentley is "the closest a car can come to having wings." Such deceptively simple statements form the backbone of a product's marketing strategy.

*Positioning: Here Embassy Suites positions itself on price/value with "You don't have to be a fat cat to enjoy the Suite Life." Alternatively, Westin Hotels and Resorts positions itself as "caring, comfortable, and civilized."*

To plan a product's position, the company first identifies the existing positions of all the products and brands currently serving its market segments. It next figures out what consumers want with respect to major product attributes. The company then selects a position based on its product's ability to satisfy consumer wants better than competitors' products. Finally, it develops a marketing program that communicates and delivers the product's position to target consumers.

**marketing mix** The set of controllable marketing variables that the firm blends to produce the response it wants in the target market.

## Developing the Marketing Mix

Once the company has decided on its positioning strategy, it is ready to begin planning the details of the marketing mix. The marketing mix is one of the major concepts in modern marketing. We define the **marketing mix** as the set of controllable marketing variables that the firm blends to produce the response it wants in the target market. The marketing mix consists of everything the firm can do to influence the demand for its product. The many possibilities can be collected into four groups of variables known as "the four *P*'s": *product, price, place,* and *promotion.*[9] The particular marketing variables under each *P* are shown in Figure 2–7.

*Product* stands for the "goods-and-service" combination the company offers to the target market. Thus, a Ford Taurus "product" consists of nuts and bolts, spark plugs, pistons, headlights, and thousands of other parts. Ford offers several Taurus styles and dozens of optional features. The car comes fully serviced and with a comprehensive warranty that is as much a part of the product as the tailpipe.

*Price* stands for the amount of money customers have to pay to obtain the product. Ford calculates suggested retail prices that its dealers might charge for each Taurus. But Ford dealers rarely charge the full sticker price. Instead, they negotiate the price with each customer, offering discounts, trade-in allowances, and credit terms to adjust for the current competitive situation and to bring the price into line with the buyer's perceptions of the car's value.

*Place* stands for company activities that make the product available to target consumers. Ford maintains a large body of independently owned dealerships that sell the company's many different models. Ford selects its dealers carefully and supports them strongly. The dealers keep an inventory of

FIGURE 2–7   The Four *P*'s of the Marketing Mix

Ford automobiles, demonstrate them to potential buyers, negotiate prices, close sales, and service cars after the sale.

*Promotion* stands for activities that communicate the merits of the product and persuade target customers to buy it. Ford spends more than $600 million each year on advertising to tell consumers about the company and its products. Dealership salespeople assist potential buyers and persuade them that Ford is the best car for them. Ford and its dealers offer special promotions—sales, cash rebates, low-financing rates—as added purchase incentives.

An effective marketing program blends all the marketing mix elements into a coordinated program designed to achieve the company's marketing objectives.[10]

## Managing the Marketing Effort

The company wants to design and put into action the marketing mix that will best achieve its objectives in its target markets. This involves four marketing management functions—*analysis, planning, implementation*, and *control*. These functions are discussed briefly below and more fully in Chapter 3.

### Marketing Analysis

Managing the marketing function begins with a complete analysis of the company's situation. The company must analyze its markets and marketing environment to find attractive opportunities and to avoid environmental threats. It must analyze company strengths and weaknesses, as well as current and possible marketing actions, to determine which opportunities it can best pursue. Marketing analysis feeds information and other inputs to each of the other marketing management functions.

### Marketing Planning

Through strategic planning, the company decides what it wants to do with each business unit. Marketing planning involves deciding on marketing strategies that will help the company attain its overall strategic objectives. A detailed marketing plan is needed for each business, product, or brand. For example, suppose Helene Curtis decides that its Suave shampoo should be built further because of its strong growth potential. Then the Suave brand manager will develop a marketing plan to carry out Suave's growth objective.

### Marketing Implementation

Good marketing analysis and planning are only a start toward successful company performance—the marketing plans must be carefully implemented. It is often easier to design good marketing strategies than put them into action.

People at all levels of the marketing system must work together to implement marketing strategy and plans. People in marketing must work closely with people in finance, purchasing, manufacturing, and other company departments. And many outside people and organizations must help with implementation—suppliers, resellers, advertising agencies, research firms, the advertising media. All must work together effectively to implement the marketing program.

The implementation process consists of five elements—*action programs*, the company's *organization structure, decision and reward systems, human resources*, and company *climate and culture*. To implement its marketing plans and strategies successfully, the company must blend these elements into a cohesive program. We will discuss these elements more fully in Chapter 3.

## Marketing Control

Many surprises are likely to occur as marketing plans are being implemented. The company needs control procedures to make certain that its objectives will be achieved. Companies want to make sure that they are achieving the sales, profits, and other goals set in their annual plans. This control involves measuring ongoing market performance, determining the causes of any serious gaps in performance, and deciding on the best corrective action to take to close the gaps. Corrective action may call for improving the ways in which the plan is being implemented or even changing the goals.

Companies should also stand back from time to time and look at their overall approach to the marketplace. The purpose is to make certain that the company's objectives, policies, strategies, and programs remain appropriate in the face of rapid environmental changes. Giant companies such as Chrysler, International Harvester, Singer, and A&P all fell on hard times because they did not watch the changing marketplace and make the proper adaptations. A major tool used for such strategic control is the *marketing audit,* which is described in Chapter 3.

## The Marketing Environment

Managing the marketing function would be hard enough if the marketer had to deal only with the controllable marketing mix variables. But the company operates in a complex marketing environment, consisting of uncontrollable forces to which the company must adapt. The environment produces both threats and opportunities. The company must carefully analyze its environment so that it can avoid the threats and take advantage of the opportunities.

Companies may think that they have few opportunities, but this is only a failure to think strategically about what business they are in and what strengths

*Reacting to the environment through analysis, planning, implementation, and control: according to Greyhound management, no company can completely shape its environment, but it can exploit the circumstances, wringing the best opportunities from them.*

they have. Every company faces many opportunities. Companies can search for new opportunities either casually or systematically. Many companies find new ideas by simply keeping their eyes and ears open to the changing marketplace. Other organizations use formal methods for analyzing the marketing environment.

Not all opportunities are right for the company. A marketing opportunity must fit the company's objectives and resources. Thus, personal computers may be an attractive industry, but not for every company. For example, we sense that personal computers would not be right for McDonald's. McDonald's seeks a high level of sales, growth, and profits from the fast-food business. And even though McDonald's has large resources, it lacks the technical know-how, industrial marketing experience, and special distribution channels needed to sell personal computers successfully.

The company's marketing environment includes forces close to the company that affect its ability to serve its consumers, such as other company departments, channel members, suppliers, competitors, and publics. It also includes broader demographic/economic forces, political/legal forces, technological/ecological forces, and social/cultural forces. The company must consider all of these forces when developing and positioning its offer to the target market. The marketing environment is discussed more fully in Chapter 5.

## ■ SUMMARY

*Strategic planning* involves developing a strategy for long-run survival and growth. Marketing helps in strategic planning, and the overall strategic plan defines marketing's role in the company. Marketers undertake the marketing management process to carry out their role in the organization.

Not all companies use formal planning or use it well. Yet formal planning offers several benefits, including systematic thinking, better coordination of company efforts, sharper objectives, and improved performance measurement, all of which can lead to improved sales and profits. Companies develop three kinds of plans—*annual plans, long-range plans,* and *strategic plans*.

Strategic planning sets the stage for the rest of company planning. The strategic planning process consists of developing the company's mission, objectives and goals, business portfolio, and functional plans.

Developing a sound *mission statement* is a challenging undertaking. The mission statement should be market-oriented, feasible, motivating, and specific if it is to direct the firm to its best opportunities. The mission statement then leads to supporting objectives and goals.

From here, strategic planning calls for analyzing the company's *business portfolio* and deciding which businesses should receive more or less resources. The company might use a formal portfolio-planning method such as the *BCG growth-share matrix*. But most companies are now designing more-customized portfolio-planning approaches that better suit their unique situations.

Beyond evaluating current *strategic business units*, management must plan for growth into new businesses and products. The *product-market expansion grid* shows four avenues for

growth. *Market penetration* involves generating more sales of current products to current customers. *Market development* involves identifying new markets for current products. *Product development* involves offering new or modified products to current markets. Finally, *diversification* involves starting businesses entirely outside current products and markets.

Each of the company's *functional departments* provides inputs for strategic planning. Once strategic objectives have been defined, management within each business must prepare a set of *functional plans* that coordinates the activities of the marketing, finance, manufacturing, and other departments. Each department has a different idea about which objectives and activities are most important. The marketing department stresses the consumer's point of view. Other functions stress different things, and this fact may generate conflict between departments. Marketing managers must understand the points of view of the company's other functions and work with other functional managers to develop a system of plans that will best accomplish the firm's overall strategic objectives.

To fulfill their role in the organization, marketers engage in the *marketing management process*. Consumers are at the center of the marketing management process. The company divides the total market into smaller segments and selects the segments it can best serve. It then designs its *marketing mix* to attract and satisfy these *target segments*. To find the best mix and put it into action, the company engages in marketing analysis, marketing planning, marketing implementation, and marketing control. Through these activities, the company watches and adapts to the marketing environment.

# QUESTIONS FOR DISCUSSION

1. What are the benefits of a "rolling" five-year plan—in other words, why should managers write five-year plans that will be changed every year?

2. In a series of job interviews, you ask three recruiters to describe the missions of their companies. One says, "To make profits." Another says, "To create customers." The third says, "To fight world hunger." What do these mission statements tell you about each company?

3. Choose a local radio station and describe what its apparent mission, objectives, and strategies are. What other things can the station do to accomplish its mission?

4. An electronics manufacturer obtains semiconductors from a company-owned subsidiary that also sells to other manufacturers. The subsidiary is smaller and less profitable than competing producers, and its growth rate has been below the industry average for five years. Into what cell of the BCG growth-share matrix does this strategic business unit fall? What should the parent company do with this SBU?

5. What market opportunities has Pizza Hut pursued in each of the four cells of the product/market expansion grid? What future opportunities would you suggest to Pizza Hut?

6. As companies become more customer- and marketing-oriented, many departments find that they must change traditional ways of doing things. How can a company's finance, accounting, and engineering departments help it become more marketing-oriented? Give examples.

7. How can organizations forecast what consumers are likely to do in the future? Choose a recently released movie or record and forecast its success. How much confidence do you have in your prediction?

8. Assume you want to start a business after graduation. What, for example, is the opportunity for a new music store selling records, tapes, and compact discs in your town? Briefly describe your target market or markets and the marketing mix you would develop for your store.

# REFERENCES

1. See Marc Beauchamp, "Under the Gun," *Forbes,* June 13, 1988, pp. 90–92; and Stewart Toy, "Can Greyhound Leave the Dog Days Behind?" *Business Week,* June 8, 1987, pp. 72–74.

2. For more on mission statements, see David A. Aaker, *Strategic Market Management,* 2nd ed. (New York: John Wiley, 1988), Chap. 3; and Laura Nash, "Mission Statements—Mirrors and Windows," *Harvard Business Review,* March-April 1988, pp. 155–56.

3. For additional reading on this and other portfolio analysis approaches, see Philippe Haspeslagh, "Portfolio Planning: Limits and Uses," *Harvard Business Review,* January-February 1982, pp. 58–73; Yoram Wind, Vijay Mahajan, and Donald J. Swire, "An Empirical Comparison of Standardized Portfolio Models," *Journal of Marketing,* Spring 1983, pp. 89–99; and Aaker, *Strategic Market Management,* Chap. 10.

4. Richard G. Hamermesh, "Making Planning Strategic," *Harvard Business Review,* July-August 1986, pp. 115–20.

5. See Daniel H. Gray, "Uses and Misuses of Strategic Planning," *Harvard Business Review,* January-February 1986, pp. 89–96.

6. H. Igor Ansoff, "Strategies for Diversification," *Harvard Business Review,* September-October 1957, pp. 113–24.

7. For more reading on marketing's role, see Paul F. Anderson, "Marketing, Strategic Planning and the Theory of the Firm," *Journal of Marketing,* Spring 1982, pp. 15–26; and Yoram Wind and Thomas S. Robertson, "Marketing Strategy: New Directions for Theory and Research," *Journal of Marketing,* Spring 1983, pp. 12–25.

8. For more reading, see Yoram Wind, "Marketing and the Other Business Functions," in *Research in Marketing,* Vol. 5, Jagdish N. Sheth, ed. (Greenwich, CT: JAI Press, 1981), pp. 237–56; and Robert W. Ruekert and Orville C. Walker, Jr., "Marketing's Interaction with Other Functional Units: A Conceptual Framework and Empirical Evidence," *Journal of Marketing,* January 1987, pp. 1–19.

9. The four *P* classification was first suggested by E. Jerome McCarthy, *Basic Marketing: A Managerial Approach,* (Homewood, IL: Richard D. Irwin, 1960).

10. See Benson P. Shapiro, "Rejuvenating the Marketing Mix," *Harvard Business Review,* September-October 1985, pp. 28–34.

# MAYTAG CORPORATION: EXPANDING THE APPLIANCE PORTFOLIO

"Ol Lonely," the famous Maytag Company repairman, may not have enough to do, but his employer's parent, Maytag Corporation, has been quite busy. Always one of the most profitable firms in an industry dominated by giant companies, Maytag often earns a higher return on stockholder's equity (for example, 30 percent in 1987) than any other company in its industry. For the five-year period from 1983 to 1987, Maytag's sales grew at an annual rate of over 5 percent while its net income grew at almost 9 percent. Maytag achieved record sales of $1.9 billion in 1987. Facing the 1990s, Maytag is acquiring new product lines and adjusting its portfolio in response to a changing environment.

Traditionally, Maytag has been a limited-line appliance manufacturer, and it has always marketed its washers, dryers, and dishwashers under a family name. Its strategy has simply been to make the best products and charge accordingly: thus, the company slogan—"Built to Last Longer." Maytag's products generally cost more than competitors' machines—roughly $100 more on average. With its reputation for making trouble-free appliances, Maytag has always targeted the upscale end of the market. In addition, by offering premium-priced products, Maytag has typically catered to second-time buyers. This replacement market slowed in the late 1970s but was strong again starting in 1982–1983: Even Maytags appliances wear out—typically after 10 to 12 years.

Maytag shies away from the cyclical home-builders segment—tough negotiators who, in the past, wanted well-known brands at low prices, and the new-household segment—always price-conscious because of the multitude of products they need to buy in a relatively short time period. Since the early 1980s, however, changing conditions in the appliance market have made Maytag consider whether it should change its traditional high-quality, high-priced targeting strategy.

Consumers and retailers have long regarded Maytag's laundry appliances as top-of-the-line. But the premium-quality niche for laundry and kitchen appliances targeted by both Maytag and competitor KitchenAid (long the market leader in the high-quality, high-price segment) may be eroding. While there is no solid evidence of this trend, there is an increasingly frequent feeling in the trade and among consumers that although the *quality* difference between high-priced and medium-priced laundry and kitchen appliances is becoming smaller, the *price* difference is becoming larger.

Competition, always a major factor in the appliance industry, has become even keener in recent years. A recent wave of mergers and acquisitions has dramatically changed the structure of the industry, with a few large full-line companies now producing most of the output. For example, Whirlpool, the biggest washer maker, increased its share to nearly 50

percent when it acquired KitchenAid dishwashers from Dart & Kraft.

Other trends are also reshaping the industry. First, a significant portion of each large company's output is supplied to other companies for sale under its own brand names. For example, White Consolidated Industries manufactures dryers for General Electric, Montgomery Ward, and Sears. Second, heavy investments in factory automation are being made by two of the largest appliance manufacturers, General Electric and Whirlpool, to bring down costs and increase competitiveness. Meanwhile, already low-cost producers, such as White Consolidated Industries, continue to drive for lower costs through more efficient operations. Third, appliance companies have intensified their marketing efforts, with greater emphasis being placed on quick sales stimulants such as factory rebates, special factory-authorized sales, and additional incentives for consumers, dealers, and salespeople. Finally, foreign competition now poses a serious threat.

In response to these changing market conditions, cash-rich Maytag has made several acquisitions, gambling that some of its success in washers, dryers, and dishwashers will rub off on products other than those with which it has been traditionally associated. First came the 1981 acquisition of Hardwick Stove company—a 105-year-old manufacturer of gas and electric ranges and microwave ovens. These products are sold through conventional outlets in the medium- and low-price brackets. The following year, Maytag acquired Jenn-Aire Company, known for its down-draft grill range, introduced in 1961. The range permits year-round indoor grilling by sucking fumes into a surface ventilation system that keeps them out of the house. In 1986, Magic Chef, Inc., the appliance industry's fourth largest firm, joined the Maytag portfolio. With this acquisition came a variety of products, including Magic Chef cooking equipment, Admiral refrigerators, Norge laundry equipment, and other appliances such as microwave ovens. The new product lines overlapped with Maytag's kitchen ranges, washers, and dryers.

The cooking equipment market differs markedly from the washer and dryer business. The industry is fragmented, with no brand clearly recognized as a premium product. Commenting on the recent acquisitions, Maytag Corporation's president explained that although "cooking equipment is a mature market, it is an exciting one because product innovation is changing the traditional way people cook and broadening sales opportunities."

For example, the microwave oven industry is a relatively new area of the cooking equipment market, and the product is now one of the hottest items in the appliance business. Microwave ovens first caught on in the 1950s, but their growth was slow until the early 1970s. At that time, microwaves had several problems. Cooking was uneven, meats would not brown, foil-wrapped foods could not be put in the oven, few cookbooks were available, and real or imagined radiation dangers were associated with the appliance. When such problems were overcome, sales took off: By the late 1970s, countertop microwave ovens were no longer considered a luxury. With more and more women working in the 1980s, the microwave oven's appeal has become even stronger. Sixty-five percent of U.S. households now contain microwave ovens, as compared to a 45-percent penetration for dishwashers. Industry analysts foresee an eventual penetration by microwaves comparable to that of color televisions.

Five of the forty or so producers of microwave ovens have well over 50 percent of the consumer market. Samsung, Sanyo, Goldstar, Sharp, and Matsushita are the industry's largest. Meanwhile, long-time market leaders Litton and Amana have fallen behind. Price competition and discounting are heavy, and premium prices are difficult to maintain. The microwave industry differs from Maytag's more familiar business arenas, and the acquisitions of Hardwick and Magic Chef provided only a minor position in the fast-moving microwave market.

As Maytag has continued to assimilate these new but related businesses into its portfolio of strategic business units, a recent merger has signaled a new strategic direction for the company. In 1988, Maytag Corporation merged with Chicago Pacific Corporation, best known for its Hoover vacuum cleaners and Pennsylvania House furniture lines. Hoover is an acknowledged leader in the U.S. vacuum cleaner industry, commanding a 32-percent share of the 10 million vacuum cleaners sold in this country each year. The combined sales of the two companies will exceed $3 billion per year.

Maytag, however, had a special interest in Hoover: Sixty-five percent of Hoover's revenues are generated *abroad*. Globalization in the appliance industry is a concept whose time is just now arriving. Prior to its merger with Chicago Pacific, Maytag had almost no presence in overseas appliance markets. Most appliances built by Maytag and other U.S. companies are too large or use too much water for typical international markets. Hoover, however, has for years been producing and distributing washers, dryers, refrigerators, dishwashers, and microwave ovens in foreign markets—it now operates 13 plants in eight countries. Thus, through its merger with Chicago Pacific, Maytag Corporation has taken a first major step toward globalization.

*Questions*

1. Assess Maytag Corporation's current portfolio of businesses, classifying each business unit or product line. Which units should receive more emphasis, which should receive less? What other new products might Maytag add?

2. Develop a formal mission statement for Maytag that will help to guide the company and all of its units in the future.

3. Why has Maytag been so successful in the past in marketing its laundry appliances? Should it use its traditional strategy for its new product lines? Why or why not?

# 3

# Planning, Implementing, and Controlling Marketing Programs

## CHAPTER OBJECTIVES

**After reading this chapter, you should be able to**

1. Identify the sections of a marketing plan and what each section contains
2. Explain why companies have trouble implementing marketing plans and programs
3. Describe the elements of the marketing-implementation process
4. Compare the four ways of organizing a marketing department
5. Explain the three ways in which companies control their marketing activities

During the 1970s, IBM became stodgy and bureaucratic. The highly structured, tradition-bound IBM organization was having trouble competing against smaller, more flexible competitors in fast-changing, high-growth segments. Thus, when IBM decided in the early 1980s to enter the personal computer market, industry analysts were skeptical. The strategy was sound enough—to carry the IBM name and reputation for quality and service into the fastest-growing segment of the computer market. But with personal computers, the company would be selling a very different product to very different customers—and against very different competition. Could large and slow-moving IBM successfully *plan for* and *implement* a new strategy so different from its previous strategies? Despite its great size and power, few analysts expected IBM to have much immediate impact in the personal computer market against more nimble competitors.

But the introduction of the IBM PC became a classic story of smart marketing planning and innovative implementation. IBM pulled some big surprises, swept aside traditional methods, and broke many of its own long-held rules. It set up a "special operating unit" called the Entry Systems Division (ESD) with complete responsibility for the IBM PC. This independent "company within a company" developed a culture and operating style similar to those of its smaller competitors. Free of close IBM control, ESD ignored traditions and did many "non-IBM-like" things. For example:

☐ IBM had *always* built its computers from the ground up, using only IBM electronic components. But to get the PC to the market more quickly, ESD made it from readily available components bought from outside suppliers.

☐ IBM had *always* carefully guarded its computer designs and developed its own software. Not so for the PC! To increase acceptance and sales, ESD published the PC's technical specifications to show how the machine was built. This made it easier for outside companies to design PC-compatible software. The resulting wealth of available software made the PC even more attractive to consumers. IBM machines soon became the industry standard for software producers.

□ IBM had *always* sold its products directly through its own salesforce. But for the PC, ESD used a network of independent retailers, including such large ones as Sears and Computerland.

□ Until the late 1970s, IBM had *always* been slow but sure in making product and price changes. But ESD spent millions to build modern production facilities that could turn out PCs at low cost, and it then used aggressive pricing to keep competitors off balance.

Thus, to plan and implement its strategy to enter the personal computer market, IBM made several tradition-shattering changes in its structure, operations, and tactics. And the new approach paid off. The IBM PC went from initial planning to market in just 13 months.

In less than three years, IBM claimed a 40 percent share of the overall personal computer market (60 to 70 percent in the company segment). Although using available parts and publishing designs later made it easier for copycat competitors to crank out IBM imitations, without these moves IBM would probably not have gotten to market so quickly or penetrated so deeply. And when IBM introduced its next generation System/2 personal computers in 1987, even with a dozen low-priced "clones" on the market, the venerable old IBM PC still held a 30 percent market share, compared with only 7 percent shares for nearest competitors Apple and Compaq.

The Entry Systems Division, which began as a 12-person team, has grown into a 10,000-employee division. IBM has now blended ESD into the rest of the $50 billion company. But the new approach worked so well that IBM has set up more than a dozen additional special business units to develop products for software, robotics, high-tech health care, and other fast-growing markets.[1]

In this chapter, we will look more closely at each marketing management function—*analysis, planning, implementation,* and *control.* Figure 3–1 shows the relationship between these marketing activities. The company first develops overall strategic plans. These companywide strategic plans are then translated into marketing and other plans for each division, product, and brand.

Through implementation, the company turns the strategic and marketing plans into actions that will achieve the company's strategic objectives. Marketing plans are implemented by people in the marketing organization working with others both inside and outside the company. Control consists of measuring and evaluating the results of marketing plans and activities and taking corrective action to make sure that objectives are being reached. Marketing analysis

FIGURE 3-1   The Relationship between Analysis, Planning, Implementation, and Control

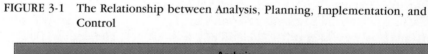
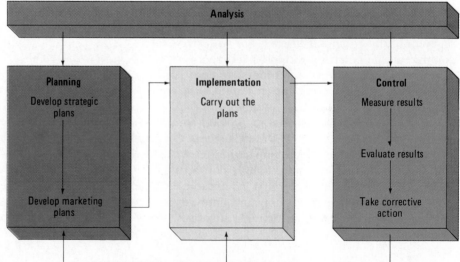

provides information and evaluations needed for all the other marketing management activities.

To review all the factors that marketers must consider when designing marketing programs, we will discuss planning first. But this does not mean that planning always comes first or that planning ends before marketers move on to the other activities. Figure 3–1 shows that planning and the other activities are closely related. Marketers must plan their analysis, implementation, and control activities; analysis provides inputs for planning, implementation, and control; control provides feedback for future planning and implementation.

In the remainder of this chapter, we will discuss marketing planning and how plans are implemented and controlled by people in the marketing department. In Chapter 4, we will examine many of the tools used in marketing analysis.

# MARKETING PLANNING

The strategic plan defines the company's overall mission and objectives. Within each business unit, functional plans must be prepared—including marketing plans. If the business unit consists of many product lines, brands, and markets, plans must be drawn up for each. Marketing plans might include product plans, brand plans, or market plans.

What does a marketing plan look like? Our discussion will focus on product or brand plans. A product or brand plan should contain the following sections: *executive summary, current marketing situation, threats and opportunities, objectives and issues, marketing strategies, action programs, budgets*, and *controls* (see Figure 3–2).

## Executive Summary

The marketing plan should open with a short summary of the main goals and recommendations to be presented in the plan. Here is a short example:

> The 1990 Marketing Plan outlines an approach to attaining a significant increase in company sales and profits over the preceding year. The sales target is $240 million, a planned 20 percent sales gain. We think this increase is attainable because of the improved economic, competitive, and distribution picture. The target operating margin is $25 million, a 25 percent increase over last year. To achieve these goals, the sales promotion budget will be $4.8 million, or 2 percent of projected sales. The advertising budget will be $7.2 million, or 3 percent of projected sales. . . . [More detail follows]

The **executive summary** helps top management to find the plan's major points quickly. A table of contents should follow the executive summary.

FIGURE 3-2   Components of a Marketing Plan

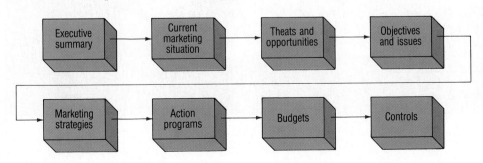

## Current Marketing Situation

The first major section of the plan describes the target market and the company's position in it. In the **current marketing situation** section, the planner provides information about the market, product performance, competition, and distribution. It includes a *market description* that defines the market, including major market segments. The planner shows market size in total and by segment for several past years and then reviews customer needs and factors in the marketing environment that may affect customer purchasing. Next, the *product review* shows sales, prices, and gross margins of the major products in the product line. A section on *competition* identifies major competitors and each of their strategies for product quality, pricing, distribution, and promotion. It also shows the market shares held by the company and each competitor. Finally, a section on *distribution* describes recent sales trends and developments in the major distribution channels.

## Threats and Opportunities

The second major section of the plan requires the manager to look ahead for major threats and opportunities that the product might face. Its purpose is to make the manager anticipate important developments that can have an impact

*Marketers must continuously plan their analysis, implementation, and control activities.*

on the firm. Managers should list as many threats and opportunities as they can imagine. Suppose a major pet foods marketer comes up with the following list:

**company marketing opportunity** An attractive arena for marketing action in which the company would enjoy a competitive advantage.

**marketing strategy** The marketing logic by which the business unit hopes to achieve its marketing objectives, including specific strategies for target markets, marketing mix, and marketing expenditure level.

□ A large competitor has just announced that it will introduce a new premium pet food line, backed by a huge advertising and sales promotion blitz.

□ Industry analysts predict that supermarket chain buyers will face more than 10,000 new grocery product introductions next year. Buyers are expected to accept only 38 percent of these new products and give each one only five months to prove itself.

□ Because of improved economic conditions over the past several years, pet ownership is increasing in almost all segments of the U.S. population.

□ The company's researchers have found a way to make a new pet food that is low in fat and calories yet highly nutritious and tasty. This product will appeal strongly to many of today's pet food buyers, who are almost as concerned about their pets' health as about their own.

□ Pet ownership and concern about proper pet care are increasing rapidly in foreign markets, especially in developing nations.

The first two items are *threats*. Not all threats call for the same attention or concern—the manager should assess likelihood of each threat and the amount of harm it could cause. The manager should then focus on the most probable and harmful threats and prepare plans in advance to meet them.

The last three items in the list are marketing opportunities. **A company marketing opportunity** is an attractive arena for marketing action in which the company could enjoy a competitive advantage. The manager should assess each opportunity according to its potential attractiveness and the company's probability of success. Figure 3–3 shows that the company should pursue only the opportunities that fit its objectives and resources. Every company has objectives based on its business mission. And each opportunity requires that the company have certain amounts of capital and know-how. Companies can rarely find ideal opportunities that fit their objectives and resources exactly. Developing opportunities involves risks. When evaluating opportunities, the manager must decide whether the expected returns justify these risks.

## Objectives and Issues

Having studied the product's threats and opportunities, the manager can now set objectives and consider issues that will affect them. The objectives should be stated as goals the company would like to reach during the plan's term. For example, the manager might want to achieve a 15 percent market share, a 20 percent pretax profit on sales, and a 25 percent pretax profit on investment. Suppose the current market share is only 10 percent. This fact poses a key issue: How can market share be increased? The manager will want to consider the major issues involved in trying to increase market share.

## Marketing Strategies

In this section of the marketing plan, the manager outlines the broad marketing strategy or "game plan" for attaining the objectives. **Marketing strategy** is the marketing logic by which the business unit hopes to achieve its marketing objectives. It consists of specific strategies for target markets, marketing mix, and marketing expenditure level. Marketing strategy should spell out the market segments on which the company will focus. These segments differ in their needs and wants, responses to marketing, and profitability. The company would be

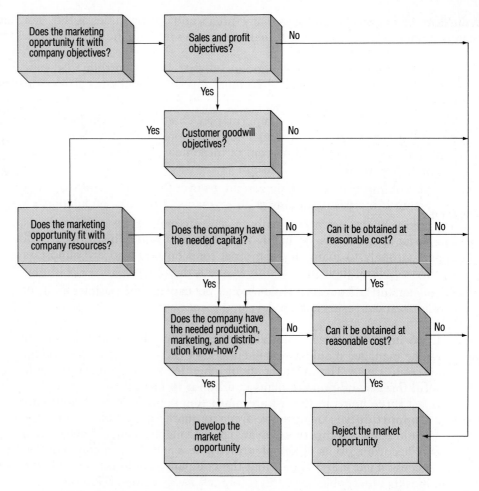

FIGURE 3-3    Evaluating a Company Marketing Opportunity in Terms of Company
Objectives and Resources

smart to put its effort and energy into those market segments it can best serve from a competitive point of view. It should develop a marketing strategy for each targeted segment.

The manager should also outline specific strategies for such marketing mix elements as new products, field sales, advertising, sales promotion, prices, and distribution. The manager should explain how each strategy responds to the threats, opportunities, and key issues spelled out earlier in the plan.

Finally, the manager should also spell out the marketing budget that will be needed to carry out the planned strategies. The manager knows that higher budgets will produce more sales but is looking for the marketing budget that will produce the best profit picture.

## Action Programs

Marketing strategies should be turned into specific action programs that answer the following questions: *What* will be done? *When* will it be done? *Who* is responsible for doing it? And *how much* will it cost? For example, the manager may want to step up sales promotion as a key strategy for winning market share. A sales promotion action plan should be drawn up to outline special offers and their dates, trade shows entered, new point-of-purchase displays, and other promotions. The action plan shows when activities will be started, reviewed, and completed.

## Budgets

Action plans allow the manager to make a supporting **marketing budget** that is essentially a projected profit-and-loss statement. On the revenue side, it shows the forecasted number of units that would be sold and the average net price. On the expense side, it shows the cost of production, physical distribution, and marketing. The difference is the projected profit. Higher management will review the budget and approve or modify it. Once approved, the budget is the basis for materials buying, production scheduling, manpower planning, and marketing operations. Budgeting can be difficult, and budgeting methods range from simple "rules of thumb" to complex computer models.[2]

## Controls

The last section of the plan outlines the controls that will be used to monitor progress. Typically, goals and budgets are spelled out for each month or quarter. This practice allows higher management to review the results each period and to spot businesses or products that are not meeting their goals. The managers of these businesses and products have to explain problems and what corrective actions they will take.

**marketing budget** A section of the marketing plan that shows projected revenues, costs, and profits.

**marketing implementation** The process that turns marketing strategies and plans into marketing actions in order to accomplish strategic marketing objectives.

# IMPLEMENTATION

Planning good strategies is only a start toward successful marketing. A brilliant marketing strategy will count for little if the company fails to implement it properly. **Marketing implementation** is the process that turns marketing

*Marketing plans and strategies are of little value until they are properly implemented.*

strategies and *plans* into marketing *actions* in order to accomplish strategic marketing objectives. Implementation involves day-to-day, month-to-month activities that effectively put the marketing plan to work. Whereas marketing planning addresses the *what* and *why* of marketing activities, implementation addresses the *who, where, when,* and *how.*

Many managers think that "doing things right" (implementation) is as important, or even more important, than "doing the right things" (strategy):

> A surprisingly large number of very successful large companies . . . don't have long-term strategic plans with an obsessive preoccupation on rivalry. They concentrate on operating details and doing things well. Hustle is their style and their strategy. They move fast and they get it right. . . . Countless companies in all industries, young or old, mature or booming, are finally learning the limits of strategy and concentrating on tactics and execution.[3]

Yet implementation is difficult—it is often easier to think up good marketing strategies than to carry them out. And managers often have trouble diagnosing implementation problems. It is usually hard to tell whether poor performance was caused by poor strategy, poor implementation, or both.[4]

## Reasons for Poor Implementation

What causes poor implementation? Why do so many companies have trouble getting their marketing plans to work effectively? Several factors cause implementation problems.

### Isolated Planning

The company's strategic plans are often set by top management or high-level "professional planners" who have little direct contact with the marketing managers who must implement the plans. Central strategic planning can provide benefits—strong central leadership, better coordination of strategies across business units, and more emphasis on long-term strategic thinking and performance. But central planning also leads to several problems. First, top-level managers and planners are concerned with broad strategy and may prepare plans that are too general. Or they may not understand the practical problems faced by line managers and may produce unrealistic plans. Second, lower-level managers who did not prepare the plans may not fully understand them. Finally, managers who face day-to-day operations may resent what they see as unrealistic plans made up by "ivory-tower" planners.

Many companies have realized that high-level managers and planners cannot plan strategies *for* marketing managers. Instead, planners must help marketing managers find their *own* strategies. Many companies are cutting down their large central planning staffs and are giving more planning responsibility to lower-level managers. In these companies, top management and strategy planners are not isolated—they work directly with line managers to design more workable strategies.[5]

### Trade-offs between Long-Term and Short-Term Objectives

Company marketing strategies often cover *long-run* activities over the next three to five years. But the marketing managers who implement these strategies are usually rewarded for *short-run* sales, growth, or profits. When choosing between long-run strategy and short-run performance, managers usually favor the more-rewarding short-run results. One study found many examples of such harmful trade-offs. For example, one company designed a marketing strategy that stressed product availability and customer service. But to increase short-term profit, operating managers cut costs by reducing inventories and service staff. These managers met short-run performance goals and received high evaluations, but their actions hurt the company's long-run strategy.[6]

Some companies are taking steps to attain a better balance between short- and long-run goals. They are making managers more aware of strategic goals, evaluating managers on both long-run and short-run performance, and rewarding managers for reaching long-run objectives.

### Natural Resistance to Change

As a rule, the company's current operations have all been designed to implement past plans and strategies. New strategies requiring new company patterns and habits may be resisted. And the more different the new strategy from the old, the greater the resistance to implementing it. For very different strategies, implementation may cut across traditional organization lines within the company. For example, when one company tried to implement a strategy of developing new markets for an old product line, its established salesforce resisted strongly. The company had to create an entirely new sales division in order to develop the new markets.

### Lack of Specific Implementation Plans

Some marketing plans are poorly implemented because the planners fail to make detailed implementation plans. They leave the details to managers, and the result is poor implementation or no implementation at all. Planners cannot simply assume that their plans will be implemented. They must prepare a detailed implementation plan that shows the specific activities needed to put the plan into action. They must also develop timetables and assign major implementation tasks to individual managers.

## The Implementation Process

People at all levels of the marketing system must work together to implement marketing plans and strategies. People in the marketing department, in other company departments, and in outside organizations—all can help or hinder marketing implementation. The company must find ways to coordinate all these actors and their activities.

The implementation process is shown in Figure 3–4.[7] The figure shows that marketing strategy and marketing performance are linked by an implementation system consisting of five related elements: *action programs*, an *organization structure, decision and reward systems, human resources,* and *managerial climate and company culture.*

### The Action Program

To implement marketing plans, people at all company levels make decisions and perform tasks. At Procter & Gamble, implementation of a plan to introduce a stream of high-quality new products requires day-to-day decisions and actions by thousands of people both inside and outside the organization. In the marketing organization, marketing researchers test new-product concepts and scan the marketplace for new-product ideas. For each new product, marketing managers make decisions about target segments, branding, packaging, pricing, promoting, and distributing. Salespeople are hired, trained and retrained, directed, and motivated.

Marketing managers work with other company managers to get support for promising new products. They talk with engineering about product design. They talk with manufacturing about production and inventory levels. They talk

**action program** A detailed program that shows what must be done, who will do it, and how decisions and actions will be coordinated to implement marketing plans and strategy.

**organization structure** A structure that breaks up the company's work into specialized jobs, assigns these jobs to people and departments, and then coordinates the jobs by defining formal ties between people and departments and by setting lines of authority and communication.

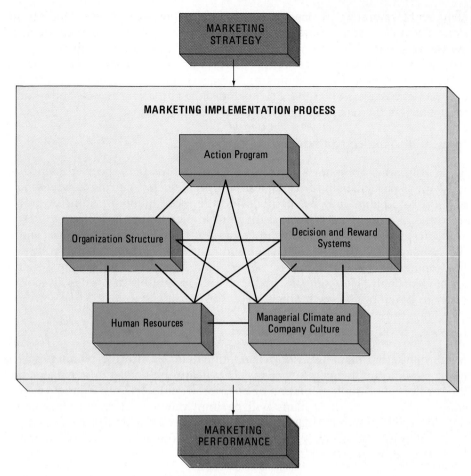

FIGURE 3-4   The Marketing Implementation Process

with finance about funding and cash flows, with the legal staff about patents and product-safety issues, and with personnel about staffing and training needs. Marketing managers also work with outside people. They meet with advertising agencies to plan ad campaigns and with the media to obtain publicity support. The salesforce urges retailers to advertise the new products, give them ample shelf space, and use company displays.

The **action program** pulls all of these people and activities together. It identifies the decisions and actions needed to implement the marketing program. It also gives responsibility for these decisions and actions to specific people in the company. Finally, the action program gives a timetable that states when decisions must be made and when actions must be taken. The action program shows what must be done, who will do it, and how decisions and actions will be coordinated to reach the company's marketing objectives.

### The Organization Structure

The company's formal **organization structure** plays an important role in implementing marketing strategy. The structure breaks up the company's work into well-defined jobs, assigns these jobs to people and departments, and allows efficiency through specialization. The structure then coordinates these specialized jobs by defining formal ties between people and departments and by setting lines of authority and communication.

Companies with different strategies need different organization structures. A small firm developing new products in a fast-changing industry might need a flexible structure that encourages individual action—a *decentralized* structure with ample informal communication. A more established company in more stable markets might need a structure that provides more integration—a more *centralized* structure with well-defined roles and communication "through proper channels."[8]

In their study of successful companies, Peters and Waterman found that they had many common structural characteristics that led to successful implementation.[9] For example, their structures tended to be more *informal*—United Airlines' MBWA (management by walking around), IBM's "open-door" policy, 3M's "clubs" to create small-group interaction. The successful companies' structures were *decentralized*, with small independent divisions or groups to encourage innovation. Structures also tended to be *simple* and *lean*. These simple structures are more flexible and allow the companies to adapt more quickly to changing conditions.

The excellent companies also have lean staffs, especially at higher levels. According to Peters and Waterman:

> Indeed, it appears that most of our excellent companies have comparatively few people at the corporate level, and that what staff there is tends to be out in the field solving problems rather than in the home office checking on things. The bottom line is fewer administrators, more operators.[10]

In recent years, many large companies—General Motors, Polaroid, Du Pont, General Electric, Lever Brothers, and others—have cut back unneeded layers of management and restructured their organizations to reduce costs and increase marketing flexibility.

Some of the Peters and Waterman's conclusions have been questioned because the study focused on high-technology and consumer-goods companies operating in rapidly changing environments.[11] The structures used by these companies may not be right for other types of firms in different situations. And many of the study's excellent companies will need to change their structures as their strategies and situations change. For example, the informal structure that made Hewlett-Packard so successful at the time of the study has caused problems for HP in recent years. The company has recently moved toward a more formal structure (see Marketing Highlight 3-1).

## Decision and Reward Systems

**Decision and reward systems** include formal and informal operating procedures that guide such activities as planning, information gathering, budgeting, recruiting and training, control, and personnel evaluation and rewards. Poorly designed systems can work against implementation; well-designed systems can help implementation. Consider a company's compensation system. If it compensates managers for short-run results, they will have little incentive to work toward long-run objectives. Many companies are designing compensation systems that will overcome this problem. Here is an example:

> One company was concerned that its annual bonus system encouraged managers to ignore long-run objectives and focus on annual performance goals. To correct this, the company changed its bonus system to include rewards for both annual performance and for reaching "strategic milestones." Under the new plan, each manager works with planners to set two or three strategic objectives. At the end of the year, the manager's bonus is based on both operating performance and on reaching the strategic objectives. Thus the bonus system encourages managers to achieve more balance of the company's long- and short-run needs.[12]

**decision and reward systems**
Formal and informal operating procedures that guide such activities as planning, information gathering, budgeting, recruiting and training, control, and personnel and rewards.

# Marketing Highlight 3–1

## HEWLETT-PACKARD'S STRUCTURE EVOLVES

In 1939, two engineers—Bill Hewlett and Dave Packard—started Hewlett-Packard in a Palo Alto garage to build test equipment. At the start, Bill and Dave did everything themselves, from designing and building their equipment to marketing it. As the firm grew out of the garage and began to build more and different types of test equipment, Hewlett and Packard could no longer make all the necessary operating decisions by themselves. They assumed roles as top managers and hired functional managers to run various company activities. These managers were relatively autonomous but still closely tied to the owners.

By the mid-1970s, Hewlett-Packard's 42 divisions employed more than 1,200 people. The company's structure evolved to support its heavy emphasis on innovation and autonomy. The structure was loose and decentralized. Each division operated as an autonomous unit and was responsible for its own strategic planning, product development, marketing programs, and implementation.

In 1982, Peters and Waterman, in their *In Search of Excellence,* cited HP's informal and decentralized structure as a major reason for the company's continued excellence. They praised HP's unrestrictive structure and high degree of informal communication (its MBWA style— management by walking around). Peters and Waterman noted that the HP structure decentralized decision making and responsibility. In the words of one HP manager:

> Hewlett-Packard [should not] have a tight, military-type organization, but rather . . . give people the freedom to work toward [overall objectives] in ways they determine best for their own areas of responsibility.

The structure also decentralized authority and fostered autonomy:

> The sales force does not have to accept a product developed by a division unless it wants it. The company cites numerous instances in which several million dollars of development funds were spent by a division, at which point the sales force said, "No thanks."

But in recent years, although still profitable, Hewlett-Packard has met with some problems in the fast-changing microcomputer and minicomputer markets. According to *Business Week:*

Hewlett-Packard's famed innovative culture and decentralization spawned such enormously successful products as its 3000 minicomputer, the handheld scientific calculator, and the ThinkJet nonimpact printer. But when a new climate required its fiercely autonomous divisions to cooperate in product development and marketing, HP's passionate devotion to the "autonomy and entrepreneurship" that Peters and Waterman advocate became a hindrance.

Thus Hewlett-Packard is finding that it must change its structure and culture to bring them in line with its changing situation. As *Business Week* puts it:

> To regain its stride, HP is being forced to abandon attributes of excellence for which it was praised. Its technology-driven, engineering-oriented culture, in which decentralization and innovation were a religion and entrepreneurs were the gods, is giving way to a marketing culture and growing centralization.

Sources: Based on information in Donald F. Harvey, *Business Policy and Strategic Management* (Columbus, OH: Charles E. Merrill, 1982), pp. 269–70; "Who's Excellent Now?" *Business Week,* November 5, 1984, pp. 76–78; and Thomas J. Peters and Robert H. Waterman, Jr., *In Search of Excellence: Lessons from America's Best-Run Companies* (New York: Harper & Row, 1982).

*Hewlett-Packard began in this garage in 1939; it now operates around the world.*

## Human Resources

**human resources** The people with needed skills, motivation, and personal characteristics who fill out the organization structure.

**managerial climate** The company climate resulting from the way managers work with others in the company.

**company culture** A system of values and beliefs shared by people in an organization—the company's collective identity and meaning.

Marketing strategies are implemented by people, so successful implementation requires careful **human resources** planning. At all levels, the company must fill its structure and systems with people who have the needed skills, motivation, and personal characteristics. Company personnel must be recruited, assigned, trained, and maintained.

The selection and development of executives and other managers are especially important for implementation. Different strategies call for managers with different personalities and skills. New-venture strategies need managers with entrepreneurial skills; holding strategies require managers with organizational and administrative skills; and retrenchment strategies call for managers with cost-cutting skills. Thus, the company must carefully match its managers to the needs of the strategies to be implemented.

In recent years, more and more companies have recognized the importance of good people planning. Systematic, long-run human resources planning can give the company a strong competitive advantage.[13]

## Managerial Climate and Company Culture

The company's managerial climate and company culture can make or break marketing implementation. **Managerial climate** involves the way company managers work with others in the company. Some managers take command, delegate little authority, and keep tight controls. Others delegate a lot, encourage their people to take the initiative, and communicate informally. No one managerial style is best for all situations. Different strategies may require different leadership styles, and which style is best varies with the company's structure, tasks, people, and environment.[14]

**Company culture** is a system of values and beliefs shared by people in an organization. It is the company's collective identity and meaning. The culture informally guides the behavior of people at all company levels. Peters and Waterman found that excellent companies have strong and clearly defined cultures:

> Without exception, the dominance and coherence of culture proved to be an essential quality of the excellent companies. Moreover, the stronger the culture and the more it was directed toward the marketplace, the less need there was for policy manuals, organization charts, or detailed procedures and rules. In these companies, people way down the line know what they are supposed to do in most situations because the handful of guiding values is crystal clear. . . . Everyone at Hewlett-Packard knows that he or she is supposed to be innovative. Everyone at Procter & Gamble knows that product quality is the [norm].[15]

Marketing strategies that do not fit the company's style and culture will be difficult to implement. For example, a decision by Procter & Gamble to increase sales by reducing product quality and prices would not work well. It would be resisted by P&G people at all levels who identify strongly with the company's reputation for quality. Because managerial style and culture are so hard to change, companies usually design strategies that fit their current cultures rather than try to change their styles and cultures to fit new strategies.

Table 3–1 lists some questions companies should ask about each element of the implementation system. Successful implementation depends on how well the company blends the five activities into a cohesive program that supports its strategies.

**TABLE 3-1  Questions About the Marketing Implementation System**

*Organization Structure*

What is the organization's structure?
What are the lines of authority and communication?
What is the role of task forces, committees, or similar mechanisms?

*Systems*

What are the important systems?
What are the key control variables?
How do product and information flow?

*Action Program*

What are the tasks to be performed and which are critical?
How are they accomplished, with what technology?
What strengths does the organization have?

*Human Resources*

What are their skills, knowedge, and experience?
What are their expectations?
What are their attitudes toward the firm and their jobs?

*Climate and Culture*

Are there shared values that are visible and accepted?
What are the shared values and how are they communicated?
What are the dominant management styles?
How is conflict resolved?

*Fit*

Does each component above support marketing strategy?
Do the various components fit together well to form a cohesive framework for implementing strategy?

*Source:* Adapted from David A. Aaker, *Strategic Market Management* (New York: Wiley, 1988), p. 322 © 1988, John Wiley & Sons, Inc.

# MARKETING DEPARTMENT ORGANIZATION

The company must design a marketing department that can carry out marketing analysis, planning, implementation, and control. In this section, we will focus on how marketing departments within companies are organized. If the company is very small, one person might do all the marketing work—research, selling, advertising, customer service, and other activities. As the company expands, a marketing department organization emerges to plan and carry out marketing activities. In large companies, this department contains many marketing specialists. Thus, General Mills has product managers, salespeople and sales managers, market researchers, advertising experts, and other specialists.

Modern marketing departments can be arranged in several ways. A company will set up its marketing department in the way that best helps it meet its marketing objectives.

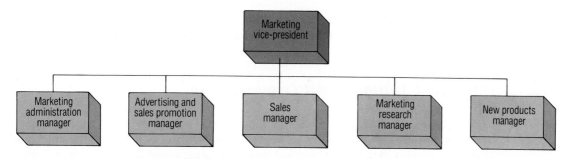

**FIGURE 3-5**   Functional Organization

## Functional Organization

The **functional organization** is the most common form of marketing organization. Marketing specialists are in charge of different marketing activities, or *functions*. Figure 3–5 shows five specialists: marketing administration manager, advertising and sales promotion manager, sales manager, marketing research manager, and new-products manager. Other specialists might include a customer service manager, a marketing planning manager, and a distribution manager.

The main advantage of a functional marketing organization is that it is simple to administer. On the other hand, this form by itself becomes less effective as the company's products and markets grow. First, it becomes difficult to make plans for each different product or market, and products that are not favorites of the functional specialists may get neglected. Second, as the functional groups compete with each other to gain more budget and status, top management may have trouble coordinating all the marketing activities.

## Geographic Organization

A company selling all across the country often uses a **geographic organization** for its salesforce. Figure 3–6 shows 1 national sales manager, 4 regional sales managers, 24 zone sales managers, 192 district sales managers, and 1,920

**functional organization** An organization structure in which marketing specialists are in charge of different marketing activities or functions such as advertising, marketing research, and sales management.

**geographic organization** An organization structure in which a company's national salesforce (and perhaps other functions) specializes by geographic area.

**FIGURE 3-6**   Geographic Organization

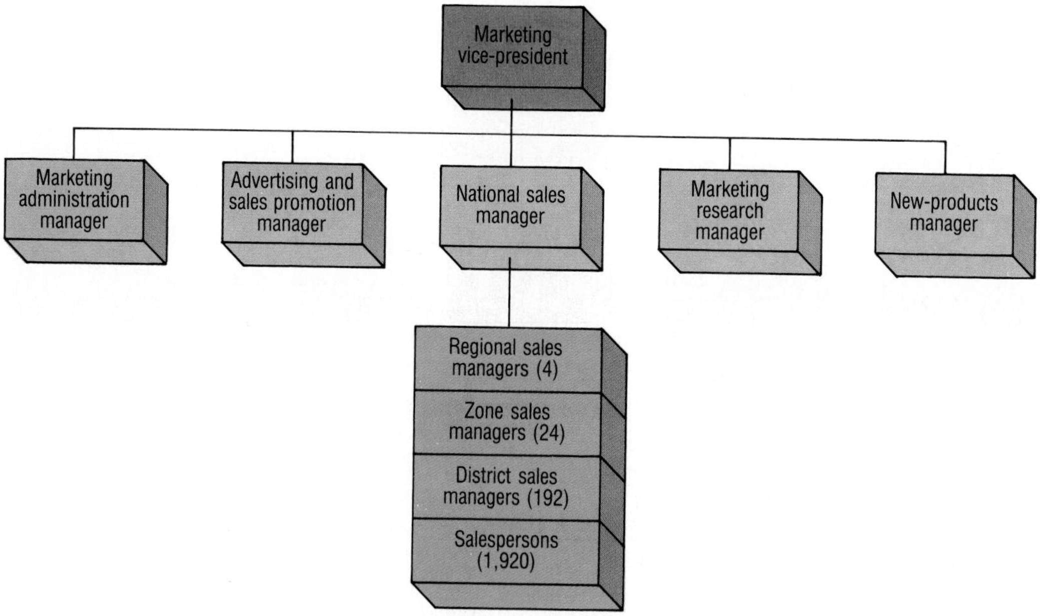

**product management organization** An organization structure in which product managers are responsible for developing and implementing marketing strategies and plans for a specific product or brand.

salespersons. Geographic organization allows salespeople to settle into a territory, get to know their customers, and work with a minimum of travel time and cost.

## Product Management Organization

Companies with many products or brands often create a **product management organization.** The product management organization is headed by a products manager who supervises several product group managers. In turn, they supervise product or brand managers in charge of specific products or brands (see Figure 3–7). The product manager's job is to develop and implement a complete strategy and marketing program for a specific product or brand. A product management organization makes sense if the company has many very different products.

Product management first appeared in the Procter & Gamble Company in 1929. A new company soap, Camay, was not doing well, and a young P&G executive was assigned to give his exclusive attention to developing and promoting this product. He was successful, and the company soon added other product managers.[16]

Since then, many firms, especially in the food, soap, toiletries, and chemical industries, have set up product management organizations. General Foods, for example, uses a product management organization in its Post Division. There are separate product group managers in charge of cereals, pet food, and beverages. Within the cereal product group, there are separate product managers for nutritional cereals, children's presweetened cereals, family cereals, and miscellaneous cereals. In turn, the nutritional cereal product manager supervises brand managers.

The product management organization has many advantages. The product manager coordinates the whole marketing mix for the product and can sense and react more quickly to product problems. Smaller brands get more attention because they have their own product manager. Finally, product management is an excellent training ground for young executives—it involves them in almost every area of company operations.

FIGURE 3-7 Product Management Organization

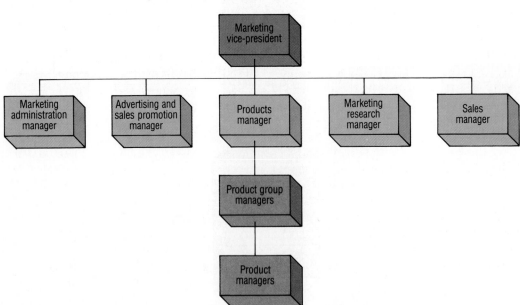

*Rethinking the role of the product manager; Campbell set up "brand sales managers."*

But a price is paid for these advantages. First, product management creates some conflict and frustration. Product managers are seldom given enough authority to carry out their responsibilities effectively. They are usually told that they are "mini-presidents" but are often treated as low-level coordinators. Second, product managers become experts in their product but rarely become experts in any functions. This hurts products that depend on a specific function, such as advertising. Third, the product management system often costs more than expected. Originally, one manager is assigned to each major product. Soon, product managers are appointed to manage even minor products. Each product manager gets an assistant brand manager and then, later, a brand assistant. With all these personnel, payroll costs climb. The company becomes saddled with a costly structure of product management people. Many consumer package goods companies today are rethinking the role of the product manager. Product managers have long tended to be home-office people who planned long-term product strategy and watched over product profitability. But with the recent swing toward regionalized marketing—increased geographic segmentation, more localized marketing, greater use of point-of-sale pricing and sales promotion—the emphasis is shifting to local markets and shorter-term strategies. To design and implement more-localized strategies effectively, already overworked product managers must now spend more time in the field. They must work with salespeople, learn what is happening in stores, and get closer to the customer. Some companies are trying new ways to deal with this problem. For example, Campbell Soup recently created "brand sales managers"—combination product managers and salespeople charged with handling brands in the field.[17]

## Market Management Organization

**market management organization** An organization structure in which market managers are responsible for developing plans for sales and profits in their specific markets.

**marketing control** The process of measuring and evaluating the results of marketing strategies and plans, and taking corrective action to ensure that marketing objectives are attained.

Many companies sell one product line to many different types of markets. For example, Smith Corona sells its electric typewriters to consumer, business, and government markets. National Steel sells its steel to the auto, railroad, construction, and public utility industries. When different markets have different needs and preferences, a **market management organization** might be best for the company.

A market management organization is similar to the product management organization shown in Figure 3–7. Market managers are responsible for developing long-range and annual plans for the sales and profits in their markets. They have to coax help from marketing research, advertising, sales, and other functions. This system's main advantage is that the company is organized around the needs of specific customer segments.

Many companies have reorganized along market lines. The Heinz Company split its marketing organization into three groups: groceries, commercial restaurants, and institutions. Each group contains further market specialists. For example, the institutional division contains separate market specialists who plan for schools, colleges, hospitals, and prisons.[18]

# MARKETING CONTROL

Because many surprises will occur during the implementation of marketing plans, the marketing department has to engage in constant marketing control. **Marketing control** is the process of measuring and evaluating the results of marketing strategies and plans and taking corrective action to ensure that marketing objectives are attained.

There are three types of marketing control (see Table 3–2). *Annual plan control* involves checking ongoing performance against the annual plan and taking corrective action when necessary. *Profitability control* involves determining the actual profitability of different products, territories, markets, and channels. *Strategic control* involves looking at whether the company's basic strategies are well matched to its opportunities.

TABLE 3–2  Types of Marketing Control

| Type of Control | Prime Responsibility | Purpose of Control | Approaches |
|---|---|---|---|
| I. Annual plan control | Top management Middle management | To examine whether the planned results are being achieved | Sales analysis Market-share analysis Marketing expense-to-sales ratios Customer attitude tracking |
| II. Profitability control | Marketing controller | To examine where the company is making and losing money | Profitability by: Product Territory Market segment Trade channel Order size |
| III. Strategic control | Top management Marketing auditor | To examine whether the company is pursuing its best marketing opportunities and doing this efficiently | Marketing audit |

## Annual Plan Control

The purpose of **annual plan control** is to ensure that the company achieves the sales, profits, and other goals set out in its annual plan. It involves the four steps shown in Figure 3–8. Management first sets monthly or quarterly goals in the annual plan. It then measures its performance in the marketplace and evaluates the causes of any differences between expected and actual performance. Finally, management takes corrective action to close the gaps between its goals and its performance. This step may require changing the action programs or even changing the goals.

What specific control tools are used by management to check on performance? The four main tools are *sales analysis, market-share analysis, marketing expense-to-sales analysis,* and *customer-attitude tracking.*

**Sales analysis** consists of measuring and evaluating actual sales in relation to sales goals. This procedure might involve finding out whether specific products and territories are producing their expected share of sales. Suppose the company sells in three territories where expected sales were 1,500 units, 500 units, and 2,000 units, respectively, adding up to 4,000 units. The actual total sales volume was 3,000 units, 25 percent below expected. A breakdown by territory shows that territories one, two, and three had sales of 1,400 units, 525 units, and 1,075 units, respectively. Thus, territory one fell short by 7 percent; territory two had a 5 percent surplus; and territory three fell short by 46 percent! Territory three is causing most of the trouble. The sales vice-president will check into territory three to see why performance there is poor.

However, company sales do not show how well the company is doing relative to *competitors.* A sales increase could be due to better economic conditions in which all companies gained rather than to improved company performance in relation to its competitors. Management thus needs to use **market-share analysis** to track the company's market share. If the company's market share goes up, it is gaining on competitors; if its market share goes down, it is losing to competitors.

Annual plan control requires making sure that the company is not overspending to achieve its sales goals. Thus, marketing control also includes **expense-to-sales analysis.** Watching the ratio of marketing expenses to sales will help keep marketing expenses in line.

Alert companies use **customer-attitude tracking** to check the attitudes of customers, dealers, and other marketing system participants. By watching changes in customer attitudes before they affect sales, management can take earlier action. The main customer-attitude tracking systems are complaint and suggestion systems, customer panels, and customer surveys.

## Profitability Control

Besides annual plan control, companies also need **profitability control** to measure the profitability of their various products, territories, customer groups, channels, and order sizes. This information will help management determine

**annual plan control** Evaluation and corrective action to ensure that the company achieves the sales, profits, and other goals set out in its annual plan.

**sales analysis** Measuring and evaluating actual sales in relation to sales goals.

**market-share analysis** Analysis and tracking of the company's market share.

**expense-to-sales analysis** Analyzing the ratio of marketing expenses to sales in order to keep marketing expenses in line.

**customer-attitude tracking** Tracking the attitudes of customers, dealers, and other marketing system participants and their effects on sales.

**profitability control** Evaluation and corrective action to ensure the profitability of various products, territories, customer groups, trade channels, and order sizes.

FIGURE 3-8 The Control Process

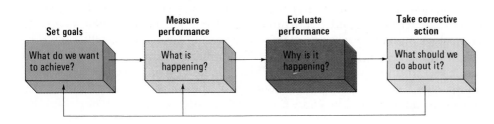

**strategic control** A critical review of the company's overall marketing effectiveness.

**marketing audit** A periodic examination of a company's environment, objectives, strategies, and activities to determine problems and opportunities and to plan actions to improve the company's marketing performance.

*Keeping track of sales and expenses.*

whether any products or marketing activities should be expanded, reduced, or eliminated.

For example, suppose a lawn mower company wants to determine the profitability of selling its lawn mowers through three types of retail channels: hardware stores, garden supply shops, and department stores. Using profitability analysis, management would first identify all the expenses involved in selling, advertising, and delivering the product. Next, it would assign these expenses to each type of channel according to the effort and dollars spent on each channel. Finally, a profit-and-loss statement would be prepared for each channel to see how much each is contributing to overall company profits.

If the analysis shows that one of the channels is unprofitable, the company can take one of many corrective actions. Suppose the company finds that it is actually losing money selling through garden supply shops. It might eliminate only the weakest garden supply shops. Or it might offer a program to train people in these shops to sell lawn mowers more effectively. Or it could cut channel costs by reducing the sales calls and promotional aid going to garden supply shops. As a last resort, it could drop the channel altogether.

## Strategic Control

From time to time, companies need **strategic control** to critically review their overall marketing effectiveness. Marketing strategies and programs can quickly become out-of-date. Thus, each company should occasionally reassess its overall approach to the marketplace, using a tool known as the marketing audit.[19] A **marketing audit** is a comprehensive, systematic, independent, and periodic examination of a company's environment, objectives, strategies, and activities to determine problems and opportunities and to plan actions to improve the company's marketing performance.

The marketing audit covers *all* the major marketing areas of a business, not just a few trouble spots. It is normally conducted by an objective and experienced outside party who is independent of the marketing department. The marketing audit should be carried out periodically, not simply when there is a crisis. It promises benefits for the successful company as well as for the company in trouble.

The marketing auditor should be given freedom to interview managers, customers, dealers, salespeople, and others who might throw light on marketing performance. Table 3–3 lists the kinds of questions the marketing auditor might ask. Not all of these questions are important in every situation. The auditor will develop a set of findings and recommendations based on this information. The findings may come as a surprise—and sometimes as a shock—to management. Management then decides which recommendations make sense and how and when to implement them.[20]

TABLE 3–3   Parts of the Marketing Audit

*Part I—Marketing Environment Audit*

The Macroenvironment
A. Demographic
   1. What major demographic developments and trends pose opportunities or threats to this company?
   2. What actions has the company taken in response to these developments and trends?
B. Economic
   1. What major developments in income, prices, savings, and credit will impact the company?
   2. What actions has the company taken in response to these developments and trends?
C. Natural
   1. What is the outlook for the cost and availability of natural resources and energy needed by the company?
   2. What concerns have been expressed about the company's role in pollution and conservation, and what steps has the company taken?
D. Technological
   1. What major changes are occurring in technology? What is the company's position in technology?
   2. What major generic substitutes might replace this product?
E. Political
   1. What laws now being proposed could affect marketing strategy and tactics?
   2. What federal, state, and local actions should be watched? What is happening in pollution control, equal employment opportunity, product safety, advertising, price control, and other areas that affect marketing strategy?
F. Cultural
   1. What is the public's attitude toward business and toward the products produced by the company?
   2. What changes in consumer and business life styles and values might affect the company?

The Task Environment
A. Markets
   1. What is happening to market size, growth, geographic distribution, and profits?
   2. What are the major market segments?
B. Customers
   1. How do customers rate the company and its competitors on reputation, product quality, service, salesforce, and price?
   2. How do different customer segments make their buying decisions?
C. Competitors
   1. Who are the major competitors? What are their objectives and strategies, their strengths and weaknesses, their sizes and market shares?
   2. What trends will affect future competition for this product?
D. Distribution and Dealers
   1. What are the main channels for bringing products to customers?
   2. What are the efficiency levels and growth potentials of the different channels?
E. Suppliers
   1. What is the outlook for the availability of key resources used in production?

*(Continued)*

TABLE 3–3   *(Continued)*

2. What trends are occurring among suppliers in their patterns of selling?

F. Marketing Service Firms
   1. What is the cost and availability outlook for transportation services, warehousing facilities, and financial resources?
   2. How effectively is the advertising agency performing?

G. Publics
   1. What publics provide particular opportunities or problems for the company?
   2. What steps has the company taken to deal effectively with each public?

## Part II—Marketing Strategy Audit

A. Business Mission
   1. Is the business mission clearly stated in market-oriented terms? Is it feasible?

B. Marketing Objectives and Goals
   1. Are the corporate and marketing objectives stated in the form of clear goals to guide marketing planning and performance measurement?
   2. Are the marketing objectives appropriate, given the company's competitive position, resources, and opportunities?

C. Strategy
   1. What is the core marketing strategy for achieving the objectives? Is it sound?
   2. Are enough resources (or too many) budgeted to accomplish the marketing objectives?
   3. Are the marketing resources allocated optimally to market segments, territories, and products?
   4. Are the marketing resources allocated optimally to the major elements of the marketing mix—such as product quality, service, salesforce, advertising, promotion, and distribution?

## Part III—Marketing Organization Audit

A. Formal Structure
   1. Does the marketing officer have adequate authority and responsibility over company activities that affect the customer's satisfaction?
   2. Are the marketing activities optimally structured along functional, product, end user, and territorial lines?

B. Functional Efficiency
   1. Are there good communication and working relations between marketing staff and sales?
   2. Is the product management system working effectively? Are product managers able to plan profits or only sales volume?
   3. Are there any groups in marketing that need more training, motivation, supervision, or evaluation?

C. Interface Efficiency
   1. Are there any problems between marketing and manufacturing, R&D, purchasing, or financial management that need attention?

## Part IV—Marketing Systems Audit

A. Marketing Information System
   1. Is the marketing intelligence system producing accurate, sufficient, and timely information about marketplace developments?
   2. Is marketing research being adequately used by company decision makers?

B. Marketing Planning System
   1. Is the marketing planning system effective?
   2. Are sales forecasting and marketing potential measurement soundly carried out?
   3. Are sales quotas set on a proper basis?

C. Marketing Control System
   1. Are control procedures adequate to ensure that the annual plan objectives are being achieved?

*(Continued)*

TABLE 3–3   *(Continued)*

2. Does management periodically analyze the profitability of products, markets, territories, and channels of distribution?

3. Are marketing costs being examined periodically?

D. New-Product Development System

1. Is the company well organized to gather, generate, and screen new-product ideas?

2. Does the company do adequate concept research and business analysis before investing in new ideas?

3. Does the company carry out adequate product and market testing before launching new products?

*Part V—Marketing Productivity Audit*

A. Profitability Analysis

1. What is the profitability of the company's different products, markets, territories, and channels of distribution?

2. Should the company enter, expand, contract, or withdraw from any business segments, and what should be the short- and long-run profit consequences?

B. Cost-Effectiveness Analysis

1. Do any marketing activities seem to have excessive costs? Can cost-reducing steps be taken?

*Part VI—Marketing Function Audits*

A. Products

1. What are the product line objectives? Are these objectives sound? Is the current product line meeting the objectives?

2. Are there products that should be phased out?

3. Are there new products that are worth adding?

4. Would any products benefit from quality, feature, or style modifications?

B. Price

1. What are the pricing objectives, policies, strategies, and procedures? To what extent are prices set on cost, demand, and competitive criteria?

2. Do the customers see the company's prices as being in line with the value of its offer?

3. Does the company use price promotions effectively?

C. Distribution

1. What are the distribution objectives and strategies?

2. Is there adequate market coverage and service?

3. Should the company consider changing its degree of reliance on distributors, sales representatives, and direct selling?

D. Advertising, Sales Promotion, and Public Relations

1. What are the organization's advertising objectives? Are they sound?

2. Is the right amount being spent on advertising? How is the budget determined?

3. Are the ad themes and copy effective? What do customers and the public think about the advertising?

4. Are the advertising media well chosen?

5. Is sales promotion used effectively?

6. Is there a well-conceived public relations program?

E. Salesforce

1. What are the organization's salesforce objectives?

2. Is the salesforce large enough to accomplish the company's objectives?

3. Is the salesforce organized along the proper principles of specialization (territory, market, product)?

4. Does the salesforce show high morale, ability, and effort?

5. Are the procedures adequate for setting quotas and evaluating performances?

6. How is the company's salesforce rated in relation to competitors' salesforces?

# SUMMARY

This chapter examines how marketing strategies are planned, implemented, and controlled.

Each business has to prepare marketing plans for its products, brands, and markets. The main components of a *marketing plan* are executive summary, current marketing situation, threats and opportunities, objectives and issues, marketing strategies, action programs, budgets, and controls. It is often easier to plan good strategies than to carry them out. To be successful, companies must implement the strategies effectively. *Implementation* is the process that turns marketing strategies into marketing actions. Several factors can cause implementation failures—isolated planning, trade-offs between long- and short-term objectives, natural resistance to change, and a lack of detailed implementation plans.

The implementation process links marketing strategy and plans with marketing performance. The process consists of five related elements. The *action program* identifies crucial tasks and decisions needed to implement the marketing plan, assigns them to specific people, and sets up a timetable. The *organization structure* defines tasks and assignments and coordinates the efforts of the company's people and units. The company's *decision and reward systems* guide activities such as planning, information, budgeting, training, control, and personnel evaluation and rewards. Well-designed action programs, organization structures, and systems can encourage good implementation.

Successful implementation also requires careful *human resources planning*. The company must recruit, allocate, develop, and maintain good people. It must carefully match its managers to the requirements of the marketing programs being implemented. The company's managerial climate and company culture can make or break implementation. *Company climate and culture* guide people in the company—good implementation relies on strong, clearly defined cultures that fit the chosen strategy.

Each element of the implementation system must fit company marketing strategy. Moreover, successful implementation depends on how well the company blends the five elements into a cohesive program that supports its strategies.

Most of the responsibility for implementation goes to the company's marketing department. Modern marketing departments are organized in a number of ways. The most common form is the *functional organization*, in which marketing functions are headed by separate managers reporting to the marketing vice-president. The company might also use a *geographic organization*, in which its salesforce or other functions specialize by geographic area. Another form is the *product management organization*, in which products are assigned to product managers who work with functional specialists to develop and implement their plans. A final form is the *market management organization*, in which major markets are assigned to market managers who work with functional specialists.

Marketing organizations carry out three types of marketing control. *Annual plan control* involves monitoring current marketing results to make sure that the annual sales and profit goals will be achieved. The main tools are *sales analysis, market-share analysis, marketing expense-to-sales analysis,* and *customer-attitude tracking*. If underperformance is detected, the company can implement several corrective measures.

*Profitability control* calls for determining the actual profitability of the firm's products, territories, market segments, and channels. *Strategic control* makes sure that the company's marketing objectives, strategies, and systems fit with the current and forecasted marketing environment. It uses the *marketing audit* to determine marketing opportunities and problems and to recommend short-run and long-run actions to improve overall marketing performance.

# QUESTIONS FOR DISCUSSION

1. A junior member of your staff wonders how a 100- or 200-page marketing plan can be condensed into a useful one-page executive summary. What should go into the summary? What should be left out?

2. Describe some of the threats and opportunities facing the fast-food business. How should McDonald's and other chains respond to these threats and opportunities?

3. Overall, which is the most important part of the marketing management process—planning, implementation, or control?

4. What steps can companies take to avoid poor implementation of marketing strategies?

5. Which is easier to change—organization structure or company culture? Which has the greater impact on how well plans are implemented?

6. IBM sells a wide range of information processing systems to individuals and organizations in the United States and around the world. What organization should IBM use for its marketing department—functional, geographic, product-management, or market-management?

7. A friend who owns a restaurant thinks that it is less profitable than it ought to be. How could marketing control help your friend's restaurant be more successful?

8. Why should a public university conduct a periodic marketing audit? Describe briefly how you would conduct an audit of your school and what you think the audit would reveal.

1. For more information, see "How the PC Project Changed the Way IBM Thinks," *Business Week,* October 3, 1983, pp. 86–90; Peter Nulty, "IBM, Clonebuster," *Fortune,* April 27, 1987, p. 225; and Geoff Lewis, "If the PS/2 Is a Winner, Why Is IBM So Frustrated?" *Business Week,* April 11, 1988, pp. 82–83.

2. For an interesting discussion of marketing budgeting methods and processes, see Nigel F. Piercy, "The Marketing Budgeting Process: Marketing Management Implications," *Journal of Marketing,* October 1987, pp. 45–59.

3. Amar Bhide, "Hustle as Strategy," *Harvard Business Review,* September-October 1986, p. 59.

4. For more on diagnosing implementation problems, see Thomas V. Bonoma, "Making Your Marketing Strategy Work," *Harvard Business Review,* March-April 1984, pp. 70–71.

5. See "The New Breed of Strategic Planner: Number-Crunching Professionals Are Giving Way to Line Managers," *Business Week,* September 17, 1984, p. 62; and Michael Goold and Andrew Campbell, "Many Best Ways to Make Strategy," *Harvard Business Review,* November-December 1987, pp. 70–76.

6. See Ray Stata and Modesto A. Maidique, "Bonus System for Balanced Strategy," *Harvard Business Review,* November-December 1980, pp. 156–63.

7. This figure is styled after several models of organizational design components. For example, see Jay R. Galbraith, *Organizational Design* (Reading, MA: Addison-Wesley, 1977); Peter Lorange, *Implementation of Strategic Planning* (Englewood Cliffs, NJ: Prentice Hall, 1982), p. 95; David A. Aaker, *Strategic Market Management* (New York: John Wiley, 1988), Chap. 17; and Carl R. Anderson, *Management: Skills, Functions, and Organization Performance* (Dubuque, IA: Wm. C. Brown, 1984), pp. 409–13.

8. For an extensive discussion of the organizational structures and processes best suited for implementing different business strategies, see Orville C. Walker, Jr., and Robert W. Ruekert, "Marketing's Role in the Implementation of Business Strategies: A Critical Review and Conceptual Framework," *Journal of Marketing,* July 1987, pp. 15–33.

9. See Thomas J. Peters and Robert H. Waterman, *In Search of Excellence: Lessons from America's Best-Run Companies* (New York: Harper & Row, 1982). For an excellent summary of the study's findings on structure, see Aaker, *Strategic Market Management,* pp. 154–57.

10. Peters and Waterman, *In Search of Excellence,* p. 311.

11. See "Who's Excellent Now?" *Business Week,* November 5, 1984, pp. 76–78; and Daniel T. Carroll, "A Disappointing Search for Excellence," *Harvard Business Review,* November-December 1983, pp. 78–79ff.

12. This example is adapted from Robert M. Tomasko, "Focusing Company Reward Systems to Help Achieve Business Objectives," *Management Review* (New York: AMA Membership Publications Division, American Management Association, October 1982), pp. 8–12.

13. For more on human resources planning, see D. Quinn Mills, "Planning with People in Mind," *Harvard Business Review,* July-August 1985, pp. 97–105; and John Hoerr, "Human Resources Managers Aren't Corporate Nobodies Anymore," *Business Week,* December 2, 1985, pp. 58–59.

14. For an interesting discussion of management styles, see J. S. Ninomiya, "Wagon Masters and Lesser Managers," *Harvard Business Review,* March-April 1988, pp. 84–90.

15. Peters and Waterman, *In Search of Excellence,* pp. 75–76. For more on organizational culture and marketing management, see Rohit Deshpande and Frederick E. Webster, Jr., "Organizational Culture and Marketing: Defining the Research Agenda," *Journal of Marketing,* January 19, 1989, pp 3-15.

16. Joseph Winski, "One Brand, One Manager," *Advertising Age,* August 20, 1987, pp. 86ff.

17. See Al Urbanski, "Repackaging the Brand Manager," *Sales & Marketing Management,* April 1987, pp. 42–45. Also see Lenore Skenazy, "Brand Managers Shelved?" *Advertising Age,* July 13, 1987, p. 81.

18. For a more complete discussion of marketing organization approaches and issues, see Robert W. Ruekert, Orville C. Walker, Jr., and Kenneth J. Roering, "The Organization of Marketing Activities: A Contingency Theory of Structure and Performance," *Journal of Marketing,* Winter 1985, pp. 13–25.

19. For details, see Philip Kotler, *Marketing Management: Analysis, Planning, Implementation, and Control* (Englewood Cliffs, NJ: Prentice Hall, 1988), Chap. 25.

20. For good discussions of broad conceptual issues in marketing control, see Bernard J. Jaworski, "Toward a Theory of Marketing Control: Environmental Context, Control Types, and Consequences," *Journal of Marketing,* July 1988, pp. 23–29; and Kenneth A. Merchant, "Progressing toward a Theory of Marketing Control: A Comment," *Journal of Marketing,* July 1988, pp. 40–44.

## Case 3

# CLARION COSMETICS: MAKING THE MASS MARKET BLUSH

Looking back on it, the idea was a natural. Noxell launched Clarion—a slick color cosmetic line of the sort which one normally finds in department stores but which Noxell sold through mass-market outlets at moderate prices. And the plan has worked out beautifully. In one year, Clarion bounded into U.S. drug chains, enticed customers with personalized computer analysis, stunned competitors with an aggressive ad campaign, and emerged as the most successful cosmetic introduction in over a decade. Now, however, Noxell faces adjustments in its marketing plans in order to ensure Clarion's continued success.

Initially positioned as a makeup line for those with sensitive skin, the high-flying Clarion ended 1987 with $50 million in sales and a 5-percent share of the mass cosmetics market. Thus, in only its first year, it almost caught up with Almay, the longtime leader in hypoallergenic makeup that claims a 5.2-percent share.

However, such dramatic success came despite some early concerns. Although the wizardry of computers interacting with customers and providing advice on the individual customer's ideal look was popular in department stores, the concept might have proved unwieldy for other types of outlets. In drugstores and discount chains, for example, the shelf and counter space needed by the apparatus is scarce. In addition, Noxell managers initially worried about just who in such mass outlets could oversee Clarion's expensive product line and computer workings. At department stores, the sales staff had the motivation and skill to perform this complex role. But in the $3 billion mass-cosmetic market, the mode of sell is strictly "pegboard": Most products are selected by the customer from a display rack with little, if any,

assistance from a salesperson. Finally, Noxell was concerned that Clarion might eat into the sales of its best-selling Cover Girl line. Although Clarion had a different positioning, a 25-percent higher price tag, and a supposed appeal to audiences older than Cover Girl's teen and young-adult buyers, the Clarion line still resembled Noxell's bread-and-butter brand in some ways.

Nevertheless, Noxell saw a marketing opportunity. The company already enjoyed a good reputation in the industry because of its Cover Girl cosmetics and Noxzema skin products. As yet, no one else was selling a slickly packaged and advertised line of color cosmetics for sensitive skin. Almay, the segment leader, seemed to be wandering, and its product line and marketing were dull. Moreover, Almay was experiencing internal turmoil: International Playtex, which had originally owned the brand, had undergone a restructuring and had finally sold Almay in 1986 to the Revlon Group—which itself had just changed hands. The market appeared ripe. Noxell had only to look at the amazing success of Clinique, a top-selling, pricey line of fragrance-free cosmetics sold through department stores, to see that there was a broad market for hypoallergenic products. With all this in mind, Noxell launched Clarion in 1987 as a "sensitive-skin makeup with a strong beauty image," says Peter M. Troup, Noxell's senior vice president of marketing.

The Clarion line of cosmetics was based on the four color groups (popularized by the book *Color Me Beautiful*) and Clarion's personalized computer. The computer—first in the mass market—lent a touch of science and reassured women that they were making the right purchases without a cosmetician's help. An exciting new

merchandising technique, the Clarion Personalized Color System works as easily as a cash machine. Women answer questions about their skin type, complexion, hair, and eye color. The computer then recommends specific Clarion products and color groups from which they can choose.

Clarion's marketing strategy—"to look like an important, mainstream cosmetic immediately"—differed from strategies for previous new products. Instead of one product at a time, Noxell launched the 85-item Clarion collection all at once. It used aggressive advertising to help establish Clarion as an important brand. During the first nine months of 1987, Noxell spent about $15 million on advertising for Clarion, making it the third most heavily advertised brand (behind Cover Girl and Maybelline, both spending about $35 million per year). Noxell far outspent other competitors, including Revlon's Almay, Cosmair's L'Oréal, and Max Factor brands.

In addition, Clarion's message was dramatically and immediately communicated using prime-time television specials such as the *American Music* and *Emmy Awards* and high-rated women-appeal programs such as *Dynasty, Dallas, Moonlighting,* and *Family Ties.* Print ads ran in beauty and fashion magazines, such as *Mademoiselle, Glamour, Vogue,* and *Cosmopolitan,* which provided beauty and fashion authority, and in women's service magazines, such as *Good Housekeeping, McCall's, Redbook,* and *New Woman,* which allowed Noxell to reach the mass audience to which Clarion appealed. *Working Woman* was also used to capture the intelligent woman who appreciates a high-quality product in the mass marketplace.

Because the overall color cosmetic

market grew only modestly in 1987, the new Clarion had to take market share away from competitors—and it did just that. The product became an immediate success and sales soared. At the same time, the company insists that it did not cannibalize sales of its own Cover Girl line, which Noxell claims also gained substantial sales growth in the same year. Noxell's aim, says Troup, is now to make Clarion "the third or fourth largest brand behind Cover Girl" in the mass market. Based on units sold, Cover Girl leads with a 21-percent share, followed by Maybelline with 18 percent and Revlon with 17 percent.

Clarion's comely performance and Noxell's deep pockets have sent competitors back to powder their noses. As a direct reaction to Clarion, competitors have launched their own brands. For example, in late 1986, Maybelline introduced Ultra Performance Pure Makeup, a single foundation for sensitive skin. Even Revlon got into the act—in June 1987, it launched fragrance-free and non-irritating New Complexion makeup and press powder.

Many in the industry have dubbed Clarion "the mass-marketer's answer to Clinique"—a label that Noxell does not mind at all. However, while marketer Troup says he "admires" Clinique, he adds that Clarion is positioned at a "broader target than hypoallergenic." Noxell's research shows that more than half of all women identify with sensitive skin: "We feel that more women can relate to 'sensitive skin' than can relate to 'hypoallergenic,'" says Troup. In fact, Clarion never uses the word "hypoallergenic" in its advertising—instead, it uses "Ultra Pure," "fragrance-free," or "sensitivity-tested." The theme line—"Makeup so pure, even women with sensitive skin can wear it. And so beautiful, every woman will want to"—reaches women who want beauty as well as pure makeup.

Thanks to the good channel relations that Noxell has forged through close salesforce supervision of Cover Girl, Clarion has found ready acceptance in chain drugstores. Noxell designed a good-looking display that would hold both Clarion products and the easy-to-use computer. Consumers such as Joni Dietrich of North Brunswick, N.J., found the computer worked as a "gimmick" to lure her to the brand and to make multiple purchases: "I thought it was rather clever," she says, "so I tried it, and I ended up buying more than just blush: I bought all the things that matched it."

In the first-ever award listing in Goldman Sach's winter 1988 *Fragrance and Cosmetic Buyer Survey,* Clarion and Noxell cleaned up. Clarion was named 1987's "Best New Product," Noxell was voted overwhelmingly as "Best All-Around Vendor," and the company won "Best Salesforce" by a landslide. Troup notes that "the sensitive-skin category in the cosmetic market is the fastest growing." And, he adds immodestly, "one of the reasons is because we're in there." As he puts it, "We're a beauty product first and foremost." And in 1987, at least, Clarion was a pretty sight, indeed.

For all of its success, however, Noxell detects some warning signs. Some analysts think that Clarion sales slowed when retailers moved the products from free-standing display units to traditional wall displays. Others believe that Clarion is missing some repeat purchases. Troup admits that with the initial heavy sell-in, "maybe there was some sluggishness" with repeat purchases. In addition, some buyers, in their enthusiasm, probably overpurchased. In hindsight, he says the company might have been better off controlling distribution more closely. The problem has been corrected, and, he adds, Clarion's sales in chain drugstores are now second only to Cover Girl.

The company also had some problems with Clarion's original ad campaign, which communicated a rather murky message. By urging buyers to "discover how pure beautiful color can be," Noxell promoted Clarion for both sensitive skin and cosmetic fashion, thereby diluting both positions. To fix these problems, Noxell switched Clarion to a new advertising agency, Leo Burnett. New ads now tap into the idea of personalization. They highlight the Clarion computer with a new tag line: "Looking Great. And Knowing It!" The new campaign downplays the ideas of hypoallergenic and UltraPure, themes that were emphasized in Clarion's first campaign. Instead, because the currently large number of hypoallergenic products no longer makes the original positioning unique, the benefits of personalized color have now been given a stronger supporting role in Clarion advertising.

According to retailers, analysts, and competitors alike, Noxell's commitment to marketing, and its proven success with Cover Girl, have earned the company respect in the trade. "If Noxell's behind it," says one divisional merchandise manager, "they're going to do whatever they can to keep the line going."

## Questions

1. What is Clarion's current marketing situation? Describe major market segments and competitors.

2. Evaluate the current marketing plan for Clarion. How has it changed from the initial plan and why?

3. What factors are most important in the successful implementation of the Clarion marketing plan?

4. What threats and opportunities should Noxell consider in planning future marketing programs for the Clarion line? What types of control should Noxell use to measure and evaluate the performance of Clarion?

# 4

# Marketing Research and Information Systems

## CHAPTER OBJECTIVES

**After reading this chapter, you should be able to**

1. Explain the importance of information to the company
2. Define the marketing information system and discuss its parts
3. Describe the four steps in the marketing research process
4. Identify the different kinds of information a company might use
5. Compare the advantages and disadvantages of various methods of collecting information

In 1985, the Coca-Cola Company made a spectacular marketing blunder. After 99 successful years, it set aside its longstanding rule—"don't mess with Mother Coke"—and dropped its original formula Coke! In its place came *New* Coke with a sweeter, smoother taste. The company boldly announced the new taste with a flurry of advertising and publicity.

At first, amid the introductory fanfare, New Coke sold well. But sales soon went flat, and a stunned public reacted. Coke began receiving sacks of mail and over 1,500 phone calls each day from angry consumers. A group called "Old Cola Drinkers" staged protests, handed out T-shirts, and threatened a class-action suit unless Coca-Cola brought back the old formula. Most marketing experts predicted that New Coke would be the "Edsel of the Eighties."

After just three months, the Coca-Cola Company brought old Coke back. Now called "Coke Classic," it sold side by side with New Coke on supermarket shelves. The company said that New Coke would remain its "flagship" brand, but consumers had a different idea. By the end of 1985, Classic was outselling New Coke in supermarkets by two to one.

By mid-1986, the company's two largest fountain accounts, McDonald's and Kentucky Fried Chicken, had returned to serving Coke Classic in their restaurants.

Quick reaction saved the company from potential disaster. It stepped up efforts for Coke Classic and slotted New Coke into a supporting role. By 1987, Coke Classic was again the company's main brand—and the country's leading soft drink. New Coke became the company's "attack brand"—its Pepsi stopper. With computer-enhanced star Max Headroom leading the charge, company ads boldly compared New Coke's taste with Pepsi's. Still, New Coke managed only a 2 percent market share. By 1989, Coke Classic was outselling New Coke ten to one. Coca-Cola cut the brand's ad budget in half and most experts are predicting that the company will allow New Coke to simply fade away.

Why was New Coke introduced in the first place? What went wrong? Many analysts blame the blunder on poor marketing research.

In the early 1980s, although Coke was still the leading soft drink, it was slowly losing market share to

Pepsi. For years, Pepsi had successfully mounted the "Pepsi Challenge," a series of televised taste tests showing that consumers preferred the sweeter taste of Pepsi. By early 1985, although Coke led in the overall market, Pepsi led in share of supermarket sales by 2 percent. (That doesn't sound like much, but 2 percent of the huge soft-drink market amounts to $600 million in retail sales!) Coca-Cola had to do something to stop the loss of its market share—and the solution appeared to be a change in Coke's taste.

Coca-Cola began the largest new-product research project in the company's history. It spent over two years and $4 million on research before settling on a new formula. It conducted some 200,000 taste tests—30,000 on the final formula alone. In blind tests, 60 percent of consumers chose the new Coke over the old, and 52 percent chose it over Pepsi. Research showed that New Coke would be a winner and the company introduced it with confidence. So what happened?

Looking back, we can see that Coke's marketing research was too narrowly focused. The research looked only at taste; it did not explore consumers' feelings about dropping the old Coke and replacing it with a new version. It took no account of the *intangibles*—Coke's name, history, packaging, cultural heritage, and image. But to many people, Coke stands beside baseball, hot dogs, and apple pie as an American institution; it represents the very fabric of America. Coke's symbolic meaning turned out to be more important to many consumers than its taste. More complete marketing research could have detected these strong emotions.

Coke's managers may also have used poor judgment in interpreting the research and planning strategies around it. For example, they took the finding that 60 percent of consumers preferred New Coke's taste to mean that the new product would win in the marketplace—as when a political candidate wins with 60 percent of the vote. But it also meant that 40 percent still liked the old Coke. By dropping the old Coke, the company trampled the taste buds of the large core of loyal Coke drinkers who didn't want a change. The company might have been wiser to leave the old Coke alone and introduce New Coke as a brand extension, as was later done successfully with Cherry Coke.

The Coca-Cola Company has one of the largest, best-managed, and most-advanced marketing research operations in America. Good marketing research has kept the company atop the rough-and-tumble soft drink market for decades. But marketing research is far from an exact science. Consumers are full of surprises, and figuring them out can be awfully tough. If Coca-Cola can make a large marketing research mistake, any company can.[1]

In carrying out marketing analysis, planning, implementation, and control, marketing managers need information at almost every turn. They need information about customers, competitors, dealers, and other forces in the marketplace. One marketing executive put it this way: "To manage a business well is to manage its future; and to manage the future is to manage information."[2]

During the past century, most companies were small and knew their customers firsthand. Managers picked up marketing information by being around people, observing them, and asking questions. During this century, however, many factors have increased the need for more and better information. As companies become national or international in scope, they need more information on larger, more distant markets. As incomes increase and buyers become more selective, sellers need better information about how buyers respond to different products and appeals. As sellers use more complex marketing approaches and face more competition, they need information on the effectiveness of their marketing tools. Finally, in today's more rapidly changing environments, managers need more up-to-date information to make timely decisions.

The supply of information has also increased greatly. John Neisbitt suggests that the United States is undergoing a "megashift" from an industrial to an information-based economy.[3] He found that over 65 percent of the U.S. work force is now employed in producing or processing information, compared with only 17 percent in 1950. Using improved computer systems and other technologies, companies can now provide information in great quantities. In fact, today's managers sometimes receive too much information. For example, one study found that with all the companies offering data, and with all the

Marketing intelligence can be gathered from many sources. Much intelligence can be collected from the company's own personnel—executives, engineers and scientists, purchasing agents, and the salesforce. But company people are often busy and fail to pass on important information. The company must "sell" its people on their importance as intelligence gatherers, train them to spot new developments, and urge them to report intelligence back to the company.

The company must also get suppliers, resellers, and customers to pass along important intelligence. Information on competitors can be obtained from what they say about themselves in annual reports, speeches and press releases, and advertisements. The company can also learn about competitors from what others say about them in business publications and at trade shows. Or a company can watch what competitors do—it can buy and analyze their products, monitor their sales, and check for new patents (see Marketing Highlight 4–1).

Companies also buy intelligence information from outside suppliers. The

employees to spill the beans . . . Often applicants have toiled in obscurity or feel that their careers have stalled. They're dying to impress somebody.

□ *Getting Information from People Who Do Business with Competitors.* Key customers can keep the company informed about competitors and their products:

For example, a while back Gillette told a large Canadian account the date on which it planned to begin selling its new Good News disposable razor in the United States. The Canadian distributor promptly called Bic and told it about the impending product launch. Bic put on a crash program and was able to start selling its razor shortly after Gillette did.

Intelligence can also be gathered by infiltrating customers' business operations:

Companies may provide their engineers free of charge to customers . . . The close, cooperative relationship that the engineers on loan cultivate with the customer's design staff often enables them to learn what new products competitors are pitching.

□ *Getting Information from Published Materials and Public Documents.*

Keeping track of seemingly meaningless published information can provide competitor intelligence. For example, the types of people sought in help-wanted ads can indicate something about a competitor's new strategies and products. Government agencies are another good source. For example:

Although it is often illegal for a company to photograph a competitor's plant from the air there are legitimate ways to get the photos . . . Aerial photos often are on file with the U.S. Geological Survey or Environmental Protection Agency. These are public documents, available for a nominal fee.

□ *Getting Information by Observing Competitors or Analyzing Physical Evidence.* Companies can get to know competitors better by buying their products or examining other physical evidence:

Companies increasingly buy competitors' products and take them apart to . . . determine costs of production and even manufacturing methods.
In the absence of better information on market share and the volume of product competitors are shipping, companies have measured the rust on rails of

railroad sidings to their competitors' plants or have counted the tractor-trailers leaving loading bays.

Some companies even buy their competitors' garbage:

Once it has left the competitor's premises, refuse is legally considered abandoned property. While some companies now shred the paper coming out of their design labs, they often neglect to do this for almost-as-revealing refuse from the marketing or public relations departments.

Although most of these techniques are legal and some are considered shrewd competitiveness, many involve questionable ethics. The company should take advantage of publicly available information but avoid practices that might be considered illegal or unethical. A company does not have to break the law or accepted codes of ethics to get good intelligence information.

*Source:* Based on Steven Flax, "How to Snoop on Your Competitors," *Fortune,* May 14, 1984, pp. 29–33. © 1984 Time Inc. All rights reserved.

**marketing research** The function that links the consumer, customer, and public to the marketer through information—information used to identify and define marketing opportunities and problems; to generate, refine, and evaluate marketing actions; to monitor marketing performance; and to improve understanding of the marketing process.

A. C. Nielsen Company sells data on brand shares, retail prices, and percentages of stores stocking different brands. The Market Research Corporation of America sells reports on weekly movements of brand shares, sizes, prices, and deals. For a fee, companies can subscribe to one or more of over 3,000 online databases or information-search services. For example, the *Adtrack* online database tracks all the advertisements of a quarter page or larger from 150 major consumer and business publications. Companies can use these data to assess their own and competitors' advertising strategies and styles, shares of advertising space, media usage, and ad budgets. The *Donnelly Demographics* database provides demographic data from the U.S. census plus Donnelly's own demographic projections by state, city, or zip code. Companies can use it to measure markets and develop segmentation strategies. The *Electronic Yellow Pages,* containing listings from nearly all the nation's 4,800 phone books, is the largest directory of American companies available. A firm like Burger King might use this database to count McDonald's restaurants in different geographic locations. A readily available online database exists to fill almost any marketing information need.[8]

Marketing intelligence can work in two directions, so companies must sometimes take steps to protect themselves from the snooping of competitors. For example, Kellogg had treated the public to tours of its Battle Creek plant since 1906 but recently closed its newly upgraded plant to outsiders to prevent competitors from getting any intelligence on its high-tech equipment. In its corporate offices, Du Pont displays a poster showing two people at a lunch table and warns, "Be careful in casual conversation. Keep security in mind."[9]

Some companies set up an office to collect and circulate marketing intelligence. The staff scans major publications, summarizes important news, and sends news bulletins to marketing managers. It develops a file of intelligence information and helps managers to evaluate new information. These services greatly improve the quality of information available to marketing managers.

## Marketing Research

Managers cannot always wait for information to arrive in bits and pieces from the marketing intelligence system. They often require formal studies of specific situations. For example, Hewlett-Packard wants to know how many and what kinds of people or companies will buy its new ultralight personal computer. Or Barat College in Lake Forest, Illinois, needs to know what percentage of its target market has heard of Barat, what they know, how they heard about Barat, and how they feel about Barat. In such situations, the marketing intelligence system will not provide the detailed information needed. And managers normally do not have the skill or time to obtain the information on their own. They need formal marketing research.

We define **marketing research** as the function that links the consumer, customer, and public to the marketer through information—information used to identify and define marketing opportunities and problems; to generate, refine, and evaluate marketing actions; to monitor marketing performance; and to improve understanding of the marketing process.[10] Marketing research specifies the information needed to address marketing issues, designs the method for collecting information, manages and implements the data-collection process, analyzes the results, and communicates the findings and their implications.

A recent survey found that marketing researchers engage in a wide variety of activities, ranging from analyses of sales and market shares to studies of social values and policies (see Table 4–1). The ten most common activities are measurement of market potentials, market-share analysis, the determination of

TABLE 4–1  Research Activities of 599 Companies

| Type of Research | Percent Doing It | Type of Research | Percent Doing It |
|---|---|---|---|
| *Advertising Research* | | *Product Research* | |
| A. Motivation research | 47 | A. New product acceptance and potential | 76 |
| B. Copy research | 61 | B. Competitive product studies | 87 |
| C. Media research | 68 | C. Testing of existing products | 80 |
| D. Studies of ad effectiveness | 76 | D. Packaging research: design or physical | 65 |
| E. Studies of competitive advertising | 67 |     characteristics | |
| *Business Economics and Corporate Research* | | *Sales and Market Research* | |
| A. Short-range forecasting (up to 1 year) | 89 | A. Measurement of market potentials | 97 |
| B. Long-range forecasting (over 1 year) | 87 | B. Market-share analysis | 97 |
| C. Studies of business trends | 91 | C. Determination of market characteristics | 97 |
| D. Pricing studies | 83 | D. Sales analysis | 92 |
| E. Plant and warehouse location studies | 68 | E. Establishment of sales quotas, territories | 78 |
| F. Acquisition studies | 73 | F. Distribution channel studies | 71 |
| G. Export and international studies | 49 | G. Test markets, store audits | 59 |
| H. MIS (Management Information System) | 80 | H. Consumer panel operations | 63 |
| I. Operations research | 65 | I. Sales compensation studies | 60 |
| J. Internal company employees | 76 | J. Promotional studies of premiums, coupons, sampling, deals, etc. | 58 |
| *Corporate Responsibility Research* | | | |
| A. Consumer "right to know" studies | 18 | | |
| B. Ecological impact studies | 23 | | |
| C. Studies of legal constraints on advertising and promotion | 46 | | |
| D. Social values and policies studies | 39 | | |

*Source:* Dik Warren Twedt, ed., *1983 Survey of Marketing Research* (Chicago: American Marketing Association, 1983), p. 41.

market characteristics, sales analysis, studies of business trends, short-range forecasting, competitive product studies, long-range forecasting, marketing information systems studies, and pricing studies.

Every marketer needs research. A company can do marketing research in its own research department or have some or all of it done outside. Whether a company uses outside firms depends on the skills and resources within the company. Most large companies have their own marketing research departments. A company with no research department will have to buy the services of research firms. But even companies with their own departments often use outside firms to do special research tasks or special studies.

## The Marketing Research Process

This section describes the four steps in the marketing research process, shown in Figure 4–2: *defining the problem and research objectives, developing the*

FIGURE 4-2  The Marketing Research Process

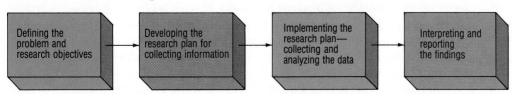

**exploratory research** Marketing research to gather preliminary information that will help to better define problems and suggest hypotheses.

**descriptive research** Marketing research to better describe marketing problems, situations, or markets—such as the market potential for a product or the demographics and attitudes of consumers.

**causal research** Marketing research to test hypotheses about cause-and-effect relationships.

*research plan, implementing the research plan,* and *interpreting and reporting the findings.*

## Defining the Problem and Research Objectives

The marketing manager and the researcher must work together closely to define the problem carefully and agree on research objectives. The manager best understands the decision for which information is needed; the researcher best understands marketing research and how to obtain the information.

Managers must know enough about marketing research to help in the planning and to interpret research results. If they know little about marketing research, they may obtain the wrong information, accept wrong conclusions, or ask for information that costs too much. Experienced marketing researchers who understand the manager's problem should also be involved at this stage. The researcher must be able to help the manager define the problem and to suggest ways that research can help the manager make better decisions.

Defining the problem and research objectives is often the hardest step in the research process. The manager may know that something is wrong, but not the specific causes. For example, managers of a discount retail store chain hastily decided that falling sales were caused by poor advertising and ordered research to test the company's advertising. When this research showed that current advertising was reaching the right people with the right message, the managers were puzzled. It turned out that the chain was not delivering what the advertising promised. More careful problem definition would have avoided the cost and delay of doing advertising research. It would have suggested research on the real problem of consumer reactions to the products, service, and prices offered in the chain's stores.

When the problem has been carefully defined, the manager and researcher must set the research objectives. A marketing research project might have one of three types of objectives. Sometimes the objective is **exploratory**—to gather preliminary information that will help to better define the problem and suggest hypotheses. Sometimes the objective is **descriptive**—to describe things such as the market potential for a product or the demographics and attitudes of consumers who buy the product. Sometimes the objective is **causal**—to test hypotheses about cause-and-effect relationships. For example, would a 10 percent decrease in tuition for a private college result in more than the increase in enrollments needed to break even financially? Managers often start with exploratory research and later follow with descriptive or causal research.

The statement of the problem and research objectives will guide the entire research process. The manager and researcher should put the statement in writing to be certain that they agree on the purpose and expected results of the research.

## Developing the Research Plan

The second step of the marketing research process calls for determining the information needed, developing a plan for gathering it efficiently, and presenting the plan to marketing management. The plan outlines sources of secondary data and spells out the specific research approaches, contact methods, sampling plans, and instruments that researchers will use to gather primary data.

***Determining Specific Information Needs*** ▪ Research objectives must be translated into specific information needs. For example, suppose Campbell decides to do research to find out how consumers will react to a new bowl-shaped plastic container that costs more but allows consumers to heat the soup in a microwave oven and eat it without using dishes. This research might call for the following specific information:

□ The demographic, economic, and life-style characteristics of current soup users. (Busy working couples might find the convenience of the new package worth the price; families with children might want to pay less and wash the pan and bowls.)

□ Consumer-usage patterns for soup—how much soup they eat, where, and when. (The new package might be ideal for adults eating lunch on the go but less convenient for parents feeding lunch to several children.)

□ The number of microwave ovens in consumer and commercial markets. (The number of microwaves in homes and business lunchrooms will limit the demand for the new container.)

□ Retailer reactions to the new package. (Failure to get retailer support could hurt sales of the new package.)

□ Forecasts of sales of both new and current packages. (Will the new package increase Campbell's profits?)

Campbell managers will need these and many other types of information to decide whether or not to introduce the new product.

**secondary data** Information that already exists somewhere, having been collected for another purpose.

**primary data** Information collected for the specific purpose at hand.

***Surveys of Secondary Information*** ▪ To meet the manager's information needs, the researcher can gather secondary data, primary data, or both. **Secondary data** consist of information that already exist somewhere, having been collected for another purpose. **Primary data** consist of information collected for the specific purpose at hand.

Researchers usually start by gathering secondary data. Table 4–2 on page 90 shows the many secondary data sources, including *internal* and *external* sources.[11] Secondary data can usually be obtained more quickly and at a lower cost than primary data. For example, a visit to the library might provide all the information Campbell needs on microwave oven usage at almost no cost. A study to collect primary information might take weeks or months and cost thousands of dollars. Also, secondary sources can sometimes provide data that an individual company cannot collect on its own—information that is not directly available or would be too expensive to collect. For example, it would be too expensive for Campbell to conduct a continuing retail store audit to find out about the market shares, prices, and displays of competitors' brands. But it can buy the Nielsen Retail Index, which provides this information from regular audits of 1,300 supermarkets, 700 drug stores, and 150 mass merchandisers.[12]

Secondary data also present problems. The needed information may not exist—researchers can rarely obtain all the data they need from secondary sources. For example, Campbell will not find existing information about consumer reactions to a new package that it has not yet placed on the market. Even when data can be found, they might not be very usable. The researcher must evaluate secondary information carefully to make certain it is *relevant*, *accurate*, *current*, and *impartial*.

Secondary data provide a good starting point for research and often help to define problems and research objectives. In most cases, however, secondary sources cannot provide all the needed information, and the company must collect primary data.

***Planning Primary Data Collection*** ▪ Good decisions require good data. Just as researchers must carefully evaluate the quality of secondary information they obtain, they must also take great care in collecting primary data to ensure that they provide marketing decision makers with relevant, accurate, current, and unbiased information. Table 4–3 on page 91 shows that designing a plan for primary data collection calls for a number of decisions on *research approaches*, *contact methods*, *sampling plan*, and *research instruments*.

**TABLE 4-2  Sources of Secondary Data**

### A. Internal Sources

Internal sources include company profit-and-loss statements, balance sheets, sales figures, sales call reports, invoices, inventory records, and prior research reports.

### B. Government Publications

*Statistical Abstract of the United States,* updated annually, provides summary data on demographic, economic, social, and other aspects of the American economy and society.

*County and City Data Book,* updated every three years, presents statistical information for counties, cities, and other geographical units on population, education, employment, aggregate and median income, housing, bank deposits, retail sales, etc.

*U.S. Industrial Outlook* provides projections of industrial activity by industry and includes data on production, sales, shipments, employment, etc.

*Marketing Information Guide* provides a monthly annotated bibliography of marketing information.

Other government publications include the *Annual survey of Manufacturers; Business Statistics; Census of Manufacturers; Census of Population; Census of Retail Trade, Wholesale Trade, and Selected Service Industries; Census of Transportation; Federal Reserve Bulletin; Monthly Labor Review; Survey of Current Business;* and *Vital Statistics Report.*

### C. Periodicals and Books

*Business Periodicals Index,* a monthly, lists business articles appearing in a wide variety of business publications.

*Standard and Poor's Industry Surveys* provide updated statistics and analyses of industries.

*Moody's Manuals* provide financial data and names of executives in major companies.

*Encyclopedia of Associations* provides information on every major trade and professional association in the United States.

Marketing journals include the *Journal of Marketing, Journal of Marketing Research,* and *Journal of Consumer Research.*

Useful trade magazines include *Advertising Age, Chain Store Age, Progressive Grocer, Sales and Marketing Management, Stores.*

Useful general business magazines include *Business Week, Fortune, Forbes,* and *Harvard Business Review.*

### D. Commercial Data

Here are just a few of the dozens of commercial research houses selling data to subscribers:

*A. C. Nielsen* provides data on products and brands sold through retail outlets (Retail Index Services), supermarket scanner data (Scantrack), data on television audiences (Media Research Services), and others.

*Arbitron/SAMI/Burke* provides television and radio audience data (Arbitron), product movement reports based on warehouse withdrawals data from supermarkets and drugstores (SAMI reports), and supermarket scanner data (Samscan).

*Information Resources, Inc.* provides supermarket scanner data for test marketing purposes (BehaviorScan) and for tracking grocery product movement (InfoScan).

*Simmons Market Research Bureau (MRB Group)* provides annual reports covering television markets, sporting goods, and proprietary drugs, giving demographic data by sex, income, age, and brand preferences.

*I.M.S. International* provides reports on the movement of pharmaceuticals, hospital laboratory supplies, animal health products, and personal care products.

*NFO Research* provides data for the beverage industry (SIPS), mail order (MOMS), and carpet and rug industries (CARS).

**TABLE 4–3**   Planning Primary Data Collection

| Research Approaches | Contact Methods | Sampling Plan | Research Instruments |
|---|---|---|---|
| Observation | Mail | Sampling unit | Questionnaire |
| Survey | Telephone | Sample size | Mechanical instruments |
| Experiment | Personal | Sampling procedure | |

***Research Approaches*** ▪ **Observational research** is the gathering of primary data by observing relevant people, actions, and situations. For example:

- ◻ A food-products manufacturer sends researchers into supermarkets to find out the prices of competing brands or how much shelf space and display support retailers give its brands.
- ◻ A bank evaluates possible new-branch locations by checking traffic patterns, neighborhood conditions, and the locations of competing branches.
- ◻ A maker of personal care products pretests its ads by showing them to people and measuring eye movements, pulse rates, and other physical reactions.
- ◻ A department store chain sends observers posing as customers to its stores to check on store conditions and customer service.
- ◻ A museum checks the popularity of various exhibits by noting the amount of floor wear around them.

Several companies sell information collected through *mechanical* observation. For example, the A. C. Nielsen Company attaches "people meters" to television sets in selected homes to record who watches which programs. Nielsen then provides summaries of the size and demographic makeup of audiences for different television programs. The television networks use these ratings to judge program popularity and to set charges for advertising time. Advertisers use the ratings when selecting programs for their commercials.[13]

Checkout scanners in retail stores also provide mechanical observation data. These scanners record consumer purchases in detail. Several companies collect and process scanner data for client companies. For example, the Information Resources, Inc., BehaviorScan service maintains panels of consumer households in major markets. Each household receives an identification number. When household members shop for groceries, they give their identification number to the checkout clerk. All the information about the family's

*Commercial data: InfoScan provides data for tracking grocery product movement.*

**survey research** The gathering of primary data by asking people questions about their knowledge, attitudes, preferences, and buying behavior.

**experimental research** The gathering of primary data by selecting matched groups of subjects, giving them different treatments, controlling related factors, and checking for differences in group responses.

purchases—brands bought, package sizes, prices paid—is recorded by the scanner and immediately entered by computer into the family's purchase file. The file also contains information about the household, such as income and age of children. Finally, the system monitors in-store factors that might affect buying, such as special price promotions and shelf displays. Thus, BehaviorScan provides companies with quick and detailed information about how their products are selling, who is buying them, and what factors affect purchase.[14]

Observational research can also be used to obtain information that people are unwilling or unable to provide. In some cases, observation may be the only way to obtain the needed information. On the other hand, some things simply cannot be observed—things such as feelings, attitudes and motives, or personal behavior. Long-run or infrequent behavior is also difficult to observe. Because of these limitations, researchers often use observation along with other data-collection methods.

**Survey research** is the approach best suited for gathering *descriptive* information. A company that wants to know about people's knowledge, attitudes, preferences, or buying behavior can often find out by asking them directly. Survey research can be structured or unstructured. *Structured* surveys use formal lists of questions asked of all respondents in the same way. *Unstructured* surveys let the interviewer probe respondents and guide the interview according to their answers.

Survey research can be direct or indirect. In the *direct* approach, the researcher asks direct questions about behavior or thoughts—for example, "Why don't you buy clothes at K mart?" By contrast, the researcher might use the *indirect* approach by asking, "What kinds of people buy clothes at K mart?" From the response to this indirect question, the researcher may be able to discover why the consumer avoids K mart clothing—in fact, it may suggest reasons the consumer is not consciously aware of.

Survey research is the most widely used method for primary data collection, and it is often the only method used in a research study. The major advantage of survey research is its flexibility. It can be used to obtain many different kinds of information in many different marketing situations. Depending on the survey design, it may also provide information more quickly and at lower cost than observational or experimental research.

However, survey research also has some problems. Sometimes people are unable to answer survey questions because they cannot remember or never thought about what they do and why. Or people may be unwilling to answer questions asked by unknown interviewers or about things they consider private. Busy people may not take the time. Respondents may answer survey questions even when they do not know the answer in order to appear smarter or more informed. Or they may try to help the interviewer by giving pleasing answers. Careful survey design can help to minimize these problems.

Whereas observation is best suited for exploratory research and surveys for descriptive research, **experimental research** is best suited for gathering *causal* information. Experiments involve selecting matched groups of subjects, giving them different treatments, controlling unrelated factors, and checking for differences in group responses. Thus, experimental research tries to explain cause-and-effect relationships. Observation and surveys can be used to collect information for experimental research.

Researchers at McDonald's might use experiments before adding a new sandwich to the menu to answer such questions as the following:

- How much will the new sandwich increase McDonald's sales?
- How will the new sandwich affect the sales of other menu items?
- Which advertising approach would have the greatest effect on sales of the sandwich?

□ How would different prices affect the sales of the product?

□ Should the new item be targeted toward adults, children, or both?

For example, to test the effects of two different prices, McDonald's could set up the following simple experiment. It could introduce the new sandwich at one price in its restaurants in one city and at another price in restaurants in another city. If the cities are similar, and if all other marketing efforts for the sandwich are the same, then differences in sales in the two cities could be related to the price charged. More complex experiments could be designed to include other variables and other locations.

**Contact Methods** ▪ Information can be collected by mail, telephone, or personal interview. Table 4–4 shows the strengths and weaknesses of each of these contact methods.

*Mail questionnaires* have many advantages. They can be used to collect large amounts of information at a low cost per respondent. Respondents may give more honest answers to more personal questions on a mail questionnaire than to an unknown interviewer in person or over the phone. No interviewer is involved to bias the respondent's answers.

However, mail questionnaires also have some disadvantages. They are not very flexible—they require simple and clearly worded questions; all respondents answer the same questions in a fixed order; and the researcher cannot adapt the questionnaire based on earlier answers. Mail surveys usually take longer to complete, and the response rate—the number of people returning completed questionnaires—is often very low. Finally, the researcher often has little control over the mail questionnaire sample—even with a good mailing list, it is often hard to control *who* at the mailing address fills out the questionaire.

*Telephone interviewing* is the best method for gathering information quickly, and it provides greater flexibility than mail questionnaires. Interviewers can explain questions that are not understood. Depending on the respondent's answers, they can skip some questions or probe further on others. Telephone interviewing also allows greater sample control. Interviewers can ask to speak to respondents with the desired characteristics or even by name, and response rates tend to be higher than with mail questionnaires.

But telephone interviewing also has drawbacks. The cost per respondent is higher than with mail questionnaires, and people may not want to discuss personal questions with an interviewer. Using an interviewer increases flexibility but also introduces interviewer bias. The way interviewers talk, small differences in how they ask questions, and other differences may affect respondents' answers. Finally, different interviewers may interpret and record respons-

TABLE 4–4  Strengths and Weaknesses of the Three Contact Methods

|  | Mail | Telephone | Personal |
|---|---|---|---|
| 1. Flexibility | Poor | Good | Excellent |
| 2. Quantity of data that can be collected | Good | Fair | Excellent |
| 3. Control of interviewer effects | Excellent | Fair | Poor |
| 4. Control of sample | Fair | Excellent | Fair |
| 5. Speed of data collection | Poor | Excellent | Good |
| 6. Response rate | Poor | Good | Good |
| 7. Cost | Good | Fair | Poor |

*Source:* Adapted with permission of Macmillan Publishing Company from *Marketing Research: Measurement and Method*, 4th ed., by Donald S. Tull and Del I. Hawkins. Copyright © 1987 by Macmillan Publishing Company.

**focus-group interviewing** Personal interviewing that consists of inviting six to ten people to gather for a few hours with a trained interviewer to talk about a product, service, or organization.

es differently, and under time pressures some interviewers might even cheat by recording answers without asking questions.

*Personal interviewing* takes two forms—individual and group interviewing. *Individual interviewing* involves talking with people in their homes or offices, on the street, or in shopping malls. The interviewer must gain their cooperation, and the time involved can range from a few minutes to several hours. Sometimes a small payment is given to people in return for their time.

*Group interviewing* consists of inviting six to ten people to gather for a few hours with a trained interviewer to talk about a product, service, or organization. The interviewer needs objectivity, knowledge of the subject and industry, and some understanding of group and consumer behavior. The participants are normally paid a small sum for attending. The meeting is held in a pleasant place and refreshments are served to make things informal. The interviewer starts with broad questions before moving to more specific issues and encourages free and easy discussion, hoping that group interactions will bring out actual feelings and thoughts. At the same time, the interviewer "focuses" the discussion—hence the name **focus-group interviewing.** The comments are recorded through written notes or on videotapes that are studied later. Focus-group interviewing has become one of the major marketing research tools for gaining insight into consumer thoughts and feelings.

Personal interviewing is quite flexible and can be used to collect large amounts of information. Trained interviewers can hold a respondent's attention for a long time and can explain difficult questions. They can guide interviews, explore issues, and probe as the situation requires. Personal interviews can be used with any type of questionnaire. Interviewers can show subjects actual products, advertisements, or packages and observe reactions and behavior. In most cases, personal interviews can be conducted fairly quickly.

The main drawbacks of personal interviewing are costs and sampling problems. Personal interviews may cost three or four times as much as telephone interviews. Group interview studies usually use small sample sizes to keep time and costs down, and it may be hard to generalize from the results. Because interviewers have more freedom in personal interviews, there is a greater problem of interviewer bias.

Which contact method is best depends on what information the researcher wants and on the number and types of respondents to be contacted. Advances in computers and communications have had an impact on methods of obtaining information. For example, most research firms now do Computer Assisted Telephone Interviewing (CATI) with a combination of WATS (Wide Area

*Researchers watch a focus group session.*

**sample** A segment of the population selected for marketing research to represent the population as a whole.

*Computer assisted telephone interviewing (CATI): the interviewer enters respondent's answers directly into the computer.*

Telephone Service) lines and data-entry terminals. The interviewer reads a set of questions from a video screen and types the respondent's answers right into the computer. This procedure eliminates data editing and coding, reduces errors, and saves time. Other research firms set up terminals in shopping centers— respondents sit down at a terminal, read questions from a screen, and type their own answers into the computer.

*Sampling Plan* ▪ Marketing researchers usually draw conclusions about large groups of consumers by studying a small sample of the. total consumer population. A **sample** is a segment of the population selected to represent the population as a whole. Ideally, the sample should be representative so that the researcher can make accurate estimates of the thoughts and behaviors of the larger population.

Designing the sample calls for three decisions. First, *who* is to be surveyed (what *sampling unit*)? The answer to this question is not always obvious. For example, to study the decision-making process for a family automobile purchase, should the researcher interview the husband, wife, other family members, dealership salespeople, or all of these? The researcher must determine what information is needed and who is most likely to have it.

Second, *how many* people should be surveyed (what *sample size*)? Large samples give more reliable results than small samples. However, it is not necessary to sample the entire target market or even a large portion to get reliable results. If well chosen, samples of less than one percent of a population can often give good reliability.

Third, *how* should the people in the sample be *chosen* (what *sampling procedure*)? They might be chosen at random from the entire population (a *probability sample*). Or the research might select people who are easiest to obtain information from (a *convenience sample*). Or the researcher might interview a specified number of people in each of several demographic groups (a *quota sample*). These and other ways of drawing samples have different costs and time limitations, as well as different accuracy and statistical properties. Which method is best depends on the needs of the research project.

*Research Instruments* ▪ In collecting primary data, marketing researchers have a choice of two main research instruments—the *questionnaire* and *mechanical devices*.

The *questionnaire* is by far the most common instrument. Broadly speaking, a questionnaire consists of a set of questions presented to a respondent for his or her answers. The questionnaire is very flexible—there are many ways to ask questions. Questionnaires must be carefully developed and tested before they can be used on a large scale. We can usually spot several errors in a carelessly prepared questionnaire (see Marketing Highlight 4–2).

In preparing a questionnaire, the marketing researcher must decide what questions to ask, the form of the questions, the wording of the questions, and the ordering of the questions. Questionnaires frequently leave out questions that should be answered and include some that cannot be answered, will not be answered, or need not be answered. Each question should be checked to see that it contributes to the research objectives.

The *form* of the question can influence the response. Marketing researchers distinguish between closed-end and open-end questions. *Closed-end questions* include all the possible answers, and subjects make choices among them. Examples include multiple-choice questions and scale questions. *Open-end questions* allow respondents to answer in their own words. In a survey of airline users, Delta might simply ask, "What is your opinion of Delta Airlines?" Or it might ask people to complete a sentence: "When I choose an airline, the most important consideration is. . . ." These and other kinds of open-end questions often reveal more than closed-end questions because respondents are not limited in their answers. Open-end questions are especially useful in exploratory research in which the researcher is trying to find out *what* people think but not measuring *how many* people think in a certain way. Closed-end questions, on the other hand, provide answers that are easier to interpret and tabulate.

Care should also be used in the *wording* of questions. The researcher should use simple, direct, unbiased wording. The questions should be pretested before they are widely used. Care should also be used in the *ordering* of

# Marketing Highlight 4–2

## A "QUESTIONABLE" QUESTIONNAIRE

Suppose the following questionnaire had been prepared by a summer camp director to be used in interviewing parents of prospective campers. How do you feel about each question?

1. What is your income to the nearest hundred dollars?
   *People don't necessarily know their income to the nearest hundred dollars nor do they want to reveal their income that closely. Furthermore, a questionnaire should never open with such a personal question.*

2. Are you a strong or a weak supporter of overnight summer camping for your children?
   *What do "strong" and "weak" mean?*

3. Do your children behave themselves well in a summer camp?
   Yes ( ) No ( )
   *"Behave" is a relative term. Besides, will people want to answer this? Furthermore, is "yes" or "no" the best way to allow a response to the question? Why is the question being asked in the first place?*

4. How many camps mailed literature to you last April? This April?
   *Who can remember this?*

5. What are the most salient and determinant attributes in your evaluation of summer camps?
   *What are "salient" and "determinant attributes"? Don't use big words on me.*

6. Do you think it is right to deprive your child of the opportunity to grow into a mature person through the experience of summer camping?
   *Loaded question. How can one answer "yes," given the bias?*

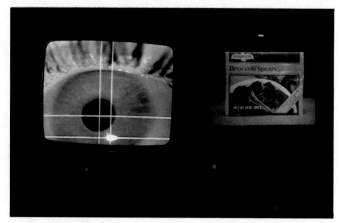

*Mechanical research instruments: eye cameras determine where eyes land and how long they linger on a given item.*

questions. The first question should create interest if possible. Difficult or personal questions should be asked last so that respondents do not become defensive. The questions should come up in a logical order.

Although questionnaires are the most common research instrument, *mechanical instruments* are also used. We discussed two mechanical instruments—people meters and supermarket scanners—earlier in the chapter. Another group of mechanical devices measures subjects' physical responses. For example, a galvanometer measures the strength of interest or emotions aroused by a subject's exposure to an ad or picture. The galvanometer detects the minute degree of sweating that accompanies emotional arousal. The tachistoscope flashes an ad to a subject at an exposure range from less than one-hundredth of a second to several seconds. After each exposure, the respondents describe everything they recall. Eye cameras are used to study respondents' eye movements and determine at what points their eyes land first and how long they linger on a given item.

***Presenting the Research Plan*** ▪ At this stage, the marketing researcher should summarize the plan in a *written proposal*. A written proposal is especially important when the research project will be large and complex or when an outside firm carries it out. The proposal should cover the management problems addressed and the research objectives, the information to be obtained, the sources of secondary information or methods for collecting primary data, and the way the results will help management decision making. The proposal should also include research costs. A written research plan or proposal makes sure that the marketing manager and researchers have considered all the important aspects of the research and that they agree on why and how the research will be done.

### Implementing the Research Plan

The researcher next puts the marketing research plan into action. This involves collecting, processing, and analyzing the information. Data collection can be carried out by the company's marketing research staff or by outside firms. The company keeps more control over the collection process and data quality by using its own staff. However, outside firms that specialize in data collection can often do the job more quickly and at lower cost.

The data-collection phase of the marketing research process is generally the most expensive and the most subject to error. The researcher should watch fieldwork closely to make sure that the plan is correctly implemented and to guard against problems with contacting respondents, respondents who refuse to cooperate or who give biased or dishonest answers, and interviewers who make mistakes or take shortcuts.

The collected data must be processed and analyzed to pull out important information and findings. Data from questionnaires are checked for accuracy and completeness and coded for computer analysis. The researcher then applies standard computer programs to prepare tabulations of results and to compute averages and other measures for major variables.

### Interpreting and Reporting the Findings

The researcher must now interpret the findings, draw conclusions, and report them to management. The researcher should not try to overwhelm managers with numbers and fancy statistical techniques. Rather, the researcher should present major findings that are useful in the major decisions faced by management.

However, interpretation should not be left only to the researchers. They are often experts in research design and statistics, but the marketing manager knows more about the problem and the decisions that must be made. In many cases, findings can be interpreted in different ways, and discussions between researchers and managers will help highlight the best interpretations. The manager will also want to check that the research project was properly carried out and that all the necessary analysis was done. Or, after seeing the findings, the manager may have additional questions that can be answered using the collected research data. Finally, the manager is the one who must ultimately decide what action the research suggests. The researchers may even make the data directly available to marketing managers so that they can perform new analyses and test new relationships on their own.

Interpretation is an important phase of the marketing process. The best research is meaningless if the manager blindly accepts wrong interpretations from the researcher. Similarly, managers may have biased interpretations—they tend to accept research results that show what they expected and to reject those that they did not expect or hope for. Thus, managers and researchers must work together closely when interpreting research results, and both share responsibility for the research process and resulting decisions (see Marketing Highlight 4–3).

### Marketing Research in Smaller Organizations

In this section, we have looked at the marketing research process—from defining research objectives to interpreting and reporting results—as a lengthy, formal process carried out by large marketing companies. But many small businesses and nonprofit organizations also use marketing research. Almost any organization can find informal, low-cost alternatives to the formal and complex marketing research techniques used by research experts in large firms (see Marketing Highlight 4–4).

## Information Analysis

Information gathered by the company's marketing intelligence and marketing research systems often requires more analysis, and sometimes managers may need more help to apply it to marketing problems and decisions. This help may include more-advanced statistical analysis to learn more about both the relationships within a set of data and their statistical reliability. Such analysis allows managers to go beyond means and standard deviations in the data and to answer such questions as the following:

- What are the major variables affecting my sales and how important is each one?
- If I raised my price 10 percent and increased my advertising expenditures 20 percent, what would happen to sales?
- What are the best predictors of consumers who are likely to buy my brand versus my competitors' brand?
- What are the best variables for segmenting my market, and how many segments exist?

Information analysis might also involve a collection of mathematical models that will help marketers make better decisions. Each model represents some real system, process, or outcome. These models can help answer the questions of *what if* and *which is best*. In the past 20 years, marketing scientists have developed numerous models to help marketing managers make better marketing mix decisions, design sales territories and sales-call plans, select sites for retail outlets, develop optimal advertising mixes, and forecast new-product sales.[15]

# Marketing Highlight 4–3

## DELICARE: A CASE OF RESEARCH MALPRACTICE?

In early 1986, Beecham Products launched Delicare, its new cold-water detergent for delicate fabrics, with much confidence. Yankelovich Clancy Shulman, a large research firm, had conducted simulated test market research and predicted that Delicare would quickly surpass market leader Woolite, capturing a 45 to 52 percent market share. Beecham paid $75,000 for the research and spent over $6 million on introductory advertising for the product. Yet in the end, Delicare leveled off at less than 20 percent of the market, far short of the 30 percent Beecham needed to recoup its investment. Beecham claimed that Yankelovich's faulty forecasts had caused it to suffer huge losses. In a move that rocked the marketing research industry, Beecham sued Yankelovich for negligence and marketing malpractice, seeking $24 million in damages.

Simulated test markets like the one used in the Delicare research provide a quick and inexpensive method for estimating consumer responses to a new product. Sample consumers view ads for the new product and others, then shop in a simulated store containing a variety of products. The researcher keeps track of how many consumers buy the new product being tested and how many buy competing products. The data are fed into a sophisticated computer model which projects national sales from the results of the simulated test market. The Yankelovich model based its Delicare prediction on an important underlying statistic obtained from Beecham—the percentage of all U.S. homes that use a delicate fabric detergent. Beecham claims it told Yankelovich to use a 30 percent figure but that the research firm used 75 percent. Yankelovich, however, claims that Delicare failed because Beecham provided inaccurate information, stopped advertising too soon, and ran ads different from those used in the research.

The Delicare case was eventually settled out of court. Although no details of the settlement were revealed, the Delicare case makes an important point for marketing managers and researchers—*both* must be closely involved in the entire research process. Beecham and Yankelovich managers share the blame for the Delicare research failure. If, as Yankelovich claims, Beecham provided inaccurate information, the researchers should have checked the data more carefully. And Beecham's marketers, rather than simply accepting the highly optimistic Delicare forecasts, should have reviewed the research outcomes and interpretations more critically. Ultimately, Beecham must take responsibility for its own marketing decisions. But if the company had worked more closely with Yankelovich throughout the research process, it might have avoided its Delicare fiasco.

*Sources:* See Matt Rothman, "A Case of Malpractice—in Marketing Research?" *Business Week*, August 10, 1987, pp. 28–29; Annetta Miller and Dody Tsiantar, "A Test for Market Research," *Newsweek*, December 18, 1987, pp. 32–33; and Ted Knutson, "Marketing Malpractice Causes Concern," *Marketing News*, October 10, 1988, pp. 1, 7.

## MARKETING RESEARCH IN SMALL BUSINESSES AND NONPROFIT ORGANIZATIONS

Managers of small businesses and nonprofit organizations often think that marketing research can be done only by experts in large companies with big research budgets. But many of the marketing research techniques discussed in this chapter can also be used less formally by smaller organizations—and at little or no expense.

Managers of small businesses and nonprofit organizations can obtain good marketing information simply by *observing* things around them. For example, retailers can evaluate new locations by observing vehicle and pedestrian traffic. They can visit competing stores to check on facilities and prices. They can evaluate their customer mix by recording how many and what kinds of customers shop in the store at different times. Competitor advertising can be monitored by collecting advertisements from local media.

Managers can conduct informal *surveys* using small convenience samples. The director of an art museum can learn what patrons think about new exhibits by conducting informal "focus groups"—inviting small groups to lunch and having discussions on topics of interest. Retail salespeople can talk with customers visiting the store; hospital officials can interview patients. Restaurant managers might make random phone calls during slack hours to interview consumers about where they eat out and what they think of various restaurants in the area.

Managers can also conduct their own simple *experiments*. For example, by changing the themes in regular fund-raising mailings and watching results, a nonprofit manager can find out much about which marketing strategies work best. By varying newspaper advertisements, a store manager can learn the effects of things such as ad size and position, price coupons, and media used.

Small organizations can obtain most of the secondary data available to large businesses. In addition, many associations, local media, chambers of commerce, and government agencies provide special help to small organizations. The U.S. Small Business Administration offers dozens of free publications giving advice on topics ranging from planning advertising to ordering business signs. Local newspapers often provide information on local shoppers and their buying patterns.

Sometimes volunteers and colleges are willing to help carry out research. Nonprofit organizations can often use volunteers from local service clubs and other sources. Many colleges are seeking small businesses and nonprofit organizations to serve as cases for projects in marketing research classes.

Thus, secondary data collection, observation, surveys, and experiments can be used effectively by small organizations with small budgets.

Although such informal research is less complex and costly, it must still be done carefully. Managers must carefully think through the objectives of the research, formulate questions in advance, recognize the biases introduced by smaller samples and less-skilled researchers, and conduct the research systematically. If carefully planned and implemented, such low-cost research can provide reliable information for improving marketing decision making.

# DISTRIBUTING INFORMATION

Marketing information has no value until managers use it to make better marketing decisions. The information gathered through marketing intelligence and marketing research must be distributed to the right marketing managers at the right time. Most companies have centralized marketing information systems that provide managers with regular performance reports, intelligence updates, and reports on the results of studies. Managers need these routine reports for making regular planning, implementation, and control decisions. But marketing managers may also need nonroutine information for special situations and on-the-spot decisions. For example, a sales manager having trouble with a major customer may want a summary of the account's sales and profitability over the past year. Or a retail store manager who has run out of a best-selling product may want to know the current inventory levels in the chain's other stores. In companies with centralized information systems, these managers must request the information from the MIS staff and wait; often, the information arrives too late to be useful.

Recent developments in information handling have caused a revolution in information distribution. With recent advances in microcomputers, software, and communications, many companies are decentralizing their marketing information systems. They are giving managers direct access to information stored in the system.[16] In some companies, marketing managers can use a microcomputer to tie in to the company's information network. From any location, they can obtain information from internal records or outside information services, analyze the information using statistical packages and models, prepare reports on a word processor, and communicate with others in the network through telecommunications (see Marketing Highlight 4-5).

Such systems offer exciting prospects. They allow the managers to get the information they need directly and quickly and to tailor it to their own needs. As more managers develop the skills needed to use such systems—and as improvements in technology make them more economical—more and more marketing companies will use decentralized marketing information systems.

# Marketing Highlight 4-5

## INFORMATION NETWORKS: DECENTRALIZING THE MARKETING INFORMATION SYSTEM

New information technologies are making it possible to help managers obtain, process, and send information directly through machines rather than relying on the services of information specialists. The last decade's centralized information systems are giving way to systems that take information management out of the hands of staff specialists and put it into the hands of managers. Many companies are developing *information networks* that link separate technologies such as word processing, data processing, and image processing into a single system.

For example, envision the working day of a future marketing manager. On arriving at work, the manager turns to a desk-top computer and reads any messages that arrived during the night, reviews the day's schedule, checks the status of an ongoing computer conference,

reads several intelligence alerts, and browses through abstracts of relevant articles from the previous day's business press. To prepare for a late-morning meeting of the new-products committee, the manager calls up a recent marketing research report from microfilm storage to the screen, reviews relevant sections, edits them into a short report, sends copies electronically to other committee members who are also connected to the information network, and has the computer file a copy on microfilm. Before leaving for the meeting, the manager uses the computer to make lunch reservations at a favorite restaurant and to buy airline tickets for next week's trip to Chicago.

The afternoon is spent preparing sales and profit forecasts for the new product discussed at the morning meeting. The manager obtains test-market data from

company data banks and information on market demand, sales of competing products, and expected economic conditions from external data bases to which the company subscribes. These data are used as inputs for the sales-forecasting model stored in the company's model bank. The manager "plays" with the model to see how different assumptions affect predicted results.

At home later that evening, the manager uses a laptop personal computer to contact the network, prepare a report on the product, and send copies to the computers of other involved managers, who can read them first thing in the morning. When the manager logs off, the computer automatically sets the alarm clock and puts out the cat.

*An advanced office network ties the manager directly into the company's information system.*

## SUMMARY

In carrying out their marketing responsibilities, marketing managers need a great deal of information. Despite the growing supply of information, managers often lack enough information of the right kind or have too much of the wrong kind. To overcome these problems, many companies are taking steps to improve their marketing information systems.

A well-designed *marketing information system* begins and ends with the user. It first *assesses information needs* by interviewing marketing managers and surveying their decision environment to determine what information is desired, needed, and feasible to offer.

The MIS next *develops information* and helps managers to use it more effectively. *Internal records* provide information on sales, costs, inventories, cash flows, and accounts receivable and payable. Such data can be obtained quickly and cheaply but must often be adapted for marketing decisions. The *marketing intelligence system* supplies marketing executives with everyday information about developments in the external marketing environment. Intelligence can be collected from company employees, customers, suppliers, and resellers or by monitoring published reports, conferences, advertisements, competitor actions, and other activities in the environment.

*Marketing research* involves collecting information relevant to a specific marketing problem facing the company. Every marketer needs marketing research, and most large compa-

nies have their own marketing research departments. Marketing research involves a four-step process. The first step consists of the manager and researcher carefully *defining the problem and setting the research objectives*. The objective may be *exploratory, descriptive,* or *causal*. The second step consists of *developing the research plan* for collecting data from primary and secondary sources. *Primary data collection* calls for choosing a *research approach* (observation, survey, experiment), choosing a *contact method* (mail, telephone, personal), designing a *sampling plan* (whom to survey, how many to survey, and how to choose them), and developing *research instruments* (questionnaire, mechanical). The third step consists of *implementing the marketing research plan* by collecting, processing, and analyzing the information. The fourth step consists of *interpreting and reporting the findings*. Further information analysis helps marketing managers to apply the information and provides advanced statistical procedures and models to develop more rigorous findings from the information.

Finally, the marketing information system distributes information gathered from internal sources, marketing intelligence, and marketing research to the right managers at the right times. More and more firms are decentralizing their information systems through *distributed processing networks* that allow managers to have direct access to information.

## QUESTIONS FOR DISCUSSION

1. What are some kinds of information that managers want? What kinds of information is a marketing information system likely to *provide?*

2. As a salesperson calling on industrial accounts, you would learn a lot that could help decision makers in your company. What kinds of information would you

pass on? How would you decide whether something is worth reporting?

3. List some internal and environmental factors that can influence the focus and scope of a company's marketing research program.

4. The president of a campus organization has asked you to investigate its declining membership. How would you apply the four steps in the marketing research process to this project?

5. You are a research supplier, designing and conducting studies for a variety of companies. What is the *most* important thing you can do to ensure that your clients will get their money's worth from your services?

6. What research problem did Coca-Cola appear to be investigating prior to the introduction of New Coke? What problem *should* Coke have investigated?

7. What type of research would be appropriate in the following situations?

    a. Kellogg wants to investigate the impact of children on parents' decisions to buy breakfast foods.

    b. Your college bookstore wants some insights into students feelings about its merchandise, prices, and services.

    c. McDonald's must decide where best to locate a new outlet in a fast-growing suburb.

    d. Gillette wants to determine whether a new line of children's deodorant will be profitable.

8. Focus-group interviewing is a widely used—and widely criticized—research technique. What are the advantages and disadvantages of focus groups? What kinds of questions can focus groups investigate?

9. A recently completed study shows that most customers use more of your company's brand of shampoo than they need in order to clean their hair. Company advertising encourages overuse, which wastes customers' money but increases sales. Although you suggested to the product manager that the advertising be modified, no changes were made. Assuming you are in the research department, what should you do now?

## REFERENCES

1. Based on numerous sources, including "Coke 'Family' Sales Fly as New Coke Stumbles," *Advertising Age*, January 17, 1986, p. 1; Jack Honomichl, "Missing Ingredients in 'New' Coke's Research," *Advertising Age*, July 22, 1985, p. 1; and Patricia Winters, "For New Coke, What Price Success?" *Advertising Age*, March 20, 1989, pp. 51–52.

2. Marion Harper, Jr., "A New Profession to Aid Management," *Journal of Marketing*, January 1961, p. 1.

3. John Neisbitt, *Megatrends: Ten New Directions Transforming Our Lives* (New York: Warner Books, 1984).

4. "Harnessing the Data Explosion," *Sales and Marketing Management*, January 1987, p. 31.

5. Neisbitt, *Megatrends*, p. 16.

6. Donald S. Tull and Del I. Hawkins, *Marketing Research: Measurement and Method*, 4th ed. (New York: Macmillan, 1987), pp. 40–41, 750–60.

7. See "Business Is Turning Data into a Potent Strategic Weapon," *Business Week*, August 22, 1983, p. 92.

8. See Tim Miller, "Focus: Competitive Intelligence," *Online Access Guide*, March/April 1987, pp. 43–57.

9. Ibid., p. 46.

10. The American Marketing Association officially adopted this definition in 1987.

11. For an excellent annotated reference to major secondary sources of business and marketing data, see Thomas C. Kinnear and James R. Taylor, *Marketing Research: An Applied Approach* (New York: McGraw-Hill, 1983), pp. 146–56, 169–84. Also see "Top 50 Research Companies Profiled," *Advertising Age*, May 23, 1988, pp. S8-S19.

12. Ibid., p. 150.

13. See Jack Honomichl, "Collision Course: Stakes High in People-Meter War," *Advertising Age*, July 27, 1987, pp. 1, 68; and Brian Dumaine, "Who's Gypping Whom in TV Ads?" *Fortune*, July 6, 1987, pp. 78–79.

14. See Leonard M. Lodish and David J. Reibstein, "New Gold Mines and Minefields in Market Research," *Harvard Business Review*, January-February 1986, pp. 168–82; and Joe Schwartz, "Back to the Source," *American Demographics*, January 1989, pp. 22–26.

15. For more on statistical analysis, consult a standard text, such as Tull and Hawkins, *Marketing Research*. For a review of marketing models, see Gary L. Lilien and Philip Kotler, *Marketing Decision Making: A Model Building Approach* (New York: Harper & Row, 1983); also see John D. C. Little, "Decision Support Systems for Marketing Managers," *Journal of Marketing*, Summer 1979, pp. 9–26.

16. See Peter Nulty, "How Personal Computers Change Managers' Lives," *Fortune*, September 3, 1984, pp. 38–48; "Marketing Managers No Stranger to the PC," *Sales & Marketing Management*, May 13, 1985; and "Make Way for the Salesman's Best Friend," *Sales & Marketing Management*, February 1988, pp. 53–56.

# FAMILY SERVICE, INC.: MARKETING RESEARCH IN A SOCIAL SERVICE AGENCY

Family Service was established in 1941 as a private nonprofit organization. In 1942, the agency obtained United Way funding for the addition of a school lunch program. Since that time, the agency has undergone a series of name changes in an attempt to reflect changes in its service offerings. In 1983, the agency once again operated under the name of Family Service, Inc., and its services now include counseling, family-life education, and home health care.

During 1983, Ann Marek, director of community affairs, became concerned about the community's lack of knowledge regarding available services. However, before embarking on an awareness campaign, she felt it necessary to assess the community's attitudes and perceptions toward Family Service as well as attitudes and perceptions toward other agencies offering similar services.

Marek arranged for a local graduate student in marketing to assist with the project. Since the home health market was extremely competitive, the project would involve a market-research survey of the general public with emphasis on home health services. Marek felt it was also important to survey physicians because many of Family Service's home health clients were referred by their doctors.

Telephone interviewing yielded 184 completed interviews from a random sample of 400 names drawn from the residence pages of the telephone directory. Respondents were first asked how they would rate the services provided by voluntary organizations in general. Ratings were on a scale of 1 to 5, 5 being high and 1 low. The results are shown in Table 1.

Respondents were then asked if they were aware of several specific organizations. Awareness did not mean knowledge of services—only that respondents were aware of the organizations' existence. Respondents were then asked to rate (on a scale of 1 to 5) the overall performance of all organizations of which they were aware. The results are shown in Table 2. The 75 respondents aware of Family Service were also asked what they considered to be the most important criterion in selecting a provider of counseling, home health, and educational services. The results are shown in Table 3.

Telephone interviewing produced 102 completed interviews from a random list of 350 physicians. Each doctor was asked first to rate the efforts of home health organizations in general (scales of 1 to 5). The mean response was 3.82, with 80 no responses.

Physicians were then asked if they were aware of several specific organizations. If aware of an organization, he or she was also asked to rate the performance of that organization. The results are shown in Table 4.

**TABLE 1    Overall Rating of Voluntary Organizations**

| Rating | Number |
|---|---|
| Excellent (5) | 38 |
| Good (4) | 87 |
| Fair (3) | 14 |
| Poor (2) | 1 |
| Very poor (1) | 1 |
| No rating | 43 |
| Mean = 4.13 | |
| Standard deviation = .781 | |

**TABLE 2    Awareness and Ratings of Specific Organizations**

| Organization | No. Aware | No. Rated | Mean Rating |
|---|---|---|---|
| United Way | 160 | 128 | 3.70 |
| North Texas Home Health Services | 36 | 23 | 4.00 |
| Crisis Intervention | 118 | 79 | 3.84 |
| Family Service | 75 | 48 | 3.90 |
| Meals on Wheels | 170 | 138 | 4.59 |
| Parenting Guidance Center | 100 | 69 | 4.12 |
| Visiting Nurses Association | 107 | 72 | 4.31 |
| Mental Health/Mental Retardation | 154 | 108 | 4.11 |
| Home Health Services of Tarrant County | 69 | 41 | 3.93 |

The interviewer noted that although several doctors had heard of an organization, they did not know enough about it to rate it. Others, however, said that although they knew of an organization and had actually referred patients to it, they were unable to give a rating because they did not know how well the organization had served the patients.

Doctors were also asked to which home health organizations they usually referred their patients. Of the 102 interviewed physicians, 15 reported that they never referred to home health agencies. Of the remaining 87, 25 could not name any specific agency. Several of these 25 stated that they did not make the actual referral—that although they prescribed the needed services, a nurse or the hospital discharge planner actually selected the provider.

## Questions

1. How does the general public view Family Service and the other agencies?

2. What are the marketing implications of Table 3?

3. How do physicians view Family Service and other similar agencies?

4. What is the importance of the discrepancy between the number of physicians who were aware of an organization and the number who rated the organization?

5. What are the marketing implications of the 25 doctors who could not name the agency or agencies to which their patients were referred?

6. What recommendations would you make to Family Service?

*Source:* This case was prepared by Donna Legg, Texas Christian University. Used with permission.

TABLE 3   Criteria for Selecting Provider of Services

| Criteria | No. of Responses |
|---|---|
| Quality | 5 |
| Accreditation | 3 |
| Cost | 5 |
| Recommendations* | 23 |
| Image/reputation | 8 |
| Credentials/knowledge of staff | 9 |
| Supportive staff | 1 |
| Success rate | 2 |
| Needs/benefits | 2 |
| Tradition | 1 |
| Confidentiality | 1 |
| Communication | 1 |
| Christian organization | 1 |
| Don't know | 13 |

*Many respondents specified recommendations from doctors, ministers, school counselors, friends, and relatives

TABLE 4   Physicians' Awareness and Ratings of Specific Organizations

| Organization | No. Aware | No. Rated | Mean Rating |
|---|---|---|---|
| United Way | 94 | 75 | 3.68 |
| North Texas Home Health Services | 52 | 35 | 3.86 |
| Crisis Intervention | 65 | 35 | 4.03 |
| Family Service | 50 | 38 | 3.71 |
| Meals on Wheels | 89 | 68 | 4.25 |
| Parenting Guidance Center | 50 | 28 | 4.00 |
| Visiting Nurses Association | 78 | 61 | 3.95 |
| Mental Health/Mental Retardation | 91 | 64 | 3.63 |
| Home Health Services of Tarrant County | 57 | 41 | 3.76 |

# 5

# The Marketing Environment

## CHAPTER OBJECTIVES

**After reading this chapter, you should be able to**

1. **Describe the environmental forces that affect the company's ability to serve its customers**
2. **Explain how changes in the demographic and economic environments affect marketing decisions**
3. **Identify the major trends in the firm's natural and technological environments**
4. **Explain the key changes that occur in the political and cultural environments**

In 1894, vegetarian Will Kellogg of Battle Creek, Michigan, found a way to make nutritious wheat meal more appealing to patients in his brother's sanitarium. He invented a process to convert the unappetizing wheat meal into attractive, tasty little cereal flakes. The crunchy flakes quickly became popular. In 1906, Will founded the Kellogg Company to sell his cereal to the world at large, and the breakfast table would never again be the same. Will Kellogg's modest invention spawned the giant ready-to-eat cereal industry, in which half a dozen large competitors now battle for shares of $5.4 billion in yearly sales. Since the very beginning, the Kellogg Company has been atop the heap, leading the industry with innovative technology and marketing.

During the 1950s and 1960s, Kellogg and other cereal makers prospered. The post-World War II baby boom created lots of kids, and kids eat lots of cereal. As the baby-boom generation passed through its childhood and teen years, cereal sales grew naturally with increases in the child population. Kellogg and its competitors focused heavily on the glut of young munchers. They offered presweetened cereals in fetching shapes and colors, pitched by memorable animated characters. Remember Tony the Tiger,

Toucan Sam, the Trix Rabbit, Sugar Bear, and Snap, Crackle, and Pop?

But by 1980, the marketing environment had changed. The aging baby boomers, concerned about their spreading waistlines and declining fitness, launched a national obsession with clean living and good nutrition. They began giving up the cereals they'd loved as kids, and industry sales growth flattened. After decades of riding natural market growth, Kellogg and its competitors now had to fight for profitable shares of a stagnant market. But through the good years, Kellogg had grown complacent and sluggish. The company stumbled briefly in the early 1980s, and its market share dropped off. Some analysts claimed that Kellogg was a company "past its prime."

To counter slow cereal industry growth, most of Kellogg's competitors—General Mills, General Foods, Quaker Oats, Ralston-Purina—diversified broadly into faster-growing nonfood businesses. But Kellogg chose a different course. It implemented an aggressive marketing strategy to revive industry sales by persuading the nation's 80 million baby boomers to eat cereal again.

Kellogg advertised heavily to reposition its old products and bring them more in line with changing adult life styles. New ad campaigns for the company's old brands stressed taste and nutrition. For example, a Kellogg's Corn Flakes ad shows adults discussing professional athletes who eat the cereal. In another spot, a young medical student tells his mother that Rice Crispies have more vitamins and minerals than her oatmeal. In a Frosted Flakes ad, consumers sitting at a breakfast table, their features obscured by shadows, confess that they still eat the Frosted Flakes they loved as kids. "That's OK," they're told. "Frosted Flakes have the taste adults have grown to love."

Beyond repositioning the old standards, Kellogg invested heavily in new brands aimed at adult taste buds and life styles. Crispix, Raisin Squares, the Nutri-Grain line, Mueslix, and many other innovative adult Kellogg brands sprouted on grocers' shelves. But the heart of Kellogg's push to capture the adult market was its growing line of high-fiber bran cereals—All-Bran, 40 Percent Bran Flakes, Bran Buds, Raisin Bran, and Cracklin' Oak Bran. Kellogg's advertising made some serious health pitches for these brands, tying them to high-fiber, low-fat diets and healthy living. One long-running ad campaign even linked Kellogg's All-Bran with reduced risks of cancer.

The controversial campaign drew sharp criticism from competitors, strong praise from the National Cancer Institute, and sales from consumers. At the same time, Kellogg did not make such strong claims for all its bran products. For example, its ads for Bran Flakes stated simply: "You take care of the outside; Kellogg's 40 Percent Bran Flakes will help you take care of the inside."

Kellogg's aggressive reaction to its changing marketing environment paid off handsomely. The company's high-powered marketing attack more than doubled the growth rate for the entire cereal industry. And while diversified competitors are now spending time and money fixing or unloading their nonfood businesses, Kellogg remains sharply focused on cereals. In only four years, Kellogg's overall market share grew from 35 percent to 42 percent, and the company's share of the fast-growing bran segment exceeds 50 percent. Five of the nation's seven best-selling cereals are Kellogg brands, and Kellogg is once again one of America's most profitable companies. As Tony the Tiger would say, at Kellogg things are going *G-r-r-reat!*[1]

**marketing environment** The actors and forces outside marketing that affect marketing management's ability to develop and maintain successful transactions with its target customers.

**microenvironment** The forces close to the company that affect its ability to serve its customers—the company, market channel firms, customer markets, competitors, and publics.

**macroenvironment** The larger societal forces that affect the whole microenvironment—demographic, economic, natural, technological, political, and cultural forces.

The marketing environment consists of uncontrollable forces that surround the company. To be successful, a company must adapt its marketing mix to trends and developments in this environment.

A company's **marketing environment** consists of the actors and forces outside marketing that affect marketing management's ability to develop and maintain successful transactions with its target customers. The changing and uncertain marketing environment deeply affects the company. Instead of changing slowly and predictably, the environment can produce major surprises and shocks. How many managers at Gerber Foods foresaw the end of the baby boom? Which auto companies foresaw the huge impact that consumerism and environmentalism would have on their business decisions? Who in the American electronics industry foresaw the dominance of Japanese and other foreign competitors in world markets? The marketing environment offers both opportunities and threats, and the company must use its marketing research and marketing intelligence systems to watch the changing environment.

The marketing environment is made up of a *microenvironment* and a *macroenvironment*. The **microenvironment** consists of the forces close to the company that affect its ability to serve its customers—the company, its marketing channel firms, its customer markets, its competitors, and its publics. The **macroenvironment** consists of the larger societal forces that affect the whole microenvironment—demographic, economic, natural, technological, political, and cultural forces. We will look first at the company's microenvironment and then at its macroenvironment.

## THE COMPANY'S MICROENVIRONMENT

The job of marketing management is to create attractive offers for target markets. However, marketing management's success will be affected by the rest of the company, and by middlemen, competitors, and various publics. These

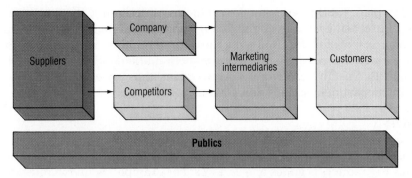

FIGURE 5–1   Major Actors in the Company's Microenvironment

actors in the company's microenvironment are shown in Figure 5–1. Marketing managers cannot simply focus on the target market's needs: They must also watch all actors in the company's microenvironment. We will look at the company, suppliers, middlemen, customers, competitors, and publics and illustrate the role and impact of these actors by referring to the Schwinn Bicycle Company, a major U.S. bicycle producer.

## The Company

In making marketing plans, marketing management at Schwinn takes other company groups into account—groups such as top management, finance, research and development (R&D), purchasing, manufacturing, and accounting. All these interrelated groups form Schwinn's microenvironment (see Figure 5-2).

Top management at Schwinn consists of the bicycle division's general manager, the executive committee, the chief executive officer, the chairman of the board, and the board of directors. These higher levels of management set the company's mission, objectives, broad strategies, and policies. Marketing managers must make decisions within the plans made by top management. And marketing plans must be approved by top management before they can be implemented.

Marketing managers must also work closely with other company departments. Finance is concerned with finding and using funds to carry out the

FIGURE 5–2   Company Microenvironment

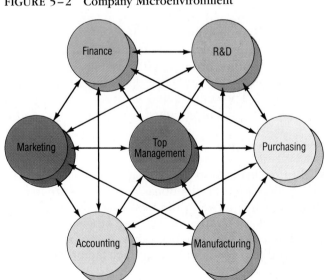

**suppliers** Firms and individuals that provide the resources needed by the company and its competitors to produce goods and services.

**marketing intermediaries** Firms that help the company to promote, sell, and distribute its goods to final buyers; they include middlemen, physical distribution firms, marketing services agencies, and financial intermediaries.

**middlemen** Distribution channel firms that help the company find customers or make sales for them.

**physical distribution firms** Warehouse, transportation, and other firms that help a company to stock and move goods from their points of origin to their destinations.

marketing plan. R&D focuses on the problems of designing safe and attractive bicycles. Purchasing worries about getting supplies and materials, while manufacturing is responsible for producing the desired number of bicycles. Accounting has to measure revenues and costs to help marketing know how well it is achieving its objectives. All these departments thus have an impact on the marketing department's plans and actions.

## Suppliers

**Suppliers** are firms and individuals that provide the resources needed by the company to produce its goods and services. For example, Schwinn must obtain steel, aluminum, rubber tires, gears, seats, and other materials to produce bicycles. It must also obtain labor, equipment, fuel, electricity, computers, and other factors of production.

Supplier developments can seriously affect marketing. Marketing managers must also watch supply availability. Supply shortages, labor strikes, and other events can cost sales in the short run and damage customer goodwill in the long run. Marketing managers also need to watch the price trends of their key inputs. Rising supply costs may force price increases that can harm the company's sales volume.

## Marketing Intermediaries

**Marketing intermediaries** are firms that help the company to promote, sell, and distribute its goods to final buyers. They include *middlemen, physical distribution firms, marketing service agencies,* and *financial intermediaries.*

### Middlemen

**Middlemen** are distribution channel firms that help the company find customers or make sales to them. These include wholesalers and retailers who buy and resell merchandise (they are often called *resellers*). Schwinn's primary method of marketing bicycles is to sell them to hundreds of independent dealers who resell them at a profit.

Why does Schwinn use middlemen? Middlemen perform important functions more cheaply than Schwinn can by itself. They stock bicycles where customers are located. They show and deliver bicycles when consumers want them. They advertise bikes and negotiate terms of sale. Schwinn finds it better to work through independent middlemen than to own and operate its own massive system of outlets.

Selecting and working with middlemen is not easy. No longer do manufacturers have many small, independent middlemen from which to choose. They now face large and growing middlemen organizations. More and more bicycles are being sold through large corporate chains (such as Sears and K mart) and large wholesaler, retailer, and franchise-sponsored voluntary chains. These groups often have enough power to dictate terms or even shut the manufacturer out of large markets. Manufacturers must work hard to get "shelf space."

### Physical Distribution Firms

**Physical distribution firms** help the company to stock and move goods from their points of origin to their destinations. Warehouses are firms that store and protect goods before they move to the next destination. Transportation firms include railroads, truckers, airlines, barges, and other companies that specialize in moving goods from one location to another. A company has to decide on the best ways to store and ship goods, balancing such factors as cost, delivery, speed, and safety.

**marketing services agencies**
Marketing research firms, advertising agencies, media firms, marketing consulting firms, and other service providers that help a company to target and promote its products to the right markets.

**financial intermediaries** Banks, credit companies, insurance companies, and other businesses that help finance transactions or insure against the risks associated with the buying and selling of goods.

*Middlemen perform important functions for Schwinn. They stock, display, promote, sell, service, and deliver Schwinn's bicycles.*

### Marketing Services Agencies

**Marketing services agencies**—marketing research firms, advertising agencies, media firms, and marketing consulting firms—help the company to target and promote its products to the right markets. When the company decides to use one of these agencies, it must choose carefully, since these firms vary in creativity, quality, service, and price. The company has to review the performance of these firms regularly and consider replacing those that no longer perform well.

### Financial Intermediaries

**Financial intermediaries** include banks, credit companies, insurance companies, and other businesses that help finance transactions or insure against the risks associated with the buying and selling of goods. Most firms and customers depend on financial intermediaries to finance their transactions. The company's marketing performance can be seriously affected by rising credit costs, limited credit, or both. For this reason, the company has to develop strong relationships with important financial institutions.

## Customers

The company must study its customer markets closely. The company can operate in five types of customer markets. These are shown in Figure 5–3 and defined below:

- □ *Consumer markets:* individuals and households that buy goods and services for personal consumption
- □ *Industrial markets:* organizations that buy goods and services for further processing or for use in their production process

**public** Any group that has an actual or potential interest in or impact on an organization's ability to achieve its objectives.

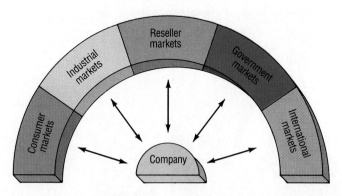

FIGURE 5-3 Basic Types of Customer Markets

□ *Reseller markets:* organizations that buy goods and services in order to resell them at a profit

□ *Government markets:* government agencies that buy goods and services in order to produce public services or transfer these goods and services to others who need them

□ *International markets:* foreign buyers, including consumers, producers, resellers, and governments

Schwinn sells bicycles in all these markets. It sells some bicycles directly to consumers through factory outlets. It sells bicycles to producers who use them to deliver goods or to get from one place to another in their large plant complexes. It sells bicycles to wholesalers and retailers who resell them to consumer and producer markets. It sells bicycles to government agencies. And it sells bicycles to foreign consumers, producers, resellers, and governments. Each market type has special characteristics that call for careful study by the seller.

## Competitors

Every company faces a wide range of competitors. The marketing concept states that to be successful, a company must satisfy the needs and wants of consumers better than its competitors do. Thus, marketers must do more than simply adapt to the needs of target consumers: They must also adapt to the strategies of competitors who are serving the same target consumers. Companies must gain strategic advantage by strongly positioning their offerings against competitors' offerings in the minds of consumers.

No single competitive marketing strategy is best for all companies. Each firm must consider its own size and industry position compared with those of its competitors. Large firms with dominant positions in an industry can use certain strategies that smaller firms cannot afford. But being large is not enough. There are winning strategies for large firms, but there are also losing strategies. And small firms can find strategies that give them better rates of return than large firms. Both large and small firms must find marketing strategies that best position them against competitors in their markets.

## Publics

The company's marketing environment also includes various publics. A **public** is any group that has an actual or potential interest in or impact on an organization's ability to achieve its objectives. Every company is surrounded by seven types of publics (see Figure 5-4):

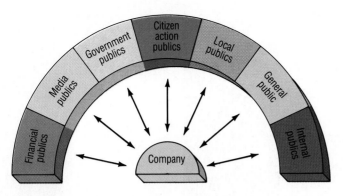

FIGURE 5–4    Types of Publics

- *Financial publics.* Financial publics influence the company's ability to obtain funds. Banks, investment houses, and stockholders are the major financial publics. Schwinn seeks the goodwill of these groups by issuing annual reports and showing the financial community that its house is in order.

- *Media publics.* Media publics are those that carry news, features, and editorial opinion. They include newspapers, magazines, and radio and television stations. Schwinn is interested in getting more and better media coverage.

- *Government publics.* Management must take government developments into account. Schwinn's marketers consult the company's lawyers on issues of product safety, truth-in-advertising, dealers' rights, and other matters. Schwinn may consider joining with other bicycle manufacturers to lobby for better laws.

- *Citizen-action publics.* A company's marketing decisions may be questioned by consumer organizations, environmental groups, minority groups, and others. For example, parent groups are lobbying for greater safety in bicycles, which are the nation's number-one hazardous product. Schwinn has the opportunity to be a leader in product-safety design. Schwinn's public relations department can help it stay in touch with consumer groups.

- *Local publics.* Every company has local publics such as neighborhood residents and community organizations. Large companies usually appoint a community relations officer to deal with the community, attend meetings, answer questions, and contribute to worthwhile causes.

- *General public.* A company should be concerned about the general public's attitude toward its products and activities. The public's image of the company affects its buying. To build a strong "corporate citizen" image, Schwinn will lend its officers to community fund drives, make large contributions to charity, and set up systems for consumer-complaint handling.

- *Internal publics.* A company's internal publics include blue-collar workers, white-collar workers, volunteers, managers, and the board of directors. Large companies use newsletters and other means to inform and motivate their internal publics. When employees feel good about their company, their positive attitude spills over to external publics.

A company can prepare marketing plans for its major publics as well as its customer markets. Suppose the company wants some response from a particular public, such as its goodwill, favorable word of mouth, or donations of time or money. The company would have to design an offer to this public attractive enough to produce the desired response.

*In these corporate image ads, NCR communicates with its customer, employee, shareholder, supplier, and community publics (which it calls stakeholders).*

---

## THE COMPANY'S MACROENVIRONMENT

The company and its suppliers, marketing intermediaries, customers, competitors, and publics all operate in a larger macroenvironment of forces that shape opportunities and pose threats to the company. The company must carefully watch and respond to these forces. The macroenvironment consists of the six major forces shown in Figure 5–5. The remaining sections of this chapter will examine these forces and show how they affect marketing plans.

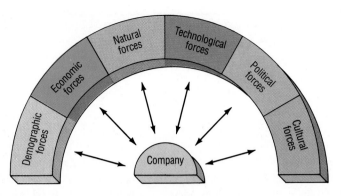

FIGURE 5–5   Major Forces in the Company's Macroenvironment

## Demographic Environment

**Demography** is the study of human populations in terms of size, density, location, age, sex, race, occupation, and other statistics. The demographic environment is of major interest to marketers because it involves people, and people make up markets. The most important demographic trends in the United States are described below.

### Changing Age Structure of the U.S. Population

The U.S. population stood at over 240 million in 1989 and may reach 300 million by the year 2020. The single most important demographic trend in the United States is the changing *age structure* of the population. The U.S. population is getting older for two reasons. First, there is a slowdown in the *birthrate,* so there are fewer young people to pull the population's average age down. Second, *life expectancy* is increasing, so there are more older people to pull the average age up.

During the **baby boom** that followed World War II and lasted until the early 1960s, the annual birthrate reached an all-time high. The baby boom created a huge "bulge" in the U.S. age distribution—75 million baby boomers now account for more than one-third of the nation's population. And as the baby-boom generation ages, it pulls the average age up with it. Because of its sheer size, most major demographic and socioeconomic changes occurring during the next half decade will be tied to the baby-boom generation (see Marketing Highlight 5–1).

The baby boom was followed by a "birth dearth," and by the mid-1970s the birthrate had fallen sharply. This decrease was caused by smaller family sizes resulting from Americans' desire to improve personal living standards, from the increasing desire of women to work outside the home, and from improved birth control. Although family sizes are expected to remain smaller, the birthrate is climbing again as the baby-boom generation moves through the childbearing years and creates a second but smaller baby boom (the "echo boom"). The birthrate will then decline in the 1990s.[2]

The second factor in the general aging of the population is increased life expectancy. Current average life expectancy is 76 years-a 27-year increase since 1900. Increasing life expectancy and the declining birthrate are producing an aging population. The U.S. median age is now 32 and is expected to reach 36 by the year 2000 and 40 by 2030.[3]

The changing age structure of the population will result in different growth rates for various age groups over the decade, and these differences will strongly affect marketers' targeting strategies. Growth trends for six age groups are summarized below.[4]

## THE BABY BOOMERS

The postwar baby boom, which began in 1946 and ran through the early 1960s, produced 75 million babies. Since then, the baby boomers have become one of the biggest forces shaping the marketing environment. The boomers have presented a moving target, creating new markets as they grew through their infant, preadolescent, teen-age, young-adult, and now middle-age years. They created markets for baby products and toys in the 1950s; jeans, records, and cosmetics in the 1960s; fun and informal fashions in the 1970s; and fitness, new homes, and childcare in the 1980s.

Today, the baby boomers are starting to gray at the temples and spread at the waist. And they are reaching their peak earning and spending years—the boomers account for a third of the population but make up 40 percent of the work force and earn over half of all personal income. They are settling into home ownership, starting to raise families, and maturing into the most affluent generation in history. Thus, they constitute a lucrative market for housing, furniture and appliances, low-cal foods and beverages, physical fitness products, high-priced cars, convenience products, and financial services.

Baby boomers cut across all walks of life. But marketers have recently paid the most attention to the small upper crust of the boomer generation—its more educated, mobile, and wealthy segments. These segments have gone by many names. In the early to mid-1980s, they were called "yuppies" (young urban professionals), "yumpies" (young upwardly mobile professionals), "bumpies" (black upwardly mobile professionals), and "yummies" (young upwardly mobile mommies). These groups were replaced by the "DINKs"—dual-income, no-kids couples. Typically, DINKs work long hours, make hefty incomes, spend money to save time, and buy lavishly:

The members of this . . . species can best be spotted after 9 p.m. in gourmet groceries, their Burberry-clothed arms reaching for arugula or a Le Menu frozen flounder dinner. In the parking lot, they slide into their BMWs and lift cellular phones to their ears before zooming off to their architect-designed homes in the exurbs. . . . Then they consult the phone-answering machine, pop dinner into the microwave and finally sink into their Italian leather sofa to watch a videocassette of, say, last week's *L.A. Law* or *Cheers* on their high-definition, large-screen stereo television.

As we move into the 1990s, yuppies and DINKS are giving way to a new breed. The boomers are evolving from the "youthquake generation" to the "backache generation"—they're slowing up, having children, and settling down. They are approaching life with a new reasonableness in the way they live, think, eat, and spend. They have shifted their focus from the outside world to the inside world. Staying home with the family and being "couch potatoes" is becoming their favorite way to spend an evening. Upscale boomers still exert their affluence, but they indulge themselves in more subtle and sensible ways. They spend heavily on convenience and high-quality products, but they have less of a taste for lavish or conspicuous buying.

Some marketers think that upscale boomers are tiring of all the attention or that focusing on affluent boomer groups is diverting companies from other profitable segments. Some are using subtler approaches that avoid stereotyping these consumers or tagging them as yuppies, DINKS, or something else. But whatever you call them, you can't ignore them. The baby boomers have been the most potent market force for the last 40 years, and they will continue to be for the next forty.

*Sources:* See Faye Rice, "Wooing the Aging Baby Boomers," *Fortune,* February 1, 1988, pp. 68–77; Jeremy Schlosberg, "Sitting Pretty," *American Demographics,* May 1988, pp. 24–27; and Faye Rice, "Yuppie Spending Gets Serious," March 27, 1989, pp. 147–49. The quoted material is from Martha Smilgis, "Here Come the DINKs," *Time,* April 20, 1987, p. 75.

*The baby boomers: a prime target for marketers.*

□ *Children.* The number of preschoolers will increase through 1990, then taper off slightly through the 1990s as the baby boomers move out of childbearing years. Markets for children's toys and games, clothes, furniture, and food are enjoying a short "boom" after years of "bust." Sony and other electronics firms are now offering products designed for children. Many retailers are adding new children's brands. For example, Sears has joined with McDonald's to market McKid's clothing. Other retailers are opening separate children's clothing chains, such as GapKids, Kids 'R' Us, and Esprit Kids. Such markets will continue to grow through the coming decade but will again decrease as the century closes.[5]

□ *Youths.* The number of 10- to 19-year-olds will drop through the early 1990s, then begin to increase again at the end of the century. This age group buys or strongly influences purchases of health and beauty aids, clothing, food, bikes, VCRs, stereo equipment, autos, family travel, entertainment, college educations, and other products and services.

□ *Young adults.* This group will decline during the 1990s as the "birth dearth" generation moves in. Marketers who sell to the 20-to-34 age group—furniture makers, life insurance companies, sports equipment manufacturers—can no longer rely on increasing market size for increases in sales. They will have to work for bigger shares of smaller markets.

□ *Early middle age.* The baby-boom generation will continue to move into the 35-to-49 age group, creating huge increases. For example, the number of 40- to 44-year-olds will increase by 50 percent. This group is a major market for larger homes, new automobiles, clothing, entertainment, and investments.

□ *Late middle age.* The 50-to-64 age group will continue to shrink until the end of the century. Then it will begin to increase as the baby boomers move in. This group is a major market for eating out, travel, clothing, recreation, and financial services.

□ *Retirees.* Between 1980 and 2000, the over-65 age group will have increased by over one-third. By the year 2000, this group will comprise almost 13 percent of all Americans; by 2020, there will be twice as many elderly as there are teen-agers. This group has a demand for retirement communities, quieter forms of recreation, single-portion food packaging, life-care and health-care services, and travel.

Thus, the changing age structure of the U.S. population will strongly affect future marketing decisions. In particular, the baby-boom generation will continue to be a prime target for marketers.

### The Changing American Family

The American ideal of the two-children, two-car suburban family has lately been losing some of its luster. There are many forces at work.[6] People are marrying later and having fewer children. Although 96 percent of all Americans will marry, the average age of couples marrying for the first time has been rising over the years. Couples with no children under 18 make up almost half of all families. And of those families that have children, the average number of children is under 2, down from 3.5 in 1955.

There has also been an increase in the number of working mothers. Since 1960, the percentage of mothers of children under age 18 who hold some kind of job has increased from about 25 percent to over 64 percent. Their incomes contribute 40 percent of their household incomes and influence the purchase of higher-quality goods and services. Marketers of tires, automobiles, insurance, travel, and financial services are increasingly directing their advertising to working women. All this activity is accompanied by a shift in the traditional

*Lipton and other companies target smaller households with single serve or individually portioned packaging.*

roles and values of husbands and wives, with the husband assuming more domestic functions such as shopping and child care. As a result, husbands are becoming more of a target market for food and household appliance marketers.

Finally, the number of nonfamily households is increasing. Many young adults leave home and move into apartments. Other adults choose to remain single. Still others are divorced or widowed people living alone. By 2000, 47 percent of all households will be nonfamily or single-parent households—the fastest-growing categories of households. These groups have their own special needs. For example, they need smaller apartments; inexpensive and smaller appliances, furniture, and furnishings; and food that is packaged in smaller sizes.

### Geographic Shifts in Population

Americans are a mobile people, with about 17 percent, or 41 million people, moving each year. Among the major trends are the following:[7]

□ *Movement to the Sunbelt states.* During the 1980s, the populations in the West and South grew. On the other hand, most of the Midwest and Northeast states lost population (see Figure 5–6). These population shifts interest marketers because people in different regions buy differently. For example, the movement to the Sunbelt states will lessen the demand for warm clothing and home heating equipment and increase the demand for air conditioning.

□ *Movement from rural to urban areas.* Except for a short period during the early 1970s, Americans have been moving from rural to metropolitan

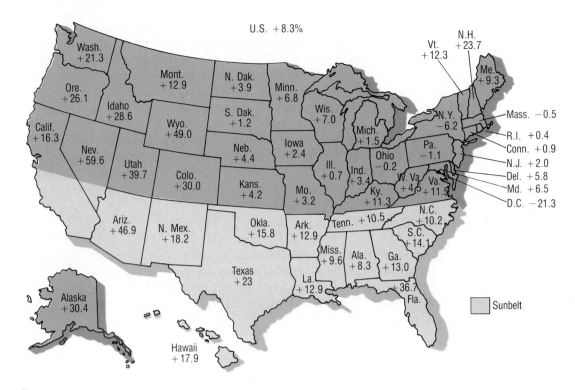

FIGURE 5–6    Population Growth Rates: 1980–1990

areas for over a century. The metropolitan areas show a faster pace of living, more commuting, higher incomes, and greater variety of goods and services than can be found in the small towns and rural areas that dot America. The largest cities, such as New York, Chicago, and San Francisco, account for most of the sales of expensive furs, perfumes, luggage, and works of art. These cities also support the opera, ballet, and other forms of "high culture."

□ *Movement from the city to the suburbs.* In the 1950s, Americans made a massive exit from the cities to the suburbs. Big cities became surrounded by even bigger suburbs. The U.S. Census Bureau calls sprawling urban areas *MSAs* (Metropolitan Statistical Areas).[8] Companies use MSAs in researching the best geographical segments for their products and in deciding where to buy advertising time. MSA research shows, for example, that people in Seattle buy more toothbrushes per capita than in any other U.S. city, people in Salt Lake City eat more candy bars, folks from New Orleans use more ketchup, and those in Miami drink more prune juice.[9]

Americans living in the suburbs engage in more casual, outdoor living, greater neighbor interaction, higher incomes, and younger families. Suburbanites buy station wagons, home workshop equipment, garden furniture, lawn and gardening tools, and outdoor cooking equipment.

## A Better-Educated and More White-Collar Population

The population is becoming better educated. In 1950, only half of all U.S. adults had gone beyond the ninth grade. By 1985, 72 percent of all Americans age 18 had completed high school. And by 1990 more than 20 percent of Americans over 24 will have completed college.[10] The rising number of educated people will increase the demand for quality products, books, magazines, and travel. It suggests a decline in television viewing, because college-educated consumers watch less TV than the population at large.

**economic environment** Factors that affect consumer buying power and spending patterns.

The work force is also becoming more white-collar. Between 1950 and 1985, the proportion of white-collar workers rose from 41 to 54 percent, that of blue-collar workers declined from 47 to 33 percent, and that of service workers increased from 12 to 14 percent. Through 1995, the most growth will come in the following occupational categories: computers, engineering, science, medicine, social service, buying, selling, secretarial, construction, refrigeration, health service, personal service, and protection.[11]

Demographic trends are highly reliable for the short and intermediate run. There is little excuse for a company's being suddenly surprised by a demographic development. Companies can easily list the major demographic trends and then spell out what the trends mean for them.

## Economic Environment

The **economic environment** consists of factors that affect consumer purchasing power and spending patterns. Markets require buying power as well as people. Total buying power depends on current income, prices, savings, and credit. Marketers should be aware of major trends in income and of changing consumer spending patterns.

### Changes in Income

Real income per capita declined during the 1970s and early 1980s as inflation, high unemployment, and increased taxes reduced the amount of money people had to spend. As a result, many Americans turned to more cautious buying. For example, they bought more store brands and fewer national brands to save money. Many companies introduced economy versions of their products and turned to price appeals in their advertising. Some consumers postponed purchases of durable goods, while others purchased them out of fear that prices would be 10 percent higher the next year. Many families began to feel that a large home, two cars, foreign travel, and private higher education were beyond their reach.

In recent years, however, economic conditions have improved. And current projections suggest that real income will rise modestly through the mid-1990s. This increase will largely result from rising income in certain important segments.[12] The baby-boom generation will be moving into its prime wage-earning years, and the number of small families headed by dual-career couples will increase greatly. These more affluent groups will demand higher quality and better service—and they will be willing and able to pay for it. They will spend more on timesaving products and services, travel and entertainment, physical fitness products, cultural activities, and continuing education.

Marketers should pay attention to *income distribution* as well as average income. Income distribution in the United States is still very skewed. At the top are *upper-class* consumers whose spending patterns are not affected by current economic events and who are a major market for luxury goods. There is a comfortable *middle class* that is somewhat careful about its spending but can still afford the good life some of the time (see Marketing Highlight 5–2). The *working class* must stick close to the basics of food, clothing, and shelter and must try hard to save. Finally, the *underclass* (persons on welfare and many retirees) have to count their pennies when making even the most basic purchases.

### Changing Consumer Spending Patterns

Table 5–1 shows the proportion of total expenditures that households at different income levels spend on major categories of goods and services. Food, housing, and transportation use up most household income. However, consum-

## THE HIGH-LIVING MIDDLE CLASS

Some 3.3 million American households have incomes that enable them to live affluent or rich lives. But far more—26 million—partake of the good life some of the time, treating themselves to Godiva chocolates, Giorgio Armani cologne, and long weekends in St. Thomas and Jamaica. They are the Joneses of the 1980s, and most have incomes of less than $40,000.

Market researchers at Grey Advertising, a New York agency with billings of $2 billion a year, discovered this new mass of "ultra consumers" while trying to figure out who has been buying so many $380 Burberry raincoats, $250 Louis Vuitton purses, and $200 Mont Blanc fountain pens. There simply aren't enough affluent or near-affluent Americans to account for all the spending on luxury goods.

The ad agency interviewed people across the country between the ages of 21 and 50 with household incomes of more than $25,000 a year, a slice representing about a quarter of the adult population. Of those surveyed, just over half said they bought the top of the line whenever they could afford it. Only 5 percent of these ultra consumers had incomes above $75,000, *Fortune's* minimum for an affluent life style.

The vast majority of these folks obviously aren't in the market for Rolls-Royces or complete designer wardrobes. But they do *rent* limos from time to time and are devotees of designer-label accessories like Hermès scarves and Gucci loafers. "This is more an attitude of the mind than the pocketbook," says Barbara Feigin, an executive vice-president at Grey.

Wanting it all has long been a hallmark of the middle class. Ultra consumers also want the best. Buying the best is a way to set themselves apart and bolster their self-image. Madison Avenue strives to reinforce that desire. Ads for premium-priced products as varied as Ultress hair coloring and Mitsubishi cars have a cloying sameness: sensual, provocative, and elegant, no matter what's for sale.

Since they cannot afford across-the-board extravagance, most ultra consumers splurge on a few items and scrimp elsewhere. They get by with fewer clothes to afford the Toshiba DX-7 digital VCR with hi-fi sound and do without the new bed so they can sleep between all-cotton sheets. "They don't have all that many wonderful things at once," says Feigin. Small doses of opulence must suffice.

*Source:* Reprinted with permission from Jaclyn Fierman. "The High-Living Middle Class, *Fortune,* April 13, 1987, p. 28.

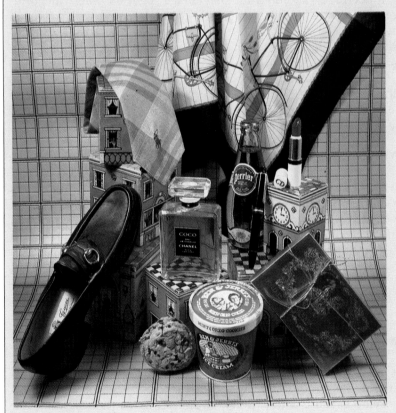

*The comfortable middle class partakes of the good life some of the time.*

**Engel's laws** Differences noted over a century ago by Ernst Engel in how people shift their spending across food, housing, transportation, health care, and other goods and services categories as family income rises.

**natural environment** Natural resources that are needed as inputs by marketers or are affected by marketing activities.

**TABLE 5–1** Distribution of Consumer Spending for Different Income Levels

| | Income Level | | |
|---|---|---|---|
| Expenditure | $10,000–$15,000 | $20,000–$30,000 | OVER $40,000 |
| Food | 17.3% | 15.5% | 13.0% |
| Housing | 22.4 | 21.9 | 22.3 |
| Utilities | 9.3 | 7.8 | 5.9 |
| Clothing | 4.8 | 4.9 | 6.2 |
| Transportation | 21.2 | 21.1 | 20.0 |
| Health Care | 5.6 | 4.0 | 3.2 |
| Entertainment | 4.0 | 4.6 | 5.5 |
| Personal Care | 1.0 | .9 | .9 |
| Reading | .7 | .7 | .6 |
| Education | 1.1 | 1.0 | 1.4 |
| Tobacco | 1.6 | 1.2 | .6 |
| Alcohol | 1.6 | 1.4 | 1.3 |
| Contributions | 2.6 | 3.7 | 4.5 |
| Insurance and Pensions | 5.3 | 9.9 | 13.2 |
| Other | 1.4 | 1.4 | 1.3 |

*Source: Consumer Expenditure Survey: Interview Survey, 1984,* U.S. Department of Labor, Bureau of Labor Statistics, Bulletin 2267, August 1986, pp. 18–21.

ers at different income levels have different spending patterns. Some of these differences were noted over a century ago by Ernst Engel, who studied how people shifted their spending as their income rose. He found that as family income rises, the percentage spent on food declines, the percentage spent on housing remains constant (except for such utilities as gas, electricity, and public services, which decrease), and both the percentage spent on other categories and that devoted to savings increase. **Engel's laws** have generally been supported by later studies.

Changes in such major economic variables as income, cost of living, interest rates, and savings and borrowing patterns have a large impact on the marketplace. Companies watch these variables using economic forecasting. Businesses do not have to be wiped out by an economic downturn or caught short in a boom. With adequate warning, they can take advantage of changes in the economic environment.

## Natural Environment

The **natural environment** involves natural resources that are needed as inputs by marketers or are affected by marketing activities. During the 1960s, public concern grew over damage to the natural environment due to the industrial activities of modern nations. Popular books raised concerns about shortages of natural resources and about the damage to water, earth, and air caused by certain industrial activities. Watchdog groups such as the Sierra Club and Friends of the Earth sprang up, and legislators proposed measures to protect the environment. Marketers should be aware of four trends in the natural environment.

### Shortages of Raw Materials

Air and water may seem to be infinite resources, but some groups see a long-run danger. Environmental groups have lobbied for a ban on certain propellants used in aerosol cans because of their potential damage to the ozone layer. Water shortage is already a problem in some parts of the world.

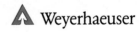
*Protecting the natural environment: Weyerhauser makes a commitment to environmental excellence.*

Renewable resources, such as forests and food, have to be used wisely. Companies in the forestry business are required to reforest timberlands in order to protect the soil and to ensure enough wood supplies to meet future demand. Food supply can be a major problem because the amount of farmable land is limited and because more and more of it is being developed for urban areas.

Nonrenewable resources, such as oil, coal, and various minerals, pose a serious problem:

> . . . it would appear at present that the quantities of platinum, gold, zinc, and lead are not sufficient to meet demands. . . . Silver, tin, and uranium may be in short supply even at higher prices by the turn of the century. By the year 2050, several more minerals may be exhausted if the current rate of consumption continues.[13]

The marketing implications are many. Firms using scarce minerals face large cost increases even if the materials do remain available. They may not find it easy to pass these costs on to the consumer. Firms engaged in research and development and in exploration can help by developing new sources and materials.

### Increased Cost of Energy

One nonrenewable resource, oil, has created the most serious problem for future economic growth. The major industrial economies of the world depend heavily on oil, and until economical energy substitutes can be developed, oil will

**technological environment** Forces that create new technologies, creating new product and market opportunities.

*As energy costs increase companies search for alternatives. Here, General Motors experiments with a solar-powered car.*

continue to dominate the world political and economic picture. Large increases in the price of oil during the 1970s (from $2 per barrel in 1970 to $34 per barrel in 1982) created a frantic search for alternative forms of energy. Although oil prices have now dropped to under $20 per barrel, coal is again popular, and many companies are searching for practical ways to harness solar, nuclear, wind, and other forms of energy. In fact, hundreds of firms are already putting out products that use solar energy for heating homes and other uses.

### Increased Levels of Pollution

Industry will almost always damage the quality of the natural environment. Consider the disposal of chemical and nuclear wastes, the dangerous mercury levels in the ocean, the quantity of DDT and other chemical pollutants in the soil and food supply, and the littering of the environment with nonbiodegradable bottles, plastics, and other packaging materials.

On the other hand, public concern creates a marketing opportunity for alert companies. It creates a large market for pollution-control solutions such as scrubbers and recycling centers. It leads to a search for new ways to produce and package goods that do not cause environmental damage.

### Government Intervention in Natural Resource Management

Various government agencies play an active role in environmental protection. For example, the Environmental Protection Agency (EPA) was set up in 1970 to deal with pollution. The EPA sets and enforces pollution standards and conducts research on the causes and effects of pollution.

Marketing management must pay attention to the natural environment. Business can expect strong controls from government and pressure groups. Instead of opposing regulation, business should help develop solutions to the material and energy problems facing the nation.

## Technological Environment

Perhaps the most dramatic force now shaping our destiny is technology. The **technological environment** consists of forces that affect new technology, creating new product and market opportunities. Technology has released such wonders as penicillin, open-heart surgery, and supercomputers. It has also released such horrors as the hydrogen bomb, nerve gas, and the submachine gun. It has released such mixed blessings as the automobile, television, and white bread. Our attitude toward technology depends on whether we are more impressed with its wonders or its blunders.

Every new technology replaces an older technology. Transistors hurt the vacuum-tube industry, xerography hurt the carbon-paper business, the automobile hurt the railroads, and television hurt the movies. When older industries fought or ignored new technologies, their businesses declined.

New technologies create new markets and opportunities. The marketer should watch the following trends in technology.

### Faster Pace of Technological Change

Many of today's common products were not available even a hundred years ago. Abraham Lincoln did not know about automobiles, airplanes, phonographs, radios, or the electric light. Woodrow Wilson did not know about television, aerosol cans, home freezers, automatic dishwashers, room air conditioners, antibiotics, or electronic computers. Franklin Delano Roosevelt did not know about xerography, synthetic detergents, tape recorders, birth control pills, or earth satellites. And John F. Kennedy did not know about personal computers, compact disk players, digital watches, VCRs, or word processors. Companies that do not keep up with technological change will soon find their products out-of-date. And they will miss new product and market opportunities.

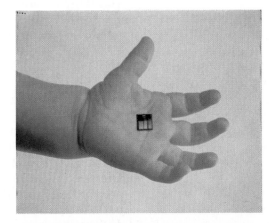
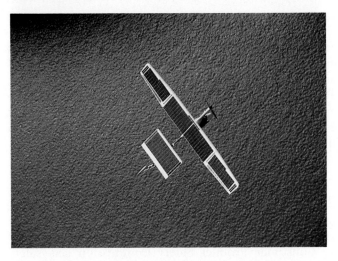

*Technology brings exciting new products and services.*

### Unlimited Opportunities

Scientists today are working on a wide range of new technologies that will revolutionize our products and production processes. The most exciting work is being done in biotechnology, miniature electronics, robotics, and materials science.[14] Scientists today are working on the following promising new products and services:

| | | |
|---|---|---|
| Practical solar energy | Commercial space shuttle | Effective superconductors |
| Cancer cures | Tiny but powerful supercomputers | Electric cars |
| Chemical control of mental health | Household robots that do cooking and cleaning | Electronic anesthetic for pain killing |
| Desalinization of seawater | Nonfattening, tasty, nutritious foods | Voice- and gesture-controlled computers |

Scientists also speculate on fantasy products, such as small flying cars, three-dimensional televisions, space colonies, and human clones. The challenge in each case is not only technical but commercial—to make *practical, affordable* versions of these products.

### High R&D Budget

The United States leads the world in research-and-development spending. In 1987, R&D expenditures exceeded $123 billion and have been increasing rapidly in recent years.[15] The federal government supplied almost half of total R&D funds. Government research can be a rich source of new product and service ideas (see Marketing Highlight 5–3).

Some companies also spend heavily on R&D. For example, General Motors spends a whopping $4.4 billion a year; IBM spends $4.0 billion; Ford and AT&T each spend about $3.5 billion.[16] Today's research is usually carried out by research teams rather than by lone inventors like Thomas Edison, Samuel Morse, or Alexander Graham Bell. Managing company scientists is a major challenge. They often resent too much cost control. They are often more interested in solving scientific problems than in coming up with marketable products. Companies are adding marketing people to R&D research teams to try to obtain a stronger marketing orientation.

### Concentration on Minor Improvements

As a result of the high cost of developing and introducing new technologies and products, many companies are making minor product improvements instead of gambling on major innovations. Even basic research companies like Du Pont, Bell Laboratories, and Pfizer are being cautious. Most companies are content to put their money into copying competitors' products, making minor feature and style improvements, or offering simple extensions of current brands. Much research is thus defensive rather than offensive.

### Increased Regulation

As products become more complex, the public needs to know that they are safe. Thus, government agencies investigate and ban potentially unsafe products. The Federal Food and Drug Administration has set up complex regulations for testing new drugs. The Consumer Product Safety Commission sets safety standards for consumer products and penalizes companies that fail to meet them. Such regulations have resulted in much higher research costs and in

## NASA: AN IMPORTANT SOURCE OF TECHNOLOGY FOR BUSINESS

Since 1958, the National Aeronautics and Space Administration (NASA) has sponsored billions of dollars' worth of aerospace research that has brought us thousands of new products. In 1962, NASA set up a program to help pass its aerospace technology along to other state and federal government agencies, public institutions, and private industry. Nine NASA applications centers across the country provide information about existing NASA technology and help in applying it.

NASA-backed aerospace research has had a great impact on industrial and consumer products. For example, NASA's need for small space systems resulted in startling advances in microcircuitry, which in turn revolutionized consumer and industrial electronics with new products ranging from home computers and video games to computerized appliances and medical systems. NASA was the first to develop communications satellites, which now carry over two-thirds of all overseas communications traffic. Here are just a few of countless other applications.

□ NASA's need for lightweight and very thin reflective materials led to research that changed the previously small-scale plastics metalization business into a flourishing industry. Using such technology, the Metalized Products Division of King-Seeley Thermos Company now makes a large line of consumer and industrial products ranging from "insulated outdoor garments to packaging materials for frozen foods, from wall coverings to aircraft covers, from bedwarmers to window shades, labels to candy wrappings, reflective blankets to photographic reflectors."

□ NASA's efforts to develop tasty, nutritional, lightweight, compactly packaged, nonperishable food for astronauts in outer space have found many applications in the food industry. Many commercial food firms are now producing astronaut-type meals for public distribution—freeze-dried foods and "retort-pouch" meals that can be used for a number of purposes.

□ NASA's need for a superstrong safety net to protect people working high in the air on space shuttles led to a new fiber. A relatively small net made of this fiber's twine can support the average-size automobile. The twine is now used to make fishing nets more than a mile long and covering more than 86 acres. The twine is thinner and denser than nylon cord, so the new nets offer less water resistance, sink faster, go deeper, and offer 30 percent productivity gains.

□ A portable X-ray machine developed by NASA uses less than 1 percent of the radiation required by conventional X-ray devices. About the size of a thermos, the unit gives instant images and is ideal for use in emergency field situations such as on-the-spot scanning for bone injuries to athletes. It can also be used for instant detection of product flaws or for security uses such as examining parcels in mailrooms and business entrances.

□ Special high-intensity lights developed by NASA to simulate the effect of sunlight on spacecraft resulted in several types of flashlights for professional and home use. One such hand-held light, which operates on a 12-volt auto or boat battery, is 50 times brighter than a car's high-beam headlights and projects a beam of light more than a mile. As a signal, it can be seen for over 30 miles.

□ Bioengineering and physiological research to design cooling systems for astronaut space clothing has led to numerous commercial and consumer products—cooler athletic clothing, lightweight and heat-resistant clothing for firefighters, survival gear for hikers and campers, and dozens of others.

*Source:* Based on information found in *Spinoff* (Washington, DC: U.S. Government Printing Office), various issues between 1977 and 1986.

longer times between new-product ideas and their introductions. Marketers must be aware of these regulations when seeking and developing new products.

Technological change faces opposition from those who see it as threatening nature, privacy, simplicity, and even the human race. Various groups have opposed the construction of nuclear plants, high-rise buildings, and recreational facilities in national parks.

Marketers need to understand the changing technological environment and how new technologies can serve human needs. They need to work closely

**political environment** Laws, government agencies, and pressure groups that influence and limit various organizations and individuals in a given society.

with R&D people to encourage more market-oriented research. They must be alert to the possible negative aspects of any innovation that might harm users or arouse opposition.

## Political Environment

Marketing decisions are strongly affected by developments in the political environment. The **political environment** is made up of laws, government agencies, and pressure groups that influence and limit various organizations and individuals in a given society. We will look at the main political trends and what they mean to marketing management.

### Legislation Regulating Business

Legislation affecting business has increased steadily over the years. This legislation has been enacted for a number of reasons. The first is to *protect companies* from each other. Business executives all praise competition but try to neutralize it when it threatens them:

> Until recently, antitrust worries kept IBM from playing too rough in the computer industry. Through the sixties and seventies the company had fought off antitrust suits and federal attempts to break it up. IBM took it easy on competitors by selling a product for four or five years and holding prices stable. This let competitors survive profitably against the industry giant. "As long as they came out with products fairly soon after IBM did, they could look forward to a few years of easy money." But in the late seventies, a more favorable regulatory climate let IBM flex its marketing muscle. IBM flooded the market with new products and made deep price cuts in all major market segments. The result was devastating to many of IBM's big, traditional rivals. Fearing total domination by IBM, competitors screamed loudly. Charging IBM with harmful competitive practices, they filed antitrust suits and urged federal regulators to step in and restore industry competitive balance.[17]

So laws are passed to define and prevent unfair competition. These laws are enforced by the Federal Trade Commission and the Antitrust Division of the Attorney General's office.

The second purpose of government regulation is to *protect consumers* from unfair business practices. Some firms, if left alone, would make bad products, tell lies in their advertising, and deceive consumers through packaging and pricing. Unfair consumer practices have been defined and are enforced by various agencies. Many managers see purple with each new consumer law. Others welcome consumer protection and look for the opportunities it presents. The third purpose of government regulation is to *protect the interests of society* against unrestrained business behavior. Profitable business activity does not always create a better quality of life. Regulation arises to make certain that firms take responsibility for the social costs of their production or products.

New laws and their enforcement will continue or increase. Business executives must watch these developments when planning their products and marketing programs. Marketers need to know about the major laws protecting competition, consumers, and society. The main federal laws are listed in Table 5–2. Marketers should also know the state and local laws that affect their local marketing activities.[18]

TABLE 5-2   Milestone U.S. Legislation Affecting Marketing

**Sherman Antitrust Act (1890)**
Prohibits (a) "monopolies or attempts to monopolize" and (b) "contracts, combinations, or conspiracies in restraint of trade" in interstate and foreign commerce.

**Federal Food and Drug Act (1906)**
Forbids the manufacture, sale, or transport of adulterated or fraudulently labeled foods and drugs in interstate commerce. Supplanted by the Food, Drug, and Cosmetic Act, 1938; amended by Food Additives Amendment in 1958 and the Kefauver–Harris Amendment in 1962. The 1962 amendment deals with pretesting of drugs for safety and effectiveness and labeling of drugs by generic name.

**Meat Inspection Act (1906)**
Provides for the enforcement of sanitary regulations in meat-packing establishments, and for federal inspection of all companies selling meats in interstate commerce.

**Federal Trade Commission Act (1914)**
Establishes the commission, a body of specialists with broad powers to investigate and to issue cease-and-desist orders to enforce Section 5, which declares that "unfair methods of competition in commerce are unlawful."

**Clayton Act (1914)**
Supplements the Sherman Act by prohibiting certain specific practices (certain types of price discrimination, tying clauses and exclusive dealing, intercorporate stockholdings, and interlocking directorates) "where the effect . . . may be to substantially lessen competition or tend to create a monopoly in any line of commerce." Provides that violating corporate officials can be held individually responsible; exempts labor and agricultural organizations from its provisions.

**Robinson–Patman Act (1936)**
Amends the Clayton Act. Adds the phrase "to injure, destroy, or prevent competition." Defines price discrimination as unlawful (subject to certain defenses) and provides the FTC with the right to establish limits on quantity discounts, to forbid brokerage allowances except to independent brokers, and to prohibit promotional allowances or the furnishing of services or facilities except where made available to all "on proportionately equal terms."

**Miller–Tydings Act (1937)**
Amends the Sherman Act to exempt interstate fair-trade (price fixing) agreements from antitrust prosecution. (The McGuire Act, 1952, reinstates the legality of the nonsigner clause.)

**Wheeler–Lea Act (1938)**
Prohibits unfair and deceptive acts and practices regardless of whether competition is injured; places advertising of foods and drugs under FTC jurisdiction.

**Antimerger Act (1950)**
Amends Section 7 of the Clayton Act by broadening the power to prevent intercorporate acquisitions where the acquisition may have a substantially adverse effect on competition.

**Automobile Information Disclosure Act (1958)**
Prohibits car dealers from inflating the factory price of new cars.

**National Traffic and Safety Act (1958)**
Provides for the creation of compulsory safety standards for automobiles and tires.

**Fair Packaging and Labeling Act (1966)**
Provides for the regulation of the packaging and labeling of consumer goods. Requires manufacturers to state what the package contains, who made it, and how much it contains. Permits industries' voluntary adoption of uniform packaging standards.

**Child Protection Act (1966)**
Bans sale of hazardous toys and articles. Amended in 1969 to include articles that pose electrical, mechanical, or thermal hazards.

**Federal Cigarette Labeling and Advertising Act (1967)**
Requires that cigarette packages contain the following statement: "Warning: The Surgeon General Has Determined That Cigarette Smoking Is Dangerous to Your Health."

**Truth-in-Lending Act (1968)**
Requires lenders to state the true costs of a credit transaction, outlaws the use of actual or threatened violence in collecting loans, and restricts the amount of garnishments. Established a National Commission on Consumer Finance.

**National Environmental Policy Act (1969)**
Establishes a national policy on the environment and provides for the establishment of

(continued)

TABLE 5–2 continued

the Council on Environmental Quality. The Environmental Protection Agency was established by Reorganization Plan No. 3 of 1970.

**Fair Credit Reporting Act (1970)**
Ensures that a consumer's credit report will contain only accurate, relevant, and recent information and will be confidential unless requested for an appropriate reason by a proper party.

**Consumer Product Safety Act (1972)**
Establishes the Consumer Product Safety Commission and authorizes it to set safety standards for consumer products as well as exact penalties for failure to uphold the standards.

**Consumer Goods Pricing Act (1975)**
Prohibits the use of price maintenance agreements among manufacturers and resellers in interstate commerce.

**Magnuson–Moss Warranty/FTC Improvement Act (1975)**
Authorizes the FTC to determine rules concerning consumer warranties and provides for consumer access to means of redress, such as the "class action" suit. Also expands FTC regulatory powers over unfair or deceptive acts or practices.

**Equal Credit Opportunity Act (1975)**
Prohibits discrimination in a credit transaction because of sex, marital status, race, national origin, religion, age, or receipt of public assistance.

**Fair Debt Collection Practice Act (1978)**
Makes it illegal to harass or abuse any person and make false statements or use unfair methods when collecting a debt.

**FTC Improvement Act (1980)**
Provides the House of Representatives and Senate jointly with veto power over FTC Trade Regulation Rules. Enacted to limit FTC's powers to regular "unfairness" issues.

## Changing Government Agency Enforcement

To enforce the laws, Congress established several federal regulatory agencies—the Federal Trade Commission, the Food and Drug Administration, the Interstate Commerce Commission, the Federal Communications Commission, the Federal Power Commission, the Civil Aeronautics Board, the Consumer Product Safety Commission, the Environmental Protection Agency, and the Office of Consumer Affairs. These agencies can have a major impact on a company's marketing performance. Government agencies have some discretion in enforcing the laws. From time to time, they appear to be overly eager and unpredictable. They are dominated by lawyers and economists who often lack a practical sense of how business and marketing works. In recent years, the Federal Trade Commission has added staff marketing experts to better understand complex business issues. The degree of enforcement lessened during the 1980s under the Reagan administration, which initiated a strong trend toward deregulation.

## Growth of Public Interest Groups

The number and power of public interest groups have increased during the past two decades. The most successful is Ralph Nader's Public Citizen group, which watchdogs consumer interests. Nader lifted consumerism into a major social force, first with his successful attack on unsafe automobiles (resulting in the passage of the National Traffic and Motor Vehicle Safety Act of 1962), and then through investigations into meat processing (resulting in the passage of the Wholesome Meat Act of 1967), truth-in-lending, auto repairs, insurance, and X-ray equipment. Hundreds of other consumer interest groups—private and governmental—operate at the national, state, and local levels. Other groups that marketers need to consider are those seeking to protect the environment and to advance the "rights" of women, blacks, senior citizens, and others.

*Secondary cultural values: the shift toward physical fitness and well-being has created a need for new products and services.*

## Cultural Environment

The **cultural environment** is made up of institutions and other forces that affect society's basic values, perceptions, preferences, and behaviors. People grow up in a particular society that shapes their basic beliefs and values. They absorb a world view that defines their relationships to themselves and others. The following cultural characteristics can affect marketing decision making.

### Persistence of Cultural Values

People in a given society hold many beliefs and values. Their core beliefs and values have a high degree of persistence. For example, most Americans believe in working, getting married, giving to charity, and being honest. These beliefs shape more specific attitudes and behaviors found in everyday life. *Core* beliefs and values are passed on from parents to children and are reinforced by schools, churches, business, and government.

*Secondary* beliefs and values are more open to change. Believing in marriage is a core belief; believing that people should get married early is a secondary belief. Marketers have some chance of changing secondary values but little chance of changing core values. For example, family-planning marketers could argue more effectively that people should get married later than that they should not get married at all.

### Subcultures

Each society contains subcultures—groups of people with shared value systems based on common life experiences or situations. Episcopalians, teen-agers, and working women all represent separate subcultures whose members share common beliefs, preferences, and behaviors. To the extent that subcultural groups show different wants and buying behavior, marketers can choose subcultures as target markets.

### Shifts in Secondary Cultural Values

Although core values are fairly persistent, cultural swings do take place. Consider the impact of popular music groups, movie personalities, and other culture heroes on young people's hair styling, clothing, and sexual norms. Marketers want to predict cultural shifts in order to spot new opportunities or threats. Several firms offer "futures" forecasts in this connection.

The major cultural values of a society are expressed in people's relationships to themselves and others, to institutions, society, nature, and the universe.

***People's Relation to Themselves*** ▪ People vary in their emphasis on serving themselves versus serving others. In the 1960s and 1970s, many people focused on self-satisfaction. Some were pleasure seekers, wanting fun, change, and escape. Others sought self-realization by joining therapeutic or religious organizations.

The marketing implications of a "me-society" are many. People use products, brands, and services as a means of self-expression. They buy their "dream cars" and take their "dream vacations." They spend more time in outdoor health activities (jogging, tennis), in thought, and on arts and crafts. The leisure industry (camping, boating, arts and crafts, sports) faces good growth prospects in a society where people seek self-fulfillment.

***People's Relation to Others*** ▪ More recently, observers have noted a shift from a "me-society" to a "we-society" in which more people want to be with and serve

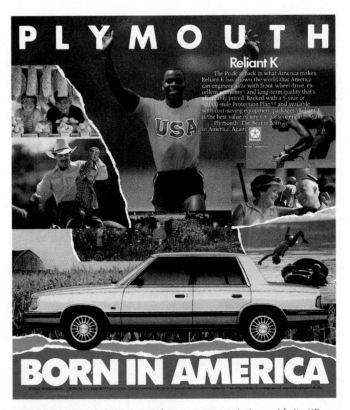

*Plymouth responded to renewed consumer patriotism with its "Born in America" theme.*

others. A recent survey showed that more people are becoming involved in charity, volunteer work, and social service activities.[19] This suggests a bright future for "social support" products and services that improve direct communication between people, such as health clubs, vacations, and games. It also suggests a growing market for "social substitutes"—things that allow people who are alone to feel that they are not, such as VCRs and computers.

*People's Relation to Institutions* ▪ People vary in their attitudes toward corporations, government agencies, trade unions, universities, and other institutions. Most people accept these institutions, although some people are highly critical of particular ones. By and large, people are willing to work for major institutions and expect them, in turn, to carry out society's work. There has been, however, a decline in institutional loyalty. People are giving a little less to these institutions and trusting them less.

Several marketing implications follow. Organizations need to find new ways to win consumer confidence. They need to review their advertising communications to make sure their messages are honest. They need to review their various activities to make sure that they are coming across as "good corporate citizens." More companies are linking themselves to worthwhile causes, measuring their images among important publics, and using public relations to build more positive images.

*People's Relation to Society* ▪ People vary in their attitudes toward their society, from patriots who defend it, to reformers who want to change it, to discontents who want to leave it. The trend through the 1960s and 1970s was toward declining patriotism and more criticism of the country's direction. The 1980s, however, saw an increase in patriotism. People's orientation to their society will influence their consumption patterns, levels of savings, and attitudes toward the marketplace.

Marketers need to watch consumers' changing social orientations and adapt their strategies accordingly. For example, U.S. companies have responded to renewed consumer patriotism with "made in America" themes and flag-waving promotions. At Chrysler, "the pride is back, born in America." A Sears catalog cover contained a photograph of the Statue of Liberty and the message "Thank You, America." The American textile industry blitzed consumers with a $40 million "Crafted with Pride in the USA" advertising campaign featuring Bob Hope, Diahann Carroll, Cathy Lee Crosby, and other celebrities insisting that "made in USA" matters.[20]

*People's Relation to Nature* ▪ People vary in their attitudes toward the natural world. Some feel ruled by it, others feel in harmony with it, and still others seek to master it. A long-term trend has been people's growing mastery over nature through technology and the belief that nature is bountiful. More recently, however, people have recognized that nature can be destroyed or spoiled by human activities.

Love of nature is leading to more camping, hiking, boating, fishing, and other outdoor activities. Business has responded with hiking gear, camping equipment, better insect repellents, and other products for nature enthusiasts. Tour operators are offering more tours to wilderness areas. Food producers have found growing markets for "natural" products such as natural cereal, natural ice cream, and health foods. Marketing communicators are using appealing natural backgrounds in advertising their products.

*People's Relation to the Universe* ▪ Finally, people vary in their beliefs about the origin of the universe and their place in it. Most Americans practice religion, but religious conviction and practice have been dropping off through the years. Church attendance has been falling steadily, with the exception of certain

**environmental management perspective** A management perspective in which the firm takes aggressive actions to affect the publics and forces in its marketing environment rather than simply watching and reacting to it.

evangelical movements that are reaching out to bring people back to organized religion. As people lose their religious orientation, they seek to enjoy their life on earth as fully as possible. They seek goods and experiences that offer fun and pleasure. In the meantime, religious institutions start turning to marketers for help in reworking their appeals so they can compete with the worldly attractions of modern society.

In summary, cultural values are showing the following long-run trends:

| | |
|---|---|
| "Me society" ⟶ | "We society" |
| Postponed satisfaction ⟶ | Immediate satisfaction |
| Hard work ⟶ | The "easy life" |
| Formal relationships ⟶ | Informal relationships |
| Religious orientation ⟶ | Worldly, nonreligious orientation |

# RESPONDING TO THE MARKETING ENVIRONMENT

Many companies view the marketing environment as an "uncontrollable" element to which they must adapt. They passively accept the marketing environment and do not try to change it. They analyze environmental forces and design strategies that will help the company avoid the threats and take advantage of the opportunities the environment provides.

Other companies take an **environmental management perspective.**[21] Rather than simply watching and reacting, these firms take aggressive actions to affect the publics and forces in their marketing environment. Thus, companies hire lobbyists to influence legislation affecting their industries and stage media events to gain favorable press coverage. They run "advertorials" (ads expressing editorial points of view) to shape public opinion. They press lawsuits and file complaints with regulators to keep competitors in line. And they form contractual agreements to better control their distribution channels. The following example shows how one company overcame a seemingly uncontrollable environmental constraint:

> Citicorp, the U.S. banking giant, had been trying for years to start full-service banking in Maryland. It had only credit card and small service operations in the state. Under Maryland law, out-of-state banks could provide only certain services and were barred from advertising, setting up branches, and other types of marketing. In March 1985, Citicorp offered to build a major credit card center in Maryland that would create 1,000 white-collar jobs and further offered the state $1 million in cash for the property where it would locate. By imaginatively designing a proposal to benefit Maryland, Citicorp became the first out-of-state bank to provide full banking services there.[22]

Marketing management cannot always affect environmental forces—in many cases, it must settle for simply watching and reacting to the environment. For example, a company would have little success trying to influence geographic population shifts, the economic environment, or major cultural values. But whenever possible, smart marketing managers take a proactive rather than reactive approach to the marketing environment.

# SUMMARY

The company must start with the *marketing environment* in searching for opportunities and monitoring threats. The marketing environment consists of all the actors and forces that affect the company's ability to transact effectively with the target market. The company's marketing environment can be divided into the microenvironment and the macroenvironment.

The *microenvironment* consists of five components. The first is the company's *internal environment*—its several departments and management levels—as it affects marketing management's decision making. The second component includes the *marketing channel firms* that cooperate to create value: the suppliers and marketing intermediaries (middlemen, physical distribution firms, marketing-service agencies, financial intermediaries). The third component consists of the five types of *markets* in which the company can sell: the consumer, producer, reseller, government, and international markets. The fourth component consists of the *competitors* facing the company. The fifth component consists of all the *publics* that have an actual or potential interest in or impact on the organization's ability to achieve its objectives: financial, media, government, citizen-action, and local, general, and internal publics.

The company's *macroenvironment* consists of major forces that shape opportunities and pose threats to the company: demographic, economic, natural, technological, political, and cultural.

The *demographic environment* shows a changing age structure in the U.S. population, a changing American family, geographic population shifts, and a better-educated and more white-collar population. The *economic environment* shows changing real income and changing consumer spending patterns. The *natural environment* shows coming shortages of certain raw materials, increased energy costs, increased pollution levels, and increasing government intervention in natural resource management. The *technological environment* shows rapid technological change, unlimited innovational opportunities, high R&D budgets, concentration on minor improvements rather than major discoveries, and increased regulation of technological change. The *political environment* shows increasing business regulation, strong government agency enforcement, and the growth of public-interest groups. The *cultural environment* shows long-run trends toward a "we-society," immediate satisfaction, the "easy life," informal relationships, and a more worldly, nonreligious orientation.

# QUESTIONS FOR DISCUSSION

1. Some companies purchase in such large volumes that they can dictate terms to their suppliers. What are the advantages and disadvantages of marketing to companies that can "make or break" you as a supplier?

2. How would an automobile manufacturer's marketing mix vary for different types of customer markets? Compare marketing mixes in the consumer, industrial, reseller, government, and international automobile markets.

3. You are communications director for a small regional airline. What publics might be affected by a report that your company had a considerably less frequent maintenance schedule than your competitors? How would you respond to this report?

4. What environmental trends will affect the success of the Walt Disney company through the 1990s? If you were in charge of marketing at Disney, what plans would you make to deal with these trends?

5. Immigration is an important component of U.S. population growth. Currently, there is one legal immigrant for every six or seven people born in the United States—twice the ratio of only 20 years ago. How will this trend affect marketing over the next 5 years? Over the next 50 years?

6. Recent life-style studies show a growing feeling that "meal preparation should take as little time as possible." What products and businesses are being affected by this trend? What future marketing opportunities does it suggest?

7. If Union Carbide developed a battery that made electric cars feasible, how do you think U.S. auto manufacturers would respond to this technological development? What kind of company would be the first to market an electric car to the general public?

8. A major alcoholic beverage marketer plans to introduce an "adult soft drink"—a socially acceptable drink that would be cheaper and lower in alcohol than wine coolers. What cultural and other factors might affect the success of this product?

9. Discuss steps that a hospital could take to "manage" its different environments.

# REFERENCES

1. For more information, see "Kellogg: Snap, Crackle, Profits," *Dun's Business Month,* December 1985, pp. 32–33; Russell Mitchell, "The Health Craze has Kellogg Feeling G-r-r-reat," *Business Week,* March 30, 1987, pp. 52–53; J. S. Richards, "Cereal Makers Reposition Products to Lure Adults," *Adweek,* May 26, 1986, p. 29; Patricia Sellers, "How King Kellogg Beat the Blahs," *Fortune,* August 19, 1988, pp. 54-64; and Wendy Zellver, "Kellogg Rides the Health Craze," *Fortune,* Special 1989 Business Week Top 1000 Issue, May 1989, pp. 28–31.

2. See "The Mommy Boom," *Sales & Marketing Management,* April 1988, p. 10.

3. See Richard Kern, "USA 2000," *Sales & Marketing Management,* October 27, 1986, pp. 8–29.

4. See Kern, "The Year 2000: A Demographic Profile of Consumer Market," *Marketing News,* May 25, 1984, Sec. 1, pp. 8–10; and Kern, "USA 2000," pp. 10–12.

5. See Paul B. Brown, Pete Engardio, Kirven Ringe, and Steve Klinkerman, "Bringing Up Baby: A New Kind of Marketing Boom," *Business Week,* April 22, 1985, pp. 58–65; Jonathan B. Levine and Amy Dunkin, "Toddlers in $90 Suits? You Gotta Be Kidding," *Business Week,* September 21, 1987, pp. 52–54; and Horst H. Stipp, "Children as Consumers," *American Demographics,* February 1988, pp. 27–32.

6. For more reading, see Paul C. Glick, "How American Families Are Changing," *American Demographics,* January 1984, pp. 21–25; Fabian Linden, "In the Rearview Mirror," *American Demographics,* April 1987, pp. 4–5; Kern, "USA 2000," pp. 16–17; and Judith Waldrop, "America's Households," *American Demographics,* March 1989, pp. 20–32.

7. See Joe Schwartz, "On the Road Again," *American Demographics,* April 1987, pp. 39–42; "Americans Keep Going West—and South," *Business Week,* May 16, 1988, p. 30; and Judith Waldrop, "2010," *American Demogaphics,* February 1989, pp. 18–21.

8. The MSA (Metropolitan Statistical Area) concept classifies heavily populated areas as MSAs or PMSAs (Primary Metropolitan Statistical Areas). MSAs and PMSAs are defined in the same way, except that PMSAs are also components of larger "megalopolies" called CMSAs (Consolidated Metropolitan Statistical Areas). MSAs and PSMAs are areas consisting of (1) a city of at least 50,000 in population, or (2) an urbanized area of at least 50,000 with a total metropolitan area of at least 100,000. See Richard Kern, "You Say Potato and I Say ADIMSADMAPMSA," *Sales & Marketing Management,* December 1988, p. 8.

9. See Thomas Moore, "Different Folks, Different Strokes," *Fortune,* September 16, 1985, pp. 65–68.

10. "The Year 2000: A Demographic Profile," *Marketing News,* May 25, 1984, Sec. 1, p. 10.

11. See Linden, "In the Rearview Mirror," p. 4. For more reading, see Bryant Robey and Cheryl Russell, "A Portrait of the American Worker," *American Demographics,* March 1984, pp. 17–21.

12. See Thomas G. Exter, "Where the Money Is," *American Demographics,* March 1987, pp. 26–32; William Lazer, "How Rising Affluence Will Reshape Markets," *American Demographics,* February 1984, pp. 17–20; Kern, "USA 2000," p. 19; and Bickley Townsend, "Dollars and Dreams," *American Demographics,* December 1987, pp. 10, 55.

13. *First Annual Report of the Council on Environmental Quality* (Washington, DC: Government Printing Office, 1970), p. 158.

14. See Gene Bylinsky, "Technology in the Year 2000," *Fortune,* July 18, 1988, pp. 92–98.

15. See "America's R&D Performance: A Mixed Review," *Business Week,* April 20, 1987, p. 59; Sana Siwolop, "Research Spending Is Building Up to a Letdown," *Business Week,* June 22, 1987, pp. 139–40; and Stuart Gannes, "The Good News About U.S. R&D," *Fortune,* February 1, 1988, pp. 48–56.

16. See "R&D Scoreboard," *Business Week,* June 20, 1988, pp. 139-40.

17. See Bro Uttal, "Is IBM Playing Too Rough?" *Fortune,* December 10, 1984, pp. 34–37; and "Personal Computers: IBM Will Keep Knocking Heads," *Business Week,* January 10, 1985, p. 67.

18. For a summary of legal developments in marketing, see Louis W. Stern and Thomas L. Eovaldi, *Legal Aspects of Marketing Strategy: Antitrust and Consumer Protection Issues* (Englewood Cliffs, NJ: Prentice Hall, 1984).

19. See Bill Barol, "The Eighties Are Gone," *Newsweek,* January 14, 1988, p. 48; Natalie de Combray, "Volunteering in America," *American Demographics,* March 1987, pp. 50–52; and Annetta Miller, "The New Volunteerism," *Newsweek,* February 8, 1988, pp. 42–43.

20. See Kenneth Dreyfack, "Draping Old Glory Around Just About Everything," *Business Week,* October 27, 1986, pp. 66–67; and Pat Sloan, "Ads Go All-American," *Advertising Age,* July 28, 1986, pp. 3, 52.

21. See Carl P. Zeithaml and Valerie A. Zeithaml, "Environmental Management: Revising the Marketing Perspective," *Journal of Marketing,* Spring 1984, pp. 46–53.

22. Philip Kotler, "Megamarketing," *Harvard Business Review,* March-April 1986, p. 117.

## CAMPBELL: RESPONDING TO A SOUPED-UP MARKETING ENVIRONMENT

At many Campbell Soup factories, soup is still cooked the old-fashioned way. Sightseers peeking through factory windows might see workers pushing large trays of carrots to be dumped into big kettles—much as they did back in 1910. This is not to say, of course, that Campbell is not moving to retool plants and develop more efficient ways to make soup. But although the old-fashioned way of cooking soup may be growing out of date, Americans' affection for and loyalty to the Campbell name is not—Campbell is the second most powerful brand name in America (behind only Coca-Cola). However, despite this continuing consumer love affair with its name, Campbell faces stiff challenges in the 1990s. Increased competition, shifting demographics, and changing consumer lifestyles provide constant opportunities for and threats to Campbell's market share. In order to maintain its long-term success, Campbell must react aggressively to its changing environment.

Campbell has marketed canned soup under its familiar red-and-white label for almost 100 years. Although Campbell's share of the $2.2 billion total soup market has shrunk from about 80 percent in the early 1970s to about 60 percent today, the company remains strong in the canned soup segment, with an 84-percent share. Recognizing that environmental and competitive changes may cause a decline in both the size of the overall canned soup market and the company's share of it, Campbell's new marketing-minded management is seeking both new market opportunities and new marketing approaches for old product lines. Although Campbell markets brands in other food categories—for example, its Pepperidge Farm, Vlasic, Prego, and LeMenu product lines—the soup business remains of special interest because of its historical importance to the company.

But the soup business just isn't what it used to be. For one thing, new soup products have flooded the market—170 in 1987 alone. Competition has stiffened, arising from such previously unimportant contenders as Progresso, Lipton, and the Japanese noodle makers Marachun and Nissin Foods. In the growing soup war, the weapon of choice has been line extensions—product variations retaining an established brand name. For example, to compete with Lipton, Campbell introduced a dehydrated soup under its own brand name rather than develop a separate brand name. With this strategy, companies try to thwart competition by attempting to satisfy every imaginable customer preference.

In addition to line extensions, the industry has in recent years created whole new categories of soups. Originally, there was canned soup, which was eventually followed by dehydrated soup. Although canned soup still accounts for 75 percent of the total market, excitement in the dehydrated category has been renewed with the startling growth of Japanese ramen noodle-style soups. More recently, microwavable soups (such as Campbell's Chunky Microwavable Soups and Fantastic Foods' "Fantastic Noodles") and new frozen/refrigerated soups (such as Chef San Francisco's Chilled Soups and Seatech's California Style Clam Chowder) have grown fast in popularity.

Changes in American lifestyles, along with other significant environmental changes, also present both many threats and opportunities. To increase the overall consumption of prepared soups and its share of this market in a vastly different and rapidly changing environment, Campbell must completely rethink its marketing strategy.

The three most important trends affecting the soup market are the aging of the population, its evolving ethnic composition, and its various lifestyle changes. The aging of the population will strongly influence American food-consumption patterns. By the year 2000, the average age of the population will jump to about 37—up from an average age of 28 in 1970. Baby boomers will continue to be the biggest demographic group, and their impact will be enormous. For one thing, with fewer opportunities to job-hop in middle age, they will settle down. In addition, their tastes will change with age, and they will be increasingly concerned with health and fitness.

The ethnic composition of the U.S. population is also changing. For example, the number of Hispanics—primarily Mexican—is growing at five times the national rate. The Hispanic segment will increase 30 percent in size by the year 2000. Although Hispanics are culturally and economically diverse, there are some identifiable features in their overall spending patterns. For example, they spend more per week on food than do members of other ethnic groups. They are also more family-oriented and brand-loyal. Marketers in many product categories are thus busy tailoring their products and promotions to meet the needs of this growing segment of the population.

In addition to the shifting demographic characteristics of the U.S. market, profound changes in lifestyle are occurring. The increasing number of dual-career and single-parent households has raised the demand for convenience products and packaging. For example, analysts predict that the $50-billion market for takeout foods will double in the next decade.

These and other recent trends present new challenges to Campbell's soup business. Campbell's short-run problem is how to make soup more attractive in the current environment. Toward this end,

(continued)

Campbell has recently advertised itself as the "well-being company" and promoted its foods as conducive to good health: One campaign even presented soup as health insurance. The slogan "Soup is Good Food" has also become a familiar part of the company's advertising. Efforts by Campbell to increase the consumption of soup also include promoting it for different occasions (eating it for breakfast), other uses (cooking sauces), and creative cookery (mixing two or more soups). And although most of Campbell's soups are condensed and must be diluted, the company created the ready-to-eat Chunky Soup line for people who want to make soup an entire meal.

In keeping with the changing times, Campbell has also developed many other new products. In fact, Campbell introduced more new products between 1982 and 1987 than any other food company. In addition to the classic red-and-white labeled soups and Campbell's Chunky Soup (introduced in 1970), other recent entries include:

□ *Canned Soups*
"Cooking Soups"—ingredient soups for recipes packaged with the traditional red-and-white label
Golden Classics—restaurant-style soups for the premium-price segment
Special Request—soups with one third less salt for those interested in reduced sodium
Creamy Natural—upscale, creamy condensed soups with no additives
Home Cookin'—hearty soups for the ready-to-eat category

□ *Dehydrated Soups*
Quality Soup & Recipe Mix—dry soups and recipe mixes to compete with the Lipton classic
Noodle Nest—ramen-style noodle soups
Campbell's Cup—individual servings of instant soup

□ *Microwavable Soups*
Chunky Microwavable Soup—shelf-stable microwavable soups in plastic bowls
Souper-Combos—frozen, single-serve combinations of soups and sandwiches

Recently, Campbell broke with industry tradition and introduced new soup products under some of its brand names in other food categories. For example, to meet the challenge from Progresso, Campbell introduced a ready-to-serve soup under the Prego name. Under its Pepperidge Farm label, it now sells a line of ultrafancy soups starting at $2 per can. Finally, under the Casera brand name (which means "home-cooked" in Spanish), Campbell now markets 50 food products—including soups—aimed at Hispanics of Caribbean origin. Under this branding strategy, consumers are often unaware that these brands are made by Campbell.

It should be noted, however, that along with its successes, Campbell has marketed several products that later fizzled. Fresh Chef—a line of refrigerated salads, soups, and sauces—flopped because of its limited shelf life and distribution and packaging problems. In general, the fresh/refrigerated category has had problems because of spoilage, distribution headaches, and prices that consumers find hard to swallow.

Campbell is also phasing in new forms

of packaging. Company management believes that the future of food packaging lies in more attractive and more convenient containers, such as plastic, aseptic boxes, and microwavable dishes. It is searching for suitable new packages and plans eventually to phase them in alongside its familiar canned soup.

Campbell managers have mixed feelings about new packaging. The company's Director of Packaging notes that "deep down everybody feels good about the can. We don't want to muck it up by changing that good solid conservative image." Obviously, exchanging the familiar tin can for a dud could be disastrous. On the other hand, consumers have many objections to cans. As Campbell's Director of Marketing Research puts it, "The can isn't as user-friendly as it used to be." In consumer preference surveys, he continues, canned soup "is being battered and beaten." One major objection to the can is inconvenience: It requires using a can opener, mixing in water if the soup is condensed, heating in a pot, and washing the pot. Other objections center on health. Younger people, in particular,

oppose the use of artificial ingredients and preservatives. They also believe that nutrients are lost in the cooking and canning process. Others contend that the salt content of canned soup is too high. A final objection comes from the rapidly growing segment of U.S. households—now over 40 percent—that use microwave ovens not designed for metal containers.

The can, however, does have some advantages. For one thing, it allows for extended shelf life (although this edge is being eroded by technological advances in plastic). The rigid tin can also protects its contents from physical damage better than almost any other package form. Lighter and less expensive cans are now being made. Finally, despite rapid changes in packaging technology, major food processors are reluctant to switch to radically new packaging systems. The answers to the basic questions of what, where, when, and how to change packaging depend on such factors as technical feasibility, economic soundness, and, most importantly, market acceptance. Eventually, alternative packaging could capture 80 percent or more of the canned soup market. But "the can is going to be

around for a long time," according to one Campbell executive.

Thus, moving into the next decade, Campbell's complex and fast-changing environment will present constant challenges. How company management handles those challenges will be critical to Campbell's future.

*Questions*

1. Assess Campbell's recent responses to environmental forces affecting the market for soup.

2. Is there a market for "well-being" products? To develop the "well-being" strategy, how should new and existing product opportunities be evaluated?

3. Which new product and packaging ideas should Campbell develop as part of the "well-being" strategy?

# 6

# Consumer Markets and Consumer Buying Behavior

## CHAPTER OBJECTIVES

After reading this chapter, you should be able to

1. Define the consumer market and construct a simple model of consumer buying behavior
2. Name the four major factors that influence consumer buying behavior
3. List the stages in the buyer decision process
4. Describe the adoption process for new products

Top managers at Porsche spend a great deal of time thinking about customers. They want to know who their customers are, what they think and how they feel, and why they buy a Porsche rather than a Jaguar, a Ferrari, or a big Mercedes coupe. These are difficult questions—even Porsche owners themselves don't know exactly what motivates their buying. But management needs to put top priority on understanding customers and what makes them tick.

Porsche appeals to a very narrow segment of financially successful people—achievers who set very high goals for themselves and then work doggedly to meet them. They expect no less from "their hobbies, or the clothes they wear, or the restaurants they go to, or the cars they drive." These achievers see themselves not as a regular part of the larger world, but as exceptions. They buy Porsches because the car mirrors their self-image—it stands for the things owners like to see in themselves and in their lives.

Most of us buy what Porsche executives call utility vehicles—"cars to be used: to go to work, to deliver the kids, to go shopping." We base buying decisions on facts like price, size, function, fuel economy, and other practical considerations. But a Porsche is a non-utility car—one to be enjoyed, not just used. Porsche buyers are moved not by facts, but by feelings. They are trying to match their dreams. To most Porsche owners, a car is more than mere transportation. It's like a piece of clothing, "something the owner actually wears and is seen in. . . . It's a very personal relationship, one that has to do with the way the car sounds, the way it vibrates, the way it feels." People buy Porsches because they enjoy driving the car, just being in it. "Just to get there, they could do it a lot less expensively. The car is an expression of themselves." Surprisingly, many Porsche owners are not car enthusiasts—they are not interested in racing or learning how to drive a high-performance car. They simply like the way a Porsche makes them feel or what the car tells others about their achievements, life styles, and stations in life.

A Porsche costs a lot of money, but price isn't much of an issue with most buyers. The company deals often with people who can buy anything they want. To many Porsche owners, the car is a hobby. In fact, Porsche's competition comes not just from other cars, but from such things as sailboats, summer homes, and airplanes. But ''most of those objects require a lot of one thing these folks don't have, and that's time. If you have a Porsche and make *it* your hobby, you can enjoy it every day on your way to work and on your way to the airport, something you can't do with a sailboat or summer home.''

Porsche has traditionally worked hard to meet its buyers' expectations. But in the mid-1980s, the company made a serious marketing blunder—it shifted toward *mass* rather than *class* marketing. It increased its sales goal by nearly 50 percent, to 60,000 cars a year. To meet this volume goal, Porsche emphasized lower-priced models that sold for as little as $20,000. Moreover, after decades of priding itself on progressive engineering, high performance, and tasteful, timeless styling, the company allowed its models to grow out-of-date. These moves tarnished Porsche's exclusive image and confused its loyal but demanding customers. At the same time, Porsche was battered by a falling U.S. dollar and increasingly fierce competition from Nissan, Toyota, BMW, and other rivals pushing new luxury sports cars. As a result, Porsche's sales plunged by 51 percent in 1988.

Porsche then fought to rebuild its damaged image and to regain rapport with its customers. It revamped its model lines, once again targeting the high end of the market—the 1989 models started at $40,000 and ranged up to $75,000. It set its sales goal at a modest 40,000 cars a year—less than a month's production at Chevrolet. The company now looks for only moderate but profitable growth; it wants to make one less Porsche than the demand. According to one executive, ''we aren't looking for volume . . . we're searching for exclusivity.'' Porsche does all it can to make Porsche ownership very special. It has even hired a representative to sell its cars to celebrities, executives of large companies, top athletes, and other notables. Having high-profile individuals driving Porsches and talking to their friends about them at cocktail parties is the best advertising the company could get.

Thus, understanding Porsche buyers is an essential but difficult task—the company must carefully craft the car and its image to match buyer needs and desires. But buyers are moved by a complex set of deep and subtle motivations. Their behavior springs from deeply held values and attitudes, from their view of the world and their place in it, from what they think of themselves and what they want others to think of them, from rationality and common sense and from whimsy and impulse. The chief executive at Porsche sums it up this way: ''If you really want to understand our customers, you have to understand the phrase, 'If I were going to be a car, I'd be a Porsche'.''[1]

---

**consumer buying behavior** The buying behavior of final consumers—individuals and households who buy goods and services for personal consumption.

**consumer market** The set of all final consumers—individuals and households who buy goods and services for personal consumption.

The Porsche example shows that many different factors affect consumer buying behavior. Marketers have to be extremely careful in analyzing consumer behavior. Consumers often turn down what appears to be a winning offer. If they do not vote for a product, the product loses. New plants and equipment might as well have been built on quicksand. Polaroid discovered this when it lost $170 million on its Polarvision instant home movie system. So did Ford when it launched the famous (or infamous) Edsel, losing a cool $350 million in the process. And so did RCA when it swallowed a huge $580 million loss on its SelectaVision videodisc player. Buying behavior is never simple, yet understanding it is the essential task of marketing management.

This chapter and the next will explore the dynamics of *consumer buying behavior* and the *consumer market*. **Consumer buying behavior** refers to the buying behavior of final consumers—individuals and households who buy goods and services for personal consumption. All of these final consumers combined make up the **consumer market.** The American consumer market consists of more than 240 million people who annually consume over $2 trillion of goods and services—that's almost $9,000 worth for every man, woman, and child. Each year, this market grows by several million people and over $100 billion, making it one of the most attractive consumer markets in the world.

American consumers vary tremendously in age, income, education level, and tastes. And they buy an incredible variety of goods and services. We will now look at how consumers make their choices among these products.

*The attractive American consumer market: the annual consumption of an American family of four.*

# MODEL OF CONSUMER BEHAVIOR

Consumers make many buying decisions every day. Most large companies research consumer buying decisions in great detail. They want to answer questions about what consumers buy, where they buy, how and how much they buy, when they buy, and why they buy (see Marketing Highlight 6–1). Marketers can study consumer purchases to find answers to questions about what they buy, where, and how much. But learning about the *whys* of consumer buying behavior and the buying-decision process is not so easy—the answers are often locked deep within the consumer's head.

The central question is this: How do consumers respond to various marketing stimuli the company might use? The company that really understands how consumers will respond to different product features, prices, and advertising appeals has a great advantage over its competitors. Therefore, companies and academics have heavily researched the relationship between marketing stimuli and consumer response. Their starting point is the stimulus-response model of buyer behavior shown in Figure 6–1. This figure shows that marketing and other stimuli enter the consumer's "black box" and produce certain responses. Marketers must figure out what is in the buyer's "black box."[2]

On the left, marketing stimuli consist of the four *P*'s—product, price, place, and promotion. Other stimuli include major forces and events in the

FIGURE 6–1  Model of Buyer Behavior

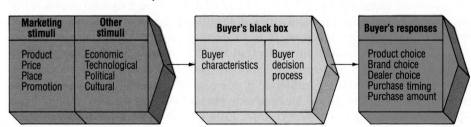

## THE WHATS AND WHYS OF CONSUMER BUYING

No one knows better than Mom, right? But does she know how much underwear you own? Jockey International does. Or the number of ice cubes you put in a glass? Coca-Cola knows that one. Or how about which pretzels you usually eat first, the broken ones or the whole ones? Try asking Frito-Lay. Big companies know the whats, wheres, hows, and whens of their consumers. They figure out all sorts of things about us that we don't even know ourselves. To marketers, this isn't trivial pursuit—knowing all about the customer is the cornerstone of effective marketing. Most companies research us in detail and amass mountains of facts about us.

Coke knows that we put 3.2 ice cubes in a glass, see 69 of its commercials every year, and prefer cans to pop out of vending machines at a temperature of 35 degrees. One million of us drink Coke with breakfast every day. Kodak knows that amateur photographers muff more than two billion pictures every year. This fact led to the disk camera, which helped eliminate almost half of our out-of-focus and overexposed shots and became one of the most successful cameras in Kodak's history.

Each new day brings piles of fresh research reports detailing our buying habits and preferences. Did you know that 38 percent of Americans would rather have a tooth pulled than take their car to a dealership for repairs? We each spend $20 a year on flowers; Arkansas has the lowest consumption of peanut butter in the U.S.; and if you send a husband and a wife to the store separately to buy beer, there is a 90 percent chance they will return with different brands.

Nothing about our behavior is sacred. Procter & Gamble once conducted a study to find out whether most of us fold or crumple our toilet paper. Abbott Laboratories figured out that one in four of us has "problem" dandruff, and Kimberly Clark, which makes Kleenex, has calculated that the average person blows his or her nose 256 times a year.

It's not that Americans are all that easy to figure out. A few years ago, Campbell Soup gave up trying to learn our opinions about the ideal-sized meatball after a series of tests showed us preferring one so big it wouldn't fit in the can.

Hoover hooked up timers and other equipment to vacuum cleaners in people's homes and found out that we spend about 35 minutes each week vacuuming, sucking up about eight pounds of dust each year and using six bags. Banks know that we write about twenty-four checks a month, and pharmaceutical companies know that all of us together take 52 million aspirins and 30 million sleeping pills a year. In fact, almost everything we swallow is closely monitored by someone. Each year, we consume 156 hamburgers, 95 hot dogs, 283 eggs, five pounds of yogurt, nine pounds of cereal, and two pounds of peanut butter. We spend 90 minutes a day preparing our food and 40 minutes a day eating it. Then we down $650 million of antacid to help digest it.

Of all businesses, however, the prize for research thoroughness may go to toothpaste makers. Among other things, they know that our favorite toothbrush color is blue and that only 37 percent of us are using one that's more than six months old. About 47 percent of us put water on our brush before we apply the paste, 15 percent of us put water on after the paste, and 24 percent of us do both. Fourteen percent don't wet the brush at all.

Thus, most big marketing companies have answers to all the what, where, when, and how questions about their consumers' buying behavior. Seemingly trivial facts add up quickly and provide important input for designing marketing strategies. But to influence consumer behavior, marketers need the answer to one more question: Beyond knowing the whats and wherefores of behavior, they need to know the *whys*—what *causes* our buying behavior? That's a much harder question to answer.

*Source:* Adapted from John Koten, "You Aren't Paranoid If You Feel Someone Eyes You Constantly," *The Wall Street Journal,* March 29, 1985, pp. 1, 22.

buyer's environment—economic, technological, political, and cultural. All these stimuli enter the buyer's black box, where they are turned into a set of observable buyer responses shown on the right—product choice, brand choice, dealer choice, purchase timing, and purchase amount.

The marketer wants to understand how the stimuli are changed into responses inside the consumer's black box. The black box has two parts. First, the buyer's characteristics influence how he or she perceives and reacts to the stimuli. Second, the buyer's decision process itself affects the buyer's behavior. This chapter looks first at buyer characteristics as they affect buying behavior. It then looks at the buyer decision process.

# PERSONAL CHARACTERISTICS AFFECTING CONSUMER BEHAVIOR

Consumer purchases are strongly influenced by cultural, social, personal, and psychological characteristics. These factors are shown in Figure 6–2. For the most part, although they cannot be controlled by the marketer, they must be taken into account. We want to examine the influence of each factor on a buyer's behavior.

We will illustrate these characteristics for the case of a hypothetical consumer named Jennifer Smith. Jennifer Smith is a married college graduate who works as a brand manager in a leading consumer packaged-goods company. She currently wants to find a new leisure-time activity that will offer some contrast to her working day. This need has led her to consider buying a camera and taking up photography. Many characteristics in her background will affect the way she goes about looking at cameras and choosing a brand.

## Cultural Factors

Cultural factors exert the broadest and deepest influence on consumer behavior. We will look at the role played by the buyer's *culture, subculture,* and *social class.*

### Culture

**Culture** is the most basic cause of a person's wants and behavior. Human behavior is largely learned. Growing up in a society, a child learns basic values, perceptions, wants, and behaviors from the family and other key institutions. Thus, an American child normally learns or is exposed to the following values: achievement and success, activity and involvement, efficiency and practicality, progress, material comfort, individualism, freedom, external comfort, humanitarianism, youthfulness, and fitness and health.[3]

Jennifer Smith's wanting a camera is a result of being raised in a modern society in which camera technology and a whole set of consumer learnings and values have developed. Jennifer knows what cameras are. She knows how to read instructions on how to operate cameras, and her society has accepted the idea of women photographers. In another culture—say, a primitive tribe in central Australia—a camera may mean nothing. It may simply be a curiosity.

**culture** The set of basic values, perceptions, wants, and behaviors learned by members of society from family and other important institutions.

FIGURE 6–2 Factors Influencing Behavior

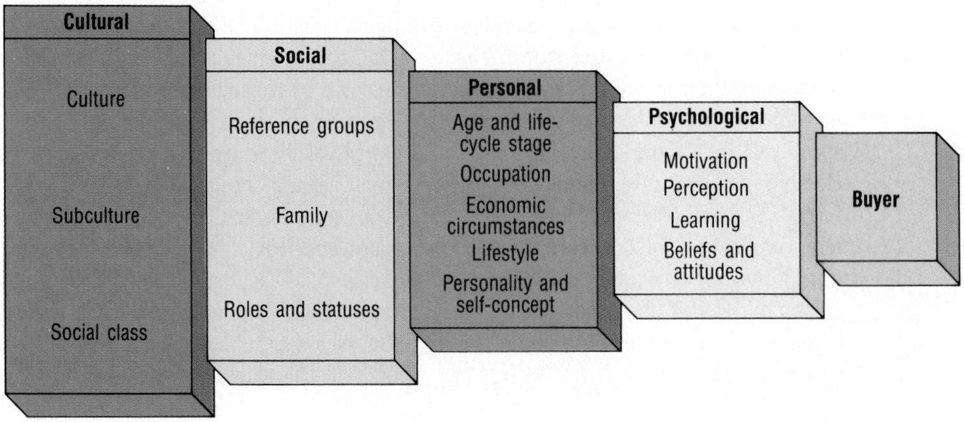

Marketers are always trying to spot *cultural shifts* in order to imagine new products that might be wanted. For example, the cultural shift toward greater concern about health and fitness has created a huge industry for exercise equipment and clothing, lighter and more natural foods, and health and fitness services. The shift toward informality has resulted in more demand for casual clothing, simpler home furnishings, and lighter entertainment. And the increased desire for leisure time has resulted in more demand for convenience products and services such as microwave ovens and fast food. It has also created a huge catalog-shopping industry. More than 6,500 catalog companies—ranging from giant retailers like Sears and Spiegel to specialty retailers like L. L. Bean, Sharper Image, Royal Silk, and Lands' End—bombard American households with 8.5 billion catalogs each year.

# Marketing Highlight 6–2

## MARKETERS TARGET IMPORTANT SUBCULTURE GROUPS

When subcultures grow large and affluent enough, companies often design special marketing programs to serve their needs. Here are examples of three such important subculture groups.

□ *Hispanic consumers.* For years, marketers have viewed the Hispanic market—Americans of Mexican, Cuban, and Puerto Rican descent—as small and poverty-stricken, but these perceptions are badly out of date. Expected to number 40 million by the year 2000, Hispanics are the second largest and fastest-growing U.S. minority. Annual Hispanic purchasing power totals $134 billion. Over half of all Hispanics live in one of six metropolitan areas—Los Angeles, New York, Miami, San Antonio, San Francisco, and Chicago. They are easy to reach through the growing selection of Spanish-language broadcast and print media that cater to Hispanics. Hispanics have long been a target for marketers of food, beverages, and household-care products. But as the segment's buying power increases, Hispanics are now emerging as an attractive market for pricier products such as computers, financial services, photography equipment, large

appliances, life insurance, and automobiles. Hispanic consumers tend to be brand-conscious and quality-conscious—generics don't sell well to Hispanics. Perhaps more important, Hispanics are very brand-loyal, and they favor companies that show special interest in them. Many companies are devoting larger ad budgets and preparing special appeals to woo Hispanics. Because of the segment's strong brand loyalty, companies that get the first foothold have an important head start in this fast-growing market.

□ *Black consumers.* With a total personal income of almost $205 billion annually, if the U.S. population of 30 million black Americans were a separate nation, their buying power would rank 12th in the free world. The black population in the U.S. is growing in affluence and sophistication. Blacks spend relatively more than whites on clothing, personal care, home furnishings, and fragrances and relatively less on medical care, food, transportation, education, and recreation. Blacks place more importance than whites on brand names, are more brand loyal, do less

"shopping around," and shop more at neighborhood stores. In recent years, many large companies—Sears, McDonald's, Procter & Gamble, Coca-Cola—have stepped up their efforts to tap this lucrative market. They employ black-owned advertising agencies, use black models in their ads, and place ads in black consumer magazines. Some companies develop special products, packaging, and appeals for the black consumer market.

□ *Mature consumers.* As the U.S. population ages, "mature" consumers—those 65 and older—are becoming a very attractive market. The seniors market will grow to over 40 million consumers by the year 2000. Seniors are better off financially—they spend about $200 billion each year, and they average twice the disposable income of consumers in the under-35 group. Seniors have long been the target of the makers of laxatives, tonics, and denture products. But many marketers know that not all seniors are poor and feeble. Most are healthy and active, and they have many of the same needs and wants as younger consumers. Because seniors have more time and money, they are an ideal market for

## Subculture

Each culture contains smaller **subcultures,** or groups of people with shared value systems based on common life experiences and situations. Nationality groups such as the Irish, Polish, Italians, and Hispanics are found within larger communities and have distinct ethnic tastes and interests. Religious groups such as Catholics, Mormons, Presbyterians, and Jews are subcultures with their own preferences and taboos. Racial groups such as blacks and Asians have distinct culture styles and attitudes. Geographical areas such as the South, California, and New England are distinct subcultures with characteristic life styles. Many of these subcultures make up important market segments, and marketers often design products and marketing programs tailored to the needs of these segments (see Marketing Highlight 6–2).[4]

**subculture** A group of people with shared value systems based on common life experiences and situations.

exotic travel, restaurants, high-tech home entertainment products, leisure goods and services, designer furniture and fashions, financial services, and life- and health-care services. Their desire to look as young as they feel makes seniors good candidates for specially designed cosmetics and personal-care products, health foods, and home physical fitness products. Several companies are hotly pursuing the seniors market. For example, the Sears 40,000-member "Mature Club" offers older consumers 25 percent discounts on everything from eyeglasses to lawn mowers. Southwestern Bell publishes the "Silver Pages," crammed full of ads offering discounts and coupons to 20 million seniors in 90 markets. To appeal more to mature consumers, McDonald's employs older people as hosts and hostesses in its restaurants and casts them in its ads. As the seniors segment grows in size and buying power, and as the stereotypes of seniors as doddering, creaky, impoverished shut-ins fade, more and more marketers will develop special strategies for this important market.

*Marketers target important subculture groups such as Hispanic, black, and senior consumers.*

respects.[5] Purchases of products that are bought and used privately are not much affected by group influences because neither the product nor the brand will be noticed by others. If Jennifer Smith buys a camera, both the product and the brand will be visible to others whom she respects, and her decision to buy the camera and her brand choice may be strongly influenced by some of her groups. Friends who belong to a photography club may influence her to buy a good camera.

### Family

Family members can have a strong influence on the buyer's behavior. The family is the most important consumer-buying organization in society, and it has been researched extensively. Marketers are interested in the roles and influence of the husband, wife, and children in the purchase of different products and services.

Husband-wife involvement varies widely by product category and by stage in the buying process. And buying roles change with evolving consumer life styles. The wife has traditionally been the main purchasing agent for the family, especially in the areas of food, household products, and clothing. But this situation is changing with the increased number of working wives and the willingness of husbands to do more of the family purchasing. For example, women now buy about 45 percent of all cars and men account for about 40 percent of food-shopping dollars.[6]

In the case of expensive products and services, husbands and wives more often make joint decisions. In the case of Jennifer Smith buying a camera, her husband will play an influencer role. He may have an opinion about her buying a camera and the kind of camera to buy. At the same time, she will be the primary decider, purchaser, and user.[7]

### Roles and Status

A person belongs to many groups—family, clubs, organizations. The person's position in each group can be defined in terms of both *role* and *status*. With her

*Family buying: depending on the product and situation, individual family members exert different amounts of influence.*

parents, Jennifer Smith plays the role of daughter; in her family, she plays the role of wife; in her company, she plays the role of brand manager. A **role** consists of the activities people are expected to perform according to the persons around them. Each of Jennifer's roles will influence some of her buying behavior.

Each role carries a **status** reflecting the general esteem given to it by society. For example, the role of brand manager has more status in our society than the role of daughter. As a brand manager, Jennifer will buy the kind of clothing that reflects her role and status. People often choose products that show their status in society. Thus, a company president will drive a Mercedes or Cadillac and wear expensive clothes. An office worker will drive a Taurus or Toyota and wear less-expensive clothes.

**role** The activities people are expected to perform according to the persons around them.

**status** The general esteem given to a role by society.

**family life cycle** The stages through which families might pass as they mature over time.

## Personal Factors

A buyer's decisions are also influenced by personal characteristics such as the buyer's *age and life-cycle stage, occupation, economic situation, life style,* and *personality and self-concept.*

### Age and Life-Cycle Stage

People change the goods and services they buy over their lifetimes. For instance, they eat baby food in their early years, most foods in their growing and mature years, and special diets in their later years. Their taste in clothes, furniture, and recreation is also age-related.

Buying is also shaped by the stage of the **family life cycle**—the stages through which families might pass as they mature over time. The stages of the family life cycle are listed in Table 6-2. Marketers often define their target markets in terms of life-cycle stage and develop appropriate products and marketing plans.

Psychological life-cycle stages have also been identified.[8] Adults experience certain passages or transformations as they go through life. Thus, Jennifer Smith may move from being a satisfied brand manager and wife to being an unsatisfied person searching for a new way to fulfill herself. In fact, such a change may have stimulated her strong interest in photography. Marketers should pay attention to

TABLE 6-2 Family Life-Cycle Stages

| *Young:* | *Middle-Aged:* | *Older:* |
|---|---|---|
| Single | Single | Older married |
| Married without children | Married without children | Older unmarried |
| Married with children | Married with children | |
|    Infant children;<br>    Young children;<br>     Adolescent children |    Young children;<br>    Adolescent children | |
| Divorced with children | Married without<br>  dependent children | |
| | Divorced without children | |
| | Divorced with children | |
| |    Young children;<br>    Adolescent children | |
| | Divorced without<br>  dependent children | |

*Sources:* Adapted from Patrick E. Murphy and William A. Staples, "A Modernized Family Life Cycle," *Journal of Consumer Research*, June 1979, p. 16. Also see Janet Wagner and Sherman Hanna, "The Effectiveness of Family Life Cycle Variables in Consumer Expenditure Research," *Journal of Consumer Research*, December 1983, pp. 281–91.

**life style** A person's pattern of living as expressed in his or her activities, interests, and opinions.

**psychographics** The technique of measuring life styles and developing life-style classifications; it involves measuring the major AIO dimensions (activities, interests, opinions).

the changing buying interests that might be associated with these adult passages.

## Occupation

A person's occupation affects the goods and services bought. A blue-collar worker will buy work clothes, work shoes, lunch boxes, and bowling recreation. A company president will buy expensive clothes, air travel, country club membership, and a large sailboat. Marketers try to identify the occupational groups that have an above-average interest in their products and services. A company can even specialize in making products needed by a given occupational group.

## Economic Situation

A person's economic situation will greatly affect product choice. Jennifer Smith can consider buying an expensive Nikon if she has enough spendable income, savings, or borrowing power. Marketers of income-sensitive goods closely watch trends in personal income, savings, and interest rates. If economic indicators point to a recession, marketers can take steps to redesign, reposition, and reprice their products.

## Life Style

People coming from the same subculture, social class, and even occupation may have quite different life styles. **Life style** is a person's pattern of living as expressed in his or her activities, interests, and opinions. Life style captures something more than the person's social class or personality. It profiles a person's whole pattern of acting and interacting in the world.

The technique of measuring life styles is known as **psychographics.**[9] It involves measuring the major dimensions shown in Table 6–3. The first three are known as the *AIO dimensions* (activities, interests, opinions). Several research firms have developed life-style classifications. The best known is the *Values and Life Styles (VALS)* typology, which now classifies the American public into eight life-style groups, including "fulfilleds," "believers" (formerly "belongers"), "actualizers," "achievers," "strivers," "strugglers," "experiencers," and "makers."[10] A person may progress through several of these life-style groups over the course of a lifetime.

Several companies have used the VALS typology to improve their marketing strategies. For example, based on VALS, Merrill Lynch changed its ad theme

TABLE 6–3    Life-Style Dimensions

| Activities | Interests | Opinions | Demographics |
|---|---|---|---|
| Work | Family | Themselves | Age |
| Hobbies | Home | Social issues | Education |
| Social events | Job | Politics | Income |
| Vacation | Community | Business | Occupation |
| Entertainment | Recreation | Economics | Family size |
| Club membership | Fashion | Education | Dwelling |
| Community | Food | Products | Geography |
| Shopping | Media | Future | City size |
| Sports | Achievements | Culture | Stage in life cycle |

*Source:* Joseph T. Plummer, "The Concept and Application of Life-Style Segmentation," *Journal of Marketing,* January 1974, p. 34.

## When you're looking for a bank that reaches farther out...Look to the Leader.™

Bank of America, California's leading business bank, helps you reach every major marketplace in the world.

Leading California companies today are stretching farther out into an ever-shrinking world. For new markets. For raw materials. If you have your sights set on the world, you need a bank that's been over the course.

**The best of both worlds.**

California's leading business bank is also a leader in international banking. We have more than 110 branches in 77 countries. We offer services from foreign exchange and letters of credit to complex merger and acquisition services. We already work with Wallace Berrie & Company, Inc., who import Smurfs® and we help the California Almond Growers Exchange export almonds to 88 foreign countries.

**California companies need smooth sailing around the world.**

Our local corporate bankers can provide access to our global network of facilities and services. They are backed by the resources and experience of California's largest business bank. So, when you're looking for a bank that reaches farther out, look to Bank of America.

**Look to the Leader.™**

**Bank of America**

*Point Loma, San Diego, California*

*Life style: this Bank of America ad targets achievers.*

**personality** The unique psychological characteristics that lead to relatively consistent and lasting individual responses to one's own environment.

from "Bullish on America" (with ads showing a herd of bulls) to "A Breed Apart" (with ads showing a single bull taking its own lead). VALS analysis showed that the original ads attracted "belongers"—traditional people who are content to follow the lead of others. But the heavy investors Merrill Lynch wanted to reach are "achievers"—hard-working, successful people who do not want to be part of the crowd—they want to stand out. Thus, the "breed apart" theme, featuring a single, independent bull, had a greater impact on Merrill Lynch's target market.[11] In another example, Bank of America found that the businessmen they were targeting consisted mainly of "achievers" who were strongly competitive individualists. The bank designed highly successful ads showing men taking part in solo sports such as sailing, jogging, and water skiing.[12]

The life-style concept, when used carefully, can help the marketer gain an understanding of changing consumer values and how they affect buying behavior.[13] Jennifer Smith, for example, can choose to live the role of a capable homemaker, a career woman, or a free spirit—or all three. She plays several roles, and the way she blends them expresses her life style. If she becomes a professional photographer, this move would change her life style, in turn changing what and how she buys.

## Personality and Self-Concept

Each person's distinct personality will influence his or her buying behavior. **Personality** refers to the unique psychological characteristics that lead to

**self-concept** Self-image, or the complex mental picture people have of themselves.

**motive** (or **drive**) A need that is sufficiently pressing to direct the person to seek satisfaction of the need.

relatively consistent and lasting individual responses to one's own environment. A person's personality is usually described in terms of such traits as the following:[14]

| | | |
|---|---|---|
| Self-confidence | Ascendancy | Emotional stability |
| Dominance | Sociability | Achievement |
| Autonomy | Defensiveness | Order |
| Change | Affiliation | Adaptability |
| Deference | Aggressiveness | |

Personality can be useful in analyzing consumer behavior for some product or brand choices. For example, coffee makers have discovered that heavy coffee drinkers tend to be high on sociability. Thus, Maxwell House ads show people relaxing and socializing over a cup of steaming coffee.

Many marketers use a concept related to personality—a person's **self-concept** (also called self-image). All of us have a complex mental picture of ourselves. For example, Jennifer Smith may see herself as outgoing, creative, and active. Thus, she will favor a camera that projects the same qualities. If the Nikon is promoted as a camera for outgoing, creative, and active people, then its brand image will match her self-image.[15]

## Psychological Factors

A person's buying choices are also influenced by four major psychological factors—*motivation, perception, learning,* and *beliefs and attitudes.*

### Motivation

We know that Jennifer Smith became interested in buying a camera. Why? What is she *really* seeking? What *needs* is she trying to satisfy?

A person has many needs at any given time. Some needs are *biological,* arising from states of tension such as hunger, thirst, or discomfort. Other needs are *psychological,* arising from the need for recognition, esteem, or belonging. Most of these needs will not be strong enough to motivate the person to act at a given point in time. A need becomes a *motive* when it is aroused to a sufficient level of intensity. A **motive** (or *drive*) is a need that is sufficiently pressing to direct the person to seek satisfaction. Psychologists have developed theories of human motivation. Two of the most popular—the theories of Sigmund Freud and Abraham Maslow—have quite different meanings for consumer analysis and marketing.

***Freud's Theory of Motivation*** ▪ Freud assumes that people are largely unconscious about the real psychological forces shaping their behavior. He sees the person as growing up and repressing many urges. These urges are never eliminated or under perfect control; they emerge in dreams, in slips of the tongue, in neurotic and obsessive behavior, or ultimately in psychoses.

Thus, a person does not fully understand his or her motivation. If Jennifer Smith wants to purchase an expensive camera, she may describe her motive as wanting a hobby or career. At a deeper level, she may be purchasing the camera to impress others with her creative talent. At a still deeper level, she may be buying the camera to feel young and independent again.

Motivational researchers collect in-depth information from small samples of consumers to uncover the deeper motives for their product choices. They use various "projective techniques" to throw the ego off guard—techniques such as word association, sentence completion, picture interpretation, and role playing. Motivation researchers have reached some interesting and sometimes odd conclusions about what may be in the buyer's mind regarding certain purchases. For example:

▫ Consumers resist prunes because they are wrinkled-looking and remind people of sickness and old age.
▫ Men smoke cigars as an adult version of thumbsucking.
▫ People prefer vegetable shortening to animal fats because the latter arouse a sense of guilt over killing animals.
▫ A woman is very serious when baking a cake because, unconsciously, she is going through the symbolic act of giving birth.

Despite its sometimes unusual conclusions, motivation research remains a useful tool for marketers seeking a deeper understanding of consumer behavior.

***Maslow's Theory of Motivation*** ▪ Abraham Maslow sought to explain why people are driven by particular needs at particular times.[16] Why does one person spend lots of time and energy on personal safety and another on gaining the esteem of others? Maslow's answer is that human needs are arranged in a hierarchy, from the most pressing to the least pressing. Maslow's hierarchy of needs is shown in Figure 6–3. In order of importance, they are *physiological* needs, *safety* needs, *social* needs, *esteem* needs, and *self-actualization* needs. A person will try to satisfy the most important need first. When that important need is satisfied, it will stop being a motivator and the person will then try to satisfy the next most important need.

For example, a starving man (Need 1) will not take an interest in the latest happenings in the art world (Need 5), nor in how he is seen or esteemed by others (Need 3 or 4), nor even in whether he is breathing clean air (Need 2). But as each important need is satisfied, the next most important need will come into play.

What light does Maslow's theory throw on Jennifer Smith's interest in buying a camera? We can guess that Jennifer has satisfied her physiological, safety, and social needs; they do not motivate her interest in cameras. Her camera interest might come from a strong need for more esteem from others.

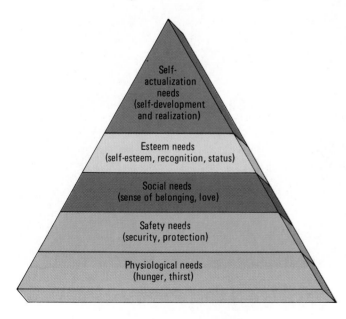

FIGURE 6–3 Maslow's Hierarchy of Needs

**perception** The process by which people select, organize, and interpret information to form a meaningful picture of the world.

**selective exposure** The tendency of people to screen out most of the information to which they are exposed.

**selective distortion** The tendency of people to adapt information to personal meanings.

Or it might come from a need for self-actualization—she wants to be a creative person and express herself through photography.

## Perception

A motivated person is ready to act. *How* the person acts is influenced by his or her *perception* of the situation. Two people with the same motivation and in the same situation may act quite differently because they perceive the situation differently. Jennifer Smith might consider a fast-talking camera salesperson loud and phony. Another camera buyer might consider the same salesperson intelligent and helpful.

Why do people have different perceptions of the same situation? All of us learn about a stimulus by the flow of information through our five senses: sight, hearing, smell, touch, and taste. However, each of us receives, organizes, and interprets this sensory information in an individual way. **Perception** is the process by which people select, organize, and interpret information to form a meaningful picture of the world.

People can form different perceptions of the same stimulus because of three perceptual processes: *selective exposure, selective distortion,* and *selective retention.*

*Selective Exposure* ▪ People are exposed to a great amount of stimuli every day. For example, the average person may be exposed to over 1,500 ads a day. It is impossible for a person to pay attention to all these stimuli; most will be screened out. **Selective exposure** means that marketers have to work especially hard to attract the consumer's attention. Their message will be lost on most people who are not in the market for the product. Moreover, even people who are in the market may not notice the message unless it stands out from the surrounding sea of other ads.

*Selective Distortion* ▪ Even stimuli that consumers do notice do not always come across in the intended way. Each person tries to fit incoming information into his or her existing mind-set. **Selective distortion** describes the tendency of

*The average person is exposed to over 1,500 ads per day—in magazines and newspapers, on radio and TV, and all around them on signs and billboards.*

people to adapt information to personal meanings. Jennifer Smith may hear the salesperson mention some good and bad points about a competing camera brand. Because she already has a strong leaning toward Nikon, she is likely to distort those points in order to conclude that Nikon is the better camera. People tend to interpret information in a way that will support what they already believe. Selective distortion means that marketers must try to understand the mind-sets of consumers and how they will affect interpretations of advertising and sales information.

*Selective Retention* ▪ People will also forget much that they learn. They tend to retain information that supports their attitudes and beliefs. Because of **selective retention,** Jennifer is likely to remember good points made about the Nikon and forget good points made about competing cameras. She remembers Nikon's good points because she "rehearses" them more whenever she thinks about choosing a camera.

These three perceptual factors—selective exposure, distortion, and retention—mean that marketers have to work hard to get their messages through. This fact explains why marketers use so much drama and repetition in sending messages to their market. Interestingly, although most marketers worry about whether their offers will be perceived at all, some consumers are worried that they will be affected by marketing messages without even knowing it (see Marketing Highlight 6–3).

## Learning

When people act, they learn. **Learning** describes changes in an individual's behavior arising from experience. Learning theorists say that most human behavior is learned. Learning occurs through the interplay of *drives, stimuli, cues, responses,* and *reinforcement.*

We saw that Jennifer Smith has a drive for self-actualization. A *drive* is a strong internal stimulus that calls for action. Her drive becomes a *motive* when it is directed toward a particular *stimulus object*—in this case a camera. Jennifer's response to the idea of buying a camera is conditioned by the surrounding cues. *Cues* are minor stimuli that determine when, where, and how the person responds. Seeing cameras in a shop window, hearing of a special sales price, and being encouraged by her husband are all cues that can influence Jennifer's *response* to the impulse to buy a camera.

Suppose Jennifer buys the camera. If the experience is *rewarding,* she will probably use the camera more and more. Her response to cameras will be *reinforced.* Then the next time she shops for a camera, binoculars, or some similar product, the probability is greater that she will buy a Nikon.

The practical significance of learning theory for marketers is that they can build up demand for a product by associating it with strong drives, using motivating cues, and providing positive reinforcement.

## Beliefs and Attitudes

Through acting and learning, people acquire their beliefs and attitudes. These in turn influence their buying behavior. A **belief** is a descriptive thought that a person has about something. Jennifer Smith may believe that a Nikon takes great pictures, stands up well under hard use, and costs $550. These beliefs may be based on real knowledge, opinion, or faith. They may or may not carry an emotional charge. For example, Jennifer Smith's belief that a Nikon camera is heavy may or may not matter to her decision.

Marketers are interested in the beliefs that people carry in their heads about specific products and services. These beliefs make up product and brand

**selective retention** The tendency of people to retain only part of the information to which they are exposed, usually information that supports their attitudes and beliefs.

**learning** Changes in an individual's behavior arising from experience.

**belief** A descriptive thought that a person has about something.

# Marketing Highlight 6-3

## SUBLIMINAL PERCEPTION: CAN CONSUMERS BE AFFECTED WITHOUT KNOWING IT?

In 1957, the words "Eat popcorn" and "Drink Coca-Cola" were flashed on a screen in a New Jersey movie theater every five seconds for one three-hundredths of a second. The researchers reported that although the audience did not consciously recognize these messages, viewers absorbed them subconsciously and bought 58 percent more popcorn and 18 percent more Coke. Suddenly, advertising agencies and consumer-protection groups became intensely interested in *subliminal perception*. People voiced fears of being brainwashed, and California and Canada declared the practice illegal. The controversy cooled when scientists failed to replicate the original results, but the issue did not die. In 1974, Wilson Bryan

Key claimed in his book *Subliminal Seduction* that consumers were still being manipulated by advertisers in print ads and television commercials.

Subliminal perception has since been studied by many psychologists and consumer researchers. None has been able to show that subliminal messages have any effect on consumer behavior. It appears that subliminal advertising simply doesn't have the power attributed to it by its critics. Most advertisers scoff at the notion of an industry conspiracy to manipulate consumers through "invisible" messages. As one advertising agency executive put it, "We have enough trouble persuading consumers using a series of up-front thirty-second ads—how could we do it in ⅓₀₀th of a second?"

While advertisers may avoid outright subliminal advertising, some critics claim that television advertising employs techniques approaching the subliminal. With more and more viewers reaching for their remote controls to avoid ads by switching channels or fast-forwarding through VCR tapes, advertisers are using new tricks to grab viewer attention and to affect consumers in ways they may not be aware of. Many ad agencies employ psychologists and neurophysiologists to help develop subtle psychological advertising strategies.

For example, some advertisers purposely try to confuse viewers, throw them off balance, or even make them uncomfortable:

[They use] film footage that wouldn't pass

---

**attitude** A person's consistently favorable or unfavorable evaluations, feelings, and tendencies toward an object or idea.

images, and people do tend to act on their beliefs. If some beliefs are wrong and prevent purchase, the marketer will want to launch a campaign to correct them.

People have attitudes regarding religion, politics, clothes, music, food, and almost everything else. An **attitude** describes a person's relatively consistent evaluations, feelings, and tendencies toward an object or idea. Attitudes put people into a frame of mind of liking or disliking things, moving toward or away from them. Thus, Jennifer Smith may hold such attitudes as "Buy the best," "The Japanese make the best products in the world," and "Creativity and self-expression are among the most important things in life." The Nikon camera therefore fits well into Jennifer's existing attitudes. A company would benefit greatly from researching the various attitudes that might bear on its product.

Attitudes are difficult to change. A person's attitudes fit into a pattern, and to change one attitude may require difficult adjustments in many others. Thus, a company should usually try to fit its products into existing attitudes rather than try to change them. There are exceptions, of course, in which the great cost of trying to change attitudes may pay off. For example:

> Honda entered the U.S. motorcycle market facing a major decision. It could either sell its motorcycles to a small number of people already interested in motorcycles or try to increase the number interested in motorcycles. The latter would be more expensive because many people had negative attitudes toward motorcycles. They associated motorcycles with black leather jackets, switchblades, and crime. Honda took the second course and launched a major campaign based on the theme "You meet the nicest people on a Honda." Its campaign worked, and many people adopted a new attitude toward motorcycles.

We can now appreciate the many individual characteristics and forces acting on consumer behavior. The person's choice is the result of the complex

muster with a junior-high film club. You have to stare at the screen just to figure out what's going on—and that, of course, is the idea. Take the ads for Wang computers. In these hazy, washed-out spots, people walk partially in and out of the camera frame talking in computer jargon. But the confusion grabs attention. . . . Even people who don't understand a word are riveted to the screen.

Other advertisers use the rapid-fire technique: Images flash by so quickly you can barely register them. Pontiac used such "machine-gun editing" in recent ads—the longest shot flashed by in one and one-half seconds, the shortest in one-quarter of a second. The ads scored high in viewer recall. Some advertisers go after our ears as well as our eyes, taking advantage of the powerful effects some sounds have on human brain waves:

Advertisers are using sounds to take advantage of the automatic systems built into the brain that force you to stop what you're doing and refocus on the screen. . . . You can't ignore these sounds. That's why commercials are starting off with noises ranging from a baby crying (Advil) to a car horn (Hertz) to a factory whistle (Almond Joy). In seeking the right sound . . . advertisers can be downright merciless. . . . Ads for Nuprin pain reliever kick off by assaulting viewers with the whine of a dentist's drill . . . to help the viewer recall the type of pain we've all experienced. Hey, thanks.

A few experts are concerned that new high-tech advertising might even hypnotize consumers, whether knowingly or not. They suggest that several techniques—rapid scene changes, pulsating music and sounds, repetitive phrases, and flashing logos—might actually start to put some viewers under.

Some critics think that such subtle, hard-to-resist psychological techniques are unfair to consumers—that advertisers can use these techniques to bypass consumers' defenses and affect them without their being aware of it. The advertisers who use these techniques, however, view them as innovative, creative approaches to advertising.

*Sources:* See Wilson Bryan Key, *Subliminal Seduction* (New York: NAL, 1974); Timothy E. Moore, "Subliminal Advertising: What You See Is What You Get," *Journal of Marketing*, Spring 1982, pp. 38–47; and Walter Weir, "Another Look at Subliminal 'Facts,'" *Advertising Age*, October 15, 1984, p. 46. Excerpts from David H. Freedman, "Why You Watch Commercials—Whether You Mean to or Not," *TV Guide*, February 20, 1988, pp. 4–7.

interplay of cultural, social, personal, and psychological factors. Many of these factors cannot be influenced by the marketer. However, they are useful in identifying interested buyers and shaping products and appeals to better serve their needs.

*Attitudes are hard to change, but it can be done. Honda's "You meet the nicest people on a Honda" campaign changes people's attitudes about who rides motorcycles.*

# THE BUYER-DECISION PROCESS

Now that we have looked at all the *influences* that affect buyers, we are ready to look at how consumers make buying *decisions*. Figure 6–4 shows that the buyer-decision process consists of five stages: *problem recognition, information search, evaluation of alternatives, purchase decision,* and *postpurchase behavior.* This model emphasizes that the buying process starts long before actual purchase and continues long after. It encourages the marketer to focus on the entire buying process rather than just the purchase decision.

This model seems to imply that consumers pass through all five stages with every purchase. But in more routine purchases, consumers skip or reverse some stages. A woman buying her regular brand of toothpaste would recognize the need and go right to the purchase decision, skipping information search and evaluation. However, we will use the model in Figure 6–4 because it shows all the considerations that arise when a consumer faces a new and complex purchase situation.

To illustrate this model, we will again follow Jennifer Smith and try to understand how she became interested in buying an expensive camera and the stages she went through to make the final choice.

## Problem Recognition

The buying process starts with the buyer recognizing a problem or need. The buyer senses a difference between his or her *actual* state and some *desired* state. The need can be triggered by *internal stimuli.* One of the person's normal needs—hunger, thirst, sex—rises to a level high enough to become a drive. From previous experience, the person has learned how to cope with this drive and is motivated toward objects that he or she knows will satisfy it.

Or a need can be triggered by *external stimuli.* Jennifer Smith passes a bakery and the sight of freshly baked bread stimulates her hunger; she admires a neighbor's new car; or she watches a television commercial for a Jamaican vacation. All of these experiences can lead her to recognize a problem or need. At this stage, the marketer needs to determine the factors and situations that usually trigger consumer problem recognition. The marketer should research consumers to find out what kinds of needs or problems arose, what brought them about, and how they led the consumer to this particular product.

Jennifer Smith might answer that she felt the need for a new hobby when her busy season at work slowed down, and she thought of cameras after talking to a friend about photography. By gathering such information, the marketer can identify the stimuli that most often trigger interest in the product and can develop marketing programs that involve these stimuli.

## Information Search

An aroused consumer may or may not search for more information. If the consumer's drive is strong and a satisfying product is near at hand, the consumer is likely to buy it at that point. If not, the consumer may simply store the need in memory and search for information bearing on it.

FIGURE 6–4  Buyer-Decision Process

*Information sources: people usually receive the most information about a product from marketer controlled sources.*

At one level, the buyer may simply have *heightened attention*. Here, Jennifer Smith simply becomes more receptive to information about cameras. She pays attention to camera ads, cameras used by friends, and camera conversations. Or Jennifer may go into *active information search,* looking for reading material, phoning friends, and gathering product information in other ways. How much searching she does will depend on the strength of her drive, the amount of information she starts with, the ease of obtaining more information, the value she places on additional information, and the satisfaction she gets from searching.

The consumer can obtain information from any of several sources. These include

- □ *Personal sources:* family, friends, neighbors, acquaintances
- □ *Commercial sources:* advertising, salespeople, dealers, packaging, displays
- □ *Public sources:* mass media, consumer-rating organizations
- □ *Experiential sources:* handling, examining, using the product

The relative influence of these information sources varies with the product and the buyer. Generally, the consumer receives the most information about a product from commercial sources—those controlled by the marketer. The most effective sources, however, tend to be personal. Commercial sources normally *inform* the buyer, but personal sources *legitimize* or *evaluate* products for the buyer. For example, doctors normally learn of new drugs from commercial sources but turn to other doctors for evaluation information.

As a result of gathering information, the consumer increases his or her awareness and knowledge of the available brands and their features. In looking for information, Jennifer Smith found out about the many camera brands available. The information also helped her drop certain brands from consideration. A company must design its marketing mix to make prospects aware of and knowledgeable about its brand. If it fails to do this, the company has lost its opportunity to sell to the customer. The company must also learn about the other brands customers consider, so that it knows its competition and can plan its own appeals.

The marketer should carefully identify consumers' sources of information and the importance of each source. Consumers should be asked how they first heard about the brand, what information they received, and the importance they place on different information sources. This information is critical in preparing effective communication to target markets.

## Evaluation of Alternatives

We have seen how the consumer uses information to arrive at a set of final brand choices. Now the question is: How does the consumer choose among alternative brands? The marketer needs to know how the consumer processes information to arrive at brand choices. Unfortunately, there is no simple and single evaluation process used by all consumers, or even by one consumer in all buying situations. There are several evaluation processes.

Certain basic concepts will help explain consumer-evaluation processes. First, we assume that each consumer sees a product as a bundle of *product attributes*. For cameras, these attributes include picture quality, ease of use, camera size, price, and other features. Consumers will vary as to which of these attributes they consider relevant. Consumers will pay the most attention to those attributes connected with their needs.

Second, the consumer will attach different *degrees of importance* to different attributes: That is, each consumer attaches importance to each attribute according to his or her unique needs and wants. Third, the consumer is likely to develop a set of *brand beliefs* about where each brand stands on each attribute. A set of beliefs about a particular brand is known as the **brand image.** Due to their experiences and the effects of selective perception, selective distortion, and selective retention, consumers' beliefs may vary from the product's true attributes.

Fourth, the consumer is assumed to have a *utility function* for each attribute. The utility function shows how the consumer expects total product satisfaction to vary with different levels of different attributes. For example, Jennifer Smith may expect her satisfaction from a camera to increase with better picture quality; to peak with a medium-weight camera as opposed to a very light or very heavy one; to be higher for a 35-mm camera than for a 135-mm camera. If we combine the attribute levels at which utilities are highest, they make up Jennifer's ideal camera. The camera would also be her preferred camera if it were available and affordable.

Fifth, the consumer arrives at attitudes toward the different brands through some *evaluation procedure*. Consumers have been found to use one or more of several evaluation procedures, depending on the consumer and the buying decision.

We will illustrate these concepts with Jennifer Smith's camera-buying situation. Suppose Jennifer has narrowed her choices to four cameras. And assume that she is primarily interested in four attributes—picture quality, ease of use, camera size, and price. Jennifer has formed beliefs about how each brand rates on each attribute. The marketer would like to be able to predict which camera Jennifer will buy.

Clearly, if one camera rated best on all attributes, we could predict that Jennifer would choose it. But brands vary in appeal. Some buyers will choose using only one attribute, and their choices are easy to predict. If Jennifer wants picture quality above everything, she will buy the camera that she thinks has the best picture quality. But most buyers consider several attributes, each with different importance. If we knew the importance Jennifer assigns to each of the four attributes, we could predict her camera choice more reliably.

How consumers go about evaluating purchase alternatives depends on the individual consumer and the specific buying situation. In some cases, consumers use careful calculations and logical thinking. In other cases, the same consumers do little or no evaluating, buying instead on impulse and relying on intuition. Sometimes consumers make buying decisions on their own; sometimes they turn to friends, consumer guides, salespeople, or even computers for advice (See Marketing Highlight 6–4).

Marketers should study buyers to find out how they actually evaluate brand alternatives. Knowing this, the marketer could take steps to influence the buyer's decision. Suppose Jennifer is inclined to buy a Nikon because she rates it high on picture quality and ease of use. What strategies might another camera maker, say Minolta, use to influence people like Jennifer? There are several. Minolta could modify its camera so that it delivers better pictures or other features that consumers like Jennifer want. It could try to change buyers' beliefs about how its camera rates on key attributes, especially if consumers currently underestimate the camera's qualities. It could try to change buyers' beliefs about Nikon and other competitors. Finally, it could try to change either the list of attributes that buyers consider or the importance attached to them. For example, it might advertise that all good cameras have about equal picture quality and that its lighter-weight, lower-priced camera is a better buy for people like Jennifer.

## Marketing Highlight 6–4

### THIS COMPUTER GIVES SHOPPERS CUSTOM-MADE ADVICE

Some people break out in a cold sweat when they have to shop. Others get cross-eyed from scanning the ratings in *Consumer Reports*. That consumers are befuddled doesn't surprise Thomas A. Williams. The Rochester Institute of Technology professor of decision sciences says he has been swamped with requests from friends who need help. So Williams is working on a high-tech solution: expert-system programs to help confused consumers shop.

Williams has tried out his computerized advisers for such products as running shoes, washing machines, touring bikes, and cars. The systems grill shoppers about their preferences, personal characteristics, and price ranges. Then they match the data with available products. If you wanted new running shoes, a system would base its recommendation on answers to questions about the anatomy of your feet, the terrain you run on, and how long and how often you run.

Williams is scouting out stores that will let customers try his systems for microcomputers and cameras. He's still not sure shoppers will welcome the electronic adviser. "The typical consumer does not approach a purchasing decision in a logical fashion," he says.

*Source:* Reprinted from the December 7, 1987, issue of *Business Week* by special permission. © 1987 by McGraw-Hill, Inc.

*To rate higher with consumers, Minolta added autofocus, motorized film control, and other features. It took major competitor Canon three years to catch up.*

## Purchase Decision

In the evaluation stage, the consumer ranks brands and forms purchase intentions. Generally, the consumer will buy the most preferred brand, but two factors can come between the purchase *intention* and the purchase *decision*. These factors are shown in Figure 6–5.[17]

The first factor is the *attitudes of others*. Suppose Jennifer Smith's husband feels strongly that Jennifer should buy the lowest-priced camera. Then the chances of Jennifer buying a more expensive camera will be reduced. How much another person's attitudes will affect Jennifer's choices depends both on the strength of the other person's attitudes toward her buying decision and on Jennifer's motivation to comply with that person's wishes. The more intense the other person's attitudes and the closer the other person is to Jennifer, the greater the effect the other person will have.

Purchase intention is also influenced by *unexpected situational factors*. The consumer forms a purchase intention based on such factors as expected family income, expected price, and expected benefits from the product. When the consumer is about to act, unexpected situational factors may arise to change the purchase intention. Jennifer Smith may lose her job, some other purchase may

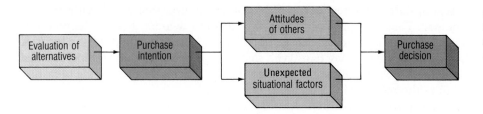

FIGURE 6–5  Steps between Evaluation of Alternatives and a Purchase Decision

become more urgent, or a friend may report being disappointed in her preferred camera.

Thus, preferences and even purchase intentions do not always result in actual purchase choice. They may direct purchase behavior but may not fully determine the outcome.

## Postpurchase Behavior

The marketer's job does not end when the product is bought. After purchasing the product, the consumer will be satisfied or dissatisfied and will engage in postpurchase actions of interest to the marketer. What determines whether the buyer is satisfied or dissatisfied with a purchase? The answer lies in the relationship between the consumer's *expectations* and the product's *perceived performance*.[18] If the product matches expectations, the consumer is satisfied; if it falls short, the consumer is dissatisfied.

Consumers base their expectations on messages they receive from sellers, friends, and other information sources. If the seller exaggerates the product's performance, consumer expectations will not be met—a situation that leads to dissatisfaction. The larger the gap between expectation and performance, the greater the consumer's dissatisfaction. This fact suggests that the seller should make product claims that faithfully represent the product's performance so that buyers are satisfied.

Some sellers might even understate performance levels to boost consumer satisfaction with a product. For example, Boeing sells aircraft worth tens of millions of dollars each—consumer satisfaction is important for repeat purchases and the company's reputation. Boeing's salespeople sell their products with facts and knowledge, not with inflated promises. In fact, salespeople tend to be conservative when they estimate their product's potential benefits. They almost always underestimate fuel efficiency—they promise a 5 percent savings that turns out to be 8 percent. Customers are delighted with better-than-expected performance; they buy again and tell other potential customers that Boeing lives up to its promises.[19]

Almost all major purchases result in **cognitive dissonance,** or discomfort caused by postpurchase conflict. Consumers are satisfied with the benefits of the chosen brand and glad to avoid the drawbacks of the brands not purchased. On the other hand, every purchase involves compromise. Consumers feel uneasy about acquiring the drawbacks of the chosen brand and about losing the benefits of the brands not purchased. Thus, consumers feel at least some postpurchase dissonance for every purchase. And they will often take steps after the purchase to reduce dissonance.[20]

Dissatisfied consumers may take any of several actions. They may return the product or complain to the company and ask for a refund or exchange. They may go to a lawyer or complain to other groups that might help them get satisfaction. Or buyers may simply stop buying the product or warn friends not to buy it. In all these cases, the seller loses something.

Marketers can take steps to reduce consumer postpurchase dissatisfaction and to help customers feel good about their purchases. Automobile companies

**new product** A good, service, or idea that is perceived by some potential customers as new.

**adoption process** The mental process through which an individual passes from first hearing about an innovation to final adoption.

can send letters to new-car owners congratulating them on having selected a fine car. They can place ads showing satisfied owners driving their new cars. They can obtain customer suggestions for improvements and list the location of available services. They can write instruction booklets that reduce dissatisfaction. They can send owners magazines full of articles describing the pleasures of owning the new car.[21]

Postpurchase communications to buyers have been shown to result in fewer product returns and order cancellations. Paying careful attention to customer dissatisfaction can help the company to spot and correct problems and increase postpurchase satisfaction for future buyers.

Understanding the consumer's needs and buying process is the foundation of successful marketing. By understanding how buyers go through problem recognition, information search, evaluation of alternatives, the purchase decision, and postpurchase behavior, the marketer can pick up many clues as to how to meet the buyer's needs. By understanding the various participants in the buying process and the major influences on their buying behavior, the marketer can develop an effective marketing program to support an attractive offer to the target market.

# BUYER-DECISION PROCESS FOR NEW PRODUCTS

We have looked at the stages buyers go through in trying to satisfy a need. Buyers may pass quickly or slowly through these stages, and some of them may even be reversed. Much depends on the nature of the buyer, the product, and the buying situation.

We will now look at how buyers approach the purchase of new products. We define **new product** as a good, service, or idea that is perceived by some potential customers as new. The new product may have been around for a while, but our interest is in how consumers learn about products for the first time and make decisions on whether to adopt them. We define **adoption process** as "the mental process through which an individual passes from first hearing about an

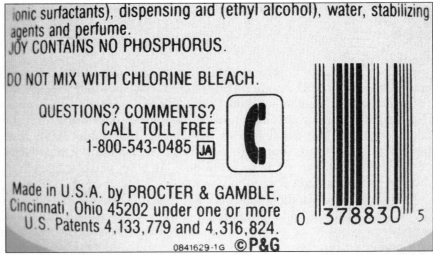

*To spot and correct post-purchase consumer dissatisfactions, Procter & Gamble puts an 800 number for customer service on every product it sells.*

innovation to final adoption."[22] We define **adoption** as the decision by an individual to become a regular user of a product.

**adoption** The decision by an individual to become a regular user of a product.

## Stages in the Adoption Process

Consumers go through five stages in the process of adopting a new product:

1. *Awareness:* The consumer becomes aware of the new product but lacks information about it.
2. *Interest:* The consumer is stimulated to seek information about the new product.
3. *Evaluation:* The consumer considers whether it would make sense to try the new product.
4. *Trial:* The consumer tries the new product on a small scale to improve his or her estimate of its value.
5. *Adoption:* The consumer decides to make full and regular use of the new product.

This model suggests that the new-product marketer should think about how to help consumers move through these stages. A manufacturer of microwave ovens may discover that many consumers in the interest stage do not move to the trial stage because of uncertainty and the large investment. If these same consumers would be willing to use a microwave oven on a trial basis for a small fee, the manufacturer should consider offering a trial-use plan with an option to buy.

## Individual Differences in Innovativeness

People differ greatly in their readiness to try new products. In each product area, there are "consumption pioneers" and early adopters. Other individuals adopt new products much later. This finding has led to a classification of people into the adopter categories shown in Figure 6-6.

After a slow start, an increasing number of people adopt the new product. The number of adopters reaches a peak and then drops off as fewer nonadopters remain. *Innovators* are defined as the first 2.5 percent of the buyers to adopt a new idea; the *early adopters* are the next 13.5 percent, and so forth.

The five adopter groups have differing values. Innovators are venturesome—they try new ideas at some risk. Early adopters are guided by respect—

FIGURE 6-6 Adopter Categorization on the Basis of Relative Time of Adoption of Innovations

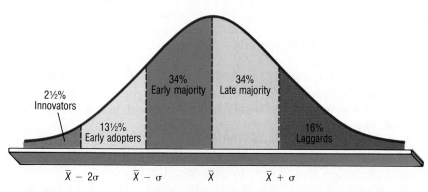

*Source:* Adapted with permission of The Free Press, a Division of Macmillan, Inc., from *Diffusion of Innovations*, 3rd ed., by Everett M. Rogers. Copyright © 1962, 1971, 1983 by The Free Press.

**personal influence** The effect of statements made by one person on another's attitude or probability of purchase.

they are opinion leaders in their communities and adopt new ideas early but carefully. The *early majority* are deliberate—although they rarely are leaders, they adopt new ideas before the average person. The *late majority* are skeptical—they adopt an innovation only after a majority of people have tried it. Finally, *laggards* are tradition-bound—they are suspicious of changes and adopt the innovation only when it has become something of a tradition itself.

This adopter classification suggests that an innovating firm should research the characteristics of innovators and early adopters and direct marketing efforts to them. For example, home computer innovators are middle-aged and higher in income and education than noninnovators, and they tend to be opinion leaders. They also tend to be more rational, more introverted, and less social.[23] In general, innovators tend to be relatively younger, better educated, and higher in income than later adopters and nonadopters. They are more receptive to unfamiliar things, rely more on their own values and judgment, and are more willing to take risks. They are less brand-loyal and more likely to take advantage of special promotions such as discounts, coupons, and samples.[24]

### Role of Personal Influence

Personal influence plays a major role in the adoption of new products. **Personal influence** describes the effect of statements made by one person on another's attitude or probability of purchase. Consumers consult each other for opinions about new products and brands, and the advice of others can strongly influence buying behavior.

Personal influence is more important in some situations and for some individuals than for others. Personal influence is more important in the evaluation stage of the adoption process than in the other stages. It has more influence on later adopters than early adopters. And it is more important in risky buying situations than in safe situations.

### Influence of Product Characteristics on Rate of Adoption

The characteristics of the new product affect its rate of adoption. Some products catch on almost overnight (frisbees), whereas others take a long time to gain acceptance (personal computers). Five characteristics are especially important in influencing an innovation's rate of adoption. We will consider these characteristics in relation to the rate of adoption of personal computers for home use.

The first characteristic is the innovation's *relative advantage*—the degree to which it appears superior to existing products. The greater the perceived relative advantage of using a personal computer—say, in preparing income taxes and keeping financial records—the sooner the personal computer will be adopted.

The second characteristic is the innovation's *compatibility*—the degree to which it fits the values and experiences of potential consumers. Personal computers, for example, are highly compatible with the life styles found in upper-middle-class homes.

The third characteristic is the innovation's *complexity*—the degree to which it is difficult to understand or use. Personal computers are complex and will therefore take a longer time to penetrate U.S. homes.

The fourth characteristic is the innovation's *divisibility*—the degree to which it may be tried on a limited basis. To the extent that people can rent personal computers with an option to buy, the product's rate of adoption will increase.

*Product characteristics affect the rate of adoption—products like home computers take a long time to gain wide acceptance.*

The fifth characteristic is the innovation's *communicability*—the degree to which the results can be observed or described to others. Because personal computers lend themselves to demonstration and description, their use will spread faster among consumers.

Other characteristics influence the rate of adoption, such as initial and ongoing costs, risk and uncertainty, and social approval. The new-product marketer has to research all these factors when developing the new product and its marketing program.

## SUMMARY ■

Markets have to be understood before marketing strategies can be developed. The consumer market buys goods and services for personal consumption. *Consumer behavior* is influenced by the *buyer's characteristics* and by the *buyer's decision process.* Buyer characteristics include four major factors: cultural, social, personal, and psychological.

*Culture* is the most basic determinant of a person's wants and behavior. Marketers try to track cultural shifts that might suggest new ways to serve consumers. *Subcultures* are "cultures within cultures" that have distinct values and life styles. Some large subcultures—Hispanics, blacks, and senior consumers—have become important target markets. *Social classes* are subcultures whose members have similar social status based on occupation, income, education, wealth, and other variables. People with different cultural, subcultural, and social-class characteristics have different product and brand preferences. Marketers may want to focus their marketing programs on the special needs of certain groups.

*Social factors* also influence a buyer's behavior. A person's *reference groups*—family, friends, social organizations, professional associations—strongly affect product and brand choices. The person's position within each group can be defined in terms of *role* and *status*. A buyer chooses products and brands that reflect his or her role and status.

The buyer's age, life-cycle stage, occupation, economic circumstances, life style, personality, and other personal characteristics influence his or her buying decisions. The needs and wants of young consumers differ from those of older consumers; the needs of young married couples differ from those of retirees; the buying habits of higher-income consumers differ from those of lower-income consumers. Consumer *life styles*—the whole pattern of acting and interacting in the world—are also an important influence on buyers' choices.

Finally, consumer buying behavior is influenced by four major psychological factors—*motivation, perception, learning,* and *attitudes.* Each of these factors provides a different perspective for understanding the workings of the buyer's "black box."

In buying something, the buyer goes through a decision process consisting of *problem recognition, information search, alternative evaluation, purchase decision,* and *postpurchase behavior.* The marketer must understand the buyer's behavior at each stage and what influences are operating upon the buyer's decision. This helps the marketer to develop effective marketing programs for the target market.

For new products, consumers respond at different rates, depending on consumer and product characteristics. Manufacturers try to bring their new products to the attention of early adopters, especially opinion leaders.

# QUESTIONS FOR DISCUSSION

1. What factors could you add to the model in Figure 6–1 to make it a more complete description of consumer behavior?

2. A new method of packaging wine in cardboard boxes offers more consumer convenience than traditional bottles: Instead of a cork, an airtight dispenser allows servings of desired amounts while keeping the remaining wine fresh for weeks. How will the factors shown in Figure 6–2 work for or against the success of this packaging innovation?

3. What does each part of the following pairs of items tell you about a person's social class:

   a. An annual income of $30,000/an annual income of $40,000?

   b. Floors covered with Oriental rugs/a house with wall-to-wall carpeting?

   c. Shopping at Sears/shopping at Neiman-Marcus?

   d. A college degree/a high-school degree?

4. Ads sponsored by Rockers Against Drunk Driving feature popular recording artists telling listeners not to drink and drive. What social factors will probably contribute to the success or failure of this campaign?

5. In designing the advertising for a soft drink, which would be more helpful—information about consumer demographics or consumer life styles? How would you use each type of information?

6. One suggestion arising from motivation research is that shaving represents a loss of masculinity to men, which is reasserted by the sting of an aftershave. Does this idea make sense? If so, what are the implications for marketing men's toiletries?

7. Which levels of Maslow's hierarchy could be appealed to in marketing the following: (a) popcorn, (b) the armed forces, (c) a college education?

8. One advertising agency president says, "Perception is reality." What does he mean by this? How is perception important to marketers?

9. How can understanding *attitudes* help in designing marketing strategies? Give examples.

10. Relate the five stages of the buyer-decision process to your most recent purchase of any kind. Now compare these stages with the steps involved in your most recent purchase of a pair of shoes.

11. When planning to go to a movie, what information sources do you use in deciding which one to see? Do you use the same sources to decide which movie to rent on videotape?

12. Describe how cents-off coupons, sweepstakes, bonus-size packs, and other forms of sales promotion can help move consumers through the five stages of the adoption *process.* Are there any drawbacks to using these techniques to promote product adoption?

13. Recently developed digital audiotape recorders allow near-perfect fidelity in recording and editing music and in playing prerecorded tapes. The first consumer-market versions of these machines cost $2000 or more, and the few available prerecorded tapes sell for more than $20. How will these factors affect the rate of adoption for this innovative product?

# REFERENCES

1. Excerpts from Peter Schutz and Jack Cook, "Porsche on Nichemanship," *Harvard Business Review,* March-April 1986, pp. 98–106. Copyright © 1986 by the President and Fellows of Harvard College; all rights reserved. Also see Mark Maremont, "Jaguar and Porsche Try to Pull Out of the Fast Lane," *Business Week,* December 12, 1988, pp. 84–86.

2. Several models of the consumer buying process have been developed by marketing scholars. The most prominent models are those of John A. Howard and Jagdish N. Sheth, *The Theory of Buyer Behavior* (New York: John Wiley, 1969); Francesco M. Nicosia, *Consumer Decision Processes* (Englewood Cliffs, NJ: Prentice Hall, 1966); James F. Engel, Roger D. Blackwell, and

Paul W. Miniard, *Consumer Behavior,* 5th ed. (New York: Holt, Rinehart & Winston, 1986); and James R. Bettman, *An Information Processing Theory of Consumer Choice* (Reading, MA: Addison-Wesley, 1979).

3. See Leon G. Schiffman and Leslie Lazar Kanuk, *Consumer Behavior,* 3d ed. (Englewood Cliffs, NJ: Prentice Hall, 1987), pp. 495–503.

4. For more on marketing to Hispanics, blacks, mature consumers, and Asians, see Ed Fitch, "Marketing to Hispanics: Is the Red Carpet Plush Enough?" *Advertising Age,* February 8, 1988, p. S1; Joe Schwartz, "Hispanics in the Eighties," *American Demographics,* January 1988, pp. 43–45; Pete Engardio, "Fast Times on Avenida Madison," *Business Week,* June 6, 1988, pp. 62–67; "Marketing to Blacks: Rising Affluence Presents Fertile Market," *Advertising Age,* August 25, 1986, pp. S1-S7; George Sternlieb and James W. Hughes, "Black Households: The $100 Billion Potential," *American Demographics,* April 1988, pp. 35–37; Peter Petre, "Marketers Mine for Gold in the Old," *Fortune,* March 31, 1986, pp. 70–78; Jeff Ostroff, "An Aging Market," *American Demographics,* May 1989, pp. 26-33; and "The Asian Market: Too Good to Be True?" *Sales & Marketing Management,* May 1988, pp. 39–42.

5. William O. Bearden and Michael J. Etzel, "Reference Group Influence on Product and Brand Purchase Decisions," *Journal of Consumer Research,* September 1982, p. 185.

6. "Do Real Men Shop?" *American Demographics,* May 1987, p. 14; and Raymond Serafin, "Carmakers Step Up Chase for Women, *Advertising Age,* May 16, 1988, p. 76.

7. For more on family decision making, see Schiffman and Kanuk, *Consumer Behavior,* pp. 397–431; Harry L. Davis, "Decision Making within the Household," *Journal of Consumer Research,* March 1976, pp. 241-60; Rosann L. Spiro, "Persuasion in Family Decision Making," *Journal of Consumer Research,* March 1983, pp. 393–402; and William J. Qualls, "Household Decision Behavior: The Impact of Husbands' and Wives' Sex Role Orientation," *Journal of Consumer Research,* September 1987, pp. 264–79.

8. See Lawrence Lepisto, "A Life Span Perspective of Consumer Behavior," in Elizabeth Hirshman and Morris Holbrook, *Advances in Consumer Research,* Vol. 12 (Provo, UT: Association for Consumer Research, 1985), p. 47.

9. See William D. Wells, "Psychographics: A Critical Review," *Journal of Marketing Research,* May 1975, pp. 196–213; W. Thomas Anderson and Linda Golden, "Lifestyle and Psychographics: A Critical Review and Recommendations," in *Advances in Consumer Research,* Vol. 11, Thomas C. Kinnear, ed. (Ann Arbor: Association for Consumer Research, 1984), pp. 405–11; Bickley Townsend, "Psychographic Glitter and Gold," *American Demographics,* November 1985, pp. 22–29; and Emanuel Demby, "Psychographics Revisited: The Birth of a Technique," *Marketing News,* January 2, 1989, p. 21.

10. See Arnold Mitchell, *The Nine American Lifestyles* (New York: Macmillan, 1983); and Judith Graham, "New VALS 2 Takes Psychological Route," *Advertising Age,* February 13, 1989, p. 24.

11. See Schiffman and Kanuk, *Consumer Behavior,* pp. 164–65; and "Emotions Important for Successful Advertising," *Marketing News,* April 12, 1985, p. 18.

12. Kim Foltz, "Wizards of Marketing," *Newsweek,* July 22, 1985, p. 44.

13. For more reading on the pros and cons of using VALS and other life-style approaches, see Lynn R. Kahle, Sharon E. Beatty, and Pamela Homer, "Alternative Measurement Approaches to Consumer Values: The List of Values (LOV) and Values and Life Styles (VALS)," *Journal of Consumer Research,* December 1986, pp. 405–9; and "Lifestyle Roulette," *American Demographics,* April 1987, pp. 24–25.

14. See Raymond L. Horton, "Some Relationships between Personality and Consumer Decision-Making," *Journal of Marketing Research,* May 1979, pp. 244–45. Also see Harold H. Kassarjian and Mary Jane Sheffet, "Personality in Consumer Behavior: An Update," in *Perspectives in Consumer Behavior,* Harold H. Kassarjian and Thomas S. Robertson, eds. (Glenview, IL: Scott Foresman, 1981), pp. 160–80; and Joseph T. Plummer, "How Personality Can Make a Difference," *Marketing News,* March-April 1984, pp. 17–20.

15. See M. Joseph Sirgy, "Self-Concept in Consumer Behavior: A Critical Review," *Journal of Consumer Research,* December 1982, pp. 287-300.

16. Abraham H. Maslow, *Motivation and Personality,* 2nd ed. (New York: Harper & Row, 1970), pp. 80–106.

17. See Jagdish N. Sheth, "An Investigation of Relationships among Evaluative Beliefs, Affect, Behavioral Intention, and Behavior," in *Consumer Behavior: Theory and Application,* John U. Farley, John A. Howard, and L. Winston Ring, eds. (Boston: Allyn & Bacon, 1974), pp. 89-114.

18. See Priscilla A. LaBarbara and David Mazursky, "A Longitudinal Assessment of Consumer Satisfaction/Dissatisfaction: The Dynamic Aspect of the Cognitive Process," *Journal of Marketing Research,* November 1983, pp. 393–404.

19. See Bill Kelley, "How to Sell Airplanes, Boeing-Style," *Sales & Marketing Management,* December 9, 1985, p. 34.

20. See Leon Festinger, *A Theory of Cognitive Dissonance* (Stanford, CA: Stanford University Press, 1957); and Schiffman and Kanuk, *Consumer Behavior,* pp. 304–5.

21. See Thomas Moore, "Would You Buy a Car from This Man?" *Fortune,* April 11, 1988, pp. 72–74.

22. The following discussion draws heavily from Everett M. Rogers, *Diffusion of Innovations,* 3rd ed. (New York: Free Press, 1983). Also see Hubert Gatignon and Thomas S. Robertson, "A Propositional Inventory for New Diffusion Research," *Journal of Consumer Research,* March 1985, pp. 849–67.

23. Mary Lee Dickerson and James W. Gentry, "Characteristics of Adopters and Non-Adopters of Home Computers," *Journal of Consumer Research,* September 1983, pp. 225–35.

24. See Schiffman and Kanuk, *Consumer Behavior,* pp. 606–17.

## CINEPLEX ODEON: BACK TO THE FUTURE

Until very recently, the movie theater industry, run by a collection of aging entrepreneurs and a few powerful public companies, has been fighting for its survival. Competition from videocassettes and cable TV caused a drastic drop in attendance during the 1970s, and movie exhibitors had for decades let their theaters decay. In a typical theater of the 1970s, the lobby carpet, blackened and musty, gave way to the concession stand, hawking watered-down Coke and $1.25 "buckets" of popcorn (the small size) covered by an anonymous oily yellow fluid. Inside the movie theater, floors covered with some mysterious glop stuck to your shoes like flypaper. Musty-smelling seats with sagging springs made you wonder what the place would really look like if the lights were not so dim. Top it off with poor quality projection, and it's no wonder that the industry fell on hard times.

Then, during the late 1970s and early 1980s, many theater owners reacted to appalling industry conditions by converting handsome old movie palaces into tiny "tenement" cinemas. To bring theaters into growing suburban neighborhoods, others built "plexes" adjacent to malls—new multiscreen theaters that were bigger and more efficient. Although such locations and facilities did save the movie theater industry, they usually lacked pizzazz—most mall complexes have no more charm than a hospital clinic. In these theaters, going to the movies offers little beyond just catching the latest flick. Gone is the moviegoing *experience* that was once a

significant part of the attraction—the escape from harsh reality that began when the customer passed through the theater door.

Since the early 1980s, however, a huge theater chain called Cineplex Odeon has been putting the flash and fantasy back into going to the movies—more than anyone has seen since the glory days of Hollywood. Its plush theaters feature art-filled lobbies, cafés, and popcorn drenched in real butter—with a price to match. Although many people maintain that showing the right movie is enough to draw in patrons, Cineplex Odeon operates under a different philosophy: Moviegoers, like restaurant patrons and department store shoppers, want to be entertained by the *environment* as much as by the *goods*. With such technologies as wide-screen 70-millimeter projection and wraparound Dolby sound, theaters can create a sense of spectacle that no TV set can match.

Prior to 1979, the movie theater business was fragmented among dozens of regional mom-and-pop operations. Many theater operators had bought into the business at dirt-cheap prices after 1948—the year an antitrust suit forced the major Hollywood studios to sell off their theaters. Granted, the new owners got great deals. But as the profits rolled in, many lost touch with their customers and let theaters deteriorate. Moreover, their share of film revenue dropped off as network television, cable, and home video ate into profits.

Since 1979, however, the industry has stabilized. Thanks to such large and

aggressive chains as General Cinema, United Artists, and Cineplex Odeon, theater patronage has remained remarkably steady and the number of movie screens has increased each year. Box-office performance still accounts for 60 percent of a film's gross revenues, and success in the television and video-rental markets depends largely on a respectable movie theater run.

To stabilize and survive, theaters have developed the lobby concession stand into an important source of revenue. To keep ticket prices down, they have marked up popcorn, soda, and candy heavily—sometimes as much as 500 percent. In addition, many theater owners, needing to refurbish, rebuild, and restore their properties, developed multiscreen theaters, creating those cramped screening rooms that moviegoers loathe. But this concept gave owners more flexibility in allocating seats to different screens—moving hits to larger capacity rooms and letting duds pay their way in small ones. Unfortunately, this trend spurred a construction craze among movie operators, and the addition of so many screens created overcapacity. With a shrinking number of moviegoers, the construction boom simply added to the industry's woes.

In meeting the changing demands of moviegoers, Cineplex Odeon has been the most innovative chain. Garth Drabinsky, a 40-year-old Canadian entertainment lawyer, started the movie chain in 1979. As chairman, president, and chief executive officer, he is the driving force behind Cineplex Odeon—a one-man marching band. His vision is to upgrade moviegoing as much as possible—and then ask customers to pay for it. Customers pay for tuxedo-clad attendants, upscale snacks, and a crisp sound system—all included in the price of their tickets. Drabinsky was thus the man who brought the $7 movie ticket to New York City—a move that aroused both the public and state officials. To encourage exhibitors to keep their prices down, the State Assembly even considered passing a law requiring theater owners to print admission prices in newspaper ads. Drabinsky was unmoved—he believes that the only alternative to the $7 price tag is run-down unkempt theaters. That's not what Cineplex Odeon is about—the desired image is that of a class act. Drabinsky builds the "Taj Mahals" of the movie-exhibition business. His theaters are clean, comfortable, and in prime locations.

Rather than appealing to the 18-to-23-year-old "youth market"—the most active moviegoing population—Cineplex Odeon went with a vengeance after the older, upscale, sophisticated baby-boomer market. When Drabinsky entered the movie business, most theaters had only one or two screens per location. By contrast, Cineplex clustered as many as 18 small-screen, limited-capacity theaters into single complexes that offered moviegoers a wide variety of films under one roof. In 1983, adding contemporary frills, it began re-creating classic movie houses. Cineplex theaters in Clearwater, Florida, Waco, Texas, and Thornhill, Ontario, now resemble the grand old movie palaces of the 1920s and 1930s.

Imagine, for example, entering the Cineplex Odeon theater in Toronto's Canada Square office complex. The spacious, circular art-deco lobby boasts a polished granite floor and recessed lighting. A thin band of neon highlights the ceiling dome. Attractive singles and couples sit reading newspapers, sipping espresso, and munching croissant sandwiches and fresh pastries at a charming café with marble tables, dapper red chairs, and thick carpets. Beyond the café is a choice of eight first-run films shown in plush auditoriums. Thus, Cineplex is determined to give patrons back the anticipation, excitement, and fantasy of the great escape that is the essence of the movies. Cineplex has brought moviegoing back to life, and consumers are responding. The Toronto-based company is the second-largest exhibitor of films in North America, operating over 500 theaters in 13 of the top 17 markets in the United States and Canada. Its number of "screens" has swollen to over 1,700; revenues quintupled in five years and profits doubled in one year. Hundreds of additional screens are planned for 1990. Cineplex's success has also forced competitors to raise their standards, resulting in the complete overhaul of an industry that had been allowed to decay.

Cineplex Odeon and other operators have had an enormous impact on the industry. Nineteen eighty-seven saw a post-World War II record year for box-office receipts. Admission revenues were up 12 percent, and attendance was up 6 percent. Of greatest interest is the fact that attendance by the over-40 age group has begun to increase. These results prove that, if they are well-treated at their favorite motion picture houses, people can be induced to leave their homes and television sets. Modern, visually stimulating, sparkling-clean theaters, staffed by a corps of customer-oriented cashiers, ushers, and confection counter attendants can provide an entertainment experience that people simply can't find at home.

Now pursuing his latest dream, Drabinsky is moving into film and TV production and distribution—he is even running a theme park. Since 1987, Cineplex Odeon has distributed such films as Prince's *Sign o' the Times* and Paul Newman's *The Glass Menagerie*. Its TV production unit made 41 episodes of *Alfred Hitchcock Presents*. The company invested $85 million in the Universal Studio theme park that it is developing jointly with MCA (which owns 49 percent of Cineplex Odeon) near Orlando, Florida. Cineplex Odeon also operates the largest film-processing lab outside of Hollywood.

Thus, entering the decade of the 1990s, the Cineplex Odeon story is still being written. See you at the movies.

*Questions*

1. What factors influence a consumer's decision to go to the movies?

2. Describe the buyer-decision process for going to the movies. How does that decision differ from the decision to stay home and watch cable television or rent a video?

3. Consider both demographic trends in the United States and the many factors that influence a consumer's decision to go to the movies. What suggestions would you make to Cineplex Odeon and other theater operators in designing future marketing strategies?

# 7
# Organizational Markets and Organizational Buyer Behavior

## CHAPTER OBJECTIVES

After reading this chapter, you should be able to

1. Explain how organizational markets differ from consumer markets
2. Identify the major factors that influence organizational buyer behavior
3. List and define the steps in the industrial buying decision process
4. Explain how resellers and government buyers make their buying decisions

Gulfstream Aerospace Corporation sells business jets with price tags as high as $16 million. Locating potential buyers isn't a problem—the organizations that can afford to own and operate multimillion dollar business aircraft are easily identified. Customers include Exxon, American Express, Seagram, Coca-Cola, General Motors, and many others, including King Fahd of Saudi Arabia. Gulfstream's more difficult problems involve reaching key decision makers, understanding their complex motivations and decision processes, analyzing what factors will be important in their decisions, and designing effective marketing approaches.

Gulfstream Aerospace recognizes the importance of *rational* motives and *objective* factors in buyers' decisions. A company buying a jet will evaluate Gulfstream aircraft on quality and performance, prices, operating costs, and service. At times, these may appear to be the only things that drive the buying decision. But having a superior product isn't enough to land the sale; Gulfstream Aerospace must also consider the more subtle *human factors* that affect the choice of a jet.

"The purchase process may be initiated by the chief executive officer (CEO), a board member (wishing to increase efficiency or security), the company's chief pilot, or through vendor efforts like advertising or a sales visit. The CEO will be central in deciding whether to buy the jet, but he or she will be heavily influenced by the company's pilot, financial officer, and perhaps by the board itself.

"Each party in the buying process has subtle roles and needs. The salesperson who tries to impress, for example, both the CEO with depreciation schedules and the chief pilot with minimum runway statistics will almost certainly not sell a plane if he overlooks the psychological and emotional components of the buying decision. 'For the chief executive,' observes one salesperson, 'you need all the numbers for support, but if you can't find the kid inside the CEO and excite him or her with the raw beauty of the new plane, you'll never sell the equipment. If you sell the excitement, you sell the jet.'

"The chief pilot, as an equipment expert, often has veto power over purchase decisions and may be able to stop the purchase of one or another brand of jet by simply expressing a negative opinion about, say, the plane's bad weather capabilities. In this sense, the pilot not only influences the decision but also serves as an information 'gatekeeper' by advising management on the equipment to select. Though the corporate legal staff will handle the purchase agreement and the purchasing department will acquire the jet, these parties may have little to say about whether or how the plane will be obtained, and which type. The users of the jet—middle and upper management of the buying company, important customers, and others—may have at least an indirect role in choosing the equipment.

"The involvement of many people in the purchase decision creates a group dynamic that the selling company must factor into its sales planning. Who makes up the buying group? How will the parties interact? Who will dominate and who submit? What priorities do the individuals have?"

In some ways, selling corporate jets to organizational buyers is like selling cars and kitchen appliances to families. Gulfstream Aerospace asks the same questions as consumer marketers: Who are the buyers and what are their needs? How do buyers make their buying decisions and what factors influence these decisions? What marketing program will be most effective? But the answers to these questions are usually different for the organizational buyer. Thus, Gulfstream Aerospace faces many of the same challenges as consumer marketers—and some additional ones.[1]

---

**organizational buying** The decision-making process by which formal organizations establish the need for purchased products and services, identifying, evaluating, and choosing among alternative brands and suppliers.

In one way or another, most large companies sell to other organizations. Many industrial companies sell *most* of their products to organizations—companies such as Xerox, Du Pont, and countless other large and small firms. Even large consumer-products companies do organizational marketing. For example, General Mills makes many familiar products for final consumers—Cheerios, Betty Crocker cake mixes, Gold Medal flour. But to sell these products to final consumers, General Mills must first sell them to the wholesale and retail organizations that serve the consumer market. General Mills also makes products, such as specialty chemicals, that are sold only to other companies.

Organizations make up a vast market. In fact, industrial markets involve many more dollars and items than do consumer markets. Figure 7–1 shows the large number of transactions needed to produce and sell a simple pair of shoes. Hide dealers sell to tanners, who sell leather to shoe manufacturers, who sell shoes to wholesalers, who in turn sell shoes to retailers, who finally sell them to consumers. Each party in the chain buys many other goods and services as well. It is easy to see why there is more organizational buying than consumer buying—many sets of *organizational* purchases were made for only one set of *consumer* purchases.

**Organizational buying** is "the decision-making process by which formal organizations establish the need for purchased products and services, and identify, evaluate, and choose among alternative brands and suppliers."[2] Companies that sell to other organizations must do their best to understand organizational buyer behavior.

FIGURE 7–1  Organizational Transactions Involved in Producing and Distributing a Pair of Shoes

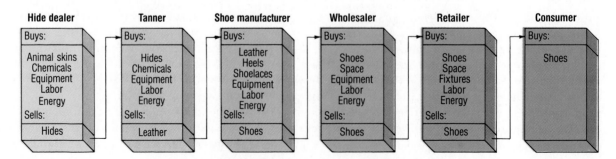

# ORGANIZATIONAL MARKETS

## Types of Organizational Markets

We will examine three types of organizational markets: the *industrial market*, the *reseller market*, and the *government market*. We identify each briefly here and discuss them in more detail later in the chapter.

### The Industrial Market

The **industrial market** consists of all the individuals and organizations acquiring goods and services that enter into the production of other products and services that are sold, rented, or supplied to others. The industrial market is *huge:* It consists of over 13 million organizations that buy more than $3 *trillion* worth of goods and services each year. (That's more money than most of us can imagine—taped end to end, three trillion one-dollar bills would wrap around the earth over 11,000 times!) Thus, the industrial market is the largest and most diverse organizational market.

### The Reseller Market

The **reseller market** consists of all the individuals and organizations that acquire goods for the purpose of reselling or renting them to others at a profit. The reseller market includes over 396,000 wholesaling firms and 1,923,000 retailing firms that combine to purchase over $2 trillion worth of goods and services a year.[3] Resellers purchase goods for resale and goods and services for conducting their operations. In their role as purchasing agents for their own customers, resellers purchase a vast variety of goods for resale—indeed, almost everything produced passes through some type of reseller.

### The Government Market

The **government market** consists of governmental units—federal, state, and local—that purchase or rent goods and services for carrying out their main functions. In 1987, governments purchased an estimated $892 billion worth of products and services. The federal government accounts for almost 41 percent of the total spent by governments at all levels, making it the nation's largest single customer.[4] Federal, state, and local government agencies buy an amazing range of products and services. They buy bombers, sculpture, chalkboards, furniture, toiletries, clothing, fire engines, vehicles, and fuel.

## Characteristics of Organizational Markets

In some ways, organizational markets are similar to consumer markets—both involve people who assume buying roles and make purchase decisions to satisfy needs. But in many ways, organizational markets differ from consumer markets.[5] The main differences are in *market structure and demand*, the *nature of the buying unit*, and the *types of decisions and the decision process*.

### Market Structure and Demand

The organizational marketer normally deals with *far fewer but far larger buyers* than the consumer marketer. For example, when Goodyear sells replacement tires to final consumers, its potential market includes the owners of 100 million American cars currently in use. But Goodyear's fate in the industrial market

**industrial market** All the individuals and organizations acquiring goods and services that enter into the production of other products and services that are sold, rented, or supplied to others.

**reseller market** All the individuals and organizations that acquire goods for the purpose of reselling or renting them to others at a profit.

**government market** Governmental units—federal, state, and local—that purchase or rent goods and services for carrying out the main functions of government.

**derived demand** Organizational demand that ultimately comes from (derives from) the demand for consumer goods.

**inelastic demand** Total demand for a product that is not much affected by price changes, especially in the short run.

depends on getting orders from one of only a few large automakers. Even in large organizational markets, a few buyers normally account for most of the purchasing.

Organizational markets are also more *geographically concentrated*. More than half the nation's industrial buyers are concentrated in seven states: New York, California, Pennsylvania, Illinois, Ohio, New Jersey, and Michigan. Organizational demand is **derived demand**—it ultimately comes from the demand for consumer goods. General Motors buys steel because consumers buy cars. If consumer demand for cars drops, so will the demand for steel and all the other products used to make cars. Thus, industrial marketers sometimes promote their products directly to final consumers to increase industrial demand (see Marketing Highlight 7–1).

Many organizational markets have **inelastic demand.** Total demand for many industrial products is not much affected by price changes, especially in the short run. A drop in the price of leather will not cause shoe manufacturers to buy much more leather unless it results in lower shoe prices that, in turn, increase consumer demand for shoes.

Finally, organizational markets have more *fluctuating demand*. The demand for many industrial goods and services tends to change more—and more quickly—than the demand for consumer goods and services. A small percentage increase in consumer demand can cause large increases in industrial

# Marketing Highlight 7–1

## HOW "NUTRASWEET" IT IS!

About 30 years ago, a G. D. Searle researcher discovered aspartame, a miracle substance that tastes like sugar, contains few calories, and is safe to eat or drink. In 1983, the FDA approved the substance, and Searle looked for the best way to market its miracle to commercial food and beverage producers. It came up with a highly effective "branded ingredient" strategy. Instead of just selling aspartame to commercial customers, Searle gave it a brand name—NutraSweet—and launched the kind of consumer marketing campaign you would expect to see for a laundry soap or soft drink. Searle marketed NutraSweet directly to consumers, even though consumers could not directly buy NutraSweet.

*The distinctive NutraSweet logo now appears on hundreds of familiar brands.*

demand. Sometimes a rise of only 10 percent in consumer demand can cause as much as a 200 percent rise in industrial demand during the next period.

## The Nature of the Buying Unit

As compared with consumer purchases, an organizational purchase usually involves *more buyers* and *more professional purchasing*. Organizational buying is often done by trained purchasing agents who spend their work lives learning how to buy better. The more complex the purchase, the more likely that several people will participate in the decision-making process. Buying committees made up of technical experts and top management are common in the buying of major goods. Organizational marketers must thus have well-trained salespeople to deal with well-trained buyers.

## Types of Decisions and the Decision Process

Organizational buyers usually face *more complex* buying decisions than consumer buyers. Purchases often involve large sums of money, complex technical and economic considerations, and interactions among many people at many levels of the buyer's organization. Because the purchases are more complex, organizational buyers may take longer to make their decisions. Thus, the

Industrial demand for NutraSweet is *derived demand*—it ultimately comes from consumer demand for products that contain NutraSweet. But before manufacturers bought the new sweetener and put it in their products, they wanted to be certain that their consumers would accept it. Thus, to build commercial demand for NutraSweet, Searle first had to create brand awareness and preference among final consumers. This meant overcoming the public's general mistrust of new sweeteners. People tended to believe the adage that if something tasted too good, it had to be bad for you. Searle needed to prove that, in the case of NutraSweet, this was not true.

Gumballs to the rescue! Searle mailed out thousands of gumballs sweetened with NutraSweet. Letters were included explaining that the new sweetener had few calories, did not promote tooth decay, and contained nothing artificial. Searle then spent millions on advertising that proclaimed, "Introducing NutraSweet: You can't buy it, but you're going to love it." The ads carried coupons offering free gumballs and other samples.

Mission accomplished. When Coca-Cola, Quaker, Kool-Aid, and other companies began to introduce NutraSweetened products, consumers responded enthusiastically to the new wonder substance. In all sorts of categories—soft drinks, fruit juices, presweetened cereals, frozen deserts, breath mints, and many others—demand increased for products displaying the distinctive red swirl 100 percent NutraSweet logo. NutraSweet became a major selling point for many new brands; it even boosted the sales of entire product categories. For example, within two years of NutraSweet's introduction, following five flat years, sales of powdered soft drinks such as Kool-Aid, Crystal Light, and iced tea mixes had jumped 20 percent. And NutraSweet revolutionized the diet soft-drink industry—products containing NutraSweet swept 22 percent of that market.

Monsanto recently acquired Searle and set up a separate subsidiary, NutraSweet Company, to market the successful product. The company now spends over $30 million a year on consumer advertising for NutraSweet, a product

consumers can't even buy. But it knows that if it convinces consumers of NutraSweet's merits, they will buy more products that contain the sweetener. If consumers buy more NutraSweetened products, manufacturers will buy more aspartame from NutraSweet Company.

The company's "branded ingredient" strategy has brought sweet success. More than 1200 brands now contain NutraSweet, and the list grows daily. NutraSweet Company rings up more than $600 million worth of sales each year. And when Monsanto's patent expires in 1992, competitors can sell aspartame—but they can't use the NutraSweet brand name consumers have learned to look for. How "NutraSweet" it is!

*Sources:* Based on "How Sweet It Is," *Management Review*, June 1985, p. 8. Also see Michael Hiestand, "Aspartame Ready to Sweeten Four New Categories," *Adweek*, January 5, 1987, p. 6; and Zachary Schiller, James E. Ellis, Reginald Rhein, and Sana Siwolop, "NutraSweet Sets Out for Fat-Substitute City," *Business Week*, February 15, 1988, pp. 100–103.

purchase of a large computer system might involve millions of dollars, thousands of technical details, dozens of people ranging from top management to lower-level users, and many months or more than a year of time.

The organizational buying process tends to be *more formalized* than the consumer buying process. Large organizational purchases usually call for detailed product specifications, written purchase orders, careful supplier searches, and formal approval. The purchase process may be spelled out in detail in policy manuals.

Finally, in the organizational buying process, buyer and seller are often much *more dependent* on each other. Consumer marketers usually stay at a distance from their customers. But organizational marketers may roll up their sleeves and work closely with their customers during all stages of the buying process—from helping customers to define their problems, to finding solutions, to supporting after-sale operation. They often customize their offerings to individual customer needs. In the short run, sales go to suppliers who meet buyers' immediate product and service needs. But organizational marketers must also build close *long-run* relationships with customers. In the long run,

Ohio University asked Honeywell to help design a communications system that will handle voice, data and video. They got one that transmits everything from...

high-tech to "Hi, Mom."

Ohio University is a leader in high technology. So it was no surprise that they knew exactly what they wanted in an integrated communications system. It would be based on fiber optics and meet their needs well into the next century.

Working together, we developed a system to serve the University's telephones and computer work stations in 110 buildings on the Athens, Ohio, campus. It can handle educational television, an energy control system, plus a security and fire detection system. It also has the growth potential to

link five regional campuses by microwave. Above all, it will give students and faculty unrivaled phone service, both local and long distance.

But Ohio University wanted more than just hardware and software. They wanted team players who knew how to make computer, communications and control systems work together, and who understood the need for continuing and conscientious service. Honeywell was the answer, because working together works. For more information, call 800-328-5111, ext. 1570.

**Together, we can find the answers.**

**Honeywell**

*Organizational marketers often roll up their sleeves and work closely with their customers during all stages of the buying process—from helping to define the problem to finding solutions, to after-sale operation. Here Honeywell tells its customers "Together, we can find the answers."*

sales are kept by companies that build lasting relationships by meeting current needs *and* thinking ahead to meet the customer's future needs.[6]

# A MODEL OF ORGANIZATIONAL BUYER BEHAVIOR

In trying to understand organizational buyer behavior, marketers must answer some hard questions. What kinds of buying decisions do organizational buyers make? How do they choose among suppliers? Who makes the decisions? What is the organizational buying-decision process? What factors affect organizational buying decisions?

At the most basic level, marketers want to know how organizational buyers will respond to various marketing stimuli. A simple model of organizational buyer behavior is shown in Figure 7–2.[7] The figure shows that marketing and other stimuli affect the organization and produce certain buyer responses. As with consumer buying, the marketing stimuli for organizational buying consist of the four *P's:* product, price, place, and promotion. Other stimuli consist of major forces in the environment: economic, technological, political, cultural, and competitive. All these stimuli enter the organization and are turned into buyer responses: product or service choice, supplier choice, order quantities, and delivery, service, and payment terms. To design good marketing mix strategies, the marketer must understand what happens within the organization to turn stimuli into purchase responses.

Within the organization, the buying activity consists of two major parts—the buying center (made up of all the people involved in the buying decision) and the buying decision process. Figure 7–2 shows that the buying center and the buying decision process are influenced by internal organizational, interpersonal, and individual factors as well as by external environmental factors.

We will now look at how the various elements in this organizational buyer behavior model apply to the specific organizational markets discussed earlier in the chapter. First, we will focus on the largest and most important organizational market—the industrial market. Later in the chapter, we will consider the special characteristics of organizational buyer behavior in the reseller and government markets.

FIGURE 7–2   A Model of Organizational Buyer Behavior

The Environment

| Marketing stimuli | Other stimuli |
| --- | --- |
| Product<br>Price<br>Place<br>Promotion | Economic<br>Technological<br>Political<br>Cultural<br>Competitive |

The Buying Organization

The buying center

Buying decision process

(Interpersonal and individual influences)

(Organizational influences)

Buyer Responses

Product or service choice
Supplier choice
Order quantities
Delivery terms and times
Service terms
Payment terms

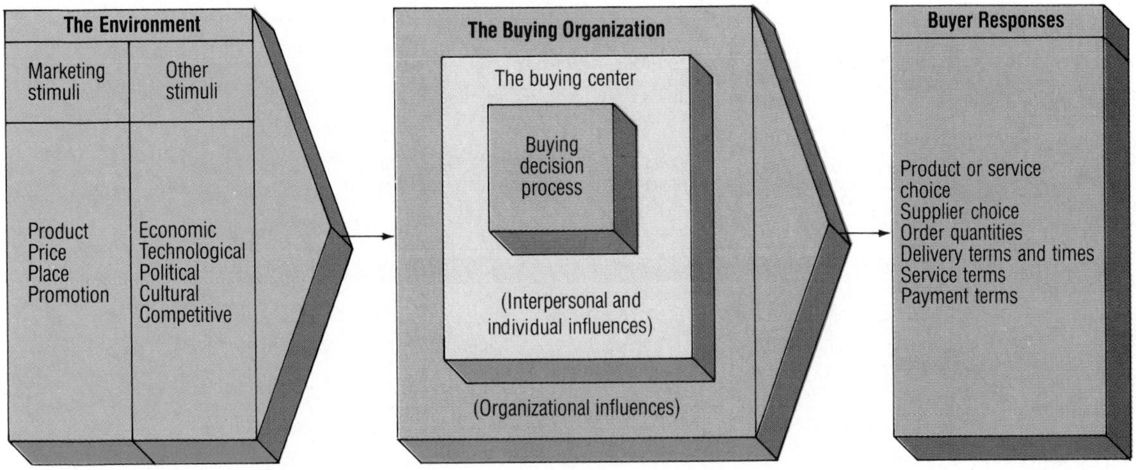

# INDUSTRIAL BUYER BEHAVIOR

**straight rebuy** An industrial buying situation in which the buyer routinely reorders something without any modifications.

**modified rebuy** An industrial buying situation in which the buyer wants to modify product specifications, prices, terms, or suppliers.

The model in Figure 7–2 suggests four questions about industrial buyer behavior: What buying decisions do industrial buyers make? Who participates in the buying process? What are the major influences on buyers? And how do industrial buyers make their buying decisions?

## What Buying Decisions Do Industrial Buyers Make?

The industrial buyer faces a whole set of decisions in making a purchase. The number of decisions depends on the type of buying situation. Here we discuss the major types of buying decisions faced by industrial buyers and the role of systems buying and selling.

### Major Types of Buying Situations

There are three major types of buying situations.[8] At one extreme is the *straight rebuy*, which is a fairly routine decision. At the other extreme is the *new task*, which may call for thorough research. In the middle is the *modified rebuy*, which requires some research. (For examples, see Figure 7–3.)

***Straight Rebuy*** ▪ In a **straight rebuy,** the buyer reorders something without any modifications. It is usually handled on a routine basis by the purchasing department. Based on past buying satisfaction, the buyer simply chooses from various suppliers on its "list." "In" suppliers try to maintain product and service quality. They often propose automatic reordering systems so that the purchasing agent will save reordering time. The "out" suppliers try to offer something new or exploit dissatisfaction so that the buyer will consider them. "Out" suppliers try to get their foot in the door with a small order and then enlarge their purchase share over time.

***Modified Rebuy*** ▪ In a **modified rebuy,** the buyer wants to modify product specifications, prices, terms, or suppliers. The modified rebuy usually involves more decision participants. "In" suppliers may become nervous and have to put their best foot forward to protect an account. "Out" suppliers see the modified

FIGURE 7–3 Three Types of Industrial Buying Situations

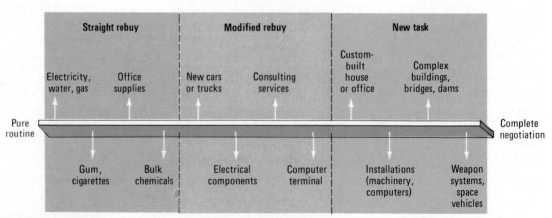

From *Marketing Principles*, 3rd ed., by Ben M. Enis. Copyright © 1980 Scott, Foresman and Company. Reprinted by permission.

rebuy situation as an opportunity to make a better offer and gain some new business.

***New Task*** ▪ The **new task** faces a company buying a product or service for the first time. The greater the cost or risk, the larger the number of decision participants and the greater their efforts to collect information. The new-task situation is the marketer's greatest opportunity and challenge. The marketer not only tries to reach as many key buying influences as possible but also provides help and information.

### The Role of Systems Buying and Selling

Many buyers prefer to buy a packaged solution to a problem and not make all the separate decisions involved. Called **systems buying,** this practice began with government buying of major weapons and communication systems. Instead of buying and putting all the components together, the government asked for bids from suppliers who would assemble the package or system. The winning supplier would be responsible for buying and assembling the components.

Sellers have increasingly recognized that buyers like to purchase in this way and have adopted the practice of systems selling as a marketing tool.[9] Systems selling has two parts. First, the supplier sells a group of interlocking products. For example, the supplier sells not only glue but applicators and dryers as well. Second, the supplier sells a system of production, inventory control, distribution, and other services to meet the buyer's need for a smooth-running operation.

Systems selling is a key industrial marketing strategy for winning and holding accounts. The contract often goes to the firm that provides the most complete system meeting the customer's needs. Consider the following:

> The Indonesian government requested bids to build a cement factory near Jakarta. An American firm's proposal included choosing the site, designing the cement factory, hiring the construction crews, assembling the materials and equipment, and turning the finished factory over to the Indonesian government. A Japanese firm's proposal included all of these services, plus hiring and training workers to run the factory, exporting the cement through their trading companies, and using the cement to build some needed roads and new office buildings in Jakarta. Although the Japanese firm's proposal cost more, it won the contract. Clearly, the Japanese viewed the problem not as one of just building a cement factory (the narrow view of systems selling) but of running it in a way that would contribute to the country's economy. They took the broadest view of the customer's needs. This is true systems selling.

## *Who Participates in the Industrial Buying Process?*

Who does the buying of the hundreds of billions of dollars worth of goods and services needed by the industrial market? The decision-making unit of a buying organization is called its **buying center,** defined as "all those individuals and groups who participate in the purchasing decision-making process, who share some common goals and the risks arising from the decisions."[10]

The buying center includes all members of the organization who play a role in the purchase decision process. This group includes the actual users of the product or service, those who make the buying decision, those who influence the buying decision, those who do the actual buying (purchasing agents), and those who control buying information.

The buying center is not a fixed and formally identified unit within the

**new task** An industrial buying situation in which the buyer purchases a product or service for the first time.

**systems buying** Buying a packaged solution to a problem without making all the separate decisions involved.

**buying center** All the individuals and units that participate in the organizational buying-decision process.

This ad recognizes the secretary as a key buying influence.

buying organization. It is a set of buying roles assumed by different people for different purchases. Within the organization, the size and makeup of the buying center will vary for different products and for different buying situations. For some routine purchases, one person—say, a purchasing agent—may assume all the buying center roles and be the only person involved in the buying decision. For more complex purchases, the buying center may include 20 or 30 people from different levels and departments in the organization. One study of organizational buying showed that the typical industrial equipment purchase involved seven people from three management levels representing four different departments.[11]

The buying center concept presents a major marketing challenge. The industrial marketer has to figure out: Who is involved in the decision? What decisions do they affect? What is their relative degree of influence? And what evaluation criteria does each decision participant use?

The buying center usually includes some obvious participants who are formally involved in the buying decision—as we saw at the beginning of the chapter, the decision to buy a corporate jet will probably involve the company's chief pilot, a purchasing agent, some legal staff, a member of top management, and others formally charged with the buying decision. It may also involve informal, less obvious participants, some of whom may actually make or strongly affect the buying decision. Sometimes, even the people in the buying center are not aware of all the buying participants. For example, the decision about which jet to buy may actually be made by a corporate board member who has an interest in flying and knows a lot about airplanes. This board member may work behind the scenes to sway the decision. Thus, many industrial buying decisions result from the complex interactions of ever-changing buying center participants.

## What Are the Major Influences on Industrial Buyers?

Industrial buyers are subject to many influences when they make their buying decisions. Some marketers assume that the major influences are economic. They think buyers will favor the supplier who offers the lowest price, the best product, or the most service. They concentrate on offering strong economic benefits to buyers. But industrial buyers also respond to personal factors:

> It has not been fashionable lately to talk about relationships in business. We're told that it has to be devoid of emotion. We must be cold, calculating, and impersonal. Don't you believe it. Relationships make the world go round. Businesspeople are human and social as well as interested in economics and investments, and salespeople need to appeal to both sides. Purchasers may claim to be motivated by intellect alone, but the professional salesperson knows that they run on both reason and emotion.[12]

Thus, industrial buyers actually respond to both economic and personal factors. When supplier offers are very similar, industrial buyers' have little basis for strictly rational choice. Because they can meet organizational goals with any supplier, buyers can bring in personal factors. When competing products differ greatly, industrial buyers are more accountable for their choice and pay more attention to economic factors.

The various groups of influences on industrial buyers—environmental, organizational, interpersonal, and individual—are listed in Figure 7–4 and described below.[13]

*Industrial buyers respond to more than just economic factors. In this ad the words stress performance but the illustration suggests a smooth, comfortable ride.*

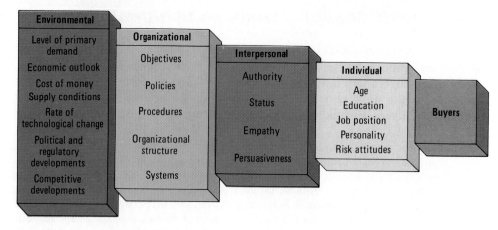

FIGURE 7–4   Major Influences on Industrial Buying Behavior

## Environmental Factors

Industrial buyers are heavily influenced by factors in the current and expected *economic environment*, such as the level of primary demand, the economic outlook, and the cost of money. As economic uncertainty rises, industrial buyers cut back on new investments and attempt to reduce their inventories.

An increasingly important environmental factor is shortages in key materials. Many companies are now more willing to buy and hold larger inventories of scarce materials. Industrial buyers are also affected by technological, political, and competitive developments in the environment. The industrial marketer must watch these factors, determine how they will affect the buyer, and try to turn these problems into opportunities.

## Organizational Factors

Each buying organization has its own objectives, policies, procedures, structure, and systems. The industrial marketer has to know these *organizational factors* as well as possible. Questions such as these arise: How many people are involved in the buying decision? Who are they? What are their evaluative criteria? What are the company's policies and limits on its buyers?

## Interpersonal Factors

The buying center usually includes many participants; each affects and is affected by the others. In many cases, the industrial marketer will not know what kinds of *interpersonal factors* and group dynamics enter into the buying process. As one writer notes: "Managers do not wear tags that say 'decision maker' or 'unimportant person.' The powerful are often invisible, at least to vendor representatives."[14]

Nor does the buying center participant with the highest rank always have the most influence. Participants may have influence in the buying decision because they control rewards and punishments, because they are well liked, because they have special expertise, or because they are related by marriage to the company president. Interpersonal factors are often very subtle. Whenever possible, industrial marketers try to understand these factors and design strategies that take them into account.

## Individual Factors

Each participant in the buying decision process brings in personal motives, perceptions, and preferences. These *individual factors* are affected by age, income, education, professional identification, personality, and attitudes toward risk. Buyers also have different buying styles. Some of the younger, higher-educated buyers may be "computer freaks" who make in-depth analyses of competitive proposals before choosing a supplier. Other buyers may be "tough guys" from the "old school" who are adept at pitting the sellers against one another for the best deal.

## How Do Industrial Buyers Make Their Buying Decisions?

We now come to the issue of how industrial buyers move through the purchasing process. We can identify eight stages of the industrial buying process.[15] They are listed in Table 7–1. The table shows that buyers facing a new-task buying situation will usually go through all the stages of the buying process. Buyers making modified or straight rebuys will skip some of the stages. We will examine these steps for the typical new-task buying situation.

### Problem Recognition

The buying process begins when someone in the company recognizes a problem or need that can be met by acquiring a specific good or service. **Problem recognition** can result from internal or external stimuli. Internally, the company may decide to launch a new product and need new equipment and materials to produce it. Or a machine may break down and need new parts. Some purchased material may turn out to be unsatisfactory and cause the company to search for another supplier. Or a purchasing manager may see a chance to get better prices or quality. Externally, the buyer may get some new ideas at a trade show, see an ad, or receive a call from a salesperson who offers a better product or a lower price.

### General Need Description

Having recognized a need, the buyer next prepares a **general need description** that describes the general characteristics and quantity of the needed item. For standard items, this process is not a serious problem. For complex items, however, the buyer will work with others—engineers, users, consultants—to define the item. The team will want to rank the importance of reliability, durability, price, and other attributes desired in the item.

**problem recognition** The stage of the industrial buying process in which someone in the company recognizes a problem or need that can be met by acquiring a good or a service.

**general need description** The stage in the industrial buying process in which the company describes the general characteristics and quantity of a needed item.

TABLE 7–1  Major Stages of the Industrial Buying Process in Relation to Major Buying Situations

| Stages of the Buying Process | Buying Situations | | |
|---|---|---|---|
| | NEW TASK | MODIFIED REBUY | STRAIGHT REBUY |
| 1. Problem recognition | Yes | Maybe | No |
| 2. General need description | Yes | Maybe | No |
| 3. Product specification | Yes | Yes | Yes |
| 4. Supplier search | Yes | Maybe | No |
| 5. Proposal solicitation | Yes | Maybe | No |
| 6. Supplier selection | Yes | Maybe | No |
| 7. Order routine specification | Yes | Maybe | No |
| 8. Performance review | Yes | Yes | Yes |

Source: Adapted from Patrick J. Robinson, Charles W. Faris, and Yoram Wind, *Industrial Buying and Creative Marketing* (Boston: Allyn & Bacon, 1967), p. 14.

**product specification** The stage of the industrial buying process in which the buying organization decides on and specifies the best technical product characteristics for a needed item.

**value analysis** An approach to cost reduction in which components are carefully studied to determine if they can be redesigned, standardized, or made by cheaper methods of production.

**supplier search** The stage of the industrial buying process in which the buyer tries to find the best vendors.

**proposal solicitation** The stage of the industrial buying process in which the buyer invites qualified suppliers to submit proposals.

The industrial marketer can help the buying company in this phase. Often, the buyer is not aware of the value of different product characteristics. An alert marketer can help the buyer define the company's needs.

### Product Specification

The buying organization next develops the item's technical **product specifications.** Often, a value-analysis engineering team will be put to work on the problem. **Value analysis** is an approach to cost reduction in which components are carefully studied to determine if they can be redesigned, standardized, or made by cheaper methods of production. Table 7-2 lists the major questions raised in value analysis. The team will decide on the best product characteristics and specify them accordingly. Sellers too can use value analysis as a tool for breaking into an account. By showing a better way to make an object, outside sellers can turn straight rebuy situations into new-task situations in which their company has a chance for the business.

### Supplier Search

The buyer now conducts a **supplier search** to find the best vendors. The buyer can look at trade directories, do a computer search, or phone other companies for recommendations. Some vendors will not be considered because they are not large enough to supply the needed quantity or because they have a poor reputation for delivery and service. The buyer will soon end up with a small list of qualified suppliers.

The newer the buying task—and the more complex and costly the item—the greater the amount of time spent in searching for suppliers. The supplier's task is to get listed in major directories and build a good reputation in the marketplace. Salespeople should watch for companies in the process of searching for suppliers and make certain that their firm is considered.

### Proposal Solicitation

In the **proposal solicitation** stage of the industrial buying process, the buyer invites qualified suppliers to submit proposals. Some suppliers will send only a catalog or a salesperson. When the item is complex or expensive, the buyer will need detailed written proposals from each potential supplier. The buyer will review the suppliers when they make their formal presentations.

Industrial marketers must therefore be skilled in researching, writing, and presenting proposals. Their proposals should be marketing documents, not just technical documents. Their presentations should inspire confidence. They should make their companies stand out from the competition.

TABLE 7–2  Questions Asked in Value Analysis

1. Does the use of the item contribute value?
2. Is its cost proportionate to its usefulness?
3. Does it need all its features?
4. Is there anything better for its intended use?
5. Can a usable part be made by a lower-cost method?
6. Can a standard product be found that will be usable?
7. Considering the quantities that are used, is the product made on proper tooling?
8. Do material, labor, overhead, and profit total its cost?
9. Will another dependable supplier provide it for less?
10. Is anyone else buying it for less?

Source: Adapted from Albert W. Frey, *Marketing Handbook*, 2d ed. (New York: Ronald Press, 1965), Sec. 27, p. 21. Copyright © 1985. Reprinted by permission of John Wiley & Sons, Inc.

## Supplier Selection

The members of the buying center now review the proposals and select a supplier or suppliers. In **supplier selection**, they will consider not only the technical competence of various suppliers but also their ability to deliver the item on time and to provide necessary services. The buying center will often draw up a list of desired supplier attributes and their relative importance. One survey of purchasing agents listed the following attributes in order of importance:[16]

| | | | |
|---|---|---|---|
| 1. | Delivery capability | 11. | Financial position |
| 2. | Quality | 12. | Attitude toward buyer |
| 3. | Price | 13. | Bidding compliance |
| 4. | Repair service | 14. | Training aids |
| 5. | Technical capability | 15. | Progress communications |
| 6. | Performance history | 16. | Management and organization |
| 7. | Production facilities | 17. | Packaging capability |
| 8. | Aid and advice | 18. | Moral/legal issues |
| 9. | Control systems | 19. | Geographic location |
| 10. | Reputation | 20. | Labor-relations record |

The members of the buying center will rate the suppliers against these attributes and identify the most attractive suppliers.

Buyers may attempt to negotiate with preferred suppliers for better prices and terms before making the final selections. In the end, they may select a single supplier or a few suppliers. Many buyers prefer multiple sources of supply: Then they will not be totally dependent on one supplier in case something goes wrong, and they will be able to compare the prices and performance of several suppliers over time.

## Order Routine Specification

The buyer now prepares an **order routine specification.** It includes the final order with the chosen supplier or suppliers, listing technical specifications, quantity needed, expected time of delivery, return policies, warranties, and so on. In the case of maintenance, repair, and operating items, buyers are increasingly using blanket contracts rather than periodic purchase orders. Writing a new purchase order each time stock is needed is expensive. Nor does the buyer want to write fewer and larger purchase orders because this practice means carrying more inventory.

A *blanket contract* creates a long-term relationship in which the supplier promises to resupply the buyer as needed and at agreed prices for a set time period. The stock is held by the seller and the buyer's computer automatically prints out an order to the seller when stock is needed. Blanket contracting leads to more single-source buying and the buying of more items from that single source. This practice locks the supplier in tighter with the buyer and makes it difficult for other suppliers to break in unless the buyer becomes dissatisfied with prices or service.

## Performance Review

In this stage, the buyer reviews supplier performance. The buyer may contact users and ask them to rate their satisfaction. The **performance review** may lead the buyer to continue, modify, or drop the seller. The seller's job is to monitor the same factors used by the buyer to make sure that the seller is giving the expected satisfaction.

**supplier selection** The stage of the industrial buying process in which the buyer reviews proposals and selects a supplier or suppliers.

**order routine specification** The stage of the industrial buying process in which the buyer writes the final order with the chosen supplier or suppliers, listing the technical specifications, quantity needed, expected time of delivery, return policies, warranties, and so on.

**performance review** The stage of the industrial buying process in which the buyer rates its satisfaction with suppliers, deciding whether to continue, modify, or drop them.

We have described the buying stages that would operate in a new-task buying situation. In the modified rebuy or straight rebuy situation, some of these stages will be compressed or bypassed. The eight-stage model provides a simple view of the industrial buying decision process. The actual process is usually much more complex.[17] Each organization buys in its own way, and each buying situation has unique requirements. Different buying center participants may be involved at different stages of the process. Although certain buying-process steps usually occur, buyers do not always follow them in the same order, and they may add other steps. Often, buyers repeat certain stages more than once.

# RESELLER BUYER BEHAVIOR

In most ways, reseller buyer behavior is like industrial buyer behavior. Reseller organizations have buying centers whose participants interact to make a variety of buying decisions. They have a buying-decision process that starts with problem recognition and ends with decisions about which products to buy from which suppliers and under what terms. The buyers are affected by a wide range of environmental, organizational, interpersonal, and individual factors. But there are some important differences between industrial and reseller buying behavior. Resellers differ in the types of buying decisions they make, who participates in the buying decision, and how they make their buying decisions.

## What Buying Decisions Do Resellers Make?

Resellers serve as purchasing agents for *their* customers, so they buy products and brands they think will appeal to their customers. They have to decide what product assortment to carry, what vendors to buy from, and what prices and terms to negotiate. The assortment decision is primary, and it positions the reseller in the marketplace. The reseller's assortment strategy will strongly affect its choice of which products to buy and which suppliers to buy from.

Resellers can carry products from one supplier, several related products or lines from a few suppliers, or a scrambled assortment of unrelated products from many suppliers. Thus, a retail store might carry only Kodak cameras; many brands of cameras; cameras, radios, and stereo equipment; or all of these plus stoves and refrigerators. The reseller's assortment will affect its customer mix, marketing mix, and supplier mix.

## Who Participates in the Reseller Buying Process?

Who does the buying for wholesale and retail organizations? The reseller's buying center may include one or many participants assuming different roles. Some will have formal buying responsibility, and some will be behind-the-scenes influencers. In small "mom and pop" firms, the owner usually takes care of buying decisions. In large reseller firms, buying is a specialized function and a full-time job. The buying center and buying process vary for different types of resellers.

Consider supermarkets. In the headquarters of a supermarket chain, specialist buyers have the responsibility for developing brand assortments and listening to new-brand presentations made by salespeople. In some chains, these buyers have the authority to accept or reject new items. In many chains, however, they are limited to screening "obvious rejects" and "obvious accepts"; otherwise, they must bring new items to the chain's buying committee for approval. However, even when an item is accepted by a buying committee, chain-store managers may not carry it. Altogether, food producers offer the nation's supermarkets over 10,000 new products each year, and store space does not permit more than 38 percent to be accepted.[18] Thus, the producers face a major challenge in trying to get new items into stores.

## How Do Resellers Make Their Buying Decisions?

For new items, resellers use roughly the same buying process described for industrial buyers. For standard items, resellers simply reorder goods when the inventory gets low. The orders are placed with the same suppliers as long as their terms, goods, and services are satisfactory. Buyers will try to renegotiate prices if their margins drop due to rising operating costs. In many retail lines, the profit margin is so low (1 to 2 percent on sales in supermarkets, for example) that a sudden drop in demand or rise in operating costs will drive profits into the red.

Resellers consider many factors besides costs when choosing products and suppliers. For example, a panel of supermarket buyers listed the following as important factors when choosing new products for their stores:[19]

□ The product's pricing and profit margins
□ The product's uniqueness and the strength of the product category

*Selling to resellers: In this ad to discount retailers, L'eggs lists plenty of reasons why its new line of Little L'eggs for children will increase the retailer's margins and open up new markets. It offers an innovative design, 5 to 1 consumer preference, 96 percent consumer name recognition, and a 57 percent gross margin.*

□ The seller's intended positioning and marketing plan for the product

□ Test-market evidence of consumer acceptance of the product

□ Advertising and sales-promotion support for the product

□ The selling company's reputation

Thus, sellers stand the best chance when they can report a promising product, show strong evidence of consumer acceptance, present a well-designed advertising and sales-promotion plan, and provide strong financial incentives to the retailer.

Sellers are facing increasingly advanced buying on the part of resellers. They need to understand resellers' changing needs and to develop attractive offers that help resellers serve their customers better. Table 7–3 lists several marketing tools used by sellers to make their offer to resellers more attractive.

# GOVERNMENT BUYER BEHAVIOR

The government market offers large opportunities for many companies. Altogether, federal, state, and local governments contain more than 82,000 buying units. Some companies sell to governments only occasionally or not at all. Others rely on the government market for a large portion of their sales (see Marketing Highlight 7–2).

Government buying and industrial buying are similar in many ways. But there are also differences that must be understood by companies wishing to sell products and services to governments.[20] To succeed in the government market, sellers must locate key decision makers, identify the factors that affect buyer behavior, and understand the buying decision process.

## Who Participates in the Government Buying Process?

Who does the buying of $892 billion of goods and services each year? Government buying organizations are found at the federal, state, and local levels. The federal level is the largest, and its buying units operate in both the civilian and military sectors.

TABLE 7–3   Vendor Marketing Tools Used with Resellers

*Cooperative advertising,* where the vendor agrees to pay a portion of the reseller's advertising costs for the vendor's product.

*Preticketing,* where the vendor places a tag on each product listing its price, manufacturer, size, identification number, and color; these tags help the reseller reorder merchandise as it is being sold.

*Stockless purchasing,* where the vendor carries the inventory and delivers goods to the reseller on short notice.

*Automatic reordering systems,* where the vendor supplies forms and computer links for automatic reordering of merchandise by the reseller.

*Advertising aids,* such as glossy photos, broadcast scripts.

*Special prices* for storewide promotion.

*Return and exchange priveleges* for the reseller.

*Allowances for merchandise markdowns* by the reseller.

*Sponsorship of in-store demonstrations.*

## ZENITH TARGETS THE GOVERNMENT MARKET

In 1979, Zenith entered the already overcrowded personal computer market. Like IBM, Tandy, AT&T, and several other competitors, Zenith targeted its line of IBM-compatibles at the business and retail markets. But Zenith lacked IBM's marketing muscle; it couldn't sustain the big-budget advertising and marketing campaign needed to challenge big rivals head-on. So in 1981, after limping along for two years, Zenith changed its strategy. It targeted two specialty markets—higher education and the federal government, markets previously overlooked by IBM and the others. By focusing on these segments, Zenith could avoid expensive advertising and costly direct competition.

Cracking the huge government market, however, took lots of effort and investment, patience, and positive thinking. Zenith set up a government salesforce to handle the special needs of the government market. The new salesforce had to learn its way through the complex, convoluted federal government bidding process and how to cut through seemingly endless red tape, bureaucracy, and paperwork. Zenith made

its proposals more appealing to cost-conscious government buyers by using the money it saved on advertising to heavily discount its prices. It took Zenith almost two years to land its first government contract, a $29 million order from the Air Force in 1983 for 6,000 personal computers. Although government business began as a trickle, the trickle soon turned into a flood.

In October 1984, Zenith got a $100 million contract to supply the Navy, Air Force, and Marines with "Tempest-grade" personal computers—machines specially shielded against electronic eavesdropping. In February 1986, Zenith beat out IBM and other large competitors to get the government's largest ever personal computer order, a $242 million contract for more than 200,000 units. That contract may eventually grow to bring in over $500 million worth of business. Also in 1986, Zenith edged out IBM and Data General to win a $27 million contract from the Internal Revenue Service for 15,000 of the company's acclaimed new laptop models. The company has also won contracts from the U.S. Department of

Health and Human Services and several other government agencies. The Army and Air Force Post Exchange Systems (PXs) carry Zenith products, and the company supplies computers to students and faculty at the Army, Air Force, and Naval academies. Zenith has even broken into the state government market, with contracts from the states of Florida, Kansas, and Massachusetts.

Thus, Zenith's strategy to target the government market has met with staggering success. Zenith is now the federal government's largest personal computer supplier and the world's second-largest producer of IBM-compatibles. Between 1982 and 1986, while most of the personal computer industry slid downward and many competitors failed, Zenith's yearly computer sales grew by over 550 percent, to $548 million. When IBM's sales through retail stores slowed under the onslaught of cheap Asian clones, Zenith was having trouble keeping up with orders from government agencies. By 1988, an estimated one-half of all Zenith's computer sales came from the government market.

By focusing on the government market, Zenith quietly established itself as a major contender in the highly competitive personal computer market. Now, using its success in the government market as a foundation, Zenith is challenging for a share of the larger retail and business markets.

*Sources:* See Thayer C. Taylor, "The PC Fight: Zenith Battles the Heavyweights," *Sales & Marketing Management,* November 1986, pp. 51-55; Kenneth Dreyfack, "Zenith's Side Road to Success in Personal Computers," *Business Week,* December 8, 1986, pp. 100-101; "Zenith Is Doing Quite Well, Thank You—In Personal Computers," *Business Week,* July 11, 1988, p. 80; and Louis Therrien, "Zenith's TV Picture Is Getting Brighter—For Now," *Business Week,* February 27, 1989, p. 41.

*By focusing on the government market, Zenith established itself as a major contender in the microcomputer market.*

The federal civilian buying establishment consists of seven categories: departments (such as Commerce), administrations (General Services Administration), agencies (Environmental Protection Agency), boards (Railroad Retirement Board), commissions (Federal Communications Commission), executive offices (Bureau of the Budget), and miscellaneous organizations (Tennessee Valley Authority). No single agency buys for all the government's needs, and no single buyer purchases all of any single item of supplies, equipment, or services. Many agencies control a large percentage of their own buying, particularly for industrial products and specialized equipment. At the same time, the General Services Administration plays a major role in centralizing the buying of commonly used items in the civilian section (office furniture and equipment, vehicles, fuels) and in standardizing buying procedures for other agencies.

Federal military buying is carried out by the Defense Department, largely through the Defense Supply Agency and the army, navy, and air force. In an effort to reduce costly duplication, the Defense Supply Agency was set up in 1961 to buy and distribute supplies used by all military services. It operates six supply centers, which specialize in construction, electronics, fuel, personnel support, industrial products, and general supplies. The trend has been toward "single managers" for major product classifications. Each service branch buys equipment and supplies in line with its own mission. For example, the Army Department has offices that acquire its own material, vehicles, medical supplies and services, and weapons.

State and local buying agencies include school districts, highway departments, hospitals, housing agencies, and many others. Each has its own buying process that sellers have to master.

The various government agencies may all be potential targets for sellers who wish to sell to this large market. But sellers should study the purchasing patterns of different agencies. Agencies differ in quality requirements and the amount of marketing effort needed to make a sale. Some agencies buy standardized products while others buy mostly customized ones. Sellers should target agencies and buying centers that match their strengths and objectives.[21]

## What Are the Major Influences on Government Buyers?

Like consumer and industrial buyers, government buyers are affected by environmental, organizational, interpersonal, and individual factors. A unique thing about government buying is that it is carefully watched by outside publics. One watchdog is Congress, and certain members of Congress have made a career out of exposing government waste. Another watchdog is the Bureau of the Budget, which checks on government spending and seeks to improve efficiency. Many private groups also watch government agencies to see how they spend the public's money.

Because spending decisions are subject to public review, government organizations are buried in paperwork. Elaborate forms must be filled out and signed before purchases are approved. The level of bureaucracy is high, and marketers have to find a way to cut through the red tape.

Noneconomic criteria are also playing a growing role in government buying. Government buyers are asked to favor depressed business firms and areas, small-business firms, and business firms that avoid race, sex, or age discrimination. Sellers need to keep these factors in mind when deciding to seek government business.

## How Do Government Buyers Make Their Buying Decisions?

Government buying practices often seem complex and frustrating to suppliers. Suppliers have voiced many complaints about government purchasing procedures. These include too much paperwork, bureaucracy, needless regulations, emphasis on low-bid prices, decision-making delays, frequent shifts in buying personnel, and too many policy changes. Yet the ins and outs of selling to the government can often be mastered in a short time. The government is generally helpful in providing information about its buying needs and procedures. Government is often as anxious to attract new suppliers as the suppliers are to find customers.

For example, the Small Business Administration prints a booklet entitled *U.S. Government Purchasing, Specifications, and Sales Directory,* which lists thousands of items most frequently purchased by the government and the specific agencies most frequently buying them. The Government Printing Office issues the *Commerce Business Daily,* which lists major current purchases and recent contract awards, both of which can provide leads to subcontracting markets. In several major cities, the General Services Administration operates Business Service Centers with staffs to provide a complete education on the way government agencies buy and the steps that suppliers should follow. Various trade magazines and associations provide information on how to reach schools, hospitals, highway departments, and other government agencies.

Government buying procedures fall into two types: the *open bid* and the *negotiated contract.* Open-bid buying means that the government office invites bids from qualified suppliers for carefully described items, generally awarding a contract to the lowest bidder. The supplier must consider whether it can meet the specifications and accept the terms. For standard items, such as fuel or school supplies, the specifications are not a hurdle. But specifications may be a hurdle for nonstandard items. The government office is usually required to award the contract to the lowest bidder on a winner-take-all basis. In some cases, allowance is made for the supplier's better product or reputation for completing contracts.

In negotiated contract buying, the agency works with one or more companies and negotiates a contract with one of them covering the project and contract terms. This occurs primarily with complex projects—those involving major research and development costs and risks or those for which there is little competition. The contract can be reviewed and renegotiated if the supplier's profits seem too high.

Many companies that sell to the government have not been marketing-oriented—for a number of reasons. Total government spending is determined by elected officials rather than by any marketing effort to develop the market. Government buying has emphasized price, making suppliers invest their effort in technology to bring costs down. When the product's characteristics are carefully specified, product differentiation is not a marketing factor. Nor do advertising or personal selling matter much in winning bids on an open-bid basis.

More companies are now setting up separate marketing departments for government marketing efforts. J. I. Case, Eastman Kodak, and Goodyear are examples. These companies want to coordinate bids and prepare them more scientifically, to propose projects to meet government needs rather than just respond to government requests, to gather competitive intelligence, and to prepare stronger communications to describe the company's competence.

# SUMMARY

Organizations make up a vast market. There are three major types of *organizational markets*—the industrial market, the reseller market, and the government market.

In many ways, organizational markets are like consumer markets, but in other ways they are much different. Organizational markets usually have fewer and larger buyers who are more geographically concentrated. Organizational demand is *derived,* largely *inelastic,* and more *fluctuating.* More buyers are usually involved in the organizational buying decision, and organizational buyers are better trained and more professional than consumer buyers. Organizational purchasing decisions are more complex, and the buying process is more formal.

The *industrial market* includes firms and individuals that buy goods and services in order to produce other goods and services for sale or rental to others. Industrial buyers make decisions that vary with the three types of buying situations— *straight rebuys, modified rebuys,* and *new tasks.* The decision-making unit of a buying organization—the *buying center*— may consist of many persons playing many roles. The industrial marketer needs to know: Who are the major participants? In what decisions do they exercise influence? What is their relative degree of influence? What evaluation criteria does each decision participant use? The industrial marketer also needs to understand the major environmental, organizational, interpersonal, and individual influences on the buying process. The buying process itself consists of eight stages: *problem*

*recognition, general need description, product specification, supplier search, proposal solicitation, supplier selection, order routine specification,* and *performance review.* As industrial buyers become more sophisticated, industrial marketers must upgrade their marketing.

The *reseller market* consists of individuals and organizations that acquire and resell goods produced by others. Resellers have to decide on their assortment, suppliers, prices, and terms. In small wholesale and retail organizations, buying may be carried on by one or a few individuals; in large organizations, it is generally conducted by an entire purchasing department. With new items, buyers go through a buying process similar to the one shown for industrial buyers; with standard items, the buying process consists of routines for reordering and renegotiating contracts.

The *government market* is a vast one that annually purchases $892 billion worth of products and services—for defense, education, public welfare, and other public needs. Government buying practices are highly specialized and specified, with open bidding or negotiated contracts characterizing most of the buying. Government buyers operate under the watchful eye of Congress, the Bureau of the Budget, and many private watchdog groups. Thus, they tend to fill out more forms, require more signatures, and respond more slowly in placing orders.

# QUESTIONS FOR DISCUSSION

1. In what ways can your school be considered an industrial marketer? What are its products and who are its customers?

2. How does the geographic concentration of organizational markets influence the marketing efforts of firms selling to organizational buyers?

3. Which of the three major types of buying situations— straight-rebuy, modified-rebuy, and new-task—are represented by the following: (a) Chrysler's purchase of computers that adjust engine performance to changing driving conditions, (b) Volkswagen's purchase of spark plugs for its line of Jettas, and (c) Honda's purchase of light bulbs for its Acura division?

4. If a university wants to introduce polo as a varsity sport, what elements would a systems seller include in a proposal to start the program and make it succeed?

5. How could a marketer of office equipment identify the buying center for a law firm's purchase of dictation equipment for its partners?

6. What major environmental factors would affect the purchase of radar speed detectors by state and local police forces?

7. What are the advantages and disadvantages of buying from single suppliers instead of multiple suppliers?

8. NutraSweet and other companies have advertised products to the general public that consumers cannot actually buy. How does this strategy help sell products to resellers?

9. Compare the major buying influences on industrial, reseller, and government buyers.

# REFERENCES

1. Excerpts from "Major Sales: Who Really Does the Buying," by Thomas V. Bonoma (May-June 1982). Copyright © 1982 by the President and Fellows of Harvard College; all rights reserved. Also see Scott Ticer, "Why Gulfstream's Rivals are Gazing Up in Envy," *Business Week,* February 16, 1987, pp. 66–67.

2. Frederick E. Webster, Jr., and Yoram Wind, *Organizational Buying Behavior* (Englewood Cliffs, NJ: Prentice Hall, 1972), p. 2.

3. See the *1982 Census of Retail Trade* and the *1982 Census of Wholesale Trade,* U.S. Department of Commerce, Bureau of the Census, 1985.

4. *Survey of Current Business,* U.S. Department of Commerce, Bureau of Economic Analysis, Vol. 67, No. 4, April 1987.

5. However, for an argument that consumer and organizational marketing do not differ very much, see Edward F. Fern and James R. Brown, "The Industrial/Consumer Marketing Dichotomy: A Case of Insufficient Justification," *Journal of Marketing,* Fall 1984, pp. 68–77.

6. See Barbara Bund Jackson, "Build Customer Relationships That Last," *Harvard Business Review,* November-December 1985, pp. 120–28.

7. For a discussion of other organizational buyer behavior models, see Raymond L. Horton, *Buyer Behavior: A Decision-Making Approach* (Columbus, OH: Charles E. Merrill, 1984), Chap. 16.

8. Patrick J. Robinson, Charles W. Faris, and Yoram Wind, *Industrial Buying Behavior and Creative Marketing* (Boston: Allyn & Bacon, 1967). Also see Erin Anderson, Weyien Chu, and Barton Weitz, "Industrial Purchasing: An Empirical Exploration of the Buyclass Framework," *Journal of Marketing,* July 1987, pp. 71–86.

9. For more on systems selling, see Robert R. Reeder, Edward G. Brierty, and Betty H. Reeder, *Industrial Marketing: Analysis, Planning, and Control* (Englewood Cliffs, NJ: Prentice Hall, 1987), pp. 247–50.

10. Webster and Wind, *Organizational Buying Behavior,* p. 6. For more reading on buying centers, see Bonoma, "Major Sales"; and Donald W. Jackson, Jr., Janet E. Keith, and Richard K. Burdick, "Purchasing Agents' Perceptions of Industrial Buying Center Influence: A Situational Approach," *Journal of Marketing,* Fall 1984, pp. 75–83.

11. Wesley J. Johnson and Thomas V. Bonoma, "Purchase Process for Capital Equipment and Services," *Industrial Marketing Management,* 10 (1981), 258–59.

12. Clifton J. Reichard, "Industrial Selling: Beyond Price and Persistence," *Harvard Business Review,* March-April 1985, p. 128.

13. Webster and Wind, *Organizational Buying Behavior,* pp. 33–37.

14. Bonoma, "Major Sales," p. 114.

15. Robinson, Faris, and Wind, *Industrial Buying.*

16. See William A. Dempsey, "Vendor Selection and the Buying Process," *Industrial Marketing Management,* 7 (1978), 257–67.

17. Johnson and Bonoma, "Purchase Process," p. 261.

18. See Ed Fitch, "Life in the Food Chain Becomes Predatory," *Advertising Age,* May 9, 1988, p. S2.

19. "Retailers Rate New Products," *Sales & Marketing Management,* November 1986, pp. 75–77.

20. For more reading on similarities and differences between government and industrial buying, see Jagdish N. Sheth, Robert F. Williams, and Richard M. Hill, "Government and Business Buying: How Similar Are They?" *Journal of Purchasing and Materials Management,* Winter 1983, pp. 7–13.

21. See Warren H. Suss, "How to Sell to Uncle Sam," *Harvard Business Review,* November-December 1984, pp. 136–44; and Don Hill, "Who Says Uncle Sam's a Tough Sell?" *Sales & Marketing Management,* July 1988, 56–60.

# Case 7

## LOCTITE CORPORATION: NEW MARKETS FOR AN OLD PRODUCT

When studying organizational markets, it is helpful to consider all the goods and services that businesses must buy in order to provide the ultimate consumers with products they want. For example, did you know that, in one year, dishwasher manufacturers buy 585 miles of rubber hose, 3.7 million water valves, and 734,000 gallons of paint? Manufacturers buy from hundreds of suppliers—most of whom are little-known to the consumers who buy the final product. Loctite Corporation is one such supplier.

Loctite Corporation, a specialty chemical company, manufactures products that bond, seal, and prevent loosening. You may have used a product today that is held together by a Loctite product—in fact, you may now be *wearing* something that contains a Loctite product! Some Loctite adhesives are used in several sectors of the garment industry, including both clothing and shoes. Consumers may also buy Loctite products for their own use. For example, the super glues "Glue Stick" and "Quick Gel," as well as Duro household cements, are Loctite products that may be in your home.

The use of adhesives, however, is relatively new. In 1953, Trinity College Professor Vernon K. Krieble developed the original Loctite "anaerobic" adhesive. This new product competed with the more traditional means of bonding materials,

such as screws, nuts and bolts, riveting, and welding. Since that time, industrial designers and engineers have increasingly integrated Loctite products into thousands of production lines to assemble parts more quickly and efficiently. Products assembled with adhesives are lighter, safer, more reliable, and less costly. Maintenance workers also use Loctite products to prevent mechanical parts from loosening, leaking, and wearing. Loctite adhesives and sealants ensure dependability and longer machine life.

Some specific Loctite industrial products and their uses include:

- *Threadlocker adhesives:* to prevent nuts, bolts, and screws from loosening because of shock and vibration.

- *Pipe sealants:* to prevent leakage from vibration loosening and extreme temperatures or pressure

- *Engineering adhesives:* for assembly operations that require strong, durable adhesives that cure quickly at room temperature

- *Maintenance products:* to maintain, repair, and overhaul machinery and equipment.

Today, adhesives are used to bond many products, including automobiles and

airplanes. The Porsche 928, one of the world's fastest production autos, contains seven different Loctite adhesives and sealants with 24 different applications in 90 places. Lockheed now assembles and fastens airplane frames and skin parts using only adhesives, and the revolutionary Lear business jet is also held together by adhesives.

Loctite is the world's major manufacturer of anaerobic and cyanocrylate adhesives and sealants, with annual sales over $415 million and a recent growth rate of 18 percent. Its great success can be attributed in part to its sales and distribution network. Loctite management realizes the importance of using the right product for the right application. Well-trained Loctite technical service personnel serve as customer problem solvers. Sixty percent of sales are made through independent distributors and the remaining 40 percent directly to end users. In order to provide technical support for the use of its products, the company maintains close and continued contact with both its distributors and major end users.

Recently, marketing executives at Loctite met to discuss a problem product called RC601—an engineering adhesive. Because the product has shown little or no profit during the past several years, the company recently performed some marketing research on RC601, hoping to find new uses and new target markets for the product. Marketing executives are now trying to develop a new marketing strategy.

The traditional target market for RC601 has been design engineers. RC601 is a thin, liquid-retaining compound supplied in a red bottle. It fills small voids that remain when parts are bonded with cylindrical fasteners (such as bolts). Design engineers typically specify the use of RC601 in the production process to allow relaxation of machining tolerance for easier assembly and lower machining costs. In this way, RC601 compensates for the inexact fit of many parts used in numerous production processes.

Inclusion of a particular adhesive in the design of a product is typically a complex decision. Although design engineers actually make the buying decision, other individuals on the new-product development team may be involved—and agreement is not often easy. For example, purchasing agents are concerned with economy, engineers with performance, and production managers with prompt delivery. Furthermore, such factors as the complexity of the production process and the long-term commitment made by specifying the adhesive in a production plan motivate decision makers to evaluate alternatives carefully.

Because design engineers are reluctant to consider new or different products, a sales representative's primary task in selling RC601 is to persuade them to buy the product for the first time. After RC601 is specified in the design of a product and the initial sale is made, almost all product requirements are bought through local distributors. Loctite uses "Product Information Data" sheets as its primary promotion tool in marketing RC601.

Sales and profits of RC601 fell off when Loctite introduced newer products (RC609, RC620, and RC680) that appealed more to its target market. The new products have a tolerance to higher temperatures (up to 450 degrees Fahrenheit in some cases). Thus, to reverse the sales decline, Loctite marketers commissioned a marketing-research study to find new potential users and customers for RC601—in short, new target markets.

Loctite always studies its products from the customer's point of view. Marketing research showed that plant maintenance workers need a product that can keep broken-down machines running until replacement parts arrive. To meet this need, Loctite reformulated RC601 into a gel that can be applied between machinery parts to temporarily repair worn areas and restore correct fits. The new gel has clear advantages in this application. Most importantly, RC601 gets equipment ready to run in one hour—compared with twelve hours for the most commonly used alternative method. A maintenance worker can quickly repair a worn part with the gel and continue operation until a new part can be installed. The product can thus save users up to $4,000 in time and labor. Because the savings are so great, the price paid is of less importance. Buyers in this situation are more concerned with availability and performance. It is not unusual for maintenance workers to request a particular product by its brand name.

Loctite marketing executives are now trying to develop a marketing strategy for the changed product (a gel-like reformulation of RC601) and new target market (maintenance workers). They recognize that the new RC601 will probably need a new name, package, and promotion effort.

*Questions*

1. Describe the decision-making process of design engineers and maintenance workers for Loctite products. Be sure to consider the type of buying situation facing each (straight rebuy, modified rebuy, or new task), the stages of the buying process, and the members of the organization who participate in the purchase-decision process.

2. What marketing strategy would you recommend to Loctite executives for the new market segment? Your recommendation should include a name for the product, packaging ideas, pricing strategy, and promotional suggestions.

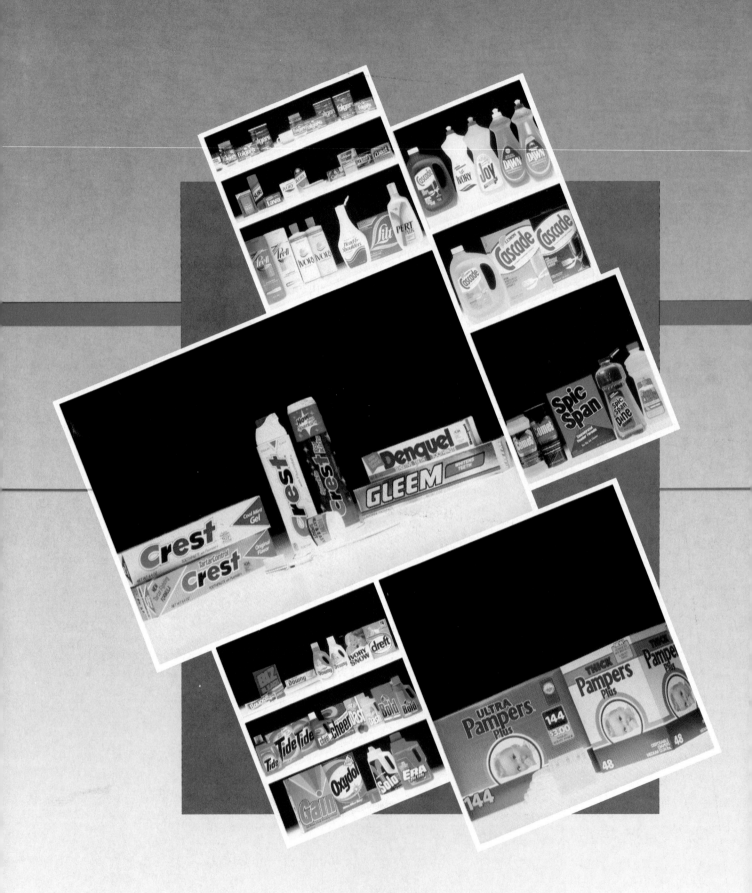

# 8

# Market Segmentation, Targeting, and Positioning

## CHAPTER OBJECTIVES

After reading this chapter, you should be able to

1. Define *market segmentation, market targeting,* and *market positioning*
2. List and discuss the major bases for segmenting consumer and industrial markets
3. Explain how companies identify attractive market segments and choose a market-coverage strategy
4. Explain how companies can position their products for maximum advantage in the marketplace

Procter & Gamble makes ten different brands of laundry detergent (Tide, Cheer, Gain, Dash, Bold 3, Dreft, Ivory Snow, Oxydol, Era, and Solo). It also sells seven brands of hand soap (Zest, Coast, Ivory, Safeguard, Camay, Kirk's, and Lava), four shampoos (Prell, Head & Shoulders, Ivory, and Pert), four liquid dishwashing detergents (Joy, Ivory, Dawn, and Liquid Cascade), four brands of toothpaste (Crest, Gleem, Complete, and Denquel), and two brands each of deodorant (Secret and Sure), coffee (Folgers and High Point), cooking oil (Crisco and Puritan), fabric softener (Downy and Bounce), cleaner (Spic & Span, Mr. Clean, and Top Job), and disposable diapers (Pampers and Luvs). Thus, P&G brands compete with one another on the same supermarket shelves.

But why would P&G introduce several brands in one category instead of concentrating its resources on a single leading brand? The answer lies in the fact that different people want different *mixes of benefits* from the products they buy. Take laundry detergents as an example. People use laundry detergents to get their clothes clean. But they also want other things from their detergents—things such as economy, bleaching power, fabric softening, fresh smell, strength or

mildness, and lots of suds. We all want *some* of these benefits from our detergent, but we may have different priorities for *each* benefit. To some people, cleaning and bleaching power are most important; to others, fabric softening is most important; still others want a mild, fresh-scented detergent. Thus, there are groups—or segments—of laundry detergent buyers, and each segment seeks a special combination of benefits.

Procter & Gamble has identified at least ten important laundry detergent segments, and it has developed a different brand designed to meet the special needs of each segment. The ten P&G brands are positioned for different segments as follows:

□ *Tide* is the "extra action," all-purpose detergent for extra-tough laundry jobs. It is a family detergent—"It gets out the dirt kids get into. Tide's in, dirt's out."

□ *Cheer* is specially formulated for use in hot, warm, or cold water. It's "all tempera-Cheer."

□ *Gain* was originally P&G's "enzyme" detergent but was repositioned as the detergent with a lingering fragrance—"for laundry so clean it's bursting with freshness."

- □ *Dash* is P&G's concentrated-powder detergent with "three powerful dirt dissolvers." It also makes less suds, so it won't clog "today's automatic washing machines."

- □ *Bold 3* originally "powered out dirt." Now it's the detergent plus fabric softener. It "cleans, softens, and controls static."

- □ *Ivory Snow* is "Ninety-nine and forty-four one-hundredths percent pure." It's the "mild, gentle soap for diapers and baby clothes."

- □ *Dreft* is also formulated for baby's diapers and clothes, and it contains borax, "nature's natural sweetener."

- □ *Oxydol* contains bleach. It's for "sparkling whites, a full-power detergent with color-safe bleach."

- □ *Era* is P&G's concentrated liquid detergent. It contains proteins to clean more stains.

- □ *Solo* is positioned as a heavy-duty liquid detergent with a fabric softener—"The convenience of a liquid plus a softer wash that doesn't cling."

By segmenting the market and having several different detergent brands, P&G has an attractive offering for consumers in all important preference groups. All P&G brands combined hold more than a 50 percent share of the laundry detergent market—much more than any single brand could obtain by itself.

---

## ■ MARKETS

**market** The set of all actual and potential buyers of a product.

The term *market* has acquired many meanings over the years. In its original meaning, a market was a location where buyers and sellers gathered to exchange goods and services. Medieval towns had market squares where sellers brought their goods and buyers shopped for them. To an economist, a market consists of all the buyers and sellers who transact over some good or service. Thus, the soft drink market consists of major sellers such as Coca-Cola, Pepsi-Cola, and Seven-Up and all the consumers who buy soft drinks. To a marketer, a **market** is the set of all actual and potential buyers of a product.

Organizations that sell to consumer and industrial markets recognize that they cannot appeal to all buyers in those markets—or at least not to all buyers in the same way. Buyers are too numerous, too widely scattered, and too varied in needs and buying practices. And different companies vary widely in their abilities to serve different segments of the market. Thus, each company has to identify the parts of the market that it can serve best. Sellers have not always practiced this philosophy. Their thinking passed through three stages:

- □ *Mass marketing.* In mass marketing, the seller mass-produces, mass-distributes, and mass-promotes one product to all buyers. At one time, Coca-Cola produced only one drink for the whole market, hoping it would appeal to everyone. The argument for mass marketing is that it should lead to the lowest costs and prices and create the largest potential market.

- □ *Product-variety marketing.* Here, the seller produces two or more products that have different features, styles, quality, sizes, and so on. Later, Coca-Cola produced several soft drinks packaged in different sizes and containers. They were designed to offer variety to buyers rather than to appeal to different market segments.

- □ *Target marketing.* Here, the seller identifies market segments, selects one or more of them, and develops products and marketing mixes tailored to each. For example, Coca-Cola now produces several soft drinks for the sugared-cola segment (Coke, Coca-Cola Classic, and Cherry Coke), the diet segment (Diet Coke and Tab), the no-caffeine segment (Caffeine Free Coke), and the non-cola segment (Minute Maid sodas).

Today's companies are moving away from mass marketing and product-variety marketing and toward target marketing. Target marketing can better help sellers find their marketing opportunities. Sellers can develop the right product for each target market. They can adjust their prices, distribution channels, and advertising to reach the target market efficiently. Instead of scattering their marketing effort (the "shotgun" approach), they can focus on the buyers who have the greater purchase interest (the "rifle" approach).

Target marketing calls for three major steps (Figure 8–1). The first is **market segmentation**—dividing a market into distinct groups of buyers who might call for separate products or marketing mixes. The company identifies different ways to segment the market and develops profiles of the resulting market segments. The second step is **market targeting**—evaluating each segment's attractiveness and selecting one or more of the market segments to enter. The third step is **market positioning**—setting the competitive positioning for the product and a detailed marketing mix. This chapter will describe the principles of market segmentation, market targeting, and market positioning.

**market segmentation** Dividing a market into distinct groups of buyers who might require separate products or marketing mixes.

**market targeting** The process of evaluating each market segment's attractiveness and selecting one or more segments to enter.

**market positioning** Formulating competitive positioning for a product and a detailed marketing mix.

# MARKET SEGMENTATION

Markets consist of buyers, and buyers differ in one or more ways. They may differ in their wants, resources, locations, buying attitudes, and buying practices. Any of these variables can be used to segment a market.

## Segmenting a Market

Because buyers have unique needs and wants, each is potentially a separate market. Ideally, then, a seller might design a separate marketing program for each buyer. For example, airplane producers such as Boeing and McDonnell-Douglas face only a few buyers and treat each as a separate market. Using such *complete* market segmentation, they customize their products and marketing programs to satisfy each specific customer.

However, most sellers do not find complete segmentation worthwhile. Instead, most sellers look for broad *classes* of buyers who differ in their product needs or buying responses. For example, General Motors has found that high- and low-income groups differ in their car-buying needs and wants. It also knows that young consumers' needs and wants differ from those of older consumers. Thus, GM has designed specific models for different income and age groups—in fact, it sells models for segments with varied *combinations* of age and income. For example, GM designed its Buick Park Avenue for older, higher-income consumers. Age and income are only two of many bases that companies use for segmenting their markets.

## Bases for Segmenting Consumer Markets

There is no single way to segment a market. A marketer has to try different segmentation variables, alone and in combination, hoping to find the best way to view the market structure. Table 8–1 outlines the major variables that might be

FIGURE 8–1   Steps in Market Segmentation, Targeting, and Positioning

**geographic segmentation** Dividing a market into different geographical units such as nations, states, regions, counties, cities, or neighborhoods.

TABLE 8-1    Major Segmentation Variables for Consumer Markets

| Variable | Typical Breakdowns |
|---|---|
| *Geographic* | |
| Region | Pacific, Mountain, West North Central, West South Central, East North Central, East South Central, South Atlantic, Middle Atlantic, New England |
| County size | A, B, C, D |
| City size | Under 5,000; 5,000–20,000; 20,000–50,000; 50,000–100,000; 100,000–250,000; 250,000–500,000; 500,000–1,000,000; 1,000,000–4,000,000; 4,000,000 or over |
| Density | Urban, suburban, rural |
| Climate | Northern, southern |
| *Demographic* | |
| Age | Under 6, 6–11, 12–19, 20–34, 35–49, 50–64, 65 + |
| Sex | Male, female |
| Family size | 1–2, 3–4, 5 + |
| Family life cycle | Young, single; young, married, no children; young, married, youngest child under 6; young married, youngest child 6 or over; older, married, with children; older, married, no children under 18; older, single; other |
| Income | Under $10,000; $10,000–$15,000; $15,000–$20,000; $20,000–$30,000; $30,000–$50,000; $50,000 and over |
| Occupation | Professional and technical; managers, officials, and proprietors; clerical, sales; craftsmen, foremen; operatives; farmers; retired; students; homemakers; unemployed |
| Education | Grade school or less; some high school; high school graduate; some college; college graduate |
| Religion | Catholic, Protestant, Jewish, other |
| Race | White, black, Asian, Hispanic |
| Nationality | American, British, French, German, Scandinavian, Italian, Latin American, Middle Eastern, Japanese |
| *Psychographic* | |
| Social class | Lower lowers, upper lowers, working class, middle class, upper middles, lower uppers, upper uppers |
| Life style | Belongers, achievers, integrateds |
| Personality | Compulsive, gregarious, authoritarian, ambitious |
| *Behavioristic* | |
| Purchase occasion | Regular occasion, special occasion |
| Benefits sought | Quality, service, economy |
| User status | Nonuser, ex-user, potential user, first-time user, regular user |
| Usage rate | Light user, medium user, heavy user |
| Loyalty status | None, medium, strong, absolute |
| Readiness stage | Unaware, aware, informed, interested, desirous, intending to buy |
| Attitude toward product | Enthusiastic, positive, indifferent, negative, hostile |

used in segmenting consumer markets. Here we will look at the major *geographic, demographic, psychographic,* and *behavior variables.*

## Geographic Segmentation

**Geographic segmentation** calls for dividing the market into different geographical units such as nations, states, regions, counties, cities, or neighborhoods. A company may decide to operate in one or a few geographical areas or to operate in all areas but pay attention to geographical differences in needs and wants. For example, General Foods' Maxwell House ground coffee is sold nationally but flavored regionally: People in the West want stronger coffee than people in the East. Campbell makes its nacho cheese soup spicier in Texas and California and sells its spicy Ranchero beans only in the South and Southwest.

S. C. Johnson & Son practices geographic segmentation for its arsenal of Raid bug killers by emphasizing the right products in the right geographic areas at the right times:

> Concerned that its dominant share of the household insecticide market had plateaued just above 40 percent, Johnson figured out where and when different bugs were about to start biting, stinging, and otherwise making people's lives miserable. The company promoted cockroach zappers in roach capitals such as Houston and New York and flea sprays in flea-bitten cities like Tampa and Birmingham. Since the program began last year, Raid has increased its market share in 16 of 18 regions and its overall piece of the $450-million-a-year U.S. insecticide market by five percentage points.[1]

Many companies today are "regionalizing" their marketing programs—localizing their products, advertising, promotion, and sales efforts to fit the needs of individual regions, cities, and even neighborhoods (see Marketing Highlight 8–1).

## Demographic Segmentation

**Demographic segmentation** consists of dividing the market into groups based on such demographic variables as age, sex, family size, family life cycle, income, occupation, education, religion, race, and nationality. Demographic factors are the most popular bases for segmenting customer groups. One reason is that consumer needs, wants, and usage rates often vary closely with demographic variables. Another is that demographic variables are easier to measure than most other types of variables. Even when market segments are first defined using other bases, such as personality or behavior, their demographic characteristics must be known in order to assess the size of the target market and to reach it efficiently. Here, we will show how certain demographic factors have been used in market segmentation.

**demographic segmentation**
Dividing the market into groups based on demographic variables such as age, sex, family size, family life cycle, income, occupation, education, religion, race, and nationality.

*Age segmentation: Colgate Junior toothpaste is specially designed for kids—it's less foamy, has a milder taste, contains sparkles, and is shaped like a star.*

## REGIONALIZATION—A PASSING FAD OR THE NEW MARKETING ERA?

For most of this century, major consumer-products companies have held fast to two mass-marketing principles—product standardization and national brand identification. They have marketed the same set of products in about the same way all across the country. But recently, Campbell Soup, Procter & Gamble, General Foods, H. J. Heinz, and other companies have tried a new approach—*regionalization.* Instead of marketing in the same way nationally to all customers, they are tailoring their products, advertising, sales promotions, and personal selling efforts to suit the needs and tastes of specific regions, cities, and even neighborhoods.

Several factors have fueled the move toward regionalization. First, the American mass market for most products has slowly broken down into a profusion of smaller fragments—the baby boomer segment here, the mature segment there; here the Hispanic market, there the black market; here working women, there single parents; here the Sun Belt, there the Rust Belt—the list goes on. Today, marketers find it difficult to create a single product or program that appeals to all of these

There's always time for a hot Southern breakfast.

Smooth, creamy Quaker® Instant Grits cook up in seconds, in the bowl or in the microwave. And that makes them right for all those mornings you just can't wait for good Southern taste. QUAKER INSTANT GRITS
The grits you love. For the way you live.™

*Regional marketing: Quaker targets the South with this ad for Quaker Instant Grits, which ran in* Southern Living *magazine.*

**age and life-cycle segmentation** Dividing a market into different age and life-cycle groups.

**sex segmentation** Dividing a market into different groups based on gender.

*Age and Life-Cycle Stage* ▪ Consumer needs and wants change with age. Some companies use **age and life-cycle segmentation,** offering different products or using different marketing approaches for different age and life-cycle segments. For example, Life Stage vitamins come in four versions, each designed for the special needs of specific age segments: chewable Children's Formula for children from 4 to 12 years old; Teen's Formula for teenagers; and two adult versions (Men's Formula and Women's Formula). Johnson & Johnson developed Affinity Shampoo for women over 40 to help overcome age-related hair changes. And McDonald's targets children, teens, adults, and seniors with different ads and media. Its ads to teens feature dance-beat music, adventure, and fast-paced cutting from scene to scene; ads to seniors are softer and more sentimental.

*Sex* ▪ **Sex segmentation** has long been used in clothing, hairdressing, cosmetics, and magazines. Recently, other marketers have noticed opportunities for sex segmentation. For example, most deodorant brands are used by men and women alike. Procter & Gamble, however, developed Secret as the brand

diverse groups. Second, improved information and marketing research technologies have also spurred regionalization. For example, data from retail store scanners allow instant tracking of product sales from store to store, helping companies pinpoint local problems and opportunities that might call for localized marketing actions. A third important factor is the increasing power of retailers. Scanners give retailers mountains of market information, and this information gives them power over manufacturers. Furthermore, competition has increased dramatically in recent years for the precious shelf space controlled by retailers. The average supermarket now carries over 300,000 stock-keeping units and about 10 new products are introduced each day. Retailers are often lukewarm about large, national marketing campaigns aimed at masses of consumers. They strongly prefer local programs tied to their own promotion efforts and aimed at consumers in their own cities and neighborhoods. Thus, to keep retailers happy and to get shelf space for their products, manufacturers must now allot more and more of their marketing budgets to local, store-by-store promotions. Campbell Soup, a pioneer in regionalization, has jumped in with both feet. For starters, Campbell has created many successful regional brands. It sells its spicy Ranchero beans in the Southwest, Creole soup in the South, and red bean soup in Hispanic areas. For Northwesterners, who like their pickles very sour, it created Zesty Pickles. These and other brands appealing to regional tastes add substantially to Campbell's annual sales. But perhaps more significantly, Campbell has reorganized its entire marketing operation to suit its regional strategy. It has divided its market into 22 regions, each with new responsibility for planning local marketing programs, and each with its own advertising and promotion budget. The company has allocated 15 to 20 percent of its total marketing budget to support local marketing; this allocation may eventually rise to 50 percent.

Within each region, Campbell sales managers and salespeople now have the authority to create advertising and promotions geared to local market needs and conditions. They use local appeals and choose whatever local advertising media work best in their areas, ranging from newspapers and radio to parking meters, shopping carts, and church bulletins. And they work closely with local retailers on displays, coupon offers, price specials, and local promotional events. For example, one sales manager recently offered Campbell's Pork & Beans at a 50-year-old-price (5 cents) to help a local retailer celebrate its 50th anniversary. Such localized efforts win retailer support and boost consumer sales.

Although regionalization offers much promise, it also presents some problems. Offering many different regional products and programs results in higher manufacturing and marketing costs. And letting area sales staffs make local marketing decisions causes some quality, planning, and control problems. Salespeople will need a lot of training and guidance.

Regionalization is still in its infancy—even Campbell has yet to implement the strategy fully. Some marketers view it as just a fad—they think companies will quickly find that the extra sales will not cover the additional costs. But others think that regionalization will revolutionize the way consumer products are marketed. Gone are the days, they say, when a company can effectively mass-market a single product using a single ad campaign all across the country. To these marketers, regionalization signals the start of a new marketing era.

*Sources:* See Christine Dugas, Mark N. Vamos, Jonathan B. Levine, and Matt Rothmann, "Marketing's New Look," *Business Week,* January 26, 1987, pp. 64–69; Al Urbanski, "Repackaging the Brand Manager," *Sales & Marketing Management,* April 1987, pp. 42–45; Scott Hume, "Execs Favor Regional Approach," *Advertising Age,* November 2, 1987, p. 36; and Joe Schwartz, "Rock Soup," *American Demographics,* April 1989, p.66.

specially formulated for a woman's chemistry and then packaged and advertised the product to reinforce the female image. The automobile industry has also begun to use sex segmentation extensively:

> With the rapid growth in the number of working women and women car owners, most automakers are now designing marketing strategies to court women buyers. Last year, women spent $30 billion on new cars and influenced the spending of another $60 billion. And they are involved in 81 percent of all new-car purchases. Thus, women have evolved as a valued target market for auto companies. Some manufacturers target women directly. For example, Chevrolet devotes 30 percent of its television advertising budget to advertisements for women. It places large advertising spreads designed especially for women consumers in such magazines as *Cosmopolitan* and *Women's Sport and Fitness.* Chevy also sponsored a nationwide series of career conferences for women. Other companies avoid direct appeals, fearing that women will be offended if they see advertising directed toward them—it sometimes comes across as condescending. Instead, companies such as Toyota, Ford, and Pontiac try to include a realistic balance of men and women in their ads without specific reference to gender.[2]

**income segmentation** Dividing a market into different income groups.

**psychographic segmentation** Dividing a market into different groups based on social class, life style, or personality characteristics.

*Income* ▪ **Income segmentation** has long been used by the marketers of such products and services as automobiles, boats, clothing, cosmetics, and travel. Many companies target affluent consumers with luxury goods and convenience services. Stores like Neiman-Marcus pitch everything from expensive jewelry, fine fashions, and exotic furs to $4 jars of peanut butter and chocolate at $20 a pound.[3]

But not all companies using income segmentation target the affluent. Many companies, such as Family Dollar stores, profitably target low-income consumers. When Family Dollar real estate experts scout locations for new stores, they look for lower-middle-class neighborhoods where people wear cheap shoes and drive old cars that drip a lot of oil. The income of a typical Family Dollar customer rarely exceeds $17,000 a year, and the average customer spends only about $6 per trip to the store. Yet the store's low-income strategy has made it one of the most profitable discount chains in the country.[4]

### Psychographic Segmentation

In **psychographic segmentation,** buyers are divided into different groups based on social class, life style, or personality characteristics. People in the same demographic group can have very different psychographic makeups.

*Social Class* ▪ We described the seven American social classes in Chapter 6 and showed that social class has a strong effect on preferences in cars, clothes, home furnishings, leisure activities, reading habits, and retailers. Many companies design products or services for specific social classes, building in features that appeal to those classes.

*Life Style* ▪ We saw in Chapter 6 that people's interest in various goods is affected by their life styles and that the goods they buy express those life styles. Marketers are increasingly segmenting their markets by consumer life styles. General Foods used life-style analysis to successfully reposition its Sanka decaffeinated coffee. For years, Sanka's market was limited by the product's staid, older image. To turn this situation around, General Foods launched an advertising campaign that positioned Sanka as an ideal beverage for today's healthy, active life styles. The campaign targeted achievers of all ages, using a classic achiever appeal that Sanka "Lets you be your best." Advertising showed people leading adventurous life styles, such as kayaking through rapids.[5]

*Redbook* magazine also targets a specific life-style segment—women whom it calls "*Redbook* Jugglers." The magazine defines the "juggler" as a 25- to 44-year-old woman who must juggle husband, family, home, and job. According to *Redbook*, this consumer makes an ideal target for marketers of health food and fitness products. She wears out more exercise shoes, swallows more vitamins, drinks more diet soda, and works out more often than other consumer groups.

*Personality* ▪ Marketers have also used personality variables to segment markets. They give their products "personalities" that correspond to consumer personalities. Successful market segmentation strategies based on personality have been used for such products as women's cosmetics, cigarettes, insurance, and liquor.[6] Honda's marketing campaign for its motor scooters provides another good example of personality segmentation:

> Honda appears to target its Spree, Elite, and Aero motor scooters at the hip and trendy 14- to 22-year-old age group. But the company actually designs ads that appeal to a much broader personality group. One ad, for example, shows a delighted child bouncing up and down on his bed while the announcer says, "You've been trying to get there all your life." The ad reminds viewers of the

euphoric feelings they got when they broke away from authority and did things their parents told them not to. And it suggests that they can feel that way again riding a Honda scooter. So while Honda seems to be targeting young consumers, the ads appeal to trend setters and independent personalities in all age groups. In fact, over half of Honda's scooter sales are to young professionals and older buyers—fifteen percent are purchased by the over-50 group. Thus, Honda is appealing to the rebellious, independent kid in all of us.[7]

### Behavior Segmentation

In **behavior segmentation,** buyers are divided into groups based on their knowledge, attitudes, uses, or responses to a product. Many marketers believe that behavior variables are the best starting point for building market segments.

*Occasions* ▪ Buyers can be grouped according to occasions when they get the idea, make a purchase, or use a product. **Occasion segmentation** can help firms build up product usage. For example, orange juice is most often consumed at breakfast, but orange growers have promoted drinking orange juice as a cool and refreshing drink at other times of the day. On the other hand, Coca-Cola's "Coke in the Morning" advertising campaign attempts to increase Coke consumption by promoting the beverage as an early morning pick-me-up. Some holidays—Mother's Day and Father's Day, for example—were originally promoted partly to increase the sale of candy, flowers, cards, and other gifts. The Curtis Candy Company promoted the "trick-or-treat" custom at Halloween to encourage every home to have candy ready for eager little callers knocking at the door.

**behavior segmentation** Dividing a market into groups based on their knowledge, attitudes, uses, or responses to a product.

**occasion segmentation** Dividing the market into groups according to occasions when buyers get the idea, make a purchase, or use a product.

*Occasion segmentation: Greyhound advertises for the holidays.*

**benefit segmentation** Dividing the market into groups according to the different benefits that consumers seek from the product.

**Benefits Sought** ▪ A powerful form of segmentation is to group buyers according to the different *benefits* that they seek from the product. **Benefit segmentation** requires finding out the major benefits people look for in the product class, the kinds of people who look for each benefit, and the major brands that deliver each benefit. One of the best examples of benefit segmentation was conducted in the toothpaste market (see Table 8–2). Research found four benefit segments: those seeking economy, protection, cosmetic, and taste benefits. Each benefit group had special demographic, behavioral, and psychographic characteristics. For example, decay-prevention seekers tended to have large families, were heavy toothpaste users, and were conservative. Each segment also favored certain brands. Most current brands appeal to one of these segments—Crest Tartar Control toothpaste stresses protection and appeals to the family segment; Aim looks and tastes good and appeals to children.

Colgate-Palmolive used benefit segmentation to reposition its Irish Spring soap. Research showed three deodorant soap benefit segments: men who prefer lightly scented deodorant soap; women who want a mildly scented, gentle soap; and a mixed, mostly male segment that wanted a strongly scented, refreshing soap. The original Irish Spring soap did well with the last segment, but Colgate wanted to target the larger middle segment. Thus, it reformulated the soap and changed its advertising to give the product more of a family appeal.[8]

Thus, companies can use benefit segmentation to clarify which benefit segment they are appealing to, its characteristics, and the major competitive brands. They can also search for new benefits and launch brands that deliver them.[9]

**User Status** ▪ Many markets can be segmented into nonusers, ex-users, potential users, first-time users, and regular users of a product. High-market-share companies are particularly interested in attracting potential users, while smaller firms will try to attract regular users. Potential users and regular users may require different kinds of marketing appeals. For example, one study found that blood donors are low in self-esteem, low risk takers, and more concerned about their health; nondonors tend to be the opposite on all three dimensions. This fact suggests that social agencies should use different marketing approaches for keeping current donors and attracting new ones.[10]

**Usage Rate** ▪ Markets can also be segmented into light-, medium-, and heavy-user groups. Heavy users are often a small percentage of the market but account for a high percentage of total buying. Figure 8–2 shows usage rates for some

TABLE 8–2   Benefit Segmentation of the Toothpaste Market

| Benefit Segments | Demographics | Behavior | Psychographics | Favored Brands |
|---|---|---|---|---|
| Economy (low price) | Men | Heavy users | High autonomy, value oriented | Brands on sale |
| Medicinal (decay prevention) | Large families | Heavy users | Hypochondriac, conservative | Crest |
| Cosmetic (bright teeth) | Teens, young adults | Smokers | High sociability, active | Aqua-Fresh, Ultra Brite |
| Taste (good tasting) | Children | Spearmint lovers | High self-involvement, hedonistic | Colgate Aim |

*Source:* Adapted from Russell I. Haley, "Benefit Segmentation: A Decision Oriented Research Tool," *Journal of Marketing*, July 1963, pp. 30–35. See also Russell I. Haley, "Benefit Segmentation: Backwards and Forwards," *Journal of Advertising Research*, February-March 1984, pp. 19–25.

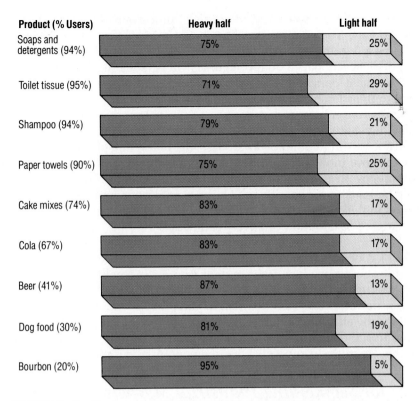

| Product (% Users) | Heavy half | Light half |
|---|---|---|
| Soaps and detergents (94%) | 75% | 25% |
| Toilet tissue (95%) | 71% | 29% |
| Shampoo (94%) | 79% | 21% |
| Paper towels (90%) | 75% | 25% |
| Cake mixes (74%) | 83% | 17% |
| Cola (67%) | 83% | 17% |
| Beer (41%) | 87% | 13% |
| Dog food (30%) | 81% | 19% |
| Bourbon (20%) | 95% | 5% |

FIGURE 8–2    Heavy and Light Users of Common Consumer Products

popular consumer products. Product users were divided into two groups—a light-user half and a heavy-user half—according to their buying rates for the specific products. Using beer as an example, the figure shows that 41 percent of the households studied buy beer. But the heavy-user half accounted for 87 percent of the beer consumed—almost seven times as much as the light-user half. Clearly, a beer company would prefer to attract one heavy user to its brand over several light users. Thus, most beer companies target the heavy beer drinker, using appeals such as Schaefer's "one beer to have when you're having more than one" or Miller Lite's "tastes great, less filling."

*Loyalty Status* ▪ A market can also be segmented by consumer loyalty. Consumers can be loyal to brands (Tide), stores (Sears), and companies (Ford). Buyers can be divided into groups according to their degree of loyalty. Some consumers are completely loyal—they buy one brand all the time. Others are somewhat loyal—they are loyal to two or three brands of a given product or favor one brand while sometimes buying others. Still other buyers show no loyalty to any brand. They either want something different each time they buy or always buy a brand on sale.

A company can learn a lot by analyzing loyalty patterns in its market. It should start by studying its own loyal customers. Colgate finds that its loyal buyers are more middle class, have larger families, and are more health conscious. These characteristics pinpoint the target market for Colgate. By studying its less-loyal buyers, the company can detect which brands are most competitive with its own. If many Colgate buyers also buy Crest, Colgate can attempt to improve its positioning against Crest, possibly by using direct-comparison advertising. By looking at customers who are shifting away from its brand, the company can learn about its marketing weaknesses. As for nonloyals, the company may attract them by putting its brand on sale.

*Buyer-Readiness Stage* ▪ At any time, people are in different stages of readiness to buy a product. Some people are unaware of the product; some are aware;

some are informed; some are interested; some want the product; and some intend to buy. The relative numbers make a big difference in designing the marketing program. For example, New York Institute of Technology recently began offering self-paced college courses via personal computer. Students can log onto their personal computers at any time and from any location to complete their lessons or "talk" to their teachers.[11] At first, potential students will be unaware of the new program. The initial marketing effort should thus employ high-awareness-building advertising and publicity using a simple message. If successful in building awareness, the marketing program should shift in order to move more people into the next readiness stage—say, interest in the program—by stressing the benefits of the "electronic university." Facilities should be readied for handling the large number of people who may be moved to enroll in the courses. In general, the marketing program must be adjusted to the changing distribution of buyer readiness.

*Attitude* ▪ People in a market can be enthusiastic, positive, indifferent, negative, or hostile about a product. Door-to-door workers in a political campaign use the voter's attitude to determine how much time to spend with the voter. They thank enthusiastic voters and remind them to vote; they spend little or no time trying to change the attitudes of negative and hostile voters. They reinforce those who are positive and try to win the vote of indifferent voters. In such marketing situations, attitudes can be effective segmentation variables.

## Bases for Segmenting Industrial Markets

Industrial markets can be segmented using many of the same variables used in consumer market segmentation. Industrial buyers can be segmented geographically or by benefits sought, user status, usage rate, loyalty status, readiness state,

*Industrial segmentation: Steelcase segments by industry, then has separate systems for dealing with large, geographically dispersed customers.*

and attitudes. Yet there are also some new variables. These include industrial customer *demographics* (industry, company size), *operating characteristics, purchasing approaches,* and *personal characteristics.*[12]

**measurability** The degree to which the size and purchasing power of a market segment can be measured.

By going after segments instead of the whole market, the company has a much better chance to deliver value to consumers and to receive maximum rewards for its close attention to segment consumer needs. Thus, Goodyear and other tire companies should decide which *industries* they want to serve. Manufacturers seeking original-equipment tires vary in their needs. Makers of luxury and high-performance cars want higher-grade tires than makers of economy models. And the tires needed by aircraft manufacturers must meet much higher safety standards than tires needed by farm tractor manufacturers.

Within the chosen industry, a company can further segment by *customer size* or *geographic location.* The company might set up separate systems for dealing with larger or multiple-location customers. For example, Steelcase, a major producer of office furniture, first segments customers into ten different industries, including banking, insurance, and electronics. Then, company salespeople work with independent Steelcase dealers to handle smaller, local or regional Steelcase customers in each segment. But many national, multiple-location customers, such as Exxon or IBM, have special needs that may reach beyond the scope of individual dealers. So Steelcase uses national accounts managers to help its dealer network handle its national accounts.

Within a certain target industry and customer size, the company can segment by *purchase approaches and criteria.* For example, government, university, and industrial laboratories typically differ in their purchase criteria for scientific instruments. Government labs need low prices (because they have difficulty getting funds to buy instruments) and service contracts (because they can easily get money to maintain instruments). University labs want equipment that needs little regular service because they do not have service people on their payrolls. Industrial labs need highly reliable equipment because they cannot afford downtime.

In general, industrial companies do not focus on one segmentation variable but use a combination of many. One aluminum company used a series of four major variables. It first looked at which *end-use* market to serve: automobile, residential, or beverage containers. Choosing the residential market, it determined the most attractive *product application:* semifinished material, building components, or mobile homes. Deciding to focus on building components, it next considered the best *customer size* to serve and chose large customers. The company further segmented the large-customer/building-components market. It saw customers falling into three *benefit* groups—those who bought on price, those who bought on service, and those who bought on quality. Because the company offered excellent service, it decided to concentrate on the service-seeking segment of the market.

## Requirements for Effective Segmentation

Clearly, there are many ways to segment a market. But not all segmentations are effective. For example, buyers of table salt could be divided into blond and brunette customers. But hair color obviously does not affect the purchase of salt. Furthermore, if all salt buyers buy the same amount of salt each month, believe all salt is the same, and want to pay the same price, the company would not benefit from segmenting this market.

To be useful, market segments must have the following characteristics:

□ **Measurability**—the degree to which the size and purchasing power of segments can be measured. Certain segmentation variables are difficult to measure. For example, there are 24 million left-handed people in the

**accessibility** The degree to which a market segment can be reached and served.

**substantiality** The degree to which a market segment is large or profitable enough.

**actionability** The degree to which effective programs can be designed for attracting and serving a given market segment.

**undifferentiated marketing** A market-coverage strategy in which a firm decides to ignore market segment differences and go after the whole market with one market offer.

U.S.—that almost equals the entire population of Canada. Yet few products are targeted toward this left-handed segment. The major problem may be that the segment is hard to identify and measure. There are no data on the demographics of lefties and the Census Bureau does not keep track of left-handedness in its surveys. Private data companies keep reams of statistics on other demographic segments, but not on left-handers.[13]

☐ **Accessibility**—the degree to which segments can be reached and served. Suppose a perfume company finds that heavy users of its brand are single women who stay out late and socialize a lot. Unless this group lives or shops at certain places and is exposed to certain media, they will be difficult to reach.

☐ **Substantiality**—the degree to which segments are large or profitable enough. A segment should be the largest possible homogeneous group worth going after with a tailored marketing program. It would not pay, for example, for an automobile manufacturer to develop cars for persons whose height is less than four feet.

☐ **Actionability**—the degree to which effective programs can be designed for attracting and serving segments. For example, although one small airline identified seven market segments, its staff was too small to develop separate marketing programs for each segment.

# MARKET TARGETING

Marketing segmentation reveals the market-segment opportunities facing the firm. The firm now has to decide how many segments to cover and how to identify the best ones.

## Three Market-Coverage Alternatives

The firm can adopt one of three market-coverage strategies: *undifferentiated marketing, differentiated marketing,* and *concentrated marketing.* These strategies are shown in Figure 8–3 and discussed below.

### Undifferentiated Marketing

Using an **undifferentiated marketing** strategy, a firm might decide to ignore market segment differences and go after the whole market with one market offer. It focuses on what is *common* in the needs of consumers rather than on what is *different.* It designs a product and marketing program that appeal to the most buyers. It relies on mass distribution and mass advertising. It aims to give the product a superior image in people's minds. An example of undifferentiated marketing is the Hershey Company's marketing some years ago of only one chocolate candy bar for everyone.

Undifferentiated marketing provides cost economies. The narrow product line keeps down production, inventory, and transportation costs. The undifferentiated advertising program keeps down advertising costs. The absence of segment marketing research and planning lowers the costs of marketing research and product management.

But most modern marketers have strong doubts about this strategy. It is difficult to develop a product or brand that will satisfy all consumers. Firms using undifferentiated marketing typically develop an offer aimed at the largest segments in the market. When several firms do this, there is heavy competition in the largest segments and less satisfaction in the smaller ones. The result is

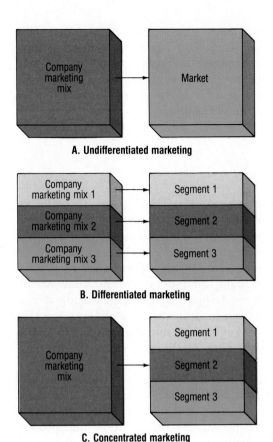

A. Undifferentiated marketing

B. Differentiated marketing

C. Concentrated marketing

FIGURE 8–3   Three Alternative
Market-Coverage Strategies

**differentiated marketing** A market-coverage strategy in which a firm decides to target several market segments and designs separate offers for each.

that the larger segments may be less profitable because they attract heavy competition. Recognition of this problem has resulted in firms being more interested in smaller segments of the market.

### Differentiated Marketing

Using a **differentiated marketing** strategy, the firm decides to target several market segments and designs separate offers for each. General Motors tries to produce a car for every "purse, purpose, and personality." By offering product and marketing variations, it hopes for higher sales and a stronger position within each market segment. It hopes that a stronger position in several segments will strengthen consumers' overall identification of the company with the product category. And it hopes for greater repeat purchasing because the company's offer better matches the customer's desire.

A growing number of firms have adopted differentiated marketing. A&P's segmentation strategy is a good example. A&P uses different food store formats to meet the needs of different customer segments:

> A&P's merchandising strategy attempts to provide a supermarket for every kind of shopper: stark black-and-white Futurestores, with the latest in gourmet departments and electronic services, for exclusive neighborhoods; conventional A&P's . . . for middle-class markets; and full-service, warehouse-style Sav-A-Centers, where shoppers have come to expect them.[14]

Differentiated marketing typically creates more total sales than undifferentiated marketing. Procter & Gamble gets a higher total market share with ten brands of laundry detergent than it could with only one. But it also increases the costs of doing business. Modifying a product to meet different market segment require-

**concentrated marketing** A
market-coverage strategy in which a
firm goes after a large share of one
or a few submarkets.

ments usually involves some R&D, engineering, or special tooling costs. It is usually more expensive to produce, say 10 units of 10 different products than 100 units of one product. Developing separate marketing plans for separate segments requires extra marketing research, forecasting, sales analysis, promotion planning, and channel management. And trying to reach different market segments with different advertising increases promotion costs. Thus, the company must weigh increased sales against increased costs when deciding on a differentiated marketing strategy.

### Concentrated Marketing

A third market-coverage strategy—**concentrated marketing**—is especially appealing when company resources are limited. Instead of going after a small share of a large market, the firm goes after a large share of one or a few submarkets. Many examples of concentrated marketing can be found. In computers, Zenith concentrates on the government and educational microcomputer segments, Cray focuses on larger, mainframe supercomputers, and Apollo targets the computer work station segment. Oshkosh Truck is the world's largest producer of airport rescue trucks and front-loading concrete mixers. Recycled Paper Products concentrates on the market for alternative greeting cards. And Vernor's concentrates on a narrow segment of the soft drink market (see Marketing Highlight 8–2).

Through concentrated marketing, the firm achieves a strong market position in the segments it serves because of its greater knowledge of segment needs and the special reputation it acquires. And it enjoys many operating economies because of specialization in production, distribution, and promotion. If the segment is chosen well, the firm can earn a high rate of return on its investment.[15]

At the same time, concentrated marketing involves higher than normal risks. The particular market segment can turn sour. For example, when young women suddenly stopped buying sportswear, it caused Bobbie Brooks's earnings to go deeply into the red. Or larger competitors may decide to enter the same segment. California Cooler's success in the wine cooler segment attracted many large competitors, causing the original owners to sell out to a larger company with more marketing resources. For these reasons, many companies prefer to diversify in several market segments.

### Choosing a Market-Coverage Strategy

Many factors need to be considered when choosing a market-coverage strategy. The best strategy depends on *company resources*. When the firm's resources are limited, concentrated marketing makes the most sense. The best strategy also depends on the degree of *product variability*. Undifferentiated marketing is more suited for uniform products such as grapefruit or steel. Products that can vary in design, such as cameras and automobiles, are more suited to differentiation or concentration. The *product's stage in the life cycle* must also be considered. When a firm introduces a new product, it is practical to launch only one version, and undifferentiated marketing or concentrated marketing makes the most sense. In the mature stage of the product life cycle, however, differentiated marketing starts making more sense. Another factor is *market variability*. If most buyers have the same tastes, buy the same amounts, and react the same way to marketing efforts, undifferentiated marketing is appropriate. Finally, *competitors' marketing strategies* are important. When competitors use segmentation, undifferentiated marketing can be suicidal. Conversely, when competitors use undifferentiated marketing, a firm can gain by using differentiated or concentrated marketing.

## VERNOR'S THRIVES IN THE SHADOWS OF THE GIANTS

You've probably never heard of *Vernor's Ginger Ale.* And if you tried it, you might not even think it tastes like ginger ale. Vernor's is "aged in oak," the company boasts, and "deliciously different." The caramel-colored soft drink is sweeter and smoother than other ginger ales you've tasted. But to many people in Detroit who grew up with Vernor's, there's nothing quite like it. They drink it cold and hot; morning, noon, and night; summer and winter; from the bottle and at the soda fountain counter. They like the way the bubbles tickle their noses. And they'll say you haven't lived until you've tasted a Vernor's float. To many, Vernor's even has some minor medicinal qualities—they use warm Vernor's to settle a child's upset stomach or to soothe a sore throat. To most Detroit adults, the familiar green and yellow packaging brings back many pleasant childhood memories.

*Vernors thrives in the shadows of the giants through concentrated marketing.*

The soft-drink industry is headed by two giants—Coca-Cola leads with a 40 percent market share and Pepsi challenges strongly with about 30 percent. Coke and Pepsi are the main combatants in the "soft-drink wars." They wage constant and pitched battles for retail shelf space. Their weapons include a steady stream of new products, heavy price discounts, an army of distributor salespeople, and huge advertising and promotion budgets.

A few "second-tier" brands—such brands as Dr Pepper, 7-Up, and Royal Crown—capture a combined 20 percent or so of the market. They challenge Coke and Pepsi in the smaller, non-cola segments. When Coke and Pepsi battle for shelf space, these second-tier brands often get squeezed. Coke and Pepsi set the ground rules, and if the smaller brands don't follow along, they risk being pushed out or gobbled up.

At the same time, a group of specialty producers who concentrate on small but loyal market segments fights for what's left of the market. While large in number, each of these small firms holds a tiny market share—usually less than one percent. Vernor's falls into this "all others" group, along with A&W root beer, Shasta sodas, Squirt, Faygo, Soho Natural Soda, Yoo-hoo, Dr Brown's Cream Soda, A. J. Canfield's Diet Chocolate Fudge Soda, and a dozen others. Whereas Dr Pepper and 7-Up merely get squeezed in the soft-drink wars, these small fry risk being crushed.

When you compare Vernor's with Coca-Cola, for example, you wonder how Vernor's survives. Coca-Cola spends more than $200 million a year advertising its soft drinks; Vernor's spends less than $1 million. Coke offers a long list of brands and brand versions—Coke, Coke Classic,

Cherry Coke, Diet Coke, Caffeine-Free Coke, Diet Cherry Coke, Caffeine-Free Diet Coke, Sprite, Tab, Mellow Yellow, Minute Maid soda, and others; Vernor's sells only two versions—original and diet. Coke's large distributor salesforce sways retailers with huge discounts and promotion allowances; Vernor's has only a small marketing budget and carries little clout with retailers. When you're lucky enough to find Vernor's at your local supermarket, it's usually tucked away on the bottom shelf with other specialty beverages. Even in Detroit, the company's stronghold, stores usually give Vernor's only a few shelf-facings, compared with 50 or 100 facings for the many Coca-Cola brands.

Yet Vernor's does more than survive—it thrives! How? Instead of going head-to-head with the bigger companies in the major soft-drink segments, Vernor's niches in the market: It concentrates on serving the special needs of loyal Vernor's drinkers. Vernor's knows that it could never seriously challenge Coca-Cola for a large share of the soft-drink market. But it also knows that Coca-Cola could never create another Vernor's ginger ale—at least not in the minds of Vernor's drinkers. As long as Vernor's keeps these special customers happy, it can capture a small but profitable share of the market. And "small" in this market is nothing to sneeze at—a one percent market share equals $380 million in retail sales! Thus, through *concentrated marketing,* Vernor's prospers in the shadows of the soft-drink giants.

*Sources:* See Betsy Bauer, "Giants Loom Larger Over Pint-Sized Soft-Drink Firms," *USA Today,* May 27, 1986, p. 5B; and Scott Ticer, "Max Headroom Speaks the Dreaded 'P-Word,'" *Business Week,* March 16, 1987, pp. 40–41.

**product position** The way the
product is defined by consumers on
important attributes—the place the
product occupies in consumers'
minds relative to competing
products.

## *Identifying Attractive Market Segments*

Suppose a firm decides on undifferentiated or concentrated marketing. It must now identify the most attractive segments to target. The company first needs to collect data on various market segments. The data would include current dollar sales, projected sales-growth rates, expected profit margins, strength of competition, and marketing channel needs. Often, the company will want to target segments with large current sales, a high growth rate, a high profit margin, weak competition, and simple marketing channel requirements. Usually, no segments will be best in all these areas, and trade-offs will have to be made. Moreover, the largest, fastest-growing segments are not always the most attractive ones for every company. The largest segment is not attractive unless the company has the skills and resources to serve its needs effectively.

After the company assesses the characteristics and requirements of the various segments, it must ask which segments best fit its own business strengths. For example, the home computer market is large and very attractive to Zenith Data Systems, but the company has had little experience selling computers to consumers and lacks the retail distribution and promotion resources needed to challenge IBM and Apple directly in the home segment. On the other hand, Zenith has developed special products and a separate salesforce for the government and higher education market segments. Thus, the company focuses on less-crowded segments in which it has the necessary business strengths to succeed. It targets the segments in which it has the greatest strategic advantage.

# MARKET POSITIONING

Once a company has decided which segments of the market it will enter, it must decide what "positions" it wants to occupy in those segments.

## *What Is Market Positioning?*

A product's **position** is the way the product is *defined by consumers* on important attributes—the place the product occupies in consumers' minds relative to competing products. Thus, Tide is positioned as an all-purpose family detergent; Era is positioned as a concentrated liquid; Cheer is positioned as the detergent for all temperatures. Hyundai and Subaru are positioned on economy; Mercedes and Cadillac are positioned on luxury; Porsche and BMW are positioned on performance.[16]

Consumers are overloaded with information about products and services. They cannot reevaluate products every time they make a buying decision. To simplify buying decision making, they organize products into categories—they "position" products, services, and companies in their minds. A product's position is the complex set of perceptions, impressions, and feelings that consumers hold for the product as compared with competing products. Consumers position products with or without the help of marketers. But marketers do not want to leave their products' positions to chance. They *plan* positions that will give their products the greatest advantage in selected target-markets, and they *design* marketing mixes to create the planned positions.

## *Positioning Strategies*

Marketers can follow several positioning strategies.[17] They can position products on specific *product attributes*—Ford Festiva advertises its low price; Saab promotes performance. Products can also be positioned on the needs they fill or the *benefits* they offer—Crest reduces cavities; Aim tastes good. Or products can be positioned according to *usage occasions*—in the summer, Gatorade can be positioned as a beverage for replacing athletes' body fluids; in the winter, it can be positioned as the drink to use when the doctor recommends plenty of liquids. Another approach is to position the product for certain classes of *users*—Johnson & Johnson improved the market share for its baby shampoo from 3 to 14 percent by repositioning the product as one for adults who wash their hair often and need a gentle shampoo.

A product can also be positioned directly *against a competitor*. For example, in ads for their personal computers, Compaq and Tandy have directly compared their products with IBM personal computers. In its famous "We're number two, so we try harder" campaign, Avis successfully positioned itself against larger Hertz. A product may also be positioned *away from competitors*—7-Up became the number-three soft drink when it was positioned as the "un-cola," the fresh and thirst-quenching alternative to Coke and Pepsi. Barbasol television ads position the company's shaving cream and other products as "great toiletries for a lot less money."

Finally, the product can be positioned for different *product classes*. For example, some margarines are positioned against butter, others against cooking oils. Camay hand soap is positioned with bath oils rather than with soap. Marketers often use a *combination* of these positioning strategies. Thus, Johnson

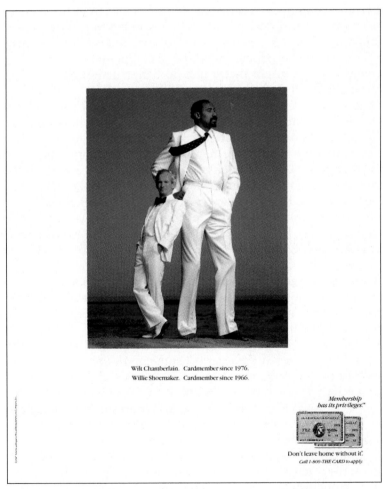

*Positioning away from competitors: American Express positions itself as a card for special people.*

**competitive advantage** An advantage over competitors gained by offering consumers lower prices than competitors or by providing more benefits that justify higher prices.

& Johnson's Affinity shampoo is positioned as a hair conditioner for women over 40 (product class *and* user). Arm & Hammer baking soda has been positioned as a deodorizer for refrigerators and garbage disposals (product class *and* usage situation).

## Choosing and Implementing a Positioning Strategy

Some firms will find it easy to choose their positioning strategy. For example, a firm well known for quality in certain segments will go for this position in a new segment if there are enough buyers seeking quality. But in many cases, two or more firms will go after the same position. Then, each will have to find other ways to set itself apart, such as promising "high quality for a lower cost" or "high quality with more technical service." That is, each firm must build a unique bundle of competitive advantages that appeal to a substantial group within the segment.

The positioning task consists of three steps: identifying a set of possible competitive advantages upon which to build a position, selecting the right competitive advantages, and effectively communicating and delivering the chosen position to the market.

A company differentiates itself from competitors by bundling competitive advantages. It gains **competitive advantage** either by offering consumers lower prices than competitors or by providing more benefits to justify higher prices.[18] Thus, the company must do a better job than competitors of keeping costs and prices down or of offering better value to consumers. The company has to compare its prices and products with those of competitors and look for possible improvements. To the extent that it can do better than its competitors, it has achieved a competitive advantage.

Not every company will find many opportunities for gaining competitive advantage. Some companies will find many minor advantages that are easily copied by competitors and therefore highly perishable. The solution for these companies is to keep identifying new potential advantages and introducing them one by one to keep competitors off-balance. These companies do not expect to gain a single major permanent advantage, but rather many minor ones that can be introduced to win market share over a period of time.

Suppose a company is fortunate enough to discover several potential competitive advantages. It must now choose the ones upon which it will build its positioning strategy. Some competitive advantages can be quickly ruled out because they are too slight, too costly to develop, or too inconsistent with the company's profile. In general, the company wants to develop those competitive advantages that are most important to consumers, that fit within its mission and resources, that give it the greatest advantage over competitors, and that competitors will find hardest to match.

Once they have chosen a position, companies must take strong steps to communicate and deliver it to target consumers. All the company's marketing mix efforts must support the positioning strategy. Positioning the company calls for concrete action, not just talk. Thus, if the company decides to build a position on better service, it should hire and train more service people, find retailers who have a good reputation for service, and develop sales and advertising messages that broadcast its superior service.

The company's positioning decisions determine who its competitors will be. When setting its positioning strategy, the company should look at its competitive strengths and weaknesses as compared with those of competitors and select a position in which it can attain a strong competitive advantage.

Sellers can take three approaches to a market. *Mass marketing* is the decision to mass-produce and mass-distribute one product and attempt to attract all kinds of buyers. *Product variety marketing* is the decision to produce two or more market offers differentiated in style, features, quality, or sizes, designed to offer variety to the market and to set the seller's products apart from competitors' products. *Target marketing* is the decision to identify the different groups that make up a market and to develop products and marketing mixes for selected target markets. Sellers today are moving away from mass marketing and product differentiation toward target marketing because this approach is more helpful in spotting market opportunities and developing more effective products and marketing mixes.

The key steps in target marketing are market segmentation, market targeting, and market positioning. *Market segmentation* is the act of dividing a market into distinct groups of buyers who might merit separate products or marketing mixes. The marketer tries different variables to see which give the best segmentation opportunities. For consumer marketing, the major segmentation variables are geographic, demographic, psychographic, and behavioral. Industrial markets can be segmented by industrial consumer demographics, operating characteristics, purchasing approaches, and personal characteristics. The effectiveness of segmentation analysis depends on finding segments that are *measurable, accessible, substantial,* and *actionable.*

Next, the seller has to target the best market segments. The first decision in choosing a market-coverage strategy is how many segments to cover. The seller can ignore segment differences *(undifferentiated marketing),* develop different market offers for several segments *(differentiated marketing),* or go after one or a few market segments *(concentrated marketing).* Much depends on company resources, product and market variability, product life-cycle stage, and competitive marketing strategies. If the company decides to enter one segment, which one should it be? Market segments can be evaluated on their objective attractiveness and on company business strengths needed to succeed in given segments.

Once a company has decided what segments to enter, it must decide on its *market-positioning* strategy—on what positions to occupy in its chosen segments. It can position its products on specific product attributes, according to usage occasion, for certain classes of users, or by product class. It can position against competitors or away from competitors. The positioning task consists of three steps: identifying a set of possible competitive advantages upon which to build a position, selecting the right competitive advantages, and effectively communicating and delivering the chosen position to the market.

# QUESTIONS FOR DISCUSSION

1. Describe how Ford has moved from mass marketing to product-variety marketing to target marketing. Can you give examples of other companies whose marketing approaches have evolved over time.

2. What variables are used in market segmentation for beer? Are the same variables used to segment the soft-drink market?

3. If you were manager of a mass-transit company, how would you use benefit segmentation to appeal to different groups of potential riders?

4. Some industrial suppliers make above-average profits by offering service, selection, and reliability—at a premium price. How do these suppliers segment the market to find customers willing to pay more for these benefits?

5. An article in *Advertising Age* reported that baseball fans prefer chocolate ice cream if their favorite team in the 1950s was the Dodgers, vanilla if their team was the Yankees, and strawberry or coffee if they rooted for the Giants. Does this relationship indicate that team preference could be a segmentation variable in marketing ice cream?

6. Are some characteristics of market segments more important than others or, are measurability, accessibility, substantiality, and actionability equally important? Why?

7. Explain which of the following marketers is likely to use undifferentiated marketing: (a) a retired home economics teacher who opens a clothing store, (b) an agricultural cooperative that promotes the use of potatoes and onions, (c) a foreign manufacturer that begins exporting automobiles to the United States, (d) an accounting firm that offers walk-in tax consulting.

8. What roles do product attributes and perceptions of attributes play in positioning a product? Can an attribute common to several competing brands contribute to a successful positioning strategy?

9. A recently developed fabric has the look and feel of cotton but is comfortably stretchable. What segment would you target with a line of casual pants made from this fabric? How would you position these pants?

# REFERENCES

1. Thomas Moore, "Different Folks, Different Strokes," *Fortune,* September 16, 1985, p. 65; and Michael Oneal, "Attack of the Bug Killers," *Business Week,* May 16, 1988, p. 81.

2. See Jesse Snyder and Raymond Serafin, "Auto Makers Set New Ad Strategy to Reach Women," *Advertising Age,* September 23, 1985, pp. 3, 86; Julie Liesse Erickson, "Marketing to Women: It's Tough to Keep Up with Changes," *Advertising Age,* March 7, 1988, p. S1; and Raymond Serafin, "Carmakers Step Up Chase for Women," *Advertising Age,* May 16, 1988, p. 76.

3. See Pat Grey Thomas, "Marketing to the Affluent," *Advertising Age,* March 16, 1987, p. S-1.

4. Steve Lawrence, "The Green in Blue-Collar Retailing," *Fortune,* May 27, 1985, pp. 74–77; and Dean Foust, "The Family Feud at Family Dollar Stores," *Business Week,* September 21, 1987, pp. 32–33.

5. Bickley Townsend, "Psychographic Glitter and Gold," *American Demographics,* November 1985, p. 22.

6. For a detailed discussion of personality and buyer behavior, see Leon G. Schiffman and Leslie Lazar Kanuk, *Consumer Behavior,* 3rd ed. (Englewood Cliffs, NJ: Prentice Hall, 1987), Chap. 4.

7. See Laurie Freeman and Cleveland Horton, "Spree: Honda's Scooters Ride the Cutting Edge," *Advertising Age,* September 5, 1985, pp. 3, 35.

8. See Schiffman and Kanuk, *Consumer Behavior,* p. 48.

9. For more reading on benefit segmentation, see Russell I. Haley, "Benefit Segmentation: Backwards and Forwards," *Journal of Advertising Research,* February-March 1984, pp. 19–25; and Russell I. Haley, "Benefit Segmentation—20 Years Later," *Journal of Consumer Marketing,* 1 (1984), 5–14.

10. See John J. Burnett, "Psychographic and Demographic Characteristics of Blood Donors," *Journal of Consumer Research,* June 1981, pp. 62-66.

11. See Mark Ivey, "Long-Distance Learning Gets an 'A' at Last," *Business Week,* May 9, 1988, pp. 108–10.

12. See Thomas V. Bonoma and Benson P. Shapiro, *Segmenting the Industrial Market* (Lexington, MA: Lexington Books, 1983).

13. See Joe Schwartz, "Southpaw Strategy," *American Demographics,* June 1988, p. 61.

14. Bill Saporito, "Just How Good Is the Great A&P?" *Fortune,* March 16, 1987, pp. 92–93.

15. See Stuart Gannes, "The Riches in Market Niches," *Fortune,* April 27, 1987, pp. 227–30.

16. For more reading on positioning, see Yoram Wind, "New Twists for Some Old Tricks," *The Wharton Magazine,* Spring 1980, pp. 34–39; David A. Aaker and J. Gary Shansby, "Positioning Your Product," *Business Horizons,* May-June 1982, pp. 56–62; and Regis McKenna, "Playing for Position," *Inc.,* April 1985, pp. 92–97.

17. See Wind, "New Twists," p. 36; and Aaker and Shansby, "Positioning Your Product," pp. 57–58.

18. See Michael Porter, *Competitive Advantage* (New York: Free Press, 1985), Chap. 2. For a good discussion of the concept of competitive advantage and methods for assessing it, see George S. Day and Robin Wensley, "Assessing Advantage: A Framework for Diagnosing Competitive Superiority," *Journal of Marketing,* April 1988, pp. 1–20.

# GATORADE: THIRSTING FOR COMPETITIVE POSITIONING

According to Larry Dykstra, manager of marketing research for Quaker Oats, the development of a focused positioning for Gatorade has allowed the company to target core users and identify secondary markets. Before Quaker acquired the beverage in 1983, Gatorade's previous owner had promoted it by portraying users as competitive athletes, adult men, teens, and caricatures of athletes.

"When we acquired Gatorade," recalls Dykstra, "it was a poorly positioned brand, with a lack of consistent focus." This position stood in contrast with the way current users were defined. "There was no message on the uses of this product or under which circumstances and occasions it was supposed to be used."

When Quaker looked at marketing research, Dykstra says the company found that Gatorade's main users were men age 19-44, that they understood the product, had a good perception of what it did, and knew when to drink it and how to use it.

Since Gatorade had been developed and marketed primarily in the South, Quaker wanted to find out if there was an opportunity to market the drink in other areas. A study of attitudes determined that the target could be expanded geographically. "We felt, based on research, that we could take a narrow, solid positioning of the product that is consistent with southern users and market the product in the North," Dykstra says.

Gatorade was positioned for physical activity enthusiasts as a drink to quench their thirst and replenish minerals lost during exercise better than other beverages did. Subsequent advertising in 1984 centered around these attributes.

In 1985, the company moved away from this core positioning by trying to joke about the product's competitive heritage—a strategy that failed. [TV ads showed people in different activity situations trying to make sports jokes.] A decision was made to go back to narrow positioning in 1986.

"In 1987, we focused in on our primary target, but there have been refinements," Dykstra explains. "We've tried to portray users as accomplished but not professional athletes." Although the drink is perceived as a "serious beverage, the ads have added a fun component by showing people enjoying it together. "We tried to show people who didn't alienate customers, but also people they could aspire to be like."

An effort also was made to portray people's *motivations* for using the product. A computer graphic that portrays thirst quenching was introduced—one which, according to Dykstra, came "across so strong we've started to change the language."

But being well-focused and consistent in developing the product over time can create other problems. "Because Gatorade is narrowly positioned in terms of users and user occasions," explains Dykstra, "growth opportunities are probably limited. So how can we go about identifying new opportunities?"

The answer was to look for opportunities consistent with the product's imagery: "About two years ago," says Dykstra, "we conducted a large study that included a sample of current users and other possible targets, such as older men and mothers with young children." Quaker also looked in terms of a vertical target: Should it target Gatorade toward runners or basketball players? "We built a large enough attitudinal study so we could look at people who considered themselves basketball players separate from those who considered themselves to be aerobic athletes. In the user section, we asked people, 'The next 10 times you're in this specific situation, are you going to use Gatorade?'"

Dykstra also felt Quaker could target mothers with active children and found this group a large market that could be targeted separately. Additionally, the company is attempting to market the

product year-round. "We found we were promoting our own seasonality, so we wanted to develop some continuity," says Dykstra.

Quaker has most recently started marketing the product to Hispanics. "We felt we could position Gatorade to them," explains Dykstra, "because they are a large growing segment, sports is important to them, and their populations are centered in areas where its presence is already well developed." An ad has been developed for this purpose and is currently being tested. "We made an effort to do it right and not offend this group," Dykstra adds. Based on qualitative findings, the TV spot's approach is conservative and narrow, focuses on sports, and includes family members. "We showed it to several focus groups and made sure the benefits translated." At the same time, efforts were made to ensure that the changes and refinements would not alienate the core users and secondary targets.

*Questions*

1. What are the major variables that might be used to segment Gatorade's consumer market?

2. Define the core and secondary targets for Gatorade.

3. Describe the position of Gatorade as defined by consumers when the brand was acquired by Quaker Oats in 1983. Trace the changes in positioning strategy from the acquisition in 1983 until 1987.

4. Evaluate the pros and cons of the current multi-segment targeting strategy.

5. Propose a marketing strategy for penetrating the pre-teen market.

*Source:* Reprinted from "Quaker Looks to Expand Market for Gatorade," *Marketing News,* Vol. 22, January 4, 1988, pp. 38, 39, published by the American Marketing Association.

# 9

# Designing Products: Products, Brands, Packaging, and Services

## CHAPTER OBJECTIVES

After reading this chapter, you should be able to

1. Define *product* and the major classifications of consumer and industrial products
2. Explain why companies use brands and identify the major branding decisions
3. Describe the roles of product packaging and labeling
4. Explain the decisions companies make when developing product lines and mixes

Each year, Revlon sells more than $1 billion worth of cosmetics, toiletries, and fragrances to consumers around the world. Its many successful perfume products make Revlon number one in the popular-price segment of the $3.7 billion fragrance market. In one sense, Revlon's perfumes are no more than careful mixtures of oils and chemicals that have nice scents. But Revlon knows that when it sells perfume, it sells much more than fragrant fluids—it sells what the fragrances will do for the women who use them.

Of course, a perfume's scent contributes to its success or failure. Fragrance marketers agree: "No smell; no sell." Most new aromas are developed by elite "perfumers" at one of 50 or so select "fragrance houses." Perfume is shipped from the fragrance houses in big, ugly oil drums—hardly the stuff of which dreams are made! Although a $180-an-ounce bottle of perfume may cost no more than $10 to produce, to perfume consumers the product is much more than a few dollars worth of ingredients and a pleasing smell.

Many things beyond the ingredients and scent add to a perfume's allure. In fact, when Revlon designs a new perfume, the scent may be the *last* element developed. Revlon first researches women's feelings about themselves and their relationships with others. It then develops and tests new perfume concepts that match women's changing values, desires, and life styles. When Revlon finds a promising new concept, it creates a scent to fit it.

Revlon's research in the early 1970s showed that women were feeling more competitive with men and that they were striving to find individual identities. For this new woman of the 1970s, Revlon created Charlie—the first of the "life-style" perfumes. Thousands of women adopted Charlie as a bold statement of independence, and it quickly became the world's best-selling perfume.

In the late 1970s, Revlon research showed a shift in women's attitudes—"women had made the equality point, which Charlie addressed. Now women were hungering for an expression of femininity." The Charlie girls had grown up; they now wanted perfumes that were subtle rather than shocking. Thus, Revlon shifted Charlie's position away from "life style" and toward "femininity and romance." It also launched a perfume for the woman of the 1980s—Jontue—which was positioned on a theme of romance.

A perfume's *name* is an important product attribute. Revlon uses such names as Charlie, Fleurs de Jontue, Ciara, and Scoundrel to create images that support each perfume's positioning. Competitors offer perfumes with such names as Obsession, Passion, Opium, Poison, Joy, White Linen, Youth Dew, and Eternity. These names suggest that the perfumes will do something more than just make you smell better. Oscar de la Renta's Ruffles perfume *began* as a name, one chosen because it created images of whimsy, youth, glamour, and femininity—all well suited to a target market of young, stylish women. Only later was a scent selected to go with the product's name and positioning.

Revlon must also carefully *package* its perfumes. To consumers, the bottle and package are the most real symbol of the perfume and its image. Bottles must feel comfortable and be easy to handle, and they must display well in stores. Most importantly, they must support the perfume's concept and image.

So when a woman buys perfume, she buys much, much more than just fragrant fluids. The perfume's image, its promises, its scent, its name and package, the company that makes it, the stores that sell it—all become a part of the total perfume product. When Revlon sells perfume, it sells more than just the tangible product—it sells life style, self-expression, and exclusivity; achievement, success, and status; femininity, romance, passion, and fantasy; memories, hopes, and dreams.[1]

---

**product** Anything that can be offered to a market for attention, acquisition, use, or consumption that might satisfy a want or need.

**core product** The problem-solving services or core benefits that consumers are really buying when they obtain a product.

**actual product** A product's parts, styling, features, brand name, packaging, and other attributes that combine to deliver core product benefits.

Clearly, perfume is more than just perfume when Revlon sells it. Revlon's great success in the rough-and-tumble fragrance world comes from developing an innovative product concept. An effective product concept is the first step in marketing mix planning.

This chapter begins with a deceptively simple question: *What is a product?* We will then look at ways to classify products in consumer and industrial markets and look for links between types of products and types of marketing strategies. Next, we will see that each product involves several decisions that go beyond basic product design—such as *branding, packaging* and *labeling,* and *product-support services.* Finally, we will move from decisions about individual products to decisions about building product lines and product mixes.

# WHAT IS A PRODUCT?

A Kennex tennis racquet, a Supercuts haircut, a Bruce Springsteen concert, a Hawaiian vacation, a GMC truck, Head skis, and a telephone answering service are all products. We define *product* as follows: A **product** is anything that can be offered to a market for attention, acquisition, use, or consumption that might satisfy a want or need; it includes physical objects, services, persons, places, organizations, and ideas.[2]

Product planners need to think about the product on three levels. The most basic level is the **core product,** which addresses the question, *What is the buyer really buying?* As illustrated in Figure 9–1, the core product stands at the center of the total product. It consists of the problem-solving services or core benefits that consumers obtain when they buy a product. A woman buying lipstick buys more than lip color. Charles Revson of Revlon saw this early: "In the factory, we make cosmetics; in the store, we sell hope." Theodore Levitt has pointed out that buyers "do not buy quarter-inch drills; they buy quarter-inch holes." Thus, when designing products, marketers must first define the core of *benefits* the product will provide to consumers.

The product planner must next build an **actual product** around the core product. Actual products may have as many as five characteristics: a *quality level, features, styling,* a *brand name,* and *packaging.* For example, Sony's Handycam Camcorder is an actual product. Its name, parts, styling, features, packaging,

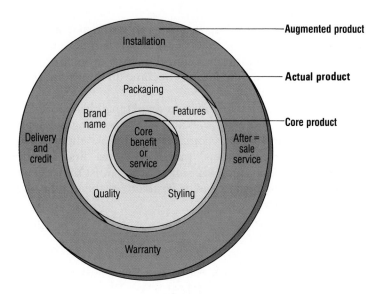

FIGURE 9–1   Three Levels of Product

and other attributes have all been carefully combined to deliver the core benefit—a convenient, high-quality way to capture important moments.

Finally, the product planner must build an **augmented product** around the core and actual products by offering additional consumer services and benefits. Sony must offer more than a camcorder—it must provide consumers with a complete solution to their picture-taking problems. Thus, when consumers buy a Sony Handycam, they get more than just the camcorder itself. Sony

*Care, tangible, and augmented product: consumers perceive this Sony Camcorder as a complex bundle of tangible and intangible features and services that deliver a core benefit—a convenient, high-quality way to capture important moments.*

**nondurable goods** Tangible goods normally consumed in one or a few uses.

**durable goods** Tangible goods that normally survive many uses.

**services** Activities, benefits, or satisfactions that are offered for sale.

**consumer goods** Goods bought by final consumers for personal consumption.

**convenience goods** Consumer goods that a customer usually buys frequently, immediately, and with a minimum of comparison and buying effort.

and its dealers might also give buyers a warranty on parts and workmanship, free lessons on how to use the camcorder, quick repair services when needed, and a toll-free telephone number to call if they have problems or questions. To the consumer, all of these augmentations become an important part of the total product.

Thus, a product is more than a simple set of tangible features. In fact, some products (a haircut or a doctor's exam) have no tangible features at all. Consumers tend to see products as complex bundles of benefits that satisfy their needs. When developing products, marketers must first identify the *core* consumer needs that the product will satisfy. They must then design the *actual* product and find ways to *augment* it in order to create the bundle of benefits that will best satisfy consumers.

# PRODUCT CLASSIFICATIONS

In seeking marketing strategies for individual products, marketers have developed several product-classification schemes based on product characteristics. We will now examine these schemes and characteristics.

## Durable Goods, Nondurable Goods, and Services

Products can be classified into three groups according to their *durability* or *tangibility*.[3] **Nondurable goods** are tangible goods normally consumed in one or a few uses: Examples include beer, soap, and salt. **Durable goods** are tangible goods that normally survive many uses: Examples include refrigerators, machine tools, and clothing. **Services** are activities, benefits, or satisfactions that are offered for sale; examples include haircuts and repairs. (Because of the growing importance of services in our society, we will look at them more closely in Chapter 19.)

## Consumer Goods

**Consumer goods** are those bought by final consumers for personal consumption. Marketers usually classify these goods based on *consumer shopping habits*. Consumer goods include *convenience, shopping, specialty,* and *unsought goods* (see Figure 9–2).[4]

**Convenience goods** are consumer goods that the customer usually buys frequently, immediately, and with a minimum of comparison and buying effort. Examples include tobacco products, soap, and newspapers. Convenience goods can be further divided into *staples, impulse goods,* and *emergency goods. Staples* are goods that consumers buy on a regular basis, such as Heinz ketchup, Crest toothpaste, or Ritz crackers. *Impulse goods* are purchased with little planning or search effort. These goods are normally available in many places because

FIGURE 9–2 Classification of Consumer Goods

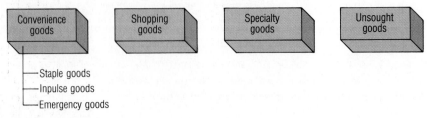

consumers seldom seek them out. Thus, candy bars and magazines are placed next to checkout counters because shoppers may not otherwise think of buying them. *Emergency goods* are purchased when a need is urgent—umbrellas during a rainstorm, boots and shovels during the first winter snowstorm. Manufacturers of emergency goods will place them in many outlets to avoid losing a sale when the customer needs these goods.

**Shopping goods** are consumer goods that the customer, in the process of selection and purchase, usually compares on such bases as suitability, quality, price, and style. Examples include furniture, clothing, used cars, and major appliances. Shopping goods can be divided into *uniform* and *non-uniform* goods. The buyer sees uniform shopping goods as similar in quality but different enough in price to justify shopping comparisons. The seller has to "talk price" to the buyer. But in shopping for clothing, furniture, and other nonuniform goods, product features are often more important to the consumer than the price. If the buyer wants a new suit, the cut, fit, and look are likely to be more important than small price differences. The seller of nonuniform shopping goods must therefore carry a wide assortment to satisfy individual tastes and must have well-trained salespeople to give information and advice to customers.

**Specialty goods** are consumer goods with unique characteristics or brand identification for which a significant group of buyers is willing to make a special purchase effort. Examples include specific brands and types of cars, stereo components, photographic equipment, and men's suits. A Jaguar, for example, is a specialty good because buyers are usually willing to travel great distances to buy one. Buyers do not normally compare specialty goods. They invest only the

**shopping goods** Consumer goods that the customer when buying, usually compares on such bases as suitability, quality, price, and style.

**specialty goods** Consumer goods with unique characteristics or brand identification for which a significant group of buyers is willing to make a special purchase effort.

*Types of consumer products: convenience, shopping, and specialty goods.*

time needed to reach dealers carrying the wanted products. Although dealers do not need convenient locations, they must let buyers know their locations.

**Unsought goods** are consumer goods that the consumer either does not know about or knows about but does not normally think of buying. New products such as smoke detectors and compact disc players are unsought goods until the consumer is made aware of them through advertising. Classic examples of known but unsought goods are life insurance and encyclopedias. By their very nature, unsought goods require a lot of advertising, personal selling, and other marketing efforts. Some of the most advanced personal-selling methods have developed out of the challenge of selling unsought goods.

## Industrial Goods

**Industrial goods** are those bought by individuals and organizations for further processing or for use in conducting a business. Thus, the distinction between a consumer good and an industrial good is based on the *purpose* for which the product is purchased. If a consumer buys a lawn mower for use around the home, the lawn mower is a consumer good. If the same consumer buys the same lawn mower for use in a landscaping business, the lawn mower is an industrial good.

Industrial goods can be classified according to how they enter the production process and according to what they cost. There are three groups: *materials and parts, capital items,* and *supplies and services* (see Figure 9–3).

**Materials and parts** are industrial goods that enter the manufacturer's product completely, either through further processing or as components. They fall into two classes: raw materials and manufactured materials and parts. *Raw materials* include farm products (wheat, cotton, livestock, fruits and vegetables) and natural products (fish, lumber, crude petroleum, iron ore). Farm products are supplied by many small producers who turn them over to marketing intermediaries who process and sell them. Natural products usually have great bulk and low unit value and require lots of transportation to move them from producer to user. There are fewer and larger producers, who tend to market them directly to industrial users.

*Manufactured materials and parts* include component materials (iron, yarn, cement, wires) and component parts (small motors, tires, castings). Component materials are usually processed further—for example, pig iron is made into steel and yarn is woven into cloth. Component parts enter the finished product completely with no further change in form, as when small motors are put into vacuum cleaners and tires are added to automobiles. Most manufactured materials and parts are sold directly to industrial users. Price and service are the major marketing factors, and branding and advertising tend to be less important.

**Capital items** are industrial goods that enter the finished product partly. They include two groups: installations and accessory equipment. *Installations* consist of buildings (factories, offices) and fixed equipment (generators, drill

FIGURE 9–3 Classification of Industrial Goods

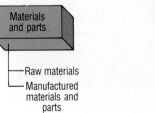

- Raw materials
- Manufactured materials and parts

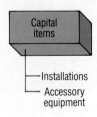

- Installations
- Accessory equipment

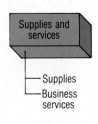

- Supplies
- Business services

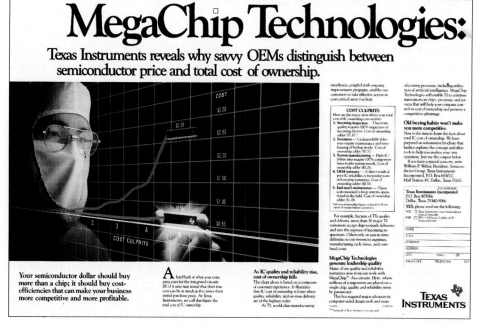
*Component parts: Texas Instruments markets semiconductor chips to manufacturers; price and reliability are important marketing factors.*

presses, large computers, elevators). Because installations are major purchases, they are usually bought directly from the producer after a long decision period.

*Accessory equipment* includes portable factory equipment and tools (hand tools, lift trucks) and office equipment (typewriters, desks). These products do not become part of the finished product. They have a shorter life than installations and simply aid in the production process. Most accessory equipment sellers use middlemen because the market is spread out geographically, the buyers are numerous, and the orders are small.

**Supplies and services** are industrial goods that do not enter the finished product at all. *Supplies* include operating supplies (lubricants, coal, typing paper, pencils) and maintenance and repair items (paint, nails, brooms). Supplies are the convenience goods of the industrial field because they are usually purchased with a minimum effort or comparison. *Business services* include maintenance and repair services (window cleaning, typewriter repair), and business advisory services (legal, management consulting, advertising). These services are usually supplied under contract. Maintenance services are often provided by small producers, and repair services are often available from the manufacturers of the original equipment.

Thus, we see that a product's characteristics will have a major affect on marketing strategy. At the same time, marketing strategy will also depend on such factors as the product's stage in its life cycle, the number of competitors, the degree of market segmentation, and the condition of the economy.

# INDIVIDUAL PRODUCT DECISIONS

We will now look at decisions relating to the development and marketing of individual products. We will look at decisions about *product attributes, branding, packaging,* and *labeling.*

**product quality** The ability of a product to perform its functions; it includes the product's overall durability, reliability, precision, ease of operation and repair, and other valued attributes.

## Product Attribute Decisions

Developing a product involves defining the benefits that the product will offer. These benefits are communicated and delivered by tangible product attributes, such as *quality*, *features*, and *design*. Decisions about these attributes will greatly affect consumer reactions toward a product. Below, we discuss the issues involved in each decision.

### Product Quality

In developing a product, the manufacturer has to choose a quality level that will support the product's position in the target market. Quality is one of the marketer's major positioning tools. **Product quality** stands for the ability of a product to perform its functions. It includes the product's overall durability, reliability, precision, ease of operation and repair, and other valued attributes. Some of these attributes can be measured objectively. From a marketing point of view, however, quality should be measured in terms of buyers' perceptions.

To some companies, improving quality means using better quality control to reduce defects that annoy consumers. But *strategic* quality management means more than this. It means gaining an edge over competitors by offering products that better serve consumers' needs and preferences for quality. As one analyst suggests, "Quality is not simply a problem to be solved; it is a competitive opportunity."[5]

The theme of quality is now attracting stronger interest among consumers and companies. A recent study of 45 fast-growing, profitable companies showed that most of them compete by marketing products that provide more value to consumers rather than ones that cost less.[6] American consumers have been impressed with the product quality in Japanese automobiles and electronics

*Product quality themes are now attracting stronger interest among consumers and companies.*

and in European automobiles, clothing, and food. Many consumers are favoring apparel that lasts and stays in style longer instead of trendy clothes. They are more interested in fresh and nutritious foods and gourmet items and less interested in soft drinks, sweets, and TV dinners. A number of companies are catering to this growing interest in quality. Ford, with its "Quality is Job 1" marketing campaign, is an excellent example of a company that mounted a quality drive and is reaping the benefits in increased market share and profitability.

Companies must do more than simply build quality into their products; they must also communicate product quality. The product's look and feel should communicate its quality level. Quality is also communicated through other elements of the marketing mix. A high price usually signals a premium-quality product. The product's brand name, packaging, distribution, and promotion also announce its quality. All of these elements must work together to communicate and support the brand's image.[7]

At the same time, we should not leap to the conclusion that the firm should design the highest quality possible. Not all customers want or can afford the high levels of quality offered in such products as a Rolls-Royce, a Sub Zero refrigerator, or a Rolex watch. The manufacturer must choose a quality level that matches target market needs and the quality levels of competing products.

## Product features

A product can be offered with varying features. A "stripped-down" model—one without any extras—is the starting point. The company can create higher-level models by adding more features. Features are a competitive tool for differentiating the company's product from competitors' products. Some companies are very innovative in adding new features. Being the first producer to introduce a needed and valued new feature is one of the most effective ways to compete.

How can a company identify new features and decide which ones to add to its product? The company should periodically survey buyers who have used the product and ask these questions: How do you like the product? What specific features of the product do you like most? What features could we add to improve the product? How much would you pay for each feature? The answers will provide the company with a rich list of feature ideas. The company can then assess each feature's *customer value* versus its *company cost*. Features that customers value little in relation to costs should be dropped; those that customers value highly in relation to costs should be added.

## Product Design

Another way to add product distinctiveness is through **product design.** Some companies have reputations for outstanding design, such as Black & Decker in cordless appliances and tools, Steelcase in office furniture and systems, and Bose in audio equipment. Many companies, however, lack a "design touch." Their product designs function poorly or are dull or common-looking. Yet design can be one of the most powerful competitive weapons in a company's marketing arsenal. Well-designed products win attention and sales:

> They stand out in the material landscape. The sleek, elegant lines of a liquid black automobile as it slips around a curve. A baby bottle carefully crafted to fit the tiny fingers of an infant. The hidden power of trim, triangular speakers as they pulsate with music. The difference is design, that elusive blend of form and function, quality and style, art and engineering.[8]

Design is a larger concept than style. *Style* simply describes the appearance of a product. Styles can be eye-catching or yawn-inspiring. A sensational style may grab attention, but it does not necessarily make the product *perform* better.

**product design** The process of designing a product's style and function and creating a product that is attractive; easy, safe, and inexpensive to use and service; and simple and economical to produce and distribute.

**brand** A name, term, sign, symbol, or design—or a combination of these—intended to identify the goods or services of one seller or group of sellers and to differentiate them from those of competitors.

**brand name** That part of a brand that can be vocalized—the utterable.

**brand mark** That part of a brand that can be recognized but is not utterable, such as a symbol, design or distinctive coloring or lettering.

*Outstanding design was the major factor in the success of Black & Decker's family of cordless power tools.*

In some cases, it might even result in worse performance: A chair may look great yet be extremely uncomfortable. Unlike style, *design* is more than skin-deep—it goes to the very heart of a product. Good design contributes to a product's usefulness as well as its looks. A good designer considers appearance but also creates products that are easy, safe, inexpensive to use and service, and simple and economical to produce and distribute.

Several companies are now waking up to the importance of design. The radical new design of the Ford Taurus—with its sleek styling, passenger comforts, engineering advances, and efficient manufacturing—has made the car a huge success. Outstanding design was a major factor in the success of Black & Decker's family of cordless power tools. And through good design, General Electric cut the number of parts in its refrigerators by 40 percent by switching to a smaller rotary compressor. This change lowered production costs for GE and increased reliability and food-storage space for consumers. All said, good design can attract attention, improve product performance, cut production costs, and give the product a strong competitive advantage in the target market.[9]

## Brand Decisions

Consumers view a brand as an important part of the product, and branding can add value to the product. For example, most consumers would perceive a bottle of White Linen perfume as a high-quality, expensive product. But the same perfume in an unmarked bottle would likely be viewed as lower in quality even if the fragrance were identical. Thus, branding decisions are an important part of product strategy.

First, we should become familiar with the language of branding. Here are some key definitions.[10] A **brand** is a name, term, sign, symbol, or design—or a combination of these—intended to identify the goods or services of one seller or group of sellers and to differentiate them from those of competitors. A **brand name** is that part of a brand which can be vocalized—the utterable. Examples are Avon, Chevrolet, Tide, Disneyland, American Express, and UCLA. A **brand mark** is that part of a brand which can be recognized but is not utterable, such as a symbol, design, or distinctive coloring or lettering. Examples are the

Pillsbury doughboy, the Metro-Goldwyn-Mayer lion, and the red K on a Kodak film box. A **trademark** is a brand or part of a brand that is given legal protection—it protects the seller's exclusive rights to use the brand name or brand mark. Finally, a **copyright** is the exclusive legal right to reproduce, publish, and sell the matter and form of a literary, musical, or artistic work.

Branding poses difficult decisions to the marketer. The key decisions are shown in Figure 9–4 and discussed below.

**trademark** A brand or part of a brand that is given legal protection.
**copyright** The exclusive legal right to reproduce, publish, and sell the matter and form of a literary, musical, or artistic work.

### Branding Decision

The company must first decide whether it should put a brand name on its product. Branding has become so strong that today hardly anything goes unbranded. Salt is packaged in branded containers, oranges are stamped with growers' names, common nuts and bolts are packaged with a distributor's label, and automobile parts—spark plugs, tires, filters—bear brand names that differ from those of the automakers. Even fruits and vegetables are branded—Sunkist oranges, Dole pineapples, and Chiquita bananas command profit margins 10 to 60 percent higher than unbranded produce. Campbell is even branding mushrooms and has started to test-market premium-priced, branded tomatoes as well as nine vegetable and fruit salads, such as a broccoli and cauliflower mix.[11]

Recently, however, there has also been a return to "nonbranding" certain consumer goods. These "generics" are plainly packaged with no manufacturer identification (see Marketing Highlight 9–1). The intent of generics is to bring down the cost to the consumer by saving on packaging and advertising.

FIGURE 9–4  An Overview of Branding Decisions

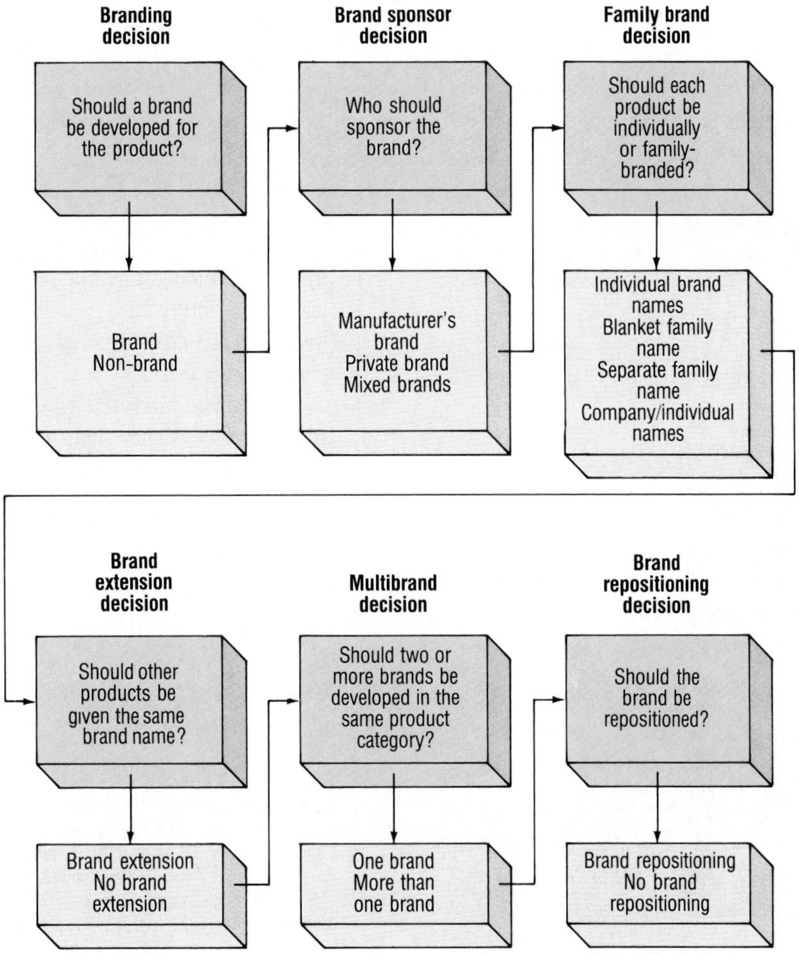

## GENERICS: THE GROWTH AND DECLINE OF "NO-BRAND, NO-FRILLS" PRODUCTS

In 1978, Jewel Food Stores shocked the grocery world by devoting an entire aisle of valuable shelf space to an assortment of low-priced, no-name products bearing only black stenciled labels: TOWELS, SUGAR, CAT FOOD. The age of "generic" products had begun. Generics are unbranded, plainly packaged, less expensive versions of common products such as spaghetti, paper towels, and canned peaches. They offer prices as much as 40 percent lower than national brands. The lower price is made possible by lower-quality ingredients, lower-cost packaging, and lower advertising costs.

Generics took brand-name manufacturers by surprise. By 1982, nearly 80 percent of all supermarkets were selling generics, and consumers could buy no-brand products in three of every four product categories. Fueled by inflation and recession, generics captured a 2.4 percent share of the grocery business and $2.8 billion in annual sales in just four years.

The price savings of generics appeal strongly to consumers, but product quality remains an important factor in their buying decisions. Generics sell better in product areas where consumers care less about quality or see little quality difference between generics and national brands. Areas such as paper products, frozen foods, peanut butter, canned vegetables, plastic bags, disposable diapers, and dog food were hardest hit by generics. Generics had less success in such areas as health and beauty aids, where consumers were less willing to trade quality for price.

Although generics are probably here to stay, it appears that their popularity peaked in 1982. Since then, the market share for generics has dropped to 1.5 percent of total grocery volume, or $1.8 billion in annual sales. This decline resulted partly from an improved economy—prices have stabilized and consumers now have more income than they did when generics exploded in the early 1980s. The decline has also resulted from better marketing strategies by brand-name manufacturers. These marketers responded by emphasizing brand image and quality. For example, when threatened by generic pet foods, Ralston-Purina increased its quality rather than reducing its price and targeted pet owners who identified strongly with their pets and cared most about quality. Kraft met the generic threat with advertising showing taste tests in which children preferred the taste of Kraft macaroni and cheese to that of the generic brand.

Another strategy is to cut costs and pass the savings along to consumers as lower prices and greater values. Or the brand-name manufacturer can introduce lower-quality, lower-priced products that compete head-on with generic products. Union Carbide, for example, produced generic garbage bags to compete with its own Glad line. Procter & Gamble introduced its line of Banner paper products. Although this line offered less quality than other P&G brands, it offered greater quality than generics and did so at a competitive price.

Brand-name marketers must continue to convince consumers that their products' higher quality is worth the extra cost. Branded products that offer large quality differences will not be hurt much by generics. Those most threatened are weak national brands and lower-price store brands that offer little additional quality. Why pay 20 to 40 percent more for a branded item when its quality is not much different from that of its generic cousin?

*Generics peaked in popularity in the early 1980s, but they are probably here to stay.*

*Sources:* See Julie Franz, "Ten Years May Be Generic Lifetime," *Advertising Age,* March 23, 1987, p. 76; Amy Dunkin, "No-Frills Products: 'An Idea Whose Time Has Gone,'" *Business Week,* June 17, 1985, pp. 64–65; and Brian F. Harris and Roger A. Strang, "Marketing in an Age of Generics," *Journal of Marketing,* Fall 1985, pp. 70–81.

Although the popularity of generics peaked in the early 1980s, the issue of whether or not to brand is very much alive today.

This situation highlights some key questions: Why have branding in the first place? Who benefits? How do they benefit? At what cost? Branding helps buyers in many ways. Brand names tell the buyer something about product quality. Buyers who always buy the same brand know that they will get the same quality each time they buy. Brand names also increase the shopper's efficiency. Imagine a buyer going into a supermarket and finding thousands of unlabeled products. Finally, brand names help call consumers' attention to new products that might benefit them—the brand name becomes the basis upon which a whole story can be built about the new product's special qualities.

Branding also gives the seller several advantages. The brand name makes it easier for the seller to process orders and track down problems. Thus, Anheuser-Busch receives an order for a hundred cases of Michelob beer instead of an order for "some of your better beer." The seller's brand name and trademark provide legal protection for unique product features that might otherwise be copied by competitors. Branding lets the seller attract a loyal and profitable set of customers. Branding helps the seller segment markets—Procter & Gamble can offer ten detergent brands, not just one general product for all consumers.

Branding also benefits society as a whole. Those favoring branding suggest that branding leads to higher and more consistent product quality. Branding also increases innovation by giving producers an incentive to look for new features that can be protected against imitating competitors. Thus, branding results in more product variety and choice for consumers. Finally, branding increases shopper efficiency, since it provides much more information about products and where to find them. While branding can be overdone in some cases, it clearly adds value to consumers and society.

*Familiar brands provide consumer information, recognition, and confidence.*

**manufacturer's brand** (or *national brand*) A brand created and owned by the producer of a product or service.

**private brand** (or *middleman, distributor,* or *dealer brand*) A brand created and owned by a reseller of a product or service.

## Brand-Sponsor Decision

In deciding to brand a product, the manufacturer has three sponsorship options. The product may be launched as a **manufacturer's brand** (also called a *national brand*). Or the manufacturer may sell the product to middlemen who put on a **private brand** (also called *middleman brand, distributor brand,* or *dealer brand*). Finally, the manufacturer may follow a *mixed-brand* strategy, selling some output under its own brand names and some under private labels. Kellogg's and IBM sell almost all their output under their own manufacturer's brand names. On the other hand, BASF Wyandotte, the world's second-largest antifreeze maker, sells its Alugard antifreeze under about 80 private brands, including K mart, True Value, Pathmark, and Rite Aid. Whirlpool sells output both under its own name and under the Sears Kenmore name.

Manufacturers' brands have dominated the American scene. Consider such well-known brands as Campbell's soup and Heinz ketchup. While most manufacturers create their own brand names, some of them "rent" well-known brand names by paying a royalty for the use of the name (see Marketing Highlight 9–2).

In recent times, however, most large retailers and wholesalers have developed their own brands. The private-label tires of Sears and J. C. Penney are as well known today as the manufacturers' brands of Goodyear and Firestone. Sears has created several names—Diehard batteries, Craftsman tools, Kenmore appliances—that buyers look for and demand. An increasing number of department stores, supermarkets, service stations, clothiers, drugstores, and appliance dealers are launching private labels.

In the fashion industry, although national brands still dominate, the use of private labels has increased dramatically in recent years. Such manufacturers as Ralph Lauren, Coach, Burberry, Esprit, and Benetton have opened stores that sell only their own labels. Traditional retailers have responded with more private-label goods. For example, Macy's now has more than 50 in-house labels, and in some categories its private labels account for up to 50 percent of sales. The Limited's private labels—including Forenza and Outback Red—represent 70 percent of the chain's sales.[12]

Despite the fact that private brands are often hard to establish and costly to stock and promote, middlemen develop private brands because they can be profitable. Middlemen can often locate manufacturers with excess capacity who will produce the private label at a low cost, resulting in a higher profit margin for the middleman. Private brands also give middlemen exclusive products that cannot be bought from competitors, resulting in greater store traffic and loyalty. For example, if K mart promotes Canon cameras, other stores that sell Canon products will also benefit. Furthermore, if K mart drops the Canon brand, it loses the benefit of its previous promotion for Canon. But if K mart promotes its private brand of Focal cameras, K mart alone benefits from the promotion. And consumer loyalty to the Focal brand becomes loyalty to K mart.

## Family-Brand Decision

Manufacturers who brand their products face several further choices. There are at least four brand-name strategies:

1. *Individual brand names.* This policy is followed by Procter & Gamble (Tide, Crest, Folger's, Pampers) and General Mills (Bisquick, Gold Medal, Betty Crocker, Nature Valley, Yoplait).
2. *A blanket family name for all products.* This policy is followed by Del Monte and General Electric.
3. *Separate family names for all products.* This policy is followed by Sears (Kenmore for appliances, Craftsman for tools, and Homart for major home installations).

# Marketing Highlight 9-2

## LICENSING BRAND NAMES FOR ROYALTIES

Manufacturers or retailers may take years and spend millions to develop consumer preference for their brands. An alternative is to "rent" names that already hold magic for consumers. The names or symbols previously created by other manufacturers, the names of celebrities, the characters introduced in popular movies and books—for a fee, any of these can provide a manufacturer's product with an instant and proven brand name. Name and character licensing has become a big business in recent years. Retail sales of licensed products jumped from $4 billion in 1977 to over $55 billion in 1987, and experts predict sales of $75 billion by 1990.

Apparel and accessories sellers are the largest users, accounting for about 35 percent of all licensing. Producers and retailers pay sizable royalties to adorn their products with the names of such fashion innovators as Bill Blass, Calvin Klein, Pierre Cardin, Gucci, and Halston, all of whom license their names or initials for everything from blouses to ties and linens to luggage. In recent years, designer labels have become so common that many retailers are discarding them in favor of their own store brands in order

to regain exclusivity, pricing freedom, and higher margins. Even less fashionable names can bring astounding success. Coca-Cola clothes by Murjani rang up $100 million in retail sales in just two years. Now, other consumer-products companies have jumped into corporate fashion licensing—Hershey, Jell-O, Burger King, McDonald's, and others.

Sellers of children's toys, games, food, and other products also make extensive use of name and character licensing. The list of characters attached to children's clothing, toys, school supplies, linens, dolls, lunch boxes, cereals, and other items is almost endless. It ranges from such classics as Disney, Peanuts, Barbie, and Flintstones characters to the Care Bears and Masters of the Universe—from the venerable Raggedy Ann and Andy to the California Raisin Advisory Board's dancing raisins.

The newest form of licensing is brand-extension licensing—renting a brand name made famous in one category and using it in a related category. Some currently successful examples include Astroturf sport shoes, Singer sewing supplies, Louisville Slugger baseball uniforms, Old Spice shaving mugs and

razors, Fabergé costume jewelry, and Winnebago camping equipment.

Licensed names or characters can add immediate distinction and familiarity to a new product and can set it apart from competitors' products. Customers debating between two similar products will most likely reach for the one with a familiar name on it. In fact, consumers often seek out products that carry their favorite names or characters.

Almost everyone is getting into the licensing act these days, even Harley-Davidson, the motorcycle maker. Over the past 80 years, the Harley-Davidson name has developed a distinct image—some people even tattoo it on their bodies. And Harley-Davidson is now licensing its name for consumer products. One toy manufacturer now markets the Harley-Davidson Big Wheel tricycle, and the company has authorized other products that meet appropriate standards of quality and taste—products ranging from wine coolers, to chocolates, to cologne.

*Sources:* See Teresa Carson and Amy Dunkin, "What's in a Name? Millions if It's Leased," *Business Week*, April 8, 1985, pp. 97–98; and Lori Kessler, "Licensing," *Advertising Age*, June 6, 1988, pp. S1-S3.

4. *Company trade name combined with individual product names.* This policy is followed by Kellogg's (Kellogg's Rice Krispies and Kellogg's Raisin Bran).

What are the advantages of an individual brand-names strategy? A major advantage is that the company does not tie its reputation to the product's acceptance. If the product fails, it does not hurt the company's name.

Using a blanket family name for all products also has some advantages. The cost of introducing the product will be less because there is no need for heavy advertising to create brand recognition and preference. Furthermore, sales will be strong if the manufacturer's name is good. Thus, new soups introduced under the Campbell brand name get instant recognition.

However, when a company produces very different products, it may not be best to use one blanket family name. Swift & Company uses separate family names for its hams (Premium) and fertilizers (Vigoro). Companies will often invent different family brand names for different quality lines within the same product class.

**brand-extension strategy** A strategy under which a new or modified product is launched under an already successful brand name.

**multibrand strategy** A strategy under which a seller develops two or more brands in the same product category.

Finally, some manufacturers want to use their company names along with an individual brand name for each product. The company name adds the firm's reputation to the product, while the individual name sets it apart from other company products. Thus, *Quaker Oats* in Quaker Oats Cap'n Crunch taps the company's reputation for breakfast cereal and *Cap'n Crunch* sets apart and dramatizes the product.

### Brand-Extension Decision

A **brand-extension** strategy is any effort to use a successful brand name to launch new or modified products. Procter & Gamble put its Ivory name on dishwashing detergent, liquid hand soap, and shampoo with excellent results, and it used the strength of the Tide name to launch unscented and liquid laundry detergents. Fruit of the Loom took advantage of its 98 percent name recognition to launch new lines of socks, men's fashion underwear, and women's underwear.[13] Brand extension saves the manufacturer the high cost of promoting new names and creates instant brand recognition of the new product. At the same time, if the new product fails, it may hurt consumer attitudes toward the other products carrying the same brand name.

### Multibrand Decision

In a **multibrand strategy,** the seller develops two or more brands in the same product category. This marketing practice was pioneered by P&G when it introduced Cheer as a competitor for its already successful Tide. Although Tide's sales dropped slightly, the combined sales of Cheer and Tide were higher. P&G now produces ten detergent brands.

Manufacturers use multibrand strategies for several reasons. First, they can gain more shelf space, thus increasing the retailer's dependence on their brands. Second, few consumers are so loyal to a brand that they will not try another. The only way to capture the "brand switchers" is to offer several brands. Third, creating new brands develops healthy competition within the manufacturer's organization. Managers of different General Motors brands compete to outperform each other. Finally, a multibrand strategy positions brands on different benefits and appeals, and each brand can attract a separate following.

### Brand-Repositioning Decision

However well a brand is initially positioned in a market, the company may have to reposition it later. A competitor may launch a brand positioned next to the company's brand and cut into its market share. Or customer wants may shift, leaving the company's brand with less demand. Marketers should consider repositioning existing brands before introducing new ones. In this way, they can build on existing brand recognition and consumer loyalty.

Repositioning may require changing both the product and its image. P&G repositioned Bold detergent by adding a fabric-softening ingredient. And Arrow added a new line of casual shirts before trying to change its image. Or a brand can be repositioned by changing only the product's image. Ivory Soap was repositioned without change from a "baby soap" to an "all natural soap" for adults who want healthy-looking skin. Similarly, Kraft repositioned Velveeta from a "cooking cheese" to a "good tasting, natural, and nutritious" snack cheese—the product remained unchanged, but Kraft used new advertising appeals to change consumer perceptions of Velveeta. When repositioning a brand, the marketer must be careful not to drop or confuse current loyal users. When shifting Velveeta's position, Kraft made certain that the product's new position was compatible with its old one. Thus, it kept loyal customers while attracting new users.[14]

What do you get after spending 75 years making America's favorite dress shirt?

"Members of the University Glee Club of New York City."

Bored.

Arrow

*Brand repositioning: long known for its dress shirts, Arrow repositioned by loosening its collar.*

## Selecting a Brand Name

The brand name should be carefully chosen. A good brand name can add greatly to a product's success. Most large marketing companies have developed a formal brand-name selection process. Finding the best brand name is a difficult task. It begins with a careful review of the product and its benefits, the target market, and proposed marketing strategies.

Among the desirable qualities for a brand name are these: (1) It should suggest something about the product's benefits and qualities. Examples: Beauty-rest, Craftsman, Sunkist, Spic and Span, Snuggles. (2) It should be easy to pronounce, recognize, and remember. Short names help—Tide, Aim, Puffs. But longer ones are sometimes effective—Love My Carpet carpet cleaner, Better Business Bureau. (3) It should be distinctive—Taurus, Kodak, Exxon. (4) It

**packaging** The activities of designing and producing the container or wrapper for a product.

should translate easily into foreign languages. Before spending $100 million to change its name to Exxon, Standard Oil of New Jersey tested the name in 54 languages in more than 150 foreign markets. It found that the name Enco referred to a stalled engine when pronounced in Japan.[15] (5) It should be capable of registration and legal protection. A brand name cannot be registered if it infringes on existing brand names. And brand names that are merely descriptive or suggestive may be unprotectable. For example, the Miller Brewing Company registered the name Lite for its low-calorie beer and invested millions to establish the name with consumers. But the courts later ruled that the terms "lite" and "light" are generic or common descriptive terms applied to beer and that Miller could not use the Lite name exclusively.[16]

Once chosen, the brand name must be protected. Many firms try to build a brand name that will eventually become identified with the product category. Such brand names as Frigidaire, Kleenex, Levi's, Jell-O, Scotch Tape, and Fiberglas have succeeded in this way. However, their very success may threaten the company's rights to the name. Originally protected brand names, cellophane, aspirin, nylon, kerosene, escalator, and shredded wheat are now names that any seller can use.[17]

## Packaging Decisions

Many products offered to the market have to be packaged. Some marketers have called packaging a fifth *P*, along with price, product, place, and promotion. Most marketers, however, treat packaging as an element of product strategy.

**Packaging** includes the activities of designing and producing the container or wrapper for a product. The package may include the product's immediate container (for example, the bottle holding Old Spice After-Shave Lotion); a secondary package that is thrown away when the product is about to be used (the cardboard box containing the bottle of Old Spice); and the shipping package necessary to store, identify, and ship the product (a corrugated box carrying six dozen bottles of Old Spice). Labeling is also part of packaging and consists of printed information appearing on or with the package.

*Packaging is an essential part of the product.*

Traditionally, packaging decisions were based mostly on cost and production factors; the primary function of the package was to contain and protect the product. In recent times, however, numerous factors have made packaging an important marketing tool. An increase in self-service means that packages must now perform many sales tasks—from attracting attention, to describing the product, to making the sale. Rising consumer affluence means that consumers are willing to pay a little more for the convenience, appearance, dependability, and prestige of better packages.[18]

Companies are also realizing the power of good packaging to create instant consumer recognition of the company or brand. The Campbell Soup Company estimates that the average shopper sees its familiar red and white can 76 times a year, creating the equivalent of $26 million worth of advertising.[19] And innovative packaging can give the company an advantage over competitors. Liquid Tide quickly attained a 10 percent share of the heavy-duty detergent market, partly because of the popularity of its container's innovative drip-proof spout and cap. The first companies to put their fruit drinks in airtight foil and paper cartons (aseptic packages) and toothpastes in pump dispensers attracted many new customers.[20] On the other hand, poorly designed packages can cause headaches for consumers and lost sales for the company (See Marketing Highlight 9–3).

In recent years, product safety has also become a major packaging concern. We have all learned how to deal with hard-to-open "child-proof" packages. And after the rash of product-tampering scares during the 1980s, most drug producers and food makers are now putting their products in tamper-resistant packages.

Developing a good package for a new product requires many decisions. The first task is to establish the packaging concept. The **packaging concept** states what the package should *be* or *do* for the product. Should the main functions of the package be to offer product protection, introduce a new dispensing method, suggest certain qualities about the product or the company, or something else? Decisions must then be made on specific elements of the package—size, shape, materials, color, text, and brand mark. These various elements must work together to support the product's position and marketing strategy. The package must be consistent with the product's advertising, pricing, and distribution.

Companies usually consider several different package designs for a new product. To select the best package, they usually test the various designs to find the one that stands up best under normal use, is easiest for dealers to handle, and receives the most favorable response from consumers. And after selecting and introducing the package, the company should check it regularly in the face of changing consumer preferences and advances in technology. In the past, a package design might last for 15 years before it needed changes. However, in today's rapidly changing environment, most companies must recheck their packaging every two or three years.

Keeping a package up-to-date usually requires only minor but regular changes—changes so subtle that they may go unnoticed by most consumers. But some packaging changes involve complex decisions, drastic action, and high cost and risk. For example, Campbell has recently been searching for a new container to replace its venerable old soup can. It has experimented with a variety of containers, such as a sealed plastic bowl that can be popped into a microwave oven to produce hot soup in a hurry with no can to open and no dishes to wash. Given Campbell's 80 percent share of the canned soup market, the potential risks and benefits of changing the package are huge. Although the change could cut Campbell's packaging costs by as much as 15 percent, revamping production facilities would cost $100 million or more. And Campbell management estimates that the change would take at least five years to implement.

**packaging concept** What the package should *be* or *do* for the product.

## THOSE FRUSTRATING, NOT-SO-EASY-TO-OPEN PACKAGES

The following letter from an angry consumer to Robert D. Stuart, then chairman of Quaker Oats, expresses beautifully the utter frustration all of us have experienced in dealing with so-called "easy-opening packages."

Dear Mr. Stuart:

I am an 86-year-old widow in fairly good health. (You may think of this as advanced age, but for me that description pertains to the years ahead. Nevertheless, if you decide to

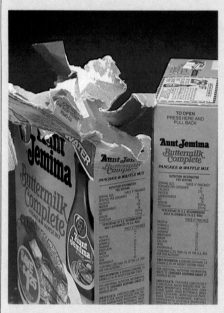

*An easy-to-open package?*

reply to this letter I wouldn't dawdle, actuarial tables being what they are.)

As I said, my health is fairly good. Feeble and elderly, as one understands these terms, I am not. My two Doberman pinschers and I take a brisk 3-mile walk every day. They are two strong and energetic animals and it takes a bit of doing to keep "brisk" closer to a stroll than a mad dash. But I manage because as yet I don't lack the strength. You will shortly see why this fact is relevant.

I am writing to call your attention to the cruel, deceptive and utterly [false] copy on your Aunt Jemima buttermilk complete pancake and waffle mix. The words on your package read, "to open—press here and pull back."

Mr. Stuart, though I push and press and groan and strive and writhe and curse and sweat and jab and push, pose and ram . . . whew!—I have never once been able to do what the package instructs—to "press here and pull back" the [blankety-blank].

It can't be done! Talk about failing strength! Have you ever tried and succeeded?

My late husband was a gun collector who among other lethal weapons kept a Thompson machine gun in a locked cabinet. It was a good thing that the cabinet was locked. Oh, the number of times I was tempted to give your package a few short bursts.

That lock and a sense of ladylike delicacy kept me from pursuing that vengeful fantasy. Instead, I keep a small cleaver in my pantry for those occasions when I need to open a package of your delicious Aunt Jemima pancakes.

For many years that whacking away with my

cleaver served a dual purpose. Not only to open the [blankety-blank] package but also to vent my fury at your sadists who willfully and maliciously did design that torture apparatus that passes for a package.

Sometimes just for the [blank] of it I let myself get carried away. I don't stop after I've lopped off the top. I whack away until the package is utterly destroyed in an outburst of rage, frustration, and vindictiveness. I wind up with a floorful of your delicious Aunt Jemima pancake mix. But that's a small price to pay for blessed release. (Anyway, the pinschers lap up the mess.)

So many ingenious, considerate (even compassionate) innovations in package closures have been designed since Aunt Jemima first donned her red bandana. Wouldn't you consider the introduction of a more humane package to replace the example of marketing malevolence to which you resolutely cling? Don't you care Mr. Stuart?

I'm really writing this to be helpful and in that spirit I am sending a copy to Mr. Tucker, president of Container Corp. I'm sure their clever young designers could be of immeasurable help to you in this matter. At least I feel it's worth a try.

Really, Mr. Stuart, I hope you will not regard me as just another cranky old biddy. I am The Public, the source of your fortunes.

Ms. Roberta Pavloff
Malvern, Pa.

*Source:* This letter was reprinted in "Some Designs Should Just Be Torn Asunder," *Advertising Age,* January 17, 1983, p. M54.

Cost remains an important packaging consideration. Developing the packaging for a new product may cost a few hundred thousand dollars and take from a few months to a year. Or, as in the Campbell example, converting to a new package may cost millions and implementing a new package design may take several years. Marketers must weigh packaging costs against both consumer perceptions of value added by the packaging and the role of packaging in helping to attain marketing objectives. In making packaging decisions, the company must also heed growing societal concerns about packaging and make decisions that serve society's interests as well as customer and company objectives (see Marketing Highlight 9–4).

# Marketing Highlight 9-4

## PACKAGING AND PUBLIC POLICY

Packaging is attracting increasing public attention. When making packaging decisions, marketers should heed the following issues.

*Fair packaging and labeling.* The public is concerned about false and potentially misleading packaging and labeling. The Federal Trade Commission Act of 1914 held that false, misleading, or deceptive labels or packages constitute unfair competition. Consumers are also concerned about confusing package sizes and shapes that make price comparisons difficult. The Fair Packaging and Labeling Act, passed by Congress in 1967, set mandatory labeling requirements, encouraged voluntary industry packaging standards, and allowed federal agencies to set packaging regulations in specific industries. The Food and Drug Administration has required processed food producers to include nutritional labeling that clearly states the amounts of protein, fat, carbohydrates, and calories contained in products, as well as their vitamin and mineral content as a percentage of the recommended daily allowance. Consumerists have lobbied for additional labeling laws to require *open dating* (to describe product freshness), *unit pricing* (to state the product cost in some standard measurement unit), *grade labeling* (to rate the quality level of certain consumer goods), and *percentage labeling* (to show the percentage of each important ingredient).

*Excessive cost.* Critics have claimed that excessive packaging on some products raises prices. They point to secondary "throwaway" packaging and question its value to the consumer. They note that the package sometimes costs more than the contents; for example, Evian moisturizer consists of five ounces of natural spring water packaged as an aerosol spray selling for $5.50. Marketers respond that they also want to keep packaging costs down but that the critics do not understand all the functions of the package.

*Scarce resources.* The growing concern over shortages of paper, aluminum, and other materials suggests that industry should try harder to reduce its packaging. For example, the growth of nonreturnable glass containers has resulted in using up to 17 times as much glass as with returnable containers. Glass and other throwaway bottles also waste energy. Some states have passed laws prohibiting or taxing nonreturnable containers.

*Pollution.* As much as 40 percent of the total solid waste in this country is made up of package material. Many packages end up as broken bottles and bent cans littering the streets and countryside. All of this packaging creates a major problem in solid waste disposal, requiring huge amounts of labor and energy.

These packaging questions have mobilized public interest in new packaging laws. Marketers must be equally concerned. They must try to design fair, economical, and ecological packages for their products.

## Labeling Decisions

Sellers may also design labels for their products, ranging from simple tags attached to products to complex graphics that are part of the package. The label might carry only the brand name or a great deal of information. Even if the seller prefers a simple label, the law may require more information.

Labels perform several functions, and the seller has to decide which ones to use. At the very least, the label *identifies* the product or brand, such as the name Sunkist stamped on oranges. The label might also *grade* the product—canned peaches are grade-labeled A, B, and C. The label might *describe* several things about the product—who made it, where it was made, when it was made, its contents, how it is to be used, and how to use it safely. Finally, the label might *promote* the product through attractive graphics.

Labels of well-known brands may seem old-fashioned after a while and need freshening up. For example, the label on Ivory Soap has been redone 18 times since the 1890s, but simply with gradual changes in the lettering. On the other hand, the label on Orange Crush soft drink was substantially changed when its competitors' labels began to picture fresh fruits and pull in more sales. Orange Crush developed a label with new symbols and much stronger, deeper colors to suggest freshness and more orange flavor.

There has been a long history of legal concerns about labels. Labels can mislead customers, fail to describe important ingredients, or fail to include needed safety warnings. As a result, several federal and state laws regulate labeling, the most prominent being the Fair Packaging and Labeling Act of 1966. Labeling has been affected in recent times by *unit pricing* (stating the price per unit of standard measure), *open dating* (stating the expected shelf life of the product), and *nutritional labeling* (stating the nutritional values in the product). Sellers should make sure their labels contain all the required information.

## Product-Support Services Decisions

Customer service is another element of product strategy. A company's offer to the marketplace usually includes some services. Services can be a minor or a major part of the total offer. In fact, the offer can range from a pure good on the one hand to a pure service on the other. In Chapter 19, we discuss services as products themselves. Here, we will discuss **product-support services—** services that augment actual products. More and more companies are using product-support services as a major tool for gaining competitive advantage.

Good customer service is good for business. It costs less to keep the goodwill of existing customers than to attract new customers or woo back lost customers. Firms that provide high-quality service usually outperform their less service-oriented competitors. A recent study by the Strategic Planning Institute compared the performance of businesses that had high customer ratings of service quality with those that had lower ratings. It found that the high-service businesses managed to charge more, grow faster, and make more profits.[21] Clearly, marketers need to think carefully about their service strategies.

### Deciding on the Service Mix

A company should design its product and support services to meet the needs of target customers. Thus, the first step in deciding what product-support services to offer is to determine both what services target consumers value and their relative importance. Customers will vary in the value they assign to different services. Some will stress credit and financing services, fast and reliable delivery, or quick installation. Others will put more weight on technical information and advice, training in product use, or after-sale service and repair.

Finding out about customers' service needs involves more than simply monitoring complaints that come in over toll-free telephone lines or on comment cards. The company should periodically survey its consumers to get ratings of current services and ideas for new ones. For example, Cadillac holds regular focus group interviews with owners and carefully watches complaints that come in to its dealerships. It recently found that buyers were most upset by repairs that were not done right the first time. As a result, the company set up a system directly linking each dealership with a group of ten engineers who can help walk mechanics through difficult repairs. Such actions helped Cadillac jump in one year from fourteenth to seventh in independent rankings of service.[22]

Products can often be designed to reduce the amount of required servicing. Thus, companies need to coordinate their product-design and service-mix decisions. For example, the Canon home copier uses a disposable toner cartridge that greatly reduces the need for service calls. Kodak and 3M are designing products that can be "plugged in" to a central diagnostic facility that performs tests, locates troubles, and fixes equipment over telephone lines. Thus, a key to successful service strategy is to design products that rarely break down and, if they do, are easily fixable with little service expense.

**Delivering Product-Support Services**

Finally, companies must decide how they want to deliver product-support services to customers. For example, consider the many ways Maytag might offer repair services on its major appliances. It could hire and train its own service people and locate them across the country. It could arrange with distributors and dealers to provide the repair services. Or it could leave it to independent companies to provide these services.

Most equipment companies start out adopting the first alternative, providing their own service. They want to stay close to the equipment and know its problems. They also find that they can make good money running the "parts and service business." As long as they are the only supplier of the needed parts, they can charge a premium price. Indeed, some equipment manufacturers make over half of their profits in after-sale service.

Over time, producers typically shift more of the maintenance and repair service to authorized distributors and dealers. These middlemen are closer to customers, have more locations, and can offer quicker if not better service. The producer still makes a profit on selling the parts but leaves the servicing cost to middlemen.

Still later, independent service firms emerge. For example, over 40 percent of all auto service work is now done outside of franchised automobile dealerships by independent garages and chains such as Midas Muffler, Sears,

*Delivering product-support services: GE backs its products with a toll-free customer service center and a fleet of service trucks ("workshops on wheels") that service GE products at customers' homes. It also provides a Quick Fix System, including parts and repair manuals for do-it-yourselfers.*

and K mart. Such independent service firms have emerged in most industries. They typically offer lower cost or faster service than the manufacturer or authorized middlemen.

Ultimately, some large customers start to handle their own maintenance and repair services. Thus, a company with several hundred personal computers, printers, and related equipment might find it cheaper to have its own service people on-site.

### The Customer Service Department

Given the importance of customer service as a marketing tool, many companies have set up strong customer service departments to handle complaints and adjustments, credit service, maintenance service, technical service, and consumer information. For example, Whirlpool, Procter & Gamble, and many other companies have set up hot lines to handle consumer complaints and requests for information. By keeping records on the types of requests and complaints, the customer service department can press for needed changes in product design, quality control, high-pressure selling, and so on. An active customer service department coordinates all the company's services, creates consumer satisfaction and loyalty, and helps the company to further set itself apart from competitors.[23]

# PRODUCT LINE DECISIONS

We have looked at product strategy decisions—branding, packaging, and services—for individual products. But product strategy also calls for building a product line. A **product line** is a group of products that are closely related either

*Product line: "We design each Olympus for a different kind of photographer."*

because they function in a similar manner, are sold to the same customer groups, are marketed through the same types of outlets, or fall within given price ranges. Thus, General Motors produces several lines of cars, Revlon produces several lines of cosmetics, and IBM produces several lines of computers. Each product line needs a marketing strategy. Marketers face a number of tough decisions on product line length and product line featuring.

**product line stretching** Increasing the product line by lengthening it beyond its current range.

## Product Line-Length Decision

Product line managers have to decide on product line length. The line is too short if the manager can increase profits by adding items; the line is too long if the manager can increase profits by dropping items. Product line length is influenced by company objectives. Companies that want to be positioned as full-line companies or are seeking high market share and market growth will carry longer lines. They are less concerned when some items fail to add to profits. Companies that are keen on high profitability will generally carry shorter lines consisting of selected items.

Product lines tend to lengthen over time. The company must plan this growth carefully. It can systematically increase the length of its product line in two ways: by *stretching* its line and by *filling* its line.

## Product Line-Stretching Decision

Every company's product line covers a certain range of the products offered by the industry as a whole. For example, BMW automobiles are located in the medium-high price range of the automobile market. Toyota focuses on the low to medium price range. **Product line stretching** occurs when a company lengthens its product line beyond its current range. As shown in Figure 9–5, the company can stretch its line downward, upward, or both ways.

### Downward Stretch

Many companies initially locate at the high end of the market and later stretch their lines downward. A company may stretch downward for any number of reasons. It may find faster growth taking place at the low end. Or it may have first

FIGURE 9–5  Product Line-Stretching Decision

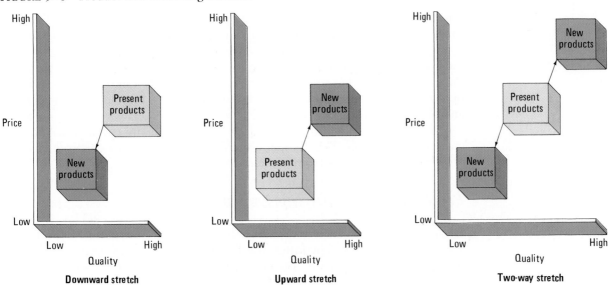

**product line filling** Increasing the product line by adding more items within the present range of the line.

**product line featuring** Selecting one or a few items in a product line to feature.

entered the high end to establish a quality image and intended to roll downward. The company may add a low-end product to plug a market hole that would otherwise attract a new competitor. Or it may be attacked at the high end and respond by invading the low end. Beech Aircraft has historically produced expensive private aircraft but has recently added less expensive planes to meet a threat from Piper, which began to produce larger planes.

### Upward stretch

Companies at the lower end of the market may want to enter the higher end. They may be attracted by a faster growth rate or higher margins at the higher end, or they may simply want to position themselves as full-line manufacturers. For example, General Electric recently added its Monogram line of high-quality built-in kitchen appliances targeted at the select few households earning more than $100,000 a year and living in homes valued at over $400,000. Sometimes, companies stretch upward in order to add prestige to their current products, as when Chrysler purchased Lamborghini, maker of exotic, handcrafted sports cars.

An upward-stretch decision can be risky. The higher-end competitors not only are well entrenched but may strike back by entering the lower end of the market. Prospective customers may not believe that the newcomer can produce quality products. Finally, the company's salespeople and distributors may lack the talent and training to serve the higher end of the market.

### Two-Way Stretch

Companies in the middle range of the market may decide to stretch their lines in both directions. Sony did this to hold off copycat competitors for its Walkman line of personal tape players. Sony introduced its first Walkman in the middle of the market. As imitative competitors moved in with lower-priced models, Sony stretched downward. At the same time, to add luster to its lower-price models and to attract more affluent consumers, Sony stretched the Walkman line upward. It now sells more than 100 models, ranging from a plain-vanilla playback-only version for $32 to a high-tech, high-quality $450 version that both plays and records. Using this two-way-stretch strategy, Sony now dominates the personal tape player market with a 30 percent share.[24]

## Product Line-Filling Decision

A product line can also be lengthened by adding more items within the present range of the line. There are several reasons for **product line filling:** reaching for extra profits, trying to satisfy dealers, trying to use excess capacity, trying to be the leading full-line company, and trying to plug holes to keep out competitors. Thus, Sony has added solar-powered and waterproof Walkmans and an ultra-light model that attaches to a sweatband for joggers, bicyclers, tennis players, and other exercisers.

However, line filling is overdone if it results in cannibalization and customer confusion. The company should make sure that new-product items are noticeably different from present items.

## Product Line-Featuring Decision

The product line manager typically selects one or a few items in the line to feature. This strategy is **product line featuring.** Sometimes, managers feature promotional models at the low end of the line to serve as "traffic builders." Thus, Sears will announce a special low-priced sewing machine to attract people. And Rolls-Royce announced an economy model selling for only $49,000—in contrast to its high-end model selling for $108,000—to bring people into its showrooms. Once the customers arrive, salespeople may try to get them to buy at the high end of the line.

At other times, managers will feature a high-end item to give the product line "class." Thus, Audimar Piguet advertises a $25,000 watch which few people buy but which acts as a "flagship" to enhance the whole line.

**product mix** The set of all product lines and items that a particular seller offers for sale to buyers.

# PRODUCT MIX DECISIONS

An organization with several product lines has a product mix. A **product mix** (also called *product assortment)* is the set of all product lines and items that a particular seller offers for sale.[25] Avon's product mix consists of four major product lines: cosmetics, jewelry, fashions, and household items. Each product line consists of several sublines. For example, cosmetics breaks down into lipstick, rouge, powder, and so on. Each line and subline has many individual items. Altogether, Avon's product mix includes 1,300 items. A large supermarket handles as many as 14,000 items; a typical K mart stocks 15,000 items; and General Electric manufactures as many as 250,000 items.

A company's product mix can be described as having a certain width, length, depth, and consistency. These concepts are illustrated in Table 9–1, which lists selected Procter & Gamble consumer products.

The *width* of P&G's product mix refers to how many different product lines the company carries. Table 9–1 shows a product mix width of six lines. (In fact, P&G produces many more lines, including mouthwashes, paper towels, and pain relievers.)

The *length* of P&G's product mix refers to the total number of items the company carries. In Table 9–1, it is 34. We can also compute the average length of a line at P&G by dividing the total length (here 34) by the number of lines (here 6). The average P&G product line as represented in Table 9–1 consists of 5.7 brands.

TABLE 9–1  Product Mix Width and Product Line Length Shown for Procter & Gamble Products

| | | | | Disposable | |
| Detergents | Toothpaste | Bar Soap | Deodorants | Diapers | Coffee |
|---|---|---|---|---|---|
| Ivory Snow | Gleem | Ivory | Secret | Pampers | Folger's |
| Dreft | Crest | Camay | Sure | Luvs | Instant Folger's |
| Tide | Complete | Lava | | | High Point Instant |
| Joy | Denquel | Kirk's | | | Folger's Flaked Coffee |
| Cheer | | Zest | | | |
| Oxydol | | Safeguard | | | |
| Dash | | Coast | | | |
| Cascade | | | | | |
| Ivory Liquid | | | | | |
| Gain | | | | | |
| Dawn | | | | | |
| Era | | | | | |
| Bold 3 | | | | | |
| Liquid Tide | | | | | |
| Solo | | | | | |

← Product mix width →

Product line length ↓

The *depth* of P&G's product mix refers to how many versions are offered of each product in the line. Thus, if Crest comes in three sizes and two formulations (paste and gel), Crest has a depth of six. By counting the number of versions within each brand, we can calculate the average depth of P&G's product mix.

The *consistency* of the product mix refers to how closely related the various product lines are in end use, production requirements, distribution channels, or in some other way. P&G's product lines are consistent insofar as they are consumer goods that go through the same distribution channels. The lines are less consistent insofar as they perform different functions for buyers.

These four dimensions of the product mix provide the handles for defining the company's product strategy. The company can increase its business in four ways. It can add new product lines, thus widening its product mix. In this way,

# Marketing Highlight 9–5

## PRODUCT DECISIONS AND PUBLIC POLICY

Marketing managers must heed various laws and regulations when making product decisions. The main areas of product concern are as follows.

*Product additions and deletions.* Under the Antimerger Act, the government may prevent companies from adding products through acquisitions if the effect threatens to lessen competition. Companies dropping products must be aware that they have legal obligations, written or implied, to their suppliers, dealers, and customers who have a stake in the discontinued product.

*Patent protection.* A firm must obey the U.S. patent laws when developing new products. A company may not make its product "illegally similar" to another company's established product. An example is Polaroid's successful suit to prevent Kodak from selling its new instant-picture camera on the grounds that it infringed on Polaroid's instant camera patents.

*Product quality and safety.* Manufacturers must comply with specific laws regarding product quality and safety. The Federal Food, Drug, and Cosmetic Act protects consumers from unsafe and adulterated food, drugs, and cosmetics. Various acts provide for the inspection of

sanitary conditions in the meat- and poultry-processing industries. Safety legislation has been passed to regulate fabrics, chemical substances, automobiles, toys, and drugs and poisons. The Consumer Product Safety Act of 1972 established a Consumer Product Safety Commission, which has the authority to ban or seize potentially hazardous products and set severe penalties for violation of the law. If consumers have been injured by a product that has been defectively designed, they can sue manufacturers or dealers. Product-liability suits are now occurring at the rate of over one million per year, with individual awards often running in the millions of dollars. This phenomenon has resulted in a huge increases in product-liability insurance premiums. For example, Piper Aircraft's insurance bill averages $75,000 for every new plane, more than the cost of producing Piper's smaller planes. The cost of liability insurance for producers of children's car seats rose from $50,000 in 1984 to over $750,000 in 1986. Some companies pass these higher rates along to consumers by raising prices. Others are forced to discontinue high-risk product lines.

*Product warranties.* Many

manufacturers offer written product warranties to convince customers of their product's quality. But these warranties are often limited and written in a language the average consumer does not understand. Too often, consumers learn that they are not entitled to services, repairs, and replacements that seem to be implied. To protect consumers, Congress passed the Magnuson-Moss Warranty Act in 1975. The act requires that full warranties meet certain minimum standards, including repair "within a reasonable time and without charge" or a replacement or full refund if the product does not work "after a reasonable number of attempts" at repair. Otherwise the company must make it clear that it is offering only a limited warranty. The law has led several manufacturers to switch from full to limited warranties and others to drop warranties altogether as a marketing tool.

*Sources:* See Michael Brody, "When Products Turn," *Fortune,* March 3, 1986, pp. 20–24; and Louis W. Stern and Thomas L. Eovaldi, *Legal Aspects of Marketing Strategy* (Englewood Cliffs, NJ: Prentice Hall, 1984), pp. 76–116.

its new lines build on the company's reputation in its other lines. Or the company can lengthen its existing product lines to become a more full-line company. Or the company can add more product versions to each product and thus deepen its product mix. Finally, the company can pursue more product line consistency—or less—depending on whether it wants to have a strong reputation in a single field or in several fields.

Thus, product strategy calls for complex decisions on product mix, product line, branding, packaging, and service strategy. These decisions must be made not only with a full understanding of consumer wants and competitors' strategies but also with increasing attention to the growing public policy affecting product decisions (see Marketing Highlight 9–5).

## SUMMARY

*Product* is a complex concept that must be carefully defined. Product strategy calls for making coordinated decisions on product items, product lines, and the product mix.

Each product item offered to customers can be looked at on three levels. The *core product* is the essential benefit the buyer is really buying. The *actual product* includes the features, styling, quality, brand name, and packaging of the product offered for sale. The *augmented product* is the actual product plus the various services offered with it, such as warranty, installation, maintenance, and free delivery.

There are several ways to classify products. For example, all products can be classified according to their durability (nondurable goods, durable goods, services). *Consumer goods* are usually classified according to consumer shopping habits (convenience, shopping, specialty, unsought goods). *Industrial goods* are classified according to their cost and how they enter the production process (materials and parts, capital items, supplies and services).

Companies have to develop strategies for the product items in their lines. They must decide on product attributes, branding, packaging, labeling, and product-support services. *Product attribute decisions* involve what product quality, features, and design the company will offer. Regarding *brands*, the company must decide whether to brand at all, whether to choose manufacturing or private branding, whether to use family brand names or individual brand names, whether to extend the brand name to new products, whether to offer several competing brands, and whether to reposition any of its brands.

Products also require *packaging decisions* to create such benefits as protection, economy, convenience, and promotion.

Marketers have to develop a packaging concept and test it to make sure that it both achieves desired objectives and is compatible with public policy.

Products also require *labeling* for identification and possible grading, description, and promotion of the product. U.S. laws require sellers to present certain minimum information on the label to inform and protect consumers.

Companies have to develop *product-support services* that are both desired by customers and effective against competitors. The company has to decide on the most important services to offer and the best ways to deliver these services. The *service mix* can be coordinated by a customer service department that handles complaints and adjustments, credit, maintenance, technical service, and customer information. *Customer service* should be used as a marketing tool to create customer satisfaction and competitive advantage.

Most companies produce not a single product but a product line. A *product line* is a group of products related in function, customer-purchase needs, or distribution channels. Each product line requires a product strategy. *Line stretching* raises the question of whether a line should be extended downward, upward, or both ways. *Line filling* raises the question of whether additional items should be added within the present range of the line. *Line featuring* raises the question of which items to feature in promoting the line.

*Product mix* describes the set of product lines and items offered to customers by a particular seller. The product mix can be described by its width, length, depth, and consistency. The four dimensions of the product mix are the tools for developing the company's product strategy.

## QUESTIONS FOR DISCUSSION

1. What are the core, tangible, and augmented products of the educational experience offered by universities?

2. How would you classify the products offered by restaurants—as nondurable goods or as services?

3. Compare the number of retail outlets for each type of consumer good (convenience, shopping, specialty, unsought) in a particular geographic area. Give examples.

4. In recent years, U.S. automakers have tried to reposition many brands at the high-quality end of the market. How well have they succeeded? What else could they do to change consumer perceptions?

5. Why are many people willing to pay more for branded products than for unbranded products? What does this fact say about the value of branding?

6. Changing an established brand name can be expensive and time-consuming. What were the benefits and drawbacks of changing the established company names "ESSO," "Bank Americard," and "Datsun" to new names—"EXXON," "VISA," and "Nissan"?

7. Think of several products you buy regularly and recommend improvements in their packaging or labeling. If the packaging change added to the product's cost, how much more would you be willing to pay for the improvement?

8. Describe some service decisions that the following marketers must make: (a) a small women's clothing store, (b) a bank, (c) a supermarket.

9. Describe the product mix of hospitals in your area. Are their mixes wide or *deep?* How could they stretch lines upward or downward?

# REFERENCES

1. See Bess Gallanis, "New Strategies Revive the Rose's Fading Bloom," *Advertising Age,* February 27, 1984, pp. M9-M11; "What Lies Behind the Sweet Smell of Success," *Business Week,* February 27, 1984, pp. 139–43; S. J. Diamond, "Perfume Equals Part Mystery, Part Marketing," *Los Angeles Times,* April 22, 1988, Sec. 4, p. 1; and Pat Sloan, Chastity Back: Sex Out, Romance In for Fragrance Market," *Advertising Age,* February 15, 1988, p. 3.

2. See *Marketing Definitions: A Glossary of Marketing Terms,* compiled by the Committee on Definitions of the American Marketing Association (Chicago: American Marketing Association, 1960).

3. The three definitions can be found in *Marketing Definitions.*

4. The first three definitions can be found in *Marketing Definitions.* For more information on product classifications, see Patrick E. Murphy and Ben M. Enis, "Classifying Products Strategically," *Journal of Marketing,* July 1986, pp. 24–42.

5. David A. Garvin, "Competing on Eight Dimensions of Quality," *Harvard Business Review,* November-December 1987, p. 109. Also see Robert Jacobson and David A. Aaker, "The Strategic Role of Product Quality," *Journal of Marketing,* October 1987, pp. 31–44.

6. Tom Peters and Perry Pascarella, "Searching for Excellence: The Winners Deliver on Value," *Industry Week,* April 16, 1984, pp. 61–62.

7. For a discussion of consumer perceptions of quality, see Valerie A. Zeithaml, "Consumer Perceptions of Price, Quality, and Value: A Means-End Model and Synthesis of Evidence," *Journal of Marketing,* July 1988, pp. 2–22.

8. Bruce Nussbaum, "Smart Design: Quality Is the New Style," *Business Week,* April 11, 1988, pp. 102–8.

9. For more on design, see Philip Kotler, "Design: A Powerful but Neglected Strategic Tool," *Journal of Business Strategy,* Fall 1984, pp. 16–21; Robert A. Abler, "The Value-Added of Design," *Business Marketing,* September 1986, pp. 96–103; and Nussbaum, "Smart Design: Quality Is the New Style."

10. The first four definitions can be found in *Marketing Definitions.*

11. See Eleanor Johnson Tracy, "Here Come Brand-Name Fruit and Veggies," *Fortune,* February 18, 1985, p. 105; and Alice Z. Cuneo, "Companies Find Brands Bear Fruit at the Farm Stand," *Advertising Age,* May 9, 1988, p. S8.

12. Walter J. Salmon and Karen A. Cmar, "Private Labels Are Back in Fashion," *Harvard Business Review,* May-June 1987, pp. 99–106.

13. See Michael Oneal, "Fruit of the Loom Escalates the Underwars," *Business Week,* February 22, 1988, pp. 114–18.

14. See Bess Gallanis, "Positioning Old Products in New Niches," *Advertising Age,* May 3, 1984, p. M50; and "Marketers Should Consider Restaging Old Brands Before Launching New Ones," *Advertising Age,* December 10, 1982, p. 5.

15. Walter Stern, "A Good Name Can Mean a Brand of Fame," *Advertising Age,* January 17, 1983, p. M53.

16. Thomas M. S. Hemnes, "How Can You Find a Safe Trademark?" *Harvard Business Review,* March-April 1985, p. 44.

17. For a discussion of legal issues surrounding the use of brand names, see Dorothy Cohen, "Trademark Strategy," *Journal of Marketing,* January 1986, pp. 61–74; and "Trademark Woes: Help Is Coming," *Sales & Marketing Management,* January 1988, p. 84.

18. See Charles A. Moldenhauer, "Packaging Designers Must Be Cognizant of Right Cues if the Consumer Base Is to Expand," *Marketing News,* March 30, 1984, p. 14; and Kate Bertrand, "Convenient and Portable Packaging Pays," *Advertising Age,* February 20, 1986, p. 16.

19. Bill Abrams, "Marketing," *The Wall Street Journal,* May 20, 1982, p. 33.

20. See Amy Dunkin, "Want to Wake Up a Tired Old Product? Repackage It," *Business Week,* July 15, 1985, pp. 130–34.

21. Bro Uttal, "Companies That Serve You Best," *Fortune,* December 7, 1987, pp. 98–116; and "Customer Service: Up the Bottom Line," *Sales & Marketing Management,* January 1989, p. 19.

22. Ibid., p. 116.

23. For more examples of how companies have used customer service as a marketing tool, see "Making Service a Potent Marketing Tool," *Business Week,* June 11, 1984, pp. 164–70; Bill Kelley, "Five Companies That Do It Right—And Make It Pay," *Sales & Marketing Management,* April 1988, pp. 57–64; and Kevin T. Higgins, "Business Marketers Make Customer Service Job for All," *Marketing News,* January 1, 1989, pp. 1-2.

24. See Amy Borrus, "How Sony Keeps the Copycats Scampering," *Business Week,* June 1, 1987, p. 69.

25. This definition can be found in *Marketing Definitions.*

# FISHER-PRICE: TOYING AROUND WITH PRODUCT DIVERSIFICATION

Dressing toddlers can be a frazzling experience. Executives at Fisher-Price Toys had that point hammered home well to them in 1983. For four hours, they peered through a one-way mirror and eavesdropped as a dozen women in Cleveland complained about battles with the zippers, buckles, buttons, and snaps on kids' clothing. "These were combat veterans who had five years experience with two children," says Stephen Muirhead, a manager in Fisher-Price's Diversified-Products Division. "They were talking about things that touch their daily lives very deeply."

In fact, however, grumpy mothers were just what Fisher-Price had hoped to find. Market research convinced the company that with its famous name and a unique design, it could find a niche in the lucrative but increasingly cutthroat children's wear market. In 1984, the Quaker Oats subsidiary rolled out its first line of preschool playwear, and there wasn't a button, zipper, or frill to be found. Nearly all the fasteners were Velcro. "Oshkosh overalls are beautifully designed," says Muirhead, "but kids being toilet trained need to be Houdini to get out of them."

Fisher-Price playwear, however, offered numerous new features: padded knees and elbows, extra-long shirttails, cuffs that can be unfurled as children grow, and big neck openings to accommodate kids' disproportionately large heads. "Fisher-Price is attacking clothing the way it does everything else," said Ken Wilcox, director of marketing administration at Tonka Corp. "The company identifies an area where kids aren't being served well and then comes up with a nearly indestructible product that's easy to use."

But it won't be an easy jump from toys to playwear. Fisher-Price is trying to break into a splintered industry where style often matters more than durability. "It's very difficult to position yourself on the basis of functionality and performance," says Peter Brown of Kurt Salmon & Associates, a management consulting firm. "Children's wear, blue jeans, and men's underwear are all advertised for their performance characteristics, but it's hard for consumers to see much difference."

Moreover, the business is becoming more crowded as other big companies are tempted by what demographers call the "baby-boom echo"—the rising number of births to women of the baby-boom generation. "Incursion of more adult brands into the kids' market is also intensifying the battle on the retail floor," says Terry Jacobs of Walter K. Levy Associates, Inc., retail marketing consultants.

Troubled by sagging sales of jeans to adults, Levi Strauss & Co. introduced "baby Levis" in the spring of 1984. The company will sell blue demin pants and diaper covers for infants, as well as tiny knit shirts proclaiming "My First Levis." Says Bill Oldenburg, general manager of the youthwear division: "We're trying to develop brand loyalty at an earlier age."

Levi predicts that by 1990 more than 8 million babies will be crawling about, an increase of 11 percent from 1983. Already, the United States has more moppets under five years—17.8 million—than in any year since 1968. What interests marketers most, though, is the growing percentage of births that are first births. That's when parents and doting grandparents tend to make their largest purchases. Kurt Salmon & Associates currently estimate the preschool clothing market at more than $6 billion a year.

"The outlook is tremendous," says Leo Goulet, president of Gerber. "There are more working mothers who have the money to spend and who are going for better-quality merchandise." The baby-food company expects sales of clothing, furniture, and other nonfood products for kids to double to $450 million in five years.

Working mothers in particular are changing the way children's wear companies design and market products. William Carter Co., for instance, is now selling Swiftly Change suits that contain more snaps to make diapering babies simpler. Fisher-Price found mothers especially interested in clothing that will enable children to dress themselves at an earlier age.

To make its playwear stand out, Fisher-Price is advertising it as "the children's clothing that mothers helped design." The company is also banking heavily on the strong pull of its brand name and its toys, which it says are in 99 percent of the homes where a child under the age of six lives. From now on, all kids featured in toy ads will be dressed in the playwear.

Fisher-Price may try to parlay its reputation for durability into kids' underwear and shoes too. "I doubt if we'll ever try to sell party dresses, though," Mr. Muirhead says. "We're not seen as very stylish or avant garde."

## Questions

1. Explain the Fisher-Price playwear in terms of the three levels of a product: core, actual, and augmented. How is product quality defined by the buyers of children's playwear?

2. What are the advantages and limitations of extending the brand-name "Fisher-Price" from toys to children's playwear?

3. Discuss the marketing research used in planning the Fisher-Price line of playwear.

4. Analyze the demographic and socioeconomic trends from 1985 to 1992 for the playwear line. Do the trends appear favorable or unfavorable for the new product line?

*Source:* Adapted from Ronald Alsop, "Fisher-Price Banks on Name, Design in Foray into Playwear." *The Wall Street Journal* August 2, 1984. Reprinted by permission of *The Wall Street Journal,* © Dow Jones & Company, Inc., 1984. All rights reserved.

# 10

# Designing Products: New-Product Development and Product Life-Cycle Strategies

## CHAPTER OBJECTIVES

After reading this chapter, you should be able to

1. List and define the steps in new-product development
2. Explain how companies find and develop new-product ideas
3. Describe the stages of the product life cycle
4. Explain how marketing strategy changes during a product's life cycle

The 3M Company markets more than 60,000 products, ranging from sandpaper, adhesives, and floppy disks to contact lenses, laser optical disks, and heart-lung machines; from coatings that sleeken boat hulls to hundreds of sticky tapes—Scotch Tape, masking tape, super-bonding tape, and even refastening disposable diaper tape. 3M views *innovation* as its path to growth and new products as its lifeblood. The company's longstanding goal is to derive an astonishing 25 percent of each year's sales from products introduced within the previous five years. More astonishing, it usually succeeds! Each year, 3M launches more than 200 new products. And last year, 32 percent of its almost $11 billion in sales came from products introduced within the past five years. Its legendary emphasis on innovation has consistently made it one of America's most admired companies.

New products don't just happen. 3M works hard to create an environment that supports innovation. It invests 6.5 percent of its annual sales in research and development—almost twice as much as the average company. Its "Innovation Task Force" seeks out and destroys corporate bureaucracy that might interfere

with new-product progress. Hired consultants help 3M find ways to make employees more inventive.

3M encourages everyone to look for new products. The company's renowned "15 percent rule" allows all employees to spend up to 15 percent of their time "bootlegging"—working on projects of personal interest whether those projects directly benefit the company or not. When a promising idea comes along, 3M forms a venture team made up of the researcher who developed the idea and volunteers from manufacturing, sales, marketing, and legal. The team nurtures the product and protects it from company bureaucracy. Team members stay with the product until it succeeds or fails and then return to their previous jobs. Some teams have tried three or four times before finally making a success out of an idea. Each year, 3M hands out "Golden Step Awards" to venture teams whose new products earned more than $2 million in U.S. sales or $4 million in worldwide sales within three years of introduction.

3M knows that it must try thousands of new-product ideas to hit one big jackpot. One well-worn slogan at 3M is, "You have to kiss a lot of frogs to find a prince." "Kissing frogs" often means making mistakes, but 3M accepts blunders and dead ends as a normal part of creativity and innovation. In fact, its philosophy seems to be: "If you aren't making mistakes, you probably aren't doing anything." But as it turns out, "blunders" have turned into some of 3M's most successful products. Old-timers at 3M love to tell the story about the chemist who accidently spilled a new chemical on her tennis shoes. Some days later, she noticed that the spots hit by the chemical had not gotten dirty. Eureka! The chemical eventually became Scotchgard fabric protector.

And then there's the one about 3M scientist Spencer Silver. Silver started out to develop a super-strong adhesive; instead he came up with one that didn't stick very well at all. He sent the apparently useless substance on to other 3M researchers to see if they could find something to do with it. Nothing happened for several years. Then Arthur Fry, another 3M scientist, had a problem—and an idea. As a choir member in a local church, Mr. Fry was having trouble marking places in his hymnal—the little scraps of paper he used kept falling out. He tried dabbing some of Mr. Silver's weak glue on one of the scraps. It stuck nicely and later peeled off without damaging the hymnal. Thus were born 3M's Post-It Notes, a product that now sells almost $100 million a year![1]

---

**new-product development** The development of original products, product improvements, product modifications, and new brands through the firm's own R&D efforts.

A company has to be good at developing new products. It also has to be good at managing them in the face of changing tastes, technologies, and competition. Every product seems to go through a life cycle—it is born, goes through several phases, and eventually dies as newer products come along that better serve consumer needs.

This product life cycle presents two major challenges. First, because all products eventually decline, the firm must find new products to replace aging ones (the problem of *new-product development*). Second, the firm must understand how its products age and adapt its marketing strategies as products pass through life-cycle stages (the problem of *product life-cycle strategies*). We will first look at the problem of finding and developing new products and then at the problem of managing them successfully over their life cycles.

## NEW-PRODUCT DEVELOPMENT STRATEGY

Given the rapid changes in tastes, technology, and competition, a company cannot rely solely on its existing products. Customers want and expect new and improved products. Competition will do its best to provide them. Every company needs a new-product development program. One expert estimates that half the profits of all U.S. companies come from products that did not even exist ten years ago.[2]

A company can obtain new products in two ways. One is through *acquisition*—by buying a whole company, a patent, or a license to produce someone else's product. The other is through **new-product development** in the company's own research and development department. As the costs of developing and introducing major new products have climbed, many large companies have decided to acquire existing brands rather than create new ones. Others have saved money by copying competitors' brands or by reviving old brands (see Marketing Highlight 10–1).

By *new products* we mean original products, product improvements, product modifications, and new brands that the firm develops through its own research and development efforts. In this chapter, we will concentrate on new-product development.

Innovation can be very risky. Ford lost $350 million on its Edsel automobile; RCA lost a staggering $580 million on its SelectaVision videodisc player; Xerox's venture into computers was a disaster; and the Concorde aircraft will

# Marketing Highlight 10–1

## GETTING AROUND THE HIGH COSTS AND RISKS OF NEW-PRODUCT DEVELOPMENT

The average cost of developing and introducing a major new product from scratch has jumped to well over $100 million. To make things worse, many of these costly new products fail. So companies are now pursuing new-product strategies that are less costly and risky than developing completely new brands. We discussed two of these strategies—*licensing* and *brand extensions*—in Chapter 9. Here we describe three other new-product strategies—*acquiring new brands, developing "me-too" products,* and *reviving old brands.*

### Acquiring New Products

Instead of building its own new products from the ground up, a company can buy another company and its established brands. The 1980s saw a dramatic flurry of big consumer companies gobbling up one another. Procter & Gamble acquired Richardson-Vicks, R. J. Reynolds bought Nabisco, Philip Morris obtained General Foods and Kraft, Nestlé absorbed Carnation, and Unilever picked up Chesebrough-Ponds.

Such acquisitions can be tricky—the company must be certain that the acquired products blend well with its own current products and that the firm has the skills and resources needed to continue to run the acquired products profitably. Acquisitions can also run into snags with government regulators. For example, even under the Reagan administration's loose antitrust policy, regulators did not allow Pepsi to acquire 7-Up or Coke to buy up Dr Pepper. Finally, such acquisitions have high price tags. Philip Morris paid $5.7 billion for General Foods, RJR coughed up $4.9 billion for Nabisco, and Nestlé forked over $3 billion for Carnation. Not many companies can afford to buy up market-winning brands.

But despite high initial outlays, buying established brands may be cheaper in the long run than paying the enormous costs of trying to create well-known brand names from scratch. And acquiring proven winners eliminates almost all the risks of new-product failure. Acquisition also provides a quick and easy way to gain access to new markets or strengthen positions in current markets. For example, by acquiring Richardson-Vicks, P&G moved immediately into the health and beauty aids market. It also strengthened its hold in the home remedies segment by getting a medicine cabinet full of such top brands as Vicks VapoRub, Formula 44D Cough Syrup, Sinex, NyQuil, and Clearasil to add to its own Pepto-Bismol and Chloraseptic brands.

### Developing "Me-Too" Products

In recent years, many companies have used "me-too" product strategies—introducing imitations of successful competitors' products. Thus, Tandy, AT&T, Zenith, and many others produce IBM-compatible personal computers. Moreover, these "clones" sometimes sell for less than half the price of the IBM models they emulate. Me-too products have also hit the fragrance industry. Several companies now offer smell-alike "knock-offs" of popular, high-priced perfumes like Obsession, Opium, Georgio, and Poison at 20 percent of the originals' prices. The success of knock-off fragrances has also inspired a wave of look-alike designer fashions and imitative versions of prestige cosmetics and hair care brands. Imitation is now fair play for products ranging from soft drinks and food to mousses and minivans.

Me-too products are often quicker and less expensive to develop—the market leader pioneers the technology and bears most of the product-development costs.

The imitative products sometimes give consumers even more value than the market-leading originals: The copycat company can build on the leader's design and technology to create an equivalent product at a lower price, or an even better product at the same or a higher price. Me-too products are also less costly and risky to introduce—they enter a proven market already developed by the market leader. Thus, while IBM invested millions to develop its personal computers and cultivate a market, the clone makers simply rode in on IBM's generous coattails.

However, a me-too strategy also has some drawbacks. The imitating company enters the market late and must battle a successful, firmly entrenched competitor. Some me-too products never take much business from the leader. Others succeed broadly and end up challenging for market leadership. Still others settle into small but profitable niches in the market created by the leader.

### Reviving Old Products

Many companies have found "new gold in the old" by reviving once-successful brands that are now dead or dying. Many old and tarnished brand names still hold magic for consumers. Often, simply reviving, reformulating, and repositioning an old brand can give the company a successful "new" product at a fraction of the cost of building new brands.

There are some classic examples of brand revivals—Arm & Hammer Baking Soda sales spurted after it was promoted as deodorizer for refrigerators, garbage disposals, cars, and kitty litter boxes. Ivory Soap reversed its sales decline in the early 1970s when it was promoted for adult use rather than just for babies. Dannon Yogurt sales rocketed when it was linked to healthy living. In recent years,

Warner-Lambert revived Black Jack gum, playing on the nostalgia of its 110-year-old name; Coca-Cola rejuvenated Fresca by adding NutraSweet and real fruit juice; and Campbell expanded the appeal of V8 Juice by tying it to today's fitness craze.

Sometimes, a dead product rises again with a new name, as happened with Nestlé's New Cookery brand of low-fat, low-sugar, low-salt entrees. Some years ago, Nestlé withdrew the product when it failed in test market—the company faulted the times, the product's name, and ordinary packaging. But New Cookery was well-suited to today's health-conscious consumers, and Stouffer, a Nestlé company, later revived the line under the Lean Cuisine brand. Lean Cuisine proved a resounding success.

*Sources:* See "Products of the Year," *Fortune,* December 9, 1985, pp. 106–12; Paul B. Brown, Zachary Schiller, Christine Dugas, and Scott Scredon, "New? Improved? The Brand-Name Mergers," *Business Week,* October 21, 1985, pp. 108–10; Kenneth Dreyfack, "The Big Brands Are Back in Style," *Business Week,* January 12, 1987, p. 74; Pat Sloan, "Knock-Offs Deliver Blows to Fragrance Market," *Advertising Age,* March 2, 1987, p. S14; and Arthur Bragg, "Back to the Future," *Sales & Marketing Management,* November 1986, pp. 61–62.

never pay back its investment. Here are several other consumer products, each launched by sophisticated companies, that failed:

□ Red Kettle soup (Campbell)

□ Cue toothpaste (Colgate)

□ Vim tablet detergent (Lever)

□ LA low alcohol beer (Anheuser-Busch)

□ PCjr personal computer (IBM)

□ Zap Mail electronic mail (Federal Express)

□ Polavision instant movies (Polaroid)

One study found that the new-product failure rate was 40 percent for consumer products, 20 percent for industrial products, and 18 percent for services. A recent study of 700 consumer and industrial firms found an overall success rate for new products of only 65 percent. Still another source estimates that of the 2,500 new products introduced each year, some 90 percent survive less than three years![3]

Why do so many new products fail? There are several reasons. A high-level executive might push a favorite idea in spite of poor marketing-research findings. Or although an idea may be good, the market size may have been overestimated. Perhaps the actual product was not designed as well as it should have been. Or maybe it was incorrectly positioned in the market, priced too high, or advertised poorly. Sometimes the costs of product development are higher than expected and sometimes competitors fight back harder than expected.

Thus, companies face a problem—although they must develop new products, the odds weigh heavily against success. The solution lies in strong new-product planning and in setting up a systematic *new-product development process* for finding and growing new products. The major steps in this process are shown in Figure 10–1 and described below.

FIGURE 10–1    Major Stages in New-Product Development

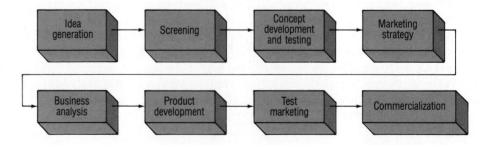

## Idea Generation

**idea generation** The systematic
search for new-product ideas.

New-product development starts with **idea generation**—the systematic search for new-product ideas. A company typically has to generate many ideas in order to find a few good ones. The search for new-product ideas should be systematic rather than haphazard. Otherwise, although the company will find many ideas, most will not be good ones for its type of business. One company spent more than a million dollars for research and development on a new product, only to have top management reject it because it did not want to get into that type of business.

Top management can avoid this error by carefully defining its new-product development strategy. It should state what products and markets to emphasize. It should state what the company wants from its new products, whether it be high cash flow, market share, or some other objective. It should state the effort to be devoted to developing original products, changing existing products, and imitating competitors' products.

To obtain a flow of new-product ideas, the company must tap many idea sources. Major sources of new-product ideas include the following:

- *Internal sources.* One study found that over 55 percent of all new-product ideas come from within the company.[4] The company can find new ideas through formal research and development. It can pick the brains of its scientists, engineers, and manufacturing people. Or company executives can brainstorm new-product ideas. The company's salespeople are another good source because they are in daily contact with customers.

- *Customers.* Almost 28 percent of all new-product ideas come from watching and listening to customers. Consumer needs and wants can be looked at through consumer surveys. The company can analyze customer questions and complaints to find new products to better solve consumer problems. Company engineers or salespeople can meet with customers to get suggestions. General Electric's Video Products Division has its design engineers talk with final consumers to get ideas for new home electronics products. National Steel has a product application center where company engineers work with automotive customers to discover customer needs that might require new products.[5] Finally, consumers often create new products on their own, and companies can benefit by finding these products and putting them on the market. Pillsbury gets promising new recipes through its annual Bake-Off—one of Pillsbury's four cake mix lines and several variations of another came directly from Bake-Off winners' recipes. About one-third of all the software IBM leases for its computers is developed by outside users.[6]

- *Competitors.* About 27 percent of new-product ideas come from analyzing competitors' products. The company can watch competitors' ads and other communications to get clues about their new products. Companies buy competing new products, take them apart to see how they work, analyze their sales, and decide whether the company should bring out a new product of its own. For example, when designing its highly successful Taurus, Ford tore down over 50 competing models, layer by layer, looking for things to copy or improve upon. It copied the Audi's accelerator pedal "feel," the Toyota Supra fuel gauge, the BMW 528e tire and jack storage system, and 400 other such outstanding features.[7]

- *Distributors and Suppliers.* Resellers are close to the market and can pass along information about consumer problems and new-product possibilities. Suppliers can tell the company about new concepts, techniques, and materials that can be used to develop new products.

**idea screening** Screening new-product ideas in order to spot good ideas and drop poor ones as soon as possible.

**product idea** An idea for a possible product that the company can see itself offering to the market.

*Pillsbury's* BAKEOFF *promotes consumer goodwill and sometimes produces new-product ideas.*

□ *Other sources.* Other idea sources include trade magazines, shows, and seminars; government agencies; new-product consultants; advertising agencies; marketing-research firms; university and commercial laboratories; and inventors.

## Idea Screening

The purpose of idea generation is to create a large number of ideas. The purpose of the succeeding stages is to *reduce* that number. The first idea-reducing stage is **idea screening.** The purpose of screening is to spot good ideas and drop poor ones as soon as possible. Product-development costs rise greatly in later stages. The company wants to go ahead only with the product ideas that will turn into profitable products.

Most companies require their executives to write up new-product ideas on a standard form that can be reviewed by a new-product committee. They describe the product, the target market, and the competition and make some rough estimates of market size, product price, development time and costs, manufacturing costs, and rate of return. They answer the following questions: Is this idea good for our particular company? Does it mesh well with the company's objectives and strategies? Do we have the people, skills, and resources to make it succeed? Many companies have well-designed systems for rating and screening new-product ideas.[8]

## Concept Development and Testing

Surviving ideas must now be developed into product concepts. It is important to distinguish between a *product idea*, a *product concept*, and a *product image*. A **product idea** is an idea for a possible product that the company can see itself offering to the market. A **product concept** is a detailed version of the idea stated in meaningful consumer terms. A **product image** is the way consumers perceive an actual or potential product.

## Concept Development

Suppose a car manufacturer figures out how to design an electric car that can go as fast as 60 miles an hour and as far as eighty miles before needing to be recharged. The manufacturer estimates that the electric car's operating costs will be about half those of a regular car.

This is a product idea. Customers, however, do not buy a product idea; they buy a product *concept*. The marketer's task is to develop this idea into some alternative product concepts, find out how attractive each concept is to customers, and choose the best one.

The following product concepts might be created for the electric car:

□ *Concept 1.* An inexpensive subcompact designed as a second family car to be used around town. The car is ideal for loading groceries and hauling children, and it is easy to enter.

□ *Concept 2.* A medium-cost, medium-size car designed as an all-purpose family car.

□ *Concept 3.* A medium-cost sporty compact appealing to young people.

□ *Concept 4.* An inexpensive subcompact appealing to conscientious people who want basic transportation, low fuel cost, and low pollution.

## Concept Testing

**Concept testing** calls for testing these concepts with a group of target consumers. The concepts may be presented through word or picture descriptions. Here is Concept 1:

> An efficient, fun-to-drive, electric-powered subcompact car that seats four. Great for shopping trips and visits to friends. Costs half as much to operate as similar gasoline-driven cars. Goes up to 60 miles an hour and does not need to be recharged for 80 miles. Priced at $8,000.

Consumers may then be asked to react to this concept by answering the questions in Table 10-1. The answers will help the company decide which

*A prototype of an electric car. This one has a top speed of 60 miles per hour and an in-city driving range of 80 miles.*

**product concept** A detailed version of the new-product idea stated in meaningful consumer terms.

**product image** The way consumers perceive an actual or potential product.

**concept testing** Testing new-product concepts with a group of target consumers to find out if the concepts have strong consumer appeal.

**marketing strategy development**
Designing an initial marketing strategy for a new product based on the product concept.

**marketing strategy statement** A statement of the planned strategy for a new product that outlines the intended target market, the planned product positioning, and the sales, market share, and profit goals for the first few years.

TABLE 10-1   Questions for Electric Car Concept Test

1. Do you understand the concept of an electric car?
2. What do you see as the benefits of an electric car compared with a conventional car?
3. Do you believe the claims about the electric car's performance?
4. Would the electric car meet all your automobile needs?
5. What improvements can you suggest in the car's various features?
6. Would you prefer an electric car to a conventional car? For what uses?
7. What do you think the price of the electric car should be?
8. Who would be involved in your purchase decision for such a car? Who would drive it?
9. Would you buy an electric car? (Definitely, probably, probably not, definitely not)

concept has the strongest appeal. For example, the last question asks about the consumer's intention-to-buy. Suppose 10 percent of the consumers said they "definitely" would buy and another 5 percent said "probably." The company could project these figures to the population size of this target group to estimate sales volume. Even then, the estimate is uncertain because people do not always carry out their stated intentions.[9]

## Marketing Strategy Development

Suppose concept 1 for the electric car tests out best. The next step is **marketing strategy development**—designing an initial marketing strategy for introducing this car into the market.

The **marketing strategy statement** consists of three parts. The first part describes the target market, the planned product positioning, and the sales, market-share, and profit goals for the first few years. Thus:

> The target market is households that need a second car for shopping trips, running errands, and visits to friends. The car will be positioned as more economical to buy and operate, and more fun to drive, than cars now available to this market. The company will aim to sell 200,000 cars in the first year, at a loss of not more than $3 million. The second year will aim for sales of 220,000 cars and a profit of $5 million.

The second part of the marketing strategy statement outlines the product's planned price, distribution, and marketing budget for the first year:

> The electric car will be offered in three colors and will have optional air conditioning and power-drive features. It will sell at a retail price of $8,000, with 15 percent off the list price to dealers. Dealers who sell over 10 cars per month will get an additional discount of 5 percent on each car sold that month. An advertising budget of $10 million will be split 50:50 between national and local advertising. Advertising will emphasize the car's economy and fun. During the first year, $100,000 will be spent on marketing research to find out who is buying the car and their satisfaction levels.

The third part of the marketing strategy statement describes the planned long-run sales, profit goals, and marketing mix strategy:

> The company intends to capture a 3 percent long-run share of the total auto market and realize an after-tax return on investment of 15 percent. To achieve this, product quality will start high and be improved over time. Price will be raised in the second and third years if competition permits. The total advertising budget will be raised each year by about 10 percent. Marketing research will be reduced to $60,000 per year after the first year.

## Business Analysis

**business analysis** A review of the sales, costs, and profit projections for a new product to find out whether these factors satisfy the company's objectives.

**product development** Developing the product concept into a physical product in order to ensure that the product idea can be turned into a workable product.

**test marketing** The stage of new-product development at which the product and marketing program are tested in more realistic market settings.

Once management has decided on its product concept and marketing strategy, it can evaluate the business attractiveness of the proposal. **Business analysis** involves a review the sales, costs, and profit projections to find out whether they satisfy the company's objectives. If they do, the product can move to the product-development stage.

To estimate sales, the company should look at the sales history of similar products and should survey market opinion. It should estimate minimum and maximum sales to learn the range of risk. After preparing the sales forecast, management can estimate the expected costs and profits for the product. The costs are estimated by the R&D, manufacturing, accounting, and finance departments. Planned marketing costs are included in the analysis. The company then uses the sales and costs figures to analyze the new product's financial attractiveness.

## Product Development

If the product concept passes the business test, it moves into **product development.** Here, R&D or engineering develop the product concept into a physical product. Up to now, it has existed only as a word description, a drawing, or perhaps a crude mockup. The product-development step, however, now calls for a large jump in investment. It will show whether the product idea can be turned into a workable product.

The R&D department will develop one or more physical versions of the product concept. It hopes to find a prototype that meets the following criteria: (1) Consumers see it as having the key features described in the product-concept statement; (2) it performs safely under normal use; and (3) it can be produced for the budgeted costs.

Developing a successful prototype can take days, weeks, months, or even years. The prototype must have the required functional features and also convey the intended psychological characteristics. The electric car, for example, should strike consumers as being well built and safe. Management must learn how consumers decide how well built a car is. Some consumers slam the door to hear its "sound." If the car does not have "solid-sounding" doors, consumers will think it is poorly built.

When the prototypes are ready, they must be tested. Functional tests are then conducted under laboratory and field conditions to make sure that the product performs safely and effectively. The new car must start well; it must be comfortable; it must be able to go around corners without overturning. Consumer tests are conducted, asking consumers to test-drive the car and rate its attributes.

## Test Marketing

If the product passes functional and consumer tests, the next step is test marketing. **Test marketing** is the stage at which the product and marketing program are introduced into more realistic market settings.

Test marketing lets the marketer get experience with marketing the product, find potential problems, and learn where more information is needed before going to the great expense of full introduction. The basic purpose of test marketing is to test the product itself in real market situations. But test marketing also allows the company to test its entire marketing program for the product—its positioning strategy, advertising, distribution, pricing, branding

**commercialization** Introducing a new product into the market.

and packaging, and budget levels. The company uses test marketing to learn how consumers and dealers will react to handling, using, and repurchasing the product. Test marketing results can be used to make better sales and profit forecasts. Thus, a good test market can provide a wealth of information about the potential success of the product and marketing program (see Marketing Highlight 10-2).

The amount of test marketing needed varies with each new product. Test marketing costs can be enormous, and test marketing takes time during which competitors may gain advantages. When the costs of developing and introducing the product are low or when management is already confident that the new product will succeed, the company may do little or no test marketing. Minor modifications of current products or copies of successful competitor products might not need testing. For example, Procter & Gamble introduced its Folger's decaffeinated coffee crystals without test marketing, and Pillsbury rolled out Chewy granola bars and chocolate-covered Granola Dipps with no standard test market. But when introducing the new product requires a large investment, or when management is not sure of the product or marketing program, the company may do a lot of test marketing. In fact, some products and marketing programs are tested, withdrawn, changed, and retested many times over a period of several years before they are finally introduced. The costs of such test markets are high, but they are often small compared with the costs of making a major mistake.

## Commercialization

Test marketing gives management the information needed to make a final decision about whether to launch the new product. If the company goes ahead with **commercialization**—introducing the new product into the market—it will face high costs. The company will have to build or rent a manufacturing facility. And it may have to spend, in the case of a new consumer packaged good, between $10 million and $100 million for advertising and sales promotion alone in the first year. For example, McDonald's spent over $5 million dollars *per week* on advertising the introduction of its McDLT sandwich.

In launching a new product, the company must make four decisions.

### When?

The first decision is whether it is the right time to introduce the new product. If the electric car will eat into the sales of the company's other cars, its introduction may be delayed. Or if the electric car can be improved further, the company may wait to launch it the following year. Or if the economy is down, the company may want to wait.

### Where?

The company must decide whether to launch the new product in a single location, a region, several regions, the national market, or the international market. Few companies have the confidence, capital, and capacity to launch new products into full national distribution. They will develop a planned *market rollout* over time. In particular, small companies may select an attractive city and put on a blitz campaign to enter the market. They may then enter other cities one at a time. Larger companies can introduce their products into a whole region and then move to the next region. Companies with national distribution networks, such as auto companies, often launch their new models in the national market.

## A TEST MARKET THAT REALLY MADE A DIFFERENCE

Some test markets do little more than confirm what management already knows. Others prune out the new-product losers—half of all test-marketed consumer products are killed before they reach national distribution. Still other test markets provide highly useful information that can save a promising product or turn an otherwise average product into a blockbuster. Here's a story about a test market that really made a difference.

After its stunning success several years ago with Dole Fruit 'n Juice Bars, Dole Foods worked feverishly to find a follow-up product with the same kind of consumer appeal. It soon came up with Fruit and Cream Bars. Before investing in a costly national rollout, Dole decided to run a test market. The company began the test market with high expectations—the Fruit and Cream brand manager predicted high sales and market share.

In the test market, Dole offered Fruit and Cream in three flavors—strawberry, blueberry, and peach—packed four to a box. Packaging modestly mentioned "100% natural" ingredients and showed a bowl of fruit and cream. Dole supported the test market with standard advertising and promotion, including television, newspaper, direct-mail, point-of-purchase, and coupon campaigns to stimulate trial and repeat purchasing. Fruit and Cream ads targeted upscale consumers aged 25 to 54 with kids, centering on the product and its taste and health appeal.

The test market quickly yielded some surprises. It showed that Fruit and Cream had much broader appeal than Dole had expected. By the end of the third month, it had become the number-one brand in the test market area. Focus groups showed that Fruit and Cream buyers saw the product as a real treat and felt they could eat it without feeling too much caloric guilt. Consumers said that Fruit and Cream's natural ingredients and natural taste made it superior to the competition. Despite dazzling sales performance, however, Dole discovered that its television advertising performed poorly—sales didn't jump when the television campaign began.

Based on the test market results, Dole made several changes in the Fruit and Cream marketing mix. It redesigned the packaging to greatly increase the size of the "100% natural" claim. And a new package picture showed cream being poured over the fruit—a subtle difference, but one that emphasized Fruit and Cream's appetite appeal. Dole created a completely new advertising campaign that focused more heavily on natural taste and created a mellow feeling. The new ads used a golden oldie song, "You're Sweet 16, Peaches and Cream," and stressed the luxury in the product. Dole also shortened the test market from one year to six months, raised its forecast of Fruit and Cream sales, and rushed to get two more flavors (banana and raspberry) ready.

With all the marketing changes, Dole was convinced that Fruit and Cream would take off like a rocket when it went national. But test markets can't predict future market events. Four new competing fruit-based novelty ice cream products came out at the same time as Fruit and Cream—two from Chiquita, one from Jell-O, and one from Minute Maid. The result was a marketer's nightmare. Fruit and Cream missed all its sales projections. But so did all the competitors, and Fruit and Cream held on, achieving a 3 percent market share instead of the expected 4 percent. The dust has now settled, and Dole expects to hit its original projections this year.

No test market can predict future competitor actions and reactions, economic conditions, changing consumer tastes, and other factors that affect a new product's success. It can only show how consumers in a selected market area react to a new product and its marketing program. But the people at Dole are still strong believers. According to the Fruit and Cream brand manager, "Without the changes we made as a result of the test market, we would have been hurt much more than we were."

*Source:* Adapted from Leslie Brennan, "Test Marketing Put to the Test," *Sales & Marketing Management,* March 1987, pp. 65–68.

*Dole Fruit and Cream Bars: test marketing really made a difference.*

### To Whom?

Within its rollout markets, the company must target its distribution and promotion to the best prospect groups. The company has already profiled the prime prospects in earlier test marketing. It must now fine-tune its market identification, looking especially for early adopters, heavy users, and opinion leaders.

### How?

The company must also develop an action plan for introducing the new product into the selected markets. It must spend the marketing budget on the marketing mix and various other activities. Thus, the electric car's launch may be supported by a publicity campaign and then by offers of gifts to draw more people to the showrooms. The company needs to prepare a separate marketing plan for each new market.

## Marketing Highlight 10–3

### PARALLEL PRODUCT DEVELOPMENT: SPEEDING NEW PRODUCTS TO MARKET

Philips, the giant Dutch consumer electronics company, marketed the first practical videocassette recorder in 1972, gaining a three-year lead on its Japanese competitors. But in the seven years that it took Philips to develop its second generation of VCR models, Japanese manufacturers had launched at least three generations of new products. A victim of its own creaky product-development process, Philips never recovered from the Japanese onslaught. Today, the company is an also-ran with only a 2 percent market share; it still loses money on VCRs. The Philips story is typical—during the last few decades, dozens of large companies have fallen victim to competitors with faster, more flexible new-product development programs. In today's fast-changing, fiercely competitive world, turning out new products too slowly can result in product failures, lost sales and profits, and crumbling market positions.

Large companies have traditionally used a "sequential product-development" approach in which new products are developed in an orderly series of steps. In a kind of relay race, each company department completes its phase of the development process before passing the new product on. The sequential process has merits—it helps bring order to risky and complex new-product development projects. But the approach can also be fatally slow.

To speed up their product-development cycles, many companies are now adopting a faster, more agile, team-oriented approach called "parallel product development." Instead of passing the new product from department to department, the company assembles a team of people from various departments that stays with the new product from start to finish. Such teams usually include representatives from marketing, finance, design, manufacturing, and legal departments, and even supplier companies. Parallel development is more like a rugby match than a relay race—team members pass the new product back and forth as they move downfield toward the common goal of a

*Ford's successful Taurus was the first American car developed using parallel product development.*

## Speeding Up New-Product Development

Many companies organize their new-product development process into an orderly sequence of steps, starting with idea generation and ending with commercialization. Under this **sequential product development** approach, one company department works individually to complete its stage of the process before passing the new product along to the next department and stage. This orderly, step-by-step process can help bring control to complex and risky projects. But it can also be dangerously slow. In fast-changing, highly competitive markets, such slow-but-sure product development can cost the company potential sales and profits at the hands of more nimble competitors. Today, in order to get their new products to market more quickly, many companies are dropping the *sequential product development* approach in favor of the faster, more flexible **parallel product development** approach. Under the new approach, various company departments work closely together, overlapping the steps in the product-development process to save time and increase effectiveness (see Marketing Highlight 10–3).

**sequential product development** A new-product development approach in which one company department works individually to complete its stage of the process before passing the new product along to the next department and stage.

**parallel product development** An approach to developing new products in which various company departments work closely together, overlapping the steps in the product-development process to save time and increase effectiveness.

speedy and successful new-product launch.

Top management gives the product-development team general strategic direction but no clear-cut product idea or work plan. It challenges the team with stiff and seemingly contradictory goals—"turn out carefully planned and superior new products, but do it quickly"—and then gives the team whatever freedom and resources it needs to meet the challenge. The team becomes a driving force that pushes the product forward. In the sequential process, a bottleneck at one phase can seriously slow or even halt the whole product-development project. In the parallel approach, if one functional area hits snags, it works to resolve them while the team moves on.

The Allen-Bradley Company, a maker of industrial controls, provides an example of the tremendous benefits gained by using parallel development. Under the old sequential approach, the company's marketing department handed off a new-product idea to designers. The designers, working in isolation, prepared concepts and passed them along to product engineers. The engineers, also working by themselves, developed expensive prototypes and handed them off to manufacturing, which tried to find a way to build the new product. Finally, after many years and dozens of costly

design compromises and delays, marketing was asked to sell the new product—which it often found to be too high-priced or sadly out-of-date. Now, Allen-Bradley has adopted the parallel product-development approach. All the company's departments work together—from beginning to end—to design and develop new products that meet customer needs and company capabilities. The results have been astonishing. For example, the company recently developed a new electrical control in just two years; under the old system, it would have taken six years.

The auto industry has also discovered the benefits of parallel product development. The approach is called "simultaneous engineering" at GM, the "team concept" at Ford, and "process-driven design" at Chrysler. The first American cars built using this process, the Ford Taurus and Mercury Sable, have been major marketing successes. Ford squeezed 14 weeks out of its product-development cycle by simply getting the engineering and finance departments to review designs at the same time instead of sequentially. It claims that such actions have helped cut average engineering costs for a project by 35 percent. In an industry that has typically taken five or six years to turn out a new model, Mazda now brags about two-to-three-year product-development

cycles—a feat that would be impossible without parallel development.

However, the parallel approach has some limitations. Superfast product development can be riskier and more costly than the slower, more orderly sequential approach. And it often creates increased organizational tension and confusion. But in rapidly changing industries facing increasingly shorter product life cycles, the rewards of fast and flexible product development far exceed the risks. Companies that get new and improved products to the market faster than competitors gain a dramatic competitive edge. They can respond more quickly to emerging consumer tastes and charge higher prices for more advanced designs. As one auto industry executive states, "What we want to do is get the new car approved, built, and in the consumer's hands in the shortest time possible. . . . Whoever gets there first gets all the marbles."

*Sources:* Hirotaka Takeuchi and Ikujiro Nonaka, "The New New Product Development Game," **Harvard Business Review**, January-February 1986, pp. 137–46; Bro Uttal, "Speeding New Ideas to Market," **Fortune**, March 2, 1987, pp. 62–65; William Jeanes, "The Idea That Saved Detroit," **Northwest**, September 1987, pp. 15–19; John Bussey and Douglas R. Sease, "Speeding Up: Manufacturers Strive to Slice Time Needed to Develop New Products," **The Wall Street Journal**, February 23, 1988, pp. 1, 24; and Brian Dumaine, "How Managers Can Succeed through Speed," **Fortune**, February 13, 1989, pp. 54-59.

# PRODUCT LIFE-CYCLE STRATEGIES

**product life cycle (PLC)** The course of a product's sales and profits over its lifetime; it involves five distinct stages—product development, introduction, growth, maturity, and decline.

After launching the new product, management wants the product to enjoy a long and happy life. Although it does not expect the product to sell forever, management wants to earn a decent profit to cover all the effort and risk that went into it. Management is aware that each product will have a life cycle, although the exact shape and length is not known in advance.

The sales and profit patterns in a typical **product life cycle (PLC)** are shown in Figure 10–2. The product life cycle is marked by five distinct stages:

1. *Product development* begins when the company finds and develops a new-product idea. During product development, sales are zero and the company's investment costs add up.

2. *Introduction* is a period of slow sales growth as the product is being introduced in the market. Profits are nonexistent in this stage because of the heavy expenses of product introduction.

3. *Growth* is a period of rapid market acceptance and increasing profits.

4. *Maturity* is a period of slowdown in sales growth because the product has achieved acceptance by most potential buyers. Profits level off or decline because of increased marketing outlays to defend the product against competition.

5. *Decline* is the period when sales fall off and profits drop.

Not all products follow this S-shaped product life cycle. Some products are introduced and die quickly. Others stay in the mature stage for a long, long time. Some enter the decline stage and are then cycled back into the growth stage through strong promotion or repositioning.

The PLC concept can describe a *product class* (gasoline-powered automobiles), a *product form* (station wagons), or a *brand* (the Ford Taurus). The PLC concept applies differently in each case. Product classes have the longest life cycles. The sales of many product classes stay in the mature stage for long time. Product forms, on the other hand, tend to have the standard PLC shape. Product forms such as the "dial telephone" and "cream deodorants" passed through a regular history of introduction, rapid growth, maturity, and decline. A specific brand's life cycle can change quickly because of changing competitive attacks and responses. The life cycles of several toothpaste brands are shown in Figure

FIGURE 10–2  Sales and Profits over the Product's Life from Inception to Demise

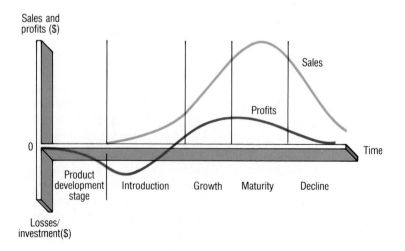

style A basic and distinctive mode of expression.
fashion A currently accepted or popular style in a given field.

*Some products stay in the maturity stage of the product life cycle for a long, long time: Kikkoman is 358 years old!*

10–3. Although teeth-cleaning products (product class) and toothpastes (product form) have enjoyed fairly long life cycles, the life cycles of specific brands have tended to be much shorter.

The PLC concept can also be applied to what are known as styles, fashions, and fads. Their special life cycles are shown in Figure 10–4. A **style** is a basic and distinctive mode of expression. For example, styles appear in homes (colonial, ranch, Cape Cod), clothing (formal, casual), and art (realistic, surrealistic, abstract). Once a style is invented, it may last for generations, coming in and out of vogue. A style has a cycle showing several periods of renewed interest.

A **fashion** is a currently accepted or popular style in a given field. For example, the "preppie look" in the clothing of the late 1970s gave way to the "loose and layered look" of the mid- to late-1980s. Fashions pass through many

FIGURE 10–3    Product Life Cycles for Selected Toothpaste Brands from 1936 to 1982

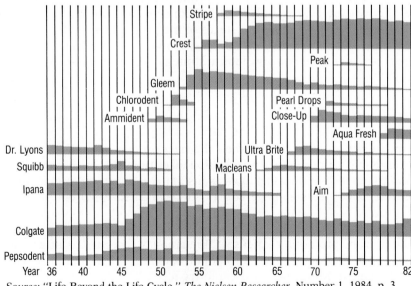

*Source:* "Life Beyond the Life Cycle," *The Nielsen Researcher*, Number 1, 1984, p. 3.

**fads** Fashions that enter quickly, are adopted with great zeal, peak early, and decline very fast.

**introduction stage** The product life-cycle stage when the new product is first distributed and made available for purchase.

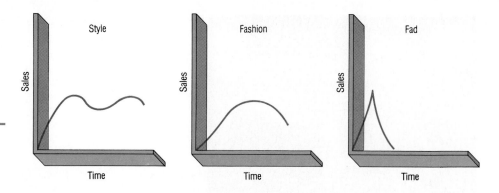

FIGURE 10-4 Marketers need to understand and predict style, fashion, and fad.

stages. First, a small number of consumers typically take an interest in something new to set themselves apart. Then, other consumers take an interest out of a desire to copy the fashion leaders. Next, the fashion becomes popular and is adopted by the mass market. Finally, the fashion fades away as consumers start moving toward other fashions that are beginning to catch their eye. Thus, fashions tend to grow slowly, remain popular for a while, then decline slowly.

**Fads** are fashions that enter quickly, are adopted with great zeal, peak early, and decline very fast. They last only a short time and tend to attract only a limited following. Fads often have a novel or quirky nature, as when people start buying Rubik's Cubes, Trivial Pursuit games, "pet rocks," or Pound Puppies. Fads appeal to people looking for excitement, a way to set themselves apart, or something to talk about to others. Fads do not survive for long because they do not normally satisfy a strong need or satisfy it well.

The PLC concept can be applied by marketers as a useful framework for describing how products and markets work. But using the PLC concept for forecasting product performance or for developing marketing strategies presents some practical problems.[10] For example, managers may have trouble identifying a product's current life-cycle stage, when it moves into the next stage, and the factors that affect how the product will move through the stages. In practice, it is difficult to forecast the sales level at each PLC stage, the length of each stage, and the shape of the PLC curve.

Using the PLC concept to develop marketing strategy can also be difficult because strategy is both a cause and a result of the product's life cycle. The product's current PLC position suggests the best marketing strategies, and the resulting marketing strategies affect product performance in later life-cycle stages. Yet when used carefully, the PLC concept can help in developing good marketing strategies for different stages of the product life cycle.

We looked at the product-development stage of the product life cycle in the first part of the chapter. We now look at strategies for each of the other life-cycle stages.

## Introduction Stage

The **introduction stage** starts when the new product is first distributed and made available for purchase. Introduction takes time, and sales growth is apt to be slow. Such well-known products as instant coffee, frozen orange juice, and powdered coffee creamers lingered for many years before they entered a stage of rapid growth.

In this stage, profits are negative or low because of the low sales and high distribution and promotion expenses. Much money is needed to attract distributors and build their inventories. Promotion spending is high to inform consumers of the new product and get them to try it.

Because the market is not generally ready for product refinements at this stage, the company and its few competitors produce basic versions of the product. These firms focus their selling on those buyers who are the readiest to buy—usually the higher-income groups. Prices tend to be on the high side because of low output, production problems, and high promotion and other expenses.

## Growth Stage

If the new product satisfies the market, it will enter a **growth stage,** in which sales will start climbing quickly. The early adopters will continue to buy, and later buyers will start following their lead, especially if they hear favorable word of mouth. Attracted by the opportunities for profit, new competitors will enter the market. They will introduce new product features, and the market will expand. The increase in competitors leads to an increase in the number of distribution outlets, and sales jump just to build reseller inventories. Prices remain where they are or fall only slightly. Companies keep their promotion spending at the same or a slightly higher level to meet competition and to continue educating the market.

Profits increase during this growth stage, as promotion costs are spread over a large volume and unit-manufacturing costs fall. The firm uses several strategies to sustain rapid market growth as long as possible. It improves product quality and adds new product features and models. It enters new market segments and new distribution channels. It shifts some advertising from building product awareness to building product conviction and purchase, and it lowers prices at the right time to attract more buyers.

The firm in the growth stage faces a trade-off between high market share and high current profit. By spending a lot of money on product improvement, promotion, and distribution, it can capture a dominant position. But it gives up maximum current profit in the hope of making this up in the next stage.

## Maturity Stage

At some point, a product's sales growth will slow down, and the product will enter a **maturity stage.** This maturity stage normally lasts longer than the previous stages, and it poses strong challenges to marketing management. Most products are in the maturity stage of the life cycle, and therefore most marketing management deals with the mature product.

*To sustain growth, Sony keeps adding new features to its Walkman line.*

**decline stage** The product life-cycle stage at which a product's sales decline.

The slowdown in sales growth results in many producers with many products to sell. In turn, this overcapacity leads to greater competition. Competitors begin marking down prices, increasing their advertising and sales promotions, and upping their R&D budgets to find better versions of the product. These steps mean a drop in profit. Some of the weaker competitors start dropping out, and the industry eventually contains only well-established competitors.

Product managers should not simply defend the product. A good offense is the best defense. They should consider modifying the market, product, and marketing mix.

### Market Modification

Here, the company tries to increase the consumption of the current product. It looks for new users and market segments, as when Johnson & Johnson targeted the adult market with its baby powder and shampoo. The manager also looks for ways to increase usage among present customers. Campbell does this by offering recipes and convincing consumers that "soup is good food." Or the company may want to reposition the brand to appeal to a larger or faster-growing segment, as Burger King did when it repositioned as "the right food for the fast times."

### Product Modification

The product manager can also change product characteristics—such as product quality, features, or style—to attract new users and more usage.

A strategy of *quality improvement* aims at increasing product performance—its durability, reliability, speed, taste. This strategy is effective when the quality can be improved, when buyers believe the claim of improved quality, and when enough buyers want higher quality.

A strategy of *feature improvement* adds new features that expand the product's usefulness, safety, or convenience. Feature improvement has been successfully used by Japanese makers of watches, calculators, and copying machines. For example, Seiko keeps adding new styles and features to its line of watches.

A strategy of *style improvement* aims to increase the attractiveness of the product. Thus, car manufacturers restyle their cars to attract buyers who want a new look. The makers of consumer food and household products introduce new flavors, colors, ingredients, or packages to revitalize consumer buying.

### Marketing Mix Modification

The product manager can also try to improve sales by changing one or more marketing mix elements. Prices can be cut to attract new users and competitors' customers. A better advertising campaign can be launched. Aggressive sales promotion—trade deals, cents-off, gifts, and contests—can be used. The company can also move into larger market channels, using mass merchandisers, if these channels are growing. Finally, the company can offer new or improved services to buyers.

## Decline Stage

The sales of most product forms and brands eventually dip. The decline may be slow, as in the case of oatmeal cereal; or rapid, as for video games. Sales may plunge to zero, or they may drop to a low level where they continue for many years. This is the **decline stage.**

Sales decline for many reasons, including technological advances, shifts in consumer tastes, and increased competition. As sales and profits decline, some firms withdraw from the market. Those remaining may reduce the number of their product offerings. They may drop smaller market segments and marginal trade channels. They may cut the promotion budget and reduce their prices further.

Carrying a weak product can be very costly to a firm, and not just in profit terms. There are many hidden costs. The weak product may take up too much of management's time. It often requires frequent price and inventory adjustments. It requires advertising and salesforce attention that might better be used to make "healthy" products more profitable. Its failing reputation can cause customer concerns about the company and its other products. The biggest cost may well lie in the future. Keeping weak products delays the search for replacements, creates a lopsided product mix, hurts current profits, and weakens the company's foothold on the future.

For these reasons, companies need to pay more attention to their aging products. The first task is to identify those products in the decline stage by regularly reviewing the sales, market shares, costs, and profit trends for each of its products. For each declining product, management has to decide whether to maintain, harvest, or drop it.

Management may decide to *maintain* its brand without change in the hope that competitors will leave the industry. For example, Procter & Gamble made good profits by remaining in the declining liquid soap business as others withdrew. Or management may decide to reposition the brand in hopes of moving it back into the growth stage of the product life cycle. Miller did this with its Miller High Life brand in the 1970s: Sales grew rapidly when it changed Miller from an upper-income, "champagne of bottled beers" position to a more middle-American one.

Management may decide to *harvest* the product, which means reducing various costs (plant and equipment, maintenance, R&D, advertising, salesforce) and hoping that sales hold up fairly well for a while. If successful, harvesting will increase the company's profits in the short run. Or management may decide to *drop* the product from the line. It can sell it to another firm or simply liquidate it at salvage value. If the company plans to find a buyer, it will not want to run down the product through harvesting.[11]

The key characteristics of each stage of the product life cycle are summarized in Table 10–2. The table also lists the marketing responses made by companies in each stage.

TABLE 10-2   Product Life Cycle: Characteristics and Responses

|  | Introduction | Growth | Maturity | Decline |
|---|---|---|---|---|
| **Characteristics** | | | | |
| Sales | Low | Fast growth | Slow growth | Decline |
| Profits | Negligible | Peak levels | Declining | Low or zero |
| Cash flow | Negative | Moderate | High | Low |
| Customers | Innovative | Mass market | Mass market | Laggards |
| Competitors | Few | Growing | Many rivals | Declining number |
| **Responses** | | | | |
| Strategic focus | Expand market | Market penetration | Defend share | Productivity |
| Mktg. expenditures | High | High (declining %) | Falling | Low |
| Mktg. emphasis | Product awareness | Brand preference | Brand loyalty | Selective |
| Distribution | Patchy | Intensive | Intensive | Selective |
| Price | High | Lower | Lowest | Rising |
| Product | Basic | Improved | Differentiated | Unchanged |

*Source:* Peter Doyle, "The Realities of the Product Life Cycle," *Quaterly Review of Marketing* (UK), Summer 1976, p. 5.

# SUMMARY

Organizations must develop new products and services. Their current products face limited life spans and must be replaced by newer products. But new products can fail—the risks of innovation are as great as the rewards. The key to successful innovation lies in strong planning and a systematic *new-product development process.*

The new-product development process consists of eight stages: *idea generation, idea screening, concept development and testing, marketing strategy development, business analysis, product development, test marketing,* and *commercialization.* The purpose of each stage is to decide whether the idea should be further developed or dropped. The company wants to minimize the chances of poor ideas moving forward and good ideas being rejected.

Each product has a *life cycle* marked by a changing set of problems and opportunities. The sales of the typical product follow an S-shaped curve made up of five stages. The cycle begins with the *product-development stage* when the company finds and develops a new-product idea. The *introduction stage* is marked by slow growth and low profits as the product is being pushed into distribution. If successful, the product enters a *growth stage* marked by rapid sales growth and increasing profits. During this stage, the company tries to improve the product, enter new market segments and distribution channels, and reduce its prices slightly. Then comes a *maturity stage* in which sales growth slows down and profits stabilize. The company seeks strategies to renew sales growth, including market, product, and marketing mix modification. Finally, the product enters a *decline stage* in which sales and profits fall off. The company's task during this stage is to identify the declining product and decide whether to maintain, harvest, or drop it. In the last case, the product can be sold to another firm or liquidated for salvage value.

# QUESTIONS FOR DISCUSSION

1. Before videotape cameras were available for home use, Polaroid introduced Polavision, a system for making home movies that did not require laboratory processing. Like most other home-movie systems, Polavision cassettes lasted only a few minutes and did not record sound. Despite the advantage of "instant developing" and heavy promotional expenditures, Polavision never gained wide acceptance. Given Polaroid's record of new-product successes, why did Polavision fail?

2. List as many new-product ideas for your favorite fast-food chain as you can. Which of these ideas have the best chance of succeeding?

3. Less than one-third of all new-product ideas come from customers. Does this low percentage conflict with the philosophy of "find a need and fill it"?

4. What factors would you consider to choose cities for test-marketing a new snack? Would your home town be a good test market?

5. NutraSweet, the NutraSweet Company's brand name for aspartame, was approved in 1981. In 1992, the company's patent expires, and other companies will be able to sell their own brands of aspartame. Describe NutraSweet's probable product life cycle from 1980 to 1999.

6. How can a company distinguish products with long life cycles from *fads* and *fashions?* What current products do you consider fads or fashions likely to disappear soon?

7. Compare the relative spending levels on promotion at the different stages of a product's life cycle. What types of promotion are best used at each stage?

8. Recent evidence suggests that consuming oatmeal—and especially oat bran—may help reduce cholesterol levels. What impact could this benefit have on the life cycle of oatmeal and oat-based products?

# REFERENCES

1. See Steven Greenhouse, "An Innovator Gets Down to Business," *The New York Times,* October 12, 1986, Sec. 3, pp. 1, 8; William Hoffer, "Spurs for Innovation," *Nation's Business,* June 1986, pp. 42–45; "Keeping the Fires Lit under the Innovators," *Fortune,* March 28, 1988, p. 45; and Russell Mitchell, "Masters of Innovation," *Business Week,* April 10, 1989, pp. 58-63.

2. See "Products of the Year," *Fortune,* December 9, 1985, pp. 106–12.

3. See David S. Hopkins and Earl L. Bailey, "New Product Pressures," *Conference Board Record,* June 1971, pp. 16–24; *New Product Management for the 1980s* (New York: Booz, Allen & Hamilton, 1982); and Christopher Knowlton, "Consumers: A Tougher Sell," *Fortune,* September 16, 1988, pp. 65-74.

4. See Leigh Lawton and A. Parasuraman, "So You Want Your New Product Planning to Be Productive," *Business Horizons,* December 1980, pp. 29–34.

5. See "Listening to the Voice of the Marketplace," *Business Week,* February 21, 1983, p. 90ff.

6. See Eric vonHipple, "Get New Products from Consumers," *Harvard Business Review,* March-April 1982, pp. 117–22.

7. Russell Mitchell, "How Ford Hit the Bullseye with Taurus," *Business Week,* June 30, 1986, pp. 69–70; and "Copycat Stuff? Hardly!" *Business Week,* September 14, 1987, p. 112.

8. For more on idea screening, see Tom W. White, "Use Variety of Internal, External Sources to Gather and Screen New Product Ideas," *Marketing News,* September 16, 1983, Sec. 2, p. 12.

9. For more on product concept testing, see William L.

Moore, "Concept Testing," *Journal of Business Research,* 10 (1982), 279–94; and David A. Schwartz, "Concept Testing Can Be Improved—and Here's How," *Marketing News,* January 6, 1984, pp. 22–23.

10. See George S. Day, "The Product Life Cycle: Analysis and Applications Issues," *Journal of Marketing,* Fall 1981, pp. 60–67; John E. Swan and David R. Rink, "Fitting Market Strategy to Varying Product Life Cycles," *Business Horizons,* January-February 1982, pp. 72–76; and Sak Onkvisit and John J. Shaw, "Competition and Product Management: Can the Product Life Cycle Help?" *Business Horizons,* July-August 1986, pp. 51–62.

11. See Laurence P. Feldman and Albert L. Page, "Harvesting: The Misunderstood Market Exit Strategy," *Journal of Business Strategy,* Spring 1985, pp. 79–85.

# Case 10

## AT&T: PLAYING IT SMART WITH A NEW PRODUCT

Whatever happened, you may ask, to quadraphonic stereo, to videodiscs, and to videotext? Answer: The first is gone, the second has been forced into a narrower market, and the last is languishing. All three were new technologies that were literally supposed to change our lives; all three had millions of dollars invested in them by well-known corporations bent not only on being first in their niche but actually creating the niche.

The question and answer are of special interest to 40-year-old Joe Griffin, who is charged with the marketing of still another product based on a new technology—the AT&T smart card. It may look like a traditional credit card, but this little slice of plastic can do more things than you ever thought of. And although Joseph E. Griffin may look like a mild-mannered middle manager, he is supersalesman, gospel spreader, alliance maker, applications developer, corporate guerrilla, publicist, production maven—and, above all, the "product champion," as he calls himself, of this very, very smart card.

Even with the AT&T name attached to it, the product looks as if it will need all the championing it can get—for several reasons. First, AT&T is a relative latecomer to the field. The earliest patents for the smart cards—which are essentially credit cards containing computer chips that provide processing power and electronic memory—were filed in France back in the early 1970s. Since then, the French have almost made smart cards a symbol of national honor. They've not only pushed the technology at home—there are more than 30 million smart cards in service in France—but they're making major inroads elsewhere in the world as well. Using the French technology, a number of U.S. companies have established a presence in this country.

Second, the AT&T card differs from traditional smart cards in that it has no electrical contact points (the points on the card's surface that come into contact with the points on the terminal during use). This absence of contact points gives the AT&T card several advantages: It has far greater durability, and it resists water, dirt, grease, and static electricity. These advantages come at a price, of course: Informed sources estimate that a non-contact card will cost anywhere from $15 to $35—compared to about $5 for a traditional smart card and about 15¢ or less for a conventional magnetic-strip credit card.

These advantages also come at the price of broad acceptance. Because the AT&T technology is unique, its smart card cannot relate to other smart card technologies, which have their own standards and ways of doing things. On the other hand, just because it comes from AT&T, it has a great deal going for it—including unrivaled experience with similar cards (AT&T has more than 40 million telephone calling cards in circulation) and a network and terminal system (telephones) already in place. AT&T is also arguably the premier communications company in the world.

So what does it *do,* this unique AT&T card? Much as a PC runs a word-processing program along with a database application and spreadsheet, the AT&T card contains an operating system with a reusable memory that permits multiple applications to coexist with the same card. The user chooses from a "menu" to switch from one application to another. All the information on the card is protected by a security system to make unauthorized access extremely difficult, if not impossible.

Yes, but what does an individual *do* with such a portable information system in his or her wallet? Well, let's say you're a sales manager about to leave on a business trip. The card contains the cash value authorized for the trip; it also contains your business credit card numbers, your airline tickets, and confirmed reservations for your hotel and rental car. In addition, the card carries ID information that gains you admittance to your company's high-security field office. Oh, yes—it can also hold important phone numbers and an electronic notebook that lets you record expenses, customer calls, salespeople appraisals, or any other information vital to your job. Or let's say you've just finished a day of trouble-shooting in the field. By dialing a certain number, you can load your findings into your company's main database; at the same time, you can get an updated list of customers whom you should see the next day.

And there are still other potential uses for smart cards—a "smart dog tag," for instance, that would provide portable personnel and payroll files, training records, and medical histories. Smart employee badges are also being tested, using the card's capability to store video images, digitized fingerprints, or voice prints.

Innovative, yes—indeed, downright creative. But a jaded marketer might well ask: Is the world really waiting—or ready—for a card this brainy?

Joe Griffin believes it is—if not exactly with open arms, then at least willing to embrace it given the right conditions. To create those conditions, he must first meet his key marketing challenge: focusing on customer needs. His second challenge is to get other people to play the game according to AT&T rules. Other players must be signed on—for instance, providers of financial, travel, and information service.

But the most immediate task, as Griffin sees it, is to spread the gospel of this new technology. His prime objective: to gain acceptance of common standards. "Remember quadraphonic sound, which was introduced in 1977?" he asks. "There were three different technologies competing with each other. Record manufacturers didn't know which one to support. The result: Quadraphonic disappeared. Another example: RCA's electromechanical videodisk versus the Philips/Pioneer optical laser disk. Their battle drew so much negative press the public didn't know which to support. Then along came home videotape, which was technically inferior but didn't have to overcome the market confusion and negative press. Griffin wants to make sure that this won't happen with his smart card: "My goal," he says, "is to sign up major players before they've made any

commitments elsewhere."

But what about the problem of AT&T's smart card technology versus that of the rest of the world? Griffin answers with another question: "How can the AT&T card meet the criteria for contact cards when our cards have no contacts? I think that, for the time being at least, there are going to be two technologies—contact and non-contact—and both will be equally valid, just as there is a standard for VHS videotape and a standard for Beta." About the future of the AT&T technology, however, Griffin is confident: "The traditional smart card is like a steam engine compared to our gas turbine."

Besides finding new constituencies for his technology, Griffin must also defend smart card's turf *inside* AT&T. "Internal critics are often the most vocal," he explains. "They'll say things like, 'We've tried that before,' or 'That doesn't belong in your group,' or 'You're just product management, we're marketing.'

"Part of the problem," he points out, "is that it's never clear who's in charge of the product. That's why the product champion has to be a corporate guerrilla. There are very few people I can fire at AT&T. I don't have a factory under my control, or legal or accounting, or any other staff departments. I have to negotiate with each of them for their time and resources. I also have to go to top management to justify funding. Eventually," Griffin concludes, "we've got to make hard decisions. Do we build the factory or not—not bricks and mortar, necessarily, but, say, giving the project a certain amount of square footage or level of staffing."

The platform for smart card technology is the E-card (for

*experimental*), recently tested by AT&T with the help of 1,000 frequent travelers. After the E-card is inserted into a specially equipped telephone (and an optional password entered), the names and phone numbers within the card's memory are displayed on a screen. When the user touches one or two keys, the number is speed-dialed and billed to one of eight designated sub-billing numbers. The card's "menu" allows the user to choose what he wants from among its contents.

Griffin describes the E-card test as successful but hedges when it comes to whether it holds the most immediate potential for the new technology: "You don't always test your best application," he explains. Certainly, he keeps plugging away at new markets for the smart card. After the so-called electronic dog tag which the military put out to bid in 1988, the next hottest market is medical systems. "Because of AIDS," Griffin explains, "this country is going to spend millions of dollars tracking our blood supply—the donor, date donated, tests performed, who administered to, and so on. People will insist that there be an information trail." Currently, he says, AT&T is meeting with several major national health care organizations on proposals to store medical information for rapid patient checkin as well as for use in emergencies.

The proportion of the gross national product devoted to health care is 10 percent and growing, and Griffin sees other opportunities for the smart card in this area. He points out that many people—the elderly in particular—often can't recall important medical events in their lives, the names of doctors who've treated them, or medications they've taken. Entire medical histories and medication data could be contained—and updated—on a smart card.

Still another promising market is corporate security badges. "Key locations within Bell Labs use them now," Griffin explains. "The smart badge tells who's in the building, for how long, and so on. In effect, the badge acts as a portable miniaturized time clock." But it goes beyond that, he says: "Access to databases can be limited and navigation quietly tracked within the computer system to monitor and permit only key individuals to gain access to certain files."

Probably the biggest market of all, however, is in financial services. Although both MasterCard and Visa have expressed varying degrees of interest in smart cards, in pilot tests both have opted for the traditional contact-point credit card. Visa, however, plans a step-by-step approach and intends by 1993 to introduce its so-called "super smart card" to upscale customers. MasterCard, on the other hand, opted for a 1989 worldwide rollout of its smart card terminals and claims banks are receptive despite the price tag of $275 to $325 per terminal. But there are doubters. Spencer Nilson, who writes a newsletter reflecting a bent for traditional magnetic-stripe technology, scoffs, "If MasterCard says they've gotten some banks to spring for the technology, they're full of baloney. In the crunch, the banks won't pay. And even if one does, so what? One bank doesn't make a technology."

Generally, experts in the smart card field are cautious. "There's not going to be any splashy application that will catch everybody's attention," comments James Kobielus of the International Center for Information Technologies, a Washington, D.C., think tank in the field of information technology. "I see two trends occurring simultaneously: first, the trend to smarts—smart toys, smart houses, smart cars, and so on; second, there's the trend to cards—ATM cards, office-admission cards, and the like. When these trends cross, and they will, we'll wind up with a collection of smart cards in our wallet, each dedicated to a different purpose. It's been said that the smart card technology is a solution looking for a problem. What I'm saying," explains Kobielus, "is that there is no single problem but a whole range of problems that smart card technology will solve."

### Questions

1. What will influence the movement of smart cards from the introductory stage of the product life cycle to the growth stage?

2. Suggest what the market for smart cards will be like for the remainder of its product life cycle.

3. The idea of storing an elderly person's medical history and medication data on a smart card is in the concept-development stage at AT&T. How should the company proceed?

4. Think of other problems that the smart card could be used to solve. Describe the consumer need, the target market, and a proposed marketing mix.

*Source:* Adapted from A. J. Vogl, "Marketing a New Technology," *Sales & Marketing Management,* July 1988, pp. 37–42.

# 11

# Pricing Products: Pricing Considerations and Approaches

## CHAPTER OBJECTIVES

After reading this chapter, you should be able to

1. Explain how marketing objectives and mix strategy, costs, and other internal company factors affect pricing decisions
2. List and explain factors outside the company that affect pricing decisions
3. Explain how price setting depends on consumer perceptions of price and on the price-demand relationship
4. Compare the three general pricing approaches

A consumer planning to buy a videocassette recorder from Sears faces a bewildering array of models and prices: The recent Sears catalog features 14 different VCR models at 12 different prices, ranging from $219.99 to $629.99. However, although consumers may have trouble choosing among different prices. Sears probably has more trouble *setting* them. Sears must consider numerous factors in its complex price-setting process. Its pricing strategy dramatically affects its profits—and perhaps even its survival.

In setting prices, Sears must first consider its overall *marketing objectives* and the role of price in the marketing mix. Should Sears price to maximize current profits on VCRs or to maximize long-run market share? Should it use a high-price/low volume strategy or a low-price/high volume strategy? The giant retailer must also consider its *costs*—the costs of making VCRs or buying them from suppliers, the costs of shipping, storing, stocking, and selling inventory, and the costs of providing customer services. Sears must price its VCRs to cover these costs plus a target profit.

However, if Sears considered only costs when setting prices it would ignore other important factors.

Beyond costs, Sears must also understand the relationship between price and *demand* for its VCRs and must set prices that match consumer value perceptions. If Sears charges more than buyer's perceived value, its VCRs will sell poorly; if it charges less, its VCRs may sell well but provide less overall revenue. Finally, Sears must consider *competitors'* VCR quality and prices. If Sears charges more for VCRs that are similar to those of its major competitors, it risks losing sales. If it sets prices much lower than those of comparable products, it will lose profit opportunities even though winning sales from competitors.

Thus, Sears sets its VCR prices on the basis of numerous factors—overall marketing objectives, costs, competitors' prices, and consumer value perceptions and demand. But setting basic prices is just the beginning. Sears must now adjust these prices to account for different buyers and different market situations. For example, because consumers vary in how they value different VCR features, Sears offers many different models for different price segments. The basic VHS 117-channel, two-head model with no extras sells for $294.97. At the other extreme, Sears' best model—a 120 channel, four-head, stereo VCR with 35-function remote control, on-screen programming, picture-in-picture capability, and multi-channel scan and freeze features—goes for $629.99. Thus, Sears offers a model to fit any consumer preference and pocketbook.

Sears also adjusts its prices for psychological impact. For example, instead of charging $300 for its basic model, Sears charges $294.97. This price suggests a bargain, and consumers will perceive the model as belonging to the under-$300 rather than the $300-and-over price range. Sears also adjusts prices to meet market conditions and competitor actions. For example, after Christmas Sears might knock $100 off the price of its best model, both to clear inventories and to boost demand. Thus, Sears must constantly adjust prices to account for buyer differences and changing market conditions. And it must do this for each of the thousands of products it sells.

Sears' pricing strategies have played a key role in the company's ups and downs over the course of ten decades. Sears originally became America's largest retailer by offering quality merchandise at affordable prices. In the late 1960s, however, the company made an important move to change its strategy: It decided to upgrade its merchandise and raise prices. When higher prices caused many loyal shoppers to switch to lower-priced competitors, Sears reacted by developing another new strategy: It initiated the practice of weekly price-off sales to make its prices more competitive. Despite this strategy of continuous sales, however, Sears continued to lose customers to K mart, Wal-Mart, and other discounters. Its market share slid 33 percent during the 1980s, and America's largest retailer found itself in big trouble.

Thus, in the spring of 1989, in what it called the biggest change in its 102-year history, Sears launched a bold new pricing strategy. Scrapping its decades-old weekly-sales approach, it adopted an *everyday low-price* strategy. Sears closed all of its 824 stores for 42 hours and retagged every piece of merchandise, slashing prices by as much as 50 percent! During the next three weeks, Sears aired its biggest-ever advertising campaign to announce the new pricing strategy. Over 2,000 television and radio ads and 900 newspaper ads proclaimed, "We've lowered our prices on over 50,000 items! Sears: your money's worth and a whole lot more."

Although Sears is betting that its new everyday low-price strategy will pull consumers back into its stores and revive sagging profits, the ploy involves substantial risks. In order to be successful with everyday low *prices*, Sears must first achieve everyday low *costs*. However, its costs have traditionally run much higher than those of its competitors—for example, Sears' selling and administrative expenses run about 30 percent of sales, as compared with about 23 percent at rival K mart. Moreover, Sears' costs have in recent years been rising faster than its sales. Beyond cost problems, Sears may face an even tougher problem in trying to change consumer perceptions of its prices and practices. For decades, Sears has conditioned customers to "hold out" for its traditional price-off sales. The rapid switch to a one-price policy and everyday low-price position could confuse consumers. Changing established consumer perceptions and buying behavior will be no doubt a long and difficult task.[1]

---

**price** The amount of money charged for a product or service or the sum of the values consumers exchange for the benefits of having or using the product or service.

All profit organizations and many nonprofit organizations must set prices on their products or services. *Price* goes by many names:

> Price is all around us. You pay *rent* for your apartment, *tuition* for your education, and a *fee* to your physician or dentist. The airline, railway, taxi, and bus companies charge you a *fare;* the local utilities call their price a *rate;* and the local bank charges you *interest* for the money you borrow. The price for driving your car on Florida's Sunshine Parkway is a *toll,* and the company that insures your car charges you a *premium.* The guest lecturer charges an *honorarium* to tell you about a government official who took a *bribe* to help a shady character steal *dues* collected by a trade association. Clubs or societies to which you belong may make a special *assessment* to pay unusual expenses. Your regular lawyer may ask for a *retainer* to cover her services. The "price" of an executive is a *salary,* the price of a salesperson may be a *commission,* and the price of a worker is a *wage.* Finally, although economists would disagree, many of us feel that *income taxes* are the price we pay for the privilege of making money.[2]

Simply defined, **price** is the amount of money charged for a product or service. More broadly, price is the sum of the values consumers exchange for the benefits of having or using the product or service.

How are prices set? Historically, prices were usually set by buyers and sellers bargaining with each other. Sellers would ask for a higher price than they expected to get, and buyers would offer less than they expected to pay. Through bargaining, they would arrive at an acceptable price. Individual buyers paid different prices for the same products, depending on their needs and bargaining skills.

Today, most sellers set *one* price to *all* buyers. This idea was helped along by the development of large-scale retailing at the end of the 19th century. F. W. Woolworth, Tiffany and Co., John Wanamaker, J. L. Hudson, and others advertised a "strictly one-price policy" because they carried so many items and had so many employees.

Historically, price has been the major factor affecting buyer choice. This is still true in poorer nations, among poorer groups, and with commodity products. However, nonprice factors have become more important in buyer-choice behavior in recent decades.

Price is the only element in the marketing mix that produces revenue; all other elements represent costs. Furthermore, pricing and price competition have been rated as the number-one problem facing marketing executives.[3] Yet many companies do not handle pricing well. The most common mistakes are: pricing that is too cost-oriented; prices that are not revised often enough to reflect market changes; pricing that does not take the rest of the marketing mix into account; and prices that are not varied enough for different product items and market segments.

In this and the next chapter, we will look at the problem of setting prices. This chapter will look at the factors marketers must consider when setting prices and at general pricing approaches. In the next chapter, we will examine pricing strategies for new-product pricing, product mix pricing, initiating and responding to price changes, and adjusting prices for buyer and situational factors.

# FACTORS TO CONSIDER WHEN SETTING PRICES

A company's pricing decisions are affected both by internal company factors and by external environmental factors. These factors are shown in Figure 11-1. *Internal factors* include the company's marketing objectives, marketing mix strategy, costs, and organization. *External factors* include the nature of the market and demand, competition, and other environmental factors.

## Internal Factors Affecting Pricing Decisions

### Marketing Objectives

Before setting price, the company must decide on its strategy for the product. If the company has selected its target market and positioning carefully, then its marketing mix strategy, including price, will be fairly straightforward. For

FIGURE 11–1    Factors Affecting Price Decisions

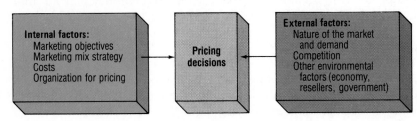

example, if General Motors decides to produce a new sports car to compete with European sports cars in the high-income segment, this decision suggests charging a high price. Motel 6 and Red Roof Inns have positioned themselves as motels that provide economical rooms for budget-minded travelers—this position requires charging a low price. Thus, pricing strategy is largely determined by past decisions on market positioning.

At the same time, the company may seek additional objectives. The clearer a firm is about its objectives, the easier it is to set price. Examples of common objectives are *survival, current profit maximization, market-share maximization,* and *product-quality leadership.*

***Survival*** ▪ Companies set *survival* as their major objective if they are troubled by too much capacity, heavy competition, or changing consumer wants. To keep a plant going, a company may set a low price, hoping to increase demand. In this case, profits are less important than survival. In recent years, many automobile dealers have resorted to pricing below cost or offering large price rebate programs in order to survive. As long as their prices cover variable costs and some fixed costs, they can stay in business until conditions change or other problems are corrected.

***Current Profit Maximization*** ▪ Many companies want to set a price that will maximize current profits. They estimate what demand and costs will be at different prices and choose the price that will produce the maximum current profit, cash flow, or return on investment. In all cases, the company wants current financial outcomes rather than long-run performance.

***Market-Share Leadership*** ▪ Other companies want to obtain the dominant market share. They believe that the company with the largest market share will enjoy the lowest costs and highest long-run profit. To become the market-share leader, they set prices as low as possible. A variation of this objective is to pursue a specific market-share gain. Say the company wants to increase its market share from 10 percent to 15 percent in one year. It will search for the price and marketing program that will achieve this goal.

***Product-Quality Leadership*** ▪ A company might decide it wants to have the highest-quality product on the market. This normally calls for charging a high price to cover the cost of high product quality and the high cost of R&D. For example, the Sub-Zero Freezer Company seeks product-quality leadership. Sub-Zero makes the Rolls-Royce of refrigerators—custom-made, built-in units that look more like hardwood cabinets or pieces of furniture than refrigerators. By offering the highest quality, Sub-Zero sells over $50 million worth of fancy refrigerators a year, priced at up to $3,000 each.[4]

***Other Objectives*** ▪ A company might also use price to attain other more specific objectives. It can set prices low to prevent competition from entering the market or set prices at competitors' levels to stabilize the market. Prices can be set to keep the loyalty and support of resellers or to avoid government intervention. Prices can be temporarily reduced to create excitement for a product or to draw more customers into a retail store. One product may be priced to help the sales of other products in the company's line. Thus, pricing may play an important role in helping to accomplish the company's objectives at many levels.

### Marketing Mix Strategy

Price is only one of the marketing mix tools that the company uses to achieve its marketing objectives. Price decisions must be coordinated with product design, distribution, and promotion decisions to form a consistent and effective

*Sub-Zero charges a premium price for its custom-made refrigerators to attain product-quality leadership.*

marketing program. Decisions made for other marketing mix variables may affect pricing decisions. For example, producers who use many resellers who are expected to support and promote their products may have to build larger reseller margins into their prices. The decision to develop a high-quality position will mean that the seller must charge a higher price to cover higher costs.

The company often makes its pricing decision first and then bases other marketing mix decisions on the price it wants to charge. For example, Hyundai, Honda, and other makers of low-budget cars discovered a market segment for affordable cars and designed models to sell within the price range that this segment was willing to pay. Here, price was a key product-positioning factor that defined the product's market, competition, and design. The intended price determined what product features could be offered and what production costs could be incurred.

Thus, the marketer must consider the total marketing mix when setting prices. If the product is positioned on nonprice factors, then decisions about quality, promotion, and distribution will strongly affect price. If price is a key positioning factor, then price will strongly affect decisions on the other marketing mix elements. In most cases, the company will consider all the marketing mix decisions together when developing the marketing program.

## Costs

Costs set the floor for the price that the company can charge for its product. The company wants to charge a price that both covers all its costs for producing,

*Ford positions its Festiva on price and economy. Jaguar positions on quality and other nonprice factors—its price adds prestige.*

distributing, and selling the product and delivers a fair rate of return for its effort and risk. A company's costs may be an important element in its pricing strategy. Many companies work to become the "low-cost producers" in their industries. Companies with lower costs can set lower prices that result in greater sales and profits (see Marketing Highlight 11–1).

A company's costs take two forms, fixed and variable. **Fixed costs** (also known as **overhead**) are costs that do not vary with production or sales level. Thus, regardless of its output, a company must pay bills each month for rent, heat, interest, and executive salaries. Fixed costs go on regardless of production level.

**fixed costs (overhead)** Costs that do not vary with production or sales level.

# Marketing Highlight 11–1

## FOOD LION'S WINNING LOW-COST, LOW-PRICE STRATEGY

The Food Lion grocery chain began operations in 1957 in a small North Carolina town. At first, despite its heavy use of trading stamps, giveaways, and other marketing gimmicks, Food Lion had trouble drawing shoppers away from more established competitors. Ten years later, the company closed 9 of its first 16 stores. In 1967, out of desperation, Food Lion slashed storewide prices by 10 percent in its remaining units. The results were startling—sales shot up by 54 percent by year's end, profits by 165 percent. The chain had found its niche and a potent competitive weapon—low prices.

Food Lion aggressively pursued this low-price, low-frills strategy and grew quickly in North Carolina. Its new slogan, LFPINC ("Lowest Food Prices in North Carolina")—featured in advertising, printed on shopping bags, and plastered to the bumpers of thousands of shoppers' cars—became a welcome and familiar sight in cities and towns around the state. In recent years, Food Lion has prospered even more. Positioned strongly as the low-price leader in most of its markets, the chain now operates almost 500 stores across the Southeast. Food Lion ads confidently claim "extra low everyday prices." And when Food Lion moves into a new town, competitors must generally drop their prices substantially to compete—a fact that Food Lion points out in its advertising. When the chain recently

entered Florida, its ads boldly asserted, "Food Lion is coming to town, and prices will be coming down!"

Food Lion's price claims are more than empty boasts. In most cases, it really does offer lower prices. Yet the chain remains highly profitable—Food Lion earns an overall net profit margin of 2.7 percent, about twice the industry average. The reason: a total dedication to cost control. The company doggedly pursues even remote opportunities to reduce costs, and its cost-cutting efforts bring big returns. For example, Food Lion pays just $650,000 for each new, no-frills store it builds—much lower than the $1 million competitors typically spend for their outlets. It saves on distribution costs by locating stores within 200 miles of one of its three modern distribution warehouses. To streamline and simplify operations, Food Lion stocks 25 percent fewer brands and sizes than other grocery stores and shuns costly extras such as fresh seafood counters, from-scratch bakeries, and flower shops. And Food Lion is itself a thrifty shopper—it ferrets out wholesaler specials and squeezes suppliers for extra savings.

Food Lion rarely overlooks a chance to economize. It recycles waste heat from refrigeration units to warm its stores and reuses banana crates as bins for cosmetics. It makes $1 million a year selling ground-up bones and fat for fertilizer. Food Lion even economizes on

its advertising. The company produces its own ads, using few paid actors and Chief Executive Tom E. Smith as advertising spokesman. Its average television spot costs only $6,000. And Food Lion saves some $8 million each year by keeping its newspaper ads smaller than those of competitors. As a result, Food Lion's advertising costs amount to one-fourth the industry average. Overall, major competitors spend an average of 21 percent of sales on their total expenses. Food Lion has kept these expenses under 14 percent of sales.

Food Lion's low-cost, low-price strategy has made it the fastest-growing and most profitable grocery chain in the nation. Over the last decade, sales have grown at an average of 30 percent per year; profits have grown 29 percent annually. Food Lion's 25 percent return on equity last year was best among the 13 top grocery chains listed in *Business Week*'s Top 1000—almost doubling the average return of the other firms. Food Lion's success hinges on a simple strategy—lower costs mean lower prices, and lower prices mean greater sales and greater profits.

*Sources:* Richard W. Anderson, "That Roar You Hear Is Food Lion," *Business Week*, August 24, 1987, pp. 65–66; "The *Business Week* Top 1000," *Business Week*, April 17, 1987, p. 146; William E. Sheeline, "Making Them Rich Down Home," *Fortune*, August 15, 1988, pp. 51–55; and various Food Lion annual reports.

**Variable costs** vary directly with the level of production. Each hand calculator produced by Texas Instruments involves costs in plastic, wires, packaging, and other inputs. These costs tend to be the same for each unit produced. They are called *variable* because their total varies with the number of units produced.

**Total costs** are the sum of the fixed and variable costs for any given level of production. Management wants to charge a price that will at least cover the total production costs at a given level of production.

The company must watch its costs carefully. If it costs the company more than competitors to produce and sell its product, the company will have to charge a higher price or make less profit, putting it at a competitive disadvantage.

### Organizational Considerations

Management must decide who within the organization should set prices. Companies handle pricing in a variety of ways. In small companies, prices are often set by top management rather than by the marketing or sales department. In large companies, pricing is typically handled by divisional or product line managers. In industrial markets, salespeople may be allowed to negotiate with customers within certain price ranges. Even here, top management sets the pricing objectives and policies and often approves the prices proposed by lower-level management or salespeople.[5] In industries where pricing is a key factor (aerospace, railroads, oil companies), companies will often have a pricing department to set the best prices or help others in setting them. This department reports to the marketing department or top management. Others who have an influence on pricing include sales managers, production managers, finance managers, and accountants.

## External Factors Affecting Pricing Decisions

### The Market and Demand

Costs set the lower limits of prices, while the market and demand set the upper limit. Both consumer and industrial buyers balance the price of a product or service against the benefits of owning it. Thus, before setting prices, the marketer must understand the relationship between price and demand for its product.

In this section, we will look at how the price-demand relationship varies for different types of markets and at how buyer perceptions of price affect the pricing decision. Then we will discuss methods for measuring the price-demand relationship.

*Pricing in Different Types of Markets* ▪ The seller's pricing freedom varies with different types of markets. Economists recognize four types of markets, each presenting a different pricing challenge.

Under **pure competition**, the market consists of many buyers and sellers trading in a uniform commodity such as wheat, copper, or financial securities. No single buyer or seller has much affect on the going market price. A seller cannot charge more than the going price because buyers can obtain as much as they need at this price. Nor would sellers charge less than the market price when they can sell all they want at that price. If price and profits rise, new sellers can easily enter the market. In a purely competitive market, marketing research, product development, pricing, advertising, and sales promotion play little or no role. Thus, sellers in these markets do not spend much time on marketing strategy.

*Monopolistic competition: in the industrial market, Stanley sets its hinges apart from dozens of other brands using both price and nonprice factors.*

**monopolistic competition** A market in which many buyers and sellers trade over a range of prices rather than a single market price.

**oligopolistic competition** A market in which there are a few sellers highly sensitive to each other's pricing and marketing strategies.

Under **monopolistic competition,** the market consists of many buyers and sellers who trade over a range of prices rather than a single market price. A range of prices occurs because sellers can differentiate their offers to the buyers. Either the physical product can be varied in quality, features, or style, or the accompanying services can be varied. Buyers see differences in sellers' products and will pay different prices. Sellers try to develop differentiated offers for different customer segments and, in addition to price, freely use branding, advertising, and personal selling to set their offers apart. Because there are many competitors, each firm is less affected by competitors' marketing strategies than in oligopolistic markets. For example, H. J. Heinz, Vlasic, and several other national brands of pickles compete with dozens of regional and local brands, all differentiated by price and nonprice factors. Because there are many competitors, each firm is less affected by competitors' marketing strategies than in oligopolistic markets.

Under **oligopolistic competition,** the market consists of a few sellers who are highly sensitive to each other's pricing and marketing strategies. The product can be uniform (steel, aluminum) or nonuniform (cars, computers). There are few sellers because it is difficult for new sellers to enter the market. Each seller is alert to competitors' strategies and moves. If a steel company slashes its price by 10 percent, buyers will quickly switch to this supplier. Other steelmakers will thus have to respond by lowering their prices or increasing their services. An oligopolist is never sure that it will gain anything permanent through a price cut. On the other hand, if an oligopolist raises its price, its competitors might not follow this lead. The oligopolist would then have to retract its price increase or risk losing customers to competitors.

**pure monopoly** A market in which there is a single seller—it may be a government monopoly, a private regulated monopoly, or a private nonregulated monopoly.

A **pure monopoly** consists of one seller. The seller may be a government monopoly (the U.S. Postal Service), a private regulated monopoly (a power company), or a private nonregulated monopoly (Du Pont when it introduced nylon). Pricing is handled differently in each case. A government monopoly can pursue a variety of pricing objectives. It might set a price below cost because the product is important to buyers who cannot afford to pay full cost. Or the price might be set either to cover costs or to produce good revenue. Or it might be set quite high to slow down consumption. In a regulated monopoly, the government permits the company to set rates that will yield a "fair return"—one that will let the company maintain and expand its operations as needed. Nonregulated monopolies are free to price at what the market will bear. However, they do not always charge the full price for a number of reasons: desire not to attract competition, desire to penetrate the market faster with a low price, fear of government regulation.

***Consumer Perceptions of Price and Value*** ▪ In the end, the consumer will decide whether a product's price is right. When setting prices, the company must consider consumer perceptions of price and the ways these perceptions affect consumers' buying decisions. Pricing decisions, like other marketing mix decisions, must be buyer-oriented:

> Pricing requires more than technical expertise. It requires creative judgment and an awareness of buyers' motivations. . . . The key to effective pricing is the same one that opens doors . . . in other marketing functions: a creative awareness of who buyers are, why they buy and how they make their buying decisions. The recognition that buyers differ in these dimensions is as important for effective pricing as it is for effective promotion, distribution, or product development.[6]

When consumers buy a product, they exchange something of value (the price) to get something of value (the benefits of having or using the product). Effective, buyer-oriented pricing involves understanding what value consumers place on the benefits they receive from the product and setting a price that fits that value. Such benefits include both actual and perceived benefits. When a consumer buys a meal at a fancy restaurant, it is easy to figure out the value of the meal's ingredients. But it is very hard, even for the consumer, to measure the value of other satisfactions such as taste, environment, relaxation, conversation, and status. Moreover, these values will vary both for different consumers and for different situations (see Marketing Highlight 11–2). Thus, the company will often find it hard to measure the values customers will attach to its product. The consumer, however, does use these values to evaluate a product's price. If the consumer perceives that the price is greater than the product's value, the consumer will not buy the product.

Marketers must thus try to look at the consumer's reasons for buying the product and set price according to consumer perceptions of the product's value. Because consumers vary in the values they assign to different product features, marketers often vary their pricing strategies for different price segments. They offer different sets of product features at different prices. For example, television manufacturers offer small, inexpensive models for consumers who want basic sets and larger, higher-priced models loaded with features for consumers who want the extras.

Buyer-oriented pricing means that the marketer cannot design a product and marketing program and then set the price. Good pricing begins with analyzing consumer needs and price perceptions. Price must be considered along with the other marketing mix variables *before* the marketing program is set.[7]

***Analyzing the Price-Demand Relationship*** ▪ Each price the company might charge will lead to a different level of demand. The relation between the price

# Marketing Highlight 11–2

## WHAT'S A HAMBURGER WORTH?

Is any hamburger worth $4? The answer seems to depend on which consumers you talk to and what they want from their burgers. Most people won't pay more than a dollar and a half (maybe two dollars) for a Big Mac or a Whopper with cheese. But there's a growing segment of consumers who seem almost eager to pay as much as $4 or $5 for a new class of burgers—gourmet burgers served at restaurants with names like Fuddrucker's, Chili's, Flaky Jakes, or J. L. Muggs.

What makes a hamburger worth $4 to some customers? For one thing, these burgers probably *are* better—they're bigger and cooked to order from fresh beef. But it's not just the hamburgers that attract customers. Upmarket burger places also offer several intangible benefits that some consumers value highly. For example, they have tables and chairs instead of plastic benches; they sell beer, wine, and cocktails; most provide table service.

The average cost for a hamburger, fries, and a beverage at Fuddrucker's runs about $6, compared with about $2.50 at a conventional fast-food restaurant. But when you add up all the values—of the hamburger, the amenities, and the atmosphere—the price of the gourmet burger seems more reasonable to some consumers than the lower prices they'd pay at McDonald's or Burger King.

So, who would pay $4 for a hamburger? You'd be surprised just how many people would. Fancy burger restaurants now pull in over $100 million in sales each year. And even conservative analysts estimate that the market will explode to $2 or $3 billion annually. Some estimate an eventual $8 billion market for $4 hamburgers.

*Source:* Adapted from Roger Neal, "Fancyburgers," *Forbes,* June 8, 1984, p. 92.

*Fuddruckers and its gourmet burger.*

charged and the resulting demand level is shown in the familiar **demand curve** in Figure 11–2A. The demand curve shows the number of units the market will buy in a given time period at different prices that might be charged. In the normal case, demand and price are inversely related: That is, the higher the price, the lower the demand. Thus, the company would sell less if it raised its price from $P_1$ to $P_2$. In short, consumers with limited budgets will probably buy less of something if its price is too high.

Most demand curves slope downward in either a straight or a curved line, as in Figure 11–2A. But for prestige goods, the demand curve sometimes slopes upward, as in Figure 11–2B. For example, one perfume company found that by raising its price from $P_1$ to $P_2$, it sold more perfume rather than less: Consumers thought the higher price meant a better or more desirable perfume. However, if the company charges too high a price $(P_3)$, the level of demand will be lower than at $P_2$.

Most companies try to measure their demand curves. The type of market makes a difference. In a monopoly, the demand curve shows the total market demand resulting from different prices. But if the company faces competition,

**demand curve** A curve showing the number of units the market will buy in a given time period at different prices that might be charged.

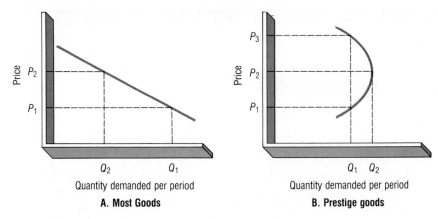

**A. Most Goods**

**B. Prestige goods**

FIGURE 11–2  Two Hypothetical Demand Schedules

its demand at different prices will depend on whether competitors' prices stay constant or change with the company's own prices. Here, we will assume that competitors' prices remain constant. Later in this chapter, we will discuss what happens when competitors' prices change. To measure a demand curve requires estimating demand at different prices. For example, Figure 11–3 shows the estimated demand curve for Quaker State Motor oil. Demand rises as the price is lowered from 73 cents to 38 cents, then drops between 38 cents and 32 cents, possibly due to consumer perceptions that the oil is too cheap and may damage the cars.

In measuring the price-demand relationship, the market researcher must not allow other factors affecting demand to vary. For example, if Quaker State also raised its advertising budget at the same time that it lowered its price, we would not know how much of the increased demand was due to the lower price and how much to the increased advertising. The same problem arises if a holiday weekend occurs when the lower price is set—more travel over the holidays causes people to buy more oil.

Economists show the impact of nonprice factors on demand through shifts in the demand curve rather than movements along it. Suppose the initial demand curve is $D_1$ in Figure 11–4. The seller is charging $P$ and selling $Q_1$ units. Now suppose the economy suddenly improves or the seller doubles its advertising budget. The higher demand is reflected through an upward shift of the demand curve from $D_1$ to $D_2$. Without changing the price, $P$, the seller's demand is now $Q_2$.

FIGURE 11–3   Demand Schedule for Quaker State Motor Oil

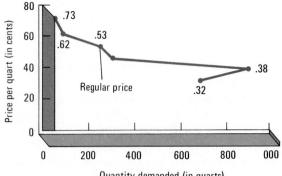

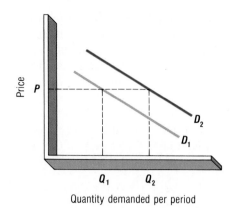

FIGURE 11–4    Effects of Promotion and Other Nonprice Variables on Demand Shown through Shifts of the Demand Curve

*Price Elasticity of Demand* ▪ Marketers also need to know **price elasticity**— how responsive demand will be to a change in price. Consider the two demand curves in Figure 11–5. In Figure 11–5A, a price increase from $P_1$ to $P_2$ leads to a relatively small drop in demand from $Q_1$ to $Q_2$. In Figure 11–5B, however, the same price increase leads to a large drop in demand from $Q'_1$ to $Q'_2$. If demand hardly varies with a small change in price, we say the demand is *inelastic*. If demand changes greatly, we say the demand is *elastic*.

What determines the price elasticity of demand? Buyers are less price-sensitive when the product is unique or when it is high in quality, prestige, or exclusiveness. They are also less price-sensitive when substitute products are hard to find or when they cannot easily compare the quality of substitutes. Finally, buyers are less price-sensitive when the total expenditure for a product is low relative to their income or when the cost is shared by another party.[8]

If demand is elastic rather than inelastic, sellers will generally consider lowering their price. A lower price will produce more total revenue. This practice makes sense as long as the extra costs of producing and selling more do not exceed the extra revenue.

## Competitors' Prices and Offers

Another external factor affecting a company's pricing decisions is competitors' prices and their possible reactions to the company's own pricing moves. A consumer considering buying a Canon camera will evaluate Canon's price and value against the prices and values of comparable products made by Nikon, Minolta, Pentax, and others. In addition, the company's pricing strategy may affect the nature of the competition it faces. If Canon follows a high-price, high-margin strategy, it may attract competition. A low-price, low-margin strategy, however, may stop competitors or drive them out of the market.

FIGURE 11–5    Inelastic and Elastic Demand

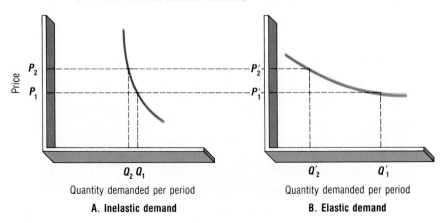

A. Inelastic demand

B. Elastic demand

The company needs to learn the price and quality of each competitor's offer. Canon might do this in several ways. It can send out comparison shoppers to price and compare Nikon, Minolta, and other competitors' products. It can get competitors' price lists and buy competitors' equipment and take it apart. It can ask buyers how they view the price and quality of each competitor's camera.

Once Canon is aware of competitors' prices and offers, it can use this information as a starting point for its own pricing. If Canon's cameras are similar to Nikon's, it will have to price close to Nikon or lose sales. If its cameras are not as good as Nikon's, Canon will not be able to charge as much. If Canon's products are better than Nikon's, it can charge more. Basically, Canon will use price to position its offer relative to that of its competitors.

### Other External Factors

When setting prices, the company must also consider other factors in its external environment. For example, *economic conditions* can have a strong impact on the results of the firm's pricing strategies. Economic factors such as inflation, boom or recession, and interest rates affect pricing decisions because they affect both the costs of producing a product and consumer perceptions of the product's price and value.

The company must consider what impact its prices will have on other parties in its environment. How will *resellers* react to various prices? The company should set prices that give resellers a fair profit, encourage their support, and help them to sell the product effectively. The *government* is another important external influence on pricing decisions. Marketers need to know the laws affecting price and make sure their pricing policies are legal. (The major laws affecting price are summarized in Marketing Highlight 11–3.)

# GENERAL PRICING APPROACHES

The price the company charges will be somewhere between one that is too low to produce a profit and one that is too high to produce any demand. Figure 11–6 summarizes the major considerations in setting price. Product costs set a floor to the price; consumer perceptions of the product's value set the ceiling. The company must consider competitors' prices and other external and internal factors to find the best price between these two extremes.

Companies set prices by selecting a general pricing approach that includes one or more of these three sets of factors. We will look at the following approaches: the *cost-based approach* (cost-plus pricing, breakeven analysis, and target profit pricing), the *buyer-based approach* (perceived-value pricing), and the *competition-based approach* (going-rate and sealed-bid pricing).

FIGURE 11–6   Major Considerations in Setting Price

| Low price | | | | High price |
|---|---|---|---|---|
| No possible profit at this price | Product costs | Competitors' prices and other external and internal factors | Consumer perceptions of value | No possible demand at this price |

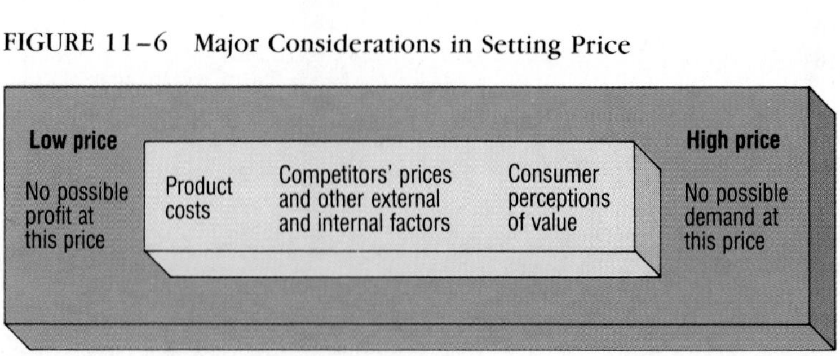

## PRICE DECISIONS AND PUBLIC POLICY

Sellers must understand the law in pricing their products. In particular, they must avoid the following practices.

*Price Fixing.* Sellers must set prices without talking to competitors. Otherwise, price collusion is suspected. Price fixing is illegal per se—that is, the government does not accept any excuses for price fixing. The only exception is where price agreements are carried out under the supervision of a government agency, as in many local milk industry agreements, in the regulated transportation industries, and in fruit and vegetable cooperatives.

*Resale Price Maintenance.* A manufacturer cannot require dealers to charge a specified retail price for its product. However, the seller can propose a manufacturer's *suggested* retail price to the dealers. The manufacturer cannot refuse to sell to a dealer who takes independent pricing action, nor punish the dealer by shipping late or denying advertising allowances. However, the manufacturer can refuse to sell to a dealer on other grounds presumably not related to the dealer's pricing.

*Price Discrimination.* The Robinson-Patman Act seeks to ensure that sellers offer the same price terms to a given level of trade. For example, every retailer is entitled to the same price terms whether the retailer is Sears or the local bicycle shop. However, price discrimination is allowed if the seller can prove its costs are different when selling to different retailers—for example, that it costs less per unit to sell a large volume of bicycles to Sears than to sell a few bicycles to a local dealer. Or the seller can discriminate in its pricing if the seller manufactures different qualities of the same product for different retailers. The seller has to prove that these differences exist and that the price differences are proportional. Price differentials may also be used to "meet competition" in "good faith," providing the firm is trying to meet competitors at its own level of competition and that the price discrimination is temporary, localized, and defensive rather than offensive.

*Minimum Pricing.* A seller is not allowed to sell below cost with the intention of destroying competition. Wholesalers and retailers in over half the states face laws requiring a minimum percentage markup over their cost of merchandise plus transportation. Designed to stop unfair-trade practices, these laws attempt to protect small merchants from larger merchants who might sell items below cost to attract customers.

*Price Increases.* Companies are free to increase their prices to any level except in times of price controls. The major exception to the freedom of pricing is regulated public utilities. Since utilities have monopoly power, their rates are regulated in the public interest. The government has also used its influence from time to time to discourage major industry price hikes during periods of shortages or inflation.

*Deceptive Pricing.* Deceptive pricing is more common in the sale of consumer goods than industrial goods, because consumers typically possess less information and buying skill. In 1958, the Automobile Information Disclosure Act required auto manufacturers to affix on auto windshields a statement of the manufacturer's suggested retail price, the prices of optional equipment, and the dealer's transportation charges. In the same year, the FTC issued its Guides Against Deceptive Pricing, warning sellers not to advertise a price reduction unless it was a saving from the usual retail price, not to advertise "factory" or "wholesale" prices unless such prices were what they claimed to be, not to advertise comparable value prices on imperfect goods, and so forth.

*Source:* See Thomas T. Nagle, *The Strategy and Tactics of Pricing* (Englewood Cliffs, NJ: Prentice Hall, 1987), pp. 321–37.

## *Cost-Based Pricing*

### Cost-Plus Pricing

**cost-plus pricing** Adding a standard markup to the cost of the product.

The simplest pricing method is **cost-plus pricing**—adding a standard markup to the cost of the product. For example, an appliance retailer might pay a manufacturer $20 for a toaster and mark it up to sell at $30—a 50 percent markup on cost. The retailer's gross margin is $10. If the store's operating costs amount to $8 per toaster sold, the retailer's profit margin will be $2.[9]

The manufacturer that made the toaster also probably used cost-plus pricing. If the manufacturer's standard cost of producing the toaster was $16, it

**breakeven pricing** Setting price to break even on the costs of making and marketing a product.

**target profit pricing** Setting price to cover the costs of making and marketing a product plus a target profit.

might have added a 25 percent markup, setting the price to the retailer at $20. Similarly, construction companies submit job bids by estimating the total project cost and adding a standard markup for profit. Lawyers and other professionals typically price by adding a standard markup to their costs. Some sellers tell their customers they will charge them cost plus a specified markup; for example, aerospace companies price this way to the government.

Markups vary greatly among different goods. Some common markups (on price, not cost) in supermarkets are 9 percent on baby foods, 14 percent on tobacco products, 20 percent on bakery products, 27 percent on dried foods and vegetables, 37 percent on spices and extracts, and 50 percent on greeting cards.[10] But these markups vary greatly around the averages. In the spices and extracts category, for example, markups on retail price range from a low of 19 percent to a high of 56 percent. Markups are generally higher on seasonal items (to cover the risk of not selling), specialty items, slower-moving items, items with high storage and handling costs, and items with inelastic demand.

Does using standard markups to set prices make logical sense? Generally, no. Any pricing method that ignores current demand and competition is not likely to lead to the best price. The retail graveyard is full of merchants who insisted on using standard markups after their competitors had gone into discount pricing.

Still, markup pricing remains popular for many reasons. First, sellers are more certain about costs than about demand. By tying the price to cost, sellers simplify pricing—they do not have to make frequent adjustments as demand changes. Second, when all firms in the industry use this pricing method, prices tend to be similar and price competition is thus minimized. Third, many people feel that cost-plus pricing is fairer to both buyers and sellers. Sellers earn a fair return on their investment but do not take advantage of buyers when buyers' demand becomes great.

### Breakeven Analysis and Target Profit Pricing

Another cost-oriented pricing approach is **breakeven pricing,** or a variation called **target profit pricing.** Here, the firm tries to determine the price at which it will break even or make the target profit it is seeking. Target pricing is used by General Motors, which prices its automobiles to achieve a 15 to 20 percent profit on its investment. This pricing method is also used by public utilities, which are constrained to make a fair return on their investment.

Target pricing uses the concept of a *breakeven chart.* A breakeven chart shows the total cost and total revenue at different levels of sales. Figure 11–7 shows a hypothetical breakeven chart. Here, fixed costs are $6 million regardless of sales volume, and variable costs are $5 per unit. *Variable costs* are added to *fixed costs* to form *total costs,* which rise with volume. The *total revenue* curve starts at zero and rises with each unit sold. The slope of the total revenue curve reflects the price. Here, the price is $15 (for example, the company's revenue is $12 million on 800,000 units, or $15 per unit).

At the $15 price, the company must sell at least 600,000 units to *break even*—that is, at this sales level, total revenues will equal total costs of $9 million. If the company wants a *target profit* of $2 million, it must sell at least 800,000 units to obtain the $12 million of total revenue needed to cover costs of $10 million plus the $2 million of target profits. On the other hand, if the company charges a higher price, say $20, it will not need to sell as many units to break even or to achieve its target profit. In fact, the higher the price, the lower the company's breakeven point.

However, as the *price* increases, *demand* decreases, and the market may

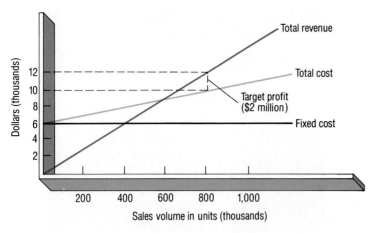

FIGURE 11-7   Breakeven Chart for Determining Target Price

perceived-value pricing Setting price based on the buyer's perceptions of value rather than on the seller's cost.

not buy even the lower volume needed to break even at the higher price. Much depends on the relationship between price and demand. For example, suppose the company calculates that, given its current fixed and variable costs, it must charge a price of $30 for the product in order to earn its desired target profit. But marketing research shows that few consumers will pay more than $25 for the product. In this case, the company will have to trim its costs in order to lower the breakeven point so that it can charge the lower price that consumers expect. Thus, although breakeven analysis and target profit pricing can help the company to determine minimum prices needed to cover expected costs and profits, they do not take the price-demand relationship into account. When using this method, the company must also consider the impact of price on the sales volume needed to realize target profits and the likelihood that the needed volume will be achieved at each possible price.

## Buyer-Based Pricing

An increasing number of companies are basing their prices on the product's perceived value. **Perceived-value pricing** uses the buyers' perceptions of value, not the seller's cost, as the key to pricing. The company uses the nonprice variables in the marketing mix to build up perceived value in the buyers' minds. Price is set to match the perceived value.

Consider the various prices different restaurants charge for the same items. A consumer who wants a cup of coffee and a slice of apple pie may pay $1.25 at a drugstore counter, $2.00 at a family restaurant, $3.50 at a hotel coffee shop, $5.00 for hotel room service, and $7.00 at an elegant restaurant. Each succeeding restaurant can charge more because of the value added by the atmosphere.

Any company using perceived-value pricing must find out the value in the buyers' minds for different competitive offers. In the last example, consumers could be asked how much they would pay for the same coffee and pie in the different surroundings. Sometimes, consumers can be asked how much they would pay for each benefit added to the offer. If the seller charges more than the buyers' perceived value, its sales will suffer. Many companies overprice their products, and those products sell poorly. Other companies underprice. Under-priced products sell very well, but they produce less revenue than they would if their price were raised to the perceived-value level.[11]

**going-rate pricing** Setting price based largely on competitors' prices rather than on company costs or demand.

**sealed-bid pricing** Setting price based on how the firm thinks competitors will price rather than on its own costs or demand—used when a company bids for jobs.

At Waterford, we take 1,120 times longer than necessary to create a glass.

While a machine can churn one out in only 45 seconds, we take over 14 hours to mouth-blow and hand-cut a single glass. But then, our goal is not efficiency, but beauty.

**Waterford**

*Perceived value: a less expensive glass would hold water, but some consumers will pay much more for the intangibles.*

## Competition-Based Pricing

### Going-Rate Pricing

In **going-rate pricing,** the firm bases its price largely on *competitors'* prices, with less attention paid to its *own* costs or demand. The firm might charge the same, more, or less than its major competitors. In oligopolistic industries that sell a commodity such as steel, paper, or fertilizer, firms normally charge the same price. The smaller firms "follow the leader": They change their prices when the market leader's prices change rather than when their own demand or cost changes. Some firms may charge a bit more or less, but they hold the amount of difference constant. Thus, minor gasoline retailers usually charge a few cents less than the major oil companies without letting the difference increase or decrease.

Going-rate pricing is quite popular. When demand elasticity is hard to measure, firms feel that the going price represents the collective wisdom of the industry concerning the price that will yield a fair return. They also feel that holding to the going price will avoid harmful price wars.

### Sealed-Bid Pricing

Competition-based pricing is also used when firms *bid* for jobs. Using **sealed-bid pricing,** a firm bases its price on how it thinks competitors will price rather than on its own costs or demand. The firm wants to win a contract, and winning the contract requires pricing lower than other firms.

Yet the firm cannot set its price below a certain level. It cannot price below cost without harming its position. On the other hand, the higher it sets its price above its costs, the lower its chance of getting the contract.

Despite the increased role of nonprice factors in the modern marketing process, *price* remains an important element in the marketing mix. Many internal and external factors influence the company's pricing decisions. Internal factors include the firm's *marketing objectives, marketing mix strategy, costs,* and *organization for pricing.*

The pricing strategy is largely determined by the company's *target market* and *positioning objectives.* Common pricing objectives include survival, current profit maximization, market-share leadership, and product-quality leadership.

Price is only one of the marketing mix tools the company uses to accomplish its objectives, and pricing decisions affect, and are affected by, product design, distribution, and promotion decisions. Price decisions must be carefully coordinated with the other marketing mix decisions when designing the marketing program.

*Costs* set the floor for the company's price—the price must cover all the costs of making and selling the product, plus a fair rate of return. Management must decide who within the organization is responsible for setting prices. In large companies, some pricing authority may be delegated to lower-level managers and salespeople, but top management usually sets pricing policies and approves proposed prices. Production, finance, and accounting managers also influence pricing.

External factors that influence pricing decisions include the nature of the market and demand, competitors' prices and offers, and other external factors such as the economy, reseller needs, and government actions. The seller's pricing options vary with different types of markets. Pricing is especially challenging in markets characterized by *monopolistic competition* or *oligopoly.*

In the end, the consumer decides whether the company has set the right price. The consumer weighs the price against the perceived values of using the product—if the price exceeds the sum of the values, consumers will not buy the product. Consumers differ in the values they assign to different product features, and marketers often vary their pricing strategies for different price segments. When assessing the *market and demand,* the company estimates the demand schedule, which shows the probable quantity purchased per period at alternative price levels. The more *inelastic* the demand, the higher the company can set its price. Demand and *consumer value perceptions* set the ceiling for prices.

Consumers compare a product's price with the prices of *competitors'* products. A company must learn the price and quality of competitors' offers and use them as a starting point for its own pricing.

The company can select one or a combination of three general pricing approaches: the *cost-based approach* (cost-plus or breakeven analysis and target profit pricing), the *buyer-based* (perceived-value) *approach,* and the *competition-based* (going-rate or sealed-bid pricing) *approach.*

# QUESTIONS FOR DISCUSSION

1. Certain "inexpensive" products that waste energy, provide few servings per container, or require frequent maintenance may *cost* much more than products selling for higher *prices.* How can marketers use cost information to gain a competitive edge in pricing and promoting products?

2. Armco, a major sheet metal producer, has developed a process for galvanizing steel sheets so that they can be painted—something previously impossible. Such sheets could be used to prevent rust in car-body parts. What price-setting factors should Armco consider in pricing this new product?

3. What different kinds of firms might have the different marketing objectives of survival, profit maximization, market-share leadership, and product-quality leadership? Give examples.

4. Which type of cost is more relevant in setting the price of a product—fixed costs or variable costs?

5. What are the major factors influencing price setting in each of these four market types—pure competition, monopolistic competition, oligopolistic competition, and pure monopoly? Give examples of these market types and describe the prices of products available in each.

6. In a supermarket, which will have the higher price elasticity of demand—hamburger or steak? If the demand for steak is elastic, what effect would raising its price have on meat department profits?

7. In test markets, Procter & Gamble replaced 16-ounce packages of regular Folgers coffee with 13-ounce "fast-roast" packages. Fast-roast processing allows Procter & Gamble to use fewer green coffee beans per pack without affecting flavor or the number of servings per package. What pricing approach was appropriate for setting the price of this coffee—cost-based, buyer-based, or competition-based?

8. You have inherited an automatic car wash with annual fixed costs of $50,000 and variable costs of $0.50 per car. You believe people will pay $1 to have a car washed. What would be your break-even volume at that price?

9. Sales of Fleischmann's gin *increased* when prices were raised 22 percent over a two-year period. What does this fact say about the demand curve and the

elasticity of demand for Fleischmann's gin? What does it suggest about perceived-value pricing in marketing alcoholic beverages?

10. Columnist Dave Barry jokes that federal law requires this message under the sticker price of new cars:

WARNING TO STUPID PEOPLE: DO NOT PAY THIS AMOUNT. Why is a car's sticker price generally higher than its actual selling price? How do car dealers set the actual prices of their cars?

# REFERENCES

1. See James E. Ellis and Brian Bremner, "Will the Big Markdown Get the Big Store Moving Again?" *Business Week*, March 13, 1989, pp. 110–14; and Kate Fitzgerald, "Sears Breaks Biggest Blitz," *Advertising Age*, February 27, 1989, pp. 2, 75.

2. See David J. Schwartz, *Marketing Today: A Basic Approach,* 3rd ed. (New York: Harcourt Brace Jovanovich, 1981), pp. 270–73.

3. See "Segmentation Strategies Create New Pressure among Marketers," *Marketing News,* March 28, 1986, p. 1.

4. Kathleen Deveny, "Sub-Zero Isn't Trembling Over a Little Competition," *Business Week,* March 3, 1986, p. 118.

5. See P. Ronald Stephenson, William L. Cron, and Gary L. Frazier, "Delegating Pricing Authority to the Sales Force: The Effects on Sales and Profit Performance," *Journal of Marketing,* Spring 1979, pp. 21-28.

6. Thomas Nagle, "Pricing as Creative Marketing," *Business Horizons,* July-August 1983, p. 19.

7. See Thomas T. Nagle, *The Strategy and Tactics of Pricing* (Englewood Cliffs, NJ: Prentice Hall, 1987), pp. 1–9.

8. Ibid., Chap. 3.

9. The arithmetic of markups and margins is discussed in Appendix A, "Marketing Arithmetic."

10. "Supermarket 1984 Sales Manual," *Progressive Grocer,* July 1984.

11. For more on value-based pricing, see John L. Forbis and Nitin T. Mehta, "Value-Based Strategies for Industrial Products," *Business Horizons,* May-June 1981, pp. 32–42; and Ely S. Lurin, "Make Sure Product's Price Reflects Its True Value," *Marketing News,* May 8, 1987, p. 8.

## SILVERADO JEWELRY: A PRICING PARADOX

Silverado Jewelry Store, located in downtown Tempe, Arizona, specializes in hand-crafted jewelry made by local Native Americans. Sheila Becker, the owner of Silverado, has just returned from a buying trip and is discussing an interesting pricing phenomenon with assistant store manager Mary Meindl.

Several months ago, the store had received a selection of mother-of-pearl stone and silver bracelets, earrings, and necklaces. Unlike the blue-green tones in typical turquoise jewelry designs, mother-of-pearl stone is pink with white marbling. In terms of size and style, the selection included a wide range of items. While some were small, round, rather simple designs, others were larger, bolder designs that were quite intricate. In addition, the collection included an assortment of traditionally styled men's studded string ties.

Sheila had purchased the mother-of-pearl selection at a very reasonable cost and was quite pleased with the distinctive product assortment. She thought the jewelry would appeal particularly to the general buyer seeking an alternative to the turquoise jewelry usually offered in shops all around Tempe. She priced the new jewelry so that shoppers would receive a good value for their money but also included a markup sufficient to cover the costs of doing business plus an average profit margin.

After the items had been displayed in the store for about a month, Sheila was disappointed in their sales. She decided to try several merchandising tactics that she had learned as a student at the University of Nevada. For example, realizing that the location of an item in the store will often influence whether or not patrons will examine merchandise, she moved the mother-of-pearl jewelry to a glass display case just to the right of the store entrance.

When sales of the mother-of-pearl merchandise still remained sluggish after the relocation, she decided to talk to store clerks about the jewelry during their weekly meeting. Suggesting that they put more effort into "pushing" this particular line, she provided them with a detailed description of the mother-of-pearl stone and supplied a short, scripted talk that they could memorize and recite for customers.

Unfortunately, this approach also failed. At this point, Sheila was preparing to leave on a buying trip. Frustrated over the sagging sales of the mother-of-pearl jewelry and anxious to reduce current inventory in order to make room for the newer selections that she would be buying, she decided to take drastic action: She would cut the mother-of-pearl prices in half. On her way out of the store, she hastily left a note for Mary Meindl. The note read:

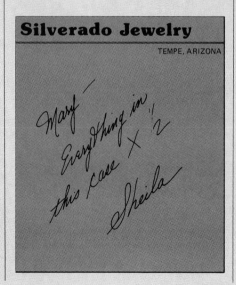

Upon her return, Sheila was pleasantly surprised to find that the entire selection of mother-of-pearl jewelry had been sold. "I really can't understand why," she commented to Mary Meindl, "but that mother-of-pearl stuff just didn't appeal to our customers. I'll have to be more careful the next time I try to increase our variety of stones." Mary responded that although she couldn't quite understand why Sheila wanted to raise the price of slow-moving merchandise, she was surprised at how quickly it had sold at higher price. Sheila was puzzled. "What higher price?" she asked. "My note said to cut the prices in half." "In *half?*" replied a startled Mary. "I thought your note said, 'Everything in this case *times two!*'" As a result, Mary had *doubled* rather than halved the prices.

*Questions*

1. Explain what happened in this situation. Why did the jewelry sell so quickly at twice its normal price?

2. What assumption had Sheila Becker made about the demand curve for the mother-of-pearl jewelry? What did the demand curve for this particular product actually look like?

3. In what type of market is Silverado Jewelry operating (pure competition, monopolistic competition, oligopolistic competition, or pure monopoly)? What leads you to this conclusion?

4. How would the concept of psychological pricing be useful to Sheila Becker? How would you advise her about future pricing decisions?

# 12

# Pricing Products: Pricing Strategies

## CHAPTER OBJECTIVES

After reading this chapter, you should be able to

1. Describe the major strategies for pricing new products
2. Explain how companies find a set of prices that maximizes the profits from the total product mix
3. Explain how companies adjust their prices to take into account different types of customers and situations
4. Tell why companies decide to change their prices

Caterpillar, Inc., the world's leading maker of heavy construction and mining equipment, has been locked in a long price war with Japanese challenger Komatsu, Ltd. In this hard-fought battle, both companies have used price to buy long-run market share even if the strategy has meant lower profits or losses in the short-run.

For over 50 years, Caterpillar has dominated the U.S. and world markets for giant construction equipment. It built a 50 percent market share by emphasizing high product quality, dependable after-sale service, and a strong dealer body. It used a premium pricing strategy—making high profit margins by convincing buyers that Cat's higher quality and trouble-free operation provided greater value and justified a higher price.

But all this began to change in the early 1980s, when Komatsu entered the U.S. market. The Japanese firm started cautiously in the United States, offering only a few products. It realized the importance of nonprice factors in the buyer's purchase decision. Like Caterpillar, Komatsu stressed high quality, and it expanded slowly to allow its parts and service capacity to keep up with sales. But Komatsu's major weapon for taking share from Caterpillar was price. A strong dollar and lower manufacturing costs allowed Komatsu to cut prices ruthlessly—its initial prices were as much as 40 percent lower than Caterpillar's. On a giant dump truck sold by Cat for $500,000, that could mean a savings of up to $200,000! Riding its strong price advantage, Komatsu targeted a 15 percent market share.

Caterpillar fought back to protect its number-one market position, and the price war was on. To support lower prices, Cat reduced its work force by a third and slashed costs by 27 percent. It vowed to meet Komatsu's prices and in some cases even initiated price cutting. With heavy discounting by both companies, manufacturer's list prices soon became meaningless. For example, a bulldozer listing for $140,000 might regularly sell for $110,000. In the battle for market share, all competitors lost out on profits. Lesser companies, such as International Harvester (Navistar) and Clark Equipment, were driven to the brink of ruin. Caterpillar and Komatsu also suffered. Starting in 1982, after 50 straight years of profits, Caterpillar lost almost $1 billion in less than three years. And Komatsu, even with its cost advantages, saw its profits decline by 30 percent.

Despite its losses, Caterpillar continued its relentless drive to cut costs and hold the line on prices. This strategy has recently begun to pay off. Thanks to an effective cost-cutting program and a falling dollar, Caterpillar has raised its prices just 5 percent a year since 1986. At the same time, it has actually improved its already vaunted quality. As a result, the company has rebounded strongly, winning back share and profits in its world markets. By contrast, facing a sharply rising yen, Komatsu has had to raise its prices seven times during the last three years. Its market share, which

peaked in 1986 at 12 percent, has now dropped to 9 percent.

Thus, the long and damaging price war appears to be coming to an end. Although fierce price competition continues, Komatsu's recent rounds of price increases may be a signal that it wants to end the fighting and return to peaceful coexistence and better profits for both companies. It hopes that Caterpillar will respond with equivalent price increases. Says the president of Komatsu America, "If they don't meet our price increases, I'll have to think of some kind of countermeasure to ensure the survival of Komatsu and our distributors. It all depends on how much our market share declines."[1]

**market-skimming pricing** Setting a high price for a new product to skim maximum revenue from the segments willing to pay the high price.

In this chapter, we will look at pricing dynamics. A company sets not a single price, but rather a *pricing structure* that covers different items in its line. This pricing structure changes over time as products move through their life cycles. The company adjusts product prices to reflect changing costs and demand and to account for variations in buyers and situations. As the competitive environment changes, the company considers *initiating* price changes at times and *responding to* them at others. This chapter will examine the major dynamic pricing strategies available to management. In turn, we will look at *new-product pricing strategies* for products in the introductory stage of the product life cycle, *product-mix pricing strategies* for related products in the product mix, *price-adjustment strategies* that account for customer differences and changing situations, and *strategies for initiating and responding to price changes.*[2]

# NEW-PRODUCT PRICING STRATEGIES

Pricing strategies usually change as the product passes through its life cycle. The introductory stage is especially challenging. We can distinguish between pricing a real product innovation that is patent-protected and pricing a product that imitates existing products.

## *Pricing an Innovative Product*

Companies bringing out an innovative patent-protected product can choose between *market-skimming* pricing and *market-penetration pricing.*

### Market-Skimming Pricing

Many companies that invent new products set high prices initially to "skim" revenues layer by layer from the market. Polaroid is a prime user of **market-skimming pricing.** On its original instant camera, it charged the highest price it could given the benefits of its new product over other products customers might buy. Polaroid set a price that made it *just* worthwhile for some segments of the market to adopt the new camera. After an initial sales slowdown, it then lowered the price to draw in the next price-sensitive layer of customers. Polaroid also used the same approach with its new Spectra camera. It introduced the Spectra at about twice the price of its previous entry in the field. After about a year, it began bringing out simpler, lower-priced versions to draw in new segments. In this way, Polaroid skimmed a maximum amount of revenue from the various segments of the market.[3]

Market skimming makes sense only under certain conditions. First, the product's quality and image must support its higher price, and enough buyers must want the product at that price. Second, the costs of producing a small volume cannot be so high that they cancel the advantage of charging more. Finally, competitors should not be able to enter the market easily and undercut the high price.

### Market-Penetration Pricing

Rather than setting a high initial price to *skim* off small but profitable market segments, other companies set a low initial price in order to *penetrate* the market quickly and deeply—to quickly attract a large number of buyers and win a large market share. Texas Instruments (TI) is a prime user of **market-penetration pricing.** TI will build a large plant, set its price as low as possible, win a large market share, realize falling costs, and then cut its price further as costs fall. Warehouse stores and discount retailers also use penetration pricing. They charge low prices to attract high volume; the high volume results in lower costs that, in turn, let the discounter keep prices low.

Several conditions favor setting a low price. The market must be highly price-sensitive so that a low price produces more market growth. Production and distribution costs must fall as sales volume increases. And the low price must help to keep out the competition.

**market-penetration pricing**
Setting a low price for a new product in order to attract a large number of buyers and a large market share.

*Market skimming: Polaroid introduced its Spectra at a high price, then brought out lower-priced versions to draw in new segments.*

**product line pricing** Setting the price steps between various products in a product line based on cost differences between the products, customer evaluations of different features, and competitors' prices.

## *Pricing an Imitative New Product*

A company that plans to develop an imitative new product faces a product-positioning problem. It must decide where to position the product on quality and price. Figure 12–1 shows nine possible price-quality strategies. If the existing market leader has taken Box 1 by producing the premium product and charging the highest price, then the newcomer might prefer to use one of the other strategies. It could design a high-quality product and charge a medium price (Box 2), design an average-quality product and charge an average price (Box 5), and so on. The newcomer must consider both the size and growth rate of the market in each box and the competitors it would face.

# PRODUCT MIX PRICING STRATEGIES

The strategy for setting a price on a product often has to be changed when the product is part of a product mix. In this case, the firm looks for a set of prices that maximize the profits on the total product mix. Pricing is difficult because the various products have related demand and costs and face different degrees of competition. We will look at four *product-mix pricing* situations.

## *Product Line Pricing*

Companies usually develop product lines rather than single products. For example, Snapper makes many different lawn mowers, ranging from simple walk-behind versions priced at $259.95, $299.95, and $399.95 to elaborate riding mowers priced at $1,000 or more. Each successive lawn mower in the line offers more features. In **product line pricing**, management must decide on the price steps to set between the various mowers.

The price steps should take into account cost differences between the mowers, customer evaluations of their different features, and competitors' prices. If the price difference between two successive lawn mowers is small, buyers will usually buy the more advanced mower, and this likelihood will increase company profits if the cost difference is smaller than the price difference. If the price difference is large, customers will generally buy the less advanced mowers.

In many industries, sellers use well-established price points for the products in their line. Thus, men's clothing stores might carry men's suits at

FIGURE 12–1   Nine Marketing Mix Strategies on Price/Quality

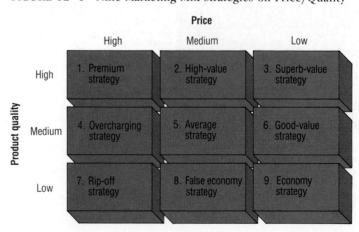

**optional-product pricing** The pricing of optional or accessory products along with a main product.

**captive-product pricing** The pricing of products that must be used along with a main product, such as blades for razors and film for cameras.

*Product-line pricing: Snapper sells a lawn mower for every pocketbook.*

three price levels: $185, $285, and $385. The customer will likely associate low-, average-, and high-quality suits with the three "price points." Even if the three prices are raised a little, men will normally buy suits at their own preferred price points. The seller's task is to establish perceived quality differences that support the price differences.

## Optional-Product Pricing

Many companies use **optional-product pricing**—offering to sell optional or accessory products along with their main product. A car buyer can order electric windows, defoggers, and cruise control. Pricing these options is a sticky problem. Automobile companies have to decide which items to build into the base price and which ones to offer as options. General Motors' normal pricing strategy is to advertise a stripped-down model for $9,000 to pull people into showrooms and then devote most of the showroom space to showing option-loaded cars at $11,000 or $12,000. The economy model is stripped of so many comforts and conveniences that most buyers reject it. When GM launched its new front-wheel drive J-cars in the early 1980s, it took a clue from Japanese automakers and included in the sticker price many useful items previously sold only as options. The advertised price then represented a well-equipped car.

## Captive-Product Pricing

Companies that make products that must be used along with a main product use **captive-product pricing.** Examples of captive products are razor blades, camera film, and computer software. Producers of the main products (razors, cameras, and computers) often price them low and set high markups on the

**two-part pricing** A strategy for pricing services in which price is broken into a fixed fee plus a variable usage rate.

**by-product pricing** Setting a price for by-products in order to make the main product's price more competitive.

**product-bundle pricing** Combining several products and offering the bundle at a reduced price.

supplies. Thus, Polaroid prices its cameras low because it makes its money on selling film. Those camera makers that do not sell film have to price their cameras higher in order to make the same overall profit.

In the case of services, this strategy is called **two-part pricing.** The price of the service is broken into a *fixed fee* plus a *variable usage rate.* Thus, a telephone company charges a monthly rate plus charges for calls beyond some minimum number. Amusement parks charge admission plus fees for food, midway attractions, and rides over a minimum. The service firm must decide how much to charge for the basic service and how much for the variable usage. The fixed amount should be low enough to induce usage of the service, and profit can be made on the variable usage fees.

## By-Product Pricing

In producing processed meats, petroleum products, chemicals, and other products, there are often by-products. If the by-products have no value and getting rid of them is costly, this fact will affect the pricing of the main product. Using **by-product pricing,** the manufacturer will seek a market for these by-products and should accept any price that covers more than the cost of storing and delivering them. This practice allows the seller to reduce the main product's price to make it more competitive.

## Product-Bundle Pricing

Using **product-bundle pricing,** sellers often combine several of their products and offer the bundle at a reduced price. Thus, theaters and sports teams sell season tickets at less than the cost of single tickets; hotels sell specially priced

*Product-bundle pricing: Hyatt offers a specially priced package.*

packages that include room, meals, and entertainment; automobile companies sell attractively priced options packages. Price bundling can promote the sales of products consumers might not otherwise buy, but the combined price must be low enough to get them to buy the bundle.[4]

---

# PRICE-ADJUSTMENT STRATEGIES

Companies usually adjust their basic prices to account for various customer differences and changing situations. We will look at the following adjustment strategies: *discount pricing and allowances, discriminatory pricing, psychological pricing, promotional pricing,* and *geographical pricing.*

## Discount Pricing and Allowances

Most companies will adjust their basic price to reward customers for certain responses, such as early payment of bills, volume purchases, and buying off-season. These price adjustments—called *discounts* and *allowances*—are described below.

### Cash Discounts

A **cash discount** is a price reduction to buyers who pay their bills promptly. A typical example is "2/10, net 30," which means that although payment is due within 30 days, the buyer can deduct 2 percent if the bill is paid within ten. The discount must be granted to all buyers meeting these terms. Such discounts are customary in many industries and help to improve the sellers' cash situation and reduce bad debts and credit-collection costs.

### Quantity Discounts

A **quantity discount** is a price reduction to buyers who buy large volumes. A typical example might be "$10 per unit for less than 100 units, $9 per unit for 100 or more units." Quantity discounts must be offered to all customers and must not exceed the seller's cost savings associated with selling large quantities. These savings include lower selling, inventory, and transportation expenses. Discounts provide an incentive to the customer to buy more from a given seller rather than buying from many sources.

### Functional Discounts

A **functional discount** (also called a **trade discount**) is offered by the seller to trade channel members who perform certain functions such as selling, storing, and record keeping. Manufacturers may offer different functional discounts to different trade channels because of the varying services they perform, but manufacturers must offer the same functional discounts within each trade channel.

### Seasonal Discounts

A **seasonal discount** is a price reduction to buyers who buy merchandise or services out of season. Seasonal discounts allow the seller to keep production steady during an entire year. Ski manufacturers will offer seasonal discounts to retailers in the spring and summer to encourage early ordering. Hotels, motels, and airlines will offer seasonal discounts in their slower selling periods.

**cash discount** A price reduction to buyers who pay their bills promptly.
**quantity discount** A price reduction to buyers who buy large volumes.
**functional discount** (or **trade discount**) A price reduction offered by the seller to trade channel members who perform certain functions such as selling, storing, and record keeping.
**seasonal discount** A price reduction to buyers who buy merchandise or services out of season.

**trade-in allowance** A price reduction given for turning in an old item when buying a new one.

**promotional allowance** A payment or price reduction to reward dealers for participating in advertising and sales-support programs.

**discriminatory pricing** Selling a product or service at two or more prices even though the difference in prices is not based on differences in costs.

## Allowances

Allowances are other types of reductions from the list price. For example, **trade-in allowances** are price reductions given for turning in an old item when buying a new one. Trade-in allowances are most common in the automobile industry and are also given for some other durable goods. **Promotional allowances** are payments or price reductions to reward dealers for participating in advertising and sales-support programs.

## Discriminatory Pricing

Companies will often adjust their basic prices to allow for differences in customers, products, and locations. In **discriminatory pricing,** the company sells a product or service at two or more prices, even though the difference in prices is not based on differences in costs. Discriminatory pricing takes several forms:

- □ *Customer-segment pricing.* Here, different customers pay different prices for the same product or service. Museums, for example, will charge a lower admission for students and senior citizens.

- □ *Product-form pricing.* Here, different versions of the product are priced differently but not according to differences in their costs. Black & Decker prices its most expensive iron at $54.98, which is $12 more than its next most expensive iron. The top model has a self-cleaning feature, yet this extra feature costs only a few more dollars to make.

- □ *Location pricing.* Here, different locations are priced differently even though the cost of offering each location is the same. For instance, a theater varies its seat prices because of audience preferences for certain locations. State universities charge higher tuition for out-of-state students.

- □ *Time pricing.* Here, prices are varied seasonally, by the month, by the day, and even by the hour. Public utilities vary their prices to commercial users by time of day and weekend versus weekday. The telephone company offers lower "off-peak" charges, and resorts give seasonal discounts.

For discriminatory pricing to be an effective strategy for the company, certain conditions must exist. The market must be segmentable and the segments must show different degrees of demand. Members of the segment paying the lower price should not be able to turn around and resell the product to the segment paying the higher price. Competitors should not be able to undersell the firm in the segment being charged the higher price. Nor should the costs of segmenting and watching the market exceed the extra revenue obtained from the price difference. The practice should not lead to customer resentment and ill will. Finally, the discriminatory pricing must be legal.

With the current deregulation taking place in certain industries, such as airlines and trucking, companies in these industries have used more discriminatory pricing. Consider the pricing used by airlines. The passengers on a plane bound from Raleigh to Los Angeles may pay as many as ten different round-trip fares for the same flight—first class, $1,512; first class—night, $1,064; first class—night, child, $851; first class—youth, $1,208; coach, $1,014; coach—night, $816; coach—night, child, $810; Super-Saver (nonrefundable fare), $238; Super-Saver (25 percent cancellation penalty), $368; and military personnel, $498. Travelers who check carefully benefit from the intense competition among different carriers flying this route.

## Psychological Pricing

Price says something about the product. For example, many consumers use price to judge quality. A $100 bottle of perfume may contain only $3 worth of scent, but some people are willing to pay $100 because the price indicates something special.

In using **psychological pricing**, sellers consider the psychology of prices and not simply the economics. A study of the relationship between price and quality perceptions of cars found that consumers perceive higher-priced cars as having higher quality.[5] By the same token, higher-quality cars are perceived to be even higher priced than they actually are! When consumers can judge the quality of a product by examining it or by calling upon past experience with it, they use price less to judge quality. But when consumers cannot judge quality because they lack the information or skill, price becomes an important quality signal (see Marketing Highlight 12–1).[6]

Another aspect of psychological pricing is **reference prices.** These are prices that buyers carry in their minds and refer to when they look at a given product. The reference price might be formed by noting current prices, remembering past prices, or assessing the buying situation. Sellers can influence or use consumers' reference prices when setting prices. For example, a company could display its product next to more expensive ones in order to imply that it belongs in the same class. Department stores often sell women's clothing in separate departments differentiated by price: Clothing found in the more expensive department is assumed to be of better quality. Companies can also influence consumers' reference prices by stating high manufacturer's suggested prices, by indicating that the product was originally priced much higher, or by pointing to a competitor's higher price.

Even small differences in price can suggest product differences. Consider a stereo priced at $300 compared with one priced at $299.95. The actual price difference is only 5 cents, but the psychological difference can be much greater. For example, some consumers will see the $299.95 as a price in the $200 range rather than the $300 range. While the $299.95 will more likely be seen as a

**psychological pricing** A pricing approach that considers the psychology of prices and not simply the economics—the price is used to say something about the product.

**reference prices** Prices that buyers carry in their minds and refer to when they look at a given product.

# Marketing Highlight 12–1

## HOW PRICE SIGNALS PRODUCT QUALITY

Heublein produces Smirnoff, America's leading brand of vodka. Some years ago, Smirnoff was attacked by another brand, Wolfschmidt, priced at one dollar less per bottle and claiming to have the same quality. Concerned that customers might switch to Wolfschmidt, Heublein considered several possible counterstrategies. It could lower Smirnoff's price by one dollar to hold on to market share; it could hold Smirnoff's price but increase advertising and promotion expenditures; or it could hold

Smirnoff's price and let its market share fall. All three strategies would lead to lower profits, and it seemed that Heublein faced a no-win situation.

At this point, however, Heublein's marketers thought of a fourth strategy—and it was brilliant. Heublein *raised* the price of Smirnoff by one dollar! The company then introduced a new brand, Relska, to compete with Wolfschmidt. Moreover, it introduced another brand, Popov, priced *lower* than Wolfschmidt. This product-line pricing

strategy positioned Smirnoff as the elite brand and Wolfschmidt as an ordinary brand. Heublein's clever strategy produced a large increase in its overall profits.

The irony is that Heublein's three brands are pretty much the same in taste and manufacturing costs. Heublein knew that a product's price signals its quality. Using price as a signal, Heublein sells roughly the same product at three different quality positions.

**promotional pricing** Temporarily pricing products below the list price—and sometimes even below cost—to increase short-run sales.

bargain price, the $300 price suggests more quality. Some psychologists even argue that each digit has symbolic and visual qualities that should be considered in pricing. Thus, 8 is round and even and creates a soothing effect, while 7 is angular and creates a jarring effect.

## Promotional Pricing

With **promotional pricing,** companies will temporarily price their products below list price—and sometimes even below cost. Promotional pricing takes several forms. Supermarkets and department stores will price a few products as *loss leaders* to attract customers to the store in the hope that they will buy other items at normal markups. Sellers will also use *special-event pricing* in certain

*Promotion pricing: companies often reduce their prices temporarily to produce sales.*

seasons to draw in more customers. Thus, linens are promotionally priced every January to attract weary Christmas shoppers back into stores. Manufacturers will sometimes offer *cash rebates* to consumers who buy the product from dealers within a specified time. The manufacturer sends the rebate directly to the customer. Rebates have recently been popular with automakers and with durable goods and small appliance producers. Some manufacturers offer *low-interest financing, longer warranties,* or *free maintenance* to reduce the consumer's "price." This practice has recently become a favorite of the auto industry. Or, the seller may simply offer *discounts* from normal prices to increase sales and reduce inventories.

**FOB-origin pricing** A geographic pricing strategy in which the customer pays the freight from the factory to the destination.
**uniform delivered pricing** A geographic pricing strategy in which the company charges the same price plus freight to all customers regardless of location.

## Geographical Pricing

A company must also decide how to price its products to customers located in different parts of the country. Should the company risk losing the business of more distant customers by charging them higher prices to cover higher shipping costs? Or should the company charge the same to all customers regardless of location? We will look at five geographical pricing strategies for the following hypothetical situation:

> The Peerless Paper Company is located in Atlanta, Georgia, and sells paper products to customers all over the United States. The cost of freight is high and affects the companies from whom customers buy their paper. Peerless wants to establish a geographical pricing policy. It is trying to determine how to price a $100 order to three specific customers: Customer A (Atlanta), Customer B (Bloomington, Indiana), and Customer C (Compton, California).

### FOB-Origin Pricing

On the one hand, Peerless can ask each customer to pay the shipping cost from the Atlanta factory to the customer's location. All three customers would pay the same factory price of $100, with Customer A paying, say, $10 for shipping, Customer B $15, and Customer C $25. Called **FOB-origin pricing,** this practice means that the goods are placed *free on board* (hence, *FOB)* a carrier, at which point the title and responsibility pass to the customer, who pays the freight from the factory to the destination.

Because each customer picks up its own cost, supporters of FOB pricing feel that this is the fairest way to assess freight charges. The disadvantage, however, is that Peerless will be a high-cost firm to distant customers. If the main competitor of Peerless happens to be in California, this competitor will no doubt outsell Peerless there. In fact, the competitor would outsell Peerless in most of the West, while Peerless would dominate the East. A vertical line could actually be drawn on a map connecting the cities where the two companies' prices plus freight charges would be roughly equal. Peerless would have the price advantage east of this line; its competitor the price advantage west of it.

### Uniform Delivered Pricing

By contrast, **uniform delivered pricing** is the exact opposite of FOB pricing. Here, the company charges the same price plus freight to all customers regardless of their location. The freight charge is set at the average freight cost. Suppose this is $15. Uniform delivered pricing therefore results in a high charge to the Atlanta customer (who pays $15 freight instead of $10) and a lower charge to the Compton customer (who pays $15 instead of $25). The Atlanta customer would prefer to buy paper from another local paper company that uses FOB-origin pricing. On the other hand, Peerless has a better chance to win the

**zone pricing** A geographic pricing strategy in which the company sets up two or more zones—all customers within a zone pay the same total price, which is higher in the more distant zones.

**basing-point pricing** A geographic pricing strategy in which the seller designates a given city as a basing point and charges all customers the freight cost from that city to the customer location, regardless of the city from which the goods are actually shipped.

**freight-absorption pricing** A geographic pricing strategy in which the company absorbs all or part of the actual freight charges in order to get desired business.

California customer. Other advantages are that uniform delivered pricing is fairly easy to administer and lets the firm advertise its price nationally.

### Zone Pricing

**Zone pricing** falls between FOB-origin pricing and uniform delivered pricing. The company sets up two or more zones. All customers within a given zone pay a single total price that is higher in the more distant zones. For example, Peerless might set up an East Zone and charge $10 freight to all customers in this zone, a Midwest Zone in which it charges $15, and a West Zone where it charges $25. In this way, the customers within a given price zone receive no price advantage from the company. Customers in Atlanta and Boston pay the same total price to Peerless. The complaint, however, is that the Atlanta customer is paying part of the Boston customer's freight cost. In addition, even though they may be within a few miles of each other, a customer just barely on the west side of the line dividing the East and Midwest pays much more than one just barely on the east side of the line.

### Basing-Point Pricing

Using **basing-point pricing,** the seller selects a given city as a "basing point" and charges all customers the freight cost from that city to the customer location regardless of the city from which the goods are actually shipped. For example, Peerless might set Chicago as the basing point and charge all customers $100 plus the freight charge from Chicago to their locations. An Atlanta customer would thus pay the freight cost from Chicago to Atlanta even though the goods were shipped from Atlanta. Using a basing-point location other than the factory raises the total price to customers near the factory and lowers the total price to customers far from it.

If all sellers used the same basing-point city, delivered prices would be the same for all customers and price competition would be eliminated. Such industries as sugar, cement, steel, and automobiles used basing-point pricing for years, but the method is less popular today. Some companies set up multiple basing points to create more flexibility: They quote freight charges from the basing-point city nearest to the customer.

### Freight-Absorption Pricing

Finally, the seller who is anxious to do business with a certain customer or geographical area might use **freight-absorption pricing.** This method involves absorbing all or part of the actual freight charges in order to get desired business. The seller might reason that if it can get more business, its average costs will fall and more than compensate for its extra freight cost. Freight-absorption pricing is used for market penetration and also to hold on to increasingly competitive markets.

# PRICE CHANGES

## Initiating Price Changes

After developing their price structures and strategies, companies may face occasions when they will want to either cut or raise prices.

## Initiating Price Cuts

Several situations may lead a firm to consider cutting its price. One is excess capacity. Here, the firm needs more business and cannot get it through increased sales effort, product improvement, or other measures. In the late 1970s, many companies dropped "follow-the-leader pricing"—charging about the same price as their leading competitors—and aggressively cut prices to boost their sales. But as the airline, construction equipment, and other industries have learned in recent years, cutting prices in an industry loaded with excess capacity may lead to price wars as competitors try to hold on to market share.

Another situation is falling market share in the face of strong price competition. Several American industries—automobiles, consumer electronics, cameras, watches, and steel—have been losing market share to Japanese competitors whose high-quality products carry lower prices than their American counterparts. Zenith, General Motors, and other American companies have resorted to more aggressive pricing action. General Motors, for example, cut its sub-compact car prices by 10 percent on the West Coast, where Japanese competition is strongest.

Companies will also cut prices in a drive to dominate the market through lower costs. Either the company starts with lower costs than its competitors or it cuts prices in the hope of gaining a market share that will cut costs through larger volume. Bausch and Lomb used an aggressive low-cost, low-price strategy to become the leader in the competitive soft contact lens market (see Marketing Highlight 12–2).

## Initiating Price Increases

On the other hand, many companies have had to *raise* prices in recent years. They do this knowing that price increases may be resented by customers, dealers, and their own salesforce. However, a successful price increase can greatly increase profits. For example, if the company's profit margin is 3 percent of sales, a 1 percent price increase will increase profits by 33 percent if sales volume is unaffected.

A major factor in price increases is cost inflation. Rising costs squeeze profit margins and lead companies to regular rounds of price increases. Companies often raise their prices by more than the cost increase in anticipation of further inflation or government price controls. Companies do not want to make long-run price agreements with customers—they fear that cost inflation will eat up their profit margins. Another factor leading to price increases is overdemand: When a company cannot supply all its customers' needs, it can raise its prices, ration products to customers, or both.

In passing price increases on to customers, the company should avoid the image of "price gouger." Price increases should be supported with a company communication program telling customers why prices are being increased. The company salesforce should help customers find ways to economize.

## Buyer Reactions to Price Changes

Whether the price is raised or lowered, the action will affect buyers, competitors, distributors, and suppliers and may interest government as well. Customers do not always put a straightforward interpretation on price changes. They may view a price *cut* in several ways. For example, what would you think if IBM suddenly cut its personal computer prices in half? You might think that these computers are about to be replaced by newer models or that they have some fault and are not selling well. You might think that IBM is in financial trouble

## BAUSCH & LOMB'S HARDBALL PRICING

Bausch & Lomb was the first company to develop and sell soft contact lenses. For many years after introducing these lenses in the early 1970s, B&L held 100 percent of the market. But in the late 1970s, as a dozen competitors entered the soft-lens market, Bausch & Lomb quickly lost its market-share dominance. To make matters worse, the company was late in developing extended-wear lenses—thinner soft lenses that can be worn for up to a

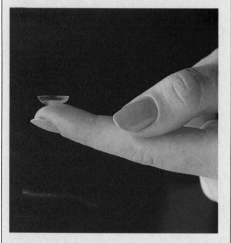

*Bausch & Lomb created the soft contact lens market, then used "hardball pricing" to hold off competitors.*

month at a time without taking them out. By the early 1980s, B&L's overall share had dropped to under 50 percent, largely because it had no share of the fast-growing extended-wear lens segment.

Bausch finally brought out its own brand of extended-wear lenses in 1983—two years after competitors' entries. To overcome its late start, B&L used all of its considerable marketing strength and a tough marketing strategy. At the heart of this strategy was aggressive low pricing. *Business Week* describes Bausch's "hardball pricing" and competitors' reactions:

[Bausch & Lomb's] entry price of $20 was 50% or more below the industry norm for extended-wear lenses. . . . [Competitor] CooperVision hit back in March with a new, top-quality lens it offered for about $15 wholesale. Bausch retaliated in April by lowering all its prices even further. Now its high-water model wholesales for $10 to $15, while its basic low-water lens lists at $8 to $13 depending on volume, and a new daily-wear lens has been introduced at a low price of $7 to $12.

Thus, shortly after entering the market, Bausch was selling its high-quality lenses for only 20 to 30 percent of competitors' previous prices. The

company's aggressive initial pricing—and its quick reactions to competitors' price thrusts—paid off well:

Within a month, B&L's sales staff had supplies of the new lenses in more than 90% of the 12,000 professional eye-care outlets in the U.S. that sell contact lenses. Within four months, Bausch captured 37% of the [extended-wear lens] market and was the No. 1 marketer.

Bausch & Lomb's low price resulted in large sales volume, which in turn lowered unit-production costs, allowing still lower prices. Bausch is now firmly positioned as the industry's low-cost, low-price producer, and its competitors face some tough decisions. Bausch's low prices have sent competitors scrambling to figure out how to respond. Those who cannot find a good answer will have to drop out of the running.

*Sources:* Excerpts from "Bausch & Lomb: Hardball Pricing Helps It to Regain Its Grip in Contact Lenses," *Business Week,* July 16, 1984, pp. 78–80. Also see Lois Therrien, "Bausch & Lomb Is Correcting Its Vision of Research," *Business Week,* March 30, 1987, p. 91.

and may not stay in the business long enough to supply future parts. You might believe that quality has been reduced. Or you might think that the price will come down even further and that it will pay to wait and see.

Similarly, a price *increase,* which would normally lower sales, may have some positive meanings for buyers. What would you think if IBM *raised* the price of its latest personal computer model? You might think that the item is very "hot" and may be unobtainable unless you buy it soon. You might think that the computer is an unusually good value or that IBM is greedy and charging what the traffic will bear.

### Competitor Reactions to Price Changes

A firm considering a price change has to worry about competitors' as well as customers' reactions. Competitors are most likely to react when the number of

*Buyer reactions to price changes: what would you think if the price of Joy was suddenly cut in half?*

firms involved is small, when the product is uniform, and when buyers are well informed.

How can a firm figure out the likely reactions of its competitors? Assume that a firm faces one large competitor. If the competitor tends to react in a set way to price changes, that reaction can be anticipated. But if the competitor treats each price change as a fresh challenge and reacts according to its own self-interest, the company will have to figure out just what makes up the competitor's self-interest at the time.

The problem is complex because the competitor can interpret a company price cut in many ways. It might think the company is trying to grab a larger market share, that the company is doing poorly and trying to boost its sales, or that the company wants the whole industry to cut prices to increase total demand.

When there are *several* competitors, the company must gauge *each* competitor's likely reaction. If all competitors behave alike, this amounts to analyzing only a typical competitor. However, if competitors do not behave alike—perhaps because of differences in size, market shares, or policies—then separate analyses are necessary. On the other hand, if some competitors will match the price change, there is good reason to expect that the rest will also match it.

## Responding to Price Changes

Here, we reverse the question and ask how a firm should respond to a price change by a competitor. The firm needs to consider several issues. Why did the competitor change the price? Was it to take more market share, to use excess

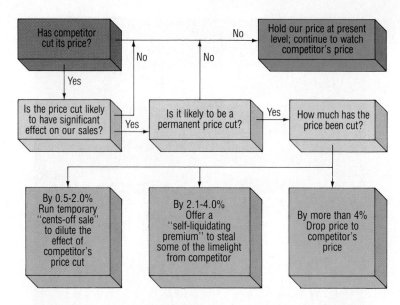

FIGURE 12–2   Price Reaction Program for Meeting a Competitor's Price Cut

*Source:* Redrawn with permission from a working paper by Raymond J. Trapp, Northwestern University, 1964.

capacity, to meet changing cost conditions, or to lead an industry-wide price change? Does the competitor plan to make the price change temporary or permanent? What will happen to the company's market share and profits if it does not respond? Are other companies going to respond? What are the competitor's and other firms' responses likely to be to each possible reaction?

Besides these issues, the company must make a broader analysis. It must consider its own product's stage in its life cycle, its importance in the company's product mix, the intentions and resources of the competitor, and possible consumer reactions to price changes.

A company cannot always make an extended analysis of its alternatives at the time of a price change. The competitor may have spent a great deal of time preparing its decision, while the company may have to react within days or even hours. About the only way to cut down reaction time is to plan ahead for both possible competitors' price changes and possible responses. Figure 12–2 shows one company's price-reaction program for meeting a competitor's possible price cut. Reaction programs for meeting price changes are often used in industries in which price changes occur often and it is important to react quickly. Examples can be found in the meatpacking, lumber, and oil industries.

# ■ SUMMARY

Pricing is a dynamic process. Companies design a *pricing structure* that covers all their products, change it over time, and adjust it to account for different customers and situations.

Pricing strategies usually change as a product passes through its life cycle. In pricing innovative products, the company can follow a *skimming policy*—initially setting high prices to "skim" the maximum amount of revenue from various segments of the market. Or it can use *penetration pricing*—setting a low initial price to win a large market share. The company can decide on one of nine price-quality strategies for introducing an imitative product.

When the product is part of a product mix, the firm searches for a set of prices that will maximize profits from the total mix. The company decides on *price zones* for items in its product line and on the pricing of *optional products, captive products,* and *by-products.*

Companies apply a variety of *price-adjustment strategies* to account for differences in consumer segments and situations. One is *geographical pricing*, whereby the company decides how to price to distant customers, choosing from such alternatives as FOB pricing, uniform delivered pricing, zone pricing, basing-point pricing, and freight-absorption pricing. A second strategy is *discount pricing and allowances*, whereby the company establishes cash discounts, quantity discounts, functional discounts, seasonal discounts, and allowances. A third strategy is *discriminatory pricing*, whereby the company sets different prices for different customers, product forms, places, or times. A fourth strategy is *psychological pricing*, whereby the company adjusts a price to better communicate a product's intended position. A fifth strategy is *promotional pricing*, whereby the company decides on loss-leader pricing, special-event pricing, and psychological discounting.

When a firm considers initiating a price change, it must consider customers' and competitors' reactions. Customers' reactions are influenced by the meaning customers see in the price change. Competitors' reactions flow from a set reaction policy or a fresh analysis of each situation. The firm initiating a price change must also anticipate the probable reactions of suppliers, middlemen, and government.

The firm that faces a price change initiated by a competitor must try to understand the competitor's intent and both the likely duration and impact of the change. If swiftness of reaction is desirable, the firm should preplan its reactions to different possible price actions by competitors.

---

# QUESTIONS FOR DISCUSSION

1. Describe which strategy—market skimming or market penetration—is used by these companies in pricing their products: (a) McDonald's, (b) Curtis Mathes (television and other home electronics), (c) Bic Corporation (pens, lighters, shavers, and related products), (d) IBM. Are these the right strategies for these companies?

2. A by-product of manufacturing tennis balls is "dead" balls—balls that do not bounce high enough to meet standards (a minimum of 53 inches when dropped from 100 inches onto a concrete surface). What strategy should be used for pricing these balls?

3. What types of discount-pricing tactics might a manufacturer of snow skis use in dealing with the retail outlets carrying its products?

4. Analyze different pricing strategies at movie theaters. To which market segments are these different strategies designed to appeal?

5. A clothing store sells men's suits at three price levels—$180, $250, and $340. If shoppers use these levels as reference prices in comparing suits, consider the effect of adding a new line of suits at a cost of $280: Would sales of the $250 suits probably increase, decrease, or stay the same?

6. A garden supply company located in New York uses catalogs to sell seeds and bulbs to gardeners in every part of the country. What geographical-pricing strategy should this company use for maximum profits?

7. Increases in the worldwide supply of cocoa have led to decreases in the price of cocoa and lowered production costs for chocolate products. What impact will this reduction have on chocolate prices? If manufacturers expect the price of cocoa to go back up next year, what approach should they take if they want to cut prices?

8. If McDonald's cut the price of a Big Mac to only 99 cents, how would competing hamburger chains probably react? Would they react the same way if the price decrease were for Chicken McNuggets rather than Big Macs?

---

# REFERENCES

1. See Bill Kelley, "Komatsu in Cat Fight," *Sales & Marketing Management,* April 1986, pp. 50–53; Jack Willoughby, "Decision Time in Peoria," *Forbes,* January 27, 1986, p. 36; Kathleen Deveny, "Going for the Lion's Share," *Business Week,* July 18, 1988, pp. 70–72; and Ronald Henkoff, "This Cat Is Acting Like a Tiger," *Fortune,* December 19, 1988, pp. 71–76.

2. For a comprehensive description and comparison of various pricing strategies, see Gerald J. Tellis, "Beyond the Many Faces of Price: An Integration of Pricing Strategies," *Journal of Marketing,* October 1986, pp. 146–60.

3. See James E. Ellis, "Spectra's Instant Success Gives Polaroid a Shot in the Arm," *Business Week,* November 3, 1986, pp. 32–34; and Thomas T. Nagle, *The Strategy and Tactics of Pricing* (Englewood Cliffs, NJ: Prentice Hall, 1987), pp. 116–117.

4. See Tellis, "Beyond the Many Faces of Price," p. 155; and Nagle, *The Strategy and Tactics of Pricing,* pp. 170–172.

5. Gary M. Erickson and Johny K. Johansson, "The Role of Price in Multi-Attribute Product Evaluations," *Journal of Consumer Research,* September 1985, pp. 195–199.

6. See Nagle, *The Strategy and Tactics of Pricing,* pp. 66–68; and Tellis, "Beyond the Many Faces of Price," pp. 152–53.

# Case 12

## EAST LINE RAILWAY: THE WISCONSIN CANNED GOODS PROJECT

Sitting in his office at the headquarters of East Line Railway, Carl Meyers was hard at work. As Marketing Analyst for the Food Products Transportation Group, Meyers was responsible for developing strategy and setting prices for the transportation of canned goods in boxcars. As one aspect of its marketing strategy in the coming year for its food-products market segment, East Line wants to increase the volume of canned goods shipped in boxcars from the Midwest to the East Coast. For starters, Meyers is targeting the market for shipments of Wisconsin canned goods to the New York City/Northern New Jersey metropolitan area—one of the biggest food-consuming areas within the East Line system.

Wisconsin canned goods consist mostly of beans, peas, and fruit. Wisconsin canners ship almost 1½-million tons of canned goods annually to the East Coast, much of it to the NY/NJ metropolitan area. In addition, a majority of Wisconsin canners are located along rail lines and have facilities for loading boxcars. Despite this fact, East Line Railway handled only 327 carloads (about 20,600 tons) from Wisconsin to the NY/NJ area in 1988. The remainder of the goods were moved by truck. Thus, Meyers saw significant potential for increasing market share.

Because a boxcar holds 126,000 pounds of canned goods (a truck holds only 42,000), East Line Railway can profitably offer the customer a significantly lower per-unit shipping price than can a trucking firm. Also, the average length of haul from Wisconsin to NY/NJ is 975 miles—well above the theoretical 300–400-mile point below

which it is harder for rail shipping to compete with truck hauling.

Trucks do in fact offer advantages over boxcars in certain situations—for example, when the shipment size is too small to fill an entire boxcar or when perishability makes speed of transit a priority. On the other hand, not only do canned goods have a relatively long shelf life, but they can be purchased in bulk and stored in large regional warehouses for shipment to stores as needed, in small lots, and mixed with other grocery commodities. Moreover, a properly loaded railcar often creates less damage than shipping by truck. Finally, shipping by train is often more convenient: Although they may have only 25 minutes to unload a truck (a job that must be done by appointment), customers can take up to three days to unload a boxcar placed at a loading dock.

Taking all these factors into account, Meyer's rule of thumb is that to be competitive, the rail price must be 15 percent lower than the equivalent truck price. This price differential covers both the cost of the longer time the product spends enroute and increased unloading costs. In 1988, the average rail rate for the 327 carloads of canned goods handled by East Line Railway from various origins in Wisconsin to the NY/NJ metropolitan area was $2.78 per hundredweight (cwt): For example, 126,000 lbs. of canned goods divided by 100 equals 1260 cwts times $2.78 per cwt equals $3,503 revenue per carload. East Line Railway's variable cost per carload ranged from $1,350 to $1,450 per carload.

Meyers used this data—plus the information contained in Figure 1 and

Table 1—to make his pricing decision. Figure 1 shows the pricing regions for the trucking industry. All customers within a given zone pay the same price per mile of truck transportation. Table 1 provides the cents-per-mile figures for a truckload of goods shipped from one price zone to another. For example, looking across the first row of Table 1, you will see that shipments within the Deep South would be charged $1.35 per mile, while shipments from the Deep South to the East Central region would be charged $.95 per mile.

For ease of comparison, Meyers usually made all the calculations "per carload." The first thing he had to decide was whether or not to revise last year's rates.

### Questions

1. What factors influence East Line Railway's share of canned goods shipments from Wisconsin to the New York/New Jersey metropolitan area?

2. What were East Line Railway's total revenues and profits from the 327 boxcars of canned goods hauled from Wisconsin to NY/NJ in 1988?

3. How does the price of shipping by truck (see Figure 1 and Table 1) compare to the current boxcar rate?

4. Taking into account costs, competition, and demand factors, what price should Meyers charge for shipments of Wisconsin canned goods to the NY/NJ area?

5. What other marketing suggestions would you make to Meyers concerning the Wisconsin Canned Goods project?

TABLE 1 Representative Over-the-Road Truck Price Levels (cents per mile)

| From: \ To: | Deep South | East Central | Florida | Mid Atl | Mid South | Mid West | New England | Rocky Mtn | South West | Texas | West Coast |
|---|---|---|---|---|---|---|---|---|---|---|---|
| Deep South | 135 | 95 | 155 | 110 | 115 | 95 | 110 | 110 | 115 | 110 | 93 |
| E. Central | 110 | 150 | 125 | 130 | 120 | 115 | 135 | 118 | 118 | 115 | 95 |
| Florida | 85 | 80 | 100 | 95 | 85 | 85 | 95 | 100 | 95 | 95 | 92 |
| Mid Atlantic | 82 | 80 | 115 | 140 | 82 | 80 | 150 | 100 | 98 | 95 | 94 |
| Mid South | 115 | 105 | 130 | 125 | 140 | 105 | 128 | 114 | 120 | 125 | 95 |
| Mid West | 112 | 110 | 130 | 132 | 118 | 130 | 135 | 125 | 125 | 122 | 100 |
| New England | 82 | 80 | 115 | 130 | 80 | 80 | 150 | 97 | 95 | 95 | 94 |
| Rocky Mtn. | 88 | 80 | 108 | 97 | 90 | 83 | 97 | 100 | 115 | 95 | 95 |
| South West | 94 | 85 | 105 | 95 | 90 | 84 | 96 | 105 | 125 | 95 | 94 |
| Texas | 90 | 85 | 115 | 95 | 95 | 82 | 95 | 100 | 120 | 105 | 92 |
| West Coast | 95 | 90 | 105 | 98 | 95 | 90 | 99 | 120 | 125 | 92 | 110 |

FIGURE 1 Major Truckload Carrier Pricing Regions

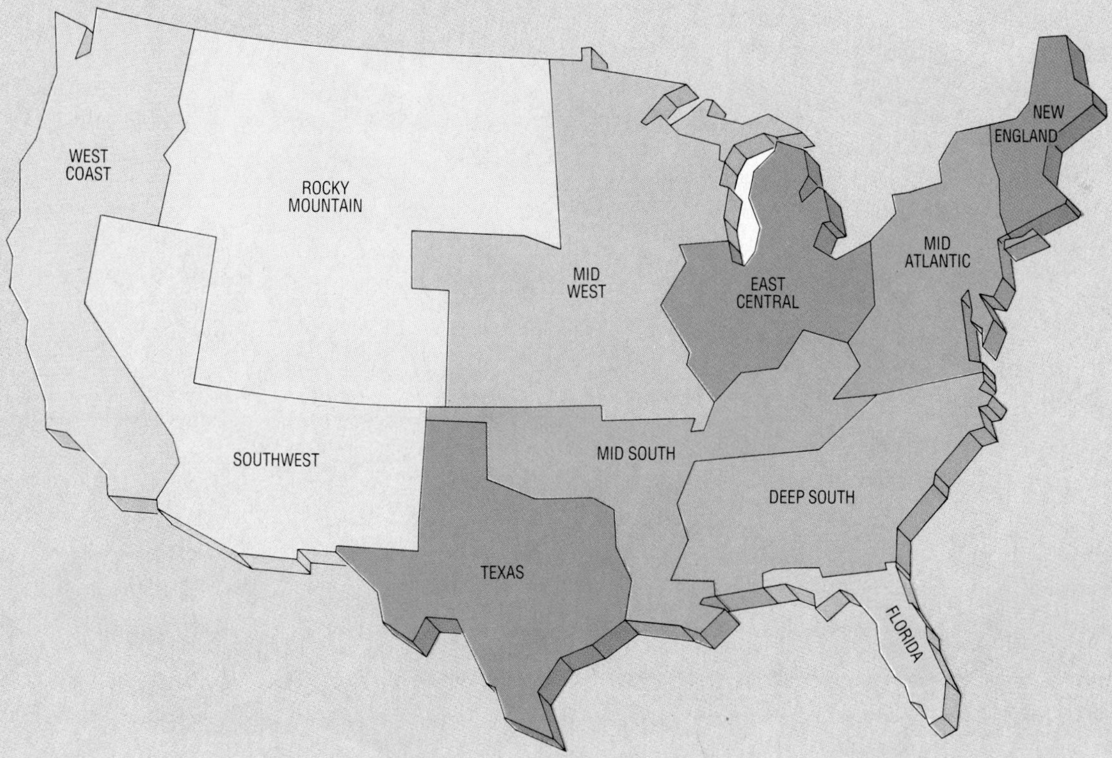

# 13

# Placing Products: Distribution Channels and Physical Distribution

## CHAPTER OBJECTIVES

**After reading this chapter, you should be able to**

1. **Explain why companies use distribution channels and the functions these channels perform**
2. **Discuss how channel members interact and how they organize to do the work of the channel**
3. **Identify the major distribution channel alternatives open to a company**
4. **Explain how companies select, motivate, and evaluate channel members**
5. **Discuss the issues firms face when setting up physical distribution systems**

Winn-Dixie Stores, the nation's fifth-largest supermarket with over $9 billion in yearly sales, is part of a complex food-industry distribution channel consisting of consumer package-goods companies, wholesale food distributors, and grocery retailers. Usually, the members of this channel work closely together toward a common goal of profitably marketing food products to consumers. But too often, distribution channels don't operate as smoothly as they should—conflicts and power struggles sometimes flare up. This fact is highlighted by a recent incident that pitted Winn-Dixie against Procter & Gamble, Pillsbury, and several of its other major suppliers.

In late 1988, Winn-Dixie stunned food producers when it announced that it would no longer accept promotional allowances on a market-by-market basis. Instead, it would expect its suppliers to adopt a uniform-pricing policy in which promotional allowances offered to any *one* of Winn-Dixie's 1260 stores would be made to *all* of its stores. In the future, the company would place chain-wide orders at the lowest available prices, even if those prices were offered in only one of its markets.

To Winn-Dixie, this new policy made good business sense. The supermarket chain claimed that most of its competitors were already attaining the lowest prices for all their stores through "diverting"—a legally questionable practice through which a retailer buys larger-than-needed quantities of a product in areas where it's on sale and then ships the excess to its stores in other areas. Many retailers routinely scour the country looking for the best prices on various grocery products. Some 5 percent of the goods on grocery store shelves get there via diverting. Winn-Dixie argued that a uniform-pricing policy would help make this time-consuming and inefficient diverting process unnecessary.

Winn-Dixie's new policy caused a furor among major package-goods marketers, most of whom are strongly wedded to regional marketing strategies (see Marketing Highlight 8–1). If they complied with Winn-Dixie's demands for uniform price allowances, they would be compelled under the law to provide the same price breaks to all of their retail customers across Winn-Dixie's 13-state trading area. This action would greatly reduce their ability to use regional marketing strategies in which prices and promotions are tailored to local competitors and conditions.

For these reasons, several of Winn-Dixie's largest and most powerful suppliers refused to go along with its demands, and the battle was joined. Procter & Gamble, Pillsbury, Campbell, Quaker, and General Foods announced that they would continue their non-standard, regional-pricing policies. Despite huge potential losses of sales and customer goodwill, Winn-Dixie began to drop selected products of these major suppliers from its shelves. In response, some of the food producers threatened retaliatory coupon blitzes in Winn-Dixie's market to boost demand for the discontinued products and to lure Winn-Dixie consumers to competing stores.

The standoff lasted for many months. But in the face of heavy pressure from some of the nation's most powerful marketers, Winn-Dixie couldn't make its new uniform-pricing policy stick. After obtaining only modest concessions from suppliers, it gracefully backed away from forcing the issue and began restoring discontinued products to its shelves.

The Winn-Dixie incident demonstrates the dynamic forces of cooperation, power, and conflict found in distribution channels. Clearly, for the good of all parties, Winn-Dixie and its suppliers must work as partners to market products to consumers. For decades, the giant food marketers have served as "senior partners" in this relationship, largely controlling marketing practices in their distribution channels. But, as more and more products compete for limited supermarket shelf space, and as scanners give retailers ever-greater leverage through market information, the balance of channel power is shifting toward grocery retailers. Increasingly, supermarket chains are taking control of the marketing process. Thus, although Winn-Dixie may not win a clear victory in this battle, it made its point. Gone are the days when the giant package-goods marketers can simply dictate channel terms and policies.[1]

Marketing channel decisions are among the most important facing management. A company's channel decisions directly affect every other marketing decision. The company's pricing depends on whether it uses mass merchandisers or high-quality specialty stores. The firm's salesforce and advertising decisions depend on how much persuasion, training, and motivation the dealers need. Whether a company develops or acquires certain new products may depend on how well those products fit the abilities of its channel members.

However, companies often pay too little attention to their distribution channels, sometimes with damaging results. For example, automobile manufacturers have lost large shares of their parts and service business to companies like NAPA, Midas, Goodyear, and others because they have resisted making needed changes in their dealer franchise networks. On the other hand, many companies have used imaginative distribution systems to gain a competitive advantage. Federal Express' creative and imposing distribution system made it the leader in the small-package delivery industry. And American Hospital Supply gained a strong advantage over its competition by linking its distribution system directly to hospitals through a sophisticated data-processing system.[2]

Distribution channel decisions often involve long-term commitments to other firms. A furniture manufacturer can easily change its advertising, prices, or promotion programs. It can scrap old product designs and introduce new ones as market tastes demand. But when it sets up a distribution channel through contracts with independent dealers, it cannot readily replace this channel with company-owned branches if conditions change. Therefore, management must design its channels carefully, with an eye on tomorrow's likely selling environment as well as today's.

In this chapter, we will examine four major distribution channel questions: *What is the nature of distribution channels? How do channel firms interact and organize to do the work of the channel? What problems do companies face in designing and managing their channels? What role does physical distribution play in attracting and satisfying customers?* In the next chapter, we will look at distribution channel issues from the viewpoint of retailers and wholesalers.

# THE NATURE OF DISTRIBUTION CHANNELS

Most producers use middlemen to bring their products to market. They try to forge a distribution channel. A **distribution channel** is the set of firms and individuals that take title, or assist in transferring title, to a good or service as it moves from the producer to the consumer or industrial user.

**distribution channel** The set of firms and individuals that take title, or assist in transferring title, to a good or service as it moves from the producer to the consumer or industrial user.

## Why Are Middlemen Used?

Why do producers give some of the selling job to middlemen? This means giving up some control over how and to whom products are sold. The use of middlemen largely boils down to their greater efficiency in making goods available to target markets. Through their contacts, experience, specialization, and scales of operation, middlemen usually offer a firm more than it can achieve on its own.

Figure 13–1 shows one way that using middlemen can provide economies. Part A shows three producers each using direct marketing to reach three customers. This system requires nine different contacts. Part B shows the three producers working through one distributor, who contacts the three customers. This system requires only six contacts. In this way, middlemen reduce the amount of work that must be done by both producers and consumers.

From the economic system's point of view, the role of middlemen is to transform the assortment of products made by producers into the assortments wanted by consumers. Producers make narrow assortments of products in large quantities. But consumers want broad assortments of products in small quantities. In the distribution channels, middlemen buy the large quantities of many producers and break them down into the smaller quantities and broader assortments wanted by consumers. Thus, middlemen play an important role in matching supply and demand.

FIGURE 13–1  How a Distributor Reduces the Number of Channel Transactions

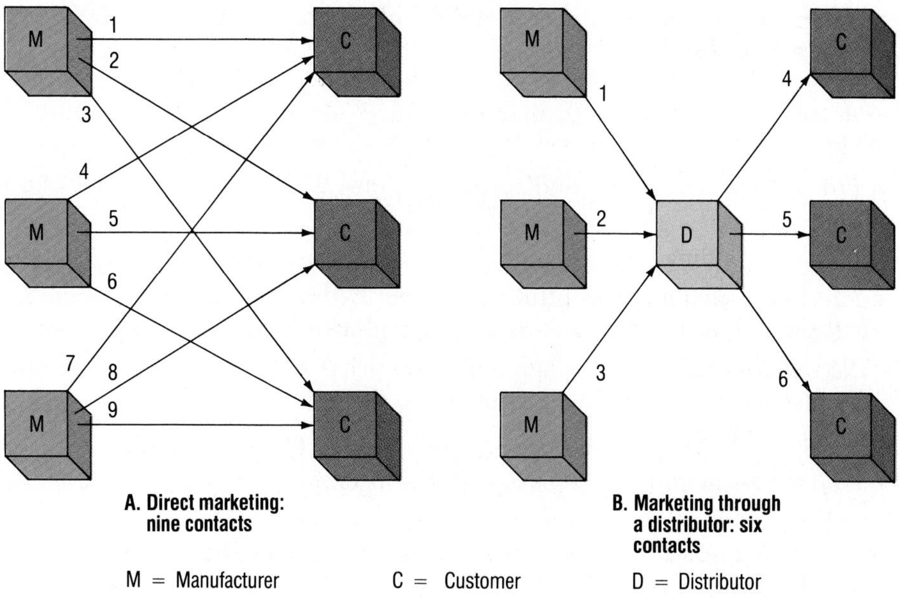

A. Direct marketing: nine contacts

B. Marketing through a distributor: six contacts

M = Manufacturer      C = Customer      D = Distributor

*From the Coca-Cola Company, to the bottler, to the retailer, to the consumer—channel members must all work together to make Coke successful.*

## Distribution Channel Functions

A distribution channel moves goods from producers to consumers. It overcomes the major time, place, and possession gaps that separate goods and services from those who would use them. Members of the marketing channel perform many key functions:

- □ *Research*—gathering information needed for planning and aiding exchange
- □ *Promotion*—developing and spreading persuasive communications about an offer
- □ *Contact*—finding and communicating with prospective buyers
- □ *Matching*—shaping and fitting the offer to the buyer's needs, including such activities as manufacturing, grading, assembling, and packaging
- □ *Negotiation*—reaching an agreement on price and other terms of an offer so that ownership or possession can be transferred
- □ *Physical distribution*—transporting and storing goods
- □ *Financing*—acquiring and using funds to cover the costs of the channel work
- □ *Risk taking*—assuming the risks of carrying out the channel work

The first five functions help to complete transactions; the last three help fulfill the completed transactions.

The question is not *whether* these functions need to be performed—they must be—but rather *who* is to perform them. All the functions have three things in common—they use up scarce resources, they can often be performed better through specialization, and they can be shifted among channel members. To the extent that the manufacturer performs them, its costs go up and its prices have to be higher. At the same time, when some functions are shifted to middlemen, the producer's costs and prices are lower, but the middlemen must add a charge to cover their work. In dividing up the work of the channel, the various functions should be assigned to the channel members who can perform them most efficiently and effectively to provide satisfactory assortments of goods to target consumers.

**channel level** A layer of middlemen who perform some work in bringing the product and its ownership closer to the final buyer.

**direct-marketing channel** A marketing channel that has no intermediary levels.

## Number of Channel Levels

Distribution channels can be described by the number of channel levels. Each layer of middlemen that performs some work in bringing the product and its ownership closer to the final buyer is a **channel level.** Because the producer and the final consumer both perform some work, they are part of every channel. We will use the *number of intermediary levels* to indicate the *length* of a channel. Figure 13–2A shows several consumer distribution channels of different lengths.

Channel 1, called a **direct-marketing channel,** has no intermediary levels. It consists of a manufacturer selling directly to consumers. For example, Avon and World Book Encyclopedia sell their products door-to-door; Franklin Mint sells collectables through mail order; Singer sells its sewing machines through

FIGURE 13–2   Consumer and Industrial Marketing Channels

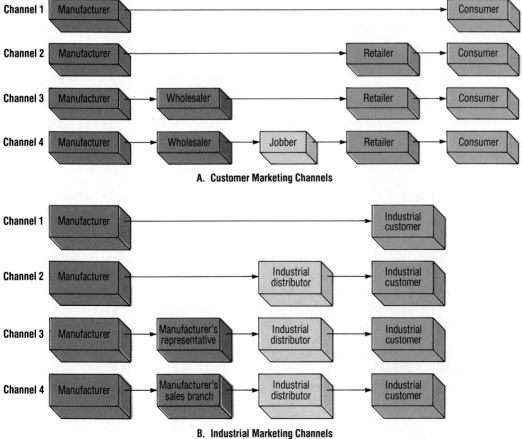

A.  Customer Marketing Channels

B.  Industrial Marketing Channels

its own stores. Channel 2 contains one middleman level. In consumer markets, this level is typically a retailer. For example, large retailers such as Sears and K mart sell televisions, cameras, tires, furniture, major appliances, and many other products that they buy directly from manufacturers. Channel 3 contains two middleman levels. In consumer markets, these levels are typically a wholesaler and a retailer. This channel is often used by small manufacturers of food, drug, hardware, and other products. Channel 4 contains three middleman levels. In the meatpacking industry, for example, jobbers usually come between wholesalers and retailers. The jobber buys from wholesalers and sells to smaller retailers who are not generally served by larger wholesalers. Distribution channels with more levels are sometimes found, but less often. From the producer's point of view, a greater number of levels means less control. And, of course, the more levels, the greater the channel's complexity.

Figure 13–2B shows some common industrial distribution channels. The industrial-goods producer can use its own salesforce to sell directly to industrial customers. It can also sell to industrial distributors who in turn sell to industrial customers. It can sell through manufacturer's representatives or its own sales branches to industrial customers, or use them to sell through industrial distributors. Thus zero-, one-, and two-level distribution channels are common in industrial goods markets.

All the institutions in the channel are connected by several types of *flows*. These include the *physical flow* of products, the *flow of ownership*, *payment flow*, *information flow*, and *promotion flow*. These flows can make even channels with only one or a few levels very complex.

# CHANNEL BEHAVIOR AND ORGANIZATION

Distribution channels are more than simple collections of firms tied together by various flows. They are complex behavioral systems in which people and companies interact to accomplish individual, company, and channel goals. Some channel systems consist of only informal interactions among loosely organized firms; others consist of formal interactions guided by strong organizational structures. And channel systems do not stand still—new types of middlemen surface and whole new channel systems evolve. Here we will look at channel behavior and at how members organize to do the work of the channel.

## Channel Behavior

A distribution channel is made up of dissimilar firms that have banded together for their common good. Each channel member is dependent on the others. A Ford dealer depends on the Ford Motor Company to design cars that meet consumer needs. In turn, Ford depends on the dealer to attract consumers, persuade them to buy Ford cars, and service cars after the sale. The Ford dealer also depends on other dealers to provide good sales and service that will uphold the reputation of Ford and its dealer body. In fact, the success of individual Ford dealers will depend on how well the entire Ford distribution channel competes with the channels of other auto manufacturers.

Each channel member plays a role in the channel and specializes in performing one or more functions. For example, IBM's role is to produce personal computers that consumers will like and to create demand through national advertising. Computerland's role is to display these computers in convenient locations, answer buyers' questions, close sales, and provide service. The channel will be most effective when each member is assigned the tasks it can do best.

Ideally, because the success of individual channel members depends on overall channel success, all channel firms should work together smoothly. They should understand and accept their roles, coordinate their goals and activities, and cooperate to attain overall channel goals. By cooperating, they can more effectively sense, serve, and satisfy the target market.

But individual channel members rarely take such a broad view. They are usually more concerned with their own short-run goals and their dealings with those firms closest to them in the channel. Cooperating to achieve overall channel goals sometimes means giving up individual company goals. Although channel members are dependent on one another, they often act alone in their own short-run best interests. They often disagree on the roles each should play—on who should do what and for what rewards. Such disagreements over goals and roles generate **channel conflict.**

*Horizontal conflict* is conflict between firms at the same level of the channel. Some Ford dealers in Chicago complain about other dealers in the city stealing sales from them by being too aggressive in their pricing and advertising or by selling outside their assigned territories. Some Pizza Inn franchisees complain about other Pizza Inn franchisees cheating on ingredients, giving poor service, and hurting the overall Pizza Inn image.

*Vertical conflict* is even more common and refers to conflicts between different levels of the same channel. For example, General Motors came into conflict with its dealers some years ago by trying to enforce policies on service, pricing, and advertising. And Coca-Cola came into conflict with some of its bottlers who agreed to bottle Dr Pepper. A large chain saw company caused conflict when it decided to bypass its wholesale distributors and sell directly to large retailers such as J. C. Penney and K mart, which then competed directly with its smaller retailers.

Some conflict in the channel takes the form of healthy competition. This competition can be good for the channel—without it, the channel could become passive and noninnovative. But sometimes, conflict can damage the channel. For the channel as a whole to perform well, each channel member's role must be specified and channel conflict must be managed. Cooperation, assigning roles, and conflict management in the channel are attained through strong channel leadership. The channel will perform better if it contains a firm, agency, or mechanism that has the power to assign roles and manage conflict.

In a large company, the formal organization structure assigns roles and provides needed leadership. But in a distribution channel made up of independent firms, leadership and power are not formally set. Traditionally, distribution channels have lacked the leadership needed to assign roles and manage conflict. In recent years, however, new types of channel organizations have appeared that provide stronger leadership and improved performance. We will now look at these organizations.[3]

**channel conflict** Disagreement among marketing channel members on goals and roles—on who should do what and for what rewards.

## Channel Organization

Historically, distribution channels have been loose collections of independent companies, each showing little concern for overall channel performance. These *conventional distribution channels* have lacked strong leadership and have been troubled by damaging conflict and poor performance.

### Growth of Vertical Marketing Systems

One of the biggest recent channel developments has been the *vertical marketing systems* that have emerged to challenge conventional marketing channels. Figure 13–3 contrasts the two types of channel arrangements.

**conventional distribution channel** A channel consisting of one or more independent producers, wholesalers, and retailers, each a separate business seeking to maximize its own profits even at the expense of profits for the system as a whole.

**vertical marketing system (VMS)** A distribution channel structure in which producers, wholesalers, and retailers act as a unified system.

**corporate VMS** A vertical marketing system that combines successive stages of production and distribution under single ownership.

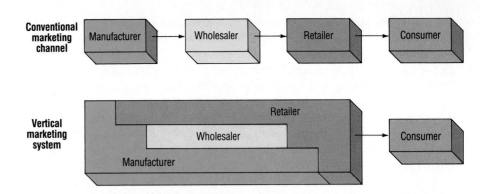

FIGURE 13-3   Comparison of Conventional Distribution Channel with Vertical Marketing System

A **conventional distribution channel** consists of one or more independent producers, wholesalers, and retailers. Each is a separate business seeking to maximize its own profits, even at the expense of profits for the system as a whole. No channel member has much control over the other members, and there are no formal means for assigning roles and resolving channel conflict.

By contrast, a **vertical marketing system (VMS)** consists of producers, wholesalers, and retailers acting as a unified system. Either one channel member owns the others, has contracts with them, or wields so much power that they all cooperate.[4] The vertical marketing system can be dominated by the producer, wholesaler, or retailer. VMSs came into being to control channel behavior and manage channel conflict. They achieve economies through size, bargaining power, and elimination of duplicated services. VMSs have become dominant in consumer marketing, serving as much as 64 percent of the total market.

We will now look at the three major types of VMSs shown in Figure 13-4. Each type uses a different means for setting up leadership and power in the channel. In a *corporate VMS*, coordination and conflict management are attained through common ownership at different levels of the channel. In a *contractual VMS*, they are attained through contractual agreements among channel members. In an *administered VMS*, leadership is assumed by one or a few dominant channel members.

*Corporate VMS* ▪ A **corporate VMS** combines successive stages of production and distribution under single ownership. For example, Sears obtains over 50 percent of its goods from companies that it partly or wholly owns. Sherwin-Williams makes paint but also owns and operates two thousand retail outlets. Giant Food Stores operates an ice-making facility, a soft-drink bottling operation, an ice cream making plant, and a bakery that supplies Giant stores with everything from bagels to birthday cakes.[5] And Gallo, the world's largest wine maker, does much more than simply turn grapes into wine:

> The [Gallo] brothers own Fairbanks Trucking Company, one of the largest intrastate truckers in California. Its 200 semis and 500 trailers are constantly hauling wine out of Modesto and raw materials back in—including . . . lime from Gallo's quarry east of Sacramento. Alone among wine producers, Gallo makes bottles—two million a day—and its Midcal Aluminum Co. spews out screw tops as fast as the bottles are filled. Most of the country's 1,300 or so wineries concentrate on production to the neglect of marketing. Gallo, by contrast, participates in every aspect of selling short of whispering in the ear of each imbiber. The company owns its distributors in about a dozen markets and probably would buy many . . . more . . . if the laws in most states did not prohibit doing so.[6]

In such corporate systems, cooperation and conflict management are handled through regular organizational channels.

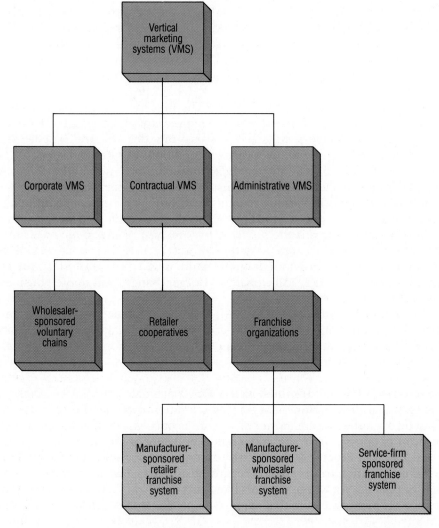

FIGURE 13–4   Conventional Distribution Channels and Vertical Marketing Systems

**contractual VMS** A vertical marketing system in which independent firms at different levels of production and distribution join together through contracts to obtain more economies or sales impact than they could achieve alone.

**wholesaler-sponsored voluntary chains** Contractual vertical marketing systems in which wholesalers organize voluntary chains of independent retailers to help them compete with large corporate chain organizations.

**retailer cooperatives** Contractual vertical marketing systems in which retailers organize a new, jointly owned business to carry on wholesaling and possibly production.

**franchise organization** A contractual vertical marketing system in which a channel member called a franchiser links several stages in the production-distribution process.

*Contractual VMS* ▪ **A contractual VMS** consists of independent firms at different levels of production and distribution who join together through contracts to obtain more economies or sales impact than they could achieve alone. Contractual VMSs have expanded rapidly in recent years. There are three types of contractual VMSs.

**Wholesaler-sponsored voluntary chains** are systems in which wholesalers organize voluntary chains of independent retailers to help them compete with large chain organizations. The wholesaler develops a program in which independent retailers standardize their selling practices and achieve buying economies that let the group compete effectively with chain organizations. Examples include the Independent Grocers Alliance (IGA), Western Auto, and Sentry Hardwares.

**Retailer cooperatives** are systems in which retailers organize a new, jointly owned business to carry on wholesaling and possibly production. Members buy most of their goods through the retailer co-op and plan their advertising jointly. Profits are passed back to members in proportion to their purchases. Nonmember retailers may also buy through the co-op but do not share in the profits. Examples include Certified Grocers, Associated Grocers, and True Value Hardware.

In **franchise organizations,** a channel member called a *franchiser* links several stages in the production-distribution process. Franchising has been the fastest-growing retailing form in recent years. Franchised businesses now account for about one-third of retail sales in the U.S. and may account for one-half by the year 2000.[7] Almost every kind of business has been franchised—from motels and fast-food restaurants to dentists and dating services, from wedding consultants and maid services to funeral homes and tub and tile refinishers. Although the basic idea is an old one, some forms of franchising are quite new.

There are three forms of franchises. The first form is the *manufacturer-sponsored retailer franchise system,* as found in the automobile industry. Ford, for example, licenses dealers to sell its cars—the dealers are independent businesspeople who agree to meet various conditions of sales and service. The second type of franchise is the *manufacturer-sponsored wholesaler franchise system,* as found in the soft-drink industry. Coca-Cola, for example, licenses bottlers (wholesalers) in various markets who buy its syrup concentrate and then carbonate, bottle, and sell the finished product to retailers in local markets. The third franchise form is the *service firm-sponsored retailer franchise system.* Here, a service firm licenses a system of retailers to bring its service to consumers. Examples are found in the auto rental business (Hertz, Avis), fast-food service business (McDonald's, Burger King), and motel business (Holiday Inn, Ramada Inn).

The fact that most consumers cannot tell the difference between contractual and corporate VMSs shows how successful contractual organizations have been in competing with corporate chains. The various contractual VMSs are discussed more fully in Chapter 14.

*Administered VMS* ▪ An **administered VMS** coordinates successive stages of production and distribution—not through common ownership or contractual ties but through the size and power of one of the parties. Manufacturers of a top brand can obtain strong trade cooperation and support from resellers. Thus, General Electric, Procter & Gamble, Kraft, and Campbell Soup can command unusual cooperation from resellers regarding displays, shelf space, promotions, and price policies. And large retailers like Sears and Toys 'R' Us can exert strong influence on manufacturers that supply the products they sell (see Marketing Highlight 13–1).

### Growth of Horizontal Marketing Systems

Another channel development is the **horizontal marketing system,** in which two or more companies at one level join together to follow a new marketing opportunity.[8] By working together, companies can combine their capital, production capabilities, or marketing resources to accomplish more than any company could accomplish working alone. Companies may work with each other on a temporary or permanent basis, or they may create a separate company.

Such horizontal marketing systems have increased dramatically in recent years, and the end is nowhere in sight. For example, the Lamar Savings Bank of Texas arranged to locate its savings offices and automated teller machines in Safeway stores. Lamar gained quicker market entry at a low cost, and Safeway was able to offer in-store banking convenience to its customers. Sears and McDonald's joined forces to market the McKids line of "Fun clothes for small fries." In this way, the companies share their marketing strengths—Sears gains the use of the well-known McDonald's logo and characters; McDonald's gains access to the huge Sears retailing system.[9]

### Growth of Multichannel Marketing Systems

In the past, many companies used a single channel to sell to a single market or market segment. Today, with the proliferation of customer segments and

## TOYS 'R' US ADMINISTERS ITS CHANNEL

Toys 'R' Us operates 360 toy supermarkets that pull in over $3 billion in annual sales and capture almost 25 percent of the huge U.S. toy market. And the giant retailer is growing explosively—some experts predict that its market share will double during the next decade. Because of its size and massive market power, Toys 'R' Us exerts strong influence on toy manufacturers—on their product, pricing, and promotion strategies and on just about everything else they do.

Critics worry that Toys 'R' Us is *too* big and influential and that it takes unfair advantage of toy producers. The reactions of Toys 'R' Us buyers can make or break a new toy. For example, Hasbro invested some $20 million to develop Nemo—a home video game system to compete with the hugely successful Nintendo system—but then quickly cancelled the project when Toys 'R' Us executives reacted negatively. Toys 'R' Us also dictates toy prices—it often frustrates and angers toy manufacturers by selling toys at far below recommended retail prices, forcing producers to settle for lower margins and profits. And some analysts have accused Toys 'R' Us of placing an unfair burden on smaller toy makers by requiring all of its suppliers to pay a fee if they want their toys to be included in Toys 'R' Us newspaper advertisements.

But other industry experts think that Toys 'R' Us helps the toy industry more than hurts it. For example, whereas other retailers feature toys only at Christmas, Toys 'R' Us has created a year-round market for toys. Moreover, its low prices mean greater overall industry sales and force producers to operate more efficiently. And Toys 'R' Us shares its extensive market data with toy producers, giving them immediate feedback on which products and marketing programs are working and which are not.

Clearly, Toys 'R' Us and the toy manufacturers need each other—the toy makers need Toys 'R' Us to market their products aggressively, and the giant retailer needs a corps of healthy producers to provide a constant stream of popular new products to fill its shelves. Through the years, both sides have recognized this interdependence. For example, in the mid-1970s, when Toys 'R' Us was threatened by bankruptcy because of the financial problems of its parent company, the Toy Manufacturers Association worked directly with banks to save the troubled retailer. The banks granted credit to Toys 'R' Us largely because several major toy manufacturers were willing to grant such credit on their own. In this action, the Toy Manufacturers Association clearly recognized that the

entire toy industry benefited by keeping Toys 'R' Us healthy.

Similarly, Toys 'R' Us has recognized its stake in seeing that toy manufacturers succeed. In recent years, as flat toy sales have plunged many large manufacturers into deep financial trouble, Toys 'R' Us has provided a strong helping hand. For example, Toys 'R' Us often helps toy manufacturers through cash shortages and other financial difficulties by granting credit and prepaying bills. In addition, the retailer's savvy buyers preview new products for toy makers, making early and valuable suggestions on possible design and marketing improvements. Such advice helped Galoob Toys convert its Army Gear line—toys that change into different weapons—from a potential flop into a top-20 seller. And on advice from Toys 'R' Us, Ohio Arts altered the advertising strategy for its Zaks plastic building toys, increasing sales by 30 percent. The president of Tyco Toys concludes, "Toys 'R' Us gets a lot of flak for being large and taking advantage of manufacturers, but I would like to have more customers who help us as much as they do."

*Sources:* Amy Dunkin, "How Toys 'R' Us Controls the Game Board," *Business Week,* December 19, 1988, pp. 58–60; and Louis W. Stern and Adel I. El-Ansary, *Marketing Channels* (Englewood Cliffs, NJ: Prentice Hall, 1988), pp. 14–15.

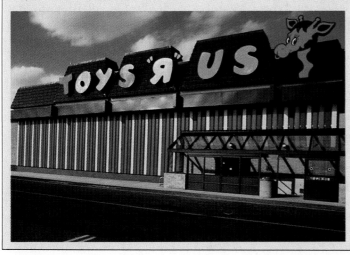

*Administered channels: large retailers like Toys 'R' Us can exert strong influence on other members of the marketing channel.*

**multimarketing** Multichannel distribution, as when a single firm sets up two or more marketing channels to reach one or more customer segments.

Just where did we get the idea kids' clothes could be more fun?

Horizontal marketing systems: Sears and McDonald's team up to sell McKids, "Fun clothes for small fries."

channel possibilities, more and more companies have adopted multichannel distribution. Such **multimarketing** occurs when a single firm sets up two or more marketing channels to reach one or more customer segments.[10] For example, General Electric sells large home appliances both through independent retailers (department stores, discount houses, catalog houses) and directly to large housing-tract builders, thus competing to some extent with its own retailers. McDonald's sells through a network of independent franchisees but owns about half of its outlets. Thus, the wholly owned restaurants compete to some extent with those owned by McDonald's franchisees.

The multimarketer gains sales with each new channel but also risks offending existing channels. Existing channels can cry "unfair competition" and threaten to drop the multimarketer unless it limits the competition or repays them in some way, perhaps by offering them exclusive models or special allowances.

In some cases, the multimarketer's channels are all under its own ownership and control. For example, J. C. Penney operates department stores, mass-merchandising stores, and specialty stores, each offering different product assortments to different market segments. Here, there is no conflict with outside channels, but the marketer might face internal conflict over how much financial support each channel deserves.

## CHANNEL DESIGN DECISIONS

We will now look at several channel-decision problems facing manufacturers. In designing marketing channels, manufacturers have to struggle between what is ideal and what is practical. A new firm usually starts by selling in a limited market area. Because it has limited capital, it typically uses only a few existing middlemen in each market—a few manufacturers' sales agents, a few wholesalers, some existing retailers, a few trucking companies, and a few warehouses.

Deciding on the best channels might not be a problem: The problem might be to convince one or a few good middlemen to handle the line.

If the new firm is successful, it might branch out to new markets. Again, the manufacturer will tend to work through the existing middlemen, although this strategy might mean using different *types* of marketing channels in different areas. In smaller markets, the firm might sell directly to retailers; in larger markets, it might sell through distributors. In one part of the country, it might grant exclusive franchises because the merchants normally work this way; in another, it might sell through all outlets willing to handle the merchandise. The manufacturer's channel system thus evolves to meet local opportunities and conditions.

Designing a channel system calls for analyzing consumer-service needs, setting the channel objectives and constraints, identifying the major channel alternatives, and evaluating them.

## Analyzing Consumer-Service Needs

Designing the distribution channel starts with finding out what services consumers in various target segments want from the channel. The necessary level of channel services depends on the answers to several questions.[11] Do consumers want to buy from nearby locations or will they buy from more distant centralized locations by traveling, phoning, or buying through the mail? The more decentralized the channel, the greater the service it provides. Do consumers want immediate delivery or are they willing to wait? Faster delivery means greater service from the channel. Do consumers value breadth of assortment or do they prefer specialization? The greater the assortment provided by the channel, the higher its service level. And finally, do consumers want many add-on services (delivery, credit, repairs, installation) or will they obtain these elsewhere? More add-on services mean a higher level of channel service.

Thus, to design an effective channel, the designer must know the service levels desired by consumers. But providing all the desired services may not be possible or practical. The company and its channel members may not have the resources or skills needed to provide all the desired services. And providing higher levels of service means higher costs for the channel and higher prices for consumers. The company must balance consumer service needs against not only the feasibility and costs of meeting these needs but also customer price preferences. The success of discount retailing shows that consumers are often willing to accept lower service levels if a lower service level means lower prices.

## Setting the Channel Objectives and Constraints

Channel objectives should be stated in terms of the desired service level of target consumers. Usually, a company can identify several segments wanting different levels of channel service. The company should decide which segments to serve and the best channels to use in each case. In each segment, the company wants to minimize the total channel cost of delivering the desired service level.

The company's channel objectives are also influenced by the nature of its products, company policies, middlemen, competitors, and environment. *Product characteristics* greatly affect channel design. For example, perishable products require more direct marketing to avoid delays and too much handling. Bulky products, such as building materials or soft drinks, require channels that minimize shipping distance and amount of handling.

*Company characteristics* also play an important role. For example, a company's size and financial situation determine which marketing functions it can handle itself and which it gives to middlemen. And a company marketing

*Product characteristics affect channel decisions: fresh flowers must be delivered quickly with a minimum of handling.*

strategy based on speedy customer delivery affects the functions that the company wants its middlemen to perform, the number of its outlets, and the choice of its transportation methods.

*Middlemen characteristics* also influence channel design. In general, middlemen differ in their abilities to handle promotion, customer contact, storage, and credit. The company may have trouble finding middlemen who are willing and able to perform the needed tasks.

When designing its channels, a company will want to consider *competitors' channels*. It may want to compete in or near the same outlets that carry competitors' products. Thus, food companies want their brands to be displayed next to competing brands; Burger King wants to locate near McDonald's. In other industries, producers may avoid the channels used by competitors. Avon decided not to compete with other cosmetics makers for scarce positions in retail stores and instead set up a profitable door-to-door selling operation.

Finally, *environmental factors* such as economic conditions and legal constraints affect channel-design decisions. For example, in a depressed economy, producers want to distribute their goods in the most economical way, using shorter channels and dropping unneeded services that add to the final price of the goods. Legal regulations prevent channel arrangements that "may tend to substantially lessen competition or tend to create a monopoly."

## Identifying the Major Alternatives

When the company has defined its channel objectives, it should next identify its major channel alternatives in terms of the *types* of middlemen, the *number* of middlemen, and the *responsibilities* of each channel member.

### Types of Middlemen

A firm should identify the types of middlemen available to carry on its channel work. For example, suppose a manufacturer of test equipment has developed an audio device that detects poor mechanical connections in any machine with moving parts. Company executives feel that this product would have a market in all industries where electric, combustion, or steam engines are made or used. This market would include such industries as aviation, automobile, railroad, food canning, construction, and oil. The company's current salesforce is small, and the problem is how best to reach these different industries. The following channel alternatives might emerge from management discussion:

□ *Company salesforce.* Expand the company's direct salesforce. Assign salespeople to territories and have them contact all prospects in the area. Or develop separate company salesforces for different industries.

□ *Manufacturer's agency.* Hire manufacturer's agencies—independent firms whose salesforces handle related products from many companies—in different regions or industries to sell the new test equipment.

□ *Industrial distributors.* Find distributors in the different regions or industries who will buy and carry the new line. Give them exclusive distribution, good margins, product training, and promotional support.

**intensive distribution** Stocking a product in as many outlets as possible.

**exclusive distribution** Giving a limited number of dealers the exclusive right to distribute a company's products in their territories.

Sometimes, a company has to develop a channel other than the one it prefers because of the difficulty or cost of using the preferred channel. Still, the decision sometimes turns out extremely well. For example, the U.S. Time Company first tried to sell its inexpensive Timex watches through regular jewelry stores. But most jewelry stores refused to carry them. The company then managed to get its watches into mass-merchandise outlets. This turned out to be a wise decision because of the rapid growth of mass merchandising.

**Number of Middlemen**

Companies also have to decide on the number of middlemen to use at each level. Three strategies are available.

*Intensive Distribution* ▪ Producers of convenience goods and common raw materials typically seek **intensive distribution**—stocking their product in as many outlets as possible. These goods must be available where and when consumers want them. For example, toothpaste, candy, and other similar items are sold in millions of outlets to provide maximum brand exposure and consumer convenience.

*Exclusive Distribution* ▪ By contrast, some producers purposely limit the number of middlemen handling their products. The extreme form of this practice is **exclusive distribution,** whereby a limited number of dealers are given the exclusive right to distribute the company's products in their territories. Exclusive distribution is often found in the distribution of new automobiles and prestige women's clothing. By granting exclusive distribution, the manufacturer hopes for stronger distributor selling support and more control over middlemen's prices, promotion, credit, and services. Exclusive distribution often enhances the product's image and allows higher markups.

*Convenience goods, such as cleaning products, are sold through every available outlet. Prestige goods, such as furs, are sold exclusively through a limited number of stores.*

***Selective Distribution*** ▪ Between intensive and exclusive distribution lies **selective distribution**—the use of more than one but less than all the middlemen who are willing to carry a company's products. The company does not have to spread its efforts over many outlets, including many marginal ones. It can develop a good working relationship with selected middlemen and expect a better-than-average selling effort. Selective distribution lets the producer gain good market coverage with more control and less cost than intensive distribution. Most television, furniture, and small appliance brands are distributed selectively.

### Responsibilities of Channel Members

The producer and middlemen need to agree on the terms and responsibilities of each channel member. They should agree on price policies, conditions of sale, territorial rights, and specific services to be performed by each party. The producer should set up a list price and a fair set of discounts for middlemen. It must define each middleman's territory and be careful where it places new resellers. Mutual services and duties need to be carefully spelled out, especially in franchise and exclusive distribution channels. For example, McDonald's provides franchisees promotional support, a record-keeping system, training, and general management assistance. In turn, franchisees must meet company standards for physical facilities, cooperate with new promotion programs, provide requested information, and buy specified food products.

## *Evaluating the Major Channel Alternatives*

Suppose a producer has identified several possible channels and wants to select the one that will best satisfy the firm's long-run objectives. Each alternative should be evaluated against *economic, control,* and *adaptive* criteria.

Using *economic criteria*, a company compares the likely profitability of different channel alternatives. It estimates the sales that each channel would produce and the costs of selling different volumes through each channel. The company must also consider *control issues*. Using middlemen usually means giving them some control over the marketing of the product, and some middlemen take more control than others. Other things being equal, the company prefers to keep as much control as possible. Finally, the company must apply *adaptive criteria*. Channels often involve long-term commitments to other firms, making it hard to adapt the channel to the changing marketing environment. The company wants to keep the channel as flexible as possible. Thus, to be considered, a channel involving a long commitment should be greatly superior on economic or control grounds.

# CHANNEL MANAGEMENT DECISIONS

Once a company has reviewed its channel alternatives and decided on the best channel design, it must implement and manage the chosen channel. Channel management calls for selecting and motivating individual middlemen and evaluating their performance over time.

## *Selecting Channel Members*

Producers vary in their ability to attract qualified middlemen. Some producers have no trouble signing up middlemen. For example, IBM has no trouble attracting retailers to sell its personal computers. In fact, it has to turn down many would-be resellers. In some cases, the promise of exclusive or selective distribution for a desirable product will draw enough applicants.

At the other extreme are producers who have to work hard to line up enough qualified middlemen. When Polaroid started, it could not get photography stores to carry its new cameras and had to go to mass-merchandising outlets. Similarly, small food producers often find it hard to get grocery stores to carry their products.

**distribution programming**
Building a planned, professionally managed vertical marketing system that meets the needs of both the manufacturer and the distributors.

## Motivating Channel Members

Once selected, middlemen must be continuously motivated to do their best. The company must sell not only *through* the middlemen but *to* them. Most producers see the problem as finding ways to gain middlemen's cooperation.[12] They use the carrot-and-stick approach. They offer such *positive* motivators as higher margins, special deals, premiums, cooperative advertising allowances, display allowances, and sales contests. At times, they will use *negative* motivators such as threatening to reduce margins, to slow down delivery, or to end the relationship altogether. A producer using this approach usually has not done a good job of studying the needs, problems, strengths, and weaknesses of its distributors.

More advanced companies try to forge long-term partnerships with their distributors through **distribution programming.** This involves building a planned, professionally managed, vertical marketing system that meets the needs of both the manufacturer *and* the distributors.[13] The manufacturer sets up a department in the marketing area called *distributor-relations planning*. Its job is to identify distributors' needs and build programs to help each distributor market the company's product. This department and the distributors jointly plan merchandising goals, inventory levels, merchandising strategies, sales training, and advertising and promotion plans. The aim is to convince distributors that they make their money by being part of an advanced vertical marketing system.

## Evaluating Channel Members

The producer must regularly check middlemen's performance against such standards as sales quotas, average inventory levels, customer delivery time, treatment of damaged and lost goods, cooperation in company promotion and training programs, and services to the customer. The company should recognize and reward middlemen who are performing well. Middlemen who are performing poorly should be helped or, as a last resort, replaced.

A company may periodically "requalify" its middlemen and prune out the weaker ones. For example, when IBM introduced its new Personal System/2 computers, it reevaluated its dealers and allowed only the best ones to carry the new models. Each IBM dealer had to turn in a business plan, send a sales and service employee to IBM training classes, and meet new sales quotas. Only about two-thirds of IBM's 2,200 dealers qualified to carry the PS/2 models.[14]

Manufacturers need to be sensitive to their dealers. Those who treat their dealers lightly risk not only losing their support but also causing some legal problems. Marketing Highlight 13–2 describes various rights and duties pertaining to manufacturers and their channel members.

## DISTRIBUTION DECISIONS AND PUBLIC POLICY

For the most part, companies are free under the law to develop whatever channel arrangements suit them. In fact, the laws affecting channels seek to ensure that the exclusionary tactics of some companies do not keep other companies from using a desired channel. Of course, this means that the company must itself avoid using such exclusionary tactics. Most channel law deals with the mutual rights and duties of channel members once they have formed a relationship.

### Exclusive Dealing

Many producers and wholesalers like to develop exclusive channels for their products. When a seller allows only certain outlets to carry its products, its strategy is called *exclusive distribution*. When the seller requires these dealers not to handle competitors' products its strategy is called *exclusive dealing*. Both parties benefit from exclusive arrangements. The seller obtains more loyal and dependable outlets. The dealers

obtain a steady source of supply and stronger seller support. But exclusive arrangements exclude other producers from selling to these dealers. This situation brings exclusive dealing contracts under the scope of the Clayton Act of 1914. They are legal as long as they do not substantially lessen competition or tend to create a monopoly and as long as both parties enter into the agreement voluntarily.

### Exclusive Territories

Exclusive dealing often includes exclusive territorial agreements. The producer may agree not to sell to other dealers in a given area, or the buyer may agree to sell only in its own territory. The first practice is normal under franchise systems as a way to increase dealer enthusiasm and commitment. And it is perfectly legal—a seller has no legal obligation to sell through more outlets than it wishes. The second practice, whereby the producer tries to keep a dealer from

selling outside its territory, has become a major legal issue.

### Tying Agreements

Producers of a strong brand sometimes sell it to dealers only if the dealers will take some or all of the rest of the line. This practice is called *full-line forcing*. Such tying agreements are not necessarily illegal, but they do violate the Clayton Act if they tend to lessen competition substantially. The practice may prevent consumers from freely choosing among competing suppliers of other brands.

### Dealers' Rights

Producers are free to select their dealers, but their right to terminate dealers is somewhat restricted. In general, sellers can drop dealers "for cause." But they cannot drop dealers, for example, if the dealers refuse to cooperate in a doubtful legal arrangement, such as exclusive dealing or tying agreements.

---

**physical distribution** The tasks involved in planning, implementing, and controlling the physical flow of materials and final goods from points of origin to points of use in order to meet the needs of customers at a profit.

# PHYSICAL DISTRIBUTION DECISIONS

We are now ready to look at *physical distribution*—how companies store, handle, and move goods so that they will be available to customers at the right time and place. Here, we will consider the *nature, objectives, systems,* and *organizational aspects* of physical distribution.

## Nature of Physical Distribution

The main elements of the physical distribution mix are shown in Figure 13–5. **Physical distribution** involves planning, implementing, and controlling the physical flow of materials and final goods from points of origin to points of use in order to meet the needs of customers at a profit. The major physical distribution cost is transportation, followed by inventory carrying, warehousing, and order processing/customer service.

Management has become concerned about the total cost of physical distribution, and experts believe that large savings can be gained in the physical

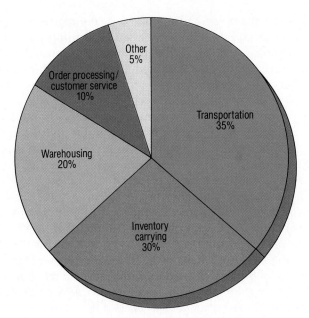

Other
5%

Order processing/
customer service
10%

Warehousing
20%

Transportation
35%

Inventory
carrying
30%

FIGURE 13–5   Costs of Physical Distribution Elements
as a Percentage of Total Physical
Distribution Costs

distribution area. Poor physical distribution decisions result in high costs. Even large companies sometimes make too little use of modern decision tools for coordinating inventory levels, transportation modes, and plant, warehouse, and store locations. For example, at least part of the blame for Sears's slow sales growth and sinking earnings over the past several years goes to its antiquated and costly distribution system. Outmoded multistory warehouses and nonauto- mated equipment have made Sears much less efficient than its competitors. Distribution costs amount to 8 percent of sales at Sears, compared with less than 3 percent at close competitors K mart and Wal-Mart.[15]

Moreover, physical distribution is more than a cost—it is a potent tool in demand creation. Companies can attract more customers by giving better service or lower prices through better physical distribution. On the other hand, companies lose customers when they fail to supply goods on time.

## The Physical Distribution Objective

Many companies state their objective as getting the right goods to the right places at the right time for the least cost. Unfortunately, no physical distribution system can *both* maximize customer service *and* minimize distribution costs. Maximum customer service implies large inventories, the best transportation, and many warehouses—all of which raise distribution costs. Minimum distribu- tion cost implies cheap transportation, low inventories, and few warehouses.

The company cannot simply let each physical distribution manager keep down his or her costs. Transportation, warehousing, and order-processing costs interact, often in an inverse way. For example, low inventory levels reduce inventory carrying costs. But they also increase costs from stockouts, back orders, paperwork, special production runs, and high-cost fast-freight ship- ments. Because physical distribution costs and activities involve strong trade- offs, decisions must be made on a total system basis.

The starting point for designing the system is to study what customers want and what competitors are offering. Customers want several things from suppli- ers: on-time delivery, sufficiently large inventories, ability to meet emergency needs, careful handling of merchandise, good after-sale service, and willingness to take back or replace defective goods. A company has to research the importance of these services to customers. For example, service-repair time is very important to buyers of copying equipment. So Xerox developed a service-delivery standard that can "put a disabled machine anywhere in the continental United States back into operation within three hours after receiving the service request." Xerox runs a service division with 12,000 service and parts personnel.

The company must also look at competitors' service standards in setting its own. It will normally want to offer at least the same level of service as competitors. But the objective is to maximize profits, not sales. The company has to look at the costs of providing higher levels of service. Some companies offer less service and charge a lower price. Other companies offer more service than competitors and charge higher prices to cover higher costs.

The company must ultimately set physical distribution objectives to guide its planning. For example, Coca-Cola wants "to put Coke within an arm's length of desire." Companies go further and define standards for each service factor. One appliance manufacturer has set the following service standards: to deliver at least 95 percent of the dealer's orders within seven days of order receipt, to fill the dealer's order with 99 percent accuracy, to answer dealer questions on order status within three hours, and to ensure that damage to merchandise in transit does not exceed 1 percent.

Given a set of objectives, the company is ready to design a physical distribution system that will minimize the cost of attaining these objectives. The major decision issues are: How should orders be handled (*order processing*)? Where should stocks be located (*warehousing*)? How much stock should be kept on hand (*inventory*)? And how should goods be shipped (*transportation*)?

## Order Processing

Physical distribution begins with a customer order. The order department prepares invoices and sends them to various departments. Items out of stock are back-ordered. Shipped items are accompanied by shipping and billing documents, with copies going to various departments.

The company and customers benefit when the steps in order processing are carried out quickly and accurately. Ideally, salespeople send in their orders daily, often using online computers. The order department quickly processes orders and the warehouse sends the goods out on time. Bills go out as soon as possible. The computer is often used to speed up the order-shipping-billing cycle. For example, General Electric operates a computer-based system that, upon receipt of a customer's order, checks the customer's credit standing and whether and where the items are in stock. The computer then issues an order to ship, bills the customer, updates the inventory records, sends a production order for new stock, and relays the message back to the salesperson that the customer's order is on its way—all in less than 15 seconds.

## Warehousing

Every company has to store its goods while they wait to be sold. A storage function is needed because production and consumption cycles rarely match. For example, Snapper, Toro, and other lawn mower makers must produce all year long and store up their product for the heavy spring and summer buying season. The storage function overcomes differences in needed quantities and timing.

A company must decide on the best number of stocking locations. The more stocking locations, the more quickly goods can be delivered to customers. However, warehousing costs go up. In making its decision about the number of its stocking locations, the company must balance the level of customer service against distribution costs.

Some company stock is kept at or near the plant and the rest located in warehouses around the country. The company might own private warehouses, rent space in public warehouses, or both. Companies have more control in owned warehouses, but they tie up their capital and are less flexible if desired locations change. Public warehouses, on the other hand, charge for rented space and provide additional services (at a cost) for inspecting goods, packaging them, shipping them, and invoicing them. In using public warehouses, companies also have a wide choice of locations and warehouse types.

Companies may use either *storage warehouses* or *distribution centers*. Storage warehouses store goods for moderate to long periods of time until they are needed. **Distribution centers** are designed to move goods rather than just store them. They are large and highly automated warehouses designed to receive goods from various plants and suppliers, take orders, fill them efficiently, and deliver goods to customers as quickly as possible. For example, Wal-Mart Stores, a regional discount chain, operates four distribution centers. One center, which serves the daily needs of 165 Wal-Mart stores, contains some 28 acres of space under a single roof. Laser scanners route up to 190,000 cases of goods per day along 11 miles of conveyor belts, and the center's 1,000 workers load or unload 310 trucks daily.[16]

Warehousing facilities and equipment technology have improved greatly in recent years. Older multistory warehouses with slow elevators and outdated materials-handling methods are facing competition from newer single-story *automated warehouses* with advanced materials-handling systems under the control of a central computer. In these warehouses, only a few employees are necessary. The computer reads orders and directs lift trucks, electric hoists, or robots to gather goods, move them to loading docks, and issue invoices. These warehouses have reduced worker injuries, labor costs, theft, and breakage and have improved inventory control.

**distribution center** A large and highly automated warehouse designed to receive goods from various plants and suppliers, take orders, fill them efficiently, and deliver goods to customers as quickly as possible.

## Inventory

Inventory levels also affect customer satisfaction. Marketers would like their companies to carry enough stock to fill all customer orders right away. However, it costs too much for a company to carry this much inventory.

*In this automated warehouse, a central computer controls an advanced material-handling system.*

Inventory costs increase at an increasing rate as the customer-service level approaches 100 percent. To justify larger inventories, management needs to know whether sales and profits will increase accordingly.

Inventory decisions involve knowing *when* to order and *how much* to order. In deciding when to order, the company balances the risks of running out of stock against the costs of carrying too much. In deciding how much to order, the company needs to balance order-processing costs against inventory-carrying costs. Larger average-order size means fewer orders and lower order-processing costs, but it also means larger inventory-carrying costs.

## *Transportation*

Marketers need to take an interest in their company's *transportation* decisions. The choice of transportation carriers affects the pricing of the products, delivery performance, and condition of the goods when they arrive—all of which will affect customer satisfaction.

In shipping goods to its warehouses, dealers, and customers, the company can choose among five transportation modes: rail, truck, water, pipeline, and air. The characteristics of each transportation mode are summarized in Table 13–1 and discussed in the following paragraphs.

### Rail

Although railroads lost share until the mid-1970s, they remain the nation's largest carrier, accounting for 37 percent of total cargo moved. Railroads are one of the most cost-effective modes for shipping large amounts of bulk products—coal, sand, minerals, farm and forest products—over long distances. In addition, railroads have recently begun to increase their customer services. They have designed new equipment to handle special categories of goods, provided flatcars for carrying truck trailers by rail (piggyback), and provided such in-transit services as the diversion of shipped goods to other destinations en route and the processing of goods en route.

### Truck

Trucks have steadily increased their share of transportation and now account for 25 percent of total cargo. They account for the largest portion of transportation *within* cities as opposed to *between* cities. Each year, trucks travel over 140

TABLE 13–1   Characteristics of Major Transportation Modes

| Transportation Mode | Intercity Cargo Volume* (%) | | | Typical Products Shipped |
|---|---|---|---|---|
| | 1965 | 1975 | 1985 | |
| Rail | 709 (43.3%) | 759 (36.7%) | 898 (37.2%) | Farm products, minerals, sand, chemicals, automobiles |
| Truck | 359 (21.9) | 454 (22.0) | 600 (24.9) | Clothing, food, books, computers, paper goods |
| Water | 262 (16.0) | 342 (16.6) | 348 (14.4) | Oil, grain, sand, gravel, metallic ores, coal |
| Pipeline | 306 (18.7) | 507 (24.5) | 562 (23.3) | Oil, coal, chemicals |
| Air | 1.9 (0.12) | 3.7 (0.19) | 6.4 (0.26) | Technical instruments, perishable products, documents |

*In billions of cargo ton-miles
*Source: Statistical Abstract of the United States,* 1986 and 1987.

*Combining modes of transportation through containerization (clockwise): piggyback, fishyback, airtruck, and trainship.*

billion miles—equal to nearly 300,000 round trips to the moon.[17] Trucks are highly flexible in their routing and time schedules. They can move goods door to door, saving shippers the need to transfer goods from truck to rail and back again at a loss of time and risk of theft or damage. Trucks are efficient for short hauls of high-value merchandise. In many cases, their rates are competitive with railway rates, and trucks can usually offer faster service.

### Water

A large amount of goods moves by ships and barges on coastal and inland waterways. By themselves, Mississippi River barges account for 15 percent of the freight shipped in the United States. The cost of water transportation is very low for shipping bulky, low-value, nonperishable products such as sand, coal, grain, oil, and metallic ores. On the other hand, water transportation is the slowest transportation mode and is sometimes affected by the weather.

### Pipeline

Pipelines are a specialized means of shipping petroleum, natural gas, and chemicals from sources to markets. Pipeline shipment of petroleum products costs less than rail shipment but more than water shipment. Most pipelines are used by their owners to ship their own products.

### Air

Although air carriers transport less than 1 percent of the nation's goods, they are becoming more important as a transportation mode. Air freight rates are much higher than rail or truck rates, but air freight is ideal when speed is

**containerization** Putting goods in boxes or trailers that are easy to transfer between two transportation modes.

needed or distant markets have to be reached. Among the most frequently air-freighted products are perishables (fresh fish, cut flowers) and high-value, low-bulk items (technical instruments, jewelry). Companies find that air freight reduces inventory levels, warehouse numbers, and packaging costs.

## Choosing Transportation Modes

Until the late 1970s, routes, rates, and service in the transportation industry were heavily regulated by the federal government. Today, most of these regulations have been eased. Deregulation has caused rapid and substantial changes. Railroads, ships and barges, trucks, airlines, and pipeline companies are now much more competitive, flexible, and responsive to the needs of their customers. These changes have resulted in better services and lower prices for shippers. But such changes also mean that marketers must do better transportation planning if they want to take full advantage of new opportunities in the changing transportation environment.[18]

In choosing a transportation mode for a product, shippers consider as many as five criteria. Table 13–2 ranks the various modes on these criteria. Thus, if a shipper needs speed, air and truck are the prime choices. If the goal is low cost, then water and pipeline might be best. Trucks appear to offer the most advantages—a fact that explains their growing share of the transportation market.

Thanks to *containerization*, shippers are increasingly combining two or more modes of transportation. **Containerization** consists of putting goods in boxes or trailers that are easy to transfer between two transportation modes.[19] *Piggyback* describes the use of rail and trucks; *fishyback*, water and trucks; *trainship*, water and rail; and *airtruck*, air and trucks. Each combination offers advantages to the shipper. For example, piggyback not only is cheaper than trucking alone but also provides flexibility and convenience.

## Organizational Responsibility for Physical Distribution

We see that decisions on warehousing, inventory, and transportation require much coordination. A growing number of companies have set up permanent committees made up of managers responsible for different physical distribution activities. These committees meet often to set policies for improving overall distribution efficiency. Some companies even have a vice-president of physical distribution who reports to the marketing vice-president, the manufacturing vice-president, or even the president. The location of the physical distribution department within the company is a secondary concern. The important thing is that the company coordinate its physical distribution and marketing activities in order to create high market satisfaction at a reasonable cost.

TABLE 13–2 Rankings of Transportation Modes (1 = Highest Rank)

|  | Speed (DOOR-TO-DOOR DELIVERY TIME) | Dependability (MEETING SCHEDULES ON TIME) | Capability (ABILITY TO HANDLE VARIOUS PRODUCTS) | Availability (NO. OF GEOGRAPHIC POINTS SERVED) | Cost (PER TON-MILE) |
|---|---|---|---|---|---|
| Rail | 3 | 4 | 2 | 2 | 3 |
| Water | 4 | 5 | 1 | 4 | 1 |
| Truck | 2 | 2 | 3 | 1 | 4 |
| Pipeline | 5 | 1 | 5 | 5 | 2 |
| Air | 1 | 3 | 4 | 3 | 5 |

*Source:* See Carl M. Guelzo, *Introduction to Logistics Management* (Englewood Cliffs, NJ: Prentice Hall, 1986), p. 46.

*Distribution channel decisions* are among the most complex and challenging decisions facing a firm. Each *channel system* creates a different level of sales and costs. Once a distribution channel has been chosen, the firm must usually stick with it for a long time. The chosen channel will strongly affect and be affected by the other elements in the marketing mix.

Each firm needs to identify alternative ways to reach its market. Available means vary from direct selling to using one, two, three, or more intermediary *channel levels*. The organizations making up the marketing channel are connected by product, title, payment, information, and promotion flows. Marketing channels face continuous and sometimes dramatic change. Three of the most important trends are the growth of *vertical, horizontal,* and *multichannel marketing systems*. These trends affect channel cooperation, conflict, and competition.

*Channel design* begins with assessing customer channel-service needs and company channel objectives and constraints. The company then identifies the major channel alternatives in terms of the *types* of intermediaries, the *number* of intermediaries, and the *channel responsibilities* of each. Each channel alternative has to be evaluated according to economic, control, and adaptive criteria. Channel management calls for selecting qualified middlemen and motivating them. Individual channel members must be evaluated regularly.

Just as the marketing concept is receiving increased recognition, more business firms are paying attention to the physical distribution concept. *Physical distribution* is an area of potentially high cost savings and improved customer satisfaction. When order processors, warehouse planners, inventory managers, and transportation managers make decisions, they affect each other's costs and ability to handle demand. The physical distribution concept calls for treating all these decisions within a unified framework. The task is to design physical distribution systems that minimize the total cost of providing a desired level of customer services.

# QUESTIONS FOR DISCUSSION

1. The Book-of-the-Month Club has been successfully marketing books by mail for over 50 years. Why do so few publishers sell their own books by mail? How has BOMC survived recent competition from B. Dalton, Waldenbooks, and other large booksellers?

2. How many channel levels are commonly used by these companies—(a) H & R Block, (b) J.C. Penney, (c) Procter & Gamble, (d) Carrier (a maker of air conditioning equipment)?

3. What organizations are needed to conduct the flows of products, ownership, payment, information, and promotion from the manufacturer to the customer? Are these organizations part of the distribution channel?

4. How is the leader chosen in a distribution channel? How much power does the leader have in getting other members to work for the overall good of the channel instead of solely for their own good?

5. Why is franchising such a fast-growing form of retail organization?

6. Why have horizontal marketing systems become more common in recent years? Suggest pairs of companies and resources that might benefit from horizontal marketing programs.

7. Describe the channel-service needs of the following groups: (a) consumers buying computers for home use, (b) retailers buying computers to resell to consumers, (c) purchasing agents buying computers for company use. What different channels would a computer manufacturer design to satisfy these different needs?

8. Which distribution strategies—intensive, selective, or exclusive—are used for the following products: (a) Piaget watches, (b) Acura automobiles, (c) Snickers candy bars?

9. How do physical distribution decisions differ from channel decisions?

10. When planning inventory levels, what consequences of running out of stock must be considered?

# REFERENCES

1. Julie Liesse Erickson and Judann Dagnoli, "Winn-Dixie, Food Giants Mend Fences," *Advertising Age,* January 9, 1989, pp. 1, 45; Judann Dagnoli and Laurie Freeman, "P&G, Pillsbury Just Say No to Big Retail Chain," *Advertising Age,* October 3, 1988, pp. 2, 68; Julie Liesse Erickson, "Grocery Chain Dumps Major Package Goods," *Advertising Age,* October 10, 1988, pp. 1, 75; Laurie Freeman and Julie Liesse Erickson, "Grocers Join Winn-Dixie," *Advertising Age,* November 7, 1988, pp. 3, 78; and "Some Deals Are Positively Diverting," *Sales & Marketing Management,* October 1988, p. 42.

2. See Louis W. Stern and Frederick D. Sturdivant, "Customer-Driven Distribution Systems," *Harvard Business Review,* July–August 1987, p. 34.

3. For an excellent summary of channel conflict and power, see Louis W. Stern and Adel I. El-Ansary, *Marketing Channels,* 2d ed. (Englewood Cliffs, NJ: Prentice Hall, 1982), Chaps. 6 and 7.

4. See Bert C. McCammon, Jr., "Perspectives for Distribution Programming," in *Vertical Marketing Systems,* Louis P. Bucklin, ed. (Glenview, IL: Scott Foresman, 1970), pp. 32–51.

5. Janet Myers, "Giant Stocks Up on Service, Vertical Integration," *Advertising Age,* April 28, 1986, p. S4.

6. Jaclyn Fierman, "How Gallo Crushes the Competition," *Fortune,* September 1, 1986, p. 27.

7. See Faye Rice, "How to Succeed at Cloning a Small Business," *Fortune,* October 28, 1985, p. 60; and Laura Zinn, "Want to Buy a Franchise? Look Before You Leap," *Business Week,* May 23, 1988, pp. 186–87.

8. This has been called "symbiotic marketing." For more reading, see Lee Adler, "Symbiotic Marketing," *Harvard Business Review,* November–December 1966, pp. 59–71; and P. "Rajan" Varadarajan and Daniel Rajaratnam, "Symbiotic Marketing Revisted," *Journal of Marketing,* January 1986, pp. 7–17.

9. See Laurie Freeman, "McKids Grow Up: Adult Clothing May Join Sears' Kids' Line," *Advertising Age,* June 1, 1987, p. 82.

10. See Robert E. Weigand, "Fit Products and Channels to Your Markets," *Harvard Business Review,* January–February 1977, pp. 95–105.

11. See Stern and Sturdivant, "Customer-Driven Distribution Systems," p. 35.

12. See Bert Rosenbloom, *Marketing Channels: A Management View* (Hinsdale, IL: Dryden Press, 1978), pp. 192–203.

13. See McCammon, "Perspectives for Distribution Programming," p. 43; and James A. Narus and James C. Anderson, "Turn Your Industrial Distributors into Partners," *Harvard Business Review,* March–April 1986, pp. 66–71.

14. See Katherine M. Hafner, "Computer Retailers: Things Have Gone from Worse to Bad," *Business Week,* June 8, 1987, p. 104.

15. Michael Oneal, "Can Sears Get Sexier but Keep the Common Touch?" *Business Week,* July 6, 1987, p. 93.

16. John Huey, "Wal-Mart: Will It Take Over the World?" *Fortune,* January 30, 1989, pp. 52–64.

17. See "Trucking," *Fortune,* November 22, 1987, p. 148.

18. See Lewis M. Schneider, "New Era in Transportation Strategy," *Harvard Business Review,* March–April 1985, pp. 118–26.

19. For more discussion, see Norman E. Hutchinson, *An Integrated Approach to Logistics Management* (Englewood Cliffs, NJ: Prentice Hall, 1987), p. 69.

# Case 13

## COMPAQ COMPUTER: A COSTLY CHANNEL CONFLICT

In February 1989, Compaq Computer abruptly ended a seven-year relationship with Businessland, the nation's largest publicly held computer store chain. With this startling decision, Compaq lost distribution in stores that accounted for 7 percent of its revenues and provided a key link to its corporate customer segment. The break ended a three-year history of disagreements between the two firms over Businessland's reported demands for preferential pricing and promotion treatment from Compaq. Instead of knuckling under to the pressure, Compaq severed the relationship.

Compaq's major competitor, IBM, which accounts for a whopping 31 percent of all Businessland sales, played a major role in the conflict. IBM had been aggressively wooing Businessland with sweetheart deals and bigger discounts than those that it offered to other IBM dealers. Using a much-disputed promotion program, IBM allowed Businessland to use IBM market-development funds to encourage sales of IBM machines over other brands. Amidst an ongoing debate over pricing discounts, IBM also began to sell PCs to Businessland and ComputerLand, the two largest chains, at

about 4 percent less than it sold them to its other dealers. The two dealers then used the extra revenue to boost commissions and run advertising.

In addition, IBM started giving money, known as "flex-funds," to computer dealers who pledged to increase sales of IBM products. Use of such funds had previously been limited to such activities as advertising and sales-training programs, but when IBM loosened its restrictions, Businessland, breaking with industry tradition, began to use these funds to supplement the commissions that it paid its 700 salespeople for selling IBM products. Finally, whereas other vendors' programs feed money back to dealers only *after* they've met sales quotas, IBM gave dealers up-front cash for the mere *promise* of increased sales. In return, Businessland pledged to boost IBM sales by as much as 50 percent. As a result, some Businessland salespeople were being paid five to ten times more commission for selling IBM than for selling Compaq.

Businessland then tried to exact special treatment from Compaq similar to that which it was getting from IBM. The chain attempted to use the IBM deal to exert pressure on Compaq to ease restrictions on its funding programs and permit similar salesforce incentives. Businessland repeatedly stressed that for Compaq to become one of its "strategic partners," the manufacturer would have to give the store chain preferential treatment. But unlike IBM, which negotiates terms on a dealer-by-dealer basis, Compaq has always had a two-tier pricing structure that it applied to all dealers and has long prided itself on its scrupulously even-handed policy toward all of its dealers. Favoring one dealer over another with special agreements simply was not consistent with the straightforward dealer strategy that had helped make Compaq so successful. Thus, when pressured by Businessland for special treatment, Compaq held fiercely to its philosophy that all dealers be treated fairly and equitably. Rather than yield to the dealer's demands, Compaq turned Businessland loose. However, conflicts between dealers and computer manufacturers are far from over. For example, Compaq expects that by publicizing IBM's discount arrangement with Businessland, it may stir other dealers into demanding the same arrangement from IBM. And what appears to be a successful coup may come back to haunt IBM. If IBM must give the same discounts to other dealers, its profits may suffer.

Although squabbles over discounts and salesforce-incentive programs are the most obvious cause of the dramatic divorce of Compaq and Businessland, there appears to be another deeper reason. Compaq's decision to separate came just weeks after Businessland publicly endorsed IBM's new Micro Channel Architecture (MCA) instead of the Extended Industry Standard Architecture (EISA) used by Compaq. A computer's architecture dictates how the computer interfaces with its peripherals, such as its printer or modem. In an effort to gain a tighter proprietary grip on new technology, IBM is trying to set a new standard for the industry—one that cannot be cloned. IBM's new MCA is much faster at transferring information between the computer and its peripherals but is not compatible with previous standards. On the other hand, the competing EISA, which has the speed of MCA, is compatible with earlier equipment.

Many analysts have speculated that the real reason for the Compaq-Businessland split was the battle over which PC-design standard would dominate. IBM has worked hard to establish the micro channel as the industry standard. It has wooed dealers by eliminating unpopular sales quotas and by hiking allowances for training and technical support. IBM reps even make joint sales calls with dealers.

However, IBM's Micro Channel design, first featured in its Personal System/2 Computers in 1987, got off to a slow start that gave Compaq—backed by eight other producers—time to propose the alternative EISA design. By jointly developing EISA, the nine computer companies hoped to challenge IBM's hold on PC-design standards. As the struggle between Compaq and IBM intensified, however, Businessland complained that EISA's challenge to MCA created confusion at the customer level, where users would have to sort out which architecture would ultimately prevail. Finally, two years after the MCA/EISA debate began, Businessland officials announced that they would emphasize the IBM standard and support EISA only when requested by customers. This decision came as a harsh blow to Compaq. Thus, the break between Compaq and Businessland may be the first indication that the success or failure of MCA versus EISA will depend on which camp musters the broadest support at the retail level.

Most industry analysts contend that Compaq will recover from the breakup faster than Businessland: Businessland accounted for 7 percent of Compaq's sales in 1988 but garnered 15 percent of its own revenues from sales of Compaq computers. Moreover, other Compaq dealers will be more than delighted to pick up Businessland's share of Compaq sales—they are already aggressively courting Businessland's former Compaq customers. Finally, buyers who prefer Compaq aren't likely to switch to IBM just in order to buy from Businessland.

Others argue, however, that the divorce will hurt Compaq more. With the split, Compaq has lost a prime channel to the corporate market. However, still others point out that corporate buyers often do not feel much loyalty to dealers. Many buyers chose Compaq as their *computer* instead of Businessland as their *vendor*—they will now seek a different dealer, not a different manufacturer.

Compaq is a savvy computer marketer. It now holds about 8 percent of the $23.2 billion U.S. personal computer market, mostly obtained by taking advantage of IBM's missteps—often churning out sleek, high-performance computers that are better and faster than Big Blue's. Moreover, while Compaq's share has grown in recent years, IBM's share has dwindled to 21 percent, down from about 31 percent in 1987. Compaq's revenues have more than tripled since 1986, and earnings have risen sixfold. So, although some analysts see Compaq's move to cut off Businessland as an uncharacteristically emotional reaction, others see it as a boldly calculated strategic move.

*Questions*

1. What functions do dealers perform in the PC market? Why are they needed?

2. What kind of channel organization does IBM have in the PC market? What kind does Compaq have?

3. How do the goals of different channel members fuel the channel conflicts discussed in the case? Who is helped or harmed by these conflicts?

4. What recommendations would you make to Compaq regarding its channel design?

This is a home furnishings store?

IKEA (👁️🗝️ ah!)

# 14

# Placing Products: Retailing and Wholesaling

## CHAPTER OBJECTIVES

**After reading this chapter, you should be able to**

1. Explain the roles of retailers and wholesalers in the distribution channel
2. Describe the major types of retailers and give examples of each
3. Identify the major types of wholesalers and give examples of each
4. Explain the marketing decisions facing retailers and wholesalers

When Scandinavian furniture giant IKEA (pronounced *eye-KEY-ah*) opened its first U.S. store in 1985, it caused quite a stir. On opening day, people flocked to the suburban Philadelphia store from as far away as Washington, D.C. Traffic on the nearby turnpike backed up for six miles, and at one point the store was so tightly packed with customers that management ordered the doors closed until the crowds thinned out. In the first week, the IKEA store packed in 150,000 people who bought over $1 million worth of furniture. When the dust had settled, the store was still averaging 50,000 customers a week.

IKEA is one of a new breed of retailers called "category killers." They get their name from their marketing strategy: carry a huge selection of merchandise in a single product category at such good prices that you destroy the competition. Category killers are now striking in a wide range of industries, including furniture, toys, records, sporting goods, housewares, and consumer electronics.

IKEA stores are about three football fields in size. Each store stocks more than 6,000 items—all furnishings and housewares, ranging from coffee mugs to leather sofas to kitchen cabinets. IKEA sells Scandinavian-design "knock-down" furniture—each item reduces to a flat-pack kit and has to be assembled at home. Consumers browse through the store's comfortable display area, where signs and stickers on each item note its price, how it is made, assembly instructions, how different pieces complement one another, and where the item is located in the adjacent warehouse. Customers wrestle desired items from warehouse stacks, haul their choices away on large trollies, and pay at giant-sized checkout counters. The store provides a reasonably priced restaurant for hungry shoppers and a supervised children's play area for weary parents. But best of all, IKEA has low prices. The store operates on the philosophy of providing a wide variety of well-designed home furnishings at prices that the majority of people can afford.

Although the first category killer, Toys 'R' Us, appeared in the late 1950s, other retailers have just recently adopted the idea. Unlike warehouse clubs and other "off-price" retailers, which offer the lowest prices but few choices within any given category, category killers offer an exhaustive selection in one line. Toys 'R' Us stocks 18,000 different toy items in football field-size stores. Huge Sportmart stores stock 100,000 sporting goods items, including 70 types of sleeping bags, 265 styles of athletic socks, 12,000 pairs of shoes, and 15,000 fishing lures. Tower Records stores carry up to 75,000 titles—25 times more than the average competitor. And Branden's, the housewares and home furnishings category killer, offers a choice of 30 different coffee pots, 25 irons, 100 patterns of bed sheets, and 800 kitchen gadgets. With such large assortments, category killers generate big sales that often allow them to charge prices as low as those of their discount competitors.

However, category killers face a few problems. IKEA has encountered occasional difficulty managing its huge inventory, sometimes overpromising or inconveniencing customers. The company's expansive stores also require large investments and huge markets. And some consumers find that they want more personal service than IKEA gives or that the savings aren't worth the work required to find products in the huge store, haul them out, and assemble them at home. Despite such problems, IKEA has prospered beyond its founders' dreams. It now has 89 stores in 19 countries racking up over $1 billion a year in sales. It recently opened a second U.S. store in the Washington, D.C., suburbs and will soon have a third in Baltimore. In all, IKEA plans to open 60 stores around the country during the next 25 years.

Most retailing experts predict great success for stores like IKEA. One retailing analyst, Wallace Epperson, Jr., "estimates IKEA will win at least a 15 percent share of any market it enters and will expand the market as it does so. If Mr. Epperson is any indication, IKEA's prospects are good. Touring IKEA in his professional capacity, Mr. Epperson couldn't resist the store. 'I spent $400,' he says. 'It's incredible.'"[1]

---

**retailing** All the activities involved in selling goods or services directly to final consumers for their personal, nonbusiness use.

**retailers** Businesses whose sales come *primarily* from retailing.

This chapter looks at *retailing* and *wholesaling*. In the first section, we look at the nature and importance of retailing, major types of store and nonstore retailers, decisions retailers make, and the future of retailing. In the second section, we discuss the same topics for wholesalers.

# RETAILING

What is retailing? We all know that Sears and K mart are retailers, but so are Avon representatives, the local Holiday Inn, and a doctor seeing patients. We define **retailing** as all the activities involved in selling goods or services directly to final consumers for their personal, nonbusiness use. Many institutions— manufacturers, wholesalers, retailers—do retailing. But most retailing is done by **retailers**—businesses whose sales come *primarily* from retailing. And although most retailing is done in retail stores, in recent years nonstore retailing—selling by mail, by telephone, by door-to-door contact, by vending machines, by numerous electronic means—has grown explosively. Because store retailing accounts for most of the retail business, we will discuss it first. Then we will look at nonstore retailing.

# STORE RETAILING

Retail stores come in all shapes and sizes, and new retail types keep emerging. They can be classified by one or more of several characteristics: *amount of service, product line sold, relative prices, control of outlets,* and *type of store cluster.* These classifications and the corresponding retailer types are shown in Table 14-1 and discussed below.

**TABLE 14-1  Different Ways to Classify Retail Stores**

| Amount Service | Product Line Sold | Relative Prices | Control of Outlets | Type of Store Cluster |
|---|---|---|---|---|
| Self-service | Specialty store | Discount store | Corporate chain | Central business district |
| Limited service | Department store | Warehouse | Voluntary chain and retailer cooperative | Regional shopping center |
| Full service | Supermarket | Catalog showroom | Consumer cooperative | Community shopping center |
| | Convenience store | | Franchise organization | Neighborhood shopping center |
| | Combination store, superstore, and hypermarket | | Merchandising conglomerate | |
| | Service business | | | |

## Amount of Service

Different products need different amounts of service, and customer-service preferences vary. Table 14-2 shows three levels of service and the types of retailers that use them.

**Self-service retailing** in this country grew rapidly during the Great Depression of the 1930s. Customers were willing to perform their own "locate-compare-select" process to save money. Today, self-service is the basis of all discount operations and is typically used by sellers of convenience goods (for example, supermarkets) and nationally branded, fast-moving shopping goods (for example, catalog showrooms such as Best Products or Service Merchandise).

**Limited-service retailers** such as Sears or J. C. Penney provide more sales assistance because they carry more shopping goods about which customers need more information. They also offer additional services such as credit and merchandise return not usually offered by low-service stores. Their increased operating costs result in higher prices.

In **full-service retailers,** such as specialty stores and first-class department

**self-service retailers** Retailers that provide very few services; customers carry out their own locate-compare-select process to save money.

**limited-service retailers** Retailers that provide limited sales assistance and additional services such as credit and merchandise return.

**full-service retailers** Retailers that assist customers in every phase of the shopping process and provide a wide variety of additional services.

**TABLE 14-2  Classification of Retailers Based on the Amount of Customer Service**

| | *Decreasing Services* ⟷ | *Increasing Services* | |
|---|---|---|---|
| | SELF-SERVICE | LIMITED SERVICE | FULL SERVICE |
| **ATTRIBUTES** | Very few services<br>Price appeal<br>Staple goods<br>Convenience goods | Small variety of services<br>Shopping goods | Wide variety of services<br>Fashion merchandise<br>Specialty merchandise |
| **EXAMPLES** | Warehouse retailing<br>Grocery stores<br>Discount retailing<br>Variety stores<br>Mail-order retailing<br>Automatic vending | Door-to-door sales<br>Department stores<br>Telephone sales<br>Variety stores | Specialty stores<br>Department stores |

*Source:* Adapted from Larry D. Redinbaugh, *Retailing Management: A Planning Approach* (New York: McGraw-Hill, 1976), p. 12.

specialty store

**specialty store** A retail store that carries a narrow product line with a deep assortment within that line.

**department store** A retail organization that carries a wide variety of product lines, each operated as a separate department managed by specialist buyers or merchandisers.

stores, salespeople assist customers in every phase of the shopping process. Full-service stores usually carry more specialty goods and slower-moving items such as cameras, jewelry, and fashions, for which customers like to be "waited on." They provide more liberal returns policies, various credit plans, free delivery, home servicing, and extras such as lounges and restaurants. More services result in much higher operating costs—costs that are passed along to customers as higher prices.

## Product Line Sold

Retailers can also be classified by the length and breadth of their product assortments. Among the most important types are the *specialty store*, the *department store*, the *supermarket*, the *convenience store*, and the *superstore*.

### Specialty Store

A **specialty store** carries a narrow product line with a deep assortment within that line. Examples include stores selling sporting goods, furniture, books, electronics, flowers, or toys. Specialty stores can be further classified by the narrowness of their product lines. A clothing store is a *single-line store*, a men's clothing store is a *limited-line store*, and a men's custom shirt store is a *superspecialty store*.

Today, specialty stores are flourishing for several reasons. The increasing use of market segmentation, market targeting, and product specialization has resulted in a greater need for stores that focus on specific products and segments. And because of changing consumer life styles and the increasing number of two-income households, many consumers have greater incomes but less time to spend shopping. They are attracted to specialty stores that provide high-quality products, convenient locations, good store hours, excellent service, and quick entry and exit.

### Department Store

A **department store** carries a wide variety of product lines—typically clothing, home furnishings, and household goods. Each line is operated as a separate department managed by specialist buyers or merchandisers. Examples of well-known department stores include Bloomingdale's (New York), Marshall Field (Chicago), and Filene's (Boston). *Specialty department stores,* which carry only clothing, shoes, cosmetics, luggage, and gift items, can also be found. Examples are Saks Fifth Avenue and I. Magnin.

Department stores grew rapidly through the first half of the century. But after World War II, they began to lose ground to other types of retailers, including discount stores, specialty store chains, and "off-price" retailers. The heavy traffic, poor parking, and general decaying of central cities, where many department stores had made their biggest investments, made downtown shopping less appealing. As a result, many department stores closed or merged with others.

Nonetheless, department stores are today waging a "comeback war." Most have opened suburban stores and many have added "bargain basements" to meet the discount threat. Still others have remodeled their stores or set up "boutiques" that compete with specialty stores. Many are trying mail-order and telephone selling. In recent years, many large department stores have been joining rather than fighting the competition by diversifying into discount and specialty stores. Dayton-Hudson, for example, operates Target (discount stores), Mervyn's (lower-price clothing), B. Dalton (books), and many other discount and specialty chains in addition to its Dayton's, Hudson's, and other department stores. These discount and specialty operations now account for more than 80 percent of total corporate sales.[2]

## Supermarket

**Supermarkets** are large, low-cost, low-margin, high-volume, self-service stores that carry a wide variety of food, laundry, and household products. Most U.S. supermarket stores are owned by supermarket chains like Safeway, Kroger, A&P, Winn-Dixie, and Jewel. Chains account for almost 70 percent of all supermarket sales.[3]

The first supermarkets introduced the concepts of self-service, customer turnstiles, and checkout counters. Supermarket growth took off in the 1930s for several reasons. The Great Depression made consumers more price-conscious, and mass automobile ownership reduced the need for small neighborhood stores. An increase in brand preselling through advertising reduced the need for salesclerks. Finally, stores selling grocery, meat, produce, and household goods in a single location allowed one-stop shopping and lured consumers from greater distances, giving supermarkets the volume needed to offset their lower margins.

However, most supermarkets today are facing slow sales growth because of slower population growth and an increase in competition from convenience stores, discount food stores, and superstores. They have also been hit hard by the rapid growth of out-of-home eating. Thus, supermarkets are looking for new ways to build their sales. Most chains now operate fewer but larger stores. They practice "scrambled merchandising," carrying many nonfood items—beauty aids, housewares, toys, prescriptions, appliances, videocassettes, sporting goods, garden supplies—hoping to find high-margin lines to improve profits.

Supermarkets are also improving their facilities and services to attract more customers. Typical improvements are better locations, improved décor, longer store hours, check cashing, delivery, and even child-care centers. Although consumers have always expected supermarkets to offer good prices, convenient locations, and speedy checkout, today's more affluent and sophisticated food buyer wants more. Many supermarkets, therefore, are "moving upscale" with the market, providing "from-scratch" bakeries, gourmet deli counters, and seafood departments.[4] Finally, to attract more customers, large supermarket chains are starting to customize their stores for individual neighborhoods. They are tailoring store size, product assortments, prices, and promotions to the economic and ethnic needs of local markets.

## Convenience Store

**Convenience stores** are small stores that carry a limited line of high-turnover convenience goods. Examples include 7-Eleven, Circle K, and Stop-N-Go Stores. These stores locate near residential areas and remain open long hours and seven days a week. Convenience stores must charge high prices to make up for higher operating costs and lower sales volume. But they satisfy an important consumer need: Consumers use convenience stores for "fill-in" purchases at off hours or when time is short, and they are willing to pay for the convenience. The number of convenience stores has increased from about 2,000 in 1957 to over 40,000 with sales of $55 billion in 1988.[5]

## Superstore, Combination Store, and Hypermarket

These three types of stores are larger than the conventional supermarket. **Superstores** are almost twice the size of regular supermarkets and carry a large assortment of routinely purchased food and nonfood items. They offer such

**supermarkets** Large, low-cost, low-margin, high-volume, self-service stores that carry a wide variety of food, laundry, and household products.

**convenience store** A small store located near a residential area, open long hours seven days a week, and carrying a limited line of high-turnover convenience goods.

**superstore** A store almost twice the size of a regular supermarket carrying a large assortment of routinely purchased food and nonfood items and offering a wide variety of services.

**combination stores** Combined food and drug stores.

**hypermarkets** Huge stores that combine supermarket, discount, and warehouse retailing.

*Hypermarkets: huge stores that combine supermarket, discount, and warehouse retailing.*

services as laundry, dry cleaning, shoe repair, check cashing, bill paying, and bargain lunch counters. Because of their wider assortment, superstore prices are 5 to 6 percent higher than those of conventional supermarkets. Many leading chains are moving toward superstores. Examples include Safeway's Pak 'N Pay and Pathmark Super Centers. Almost 80 percent of Safeway's new stores over the past several years have been superstores. In 1975, superstores accounted for only about 3 percent of total food store sales, but by 1986 they took in over 26 percent of the business.[6]

**Combination stores** are combined food and drug stores. They average about one and one-half football fields in size—about twice the size of superstores. Examples are A&P's Family Mart and Kroger-Sav-On. Combination stores take in less than 5 percent of the business done by food stores.

**Hypermarkets** are even bigger than combination stores, ranging in size up to about *six* football fields. They combine supermarket, discount, and warehouse retailing. They carry more than routinely purchased goods, also selling furniture, appliances, clothing, and many other items. The hypermarket operates like a warehouse. Products in wire "baskets" are stacked high on metal racks; forklifts move through aisles during selling hours to restock shelves. The store gives discounts to customers who carry their own heavy appliances and furniture out of the store. Examples include Bigg's in Cincinnati, Ralph's Giant Stores in Southern California, and Carrefour in Philadelphia. Hypermarkets have grown quickly in Europe and now appear to be catching on in the United States, with major retailers such as K mart and Wal-Mart now opening such giant stores. Industry experts estimate that 150 hypermarkets will be operating in the U.S. by 1990.[7]

### Service Business

For some businesses, the "product line" is actually a service. Service retailers include hotels and motels, banks, airlines, colleges, hospitals, movie theaters, tennis clubs, bowling alleys, restaurants, repair services, barber and beauty shops, and dry cleaners. Service retailers in the United States are growing faster than product retailers, and each service industry has its own retailing drama. Banks look for new ways to distribute their services, including automatic tellers, direct deposit, and telephone banking. Health organizations are changing the ways consumers get and pay for health services. The amusement industry has spawned Disney World and other theme parks. H&R Block has built a franchise network to help consumers pay as little as possible to Uncle Sam.

## Relative Prices

Retailers can also be classified according to their prices. Most retailers charge regular prices and offer normal-quality goods and customer service. Some offer higher-quality goods and service at higher prices. Here, we will look at retailers that feature low prices: discount stores, "off-price" retailers, and catalog showrooms.

### Discount Store

A **discount store** sells standard merchandise at lower prices by accepting lower margins and selling higher volume. The use of occasional discounts or specials does not make a discount store: A true discount store *regularly* sells its merchandise at lower prices, offering mostly national brands, not inferior goods. Early discount stores cut expenses by operating in warehouse-like facilities in low-rent but heavily traveled districts. They slashed prices, advertised widely, and carried a reasonable width and depth of products.

In recent years, facing intense competition from other discounters and department stores, many discount retailers have "traded up." They have improved décor, added new lines and services, and opened suburban branches—all of which has led to higher costs and prices. And as some department stores have cut their prices to compete with discounters, the distinction between many discount and department stores has become blurred. As a result, several major discount stores folded in the 1970s because they lost their price advantage. And many department store retailers have upgraded their stores and services, once again setting themselves apart from the improved discounters.

### Off-Price Retailers

When the major discount stores traded up, a new wave of **off-price retailers** moved in to fill the low-price, high-volume gap. Ordinary discounters buy at regular wholesale prices and accept lower margins to keep prices down. Off-price retailers, on the other hand, buy at less than regular wholesale prices and charge consumers less than retail. They tend to carry a changing and unstable collection of higher-quality merchandise, often leftover goods, overruns, and irregulars obtained at reduced prices from manufacturers or other retailers. Off-price retailers have made the biggest inroads in clothing, accessories, and footwear. But they can be found in all areas, from no-frills banking and discount brokerages to food stores and electronics (see Marketing Highlight 14–1).

There are three main types of off-price retailers—*factory outlets, independents,* and *warehouse clubs.* **Factory outlets** are owned and operated by manufacturers and normally carry the manufacturer's surplus, discontinued, or irregular goods. Examples are the Burlington Coat Factory Warehouse, Manhattan's Brand Name Fashion Outlet, and the well-known factory outlets of Levi Strauss, Carter's, and Ship 'n Shore. Such outlets sometimes group together in *factory outlet malls,* where dozens of outlet stores offer prices as much as 50 percent below retail on a wide range of items. The number of factory outlet malls grew from less than 60 in 1980 to over 370 in 1986.[8]

**Independent off-price retailers** either are owned and run by entrepreneurs or are divisions of larger retail corporations. Although many off-price operations are run by smaller independents, most large off-price retailer operations are owned by bigger retail chains. Examples include Loehmann's

---

**discount store** A retail institution that sells standard merchandise at lower prices by accepting lower margins and selling at higher volume.

**off-price retailers** Retailers who buy at less than regular wholesale prices and sell at less than retail.

**factory outlets** Off-price retailing operations that are owned and operated by manufacturers and normally carry the manufacturer's surplus, discontinued, or irregular goods.

**independent off-price retailers** Off-price retailing operations which either are owned and run by entrepreneurs or are divisions of larger retail corporations.

**warehouse clubs** (or **wholesale clubs**) Off-price retailers that sell a limited selection of brand-name grocery items, appliances, clothing, and a hodgepodge of other goods at deep discounts to members who pay annual membership fees.

(operated by Associated Dry Goods, owner of Lord & Taylor), Designer Depot K mart), Filene's Basement (Federated Department Stores), and T. J. Maxx (Zayre).

**Warehouse clubs** (or **wholesale clubs**) sell a limited selection of brand-name grocery items, appliances, clothing, and a hodgepodge of other goods at deep discounts to members who pay $25 to $50 annual membership fees. Examples are the Price Club, Sam's Wholesale Club, BJ's Wholesale Club, and

# Marketing Highlight 14–1

## OFF-PRICE RETAILING AT 47TH STREET PHOTO

On the surface, 47th Street Photo doesn't look like much of a retailing operation. Its main store is a small, dingy affair located above Kaplan's Delicatessen on New York's West 47th Street. Its second store, a small computer outlet located a few blocks away, is only slightly more attractive. But beneath the surface, 47th Street Photo represents the state of the art in off-price retailing—selling quality, branded merchandise at large discounts. In business for only fifteen years, 47th Street's two tiny stores annually sell more than $100 million worth of electronics products, and its sales are growing at 25 percent a year.

47th Street Photo is typical of the new discounters that emerged at retailing's low end to fill the gap created when more mature discount institutions began to

trade up their merchandise, services, and prices. 47th Street maintains a low-cost, low-margin, high-volume philosophy. It carries a huge inventory of over 25,000 fast-moving, branded electronics products—including such items as cameras and camera equipment (only 30 percent of its business), personal computers, calculators, typewriters, telephones, answering machines, and videotape machines. It keeps its costs down through low-cost, no-frills facilities, efficient operations, and smart buying. Then it offers customers the lowest prices and turns its inventory quickly.

47th Street Photo's customers endure more abrupt treatment and enjoy fewer services than they would at plusher specialty stores. Like a well-run restaurant, 47th Street gets 'em in, feeds

'em, and gets 'em out. Customers line up at the sales counter to be waited on by efficient but curt salespeople who prefer that customers know what they want before coming in. In-store product inspections and comparisons are discouraged, and salespeople offer little information or assistance.

But the price is right! 47th Street Photo regularly monitors competitor prices to be certain that its own prices support its "lowest-price" position. Price examples: Suggested retail price of the Canon PC-20 copier, $1,295; at 47th Street Photo, it's $880. Macy's offers a Brother typewriter for $400, and on a recent Sunday it's out of stock. At 47th Street the same model is $289 and, of course, in stock.

Half of 47th Street Photo's sales come from mail-order and telephone customers. Its 224-page catalog, toll-free telephone numbers, and packed ads in the *New York Times, The Wall Street Journal,* and several other business and special-interest magazines make New York's "only dopes pay retail" shopping style available to the rest of the country. Over the years, 47th Street has built a solid reputation for trustworthiness. A price is a price—no bait-and-switch, no haggling or hidden prices.

So on the surface, 47th Street Photo doesn't look like much of a retailing operation. But behind its low-overhead exterior is a gutsy, finely tuned merchandising machine.

*Source:* Adapted from John Merwin, "The Source," *Forbes,* April 9, 1984, pp. 74–78.

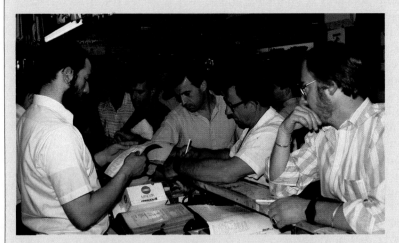

*47th Street Photo doesn't look like much, but it's a finely tuned merchandising machine.*

Pace Membership Warehouse. These wholesale clubs operate in huge, low-overhead, warehouse-like facilities and offer few frills. Often, stores are drafty in the winter and stuffy in the summer. Customers themselves must wrestle furniture, heavy appliances, and other large items into the checkout line. Such clubs make no home deliveries and accept no credit cards. But they do offer rock-bottom prices—typically 20 to 40 percent below supermarket and discount store prices.[9]

Off-price retailing blossomed during the early 1980s, and competition has stiffened in recent years as more and more off-price retailers enter the market. But the growth of off-price retailing has slowed a bit recently because of an upswing in the economy and more effective counterstrategies by department stores and regular discounters. Still, off-price retailing remains a vital and growing force in modern retailing.[10]

### Catalog Showroom

A **catalog showroom** sells a wide selection of high-markup, fast-moving, brand-name goods at discount prices. These include jewelry, power tools, cameras, luggage, small appliances, toys, and sporting goods. Catalog showrooms make their money by cutting costs and margins to provide low prices that will attract a higher volume of sales. The catalog showroom industry is led by companies such as Best Products and Service Merchandise.

Emerging in the late 1960s, catalog showrooms became one of retailing's hottest new forms. But catalog showrooms have been struggling in recent years to hold their share of the retail market. For one thing, department stores and discount retailers now run regular sales that match showroom prices. In addition, off-price retailers consistently beat catalog prices. As a result, many showroom chains are broadening their lines, doing more advertising, renovating their stores, and adding services in order to attract more business.

## Control of Outlets

About 80 percent of all retail stores are independents, and they account for two-thirds of all retail sales. Here, we will look at several other forms of ownership—the *corporate chain*, the *voluntary chain* and *retailer cooperative*, the *franchise organization*, and the *merchandising conglomerate*.

### Corporate Chain

The chain store is one of the most important retail developments of this century. **Chain stores** are two or more outlets that are commonly owned and controlled, employ central buying and merchandising, and sell similar lines of merchandise. Corporate chains appear in all types of retailing, but they are strongest in department stores, variety stores, food stores, drugstores, shoe stores, and women's clothing stores. Corporate chains gain many advantages over independents. Their size allows them to buy in large quantities at lower prices. They can afford to hire corporate-level specialists to deal with such areas as pricing, promotion, merchandising, inventory control, and sales forecasting. And chains gain promotional economies because their advertising costs are spread over many stores and a large sales volume.

### Voluntary Chain and Retailer Cooperative

The great success of corporate chains caused many independents to band together in one of two forms of contractual associations. One is the *voluntary chain*—a wholesaler-sponsored group of independent retailers that engage in group buying and common merchandising. Examples include the Independent

**catalog showroom** A retail operation that sells a wide selection of high-markup, fast-moving, brand-name goods at discount prices.

**chain stores** Two or more outlets that are commonly owned and controlled, have central buying and merchandising, and sell similar lines of merchandise.

**franchise** A contractual association between a manufacturer, wholesaler, or service organization (a franchiser) and independent businesspeople (franchisees) who buy the right to own and operate one or more units in the franchise system.

**merchandising conglomerates** Corporations that combine several different retailing forms under central ownership and share some distribution and management functions.

Grocers Alliance (IGA), Sentry Hardwares, and Western Auto. The other form of contractual association is the *retailer cooperative*—a group of independent retailers that band together to set up a jointly owned central wholesale operation and conduct joint merchandising and promotion efforts. Examples include Associated Grocers and True Value Hardware. These organizations give independents the buying and promotion economies they need to meet the prices of corporate chains.

### Franchise Organization

**A franchise** is a contractual association between a manufacturer, wholesaler, or service organization (the franchiser) and independent businesspeople (franchisees) who buy the right to own and operate one or more units in the franchise system. The main difference between a franchise and other contractual systems (voluntary chains and retail cooperatives) is that franchise systems are normally based either on some unique product or service, on a method of doing business, or on the trade name, goodwill, or patent that the franchiser has developed. Franchising has been prominent in fast foods, motels, gas stations, video stores, health and fitness centers, auto rentals, hair cutting, real estate, travel agencies, and dozens of other product and service areas.

The compensation received by the franchiser may include an initial fee, a royalty on sales, lease fees for equipment, and a share of the profits. McDonald's franchisees may pay up to $500,000 in initial start-up costs for a franchise. Then McDonald's charges a 3.5 percent service fee and a rental charge of 8.5 percent of the franchisee's volume. It also requires franchisees to go to Hamburger University for three weeks to learn how to manage the business.

### Merchandising Conglomerate

**Merchandising conglomerates** are corporations that combine several different retailing forms under central ownership and share some distribution and management functions. Examples include Federated Department Stores, Allied Stores, Dayton-Hudson, J. C. Penney, and F. W. Woolworth. For example, F. W. Woolworth, in addition to its variety stores, operates 28 specialty chains, including Kinney Shoe Stores, Afterthoughts (costume jewelry and handbags), Face Fantasies (budget cosmetics), Herald Square Stationers, Frame Scene, Foot Locker (sports shoes), and Kids Mart. Diversified retailing provides superior management systems and economies that benefit all the separate retail operations and is likely to increase through the 1990s.

## Type of Store Cluster

Most stores today cluster together to increase their customer pulling power and to give consumers the convenience of one-stop shopping. The main types of store clusters are the *central business district* and the *shopping center*.

### Central Business District

Central business districts were the main form of retail cluster until the 1950s. Every large city and town had a central business district with department stores, specialty stores, banks, and movie theaters. However, when people began to move to the suburbs, these central business districts, with their traffic, parking, and crime problems, began to lose business. Downtown merchants opened branches in suburban shopping centers, and the decline of central business districts continued. Only recently have many cities joined with merchants to try to revive downtown shopping areas by building malls and providing underground parking. Some central business districts have made a comeback; others remain in a slow and possibly irreversible decline.

A regional shopping center is like a mini-downtown.

**shopping center** A group of retail businesses planned, developed, owned, and managed as a unit.

## Shopping Center

A **shopping center** is a group of retail businesses planned, developed, owned, and managed as a unit. A *regional shopping center,* the largest and most dramatic shopping center, is like a mini-downtown. It contains from 40 to 100 or more stores and pulls customers from a wide area. Larger regional malls often have several department stores and a wide variety of specialty stores on several shopping levels. Many have added new types of retailers over the years—dentists, health clubs, and even branch libraries.

A *community shopping center* contains 15 to 50 retail stores. It normally contains a branch of a department or variety store, a supermarket, specialty stores, professional offices, and sometimes a bank. Most shopping centers are *neighborhood shopping centers* that generally contain 5 to 15 stores. They are close and convenient for consumers. They usually contain a supermarket and several service stores—a dry cleaner, self-service laundry, drugstore, barber or beauty shop, hardware store, or other stores.

Combined, all shopping centers now account for about one-third of all retail sales, but they may be reaching their saturation point. Many areas contain too many malls, and as sales-per-square-foot are dropping, vacancy rates are climbing. Some malls have even gone out of business. The current trend is toward smaller malls located in medium-size and smaller cities in fast-growing areas such as the Southwest.

# NONSTORE RETAILING

Although most goods and services are sold through stores, nonstore retailing has been growing much faster than store retailing. Nonstore retailing now accounts for more than 14 percent of all consumer purchases, and it may account for a third of all sales by the end of the century.[11] Here, we will examine

**direct marketing** Marketing through various advertising media that interact directly with consumers, generally calling for the consumer to make a direct response.

**direct-mail marketing** Direct marketing through single mailings that include letters, ads, samples, foldouts, and other "salespeople on wings" sent to prospects on mailing lists.

**catalog marketing** Selling through catalogs mailed to a select list of customers or made available in stores.

three types of nonstore retailing: *direct marketing, direct selling,* and *automatic vending.*

## Direct Marketing

**Direct marketing** uses various advertising media to interact directly with consumers, generally calling for the consumer to make a direct response.[12] We will now look at the four major forms of direct marketing: *direct-mail and catalog marketing, telemarketing, television marketing,* and *electronic shopping.*

### Direct-Mail and Catalog Marketing

**Direct-mail marketing** involves single mailings that include letters, ads, samples, foldouts, and other "salespeople on wings" sent to prospects on mailing lists. Mailing lists are developed from customer lists or obtained from mailing list houses that provide names of people fitting almost any description—the superwealthy, mobile home owners, veterinarians, pet owners, or just about anything else.

A recent study showed that direct mail and catalogs accounted for 48 percent of all direct-response offers leading to eventual orders (compared with telephone at 7 percent, circulars at 7 percent, and magazines and newspapers, each at 6 percent).[13] Direct mail is becoming increasingly popular because it permits high target market selectivity, can be personalized, is flexible, and allows easy measurements of results. Although the cost-per-thousand people reached is higher than with such mass media as television or magazines, the people who are reached are much better prospects. Over 35 percent of Americans have responded to direct-mail ads, and the number is growing. Direct mail has proved very successful in promoting books, magazine subscriptions, and insurance and is increasingly being used to sell novelty and gift items, clothing, gourmet foods, and industrial products. Direct mail is also used heavily by charities, which raised over $35 billion in 1986 and accounted for about 25 percent of all direct-mail revenues.[14]

**Catalog marketing** involves selling through catalogs mailed to a select list of customers or made available in stores. This approach is used by huge general-merchandise retailers—such as Sears, J. C. Penney, and Spiegel—that carry a full line of merchandise. But recently, the giants have been challenged by thousands of specialty catalogs with more sharply focused audiences. These smaller catalog retailers have successfully filled highly specialized market niches.

Consumers can buy just about anything from a catalog. Over 12.4 billion copies of more than 8,500 different catalogs are mailed annually, and the average household receives at least 50 catalogs per year.[15] Hanover House sends out 22 different catalogs selling everything from shoes to decorative lawn birds. Sharper Image sells $2,400 jet-propelled surf boards. The Banana Republic Travel and Safari Clothing Company features everything you would need to go hiking in the Sahara. The list of specialty catalogers is almost endless. Recently, specialty department stores such as Neiman-Marcus, Bloomingdale's, and Saks Fifth Avenue have begun sending catalogs to cultivate upper-middle-class markets for high-priced, often exotic, merchandise. Several major corporations have also developed or acquired mail-order divisions. For example, Avon now issues ten women's fashion catalogs along with catalogs for children's and men's clothes. Hershey and other food companies are investigating catalog opportunities.

Most consumers enjoy receiving catalogs and will sometimes even pay to get them. Many catalog marketers even sell their catalogs at book stores and magazine stands. Some companies—Royal Silk, Neiman-Marcus, Sears, Spie-

**telemarketing** Using the telephone to sell directly to consumers.

**television marketing** Using television to market goods directly to consumers through direct-response advertising or home shopping channels.

*Almost 12 billion catalogs are mailed out each year; the average household receives 50 catalogs annually.*

gel, and others—are also experimenting with videotape catalogs, or "videologs." Royal Silk sells 35-minute video catalogs to its customers for $5.95 and plans to market them to video stores. These tapes contain polished presentations of Royal Silk products, tell customers how to care for silk, and provide ordering information.[16]

## Telemarketing

**Telemarketing**—using the telephone to sell directly to consumers—has become the major direct marketing tool. Marketers spend an estimated $41 billion each year in telephone charges to help sell their products and services.[17] Telemarketing blossomed in the late 1960s with the introduction of inward and outward Wide Area Telephone Service (WATS). With IN WATS, marketers can use toll-free 800 numbers to receive orders from television and radio ads, direct mail, or catalogs. With OUT WATS, they can use the phone to sell directly to consumers and businesses.

During January 1982, more than 700 people dialed an 800 number every minute in response to television commercials. The average household receives 19 telephone sales calls each year and makes 16 calls to place orders. Some telemarketing systems are fully automated. For example, automatic dialing and recorded message players (ADRMPs) self-dial numbers, play a voice-activated advertising message, and take orders from interested customers on an answering machine device or by forwarding the call to an operator. Telemarketing is used in business marketing as well as consumer marketing. For example, Raleigh Bicycles used telemarketing to reduce the amount of personal selling needed for contacting its dealers. In the first year, salesforce travel costs were reduced by 50 percent, and sales in a single quarter were up 34 percent.

## Television Marketing

**Television marketing** is used in two different ways to market products directly to consumers. The first is through *direct-response advertising*. Direct-response marketers air television spots, often 60 or 120 seconds long, that persuasively describe a product and give customers a toll-free number for ordering. Direct-response advertising works well for magazines, books, small appliances, records and tapes, collectibles, and many other products. Some successful direct-response ads run for years and become classics. Dial Media's ads for Ginsu knives ran for seven years and sold almost 3 million sets of knives worth over $40 million in sales; its Armourcote cookware ads generated more than twice that much.[18]

*Home shopping channels,* another form of television direct marketing, are television programs—or even entire channels—dedicated to selling goods and services. The largest is the Home Shopping Network (HSN). With HSN, viewers tune in the Home Shopping Club, which broadcasts 24 hours a day. The program's hosts offer bargain prices on products ranging from jewelry, lamps, collectible dolls, and clothing to power tools and consumer electronics—usually obtained by HSN at closeout prices. The show is upbeat, with the hosts honking horns, blowing whistles, and praising viewers for their good taste. Viewers call an 800 number to order goods. At the other end, 400 operators handle more than 1,200 incoming lines, entering orders directly into computer terminals. Orders are shipped within 48 hours.

Sales through home shopping channels grew from $450 million in 1986 to $2 billion in 1987, and they are expected to reach $7.2 billion by 1992. More than half of all U.S. homes have access to HSN or other home shopping channels, such as Cable Value Network, Value Club of America, Home Shopping Mall, or TelShop. Sears, K mart, J. C. Penney, Spiegel, and other major retailers are now looking into the home shopping industry. Although some experts contend that TV home shopping is just a fad, most think it is here to stay.[19]

### Electronic Shopping

The major form of electronic shopping is *videotex.* Videotex is a two-way system that links consumers with the seller's computer data banks by cable or telephone lines. The videotex service makes up a computerized catalog of products offered by producers, retailers, banks, travel organizations, and others. Consumers use an ordinary television set that has a special keyboard device connected to the system by two-way cable. Or they hook into the system by telephone using a home computer. For example, a consumer wanting to buy a new compact disc player could request a list of all CD brands in the computerized catalog, compare brands, and order one using a charge card—all without leaving home.

Videotex is still a new idea. In recent years, several large videotex systems have failed because of too few subscribers or too little use. One such system called "Gateway" offered in-home shopping services and much more. Through Gateway, consumers could order goods from local and national retailers; do their banking with local banks; survey the contents of the *Los Angeles Times* the evening before the paper was printed; book airline, hotel, and car rental reservations; look at the text of an entire encyclopedia; take college courses; buy tickets to concerts and sporting events; play games, quizzes, and contests; get tips on plumbing repair, first aid, physical fitness, home decorating, and hundreds of other topics; and send messages and video greeting cards to one another. Although Gateway failed, other large companies are investing in even more promising systems. IBM and Sears have joined to form a system called "Prodigy" and Chemical Bank, Bank of America, Time, and AT&T are forming one called "Covidea." The acceptance of such electronic systems will grow as more consumers acquire cable television and personal computers and as consumers discover the wonders of electronic shopping.[20]

## Direct selling

**door-to-door retailing** Selling door-to-door, office-to-office, or at home-sales parties.

**automatic vending** Selling through vending machines.

**Door-to-door retailing,** which started centuries ago with roving peddlers, has grown into a huge industry. More than 600 companies sell either door-to-door, office-to-office, or at home-sales parties. The pioneers in door-to-door selling are the Fuller Brush Company, vacuum cleaner companies like Electrolux, and book-selling companies like World Book and Southwestern. The image of door-to-door selling improved greatly when Avon entered the industry with its Avon representative—the homemaker's friend and beauty consultant. Tupperware and Mary Kay Cosmetics helped to popularize home-sales parties, in which several friends and neighbors attend a party at a private home where products are demonstrated and sold.

The advantages of door-to-door selling are consumer convenience and personal attention. But the high costs of hiring, training, paying, and motivating the salesforce result in higher prices. Although some door-to-door companies are still thriving, door-to-door selling has a somewhat uncertain future. The increase in the number of single-person and working-couple households decreases the chances of finding a buyer at home. Home-party companies are having trouble finding nonworking women who want to sell products part-time. And with recent advances in interactive direct-marketing technology, the door-to-door salesperson may well be replaced in the future by the household telephone, television, or home computer.

## Automatic vending

**Automatic vending** is not new—in 215 B.C., Egyptians could buy sacrificial water from coin-operated devices. But this method of selling soared after World War II. Today's automatic vending uses space-age and computer technology to sell a wide variety of convenience and impulse goods—cigarettes, beverages, candy, newspapers, foods and snacks, hosiery, cosmetics, paperback books, records and tapes, T-shirts, insurance policies, and even shoeshines and fishing worms. Vending machines are found everywhere—in factories, offices, lobbies, retail stores, gasoline stations, airports, and train and bus terminals. Automatic teller machines provide bank customers with checking, savings, withdrawals, and funds-transfer services. As compared with store retailing, vending machines offer consumers 24-hour selling, self-service, and less-damaged goods. But the expensive equipment and labor required for automatic vending make it a costly channel, and prices of vended goods are often 15 to 20 percent higher than those in retail stores. Customers must also put up with aggravating machine breakdowns, out-of-stocks, and the fact that merchandise cannot be returned.

# RETAILER MARKETING DECISIONS

We will now look at the major marketing decisions retailers must make about their *target markets, product assortment and services, price, promotion,* and *place.*

## Target Market Decision

Retailers must first define their target market and then decide how they position themselves in it. Next, product assortment, services, pricing, advertising, store décor, and all other decisions must support the retailer's position.

Some retailers define their target markets quite well. For example, The

Limited initially targeted young, fashion-conscious, moderately affluent women. All aspects of the store—assortment, atmosphere, salespeople—were carefully selected to match this target consumer. Over the years, the savvy retailer has added Limited Express, Lane Bryant, Victoria's Secrets, Lerners, and other highly targeted chains to reach new segments. The Limited now operates 2,400 stores in seven different market segments with yearly sales of $2.4 billion. But too many retailers fail to define clearly their target markets and positions. They try to have "something for everyone" and end up satisfying no single market well. Even large department stores like Sears must define their major target markets so that they can design effective strategies for serving them.

A retailer should do periodic marketing research to check that it is satisfying its target customers. Consider a store that wants to attract wealthy consumers, but whose *store image* is shown by the red line in Figure 14–1. This store does not currently appeal to its target market—it must change its target market or redesign itself as a "classier" store. Suppose the store then upgrades its products, services, and salespeople and raises its prices. Some time later, a second customer survey may reveal the image shown by the blue line in Figure 14–1. The store has established a position that matches its target market choice.

## Product Assortment and Services Decision

Retailers have to decide on three major product variables: *product assortment, services mix,* and *store atmosphere.*

The retailer's *product assortment* must match what target shoppers expect. The retailer has to decide on both product assortment *width* and *depth*. Thus, a restaurant can offer a narrow and shallow assortment (small lunch counter), a narrow and deep assortment (delicatessen), a wide and shallow assortment (cafeteria), or a wide and deep assortment (large restaurant). Another product assortment element is the *quality* of the goods: The customer is interested not only in the range of choice but also in the quality of the products available.

However, no matter what the store's product assortment and quality level, there will always be competitors with similar assortments and quality. Thus, the retailer must search for other ways to *differentiate* itself from similar competitors. It can use any of several product-differentiation strategies. For one thing, it

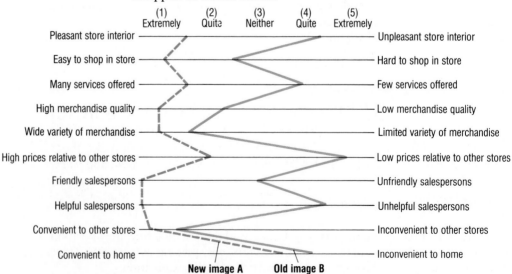

FIGURE 14–1   A Comparison between the Old and the New Image of a Store Seeking to Appeal to a Class Market

*Source:* Adapted from David W. Cravens, Gerald E. Hills, and Robert B. Woodruff, *Marketing Decision Making: Concepts and Strategy* (Homewood, IL; Richard D. Irwin, 1976), p. 234.

can offer merchandise that no other competitor carries—its own private brands or national brands on which it holds exclusives. Thus, The Limited designs most of the clothes carried by its store and Saks gets exclusive rights to carry a well-known designer's labels. Second, the retailer can feature blockbuster merchandising events—Bloomingdale's is known for running spectacular shows featuring goods from a certain country, such as India or China. Or the retailer can offer surprise merchandise, as when Loehmann's offers surprise assortments of seconds, overstocks, and closeouts. Finally, the retailer can differentiate itself by offering a highly targeted product assortment—Lane Bryant carries goods for larger women; Brookstone offers an unusual assortment of gadgets in what amounts to an adult toy store.

Retailers must also decide on a *services mix* to offer customers. The old "mom and pop" grocery stores offered home delivery, credit, and conversation—services that today's supermarkets ignore. The services mix is one of the key tools of nonprice competition for setting one store apart from another. Table 14–3 lists some of the major services that full-service retailers can offer.

The *store's atmosphere* is another element in its product arsenal. Every store has a physical layout that makes moving around in it either hard or easy. Every store has a "feel"—one store is cluttered, another charming, a third plush, a fourth somber. The store must have a planned atmosphere that suits the target market and moves customers to buy. A bank should be quiet, solid, and peaceful; a nightclub should be bright, loud, and vibrating. Increasingly, retailers are working to create shopping environments that match their target markets. Chains like the Banana Republic and Laura Ashley are turning their stores into theaters that transport customers into unusual, exciting shopping environments. Even conservative Sears divides the clothing areas within each store into six distinct "shops," each with its own selling environment designed to meet the tastes of individual segments.

## Price Decision

A retailer's prices are a key positioning factor and must be decided in relation to its target market, its product and service assortment, and its competition. All retailers would like to charge high markups and achieve high volume, but the two seldom go together. Most retailers seek *either* high markups on lower

TABLE 14–3 Typical Retail Services

| Primary Services | Supplemental Services | |
|---|---|---|
| Alterations | Baby strollers | Packaging and gift wrapping |
| Complaint handling | Bill payment | |
| Convenient store hours | Bridal registries | Product locater |
| Credit | Check cashing | Restaurants or snack counters |
| Delivery | Children's playrooms | |
| Fitting rooms | Demonstrations | Shopping consultants |
| Installation and assembly | Layaway | Shopping information |
| | Lost and found | Shows, displays, and exhibits |
| Merchandise returns and adjustments | Personal shopping | |
| | Package checkrooms | Special ordering |
| Parking | | Wheelchairs |
| Rest rooms | | |
| Service and repair | | |
| Telephone ordering | | |

*Store atmospheres: Chanel's (left) and Bergdorf Goodman (right) create very different store atmospheres to match their different target markets.*

volume (most specialty stores) *or* low markups on higher volume (mass merchandisers and discount stores). Thus, Bijan's on Rodeo Drive in Beverly Hills prices men's suits starting at $1,000 and shoes at $400—it sells a low volume but makes a hefty profit on each sale. At the other extreme, T. J. Maxx sells brand-name clothing at discount prices, settling for a lower margin on each sale but selling at a much higher volume.

Retailers must also pay attention to pricing tactics. Most retailers will put low prices on some items to serve as "traffic builders" or "loss leaders." On some occasions, they run storewide sales. On others, they plan markdowns on slower-moving merchandise. For example, shoe retailers expect to sell 50 percent of their shoes at the normal markup, 25 percent at a 40 percent markup, and the remaining 25 percent at cost.

## Promotion Decision

Retailers use the normal promotion tools—advertising, personal selling, sales promotion, and public relations—to reach consumers. Retailers advertise in newspapers, magazines, radio, and television. Advertising may be supported by circulars and direct-mail pieces. Personal selling requires careful training of salespeople in how to greet customers, meet their needs, and handle their complaints. Sales promotion may include in-store demonstrations, displays, contests, and visiting celebrities. Public relations activities—press conferences and speeches, store openings and other special events, newsletters and store magazines, public service activities, and others—are always available to retailers.

## Place Decision

Retailers often say that there are three critical factors in retailing success: *location, location,* and *location.* A retailer's location is key to its ability to attract customers. And the costs of building or leasing facilities have a major impact on the retailer's profits. Thus, site-location decisions are among the most important the retailer makes. Small retailers may have to settle for whatever locations they can find or afford. Large retailers usually employ specialists who select locations using advanced site-location methods.[21]

# THE FUTURE OF RETAILING

Several trends will affect the future of retailing. First, the slowdown in population and economic growth means that retailers will no longer enjoy sales and profit growth through natural expansion in current and new markets. Growth will have to come from increasing shares of current markets. But greater competition and new types of retailers will make it harder to improve market shares. Consumer demographics, life styles, and shopping patterns are changing rapidly. To be successful, then, retailers will have to choose target segments carefully and position themselves strongly.

Moreover, quickly rising costs will make more efficient operation and smarter buying essential to successful retailing. Thus, retail technologies are growing in importance as competitive tools. Progressive retailers are using computers to produce better forecasts, control inventory costs, order electronically from suppliers, communicate between stores, and even sell to consumers within stores. They are adopting checkout-scanning systems, in-store television, on-line transaction processing, and electronic funds transfer.

Many retailing innovations are partially explained by the **wheel of retailing** concept.[22] According to this concept, many new types of retailing forms begin as low-margin, low-price, low-status operations. They challenge established retailers that have become "fat" over the years by letting their costs and margins increase. The new retailers' success leads them to upgrade their facilities and offer more services. In turn, their costs increase, forcing them to increase their prices. Eventually, the new retailers become like the conventional retailers they replaced. The cycle begins again when still newer types of retailers evolve with lower costs and prices (see Marketing Highlight 14–2). The wheel of retailing concept seems to explain the initial success and later troubles of department stores, supermarkets, and discount stores and the recent success of off-price retailers.

New retail forms will continue to emerge to meet new consumer needs and new situations. But the life cycle of new retail forms is getting shorter. Department stores took about 100 years to reach the mature stage of the life cycle; more recent forms—such as catalog showrooms and furniture warehouse stores—reached maturity in about ten years. Retailers can no longer sit back with a successful formula. To remain successful, they must keep adapting.

**wheel of retailing concept** A concept of retailing that states that new types of retailers usually begin as low-margin, low-price, low-status operations but later evolve into higher-priced, higher-service operations, eventually becoming like the conventional retailers they replaced.

**wholesaling** All the activities involved in selling goods and services to those buying for resale or business use.

**wholesalers** Firms engaged *primarily* in wholesaling activity.

# WHOLESALING

**Wholesaling** includes all activities involved in selling goods and services to those buying for resale or business use. A retail bakery does wholesaling when it sells pastry to the local hotel. But we will call **wholesalers** firms engaged *primarily* in wholesaling activity.

Wholesalers buy mostly from producers and sell mostly to retailers, industrial consumers, and other wholesalers. But why are wholesalers used at all? For example, why would a producer use wholesalers rather than selling directly to retailers or consumers? Quite simply, wholesalers are often better at performing one or more of the following channel functions:

- *Selling and promoting.* Wholesalers' salesforces help manufacturers reach many small customers at a low cost. The wholesaler has more contacts and is often more trusted by the buyer than the distant manufacturer.
- *Buying and assortment building.* Wholesalers can select items and build assortments needed by their customers, thus saving the consumers much work.

### THE WHEEL OF RETAILING TURNS AT K MART

Over the past two decades, K mart has been the model for discount department stores and has held unswervingly to the principles of discount merchandising. But like many other discount retailers in recent years, K mart has moved away from the formula that made it the number-two retailer in the country (behind Sears). K mart is now trading up and away from its no-frills, low-price strategy toward an upscale philosophy emphasizing brand-name products, quality, and value rather than low prices. With this new strategy, K mart hopes to get more business from the increasing numbers of more affluent consumers—consumers who previously shopped at K mart only to "cherry-pick" sales items.

To establish its new image, K mart has been making gradual but sweeping changes in its merchandise assortment and store facilities. Its broadened and upgraded product assortment now includes more well-known national brands and higher-quality store brands. More store space is being devoted to fashions, sporting goods, electronics, and other higher-margin goods. K mart advertising now features fewer sales, more branded products, and more "life style" appeals.

K mart is currently spending a whopping $2.2 billion to modernize and upgrade its more than 2,000 stores. The plain fixtures and long rows of racks are being replaced. Store space is being modularized into special departments—a "Kitchen Korner," a home electronics center, a nutrition center, a hardcover-books section, and others—all to provide a more pleasing shopping environment for more discriminating shoppers.

Thus, the wheel of retailing turns at K mart. The new, upgraded K mart stores will more closely resemble Sears or J. C. Penny stores than discount stores. The new strategy could be risky—while K mart attempts to woo more upscale consumers, other discounters will emerge and try to lure away the core of price-conscious, lower-scale consumers that made K mart so successful in the first place.

But K mart understands the wheel of retailing and has taken steps to ensure that it won't be displaced at the bottom of the retailing ladder. At the same time that it is upgrading its K mart stores, the company is also moving into "off-price" and other new forms of discount retailing to pick up the low-end business that might be lost under the new upscale strategy. In recent years, for example, K mart has developed or acquired a number of discount specialty chains—Designer Depot (designer label clothing at large discounts), Garment Rack (lower-quality clothing), Accent (quality gifts and housewares at discount prices), Bishop Buffets and Furr's Cafeterias (inexpensive food), Builders Square (do-it-yourself hardware), Sports Giant (sporting goods), American Fare (hypermarkets), Pay Less Drug Stores, and other businesses that combine for about 25 percent of total company sales. And the company is considering additional discount operations in such areas as toys, jewelry, and books. Rather than falling victim to the wheel of retailing, K mart appears to be using it to advantage.

*Sources:* See Russell Mitchell, "K mart Spruces Up the Bargain Basement," *Business Week,* September 8, 1986, pp. 45–48; and Patricia Strnad, "K mart's Antonini Moves Far Beyond Retail 'Junk' Image," *Advertising Age,"* July 25, 1988, pp. 1, 67.

□ *Bulk-breaking.* Wholesalers save their customers money by buying in carload lots and breaking bulk (breaking large lots into small quantities).

□ *Warehousing.* Wholesalers hold inventories, thereby reducing the inventory costs and risks of suppliers and customers.

□ *Transportation.* Wholesalers can provide quicker delivery to buyers because they are closer than producers.

□ *Financing.* Wholesalers finance their customers by giving credit, and they finance their suppliers by ordering early and paying bills on time.

□ *Risk bearing.* Wholesalers absorb risk by taking title and bearing the cost of theft, damage, spoilage, and obsolescence.

□ *Market information.* Wholesalers give information to suppliers and customers about competitors, new products, and price developments.

□ *Management services and advice.* Wholesalers often help retailers to train their salesclerks, improve store layouts and displays, and set up accounting and inventory-control systems.

# TYPES OF WHOLESALERS

Wholesalers fall into three major groups (see Table 14–4): *merchant wholesalers, brokers and agents,* and *manufacturers' sales branches and offices.* We will now look at each of these groups of wholesalers.

## Merchant Wholesalers

**Merchant wholesalers** are independently owned businesses that take title to the merchandise they handle. They are the largest single group of wholesalers, accounting for roughly 50 percent of all wholesaling. Merchant wholesalers include two broad types: *full-service wholesalers* and *limited-service wholesalers.*

### Full-Service Wholesalers

**Full-service wholesalers** provide a full set of services such as carrying stock, using a salesforce, offering credit, making deliveries, and providing management assistance. They are either *wholesale merchants* or *industrial distributors.*

Wholesale merchants sell mostly to retailers and provide a full range of services. They vary in the width of their product line. Some carry several lines of goods to meet the needs of both general merchandise retailers and single-line retailers. Others carry one or two lines of goods in a greater depth of assortment. Examples are hardware wholesalers, drug wholesalers, and clothing wholesalers. Some specialty wholesalers carry only part of a line in great depth. Examples are health-food wholesalers, seafood wholesalers, and automotive parts wholesalers. They offer customers deeper choice and greater product knowledge.

Industrial distributors are merchant wholesalers who sell to producers rather than to retailers. They provide inventory, credit, delivery, and other services. They may carry a broad range of merchandise, a general line, or a specialty line. Industrial distributors may concentrate on such lines as maintenance and operating supplies, original-equipment goods (such as ball bearings and motors), or equipment (such as power tools and forklift trucks).

### Limited-Service Wholesalers

**Limited-service wholesalers** offer fewer services to their suppliers and customers. There are several types of limited-service wholesalers.

**merchant wholesaler** An independently owned wholesale operation that takes title to the merchandise it handles.

**full-service wholesalers** Wholesalers that provide a full set of services such as carrying stock, using a salesforce, offering credit, making deliveries, and providing management assistance.

**limited-service wholesalers** Wholesalers that offer only limited services to their suppliers and customers.

TABLE 14–4   Classification of Wholesalers

| Merchant Wholesalers | Brokers and Agents | Manufacturers' Sales Branches and Offices |
|---|---|---|
| Full-service wholesalers | Brokers | Sales branches and offices |
|   Wholesale merchants | Agents | Purchasing offices |
|   Industrial distributors | | |
| Limited-service wholesalers | | |
|   Cash-and-carry wholesalers | | |
|   Truck wholesalers | | |
|   Drop shippers | | |
|   Rack jobbers | | |
|   Producers' cooperatives | | |
|   Mail-order wholesalers | | |

*A typical Fleming Companies, Inc., wholesale food distribution center. The average Fleming Warehouse contains 500,000 square feet of floor space (with 30-foot-high ceilings), carries 16,000 different food items, and serves 150-200 retailers with a 500-mile radius.*

*Cash-and-carry wholesalers* have a limited line of fast-moving goods, sell to small retailers for cash, and normally do not deliver. A small fish store retailer, for example, normally drives at dawn to a cash-and-carry fish wholesaler and buys several crates of fish, pays on the spot, drives the merchandise back to the store, and unloads it.

*Truck wholesalers* (also called *truck jobbers)* perform a selling and delivery function. They carry a limited line of goods (such as milk, bread, or snack foods) that they sell for cash as they make their rounds of supermarkets, small groceries, hospitals, restaurants, factory cafeterias, and hotels.

*Drop shippers* operate in bulk industries such as coal, lumber, and heavy equipment. They do not carry inventory or handle the product. Once an order is received, they find a producer who ships the goods directly to the customer. The drop shipper takes title and risk from the time the order is accepted to the time it is delivered to the customer. Because drop shippers do not carry inventory, their costs are lower and they can pass some savings on to customers.

*Rack jobbers* serve grocery and drug retailers, mostly in the area of nonfood items. These retailers do not want to order and maintain displays of hundreds of nonfood items. Rack jobbers send delivery trucks to stores, and the delivery person sets up racks of toys, paperbacks, hardware items, health and beauty aids, or other items. They price the goods, keep them fresh, and keep inventory records. Rack jobbers sell on consignment—they retain title to the goods and bill the retailers only for the goods sold to consumers. Thus, they provide such services as delivery, shelving, inventory, and financing. They do little promotion because they carry many branded items that are already highly advertised.

*Producers' cooperatives,* owned by farmer-members, assemble farm produce to sell in local markets. Their profits are divided among members at the end of the year. They often try to improve product quality and promote a co-op brand name, such as Sun Maid raisins, Sunkist oranges, or Diamond walnuts.

*Mail-order wholesalers* send catalogs to retail, industrial, and institutional customers offering jewelry, cosmetics, special foods, and other small items. Their main customers are businesses in small outlying areas. They have no salesforces to call on customers. The orders are filled and sent by mail, truck, or other means.

## Brokers and Agents

*Brokers* and *agents* differ from merchant wholesalers in two ways: They do not take title to goods, and they perform only a few functions. Their main function is to aid in buying and selling, and for these services they earn a commission on the selling price. Like merchant wholesalers, they generally specialize by product line or customer type. They account for 11 percent of the total wholesale volume.

### Brokers

A **broker** brings buyers and sellers together and assists in negotiation. Brokers are paid by the parties hiring them. They do not carry inventory, get involved in financing, or assume risk. The most familiar examples are food brokers, real estate brokers, insurance brokers, and security brokers.

### Agents

**Agents** represent buyers or sellers on a more permanent basis. There are several types. *Manufacturers' agents* (also called *manufacturers' representatives)* are the most numerous agent wholesalers. They represent two or more manufacturers of related lines. They have a formal agreement with each manufacturer covering prices, territories, order-handling procedures, delivery and warranties, and commission rates. They know each manufacturer's product line and use their wide contacts to sell the products. Manufacturers' agents are used in such lines as apparel, furniture, and electrical goods. Most manufacturers' agents are small businesses, with only a few employees who are skilled salespeople. They are hired by small producers who cannot afford to maintain their own field salesforces and by large producers who want to open new territories or sell in areas that cannot support a full-time salesperson.

*Selling agents* contract to sell a producer's entire output—either the manufacturer is not interested in the doing the selling or feels unqualified. The selling agent serves as a sales department and has much influence over prices, terms, and conditions of sale. The selling agent normally has no territory limits. Selling agents are found in such product areas as textiles, industrial machinery and equipment, coal and coke, chemicals, and metals.

*Purchasing agents* generally have a long-term relationship with buyers. They make purchases for buyers and often receive, inspect, warehouse, and ship goods to the buyers. One type consists of *resident buyers* in major apparel markets—purchasing specialists who look for apparel lines that can be carried by small retailers located in small cities. They not only know a lot about their product lines and provide helpful market information to clients but can obtain the best goods and prices available.

*Commission merchants* (or *houses)* are agents that take physical possession of products and negotiate sales. They are not normally used on a long-term basis. They are used most often in agricultural marketing by farmers who do not want to sell their own output and who do not belong to cooperatives. Typically, the commission merchant will take a truckload of farm products to a central market, sell it for the best price, deduct a commission and expenses, and pay the balance to the farmer.

## Manufacturers' Sales Branches and Offices

The third major type of wholesaling is that done in **manufacturers' sales branches and offices** by sellers or buyers themselves rather than through independent wholesalers. Manufacturers' sales branches and offices account for about 31 percent of all wholesale volume. Manufacturers often set up their own

**broker** A wholesaler who does not take title to goods and whose function is to bring buyers and sellers together and assist in negotiation.

**agent** A wholesaler who represents buyers or sellers on a relatively permanent basis, performs only a few functions, and does not take title to goods.

**manufacturers' sales branches and offices** Wholesaling by sellers or buyers themselves rather than through independent wholesalers.

sales branches and offices to improve inventory control, selling, and promotion. *Sales branches* carry inventory and are found in such industries as lumber and automotive equipment and parts. *Sales offices* do not carry inventory and are most often found in dry goods and notion industries. Many retailers set up *purchasing offices* in major market centers such as New York and Chicago. These purchasing offices perform a role similar to that of brokers or agents but are part of the buyer's organization.

# WHOLESALER MARKETING DECISIONS

Like retailers, wholesalers make decisions about target markets, product assortments and services, price, promotion, and place.

## Target Market Decision

Wholesalers need to define their target markets and not try to serve everyone. They can choose a target group by size of customer (only large retailers), type of customer (convenience food stores only), need for service (customers who need credit), or other factors. Within the target group, they can identify the more profitable customers, design stronger offers for them, and build better relationships with them. They can propose automatic reordering systems, set up management-training and advising systems, or even sponsor a voluntary chain. They can discourage less profitable customers by requiring larger orders or adding service charges to smaller ones.

## Product Assortment and Services Decision

The wholesaler's "product" is its assortment. Wholesalers are under great pressure to carry a full line and stock enough for immediate delivery. But this practice can damage profits. Wholesalers today are cutting down on the number of lines they carry, choosing to carry only the more profitable ones. Wholesalers are also rethinking which services count most in building strong customer relationships and which should be dropped or charged for. The key is to find the mix of services most valued by their target customers.

## Price Decision

Wholesalers usually mark up the cost of goods by a standard percentage—say, 20 percent. Expenses may run 17 percent of the gross margin, leaving a profit margin of 3 percent. In grocery wholesaling, the average profit margin is often less than 2 percent. Wholesalers are now trying new pricing approaches. They may cut their margin on some lines in order to win important new customers. They may ask suppliers for special price breaks when they can turn them into an increase in the supplier's sales.

## Promotion Decision

Most wholesalers are not promotion-minded. Their use of trade advertising, sales promotion, personal selling, and public relations is largely scattered and unplanned. Many are behind the times in personal selling—they still see selling as a single salesperson talking to a single customer instead of a team effort to sell, build, and service major accounts. And wholesalers also need to adopt some of the nonpersonal promotion techniques used by retailers. They need to develop an overall promotion strategy and to make greater use of supplier promotion materials and programs.

## Place Decision

Wholesalers typically locate in low-rent, low-tax areas and have tended to invest little money in their buildings, equipment, and systems. As a result, their materials-handling and order-processing systems are often out-of-date. In recent years, however, large and progressive wholesalers are reacting to rising costs by investing in automated warehouses and on-line ordering systems. Orders are fed from the retailer's system directly into the wholesaler's computer, and the items are picked up by mechanical devices and automatically taken to a shipping platform where they are assembled. Many wholesalers are turning to computers to carry out accounting, billing, inventory control, and forecasting. Progressive wholesalers are adapting their services to the needs of target customers and finding cost-reducing methods of doing business.

# TRENDS IN WHOLESALING ■

Progressive wholesalers constantly watch for better ways to meet the needs of their suppliers and target customers. They recognize that, in the long run, their only reason for existence comes from increasing the efficiency and effectiveness

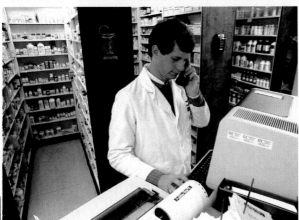

*Drug wholesaler Foremost-McKesson improved efficiency by setting up direct computer links with manufacturers and retail pharmacies.*

of the entire marketing channel. To achieve this aim, they must constantly improve their services and reduce their costs.[23]

Foremost-McKesson, a large drug wholesaler, provides an example of progressive wholesaling. To survive, it had to remain more cost-effective than its manufacturers' sales branches. Thus, the company automated 72 of its warehouses, set up direct computer links with 32 drug manufacturers, designed a computerized accounts-receivable program for pharmacists, and provided drugstores with computer terminals for ordering inventories. Thus, Foremost-McKesson delivered better value to both manufacturers and customers.

One study predicts several developments in the wholesaling industry.[24] Wholesaling companies will grow larger, primarily through acquisition, merger, and geographic expansion. Geographic expansion will require distributors to learn how to compete effectively over wider and more diverse areas. Wholesalers will be helped in this by the increased use of computerized and automated systems; by 1990, over three-fourths of all wholesalers will be using on-line order systems.

The distinction between large retailers and large wholesalers continues to blur. Many retailers now operate formats such as wholesale clubs and hypermarkets that perform many wholesale functions. In return, many large wholesalers are setting up their own retailing operations. Super Valu, Fleming, and Wettrau, all leading wholesalers, now operate their own retail outlets.

Wholesalers will continue to increase the services they provide to retailers—retail pricing, cooperative advertising, marketing- and management-information reports, accounting services, and others. Rising costs on the one hand, and the demand for increased services on the other, will put the squeeze on wholesaler profits. Wholesalers who do not find efficient ways to deliver value to their customers will soon drop by the wayside.

# SUMMARY

Retailing and wholesaling consist of many organizations bringing goods and services from the point of production to the point of use. *Retailing* includes all activities involved in selling goods or services directly to final consumers for their personal, nonbusiness use. Retailers can be classified as store retailers and nonstore retailers. *Store retailers* can be further classified by the *amount of service* they provide (self-service, limited service, or full service); *product line sold* (specialty stores, department stores, supermarkets, convenience stores, combination stores, superstores, hypermarkets, and service businesses); *relative prices* (discount stores, off-price retailers, and catalog showrooms); *control of outlets* (corporate chains, voluntary chains and retailer cooperatives, franchise organizations, and merchandising conglomerates); and *type of store cluster* (central business districts and shopping centers).

Although most goods and services are sold through stores, nonstore retailing has been growing much faster than store retailing. Nonstore retailing now accounts for more than 14 percent of all consumer purchases, and it may account for a third of all sales by the end of the century. It consists of *direct marketing* (direct-mail and catalog retailing, telemarketing, television marketing, and electronic shopping), *door-to-door selling*, and *automatic vending*. Each retailer must make deci-

sions about its target markets, product assortment and services, price, promotion, and place. Retailers need to choose target markets carefully and position themselves strongly.

*Wholesaling* includes all the activities involved in selling goods or services to those who are buying for the purpose of resale or for business use. Wholesalers perform many functions, including selling and promoting, buying and assortment building, bulk-breaking, warehousing, transporting, financing, risk bearing, supplying market information, and providing management services and advice. Wholesalers fall into three groups. *Merchant wholesalers* take possession of the goods. They include *full-service wholesalers* (wholesale merchants, industrial distributors) and *limited-service wholesalers* (cash-and-carry wholesalers, truck wholesalers, drop shippers, rack jobbers, producers' cooperatives, and mail-order wholesalers). *Agents* and *brokers* do not take possession of the goods but are paid a commission for aiding buying and selling. *Manufacturers' sales branches and offices* are wholesaling operations conducted by nonwholesalers to bypass wholesalers. Wholesaling is holding its own in the economy. Progressive wholesalers are adapting their services to the needs of target customers and are seeking cost-reducing methods of doing business.

1. In deciding where to shop, many consumers value quality of service more than such factors as price or convenience. If this trend continues, what impact will it have on full-service retailers? Will it have the same impact on self-service and limited-service retailers?

2. Which would do more to increase a convenience store's sales—an increase in the length or the breadth of its product assortment?

3. Off-price retailers provide tough price competition for other retailers. Will large retailers' growing power in distribution channels affect manufacturers' willingness to sell to off-price retailers below regular wholesale rates? For example, what policy should Sony adopt in selling to off-price retailers?

4. Postal rate hikes make it more expensive to send direct mail, catalogs, and purchased products to consumers. How are direct-mail and catalog marketers likely to respond to an increase in postage rates?

5. Which retailing innovations can be explained by the wheel-of-retailing concept? Will retailing operations continue to evolve as described by this concept?

6. A typical "country store" in a farming community sells a variety of food and nonfood items—snacks, staples, hardware, and many other types of goods. From what kinds of wholesalers do such stores obtain their products? Are they the same suppliers that a supermarket uses?

7. How would a small producer of lawn and garden tools prefer to sell its output—through a manufacturers' agent or through a selling agent?

8. When it comes to marketing decisions, are there any fundamental differences among retailers, wholesalers, and manufacturers? Give examples of the marketing decisions made by these three groups, showing key similarities and differences.

9. Why has the promotion area of marketing strategy traditionally been weak for wholesalers? How can they use promotion to improve competitive positions?

10. As the distinction between large retailers and large wholesalers becomes blurred, which strategy is likely to be more common—retailers dealing directly with manufacturers rather than through wholesalers or wholesalers setting up their own retailing operations?

# REFERENCES

1. The Quotation is from Steve Weiner, "With Big Selection and Low Prices, 'Category Killer' Stores Are a Hit," *The Wall Street Journal,* June 17, 1986, p. 33. Also see Eleanor Johnson Tracy, "Shopping Swedish-Style Comes to the U.S.," *Fortune,* January 20, 1986, p. 63; Carolyn Pfaff, "IKEA: The Supermarket of Furniture Stores," *Adweek,* May 5, 1986, pp. MM26–28; and Bill Kelley, "The New Wave from Europe," *Sales & Marketing Management,* November 1987, pp. 45–50.

2. For more on department stores, see Arthur Bragg, "Will Department Stores Survive?" *Sales & Marketing Management,* April 1986, pp. 60-64; and Anthony Ramirez, "Department Stores Shape Up," *Fortune,* September 1, 1986, pp. 50–52.

3. Julie Liesse Erickson, "Supermarket Chains Work to Fill Tall Order," *Advertising Age,* April 28, 1986, pp. S1-S2.

4. See Denise Frenner, "From Piano to Sushi Bars, Grocers Jazz Up Service," *Advertising Age,* May 4,

1987, p. S1; John Schwartz, "Super-Duper Supermarkets," *Newsweek,* June 27, 1988, pp. 40–41; and Ruth Hamel, "Food Fight," *American Demographics,* March 1989, pp.36–41.

5. See Teresa Carson, "Karl Eller's Big Thirst for Convenience Stores," *Business Week,* June 13, 1988, pp. 86–87.

6. See Mary McCabe English, "Competition Gains Ground," *Advertising Age,* April 18, 1985, p. 17; and Cynthia Valentino, "In a Fragmented Market, Grocers Cover Niches," *Advertising Age,* May 4, 1987, p. S8.

7. See "How Much Hype in Hypermarkets?" *Sales & Marketing Management,* April 1988, pp. 56–63; "Talk about Hype," *Advertising Age,* May 9, 1988, p. S26; and Todd Mason, "The Return of the Amazing Colossal Store," *Business Week,* August 22, 1988, pp. 59–61.

8. See Lois Therrien and Amy Dunkin, "The Wholesale Success of Factory Outlet Malls," *Business Week,*

February 3, 1986, pp. 92–94; and Jay A. Wedeven, "Factory-Outlet Retailers Find There's Strength in Numbers," *Marketing News,* April 25, 1988, pp. 7, 26.

9. See Amy Dunkin, Todd Mason, Lois Therrien, and Teresa Carson, "Boom Times in a Bargain Hunter's Paradise," *Business Week,* March 11, 1985, p. 116; Janice Steinberg, "Wholesale Clubs Add Some Bulk," *Advertising Age,* May 9, 1988, p. S24; and Andrew Kupfer, "The Final Word in No-Frills Shopping," *Fortune,* March 13, 1989, p. 30.

10. See Jack G. Kaikati, "Don't Discount Off-Price Retailers," *Harvard Business Review,* May-June 1985, pp. 85–92; and "Off-Pricers Grab Growing Retail Market Share," *Marketing News,* March 13, 1987, pp. 9, 14.

11. See Richard Green, "A Boutique in Your Living Room," *Forbes,* May 7, 1984, pp. 86–94.

12. See "Direct Marketing—What Is It?" *Direct Marketing,* May 1988, p. 32.

13. See Eileen Norris, "Alternative Media Try to Get Their Feet in the Door," *Advertising Age,* October 17, 1985, p. 15.

14. Arnold Fishman, "The 1986 Mail Order Guide," *Direct Marketing,* July 1987, p. 40.

15. Janice Steinberg, "Cacophony of Catalogs Fill All Niches," *Advertising Age,* October 26, 1987, pp. S1–2; and Ed Fitch, "Election-Year Frenzy Bane of Catalogers," *Advertising Age,* August 1, 1988, p. S2.

16. Elaine Santoro, "Royal Silk Shines," *Direct Marketing,* April 1987, p. 53. Also see Carol Boyd Leon, "Selling through VCR," *American Demographics,* December 1987, pp. 40–47; and Judith Graham, "Neiman-Marcus Tries Video Catalog," *Advertising Age,* March 21, 1988, p. 68.

17. Rudy Oetting, "Telephone Marketing: Where We've Been and Where We Should Be Going," *Direct Marketing,* February 1987, p. 98.

18. Jim Auchmute, "But Wait There's More!" *Advertising Age,* October 17, 1985, p. 18.

19. See Arthur Bragg, "TV's Shopping Shows: Your Next Move?" *Sales & Marketing Management,* October 1987, pp. 85–89; and Mary J. Pitzer, "A Bargain Basement Where the TV Reception Is Great," *Business Week,* May 30, 1988, p. 79.

20. See Bill Saporito, "Are IBM and Sears Crazy? Or Canny?" *Fortune,* September 28, 1987, pp. 74–80; Laura Loro, "Videotex Ventures," *Advertising Age,* May 9, 1988, p. S78; and Alison Fahey, "Prodigy Videotex Expands Its Reach," *Advertising Age,* April 24, 1989, p. 75.

21. For more on retail site location, see Lewis A. Spaulding, "Beating the Bushes for New Store Locations," *Stores,* October 1980, pp. 30–35; R. L. Davies and D. S. Rogers, eds., *Store Location and Store Assessment Research* (New York: John Wiley, 1984); and Avijit Ghosh and C. Samuel Craig, "An Approach to Determining Optimal Locations for New Services," *Journal of Marketing Research,* November 1986, pp. 354–62.

22. See Malcolm P. McNair and Eleanor G. May, "The Next Revolution of the Retailing Wheel," *Harvard Business Review,* September-October 1978, pp. 81–91.

23. See James A. Narus and James C. Anderson, "Contributing as a Distributor to Partnerships with Manufacturers," *Business Horizons,* September-October 1987.

24. See Arthur Andersen & Co., *Future Trends in Wholesale Distribution: A Time of Opportunity* (Washington, DC: Distribution Research and Education Foundation, 1982), pp. 96–101. Also see Madhav Kacker, "Wholesaling Ignored Despite Modernization," *Marketing News,* February 14, 1986, p. 35; and Joseph Weber, "Mom and Pop Move Out of Wholesaling," *Business Week,* January 9, 1989, p. 91.

## HOLLY FARMS: PUTTING THE CHICKEN BEFORE THE EGG

Holly Farms Corporation thought it had created the Cadillac of poultry with its roasted chicken. The fresh, fully cooked bird seemed just the ticket for today's busy consumers: a modern, more convenient alternative to raw chicken. It scored big in a year of test marketing.

The company began phasing in national distribution of the product in the fall of 1987. But it fared so dismally that the planned expansion into more markets was halted so that Holly Farms could reconsider its marketing strategy.

Company executives acknowledge that the "false start" for the roasted-chicken product hurt fiscal 1988 earnings. One analyst, Bonnie Rivers of Salomon Brothers, Inc., cites the blunder as a major reason she slashed her estimate for Holly Farms' profit for the year ending May 31, 1988, by 22 percent—$2.25 a share from $2.90. Higher feed and persistently low chicken prices also contributed to the lower profit projection. In fiscal 1987, the Memphis, Tennessee-based poultry and food concern had earned $71.7 million, or $4.31 a share, on revenue of $1.42 billion. Grocers are buying far less of the product than Holly Farms had hoped, he says, because they believe it does not last long enough on the shelf. Until this problem could be solved, Holly Farms decided not to expand distribution of the chicken, now available in about 50 percent of the markets nationwide.

Holly Farms' experience is a classic example of how a food company can stumble in launching a new product. Although extensive test marketing identified strong consumer support for the product (22 percent of Atlanta women surveyed said they had tried it, and of those, 90 percent said they would buy it again,) the company failed to detect the concerns and resistance of its front-line customer—the retailer.

Several retailers concur that the problem was not with the roasted chicken itself. Ray Heatherington, meat merchandising manager for Safeway

Stores, Inc.'s Northern California division, calls the product "outstanding." But his stores dropped it after several weeks because of its short shelf life.

Grocers bought far less of the product than Holly Farms had hoped because they felt it did not last long enough on the shelf. According to Holly Farms, the chicken's quality is maintained for a good 18 days. To be safe, it marked the last day sale date of 14 days after the chicken was roasted. However, it can take as long as 9 days to get the chicken to stores from the North Carolina plant Holly Farms built especially to house its fully cooked operation. That delivery time does not give grocers much lead time. To avoid being stuck with an outdated backlog, many wait until they run out before reordering.

In the case of raw chicken, shelf life is not a major factor because the product's high volume means it is sold in the first few days after delivery and grocers know from experience how much to stock.

A general suspicion of new products also probably hurt the effort. "It's a hard sell to get into the supermarket, particularly if you've got a new product that the consumers and retailers haven't seen before," says Joe Scheringer, an editor at *Grocery Marketing* magazine, and the meat department is probably the most resistant to change.

Some competitors believe Holly Farms did not do enough preliminary groundwork with retailers. Holly Farms has acknowledged that it probably did not go far enough to tailor its marketing program to each supermarket chain or spend sufficient time educating meat managers.

But the company has mended fences. "Before mounting a successful relaunch, we had to take a second look at all elements involved with this new product introduction, from production to distribution to the marketing mix," says John W. Bartelme, the new vice president of marketing for Holly Farms. The company improved its packaging system

and doubled shelf life. To shorten delivery time, Holly Farms installed a new inventory and distribution system.

After months of additional market research, which included consumer focus group testing, Holly Farms relaunched the roasted chicken in June 1988 with a new name, new packaging, and a new marketing program.

The company shifted a hefty portion of its marketing budget out of television and radio and into the grocery store in the form of promotions, coupons, in-store sampling, and contests for meat managers. Nearly two-thirds of Holly Farms' roughly $14 million in a half year's marketing expenditures for the product initially went to media advertising; spending has been reduced significantly and reallocated to other parts of the marketing mix to obtain a more effective program. This strategy has resulted in a doubling of sales for the time between June 1988 and January 1989.

Holly Farms believes that this time out, its roasted-chicken will be a blockbuster. So does Salomon Brothers' Ms. Rivers, who says, "I definitely agree with what they're doing and why they're doing it."

*Questions*

1. What criteria are used by consumers when buying a roasted chicken product? Compare those criteria to the criteria used by a retailer when deciding to stock a roasted chicken product.

2. What could Holly Farms have done prior to introducing its product to avoid its marketing blunder?

3. To overcome the problem with the grocers, what changes would you have recommended in Holly Farm's marketing strategy?

*Source:* Adapted from Arthur Buckler, "Holly Farms' Marketing Error: The Chicken That Laid An Egg," *The Wall Street Journal,* February 9, 1988. Reprinted by permission of *The Wall Street Journal,* © Dow Jones & Company, Inc., 1988. All rights reserved.

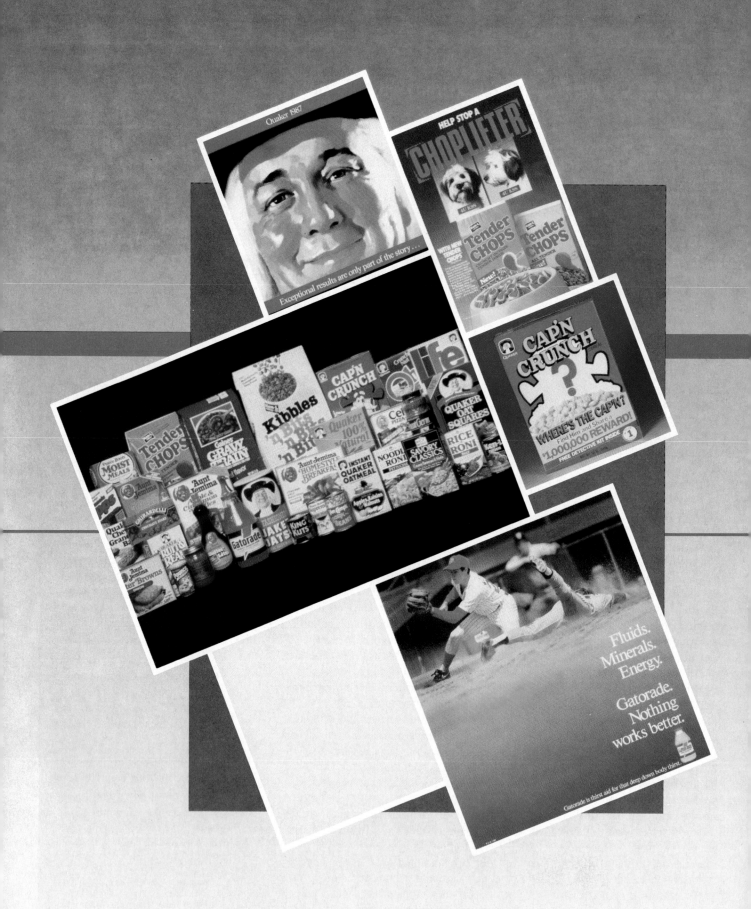

# 15

# Promoting Products: Communications and Promotion Strategy

## CHAPTER OBJECTIVES

After reading this chapter, you should be able to

1. Name and define the four tools of the promotion mix
2. Discuss the elements of the marketing communication process
3. Explain the methods for setting the promotion budget
4. Discuss the factors that affect the design of the promotion mix

Most Quaker Oats brands have become staples in American pantries. Quaker dominates the hot cereal market with a whopping 68-percent share, and its Aunt Jemima brand is tops in frozen breakfast products and pancake mixes. Quaker captures 25 percent of the huge pet food market (Gravy Train, Gainesburgers, Cycle, Ken-L Ration, Kibbles 'n Bits). Moreover, it's the number-four ready-to-eat cereal producer (Cap'n Crunch, Life, Oh!s, 100% Natural). Other leading Quaker brands include Gatorade, Van Camp's Pork and Beans, Granola Bars, and Rice-A-Roni. In all, brands with leading market shares account for over 60 percent of Quaker's nearly $4 billion in yearly sales.

A company the size of Quaker has lots to say to its many publics and several promotion tools with which to communicate what it has to say. Hundreds of Quaker employees work in advertising, personal selling, sales promotion, and publicity units around the company. A half dozen large advertising and public relations agencies aim carefully planned communications to consumers, retailers, the media, stockholders, employees, and other publics.

As consumers, we know a good deal about Quaker's advertising: Each year, Quaker bombards us with about $250 million worth of advertising telling us about its brands and persuading us to buy them. Quaker also spends heavily on consumer sales promotions such as coupons, premiums, and sweepstakes to coax us further. You may remember the "Treasure Hunt" promotion in which Quaker gave away $5 million in silver and gold coins randomly inserted in Ken-L Ration packages. Then there was the "Where's the Cap'n?" promotion: Quaker removed the picture of Cap'n Horatio Crunch from the front of its cereal boxes and then provided clues to his location on the back. Consumers who used the clues to find the Cap'n could win cash prizes. The 14-week promotion cost Quaker $18 million but increased sales by 50 percent. Consumer advertising and sales promotions work directly to create consumer demand, and this demand "pulls" Quaker products through its channel.

But consumer advertising and sales promotions account for only a small portion of Quaker's total promotion mix. The company spends many times as much on behind-the-scenes promotion activities that "push" its products toward consumers. Personal selling and trade promotions are major weapons in Quaker's battle for retailer support. The company's main objective is shelf space in over 300,000 supermarkets, convenience stores, and corner groceries across the country. Quaker's army of salespeople court retailers with strong service, trade allowances, attractive displays, and other trade promotions. They urge retailers to give Quaker products more and better shelf space and to run ads featuring Quaker brands. These push-promotion activities work closely with pull-promotion efforts to build sales and market share. The pull activities persuade consumers to look for Quaker brands; the push activities ensure that Quaker products are available, easy to find, and effectively merchandised when consumers start looking.

In addition to advertising, sales promotion, and personal selling, Quaker communicates through publicity and public relations. The company's publicity department and public relations agency place newsworthy information about Quaker and its products in the news media. They prepare annual reports to communicate with investor and financial publics and hold press conferences to communicate with media publics. Quaker sponsors many public relations activities to promote the company as a good citizen. For example, the Quaker Oats Foundation donates millions of dollars in cash and products each year to worthy causes, matches employee donations to nonprofit organizations, donates food to needy people, and supports a network of centers providing therapy for families with handicapped children.

Quaker owes much of its success to quality products that appeal strongly to millions of consumers around the world. But success also depends on Quaker's skill in telling its publics about the company and its products. All of Quaker's promotion tools—advertising, personal selling, sales promotion, and public relations—must blend harmoniously into an effective communication program to tell the Quaker story.[1]

**promotion mix** The specific mix of advertising, personal selling, sales promotion, and public relations that a company uses to pursue its advertising and marketing objectives.

Modern marketing calls for more than developing a good product, pricing it attractively, and making it available to target customers. Companies must also *communicate* with their customers. And what is communicated should not be left to chance.

To communicate well, companies often hire advertising agencies to develop effective ads, sales-promotion specialists to design sales-incentive programs, and public relations firms to develop corporate images. They train their salespeople to be friendly, helpful, and persuasive. For most companies, the question is not *whether* to communicate, but *how much to spend* and *in what ways*.

A modern company manages a complex marketing-communications system (see Figure 15–1). The company communicates with its middlemen, consumers, and various publics. Its middlemen communicate with their consumers and publics. Consumers have word-of-mouth communication with each other and with other publics. Meanwhile, each group provides feedback to every other group.

A company's total marketing communications program—called its **promotion mix**—consists of the specific blend of advertising, sales promotion, public relations, and personal selling, that the company uses to pursue its

FIGURE 15–1  The Marketing-Communications System

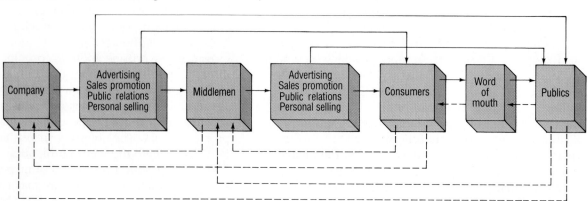

advertising and marketing objectives. The four major promotion tools are defined below:

□ **Advertising:** Any paid form of nonpersonal presentation and promotion of ideas, goods, or services by an identified sponsor.

□ **Sales promotion:** Short-term incentives to encourage purchase or sales of a product or service.

□ **Public relations:** Building good relations with the company's various publics by obtaining favorable publicity, building a good "corporate image," and handling or heading off unfavorable rumors, stories, and events.

□ **Personal selling:** Oral presentation in a conversation with one or more prospective purchasers for the purpose of making sales.[2]

Within these categories are specific tools such as sales presentations, point-of-purchase displays, specialty advertising, trade shows, fairs, demonstrations, catalogs, literature, press kits, posters, contests, premiums, coupons, and trading stamps. At the same time, communication goes beyond these specific promotion tools. The product's design, its price, the shape and color of its package, and the stores that sell it *all* communicate something to buyers. Thus, although the promotion mix is the company's primary communication activity, the entire marketing mix—promotion *and* product, price, and place—must be coordinated for greatest communication impact.

This chapter looks at two questions: *What are the major steps in developing effective marketing communication? How should the promotion budget and mix be determined?* Chapter 16 will look at mass-communication tools—advertising, sales promotion, and public relations. Chapter 17 will look at the salesforce as a communication and promotion tool.

**advertising** Any paid form of nonpersonal presentation and promotion of ideas, goods, or services by an identified sponsor.

**sales promotion** Short-term incentives to encourage purchase or sales of a product or service.

**public relations** Building good relations with the company's various publics by obtaining favorable publicity, building a good "corporate image," and handling or heading off unfavorable rumors, stories, and events.

**personal selling** Oral presentation in a conversation with one or more prospective purchasers for the purpose of making sales.

# STEPS IN DEVELOPING EFFECTIVE COMMUNICATION

Marketers need to understand how communication works. Communication involves the nine elements shown in Figure 15–2. Two elements are the major parties in a communication—*sender* and *receiver*. Another two are the major communication tools—*message* and *media*. Four are major communication functions—*encoding, decoding, response,* and *feedback*. The last element is *noise*

**FIGURE 15–2** Elements in the Communication Process

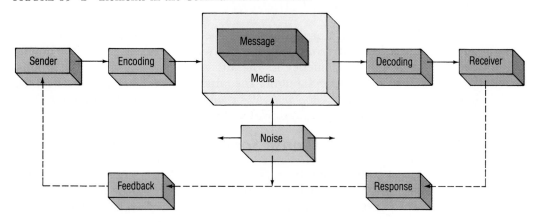

in the system. These elements are defined below and applied to a McDonald's television ad:

- □ *Sender:* The *party sending the message* to another party—McDonald's
- □ *Encoding:* The process of *putting thought into symbolic form*—McDonald's advertising agency assembles words and illustrations into an advertisement that will convey the intended message
- □ *Message:* The *set of symbols* that the sender transmits—the actual McDonald's advertisement
- □ *Media:* The *communication channels* through which the message moves from sender to receiver—in this case, television and the specific television programs McDonald's selects
- □ *Decoding:* The process by which the receiver *assigns meaning to the symbols* encoded by the sender—a consumer watches the ad and interprets the words and illustrations it contains
- □ *Receiver:* The *party receiving the message* sent by another party—the consumer who watches the McDonald's ad
- □ *Response:* The *reactions of the receiver* after being exposed to the message—any of hundreds of possible responses, such as the consumer likes McDonald's better, is more likely to eat at McDonald's next time he or she eats fast food, or does nothing
- □ *Feedback:* The part of the *receiver's response communicated back to the sender*—McDonald's research shows that consumers like and remember the ad or consumers write or call McDonald's praising or criticizing the ad or McDonald's products
- □ *Noise:* The *unplanned static or distortion* during the communication process that results in the receiver's getting a different message than the sender sent—the consumer has poor TV reception or is distracted by family members while watching the ad

This model points out the key factors in good communication. Senders need to know what audiences they want to reach and what responses they want. They must be good at encoding messages that take into account how the target audience decodes them. They must send the message through media that reach target audiences. And they must develop feedback channels so that they can assess the audience's response to the message.

Thus, the marketing communicator must make the following decisions: (1) identify the target audience, (2) determine the response sought, (3) choose a message, (4) choose the media through which to send the message, (5) select the message source, and (6) collect feedback. We will now discuss each of these communications decisions.

## Identifying the Target Audience

A marketing communicator starts with a clear target audience in mind. The audience may be potential buyers or current users, those who make the buying decision or those who influence it. The audience may be individuals, groups, special publics, or the general public. The target audience will heavily affect the communicator's decisions on *what* will be said, *how* it will be said, *when* it will be said, *where* it will be said, and *who* will say it.

## Determining the Response Sought

Once the target audience has been defined, the marketing communicator must decide what response is sought. Of course, the final response is *purchase.* But purchase is the result of a long process of consumer decision making. The marketing communicator needs to know where the target audience now stands and to what state it needs to be moved.

The target audience may be in any of six **buyer-readiness states**— *awareness, knowledge, liking, preference, conviction,* or *purchase*. These states are shown in Figure 15–3 and discussed below.

### Awareness

The communicator must first know how aware the target audience is of the product or organization. The audience may be totally unaware of it, know only its name, or know one or a few things about it. If most of the target audience is unaware, the communicator tries to build awareness—perhaps starting with just name recognition. This process can begin with simple messages repeating the name. Even then, building awareness takes time. Suppose a small Iowa college called Pottsville seeks applicants from Nebraska but has no name recognition in Nebraska. And suppose there are 30,000 high school seniors in Nebraska who may potentially be interested in Pottsville College. The college might set the objective of making 70 percent of these students aware of Pottsville's name within one year.

### Knowledge

The target audience might have company or product awareness but not know much more. Pottsville may want its target audience to know that it is a private four-year college with excellent programs in English and the language arts. Pottsville College thus needs to learn how many people in its target audience have little, some, or much knowledge about Pottsville. The college may then decide to select product knowledge as its first communication objective.

### Liking

If target audience members *know* the product, how do they *feel* about it? We can develop a scale covering degrees of liking—including dislike very much, dislike somewhat, indifferent, like somewhat, and like very much. If the audience looks unfavorably on Pottsville College, the communicator has to find out why and then develop a communications campaign to shore up favorable feelings. If the unfavorable view is based on real problems of the college, then communications alone cannot do the job. Pottsville will have to fix its problems and then communicate its renewed quality. Good public relations call for "good deeds followed by good words."

### Preference

The target audience might *like* the product but not *prefer* it to others. In this case, the communicator must try to build consumer preference. The communicator will promote the product's quality, value, performance, and other

FIGURE 15–3  Buyer-Readiness States

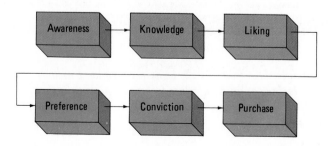

features. The communicator can check on the campaign's success by measuring audience preferences again after the campaign. If Pottsville College finds that many high school seniors like Pottsville but choose to attend other colleges, it will have to identify those areas where its offerings are better than those of competing colleges. It must then promote its advantages to build preference among prospective students.

### Conviction

A target audience might *prefer* the product but not develop a *conviction* about buying it. Thus, some high school seniors may prefer Pottsville but may not be sure they want to go to college. The communicator's job is to build conviction that going to college is the right thing to do.

### Purchase

Finally, some members of the target audience might have *conviction* but not quite get around to making the *purchase*. They may wait for more information

*Buyer readiness states: with this ad, Johnson & Johnson tries to create awareness, knowledge, and preference for its new Acuvue disposable lens. It hopes that eyecare professionals will then move consumers through the final stages toward purchase.*

or plan to act later. The communicator must lead these consumers to take the final step. Actions might include offering the product at a low price, offering a premium, or letting consumers try it on a limited basis. Thus, Pottsville might invite selected high school students to visit the campus and attend some classes. Or it might offer scholarships to deserving students.

Buyer-readiness states are important to the marketing communicator. Buyers normally pass through these stages on their way to purchase. The communicator's task is to identify the stage that most consumers are in and develop a communication campaign that will move them to the next one.

**rational appeals** Message appeals that relate to the audience's self-interest and show that the product will produce the claimed benefits.

## Choosing a Message

Having defined the desired audience response, the communicator turns to developing an effective message. Ideally, the message should get *Attention,* hold *Interest,* arouse *Desire,* and obtain *Action* (a framework known as the *AIDA model)*. In practice, few messages take the consumer all the way from awareness to purchase, but the AIDA framework does suggest the desirable qualities of a good message.

In putting the message together, the marketing communicator must solve three problems: what to say *(message content),* how to say it logically *(message structure),* and how to say it symbolically *(message format)*.

### Message Content

The communicator has to figure out an appeal or theme that will produce the desired response. There are three types of appeals. **Rational appeals** relate to the audience's self-interest. They show that the product will produce the desired benefits. Examples are messages showing a product's quality, economy, value, or performance. Thus, in ads for its Excel car, Hyundai offers "cars that make sense," stressing low price, operating economy, and sensible features. When

*A mild fear appeal: "When you get a cavity, there's no second chance."*

**emotional appeals** Message appeals that attempt to stir up negative or positive emotions that will motivate purchase.

**moral appeals** Message appeals that are directed to the audience's sense of what is right and proper.

pitching computer systems to business users, IBM salespeople talk about quality, performance, reliability, and improved productivity.

**Emotional appeals** attempt to stir up either negative or positive emotions that can motivate purchase. These include fear, guilt, and shame appeals that get people to do things they should (brush their teeth, buy new tires) or stop doing things they shouldn't (smoke, drink too much, overeat). For example, a recent Crest ad invoked mild fear when it claimed, "There are some things you just can't afford to gamble with" (cavities). So did Michelin tire ads that featured cute babies and suggested, "Because so much is riding on your tires." Communicators also use positive emotional appeals such as love, humor, pride, and joy. Thus AT&T's long-running ad theme, "Reach out and touch someone," stirs a bundle of strong emotions.

**Moral appeals** are directed to the audience's sense of what is right and proper. They are often used to urge people to support such social causes as a cleaner environment, better race relations, equal rights for women, and aid to the needy. An example is the March of Dimes appeal: "God made you whole. Give to help those He didn't."

### Message Structure

The communicator also has to decide how to handle three message-structure issues. The first is whether to draw a conclusion or leave it to the audience. Early research showed that drawing a conclusion was usually more effective. More recent research, however, suggests that in many cases, the advertiser is better off asking questions and letting buyers come to their own conclusions. The second message-structure issue is whether to present a one-sided or a two-sided argument. Usually, a one-sided argument is more effective in sales presentations—except when audiences are highly educated and negatively disposed. The third message-structure issue is whether to present the strongest arguments first or last. Presenting them first gets strong attention but may lead to an anticlimactic ending.[3]

### Message Format

The communicator also needs a strong *format* for the message. In a print ad, the communicator has to decide on the headline, copy, illustration, and color. To attract attention, advertisers can use novelty and contrast, eye-catching pictures and headlines, distinctive formats, message size and position, and color, shape, and movement. If the message is to be carried over the radio, the communicator has to choose words, sounds, and voices. The "sound" of an announcer promoting a used car should be different from one promoting quality furniture.

If the message is to be carried on television or in person, then all these elements plus body language have to be planned. Presenters plan their facial expressions, gestures, dress, posture, and hair style. If the message is carried on the product or its package, the communicator has to plan texture, scent, color, size, and shape. For example, color plays a major communication role in food preferences. When consumers sampled four cups of coffee that had been placed next to brown, blue, red, and yellow containers (all the coffee was identical, but the consumers did not know this), 75 percent felt that the coffee next to the brown container tasted too strong; nearly 85 percent judged the coffee next to the red container to be the richest; nearly everyone felt that the coffee next to the blue container was mild; and the coffee next to the yellow container was seen as weak. Thus, if a coffee company wants to communicate that its coffee is rich, it should probably use a red container along with label copy boasting the coffee's rich taste.

# Choosing Media

The communicator must now select *channels of communication*. There are two broad types of communication channels—*personal* and *nonpersonal*.

## Personal Communication Channels

In **personal communication channels,** two or more people communicate directly with each other. They might communicate face-to-face, person-to-audience, over the telephone, or even through the mail. Personal communication channels are effective because they allow for personal addressing and feedback.

Some personal communication channels are directly controlled by the communicator. For example, company salespeople contact buyers in the target market. But other personal communications about the product may reach buyers through channels not directly controlled by the company. These might include independent experts making statements to target buyers—consumer advocates, consumer buying guides, and others. Or they might be neighbors, friends, family members, and associates talking to target buyers. This last channel, known as **word-of-mouth influence,** has considerable effect in many product areas.

Personal influence carries great weight for products that are expensive, risky, or highly visible. For example, buyers of automobiles and major appliances often go beyond mass-media sources to seek the opinions of knowledgeable people.

Companies can take several steps to put personal communication channels to work for them. They can devote extra effort to selling their products to well-known people or companies, who may in turn influence others to buy. They can create *opinion leaders*—people whose opinions are sought by others—by supplying certain people with the product on attractive terms. For example, companies can work through community members such as disc jockeys, class presidents, and presidents of local organizations. And they can use influential people in their advertisements or develop advertising that has high "conversation value."

## Nonpersonal Communication Channels

**Nonpersonal communication channels** are media that carry messages without personal contact or feedback. They include mass and selective media, atmospheres, and events. **Mass and selective media** consist of print media (newspapers, magazines, direct mail), broadcast media (radio, television), and display media (billboards, signs, posters). Mass media are aimed at large, often unsegmented audiences; selective media are aimed at smaller, selected audiences. **Atmospheres** are designed environments that create or reinforce the buyer's leanings toward buying a product. Thus, lawyers' offices and banks are designed to communicate confidence and other things that might be valued by clients. **Events** are occurrences staged to communicate messages to target audiences. Public relations departments arrange press conferences, grand openings, public tours, and other events to communicate with specific audiences.

Nonpersonal communication affects buyers directly. In addition, using mass media often affects buyers indirectly by causing more personal communication. Mass communications affect attitudes and behavior through a *two-step-flow-of-communication process*. In this process, communications first flow from television, magazines, and other mass media to opinion leaders and then from these to the less active sections of the population.[4] This two-step-flow process means the effect of mass media is not as direct, powerful, and automatic as once

**personal communication channels** Channels through which two or more people communicate directly with each other, including face-to-face, person-to-audience, over the telephone, or through the mail.

**word-of-mouth influence** Personal communication about a product between target buyers and neighbors, friends, family members, and associates.

**nonpersonal communication channels** Media that carry messages without personal contact or feedback, including mass and selective media, atmospheres, and events.

**mass and selective media** Print media, broadcast media, and display media aimed at large, unsegmented audiences (mass media) or at selected audiences (selective media).

**atmospheres** Designed environments that create or reinforce the buyer's leanings toward consumption of a product.

**events** Occurrences staged to communicate messages to target audiences, such as news conferences and grand openings.

supposed. Rather, opinion leaders step between the mass media and their audiences. Opinion leaders are more exposed to mass media, and they carry messages to people who are less exposed to media.

The two-step-flow concept challenges the notion that people's buying is affected by a "trickle-down" of opinions and information from higher social classes. Because people mostly interact with others in their own social class, they pick up their fashion and other ideas from people *like themselves* who are opinion leaders. The two-step-flow concept also suggests that mass communicators should aim their messages directly at opinion leaders, letting them carry the message to others.

## Selecting the Message Source

The message's impact on the audience is also affected by how the audience views the sender. Messages delivered by highly credible sources are more persuasive. For example, pharmaceutical companies want doctors to tell about their products' benefits because doctors are very credible figures. Many food companies are now promoting to doctors, dentists, and other health-care providers to motivate these professionals to recommend their products to patients (see Marketing Highlight 15–1). Marketers also hire well-known actors and athletes to deliver their messages. Bill Cosby speaks for Jell-O, Michael J. Fox tells us about Pepsi, and basketball star Michael Jordan soars for Nike.[5]

But what factors make a source credible? The three factors most often found are expertise, trustworthiness, and likability. *Expertise* is the degree to which the communicator appears to have the *authority* needed to back the claim. Doctors, scientists, and professors rank high on expertise in their fields. *Trustworthiness* is related to how *objective and honest* the source appears to be. Friends, for example, are tursted more than salespeople. *Likability* is how *attractive* the source is to the audience; people like sources who are open, humorous, and natural. Not surprisingly, the most highly credible source is a person scoring high on all three factors—expertise, trustworthiness, and likability.

*Celebrities impart some of their own likability and trustworthiness to the products they endorse.*

## PROMOTING PRODUCTS THROUGH DOCTORS AND OTHER PROFESSIONALS

Food marketers are discovering that the best way to a consumer's stomach may be through a doctor's recommendation. Facing a deluge of health claims being made for different food products, today's more nutrition-conscious consumers often seek advice from doctors and other health-care professionals about which products are best for them. Kellogg, Procter & Gamble, Quaker, and other large food companies are increasingly recognizing what pharmaceutical companies have known for years—professional recommendations can strongly influence consumer-buying decisions. So they are stepping up promotion to doctors, dentists, and others, hoping to inform them about product benefits and motivate them to recommend the promoted brands to their patients.

Doctors receive the most attention from food marketers. For example, Cumberland Packing runs ads in medical journals for its Sweet 'N Low sugar substitute, saying, "It's one thing you can do to make your patient's diet a little easier to swallow." And Kellogg launched its "Project Nutrition" promotion to sell doctors on the merits of eating high-fiber cereal breakfasts. The promotion consists of cholesterol screenings of 100,000 Americans around the country, ads

targeting doctors in the *Journal of the American Medical Association* and the *New England Journal of Medicine,* and a new quarterly newsletter called *Health Vantage* mailed to 50,000 U.S. medical professionals. Similarly, Quaker sends out a quarterly newsletter, *Fiber Report,* to doctors nationwide; it includes articles, research reports, and feature stories about the importance of fiber in diets.

Procter & Gamble provides literature about several of its products that doctors can pass along to patients. One booklet for Citrus Hill Calcium Plus orange juice even contains a 20-cents-off coupon. And P&G actively seeks medical endorsements. Years ago, a heavily promoted American Dental Association endorsement helped make P&G's Crest the leading toothpaste brand. The company hopes that an endorsement obtained from the American Medical Women's Association will give a similar boost to its Citrus Hill calcium-fortified fruit juices.

Other professionals targeted by food companies include dentists, veterinarians, teachers, and even high school coaches. The makers of Trident gum, Equal sugar substitute, Plax mouth rinse, and dozens of other products reach dentists through colorful brochures, samples, and ads in dental journals. Quaker does extensive product sampling of its Gaines and Ken-L

Ration pet foods through veterinarians. Quaker also runs ads for Gatorade in magazines read by high school sports trainers and coaches; it sponsors a fleet of vans that comb the country, offering Gatorade information and samples in key markets. Thus, food companies actively court as spokespeople any professionals who provide health or nutrition advice to their customers.

Many doctors and other health-care providers welcome the promotions as good sources of information about healthy foods and nutrition that can help them give better advice to their patients. Others, however, do not feel comfortable recommending specific food brands; some even resent attempts to influence them through promotion. It will take a lot of time and investment to get these professionals to change their habits. But the results will be worth the effort and expense. If a company can convince key health-care providers that the product is worthy of endorsement, it will gain powerful marketing allies. As one marketer puts it, "If a doctor hands you a product to use, that recommendation carries a lot of weight."

*Sources:* See Laurie Freeman and Liesse Erickson, "Doctored Strategy: Food Marketers Push Products through Physicians," *Advertising Age,* March 28, 1988, p. 12.

## Collecting Feedback

After sending the message, the communicator must research its effect on the target audience. This involves asking the target audience whether they remember the message, how many times they saw it, what points they recall, how they felt about the message, and their past and present attitudes toward the product and company. The communicator would also like to measure behavior resulting from the message—how many people bought a product, talked to others about it, or visited the store.

Figure 15–4 shows an example of feedback measurement. Looking at Brand A, we find that 80 percent of the total market is aware of it, that 60 percent of those aware of it have tried it, but that only 20 percent of those who tried it were satisfied. These results suggest that although the communication program

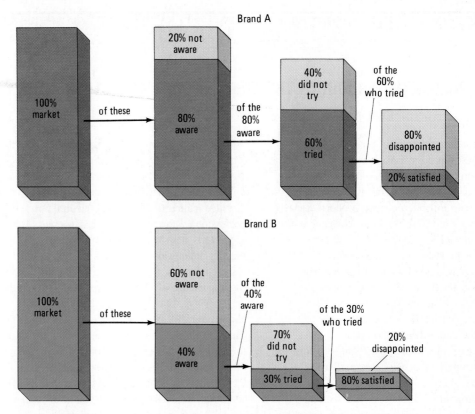

FIGURE 15-4  Current Consumer States for Two Brands

is creating *awareness*, the product fails to give consumers the *satisfaction* they expect. The company should therefore try to improve the product while staying with the successful communication program. On the other hand, we find that only 40 percent of the total market is aware of Brand B, that only 30 percent of those have tried it, but that 80 percent of those who tried it were satisfied. In this case, the communication program needs to be stronger to take advantage of the brand's power to obtain satisfaction.

# SETTING THE TOTAL PROMOTION BUDGET AND MIX

We have looked at the steps in planning and sending communications to a target audience. But how does a company decide on the total *promotion budget* and its division among the major promotional tools to create the *promotion mix?* We will now look at these questions.

## Setting the Total Promotion Budget

One of the hardest marketing decisions facing companies is how much to spend on promotion. John Wanamaker, the department store magnate, once said: "I know that half of my advertising is wasted, but I don't know which half. I spent $2 million for advertising, and I don't know if that is half enough or twice too much." Thus, it is not surprising that industries and companies vary widely in how much they spend on promotion. Promotion spending may be 20 to 30 percent of sales in the cosmetics industry and only 5 to 10 percent in the industrial machinery industry. Within a given industry, both low- and high-spending companies can be found.

How do companies decide on their promotion budget? We will look at four common methods used to set the total budget for advertising: the *affordable method,* the *percentage-of-sales method,* the *competitive-parity method,* and the *objective-and-task method.*[6]

## Affordable Method

Many companies use the **affordable method:** They set the promotion budget at what they think the company can afford. One executive has explained this method as follows: "Why it's simple. First, I go upstairs to the controller and ask how much they can afford to give this year. He says a million and a half. Later, the boss comes to me and asks how much we should spend and I say, 'Oh, about a million and a half.'"[7]

Unfortunately, this method of setting budgets completely ignores the effect of promotion on sales volume. It leads to an uncertain annual promotion budget—a fact that makes long-range market planning difficult. Although the affordable method can result in overspending on advertising, it more often results in underspending.

## Percentage-of-Sales Method

Many companies use the **percentage-of-sales method,** setting their promotion budgets at a certain percentage of current or forecasted sales. Or they budget a percentage of the sales price. Automobile companies usually budget a fixed percentage for promotion based on the planned car price. Oil companies set the budget at some fraction of a cent for each gallon of gasoline sold under their labels.

A number of advantages are claimed for the percentage-of-sales method. First, promotion spending is likely to vary with what the company can "afford." It also helps management to think about the relationship between promotion spending, selling price, and profit-per-unit. Finally, it supposedly creates competitive stability because competing firms tend to spend about the same percentage of their sales on promotion.

However, in spite of these claimed advantages, the percentage-of-sales method has little to justify it. It mistakenly views sales as the *cause* of promotion rather than as the *result.* The budget is based on availability of funds rather than on opportunities. It may prevent the increased spending sometimes needed to turn falling sales around. Because the budget varies with year-to-year sales, long-range planning is difficult. Finally, this method does not provide any basis for choosing a *specific* percentage, except past practices or what competitors are presently doing.

## Competitive-Parity Method

Other companies use the **competitive-parity method,** setting their promotion budgets to match competitors' outlays. They watch competitors' advertising or get industry promotion-spending estimates from publications or trade associations, and they then set their budgets based on the industry average.

Two arguments support this method. First, competitors' budgets represent the collective wisdom of the industry. Second, spending what competitors spend helps prevent promotion wars. Unfortunately, neither argument is valid. There are no grounds for believing that the competition has a better idea of what a company should be spending on promotion than the company itself does. Companies differ greatly, and each has its own special promotion needs. And

**affordable method** Setting the promotion budget at what management thinks the company can afford.

**percentage-of-sales method** Setting the promotion budget at a certain percentage of current or forecasted sales or as a percentage of the sales price.

**competitive-parity method** Setting the promotion budget to match competitors' outlays.

**objective-and-task
method** Developing the promotion
budget by defining specific
objectives, determining the tasks
that must be performed, and
estimating the costs of performing
these tasks.

there is no evidence that budgets based on competitive parity prevent promotion wars.

### Objective-and-Task Method

The most logical budget setting method is the **objective-and-task method.** Marketers develop their promotion budgets by (1) defining specific objectives, (2) determining the tasks that must be performed to achieve these objectives, and (3) estimating the costs of performing these tasks. The sum of these costs is the proposed promotion budget.

The objective-and-task method makes management spell out its assumptions about the relationship between dollars spent and promotion results. But it is also the most difficult method to use. It is often hard to figure out which specific tasks will achieve specific objectives. For example, suppose Sony wants 95 percent awareness for its new Walkman-size personal videocassette player during the six-month introductory period. What specific advertising messages and media schedules would Sony need in order to attain this objective? How much would these messages and media schedules cost? Sony management must consider such questions even though they are hard to answer. With the objective-and-task method, the company sets its promotion budget based on what it wants to accomplish with promotion.

## Setting the Promotion Mix

The company must now divide the total promotion budget among the major promotion tools—advertising, personal selling, sales promotion, and public relations. It must carefully blend the promotion tools into a coordinated *promotion mix* that will achieve its advertising and marketing objectives. Companies within the same industry differ greatly in how they design their promotion mixes. Avon spends most its promotion funds on personal selling and catalog marketing (its advertising is only 1.5 percent of sales), whereas Revlon spends heavily on consumer advertising (about 8 percent of sales). Electrolux sells 75 percent of its vacuum cleaners door-to-door, whereas Hoover relies more on advertising. Thus, a company can achieve a given sales level with various mixes of advertising, personal selling, sales promotion, and public relations.

Companies are always looking for ways to improve promotion by replacing one promotion tool with another one that will do the same job more economically. Many companies have replaced a portion of their field-sales activities with telephone sales and direct mail. Other companies have increased their sales-promotion spending in relation to advertising in order to gain quicker sales.

Designing the promotion mix is even more complex when one tool must be used to promote another. Thus, when McDonald's decides to run a Million Dollar Sweepstakes in its fast-food outlets (a sales promotion), it has to run ads to inform the public. When General Mills uses a consumer advertising/sales promotion campaign to back a new cake mix, it has to set aside money to promote this campaign to the resellers in order to win their support.

Many factors influence the marketer's choice of promotion tools. We will now look at these factors.

### The Nature of Each Promotion Tool

Each promotion tool—*advertising, personal selling, sales promotion,* and *public relations*—has unique characteristics and costs. Marketers have to understand these characteristics in selecting their tools.

***Advertising*** ▪ Because of the many forms and uses of advertising, it is hard to generalize about its unique qualities as a part of the promotion mix. Yet several qualities can be noted. Advertising's public nature suggests that the advertised product is standard and legitimate. Because many people see ads for the product, buyers know that purchasing the product will be publicly understood and accepted. Advertising also lets the seller repeat a message many times, and it lets the buyer receive and compare the messages of various competitors. Large-scale advertising by a seller says something positive about the seller's size, popularity, and success.

Advertising is also very expressive, letting the company dramatize its products through the artful use of print, sound, and color. On the one hand, advertising can be used to build up a long-term image for a product (such as Coca-Cola ads) and, on the other, to trigger quick sales (as when K mart advertises a weekend sale). Advertising can reach masses of geographically spread-out buyers at a low cost per exposure.

Advertising also has some shortcomings. Although it reaches many people quickly, advertising is impersonal and cannot be as persuasive as a company salesperson. Advertising is able to carry on only a one-way communication with the audience, and the audience does not feel that it has to pay attention or respond. In addition, advertising can be very costly. Although some forms, such as newspaper and radio advertising, can be done on small budgets, other forms, such as network TV advertising, require very large budgets.

***Personal selling*** ▪ Personal selling is the most effective tool at certain stages of the buying process, particularly in building up buyers' preferences, convictions, and actions. As compared with advertising, personal selling has several unique qualities. It involves personal interaction between two or more people, so each person can observe the other's needs and characteristics and make quick adjustments. Personal selling also lets all kinds of relationships spring up, ranging from a matter-of-fact selling relationship to a deep personal friendship. The effective salesperson keeps the customer's interests at heart in order to build a long-run relationship. Finally, the buyer usually feels a greater need to listen and respond, even if the response is a polite "no thank you."

These unique qualities come at a cost. A salesforce requires a longer-term commitment than advertising—advertising can be turned on and off, but salesforce size is harder to change. And personal selling is the company's most expensive promotion tool, costing industrial companies an average of $197 per sales call.[8] American firms spend up to three times as much on personal selling as they do on advertising.

***Sales promotion*** ▪ Sales promotion includes a wide assortment of tools—coupons, contests, cents-off deals, premiums, and others—and these tools have many unique qualities. They attract consumer attention and provide informa-

*With personal selling, the customer feels a greater need to listen and respond, even if the response is a polite "no thank you."*

tion that may lead the consumer to buy the product. They offer strong incentives to purchase by providing inducements or contributions that give additional value to consumers. And sales promotions invite and reward quick response. While advertising says "buy our product," sales promotion says "buy it now."

Companies use sales-promotion tools to create a stronger and quicker response. Sales promotion can be used to dramatize product offers and to boost sagging sales. However, sales-promotion effects are usually short-lived and are not effective in building long-run brand preference.

***Public Relations*** ▪ Public relations offers several unique qualities. It is very believable—news stories, features, and events seem more real and believable to readers than do ads. Public relations can reach many prospects who avoid salespeople and advertisements—the message gets to the buyers as "news" rather than as a sales-directed communication. And like advertising, public relations can dramatize a company or product.

Marketers tend to underuse public relations or use it as an afterthought. Yet a well-thought-out public relations campaign used with other promotion mix elements can be very effective and economical.

### Factors in Setting the Promotion Mix

Companies consider many factors when developing their promotion mixes. We will look at these factors below.

***Type of Product/Market*** ▪ The importance of different promotion tools varies between consumer and industrial markets. The differences are shown in Figure 15–5. Consumer goods companies usually put more of their funds in advertising, followed by sales promotion, personal selling, and then public relations. Industrial goods companies put most of their funds in personal selling, followed by sales promotion, advertising, and public relations. In general, personal selling is more heavily used with expensive and risky goods and in markets with fewer and larger sellers.

Although advertising is less important than sales calls in industrial markets, it still plays an important role. Advertising can build product awareness and knowledge, develop sales leads, and reassure buyers.

Similarly, personal selling can add a lot to consumer-goods marketing efforts. It is simply not the case that "salespeople put products on shelves and advertising takes them off." Well-trained consumer-goods salespeople can sign

FIGURE 15–5   Relative Importance of Promotion Tools in Consumer versus Industrial Markets

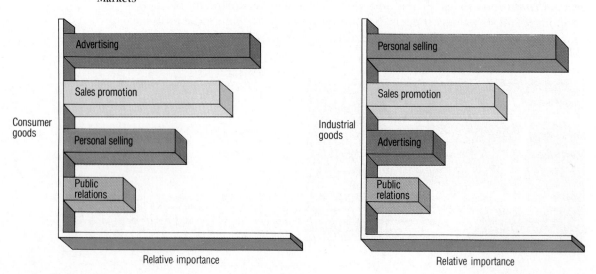

**push strategy** A promotion strategy that calls for using the sales force and trade promotion to push the product through channels.

*Advertising can play a dramatic role in industrial marketing as shown in this classic McGraw-Hill ad.*

up more dealers to carry a particular brand, convince them to give the brand more shelf space, and urge them to use special displays and promotions.

***Push versus Pull Strategy*** ▪ The promotion mix is heavily affected by whether the company chooses a *push* or a *pull* strategy. The two strategies are contrasted in Figure 15–6. A **push strategy** calls for using the salesforce and trade promotion to "push" the product through the channels. Producers promote the

FIGURE 15–6   Push versus Pull Strategy

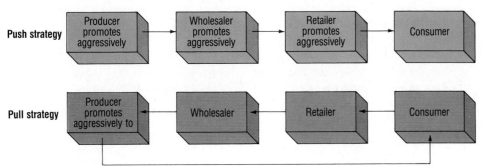

**pull strategy** A promotion strategy that calls for spending a lot of money on advertising and consumer promotion to build up consumer demand and "pull" the product through the channel.

product to wholesalers, wholesalers promote the product to retailers, and retailers promote the product to consumers.[9] A **pull strategy** calls for spending a lot of money on advertising and consumer promotion to build up consumer demand. Consumer demand then "pulls" the product through the channels. If the strategy is effective, consumers will demand the product from their retailers, who will demand it from wholesalers, who will in turn demand it from producers.

Some small industrial-goods companies use only push strategies; some direct-marketing companies use only pull. Most large companies use some combination of both. For example, Procter & Gamble uses mass-media advertising to pull its products and a large salesforce and trade promotions to push its products through the channels. In recent years, consumer goods companies have been decreasing the pull portions of their promotion mixes in favor of more push (see Marketing Highlight 15–2).

# Marketing Highlight 15–2

## CONSUMER GOODS COMPANIES ARE GETTING "PUSHY"

Consumer package-goods companies like Procter & Gamble, General Foods, Quaker, Campbell, and Gillette grew into giants by using mostly pull promotion strategies. They used massive doses of national advertising to differentiate their products, build market share, and maintain customer loyalty. But during the past two decades, these companies have gotten more "pushy," de-emphasizing national advertising and putting more of their promotion budgets into personal selling and sales promotions. Trade promotions (trade allowances, displays, cooperative advertising) now account for 37 percent of total consumer product company marketing spending; consumer promotions (coupons, cents-off deals, premiums) account for another 29 percent. That leaves only 34 percent of total marketing spending for media advertising, down from 42 percent just eight years ago.

Why are these companies shifting so heavily toward push strategies? One reason is that mass media campaigns are more expensive and less effective these days. Network television costs have risen sharply while audiences have fallen off, making national advertising less cost-effective. Companies are also

increasingly segmenting their markets and tailoring their marketing efforts more narrowly, making national advertising less suitable than localized retailer promotions. And in these days of brand extensions and me-too products, companies sometimes have trouble finding meaningful product differences to feature in advertising. So they differentiate their products through price reductions, premium offers, coupons, and other push techniques.

Another factor speeding the shift from pull to push is the greater strength of retailers. Today's retailers are larger and have more access to product sales and profit information. They now have the power to demand and get what they want—and what they want is more push. While national advertising bypasses them on its way the masses, push promotion benefits them directly. Consumer promotions give retailers an immediate sales boost, and cash from trade allowances pads retailer profits. Thus, producers must often use push just to obtain good shelf space and advertising support from important retailers.

However, many marketers are concerned that the reckless use of push

will lead to fierce price competition and a never-ending spiral of price slashing and deal making. This situation would mean lower margins, and companies would have less to invest in the research and development, packaging, and advertising needed to improve products and maintain long-run consumer preference and loyalty. If used improperly, push promotion can mortgage a brand's future for short-term gains.

Yet push strategies are very important in package-goods marketing, where success often depends more on retailer support than on the producer's advertising. And if they are well designed, push strategies can help rather than hinder in building long-run consumer preference. The company needs to blend both push and pull elements into an integrated promotion program that meets immediate consumer and retailer needs as well as long-run strategic needs.

*Sources:* Richard Edel, "No End in Sight to Promotion's Upward Spiral," *Advertising Age,* March 23, 1987, pp. S1–4; Alvin A. Achenbaum and F. Kent Mitchel, "Pulling Away from Push Marketing," *Harvard Business Review,* May-June 1987, pp. 38–40; and Len Strawzewski, "Promotional Carnival Gets Serious," *Advertising Age,* May 2, 1988, pp. S1–2.

***Buyer-Readiness State*** ▪ Promotional tools vary in their effects at the different states of buyer readiness discussed earlier in the chapter. Advertising, along with public relations, plays the major role in the awareness and knowledge states, more important than that played by "cold calls" from salespeople. Customer liking, preference, and conviction are more affected by personal selling, which is closely followed by advertising. Finally, closing the sale is mostly done with sales calls and sales promotion. Clearly, personal selling, given its high costs, should focus on the later stages of the customer buying process.

***Product Life-Cycle Stage*** ▪ The effects of different promotion tools also vary with stages of the product life cycle. In the introduction stage, advertising and public relations are good for producing high awareness, and sales promotion is useful in promoting early trial. Personal selling must be used to get the trade to carry the product. In the growth stage, advertising and public relations continue to be powerful, while sales promotion can be reduced because fewer incentives are needed. In the mature stage, sales promotion again becomes important relative to advertising. Buyers know the brands, and advertising is needed only to remind them of the product. In the decline stage, advertising is kept at a reminder level, public relations is dropped, and salespeople give the product only a little attention. Sales promotion, however, might continue strong.[10]

## Responsibility for Marketing Communications Planning

Members of the marketing department often have different views on how to split the promotion budget. The sales manager would rather hire two more salespeople than spend $100,000 on a single television commercial. The public relations manager feels that he or she can do wonders with some money shifted from advertising to public relations.

In the past, companies left these decisions to different people. No single person was responsible for thinking through the roles of the various promotion tools and coordinating the promotion mix. Today, some companies have appointed marketing communications directors who are responsible for all the company's marketing communications. This director develops policies for using different promotion tools, keeps track of all promotion spending by product, tool, and results, and coordinates the promotion mix activities when major campaigns take place.

# SUMMARY

*Promotion* is one of the four major elements of a company's marketing mix. The main promotion tools—*advertising, sales promotion, public relations*, and *personal selling*—work together to achieve the company's communication objectives.

In preparing marketing communications, the communicator has to understand the nine elements of any communication process: *sender, receiver, encoding, decoding, message, media, response, feedback*, and *noise*. The communicator's first task is to identify the target audience and its characteristics. Next, the communicator has to define the response sought, whether it be *awareness, knowledge, liking, preference, conviction*, or *purchase*. Then a message should be constructed with effective content, structure, and format. Media must be selected, both for personal communication and nonpersonal communication. The message must be delivered by a credible *source*—someone who is an expert, trustworthy, and likable.

Finally, the communicator must collect *feedback* by watching how much of the market becomes aware, tries the product, and is satisfied in the process.

The company has to decide how much to spend for promotion. The most popular approaches are to spend what the company can afford, use a percentage of sales, base promotion on competitors' spending, or base it on an analysis and costing of communication objectives and tasks.

The company has to split the *promotion budget* among the major tools to create the *promotion mix*. Companies are guided by the characteristics of each promotion tool, the type of product/market, the desirability of a *push* or a *pull* strategy, the *buyer's readiness state*, and the *product life-cycle stage*. The different promotion activities require strong coordination for maximum impact.

# QUESTIONS FOR DISCUSSION

1. Which form of marketing communication does each of the following represent: (a) a U2 t-shirt sold at a concert, (b) a *Rolling Stone* interview with George Michael arranged by his manager, (c) a scalper auctioning tickets at a Michael Jackson concert, (d) a record store selling Prince albums at a $2 discount during the week his latest movie opens?

2. The Department of Defense spends two-thirds of the U.S. government's advertising budget. How does the U.S. Army coordinate its promotion and marketing mixes in its efforts to obtain recruits?

3. Relate the six buyer-readiness states to (a) a product you bought on impulse at a grocery store and (b) your feelings about purchasing Coke, Coke Classic, and Pepsi.

4. Long-distance telephone services have tried to attract customers with both emotional appeals ("AT&T—reach out and touch someone") and rational appeals ("If your long-distance bills are too high, call MCI"). Which approach do you think is more effective?

5. Bill Cosby has appeared in ads for such products and companies as Jell-O, Coke, Texas Instruments, and E. F. Hutton. Is he a credible source for *all* these companies or does his credibility vary? Has he been chosen for his credibility or for some other characteristic?

6. How can an organization get feedback on the effects of its communication efforts? Describe the different ways in which (a) the March of Dimes and (b) Procter & Gamble can get such feedback.

7. When a decline in oil prices caused economic troubles in Texas and nearby states, Houston-based National Convenience Stores stopped advertising to cut costs. Which of the four major budgeting approaches were they following—affordable-method, percentage-of-sales-method, competive-parity-method, or objective-and-task-method? What approach would you have recommended?

8. Why do some industrial marketers advertise on national television even though their target audience is only a fraction of the people they reach with their message? List some nonconsumer-oriented TV commercials and explain what the marketers were trying to accomplish.

9. How does the number of levels in the distribution channel influence the decision to use a *push* or a *pull* strategy? What other factors may be involved in this decision?

# REFERENCES

1. See Kenneth Dreyfack, "Quaker Is Feeling Its Oats Again," *Business Week,* September 22, 1986, pp. 80–81; "Quaker Oats Co.," *Advertising Age,* September 4, 1986, p. 144–45; Richard Edel, "No End in Site for Promotion's Upward Spiral," *Advertising Age,* March 23, 1987, p. S2; and Julie Liesse Erickson, "Quaker Fortifies Oatmeal Position," *Advertising Age,* January 11, 1988, p. 54.

2. These definitions, except for *sales promotion,* are from *Marketing Definitions: A Glossary of Marketing Terms* (Chicago: American Marketing Association, 1960).

3. For more on message content and structure, see Leon G. Schiffman and Leslie Lazar Kanuk, *Consumer Behavior,* 3rd ed. (Englewood Cliffs, NJ: Prentice Hall, 1987), pp. 347–53.

4. See P. F. Lazarsfeld, B. Berelson, and H. Gaudet, *The People's Choice,* 2d ed. (New York: Columbia University Press, 1948), p. 151; and Schiffman and Kanuk, *Consumer Behavior,* pp. 571–72.

5. See Michael Oneal and Peter Finch, "Nothing Sells Like Sports," *Business Week,* August 31, 1987; and "Only One Spot, but Fox Delivers," *Advertising Age,* May 2, 1988, p. 48.

6. For a more comprehensive discussion on setting promotion budgets, see Michael L. Rothschild, *Advertising* (Lexington, MA: D. C. Heath, 1987), Chap. 20.

7. Quoted in Daniel Seligman, "How Much for Advertising?" *Fortune,* December 1956, p. 123.

8. See Richard Kern, "Unraveling the Mystery of Cost Per Call," *Sales & Marketing Management,* March 1989, p. 8.

9. For more on push strategies, see Michael Levy, John Webster, and Roger Kerin, "Formulating Push Marketing Strategies: A Method and Application," *Journal of Marketing,* Winter 1983, pp. 25–34; and Alvin A. Achenbaum and F. Kent Mitchel, "Pulling Away from Push Marketing," *Harvard Business Review,* May-June 1987, pp. 38–40.

10. For more on advertising and the product life cycle, see John E. Swan and David R. Rink, "Fitting Market Strategy to Product Life Cycles," *Business Horizons,* January-February 1982, pp. 60–67.

# Case 15

## EASTERN STATE COLLEGE: PROMOTING EDUCATION

Eastern State College is a four-year public college that had once been devoted to teacher training but had in the past ten years developed a college of business administration and a school of communications. Moreover, new programs in social work and public administration had been developed. The college has an undergraduate enrollment of approximately 2,200 male and 2,300 female students. There are about 750 male graduate and 800 female graduate students. There are only about 400 continuing-education students. The college operates on a 15-week semester and 12-week summer-session basis. Eastern State College is located in a small rural community about 40 miles from a community with a population of over 100,000. The college features a 200-acre campus, field house, student center, and relatively new men's and women's dormitories and apartments.

The curriculum at Eastern State College had developed so that the business, social-work, physics, and journalism programs had received national accreditation by their associations. The college offered master's-degree programs in the following fields: biology, business, chemistry, counseling, elementary education, English, history, mathematics, physics, reading, social science, and special education. Currently in progress was the development of a master's-degree program in computer science.

An analysis of students admitted to Eastern State found that 85 percent ranked in the top two-fifths of their high school classes. Approximately 50 percent had combined SAT scores above 1000. The middle 50 percent of students accepted for admission had SAT verbal scores between 440 and 540 and SAT mathematical scores between 475 and 585. The college accepted about 300 transfer students annually.

About 90 percent of the students had graduated from in-state high schools. The other students came from adjoining states. There were relatively few foreign students on campus, and these came primarily from South America. The estimated undergraduate enrollment by school was 40 percent in Arts and Sciences, which included the School of Communications; 35 percent in Business Administration; 15 percent in Education; and 10 percent undeclared majors. Faculty and administration consisted of about 350 people.

A faculty committee met in the Fall 1989 for the purpose of improving and extending the college's summer program, which had been experiencing a summer school enrollment decline for the past four years. The committee was designated the Summer Task Force Committee. The committee had the following tasks:

1. To identify which students were served by the summer program.

2. To revise the summer-program calendar if necessary.

3. To make more effective use of direct mail and other media.

4. To develop a logo.

5. To improve teaching and evaluation of promotional efforts.

6. To improve forecasting techniques.

Summer school enrollment was similar to fall and spring enrollment in the different schools. Students from the School of Arts and Sciences and the School of Business made up approximately 75 percent of the enrollment. However, about 60 percent of the graduate enrollment involved teacher training. The proportion of undergraduate enrollment in the School of Education had declined from 35 percent in 1983 to 15 percent by 1989. Graduate education in the regular semester had declined from 50 percent of the total to 20 percent. In the summer, graduate education enrollment had declined from 80 percent to 60 percent from 1983 to 1989. Further declines were anticipated.

Approximately 10 percent of the summer school enrollment consisted of students who lived within commuting distance of the college. Many of these students were surprised to learn that Eastern State College was not primarily a teacher-training institution. These students enrolled mostly in the newly created School of Business and in other programs in journalism and public relations. Some of the high school students who had graduated in June were taking basic core courses in order to accelerate their studies, and this enrollment source seemed to have promising potential.

The present college calendar consisted of a three-week presummer session, a six-week main session, and a three-week postsummer session. Table 1 shows the credit-hour enrollment for pre-, main-, and postsummer sessions. The graduate summer enrollment demonstrated sharp declines. Although undergraduate enrollment had stabilized in some respects, certain environmental conditions were disturbing. First of all, tuition was increased by the state legislature, and with the high costs of an education, many students needed to work full time over the summer. Second, the rising cost of gasoline might be especially burdensome for students situated in rural communities without public transportation. Third, more and more families were hard hit by reductions of state financial assistance. Finally, many Eastern State College students were first-generation college students and needed loans in order to attend college.

A number of suggestions were made regarding the summer calendar. Because there were relatively few courses offered in the evening, it was thought that more courses should be placed in the evening session. This arrangement would permit students to work during the day. Perhaps

TABLE 1   Credit Hour Production

| | 1986 | | | 1987 | | | 1988 | | | 1989 | | |
|---|---|---|---|---|---|---|---|---|---|---|---|---|
| | PRE- | MAIN- | POST- | PRE- | MAIN- | POST- | PRE- | MAIN- | POST- | PRE- | MAIN- | POST- |
| UG | 2132 | 3926 | 1182 | 2055 | 4262 | 1822 | 1700 | 4087 | 1564 | 2027 | 4065 | 1372 |
| G | 2348 | 5315 | 1264 | 2020 | 4424 | 1103 | 1779 | 3930 | 1154 | 1316 | 3297 | 876 |

the length of each session could also be extended so that classes would meet only four times a week instead of five. This schedule would give students long weekends and reduce traveling expenses. Another option was two five-week sessions. This calendar would have the effect of shortening a 12-week program to 10 weeks. Other options were a three-week—six-week—three-week plan, five-week—five-week—five-week plan, and three-week—four-week—five-week plan. Naturally, the college could continue the traditional three-week—six-week— three-week schedule. Some objections were raised concerning the four-day plan and schedules that would extend the length of each session. It was believed that perhaps students might be asked to absorb more material than could possibly be learned in a single session and that this practice could lead to instructional problems. Another instructional problem would be the longer class periods in a five-week session, an arrangement that would require the current restructuring of courses and assignments.

The impact of the current advertising of the summer announcements was also reviewed. The 1988 advertising campaign was studied in order to make effective use of financial resources. Table 2 shows newspaper advertising for the summer program in 1988. A 36-inch advertisement had been used, the cost computed by multiplying by the cost per inch. One advertisement had been taken out in each newspaper in communities where summer school students lived, and the advertisements had been staggered from April 1 to May 15. Some faculty members suggested that perhaps funds should be concentrated for newspaper advertising in areas where the majority of students lived rather than a comprehensive approach. Should this be done, newspapers 5, 6, 7, 10, and 11 would probably be eliminated. A coupon had been placed in each advertisement, and 54 coupons were received. These coupons were about equally divided among newspapers 1 through 4.

TABLE 2   Schedule of Newspaper Advertising April 1–May 15, 1988

| | | | |
|---|---|---|---|
| 1. Patriot News | 36″ / $8.96 = $ | 332.56 |
| 2. Carlisle Sentinel | 36″ / 2.70 = | 197.10 |
| 3. Public Opinion | 36″ / 2.60 = | 93.60 |
| 4. News Chronicle | 36″ / 2.80 = | 100.80 |
| 5. Gettysburg Times | 36″ / 2.36 = | 84.96 |
| 6. Herald/Mail | 36″ / 6.11 = | 219.96 |
| 7. Lewistown Sentinel | 36″ / 2.75 = | 99.00 |
| 8. York Dispatch | 36″ / 5.74 = | 206.64 |
| 9. York Record | 36″ / 4.40 = | 158.40 |
| 10. Lancaster papers | 36″ / 7.56 = | 272.16 |
| 11. PSU Daily Collegian | 36″ / 3.90 = | 133.20 |
| | | $1,888.38 |

Another $1050 was spent on direct-mail advertising. This strategy included mailing program circulars to students who had registered the previous summer and to various schools in order to attract teachers working for master's degrees. A total of about $5000 was allocated in 1988 for advertising, and $6000 would be budgeted for 1990.

There was some sentiment that perhaps television advertising should also be used, since a wide audience could be reached. Table 3 shows the audiences and costs of advertising on television.

The committee was also asked to develop a logo. Many members believed that this was a public-relations aspect of the advertising program, since a logo should reflect an image of the college. Because the football team was known as the Red Raiders, some members suggested that a picture of an Indian be used on all stationery and direct-mail pieces. Other suggestions included the use of the initials ESC in some pictorial way or a picture of the home of a former president of the United States that was well known and only a few miles away. Still others thought that a picture of one of the modern campus buildings would show the college to better advantage. The committee appointed a subcommittee to review these options.

Because the use of coupons in newspapers did not reveal much information, one problem was to develop a method to measure the effectiveness of summer program advertising. The committee was at a loss to make recommendations in this area. Another facet of developing an effective advertising program was to identify the potential market. A commercial organization could furnish a list of about 4 million college students. Students could be selected by home address, school address, geographic area, and even by field of study. A basic list would cost about $300, with added charges as the list was made more specific.

The committee believed that more information was needed about the characteristics of students who attended the previous summer session. The committee also wanted to know if special programs would stimulate summer attendance. A number of athletic conferences had been held, and these sessions were cited as examples. One member mentioned a computer workshop session of one week for recent high school graduates that had been very successful at another college. The committee session concluded with a discussion of the possible development of summer workshops.

## Questions

1. What market-targeting strategy has Eastern State College been using? Can you suggest improvements?

2. Assess ESC's promotion strategy and recommend appropriate changes.

3. Propose a detailed promotion budget for ESC's Summer School Program.

Source: Adapted from Ronald D. Michman, "Eastern State College," in Carl McDaniel, J., *Marketing*: 2nd ed. (New York: 1982) Harper and Row, pp. 606.

TABLE 3   Television Advertising

|  | Saturday Night Live | The Cosby Show | Cheers | Total |
|---|---|---|---|---|
| Total households | 67,000 | 70,000 | 63,000 | 200,000 |
| Women 18–34 | 25,000 | 21,000 | 16,000 | 62,000 |
| Men 18–34 | 26,000 | 13,000 | 15,000 | 54,000 |
| Total 18–34 | 51,000 | 34,000 | 31,000 | 116,000 |
| Three 30-second spots *Saturday Night Live* | $3840 | | | |
| One 30-second spot, *The Cosby Show* | 2000 | | | |
| One 30-second spot, *Cheers* | 2000 | | | |
| Total | $7840 + production | | | |

# 16

# Promoting Products: Advertising, Sales Promotion, and Public Relations

## CHAPTER OBJECTIVES

After reading this chapter, you should be able to

1. Define the roles of advertising, sales promotion, and public relations in the promotion mix
2. Describe the major decisions in developing an advertising program
3. Explain how sales promotion campaigns are developed and implemented
4. Explain how companies use public relations to communicate with their publics

The California raisin producers had a problem. Raisin production was booming—in fact, output was almost doubling annual sales. But consumer sales were dropping at a rate of one or two percent per month. Research by the California Raisin Advisory Board showed that although consumers knew a lot about the natural health benefits of the dark wrinkly fruit, they found it emotionally boring. To most consumers, raisins were dull, uninteresting, and, worst of all, "wimpy."

So the Advisory Board handed its advertising agency, Foote, Cone & Belding, an improbable advertising challenge—make raisins hip! The agency responded with an equally improbable advertising campaign. The first ad featured a conga line of sneaker-shod raisins singing and dancing to the 1960s hit "I Heard It Through the Grapevine." The ad quickly became the hottest 30 seconds on television, and the imaginative dancing raisins campaign has become an award-winning classic.

The plump and personable raisin characters spring to life through a technique called Claymation. An ad is first filmed using live actors, then animators carefully

sculpt purple, potato-sized clay figures to imitate the actors' expressions and movements. Using stop-action photography and making gradual changes in the clay figures—24 for each second of film—the animators simulate live action. It takes many months of tedious work to film a single 30-second ad. During the months of filming, the clay figures get droopy and dirty, so the animators sculpt a drawer full of fresh backups for each character.

Nor is the process cheap. The Advisory Board paid more than $200,000 for the first ad, plus another $120,000 for music rights. And it budgeted $7 million for the first six months of television time. But the investment paid off—the campaign was both well-liked and effective. Following the first ad, consumers clamored for more, swamping the Advisory Board and its ad agency with enthusiastic fan mail. Halloween parties that year were overrun with raisin look-alikes in black tights and plastic garbage bags. The infectious little raisin critters easily beat out the Pillsbury Doughboy, Tony the Tiger, the Keebler Elves, and other classic personalities in consumer voting for their favorite animated characters. The California Raisin

Board reacted with new ads, point-of-purchase displays featuring their raisin stars, a national contest to name the three lead raisins, a music album, television specials, a board game, and 62 licensing agreements that have hip raisins dancing on everything from T-shirts and bed sheets to pencils, lunch boxes, and watches. And the raisins have now become spokespersons for other companies and products—

Hardees, Del Monte, Post Raisin Bran, and others.

Raisins are now "cool" and sales are surging, with increases of 5 to 6 percent a month since the campaign began. The editors of *Advertising Age* chose Foote, Cone & Belding as their advertising agency of the year and the dancing raisins ad as the year's top 30-second spot.[1]

**advertising** Any paid form of nonpersonal presentation and promotion of ideas, goods, or services by an identified sponsor.

Companies must do more than make good products—they must inform consumers about product benefits and carefully position products in consumers' minds. To do this, they must skillfully use the mass-promotion tools of *advertising, sales promotion,* and *public relations.* We examine these tools in this chapter.

# ADVERTISING

We define **advertising** as any paid form of nonpersonal presentation and promotion of ideas, goods, or services by an identified sponsor. In 1987, advertising ran up a bill of more than $109 billion. The spenders included not only business firms but museums, professionals, and social organizations that advertise their causes to various target publics. In fact, the thirty-third largest advertising spender is a nonprofit organization—the U.S. government.

The top 100 national advertisers account for about one-fourth of all advertising.[2] Table 16–1 lists the top ten advertisers in 1988. Philip Morris is the leader with over $1.5 billion, or 8.5 percent of its total U.S. sales. The other major spenders are found in the auto, food, retailing, and tobacco industries. Advertising as a percentage of sales is low in the auto industry and high in food, drugs, toiletries, and cosmetics, followed by gum, candy, and soaps. Companies

TABLE 16–1   Top 10 National Advertisers

| Rank | Company | Total U.S. Advertising (MILLIONS) | Total U.S. Sales (MILLIONS) | Advertising As a Percent Of Sales |
|---|---|---|---|---|
| 1 | Philip Morris | $1,558 | $18,228 | 8.5% |
| 2 | Procter & Gamble | 1,387 | 12,423 | 11.2 |
| 3 | General Motors | 1,025 | 86,422 | 1.2 |
| 4 | Sears | 887 | 48,440* | 1.8 |
| 5 | RJR Nabisco | 840 | 11,721 | 7.2 |
| 6 | PepsiCo | 704 | 9,515 | 7.4 |
| 7 | Eastman Kodak | 658 | 8,040 | 8.2 |
| 8 | McDonald's | 650 | 10,576 | 6.1 |
| 9 | Ford | 640 | 55,302 | 1.2 |
| 10 | Anheuser-Busch | 635 | 9,019 | 7.0 |

*Worldwide sales—U.S. sales not available.

*Source:* Reprinted with permission from the September 28, 1988, issue of *Advertising Age.* Copyright 1988, Crain Communications, Inc.

spending the largest percentages of their sales on advertising were Noxell (33 percent) and Warner-Lambert (30 percent).

The roots of advertising can be traced back to early history (see Marketing Highlight 16–1). Although advertising is mostly used by private enterprise, it is employed in all the countries of the world, including socialist countries. Advertising is a good way to inform and persuade, whether the purpose is to sell Coca-Cola all over the world or to get consumers in a developing nation to drink milk or use birth control.

Organizations handle advertising in different ways. In small companies, advertising might be handled by someone in the sales department. Large companies set up advertising departments whose job is to set the advertising budget, work with the ad agency, and handle direct-mail advertising, dealer displays, and other advertising not done by the agency. Most large companies use an outside advertising agency because it offers several advantages (see Marketing Highlight 16–2).

# Marketing Highlight 16–1

## HISTORICAL MILESTONES IN ADVERTISING

Advertising goes back to the very beginnings of recorded history. Archaeologists working in the countries around the Mediterranean Sea have dug up signs announcing various events and offers. The Romans painted walls to announce gladiator fights, and the Phoenicians painted pictures promoting their wares on large rocks along parade routes. A Pompeii wall painting praised a politician and asked for the people's votes.

Another early form of advertising was the town crier. During the Golden Age in Greece, town criers announced the sale of slaves, cattle, and other goods. An early "singing commercial" went as follows: "For eyes that are shining, for cheeks like the dawn/For beauty that lasts after girlhood is gone/For prices in reason, the woman who knows/Will buy her cosmetics of Aesclyptos."

Another early advertising form was the mark that tradespeople placed on their goods, such as pottery. As the person's reputation spread by word of mouth, buyers began to look for his special mark, just as trademarks and brand names are used today. Over 1,000 years ago in Europe, Osnabruck linen was carefully controlled for quality and commanded a price 20 percent higher than unbranded Westphalian linens. As production became more centralized and markets became more distant, the mark became more important.

The turning point in the history of advertising came in the year 1450 when Johann Gutenberg invented the printing press. Advertisers no longer had to produce extra copies of a sign by hand. The first printed advertisement in the English language appeared in 1478.

In 1622, advertising got a big boost with the launching of the first English newspaper, *The Weekly Newes*. Later, Joseph Addison and Richard Steele published the *Tatler* and became supporters of advertising. Addison gave this advice to copy writers: "The great art in writing advertising is the finding out the proper method to catch the reader, without which a good thing may pass unobserved, or be lost among commissions of bankrupts." The September 14, 1710, issue of the *Tatler* contained ads for razor strops, patent medicine, and other consumer products.

Advertising had its greatest growth in the United States. Ben Franklin has been called the father of American advertising because his *Gazette,* first published in 1729, had the largest circulation and advertising volume of any paper in colonial America. Several factors led to America's becoming the cradle of advertising. First, American industry led in mass production, which created surpluses and the need to convince consumers to buy more. Second, the development of a fine network of waterways, highways, and roads allowed the transportation of goods and advertising media to the countryside. Third, the establishment in 1813 of compulsory public education increased literacy and the growth of newspapers and magazines. The invention of radio and, later, television created two more amazing media for the spread of advertising.

## HOW DOES AN ADVERTISING AGENCY WORK?

Madison Avenue is a familiar name to most Americans. It's a street in New York City where some major advertising agency headquarters are located. But most of the nation's 10,000 agencies are found outside New York, and almost every city has at least one agency, even if it's a one-person shop. Some ad agencies are huge—the largest U.S. agency, Young & Rubicam, has annual billings of over $5.4 billion.

Advertising agencies were started in the mid- to late 1800s by salespeople and brokers who worked for the media and received a commission for selling advertising space to various companies. As time passed, these salespeople began to help customers prepare their ads.

Eventually, they formed agencies and grew closer to the advertisers than to the media. Agencies offered both more advertising and more marketing services to their clients.

Even companies with strong advertising departments use advertising agencies. Agencies employ specialists who can often perform advertising tasks better than the company's own staff. Agencies also bring an outside point of view to solving a company's problems, along with lots of experience from working with different clients and situations. Agencies are paid partly from media discounts and often cost the firm very little. And because the firm can drop its agency at any time, an agency works hard to do a good job.

Advertising agencies usually have four departments: *creative,* which develops and produces ads; *media,* which selects media and places ads; *research,* which studies audience characteristics and wants; and *business,* which handles the agency's business activities. Each account is supervised by an account executive, and people in each department are usually assigned to work on one or more accounts.

Agencies often attract new business through reputation or size. Generally, however, a client invites a few agencies to make a presentation for its business and then selects one of them.

Ad agencies have traditionally been paid through commissions and some fees.

# MAJOR DECISIONS IN ADVERTISING

Marketing management must make five important decisions in developing an advertising program. These decisions are listed in Figure 16–1 and discussed below.

## Setting Objectives

The first step in developing an advertising program is to set *advertising objectives.* These objectives should be based on past decisions about the target market,

FIGURE 16–1   Major Decisions in Advertising

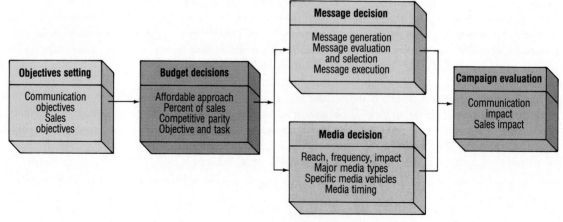

Under this system, the agency usually receives 15 percent of the media cost as a rebate. Suppose the agency buys $60,000 of magazine space for a client. The magazine bills the advertising agency for $51,000 ($60,000 less 15 percent), and the agency bills the client for $60,000, keeping the $9,000 commission. If the client bought space directly from the magazine, it would have paid $60,000 because commissions are only paid to recognized advertising agencies.

However, both advertisers and agencies have become more and more unhappy with the commission system. Larger advertisers complain that they pay more for the same services received by smaller ones simply because they place more advertising. Advertisers also believe that the commission system drives agencies away from low-cost media and short advertising campaigns. Agencies are unhappy because they perform extra services for an account without getting any more pay. As a result, the trend is now toward paying either a straight fee or a combination commission and fee. And some large advertisers are tying agency compensation to the performance of the agency's advertising campaigns. Today, only about 35 percent of companies still pay their agencies on a commission-only basis.

Another trend is also hitting the advertising agency business: In recent years, as growth in advertising spending has slowed, many agencies have tried to keep growing by gobbling up other agencies, thus creating huge agency holding companies. The largest of these agency "supergroups," Saatchi & Saatchi PLC, includes several large agencies—Saatchi & Saatchi Compton, Ted Bates Worldwide, DFS Dorland Worldwide, and others—with combined billings (the dollar amount of advertising placed for clients) exceeding $13.5 billion. Many agencies have also sought growth by diversifying into related marketing services. These new "superagencies" offer a complete list of integrated marketing and promotion services under one roof, including advertising, sales promotion, public relations, direct marketing, and marketing research.

*Sources:* See Walecia Konrad, "A Word from the Sponsor: Get Results—Or Else," *Business Week,* July 4, 1988, p. 66; Anthony Ramirez, "Do Your Ads Need a Superagency?" *Fortune,* April 27, 1987, pp. 84–89; and "U.S. and Foreign Advertising Agency Income Report," a special issue of *Advertising Age,* March 29, 1989.

positioning, and marketing mix. The marketing positioning and mix strategy defines the job that advertising must do in the total marketing program.

An **advertising objective** is a specific communication *task* to be accomplished with a specific *target* audience during a specific period of *time*. Advertising objectives can be classified as to whether their aim is to *inform, persuade,* or *remind.* Table 16–2 lists examples of these objectives. **Informative advertising** is used heavily when introducing a new product category and when the objective is to build primary demand. Thus, producers of compact disc players first informed consumers of the sound and convenience benefits of CDs. **Persuasive advertising** becomes more important as competition increases and

**advertising objective** A specific communication *task* to be accomplished with a specific *target* audience during a specific period of *time.*

**informative advertising** Advertising used to inform consumers about a new product or feature and to build primary demand.

**persuasive advertising** Advertising used to build selective demand for a brand by persuading consumers that it offers the best quality for their money.

TABLE 16–2 Possible Advertising Objectives

*Informative advertising:*

| | |
|---|---|
| Telling the market about a new product | Describing available services |
| Suggesting new uses for a product | Correcting false impressions |
| Informing the market of a price change | Reducing consumers' fears |
| Explaining how the product works | Building a company image |

*Persuasive advertising:*

| | |
|---|---|
| Building brand preference | |
| Encouraging switching to your brand | Persuading customer to purchase now |
| Changing customer's perception of product attributes | Persuading customer to receive a sales call |

*Reminder advertising:*

| | |
|---|---|
| Reminding consumers that the product may be needed in the near future | Keeping it in their minds during off-seasons |
| Reminding them where to buy it | Maintaining its top-of-mind awareness |

**comparison advertising**
Advertising that compares one brand directly or indirectly with one or more other brands.

**reminder advertising** Advertising used to keep consumers thinking about a product.

Comparison advertising: here Budget Gourmet compares itself directly to competitor Lean Cuisine.

a company's objective is to build selective demand. For example, when compact disc players became established and accepted, Sony began trying to persuade consumers that its brand offers the best quality for their money.

Some persuasive advertising has become **comparison advertising,** which compares one brand directly or indirectly with one or more other brands. For example, in its classic comparison campaign, Avis positioned itself against market-leading Hertz by claiming, "We're number two, so we try harder." Procter & Gamble positioned Scope against Listerine, claiming that minty-fresh Scope "fights bad breath and doesn't give medicine breath." Comparison advertising has also been used for such products as computers, deodorants, toothpastes, automobiles, wines, and pain relievers.

**Reminder advertising** is important for mature products—it keeps consumers thinking about the product. Expensive Coca-Cola ads on television are designed to remind people about Coca-Cola, not to inform or persuade them.

## Budget Decision

After determining its advertising objectives, the company can next set its *advertising budget* for each product. The role of advertising is to affect demand for a product: The company wants to spend the amount needed to achieve the sales goal. Four commonly used methods for setting the advertising budget were discussed in Chapter 15. Here we will describe some specific factors that should be considered when setting the advertising budget:

☐ *Stage in the product life cycle.* New products typically need large advertising budgets to build awareness and to gain consumer trial. Mature brands usually require lower budgets as a ratio to sales.

- □ *Market share.* High-market-share brands usually need more advertising spending as a percentage of sales than low-share brands. Building the market or taking share from competitors requires larger advertising spending than simply maintaining current share.
- □ *Competition and clutter.* In a market with many competitors and high advertising spending, a brand must advertise more heavily to be heard above the noise in the market.
- □ *Advertising frequency.* When many repetitions are needed to put across the brand's message to consumers, the advertising budget must be larger.
- □ *Product differentiation.* A brand that closely resembles other brands in its product class (cigarettes, beer, soft drinks) requires heavy advertising to set it apart. When the product differs greatly from competitors', advertising can be used to point out the differences to consumers.[3]

Companies such as Du Pont and Anheuser-Busch often run experiments as part of their advertising budgeting process. For example, Anheuser-Busch recently began testing a new ultrapremium beer, named "Anheuser," with no advertising at all. No major beer is likely to survive without advertising, but in this case the company wants to see if this specialty beer can make it on word-of-mouth alone. In fact, the lack of advertising might even add to the beer's allure. If the new brand succeeds without advertising, Anheuser-Busch will probably take a careful look at the over $500 million it spends each year advertising its other products.[4]

## Message Decision

A large advertising budget does not guarantee a successful advertising campaign. No matter how big the budget, advertising can succeed only if *messages* gain attention and communicate well. Good advertising messages are especially important in today's costly and cluttered advertising environment. Take the situation facing network television advertisers. They typically pay $100,000 to $200,000 for 30 seconds of advertising time during a popular prime-time TV program—even more if it is an especially popular program such as "The Cosby Show" ($380,000 per spot) or an event like the Super Bowl ($550,000!). In such cases, their ads are sandwiched in with a clutter of some 60 other commercials, announcements, and network promotions per hour.

But wait—if you are an advertiser, things get even worse! Until recently, television viewers were pretty much a captive audience for advertisers. Viewers had only a few channels to choose from. Those who found the energy to get up and change channels during boring commercial breaks usually found only more of the same on the other channels. But with the growth in cable TV, VCRs, and remote-control units, today's viewers have many more options. They can actually avoid ads by watching commercial-free cable channels. They can "zap" commercials by pushing the fast-forward button during taped programs. With remote control, they can instantly turn off the sound during a commercial or "zip" around the channel to see what else is on. Advertisers take such "zipping" and "zapping" seriously. One expert predicts that by the year 2000, 60 percent of all TV viewers may be regularly tuning out commercials.[5]

Thus, just to gain and hold attention, today's advertising messages must be better planned, more imaginative, more entertaining, and more rewarding to consumers. Creative strategy will therefore play an increasingly important role in advertising success. Advertisers go through three steps to develop a creative strategy: *message generation, message evaluation and selection,* and *message execution.*

### Message Generation

Creative people have different ways to find advertising message ideas. Many creative people start by talking to consumers, dealers, experts, and competitors. Others try to imagine consumers using the product and figure out the benefits consumers seek when buying and using it. Generally, although advertisers create many possible messages, only a few will ultimately be used.

### Message Evaluation and Selection

The advertiser must evaluate the possible messages. The appeals used in messages should have three characteristics. First, they should be *meaningful*, pointing out benefits that make the product more desirable or interesting to consumers. Second, appeals should be *distinctive*—they should tell how the product is better than competing brands. Finally, they must be *believable*. It may be hard to make message appeals believable because many consumers doubt the truth of advertising in general. One study found that, on average, consumers rate advertising messages as "somewhat unbelievable."[6]

Thus, advertisers should evaluate their advertising messages on the above factors. For example, the March of Dimes searched for an advertising theme to raise money for its fight against birth defects.[7] Twenty possible messages came out of a brainstorming session. A group of young parents was asked to rate each message for interest, distinctiveness, and believability, giving up to 100 points for each. For example, the message "Five hundred thousand unborn babies die each year from birth defects" scored 70, 60, and 80 on interest, distinctiveness, and believability, while the message "Your next baby could be born with a birth defect" scored 58, 50, and 70. The first message was thus rated higher than the second and was used in advertising.

### Message Execution

The impact of the message depends not only on *what* is said but also on *how* it is said—its message execution. The advertiser has to put the message across in a way that wins the target market's attention and interest.

The advertiser usually begins with a statement of the objective and approach of the desired ad. Here is such a statement for a Pillsbury product called 1869 Brand Biscuits:

> The objective of the advertising is to convince biscuit users that now they can buy a canned biscuit that's as good as homemade—Pillsbury's 1869 Brand Biscuits. The content of the advertising will emphasize that the biscuits look like homemade biscuits, have the same texture as homemade, and taste like homemade biscuits. Support for the "good as homemade" promise will be twofold: (1) 1869 Brand Biscuits are made from a special kind of flour (soft wheat flour) used to make homemade biscuits but never before used in making canned biscuits, and (2) the use of traditional American biscuit recipes. The tone of the advertising will be a news announcement, tempered by a warm, reflective mood coming from a look back at traditional American baking quality.

The creative people must find a style, tone, words, and format for executing the message. Any message can be presented in different *execution styles,* such as the following:

1. *Slice-of-life.* This style shows one or more people using the product in a normal setting. A family seated at the dinner table might talk about a new biscuit brand.

2. *Life style.* This style shows how a product fits in with a life style. For

Message execution styles: Cunard builds a fantasy around its cruise vacations; 9-Lives created Morris the 9-Lives cat as a personality symbol.

example, a National Dairy Board ad shows women exercising and talks about how milk adds to a healthy, active life style.

3. *Fantasy.* This style creates a fantasy around the product or its use. For instance, Revlon's first ad for Jontue showed a barefoot woman wearing a chiffon dress and coming out of an old French barn, crossing a meadow, meeting a handsome young man on a white horse, and riding away with him.

4. *Mood or image.* This style builds a mood or image around the product, such as beauty, love, or serenity. No claim is made about the product except through suggestion. Many coffee ads create moods.

5. *Musical.* This style shows one or more people or cartoon characters singing a song about the product. Many cola ads have used this format.

6. *Personality symbol.* This style creates a character that represents the product. The character might be *animated* (the Jolly Green Giant, Cap'n Crunch, Garfield the Cat) or *real* (the Marlboro man, Morris the 9-Lives Cat).

7. *Technical expertise.* This style shows the company's expertise in making the product. Thus, Hills Brothers shows one of its buyers carefully selecting coffee beans, and Gallo tells about its many years of winemaking.

8. *Scientific evidence.* This style presents survey or scientific evidence that the brand is better or better liked than one or more other brands. For years, Crest toothpaste has used scientific evidence to convince buyers that Crest is better than other brands at fighting cavities.

9. *Testimonial evidence.* This style features a highly believable or likable source endorsing the product. It could be a celebrity like Bill Cosby (Jell-O Pudding, Kodak film) or ordinary people saying how much they like a given product.

The advertiser must also choose a *tone* for the ad. Procter & Gamble always uses a positive tone: Its ads say something very positive about its own products. P&G also avoids humor that might take attention away from the message. By contrast, ads for Bud Light beer use humor and poke fun at people who order "just any light."

Memorable and attention-getting *words* must also be found. For example, the themes listed below on the left would have had much less impact without the creative phrasing on the right:

| THEME | CREATIVE COPY |
|---|---|
| □ 7-Up is not a cola. | □ "The Uncola." |
| □ Ride in our bus instead of driving your car. | □ "Take the bus, and leave the driving to us" (Greyhound). |
| □ If you drink much beer, Schaefer is a good beer to drink. | □ "The one to have when you're having more than one." |
| □ We don't rent as many cars, so we have to do more for our customers. | □ "We're number two, so we try harder" (Avis). |
| □ Hanes socks last longer than less expensive ones. | □ "Buy cheap socks and you'll pay through the toes." |
| □ Nike shoes will help you jump higher and play better basketball. | □ "Parachute not included." |

Finally, *format* elements will make a difference in an ad's impact as well as its cost. A small change in the way an ad is designed can make a big difference in its effect. The *illustration* is the first thing the reader notices, and that illustration must be strong enough to draw attention. Then the *headline* must effectively entice the right people to read the copy. The *copy*—the main block of text in the ad—must be simple but strong and convincing. Moreover, these three elements must also work effectively *together*. Even then, a truly outstanding ad will be noted by less than 50 percent of the exposed audience; about 30 percent of the exposed audience will recall the main point of the headline; about 25 percent

*Advertisements vary widely in format and the use of different components. In this award winning ad, the bold headline and illustrations effectively communicate a simple message.*

will remember the advertiser's name; and less than 10 percent will have read most of the body copy. Less than outstanding ads, unfortunately, will not achieve even these results.

## Media Decision

The advertiser next chooses advertising media to carry the message. The major steps in media selection are (1) deciding on *reach, frequency,* and *impact;* (2) choosing among major *media types;* (3) selecting specific *media vehicles;* and (4) deciding on *media timing.*

### Deciding on Reach, Frequency, and Impact

To select media, the advertiser must decide what reach and frequency are needed to achieve advertising objectives. **Reach** is a measure of the percentage of people in the target market who are exposed to the ad campaign during a given period of time. For example, the advertiser might try to reach 70 percent of the target market during the first year. **Frequency** is a measure of how many *times* the average person in the target market is exposed to the message. For example, the advertiser might want an average exposure frequency of three. The advertiser must also decide on desired **media impact**—the *qualitative value* of a message exposure through a given medium. For example, for products that need to be demonstrated, messages on television may have more impact than messages on radio because television uses sight and sound, not just sound. The same message in one magazine (say, *Newsweek)* may be more believable than in another (say, *The National Enquirer).*

Suppose the advertiser's product might appeal to a market of 1,000,000 consumers. The goal is to reach 700,000 consumers (70 percent of 1,000,000). Because the average consumer will receive three exposures, 2,100,000 exposures (700,000 × 3) must be bought. If the advertiser wants exposures of 1.5 impact (assuming 1.0 impact is the average), a rated number of exposures of 3,150,000 (2,100,000 × 1.5) must be bought. If 1,000 exposures with this impact cost $10, the advertising budget will have to be $31,500 (3,150 × $10). In general, the more reach, frequency, and impact the advertiser seeks, the higher the advertising budget will have to be.

### Choosing among Major Media Types

The media planner has to know the reach, frequency, and impact of each of the major media types. The major advertising media are summarized in Table 16–3. The major media types, in order of advertising volume, are newspapers, television, direct mail, radio, magazines, and outdoor. Each medium has advantages and limitations.

Media planners consider many factors when making their media choices. The *media habits of target consumers* will affect media choice—for example, radio and television are the best media for reaching teen-agers. So will the *nature of the product*—dresses are best shown in color magazines, and Polaroid cameras are best demonstrated on television. Different *types of messages* may require different media. A message announcing a major sale tomorrow will require radio or newspapers; a message with a lot of technical data might require magazines or direct mailings. *Cost* is also a major factor in media choice. While television is very expensive, newspaper advertising costs much less. The media planner looks at both the total cost of using a medium and at the cost per thousand exposures—the cost of reaching 1,000 people using the medium.

Ideas about media impact and cost must be reexamined regularly. For a long time, television and magazines dominated in the media mixes of national advertisers, with other media often neglected. Recently, however, the costs and

**reach** The percentage of people in the target market exposed to an ad campaign during a given period.

**frequency** The number of times the average person in the target market is exposed to an advertising message during a given period.

**media impact** The qualitative value of an exposure through a given medium.

**TABLE 16–3** Profiles of Major Media Types

| Medium | Volume In Billions | Percentage | Example of Cost | Advantages | Limitations |
|---|---|---|---|---|---|
| Newspapers | $ 29.4 | 26.8% | $29,800 for one page, weekday *Chicago Tribune* | Flexibility; timeliness; good local market coverage; broad acceptance; high believability | Short life; poor reproduction quality; small "pass along" audience |
| Television | 23.9 | 21.8% | $1,500 for thirty seconds of prime time in Chicago | Combines sight, sound, and motion; appealing to the senses; high attention; high reach | High absolute cost; high clutter; fleeting exposure; less audience selectivity |
| Direct mail | 19.1 | 17.4% | $1,520 for the names and addresses of 40,000 veterinarians | Audience selectivity; flexibility; no ad competition within the same medium; personalization | Relatively high cost; "junk mail" image |
| Radio | 7.2 | 6.6% | $700 for one minute of drive time (during commuting hours, a.m. and p.m.) in Chicago | Mass use; high geographic and demographic selectivity; low cost | Audio presentation only; lower attention than television; nonstandardized rate structures; fleeting exposure |
| Magazines | 5.6 | 5.1% | $84,390 for one page, four-color, in *Newsweek* | High geographic and demographic selectivity; credibility and prestige; high-quality reproduction; long life; good pass-along readership | Long ad purchase lead time; some waste circulation; no guarantee of position |
| Outdoor | 1.0 | 0.9% | $25,500 per month for seventy-one billboards in metropolitan Chicago | Flexibility; high repeat exposure; low cost; low competition | No audience selectivity; creative limitations |
| Other | 23.4 | 21.4% | | | |
| Total | 109.6 | 100.0% | | | |

*Source:* Columns 2 and 3 are from *Advertising Age*, June 3, 1988, p. 64. Printed with permission. Copyright © 1988. Crain Communications, Inc.

**media vehicles** Specific media within each general media type, such as specific magazines, television shows, or radio programs.

clutter (competition from competing messages) of these media have gone up, audiences have dropped, and marketers are adopting strategies beamed at narrower segments. As a result, TV and magazine advertising revenues have leveled off or declined. Advertisers are increasingly turning to alternative media, ranging from cable TV and outdoor advertising to parking meters and shopping carts (see Marketing Highlight 16–3).

Given these and other media characteristics, the media planner must decide how much of each media type to buy. For example, in launching its new biscuit, Pillsbury might decide to spend $3 million on daytime network television, $2 million on women's magazines, and $1 million on daily newspapers in 20 major markets.

### Selecting Specific Media Vehicles

The media planner must now choose the best **media vehicles**—specific media within each general media type. For example, television vehicles include "The Bill Cosby Show," "Sixty Minutes," and the "CBS Evening News." Magazine vehicles include *Newsweek, People, Sports Illustrated*, and *Reader's Digest*. If advertising is placed in magazines, the media planner must look up circulation figures and the costs of different ad sizes, color options, ad positions, and frequencies for various specific magazines. The planner then evaluates each magazine on such factors as credibility, status, reproduction quality, editorial focus, and advertising submission deadlines. The media planner decides which vehicles give the best reach, frequency, and impact for the money.

Media planners also compute the cost per thousand persons reached by a vehicle. If a full-page, four-color advertisement in *Newsweek* costs $84,000 and *Newsweek*'s readership is 3 million people, the cost of reaching each one thousand persons is $28. The same advertisement in *Business Week* may cost only $30,000 but reach only 775,000 persons—at a cost per thousand of $39. The media planner would rank each magazine by cost per thousand and favor those magazines with the lower cost per thousand for reaching target consumers.

The media planner must also consider the costs of producing ads for different media. While newspaper ads may cost very little to produce, flashy television ads may cost millions. On average, advertisers must pay $118,000 to produce a single 30-second television commercial. Timex paid a cool million to make one 30-second ad for its Atlantis 100 sports watch, and Apple Computer recently spent $6 million to produce 11 spots.[8]

The media planner must thus balance media cost measures against several media impact factors. First, costs should be balanced against the media vehicle's *audience quality*. For a baby lotion advertisement, *New Parents* magazine would have a high-exposure value; *Gentlemen's Quarterly* would have a low-exposure value. Second, the media planner should consider *audience attention*. Readers of *Vogue*, for example, typically pay more attention to ads than do readers of *Newsweek*. Third, the planner assesses the vehicle's *editorial quality*—*Time* and *The Wall Street Journal* are more believable and prestigious than *The National Enquirer*.

**continuity** Scheduling ads evenly within a given period.

**pulsing** Scheduling ads unevenly in bursts over a time period.

### Deciding on Media Timing

The advertiser must also decide how to schedule advertising over the course of a year. Suppose sales of a product peak in December and drop off in March. The firm can vary its advertising to follow the seasonal pattern, to oppose the seasonal pattern, or to be the same all year. Most firms do some seasonal advertising. Some do *only* seasonal advertising: For example, Hallmark advertises its greeting cards only before major holidays.

Finally, the advertiser has to choose the pattern of the ads. **Continuity** means scheduling ads evenly within a given period. **Pulsing** means scheduling ads unevenly over a given time period. Thus, 52 ads could either be scheduled at one per week during the year or pulsed in several bursts. Those who favor pulsing feel that the audience will learn the message more completely and that money can be saved. For example, Anheuser-Busch found that Budweiser could drop advertising in a given market with no harm to sales for at least a year and a half. Then the company could use a six-month burst of advertising and regain the past sales-growth rate. This finding led Budweiser to adopt a pulsing strategy.[9]

## *Advertising Evaluation*

The advertising program should regularly evaluate the *communication effects* and *sales effects* of advertising.

## ADVERTISERS SEEK ALTERNATIVE MEDIA

As network television costs soar and audiences shrink, many advertisers are looking for new ways to reach consumers. And the move toward regionalized strategies, focused more narrowly on specific consumer groups, has also fueled the search for alternative media to replace or supplement network television. Advertisers are shifting larger portions of their budgets to media that cost less and target more effectively.

Two media benefiting most from the shift are outdoor advertising and cable television. Billboards have undergone a resurgence in recent years. Gone are the ugly eyesores of the past; in their place, we now see cleverly designed, colorful attention-grabbers. Outdoor advertising provides an excellent way to reach important local consumer segments. For example, Anheuser-Busch sells its Budweiser, Busch, and Bud Lite beers on

billboards in black and Hispanic neighborhoods.

Cable television is also booming. Today, more than 54 percent of all U.S. households subscribe to cable, and cable TV advertising revenues exceed $1.8 billion a year. Cable systems allow narrow programming formats such as all sports, all news, nutrition programs, arts programs, and others that target select groups. Advertisers can take advantage of

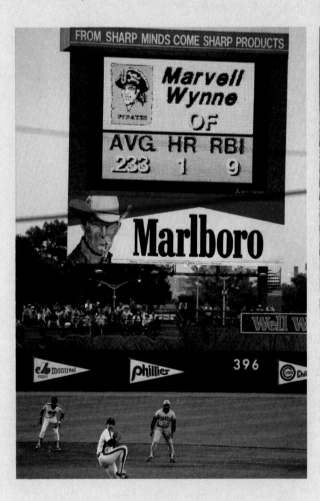

*Marketers have discovered a dazzling array of "alternative media."*

such "narrowcasting" to "rifle in" on special market segments rather than use the "shotgun" approach offered by network broadcasting.

Cable TV and outdoor advertising seem to make good sense. But increasingly, ads are popping up in far less likely places. In their efforts to find less costly and more highly targeted ways to reach consumers, advertisers have discovered a dazzling collection of "alternative media." As consumers, we are used to ads on television, in magazines and newspapers, on the radio, and along the roadways. But these days, no matter where you go or what you do, you will probably run into some new form of advertising.

Tiny billboards and miniature video screens attached to shopping carts and ads on grocery bags urge you to treat yourself to Jell-O Pudding Pops or Pampers disposable diapers. Signs atop parking meters hawk everything from Jeeps to Minolta cameras to Recipe dog food. You escape to the ballpark, only to find billboard-size video screens running Budweiser ads while a blimp with an electronic message board circles lazily overhead. You pay to see a movie at your local theater, but first you see a two-minute science fiction fantasy that turns out to be an ad for General Electric portable stereo boxes. Then the movie is full of not-so-subtle promotional plugs for Pepsi, Alka-Seltzer, MasterCard, Fritos, or one of a dozen other products. Boats cruise along public beaches flashing advertising messages for Sundown Sunscreen or Gatorade to sunbathers. Even your church bulletin carries ads for Campbell's Soup.

Some of these alternative media seem a bit farfetched, and they sometimes irritate consumers. But for many marketers, these media can save money and provide a way to hit selected consumers where they live, shop, work, and play. Of course, this may leave you wondering if there are any commercial-free havens remaining for ad-weary consumers. The back seat of a taxi, perhaps, or stalls in a public restroom? Forget it! Both have already been invaded by innovative marketers.

*Sources:* See Kim Foltz, "Ads Popping Up All Over," *Newsweek,* August 12, 1985, pp. 50–51; Ruth Hamel and Tim Schreiner, "Billboards Want Respect," *American Demographics,* July 1988, pp. 45–49; "Cable Continues to Grow in Importance," *Advertising Age,* February 20, 1989, p. C6; and Alison Leigh Cowan, "Marketers Worry as Ads Crop Up in Unlikely Places," *Raleigh News and Observer,* February 21, 1988, p. 1I.

**copy testing** Measuring the communication effect of an advertisement before or after it is printed or broadcast.

### Measuring the Communication Effect

Measuring the communication effect reveals whether an ad is communicating well. Called **copy testing,** this process can be performed before or after an ad is printed or broadcast. Before the ad is placed, the advertiser can show it to consumers, ask how they like it, and measure recall or attitude changes resulting from it. After the ad has run, the advertiser can measure how the ad affected consumer recall or product awareness, knowledge, and preference.

### Measuring the Sales Effect

What sales are caused by an ad that increases brand awareness by 20 percent and brand preference by 10 percent? The sales effect of advertising is often harder to measure than the communication effect. Sales are affected by many factors besides advertising—such as product features, price, and availability.

One way to measure sales effect is to compare past sales with past advertising expenditures. Another way is through experiments. Du Pont was one of the first companies to use advertising experiments.[10] Du Pont's paint department divided 56 sales territories into high, average, and low market-share territories. In one-third of the group, Du Pont spent the normal amount for advertising; in another third, the company spent two and one-half times the normal amount; and in the remaining third, it allotted four times the normal amount. At the end of the experiment, Du Pont estimated how many extra sales had been created by higher levels of advertising expenditure. It found that higher advertising spending increased sales at a diminishing rate and that the sales increase was weaker in its high-market-share territories.

To spend a large advertising budget wisely, advertisers must define their advertising objectives, make careful budget, message, and media decisions, and evaluate the results. Advertising also draws much public attention because of its power to affect life styles and opinions. Advertising faces increased regulation to ensure that it performs responsibly (see Marketing Highlight 16–4).[11]

# Marketing Highlight 16–4

## ADVERTISING DECISIONS AND PUBLIC POLICY

By law, companies must avoid deception or discrimination in their use of advertising. Here are the major issues:

*False advertising*. Advertisers must not make false claims, such as stating that a product cures something that it does not. Advertisers must avoid false demonstrations, such as using sand-covered plexiglass instead of sandpaper in a commercial to demonstrate that a razor blade can shave sandpaper.

*Deceptive advertising*. Advertisers must not create ads that have the capacity to deceive, even though no one may be deceived. A floor wax cannot be advertised as giving six months' protection unless it does so under typical conditions, and a diet bread cannot be advertised as having fewer calories simply because its slices are thinner. The problem is to tell the difference between deception and "puffery"—simple, acceptable exaggerations not intended to be believed.

*Bait-and-switch advertising*. The seller should not attract buyers on false pretenses. For example, let's say a seller advertises a $79 sewing machine. When consumers try to buy the advertised machine, the seller refuses to sell it, downplays its features, shows a faulty one, or promises unreasonable delivery dates, trying to switch the buyer to a more expensive machine.

*Promotional allowances and services*. The company must make promotional allowances and services available to all customers on proportionately equal terms.

# SALES PROMOTION

Advertising is joined by two other mass-promotion tools—*sales promotion* and *public relations*. **Sales promotion** consists of short-term incentives to encourage purchase or sales of a product or service. Sales promotion includes a wide variety of promotion tools designed to stimulate earlier or stronger market response. It includes **consumer promotion**—samples, coupons, rebates, prices-off, premiums, contests, trading stamps, demonstrations; **trade promotion**—buying allowances, free goods, merchandise allowances, cooperative advertising, push money, dealer sales contests; and **salesforce promotion**—bonuses, contests, sales rallies.

Sales promotion tools are used by most organizations, including manufacturers, distributors, retailers, trade associations, and nonprofit institutions. Estimates of annual sales-promotion spending run as high as $100 billion, and this spending has increased rapidly in recent years.[12] A few decades ago, the ratio of advertising to sales-promotion spending was about 60/40. Today, in many consumer packaged goods companies, the picture is reversed, with sales promotion often accounting for 60 or 70 percent of all marketing expenditures.

Sales promotions are usually used together with advertising or personal selling. Consumer promotions must usually be advertised and can add excitement and pulling power to ads. Trade and salesforce promotions support the firm's personal selling process. In using sales promotion, a company must set objectives, select the right tools, develop the best program, pretest and implement it, and evaluate the results.

## Setting Sales-Promotion Objectives

Sales-promotion objectives vary widely. Sellers may use *consumer promotions* to increase short-term sales or to help build long-term market share. The objective may be to entice consumers to try a new product, lure consumers away from competitors' products, get consumers to "load up" on a mature product, or hold and reward loyal customers. Objectives for *trade promotions* include getting retailers to carry new items and more inventory, getting them to advertise the product and give it more shelf space, and getting them to buy ahead. For the *salesforce*, objectives include getting more salesforce support for current or new products or getting salespeople to sign up new accounts.

In general, sales promotions should be **consumer franchise building**—they should promote the product's positioning and include a selling message along with the deal. Ideally, the objective is to build long-run consumer demand rather than to prompt temporary brand switching. If properly designed, every sales-promotion tool has consumer franchise-building potential.[13]

## Selecting Sales-Promotion Tools

Many tools can be used to accomplish sales-promotion objectives. The promotion planner should consider the type of market, the sales-promotion objectives, the competition, and the costs and effectiveness of each tool. The main consumer- and trade-promotion tools are described below.

### Consumer-Promotion Tools

The main consumer-promotion tools include samples, coupons, cash refunds, price packs, premiums, patronage rewards, point-of-purchase displays and demonstrations, and contests, sweepstakes, and games.

**sales promotion** Short-term incentives to encourage purchase or sales of a product or service.

**consumer promotion** Sales promotion designed to stimulate consumer purchasing.

**trade promotion** Sales promotion designed to gain reseller support and to improve reseller selling efforts.

**salesforce promotion** Sales promotion designed to motivate the salesforce and make salesforce selling efforts more effective.

**consumer franchise-building promotions** Sales promotions that promote the product's positioning and include a selling message along with the deal.

**samples** Offers of a trial amount of a product to consumers.

**coupons** Certificates that give buyers savings when they purchase specified products.

**cash refund offers** (or **rebates**) Offers to refund part of the purchase price of a product to consumers who send a "proof of purchase" to the manufacturer.

**price packs** (or **cents-off deals**) Reduced prices that are marked by the producer directly on a label or package.

**Samples** are offers of a trial amount of a product. Some samples are free; for others, the company charges a small amount to offset its cost. The sample might be delivered door to door, sent in the mail, handed out in a store, attached to another product, or featured in an ad. Sampling is the most effective—but most expensive—way to introduce a new product. For example, Lever Brothers had so much confidence in its new Surf detergent that it spent $43 million to distribute free samples to four out of every five American households.

**Coupons** are certificates that give buyers savings when they purchase specified products. Over 220 billion coupons are distributed in the U.S. each year, with a total face value of over $55 billion. Consumers redeem about 7.3 billion of these coupons, saving almost $3 billion on their shopping bills.[14] Coupons can be mailed, included with other products, or placed in ads. Several package goods companies are experimenting with point-of-sale coupon dispensing machines and computerized printers that automatically print out coupons at the cash register when certain products pass over the scanner. Coupons can stimulate sales of a mature brand and promote early trial of a new brand.

**Cash refund offers** (or **rebates**) are like coupons except that the price reduction occurs after the purchase rather than at the retail outlet. The consumer sends a "proof of purchase" to the manufacturer, who then refunds part of the purchase price by mail. Cash refunds have been used for major products such as automobiles as well as for small appliances and packaged goods.

**Price packs** (also called **cents-off deals**) offer consumers savings off the regular price of a product. The reduced prices are marked by the producer

*Companies send out over 200 billion coupons each year and spend hundreds of millions of dollars on samples.*

directly on the label or package. Price packs can be single packages sold at a reduced price (such as two for the price of one), or two related products banded together (such as a toothbrush and toothpaste). Price packs are very effective— even more so than coupons—in stimulating short-term sales.

**Premiums** are goods offered either free or at low cost as an incentive to buy a product. In its "Treasure Hunt" promotion, for example, Quaker Oats inserted $5 million of gold and silver coins in Ken-L Ration dog food packages. In its recent premium promotion, Cutty Sark scotch offered a brass tray with the purchase of one bottle of Cutty and a desk lamp with the purchase of two. A premium may come inside (in-pack) or outside (on-pack) the package. The package itself, if reusable (such as a decorative tin), may serve as a premium. Premiums are sometimes mailed to consumers who have sent in a proof of purchase, such as a box top. A *self-liquidating premium* is a premium sold below its normal retail price to consumers who request it. For example, manufacturers now offer consumers all kinds of premiums bearing the company's name: Budweiser fans can order T-shirts, hot-air balloons, and hundreds of other items with Bud's name on them at unusually low prices.

**Patronage rewards** are cash or other awards for the regular use of a certain company's products or services. For example, airlines offer "frequent flyer plans," awarding points for miles traveled that can be turned in for free airline trips. Marriott Hotels has adopted an "honored guest" plan that awards points for users of their hotels. Trading stamps are also patronage rewards in that customers receive stamps when buying from certain merchants and can redeem them for goods either at redemption centers or through mail-order catalogs.

**Point-of-purchase (POP) promotions** include displays and demonstrations that take place at the point of purchase or sale. An example is a five-foot-high cardboard display of Cap'n Crunch next to Cap'n Crunch cereal boxes. Unfortunately, many retailers do not like to handle the hundreds of displays, signs, and posters they receive from manufacturers each year. Manufacturers have thus responded by offering better POP materials, tying them in with television or print messages and offering to set them up. A good example is the award-winning Pepsi "tipping can" display. From an ordinary display of Pepsi six-packs along a supermarket aisle, a mechanically rigged six-pack begins to tip forward, grabbing the attention of passing shoppers who think the six-pack is falling. A sign reminds shoppers, "Don't forget the Pepsi!" In test market stores, the display helped get more trade support and greatly increased Pepsi sales.

**Contests, sweepstakes,** and **games** give consumers the chance to win something—such as cash, trips, or goods—by luck or through extra effort. A *contest* calls for consumers to submit an entry—a jingle, guess, suggestion—to be judged by a panel that will select the best entries. A *sweepstakes* calls for consumers to submit their names for a drawing. A *game* presents consumers with something every time they buy—bingo numbers, missing letters—that may or may not help them win a prize. A sales contest urges dealers or the salesforce to increase their efforts, with prizes going to the top performers.

### Trade-Promotion Tools

More sales-promotion dollars are directed to retailers and wholesalers (55 percent) than to consumers (45 percent)![15] Trade promotion can persuade retailers or wholesalers to carry a brand, give it shelf space, promote it in advertising, and push it to consumers. Shelf space is so scarce these days that manufacturers often have to offer price-offs, allowances, buy-back guarantees, or free goods to get on the shelf and, once there, to stay on it.

Manufacturers use several trade-promotion tools. Many of the tools used for consumer promotions—contests, premiums, displays—can also be used as

**premiums** Goods offered either free or at low cost as an incentive to buy a product.

**patronage rewards** Cash or other awards for the regular use of a certain company's products or services.

**point-of-purchase (POP) promotions** Displays and demonstrations that take place at the point of purchase or sale.

**contests, sweepstakes,** and **games** Promotional events that give consumers the chance to win something by luck or through extra effort.

**discount** A straight reduction in price on purchases during a stated period of time.

**allowance** Promotional money paid by manufacturers to retailers in return for an agreement to feature the manufacturer's products in some way.

# TIPPERS STOP TRAFFIC!

The bottle or 6-pack that asks to be put in the shopping cart!

Every 30 seconds this self-contained tipper display will appear to fall from the shelf and then slowly return to its place.

Display occupies the space of two 2-liter bottles or four 6-packs of cans.

Operates for 6 to 8 weeks on one 6-volt battery.

Works on the shelf or a rack. For a super visual effect, use multiple units on a mass display.

# AND THERE'S MORE...

*Pepsi's tipping can and tipping bottle displays grab shopper attention.*

trade promotions. Or the manufacturer may offer a straight **discount** off the list price on each case purchased during a stated period of time (also called a *price-off, off-invoice,* or *off-list*). The offer encourages dealers to buy in quantity or to carry a new item. Dealers can use the discount for immediate profit, for advertising, or for price reductions to their customers.

Manufacturers may also offer an **allowance** (usually so much off per case) in return for the retailer's agreement to feature the manufacturer's products in some way. An *advertising allowance* compensates retailers for advertising the product. A *display allowance* compensates them for using special displays.

Manufacturers may offer *free goods,* which are extra cases of merchandise, to middlemen who buy a certain quantity or who feature a certain flavor or size. They may offer *push money*—cash or gifts to dealers or their salesforce to "push" the manufacturer's goods. Manufacturers may give retailers free *specialty advertising items* that carry the company's name, such as pens, pencils, calendars, paperweights, matchbooks, memo pads, ashtrays, and yardsticks.

Many companies and trade associations organize *conventions and trade shows* to promote their products. Firms selling to the industry show their products at the trade show. Over 5,600 trade shows take place every year, drawing approximately 80 million people. Vendors get many benefits, such as finding new sales leads, contacting customers, introducing new products, meeting new customers, and selling more to present customers.

## Developing the Sales-Promotion Program

The marketer must make some other decisions in order to define the full sales-promotion program. First, the marketer must decide on the *size of the incentive*. A certain minimum incentive is necessary if the promotion is to succeed. A larger incentive will produce more sales response. Some of the large firms that sell consumer package goods have a sales-promotion manager who studies past promotions and recommends incentive levels to brand managers.

The marketer must also set *conditions for participation*. Incentives might be offered to everyone or only to select groups. A premium might be offered only to those who turn in boxtops. Sweepstakes might not be offered in certain states, to families of company personnel, or to persons under a certain age.

The marketer must then decide how to *promote and distribute the promotion* program itself. A 50-cents-off coupon could be given out in a package, at the store, by mail, or in an advertisement. Each distribution method involves a different level of reach and cost. The *length of the promotion* is also important. If the sales-promotion period is too short, many prospects who may not be buying during that time will not be able to take advantage of it. If the promotion runs too long, the deal will lose some of its "act now" force. Brand managers need to set calendar dates for the promotions. The dates will be used by production, sales, and distribution. Some unplanned promotions may also be needed, requiring cooperation on short notice.

Finally, the marketer has to decide on the *sales-promotion budget*. It can be developed in two ways. The marketer can choose the promotions and estimate their total cost. However, the more common way is to use a percentage of the total budget for sales promotion. One study found three major problems in how companies budget for sales promotion. First, they do not consider cost effectiveness. Second, instead of spending to achieve objectives, they simply extend the previous year's spending, take a percentage of expected sales, or use the "affordable approach." Finally, advertising and sales-promotion budgets are too often prepared separately.[16]

## Pretesting and Implementing

Whenever possible, sales-promotion tools should be *pretested* to find out if they are appropriate and of the right incentive size. Yet few promotions are ever tested ahead of time—70 percent of companies do not test sales promotions before starting them.[17] Nevertheless, consumer sales promotions can be quickly and inexpensively pretested. For example, consumers can be asked to rate or rank different possible promotions or promotions can be tried on a limited basis in selected geographic areas.

Companies should prepare implementation plans for each promotion, covering lead time and sell-off time. *Lead time* is the time necessary to prepare the program before launching it. *Sell-off time* begins with the launch and ends when the promotion ends.

## Evaluating the Results

Evaluation is also important. Yet many companies fail to evaluate their sales-promotion programs and others evaluate them only superficially. Manufacturers can use one of many evaluation methods. The most common method is to compare sales before, during, and after a promotion. Suppose a company has a 6 percent market share before the promotion, which jumps to 10 percent during the promotion, falls to 5 percent right after, and rises to 7 percent later on. The promotion seems to have attracted new triers and more buying from current customers. After the promotion, sales fell as consumers used up their inventories. The long-run rise to 7 percent means that the company gained some new users. If the brand's share returned to the old level, then the promotion had changed only the *timing* of demand rather than the *total* demand.

Consumer research would show the kinds of people who responded to the promotion and what they did after it. *Surveys* can provide information on how many consumers recall the promotion, what they thought of it, how many took advantage of it, and how it affected their buying. Sales promotions can also be evaluated through *experiments* that vary such factors as incentive value, length, and distribution method.

Clearly, sales promotion plays an important role in the total promotion mix. To use it well, the marketer must define sales-promotion objectives, select the best tools, design the sales-promotion program, pretest and implement it, and evaluate the results. Marketing Highlight 16–5 describes some award-winning sales-promotion campaigns.[18]

# Marketing Highlight 16–5

## AWARD-WINNING SALES PROMOTIONS

Each year, American companies bombard consumers with thousands upon thousands of assorted sales promotions. Some fizzle badly, never meeting their objectives; others yield blockbuster returns. Here are examples of some award-winning sales promotions.

### Quaker's ''Where's the Cap'n'' Contest

In this contest for kids, Quaker removed the likeness of Cap'n Crunch from the front of its cereal boxes and offered cash rewards totaling a million dollars to children who could find him. Clues to the Cap'n's whereabouts were provided inside the box, along with a free detective kit. Quaker supported the contest with large amounts of advertising during children's network television programming and in children's magazines. Coupons offering discounts on boxes of Cap'n Crunch cereal were distributed to parents. The promotion's objective: to turn around the brand's declining sales and market share. It accomplished this objective—and more. The contest became a major media event. Although it cost Quaker $18 million, brand awareness rose quickly, and Cap'n

Crunch sales increased by a dramatic 50 percent!

### 9-Lives ''Free Health Exam for Your Cat'' Offer

In this unusual premium promotion, Star-Kist Foods teamed with the American Animal Hospital Association to offer cat owners a free $15 cat physical in exchange for proofs of purchase from 9-Lives cat food products. The 1,500 AAHA members donated their services to get cat owners into the habit of regular pet checkups. Star-Kist supported the premium offer with 63 million coupons and trade discounts to boost retailer support. The promotion cost about $600,000 (excluding media). Consumers redeemed coupons at a rate 40 percent higher than normal, and Star-Kist gave out more than 50,000 free exam certificates. During the promotion, 9-Lives canned products achieved their highest share of the market in two years.

### The ''Red Baron Fly-In'' Promotion

Red Baron Pizza Service used an imaginative combination of special events,

couponing, and charitable activities to boost sales of its frozen pizza. The company re-created World War I flying ace Baron Manfred von Richthofen—complete with traditional flying gear and open-cockpit Stearman biplanes—as its company spokesperson. Red Baron pilots barnstormed 13 markets, showed the plane, did stunts, gave out coupons, and invited consumers to ''come fly with the Red Baron.'' The company donated $500 to a local youth organization in each market and urged consumers to match the gift. Trade promotions and local tie-in promotions boosted retailer support. The total budget: about $1 million. The results: For the four-week period during and after the fly-ins, unit sales in the 13 markets jumped an average of 100 percent. In the 90 days following the fly-in, sales in some markets increased as much as 400 percent.

*Sources:* See William A. Robinson, ''The Best Promotions of 1983,'' *Advertising Age,* May 31, 1984, pp. 10–12; Robinson, ''1985 Best Promotions of the Year,'' *Advertising Age,* May 5, 1986, pp. S10–11; ''A Gallery of Best Sales Promotions,'' *Advertising Age,* February 23, 1987, pp. 49–50; and ''Sales Promotions Rack Up 'Reggies,' '' *Advertising Age,* March 21, 1988, p. 26.

# PUBLIC RELATIONS

Another major mass-promotion tool is **public relations**—building good relations with the company's various publics by obtaining favorable publicity, building up a good "corporate image," and handling or heading off unfavorable rumors, stories, and events. The old name for marketing public relations was **publicity,** which was seen simply as activities to promote a company or its products by planting news about it in media not paid for by the sponsor. Public relations is a much broader concept that includes publicity and many other activities. Public relations departments use many different tools:

□ *Press relations:* Placing newsworthy information into the news media to attract attention to a person, product, or service.

□ *Product publicity:* Publicizing specific products.

□ *Corporate communications:* Creating internal and external communications to promote understanding of the firm or institution.

□ *Lobbying:* Dealing with legislators and government officials to promote or defeat legislation and regulation.

□ *Counseling:* Advising management about public issues and company positions and image.[19]

Public relations is used to promote products, people, places, ideas, activities, organizations, and even nations. Trade associations have used public relations to rebuild interest in declining commodities such as eggs, apples, milk, and potatoes. New York City's image turned around when its "I Love New York" campaign took root, bringing millions more tourists to the city. Johnson & Johnson's masterly use of public relations played a major role in saving Tylenol from extinction after its product-tampering scares. Lee Iaccoca's speeches and autobiography helped create a new winning image for Chrysler. Nations have used public relations to attract more tourists, foreign investment, and international support.

Public relations can have a strong impact on public awareness at a much lower cost than advertising. The company does not pay for the space or time in the media. It pays for a staff to develop and circulate information and manage events. If the company develops an interesting story, it could be picked up by several different media, having the same effect as advertising that would cost millions of dollars. And it would have more credibility than advertising. Public relations results can sometimes be spectacular. Consider the case of Cabbage Patch dolls:

> Public relations played a major role in making Coleco's Cabbage Patch dolls an overnight sensation. The dolls were formally introduced at a Boston press conference where local schoolchildren performed a mass-adoption ceremony for the press. Thanks to Coleco's public relations machine, child psychologists publicly endorsed the Cabbage Patch Kids, and Dr. Joyce Brothers and other newspaper columnists proclaimed that the Kids were healthy playthings. Major women's magazines featured the dolls as ideal Christmas gifts, and after a five-minute feature on the "Today" show, the Kids made the complete talk-show circuit. Marketers of other products used the hard-to-get Cabbage Patch dolls as premiums, and retailers used them to lure customers into their stores. The word spread, and every child just *had* to have one. The dolls were quickly sold out, and the great "Cabbage Patch Panic" began.

Despite its potential strengths, public relations is often described as a marketing stepchild because of its limited and scattered use. The public

**public relations** Building good relations with the company's various publics by obtaining favorable publicity, building a good "corporate image," and handling or heading off unfavorable rumors, stories, and events.

**publicity** Activities to promote a company or its products by planting news about it in media not paid for by the sponsor.

*The great "Cabbage Patch Panic."*

relations department is usually located at corporate headquarters. Its staff is so busy dealing with various publics—stockholders, employees, legislators, city officials—that public relations to support product-marketing objectives may be ignored. And marketing managers and public relations practitioners do not always talk the same language. Many public relations practitioners see their job as simply communicating. Marketing managers, on the other hand, tend to be much more interested in how advertising and public relations affect sales and profits.

However, this situation is changing. Many companies now want their public relations departments to manage all of their activities with a view toward marketing the company and improving the bottom line. Some companies are setting up special units called *marketing public relations* to support corporate and product promotion and image making directly. Many companies hire marketing public relations firms to handle their PR programs or to assist the public relations team. In a recent survey of marketing managers, three-fourths reported that their companies use marketing public relations. They found it particularly effective in building brand awareness and knowledge for both new and established products. In several cases, it proved more cost-effective than advertising.[20]

## Major Public Relations Tools

Public relations professionals use several tools. One of the major tools is *news*. PR professionals find or create favorable news about a company and its products or people. Sometimes news stories occur naturally, and sometimes the PR person can suggest events or activities that will create news. *Speeches* can also create product and company publicity. Lee Iaccoca's charismatic talks to large audiences helped to sell Chrysler cars to consumers and stock to investors. Increasingly, company executives must field questions from the media or give talks at trade associations or sales meetings, and these events can build or hurt the company's image. Another common PR tool is *special events,* ranging from

*Attractive, distinctive, memorable company logos become strong marketing tools, as they are for these PepsiCo companies.*

news conferences, press tours, grand openings, and fireworks displays to laser shows, hot-air balloon releases, multimedia presentations, and star-studded spectaculars that will reach and interest target publics.

Public relations people also prepare *written materials* to reach and influence their target markets. These materials include annual reports, brochures, articles, and company newsletters and magazines. *Audio-visual materials* such as films, slide-and-sound programs, and video and audio cassettes are increasingly being used as communication tools. *Corporate identity materials* can also help to create a corporate identity that the public immediately recognizes. Logos, stationery, brochures, signs, business forms, business cards, buildings, uniforms, and company cars and trucks—all become marketing tools when they are attractive, distinctive, and memorable.

Companies can also improve public goodwill by contributing money and time to *public-service activities*. For example, Procter & Gamble and Publishers' Clearing House held a joint promotion to aid the Special Olympics. The Publishers' Clearing House mailing included product coupons, and Procter & Gamble donated ten cents per redeemed coupon to the Special Olympics. In another example, B. Dalton Booksellers earmarked $3 million over a four-year period for the fight against illiteracy.[21]

## *Major Public Relations Decisions*

In considering when and how to use product public relations, management should set PR objectives, choose PR messages and vehicles, implement the PR plan, and evaluate the results.

### Setting Public Relations Objectives

The first task is to set *objectives* for public relations. Some years ago, the Wine Growers of California hired a public relations firm to develop a program to support two major marketing objectives: to convince Americans that wine drinking is a pleasant part of good living and to improve the image and market share of California wines among all wines. The following public relations objectives were set: develop magazine stories about wine and get them placed in top magazines (such as *Time* and *House Beautiful*) and in newspapers (food columns and feature sections); develop stories about the many health values of wine and direct them to the medical profession; and develop specific publicity for the young adult market, the college market, governmental bodies, and various ethnic communities. These objectives were turned into specific goals so that final results could be evaluated.

## Choosing Public Relations Messages and Vehicles

The organization next finds interesting stories to tell about the product. Suppose a little-known college wants more public recognition. It will search for possible stories. Do any faculty members have unusual backgrounds, or are any working on unusual projects? Are any interesting new courses being taught or any interesting events taking place on campus? Usually, this search will uncover hundreds of stories that can be fed to the press. The chosen stories should reflect the image sought by the college.

If there are not enough stories, the college could sponsor newsworthy events. Here, the organization creates news rather than finds it. Ideas might include hosting major academic conventions, inviting well-known speakers, and holding news conferences. Each event creates many stories for many different audiences.

Event creation is especially important in publicizing fund-raising drives for nonprofit organizations. Fund-raisers have developed a large set of special events such as art exhibits, auctions, benefit evenings, book sales, contests, dances, dinners, fairs, fashion shows, phonothons, rummage sales, tours, and walkathons. No sooner is one type of event created, such as a walkathon, than competitors create new versions, such as readathons, bikeathons, and jogathons.

## Implementing the Public Relations Plan

Implementing public relations requires care. Take the matter of placing stories in the media. A *great* story is easy to place—but most stories are not great and may not get past busy editors. Thus, one of the main assets of public relations people is their personal relationships with media editors. In fact, PR professionals are often ex-journalists who know many media editors and know what they want. They view media editors as a market to be satisfied so that editors will continue to use their stories.

## Evaluating Public Relations Results

Public relations results are difficult to measure because PR is used with other promotion tools and its impact is often indirect. If PR is used before other tools come into play, its contribution is easier to evaluate.

The easiest measure of publicity effectiveness is the number of exposures in the media. Public relations people give the client a "clippings book" showing all the media that carried news about the product and a summary such as the following:

> Media coverage included 3,500 column inches of news and photographs in 350 publications with a combined circulation of 79.4 million; 2,500 minutes of air time on 290 radio stations and an estimated audience of 65 million; and 660 minutes of air time on 160 television stations with an estimated audience of 91 million. If this

time and space had been purchased at advertising rates, it would have amounted to $1,047,000.[22]

However, this exposure measure is not very satisfying. It does not tell how many people actually read or heard the message, nor what they thought afterward. In addition, since the media overlap in readership and viewership, it does not give information on the *net* audience reached.

A better measure is the change in product awareness, knowledge, and attitude resulting from the publicity campaign. Assessing the change requires measuring the before-and-after levels of these measures. The Potato Board learned, for example, that the number of people who agreed with the statement "Potatoes are rich in vitamins and minerals" went from 36 percent before its public relations campaign to 67 percent after the campaign. That change represented a large increase in product knowledge.

Sales and profit impact, if obtainable, is the best measure of public relations effort. For example, 9-Lives sales increased 43 percent at the end of a major "Morris the Cat" campaign. However, advertising and sales promotion had also been stepped up, and their contribution has to be considered.

---

# SUMMARY

Three major tools of mass promotion are advertising, sales promotion, and public relations. They are mass-marketing tools as opposed to personal selling, which targets specific buyers.

*Advertising*—the use of paid media by a seller to inform, persuade, and remind consumers about its products or organization—is a strong promotion tool. American marketers spend over $109 billion each year on advertising, and it takes many forms and has many uses. *Advertising decision making* is a five-step process consisting of setting objectives, budget decision, message decision, media decision, and evaluation. Advertisers should set clear *objectives* as to whether the advertising is supposed to inform, persuade, or remind buyers. The advertising *budget* can be based on what is affordable, a percentage of sales, competitors' spending, or objectives and tasks. The *message decision* calls for designing messages, evaluating them, and executing them effectively. The *media decision* calls for defining reach, frequency, and impact goals,

choosing major media types, selecting media vehicles, and scheduling the media. Finally, *evaluation* calls for evaluating the communication and sales effects of advertising before, during, and after the advertising is placed.

*Sales promotion* covers a wide variety of short-term incentive tools—coupons, premiums, contests, buying allowances—designed to stimulate consumers, the trade, and the company's own salesforce. Sales-promotion spending has been growing faster than advertising spending in recent years. Sales promotion calls for setting sales-promotion objectives; selecting tools; developing, pretesting, and implementing the sales-promotion program; and evaluating results.

*Public relations*—which involves gaining favorable publicity and creating a favorable company image—is the least used of the major promotion tools, although it has great potential for building awareness and preference. Public relations involves setting PR objectives, choosing PR messages and vehicles, implementing the PR plan, and evaluating PR results.

---

# QUESTIONS FOR DISCUSSION

1. Is it feasible for an advertising agency to work for two competing clients at the same time? How much competition between such accounts is too much competition?

2. According to advertising expert Steuart Henderson Britt, good advertising objectives spell out the intended audience, the advertising message, the desired effects, and the criteria for determining whether the effects were achieved (for example, not just "increase awareness" but "increase awareness 20%"). Why should these components be part of the

advertising objective? What are some effects that an advertiser wants a campaign to achieve?

3. What are some benefits and drawbacks of comparison advertising? Which has more to gain from using comparison advertising—the market-leading brand or a lesser brand?

4. What impact would a 5 percent national advertising tax have on advertising budgets? How would such a tax affect advertisers, consumers, the media, and the economy?

5. Describe several ads that you think are particularly

effective and compare them with others you think are ineffective. How would you improve the less-effective ads?

6. What factors call for more *frequency* in an advertising media schedule? What factors call for more *reach?* How can you increase one without either sacrificing the other or increasing your advertising budget?

7. A certain ad states that, except for homemade cookies, Almost Home cookies are the ''moistest, chewiest, most perfectly baked cookies the world has ever tasted.'' If you think some other cookie is moister, chewier, or both, is the Almost Home claim false? Should such claims be regulated?

8. Which forms of sales promotion are most effective in getting consumers to try a product? Which are most effective in building loyalty to a product?

9. Why are many companies spending more on trade and consumer promotions than on advertising? Is heavy spending on sales promotion a good strategy for long-term profits?

10. The Graduate School of Business Administration at the University of North Carolina recently hired a public relations firm. What objectives might the school set for a public relations campaign? How can the campaign results be measured?

## REFERENCES

1. See Alice Z. Cuneo, ''FCB Creativity Bears Fruit,'' *Advertising Age,* July 6, 1987, p. 25; Joan O'C. Hamilton, ''You've Come a Long Way, Gumby,'' *Business Week,* December 8, 1986, p. 74; Cuneo, ''Hot Raisins: It's Licensed Products That Bring Big Bucks,'' *Advertising Age,* May 16, 1988, p. 30; and Marcy Magiera, ''Clamation Wiz Molds Winning Business,'' *Advertising Age,* November 14, 1988, p. 42.

2. Statistical information in this section on the size and composition of advertising draws on the September 28, 1988, special issue of *Advertising Age* on the hundred leading national advertisers.

3. See Donald E. Schultz, Dennis Martin, and William P. Brown, *Strategic Advertising Campaigns* (Chicago: Crain Books, 1984), pp. 192–97.

4. See Scott Hume, ''Anheuser Beer Arrives without Ads,'' *Advertising Age,* July 6, 1987, p. 2.

5. Christine Dugas, ''And Now, a Wittier Word from Our Sponsors,'' *Business Week,* March 24, 1986, p. 90. Also see Felix Kessler, ''In Search of Zap-Proof Commercials,'' *Fortune,* January 21, 1985, pp. 68–70; and Dennis Kneale, '' 'Zapping' of TV Ads Appears Pervasive,'' *The Wall Street Journal,* April 25, 1988, p. 29.

6. See ''Ad Quality Good, Believability Low,'' *Advertising Age,* May 31, 1984, p. 3.

7. See William A. Mindak and H. Malcolm Bybee, ''Marketing's Application to Fund Raising,'' *Journal of Marketing,* July 1971, pp. 13–18.

8. Janet Meyers and Laurie Freeman, ''Marketers Police TV Commercial Costs,'' *Advertising Age,* April 3, 1989, p. 51; and Dugas, ''And Now, a Wittier Word from Our Sponsor,'' p. 91.

9. Philip H. Dougherty, ''Bud 'Pulses' the Market,'' *New York Times,* February 18, 1975, p. 40.

10. See Robert D. Buzzell, ''E. I. Du Pont de Nemours & Co.: Measurement of Effects of Advertising,'' in his *Mathematical Models and Marketing Management* (Boston: Division of Research, Graduate School of Business Administration, Harvard University, 1964), pp. 157–79.

11. For more on the legal aspects of advertising and sales promotion, see Louis W. Stern and Thomas L. Eovaldi, *Legal Aspects of Marketing Strategy* (Englewood Cliffs, NJ: Prentice Hall, 1984), Chaps. 7 and 8.

12. Leon Strazewski, ''Promotion 'Carnival' Gets Serious,'' *Advertising Age,* May 2, 1988, pp. S1–2.

13. See Roger Strang, Robert M. Prentice, and Alden G. Clayton, *The Relationship between Advertising and Promotion in Brand Strategy* (Cambridge, MA: Marketing Science Institute, 1975), Chap. 5; and P. Rajan Varadarajan, ''Cooperative Sales Promotion: An Idea Whose Time Has Come,'' *Journal of Consumer Marketing,* Winter 1986, pp. 15–33.

14. See ''Coupons,'' *Progressive Grocer 1987 Nielsen Review,* September 1987 pp. 16–18; Lori Kesler, ''Catalina Cuts Couponing Clutter,'' *Advertising Age,* May 9, 1988, p. S30; and Alison Fahey, ''Red Letter Cut from Coupon Wars,'' *Advertising Age,* April 3, 1989, p. 38.

15. See Felix Kessler, ''The Costly Coupon Craze,'' *Fortune,* June 9, 1986, p. 83.

16. Roger A. Strang, ''Sales Promotion—Fast Growth, Faulty Management,'' *Harvard Business Review,* July-August 1976, p. 119.

17. ''Pretesting Phase of Promotions Is Often Overlooked,'' *Marketing News,* February 29, 1988, p. 10.

18. For more on sales promotion, see Don E. Schultz and William A. Robinson, *Sales Promotion Management* (Chicago: Crain Books, 1982); John Keon and Judy Bayer, "An Expert Approach to Sales Promotion Management," *Journal of Advertising Research,* June-July 1986, pp. 19–26; and Kenneth G. Hardy, "Key Success Factors for Manufacturer's Sales Promotions in Package Goods," *Journal of Marketing,* July 1986, pp. 13–23.

19. Adapted from Scott M. Cutlip, Allen H. Center, and Glen M. Brown, *Effective Public Relations,* 6th ed. (Englewood Cliffs, NJ: Prentice Hall, 1985), pp. 7–17.

20. Tom Duncan, *A Study of How Manufacturers and Service Companies Perceive and Use Marketing Public Relations* (Muncie, IN: Ball State University, December 1985).

21. For more examples, see Laurie Freeman and Wayne Walley, "Marketing with a Cause Takes Hold," *Advertising Age,* May 16, 1988, p. 34.

22. Arthur M. Merims, "Marketing's Stepchild: Product Publicity," *Harvard Business Review,* November-December 1972, pp. 111–12. Also see Katharine D. Paine, "There *Is* a Method for Measuring PR," *Marketing News,* November 6, 1987, p. 5.

# Case 16

## PILLSBURY CO.: THE "BIG CHEESE" IN THE PIZZA WARS

For generations of American consumers, the Pillsbury Doughboy has been a cute and cuddly symbol of outstanding food products. But to competitors, confronted with Pillsbury's increasingly aggressive marketing stance, the Doughboy must seem more like the monstrous marshmallow creature from *Ghostbusters*. Nearing its 120th birthday, Pillsbury has lessened its dependence on baking products and increased its emphasis on ready-to-eat convenience products. One such product is frozen pizza. Pillsbury first introduced microwavable frozen pizza under its own brand name and then acquired several large competitors, including Totino's in 1975 and Jeno's in 1985. With over 50 percent of the market, it was certainly the "Big Cheese" of frozen pizza. However, bringing the Pillsbury, Totino's, and Jeno's brands under a single corporate umbrella has been challenging, and Pillsbury's pizza sales have recently sagged: In effect, Pillsbury has been marketing against itself. Future success will depend on the company's ability both to position its various brands relative to one another and to communicate these positions to consumers.

Frozen pizza now accounts for more than $1 billion in sales annually. However, the market is growing rather slowly—at only about 1.5 percent per year. Thus, the industry has become fiercely competitive. In the battle for market share, large national competitors must increase sales by attracting buyers from each other, from small regional processors, and even from local pizzerias. Regional competitors, fighting for their existence, are increasingly cutting prices, and other heavyweights are now entering the frozen pizza field. For example, Kraft acquired its first pizza brand, Tombstone Pizza, in 1986.

Lifestyle changes also continue to influence the industry. Americans eat one billion tons of pizza annually—nearly 22.5 pounds per person. Ninety-six percent of all U.S. households now eat pizza some 30 times yearly. Although frozen pizza represents only about 30 percent of all pizza purchases, consumers eat over 70 percent of all pizza, including pizzeria pizza, at home.

Moreover, regional pizza tastes vary widely, and such variety makes it difficult for national brands to customize—a fact that makes it easier for small regional brands to survive. Regional taste differences also explain why, until recently, the frozen pizza industry was highly fragmented—that is, why there were no particularly strong national brands. At this point, the market has segmented into two distinct niches: popularly-priced and premium. The popularly-priced segment showed no growth from 1983 to 1988. The premium segment, on the other hand, grew 13 percent during the same period.

Advertising and sales-promotion trends have further influenced the competitive environment. Advertising expenditures for the industry amount to 2 percent of sales—among the lowest for food products of any kind. On the other hand, frozen pizza marketers spend a considerable amount of money at the retail level in the form of display allowances, advertising allowances, and deals to the trade. They also offer numerous consumer incentives, usually promotional price specials and coupons. Almost one-third of all frozen pizza sold uses some sort of price reduction to woo consumers. Hardly a week goes by without some special promotion for various items in the frozen pizza case.

Naturally, retailers prefer profit-producing brands. With limited

freezer cabinet space, they favor sellers who spend the most on advertising and promotion, especially trade allowances, which improve profitability directly. On the other hand, Pillsbury and other manufacturers recognize that such allowances and most other types of sales promotion are only *short-term* sales stimulators that build little long-term consumer loyalty. Nevertheless, some competitors, especially marginal manufacturers, prefer to spend for immediate sales stimulation.

As if heated competition within their own ranks weren't enough of a headache, frozen pizza marketers continue to face stiff challenges on a number of other fronts. Most formidable, perhaps, is the continued growth of home-delivery services, which expanded at a 20-percent rate for the second year in a row. Also disturbing is the fact that the consumption of "fresh" or "deli" pizzas—those made and baked at a growing number of supermarkets—soared 47 percent from 1986 to 1987. Meanwhile, 40 percent of all U.S. supermarkets now offer fresh pizza. And much of the movement to fresh pizza has been prompted by consumers' perceptions of a decline in the quality of frozen pizzas.

To understand Pillsbury's current standing in the intensely competitive frozen pizza market, one need only trace its recent pattern of acquisitions. In 1975, Pillsbury acquired Totino's, a frozen pizza company with an annual sales-growth rate of 20 percent. Within two years, Pillsbury had developed Totino's revolutionary crisp-crust technology, and the company put into action an aggressive marketing plan that made it the leader in frozen pizzas. The key aspects of the plan were product improvement, aggressive promotion, and coverage of both the high- and popularly-priced market segments.

Within three years, despite both new competitive entries sponsored by General Mills (Saluto), H.J. Heinz (La Pizzeria), Nestlé (Stouffer's), and Quaker Oats (Celeste) and more vigorous competition from over 100 smaller regional firms, Totino's was the leading brand of frozen pizza in the United States.

In 1984, Pillsbury then introduced a frozen pizza designed exclusively for microwave ovens. This product was introduced under the Pillsbury Microwave brand name, which includes other microwavable products such as pancakes and popcorn. The new Pillsbury Microwave Pizza represented a major breakthrough in microwave technology. Because microwaves are, in effect, steamers, they usually turn bread soggy. But through a patented process called "susceptor technology," Pillsbury achieved the long-sought crisp crust. Basically, the pizza is packed in an aluminum foil tray that provides heat while preventing microwave electrons from penetrating to the product itself. In essence, the package becomes its own disposable oven. Pillsbury used the same technology to create another line of frozen pizza—Pillsbury's French Bread Pizza.

Meanwhile, Jeno's, the former leader in the frozen pizza market, sought to regain leadership by introducing its own "Crisp and Tasty Crust" pizza. But Jeno's lagged Totino's by two years in product and packaging innovations. Thus, by the early 1980s, although it had increased its market share by acquiring Chef Saluto from General Mills and two regional brands, John's and Gino's, Jeno's still remained in second place.

Pillsbury then acquired archrival Jeno's in 1985. This acquisition added important market depth to Pillsbury's pizza business and provided opportunities for brand differentiation, product-quality improvements, and operating efficiencies. With such brands as Totino's, Jeno's,

Pillsbury Microwave, My Classic, Mr. P's, Fox DeLuxe, and Chef Saluto, pizza became one of the highest-volume products in Pillsbury's Consumer Foods portfolio.

Although linking Jeno's with Totino's obviously made Pillsbury a powerful force in the frozen pizza industry, it also caused problems for the company. How do you market one-time competing brands to retailers who are concerned that the absence of competition between the two will make wheeling and dealing for sales-promotion dollars more difficult? Gone, it would seem, were the days when Totino's and Jeno's, each looking for a competitive edge, bashed each other with discounts and deals to retailers. Retailers wanted to know what this situation meant for them in the long run.

One thing seemed certain: Pillsbury wanted to position its two major pizza brands so that one complemented the other. Thus, it made a number of product and pricing changes to reposition Totino's as a premium brand while retaining its popular-price position for Jeno's. Pillsbury reformulated Jeno's Crisp 'n Tasty brand—the number-two national frozen pizza line—so that it boasted a better-tasting crust and improved sauce. As for Totino's, what had been Totino's Party Pizza line in 1987—often on sale for 89 cents or even less—became Totino's Temptin' Toppings Pizza. To justify a price boost, Pillsbury reformulated the line to provide 35 percent more toppings, bigger pieces of meat, and a thicker sauce with more tomato flavor. Next, the company expanded Totino's Microwave Pizza line by adding a new full-sized (11.9-ounce to 14-ounce) product in five flavors, featuring "50 percent more pizza by weight than most other microwave pizzas." Finally, Pillsbury rolled out the premium, family-sized Totino's Pan Pizza, with nearly one pound of toppings, a

thick and chewy crust, and its own bake-and-serve pan that has an authentic pizzeria look. The line included four types of pizza available at a hefty $4.79-$5.19 each—still less than most family-sized pizzeria versions. With this product—and ads claiming "Pizza worth coming home to"—Pillsbury openly challenged eat-in and take-out pizzerias, where pan pizzas had proved far more than a flash in the pan.

Nevertheless, the new positioning strategy for its long line of frozen pizza brands failed to take hold: Pillsbury was unable to convince retailers and consumers that Totino's and Jeno's were unmistakably different—and thus damaged both. Surprisingly, the company's frozen pizza sales declined 7 percent in unit sales from 1987 to 1988. In view of the new competitive situation and changing consumer lifestyles, Pillsbury's management must now reconsider its marketing objectives and activities, especially with regard to advertising and promotion.

### Questions

1. Describe the consumer's buying-decision process for frozen pizza.

2. Describe the factors that influence a retailer's decision about which frozen pizza brands to stock and support.

3. What are the advantages and disadvantages of each type of promotional tool (advertising, consumer promotion, and trade promotion)? What role should each play in promoting Pillsbury's frozen pizza brands?

# 17
# Promoting Products: Personal Selling and Sales Management

## CHAPTER OBJECTIVES

**After reading this chapter, you should be able to**

1. Discuss the role of a company's salespeople
2. Identify the seven major salesforce management decisions
3. Explain how companies set salesforce objectives and strategy
4. Explain how companies recruit, select, and train salespeople
5. Describe how companies supervise salespeople and evaluate their effectiveness.

□ November 7: United Airlines announces it will buy 110 Boeing 737s and six Boeing 747s. Price: $3.1 billion.

□ October 22: Northwest Airlines announces it will buy 10 Boeing 747s and 10 Boeing 757s. Price: $2 billion.

□ October 9: International Lease Finance announces it will buy two Boeing 737s. Price: $50 million.

□ October 8: USAir announces it will buy two Boeing 737s. Price: $50 million.

□ October 2: Western Airlines announces it will buy 12 Boeing 737s. Price: $250 million.

□ October 1: Republic Airlines announces it will buy six Boeing 757s. Price: $240 million.

Not a bad couple of weeks' work! But you might expect such success from a company with a 60 percent share of the commercial airplane market, a company whose average order size is $34.9 million, and a company whose dedication to making a sale has been called obsessive. The company, of course, is Boeing, the $16.3 billion aerospace giant. In a field where big sales are

seldom big news, Boeing got everyone's attention when, during just six weeks, it received orders worth $6.23 billion (the sales listed above plus others).

Most of the responsibility for marketing Boeing's commercial aircraft falls on the shoulders of the company's salesforce. In some ways, selling airplanes differs from selling other industrial products. Nationwide, there are only about 55 potential customers; there are only three major competitors (Boeing, McDonnell-Douglas, and Airbus); and the high-tech product is especially complex and challenging. But in many other ways, selling commercial aircraft is like selling any other industrial product. The salespeople determine needs, demonstrate how their product fulfills needs, try to close the sale, and follow up after the sale.

To determine needs, Boeing salespeople become experts on the airlines they are responsible for, much like Wall Street analysts would. They find out where each airline wants to grow, when it wants to replace planes, and its financial situation. Then they find ways to fulfill customer needs. They run Boeing and competing planes through computer systems, simulating the airline's routes, cost per seat, and other factors to show that their planes are most efficient. And, more than likely, they'll bring in financial, planning, and technical people to answer any questions.

Then the negotiations begin. Deals are cut, discounts made, training programs offered; sometimes, top executives from both the airline and Boeing are brought in to close the deal. The selling process is nerve-rackingly slow—it can take two or three years from the day the salesperson makes the first presentation to the day the sale is announced. After getting the order, salespeople must then keep in almost constant touch to keep track of the account's equipment needs and to make certain the customer stays satisfied. Success depends on building solid, long-term relationships with customers based on performance and trust. According to one analyst, Boeing's salespeople "are the vehicle by which information is collected and contacts are made so all other things can take place."

The Boeing salesforce is made up of experienced salespeople who use a conservative, straightforward sales approach. They are smooth and knowledgeable, and they like to sell on facts and logic rather than hype and promises. In fact, they tend to undestate rather than overstate product benefits. For example, one writer notes that "they'll always underestimate fuel efficiency. They'll say it's a five percent savings, and it'll be eight." Thus, a customer thinking about making a $2 billion purchase can be certain that, after the sale, Boeing products will live up to expectations.

Boeing salespeople have a head start on the competition. They have a broad mix of excellent products to sell, and Boeing's size and reputation help them get orders. Its salespeople are proud to be selling Boeing aircraft, and their pride creates an attitude of success that is perhaps best summed up by the company's director of marketing communications: "The popular saying is that Boeing is the Mercedes of the airline industry. We think that's backward. We like to think that Mercedes is the Boeing of the auto industry."[1]

---

**salesperson** An individual acting for a company by performing one or more of the following activities: prospecting, communicating, servicing, and information gathering.

Robert Louis Stevenson once noted that "everyone lives by selling something." Salesforces are found in nonprofit as well as profit organizations. Recruiters are a college's salesforce for attracting students. Churches use membership committees to attract new members. The U.S. Agricultural Extension Service sends agricultural specialists to sell farmers on new farming methods. Hospitals and museums use fund-raisers to contact donors and raise money.

The people who do the selling go by many names: *salespeople, sales representatives, account executives, sales consultants, sales engineers, field representatives, agents, district managers,* and *marketing representatives.* Selling is one of the oldest professions in the world (see Marketing Highlight 17–1).

There are many stereotypes of salespeople. "Salesman" may bring to mind the image of Arthur Miller's pitiable Willy Loman in *Death of a Salesman* or Meredith Willson's cigar-smoking, back-slapping con man Harold Hill in *The Music Man.* Salespeople are typically pictured as outgoing and sociable—although many salespeople actually dislike unnecessary socializing. They are blamed for forcing goods on people—although buyers often search out salespeople.

Actually, the term **salesperson** covers a wide range of positions whose differences are often greater than their similarities. Here is one popular classification of sales positions:

□ Positions in which the salesperson's job is largely to *deliver* the product, such as milk, bread, fuel, or oil.

□ Positions in which the salesperson is largely an *inside order taker,* such as the department store salesperson standing behind the counter, or an *outside order taker,* such as the packing house, soap, or spice salesperson.

□ Positions in which the salesperson is not expected or permitted to take an order but only *builds goodwill or educates buyers*—the "detailer" for a pharmaceutical company who calls on doctors to educate them about the company's drug products and to urge them to prescribe these products to their patients.

# Marketing Highlight 17-1

## MILESTONES IN THE HISTORY OF SELLING

Selling goes back to the dawn of history. Paul Hermann has described a Bronze Age traveling salesman's sample case: ". . . a solid wooden box, 26 inches in length, containing in specially hollowed compartments various types of axes, sword blades, buttons, etc." Early sellers and traders were not held in high esteem. The Roman word for salesman meant "cheater," and Mercury, the god of cunning and barter, was regarded as the patron deity of merchants and traders. The buying and selling of commodities flourished over the centuries and centered in market towns. Traveling peddlers carried goods to the homes of prospective customers who were unable to get to the market towns.

The first salespeople in the United States were Yankee peddlers (pack peddlers) who carried clothing, spices, household wares, and notions in backpacks from East Coast manufacturing centers to settlers in the western frontier regions. Pack peddlers also traded with Indians, exchanging knives, beads, and ornaments for furs. Many traders came to be viewed as shrewd, unprincipled tricksters who would not think twice about putting sand in the sugar, dust in the pepper, and chicory in the coffee. They often sold colored sugar water as "medicine" guaranteed to cure all ills. In the early 1800s, some peddlers began to use horse-drawn wagons and stock heavier goods, such as furniture, clocks, dishes, weapons, and ammunition. Some wagon peddlers settled in frontier villages and opened the first general stores and trading posts.

Larger retailers traveled once or twice a year to the nearest major city to replenish their stock. Eventually, wholesalers and manufacturers hired greeters, or "drummers," who would seek out and invite retailers to visit the displays of their employers. "Drummers" would meet incoming trains and ships to beat their competitors. In time, drummers traveled to their customers' places of business. Prior to 1860, there were fewer than 1,000 traveling salespeople, many of whom were credit investigators who also took orders for goods. By 1870, there were 7,000; by 1880, 28,000; and by 1900, 93,000 traveling salespeople.

Modern selling and sales-management techniques were refined by John Henry Patterson (1844-1922), widely regarded as the father of modern selling. Patterson ran the National Cash Register Company (NCR). He asked his best salespeople to demonstrate their sales approaches to other salespeople. The best sales approach was printed in a "Sales Primer" and distributed to all NCR salespeople to be followed to the letter. This practice was the beginning of the canned sales approach. In addition, Patterson assigned his salespeople exclusive territories and sales quotas to stretch their effort. He held frequent sales meetings that served as both sales training sessions and social gatherings. He sent his salespeople regular communications on how to sell. One of the young people trained by Patterson was Thomas J. Watson, who later founded IBM. Patterson showed other companies the way to turn a salesforce into an effective tool for building sales and profits.

---

□ Positions in which the major emphasis is on *technical knowledge*—the engineering salesperson who is mostly a consultant to client companies.

□ Positions that demand the *creative sale* of tangible products, like appliances, encyclopedias, houses, or technical equipment, or of intangibles such as insurance, advertising services, or education.[2]

This list ranges from the least to the most creative types of selling. For example, the jobs at the top of the list call for servicing accounts and taking orders, while the last ones simply call for hunting down buyers and getting them to buy. We will focus on the more creative types of selling and on the process of building and managing an effective salesforce. We define **salesforce management** as the analysis, planning, implementation, and control of salesforce activities. It includes setting salesforce objectives, designing salesforce strategy, and recruiting, selecting, training, supervising, and evaluating the firm's salespeople. The major salesforce management decisions are shown in Figure 17-1 and discussed in the following sections.

**salesforce management** The analysis, planning, implementation, and control of salesforce activities.

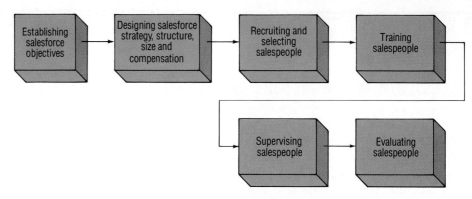

FIGURE 17–1   Major Salesforce Management Decisions

## SETTING SALESFORCE OBJECTIVES

Companies set different objectives for their salesforces. IBM's salespeople are to "sell, install, and upgrade" customer computer equipment; AT&T salespeople should "develop, sell, and protect" accounts. Salespeople usually perform one or more of many tasks. They find and develop new customers and communicate information about the company's products and services. They sell products by approaching customers, presenting their products, answering objections, and closing sales with customers. In addition, salespeople provide services to customers, carry out market research and intelligence work, and fill out sales call reports.

Some companies are very specific about their salesforce objectives and activities. One company advises its salespeople to spend 80 percent of their time with current customers and 20 percent with prospects, and 85 percent on current products and 15 percent on new products. This company believes that if

*The term "salesperson" covers a wide range of positions, from the clerk selling in a retail store to the engineering salesperson who consults with client companies.*

such norms are not set, salespeople tend to spend almost all of their time selling current products to current accounts and neglect new products and new prospects.

The old view is that salespeople should worry about sales and the company should worry about profit. However, a newer view holds that salespeople should be concerned with more than just producing *sales*—they must also know how to produce *customer satisfaction* and *company profit*. They should know how to look at sales data, measure market potential, gather market intelligence, and develop marketing strategies and plans. Salespeople need marketing-analysis skills, especially at higher levels of sales management. A market-oriented rather than a sales-oriented salesforce will be more effective in the long run.

**territorial salesforce structure** A salesforce organization that assigns each salesperson to an exclusive geographic territory in which that salesperson carries the company's full line.

# DESIGNING SALESFORCE STRATEGY

Once the company has set its salesforce objectives, it is ready to face questions of salesforce strategy, structure, size, and compensation.

## Salesforce Strategy

Every company competes with other firms to get orders from customers. Thus, it must base its strategy on an understanding of the customer-buying process. A company can use one or more of several sales approaches to contact customers. An individual salesperson can talk to a prospect or customer in person or over the phone. Or a salesperson can make a sales presentation to a buying group. A sales *team* (such as a company executive, a salesperson, and a sales engineer) can make a sales presentation to a buying group. In *conference selling*, a salesperson brings resource people from the company to meet with one or more buyers to discuss problems and opportunities. In *seminar selling*, a company team conducts an educational seminar for technical people in a customer company about state-of-the-art developments.

Thus, the salesperson often acts as an "account manager" who arranges contacts between people in the buying and selling companies. Because salespeople need help from others in the company, selling calls for teamwork. Others who might assist salespeople include top management, especially when major sales are at stake; technical people who provide technical information to customers; customer service representatives who provide installation, maintenance, and other services to customers; and office staff such as sales analysts, order processors, and secretaries.

## Salesforce Structure

The company must also decide how to structure its salesforce. This decision is simple if the company sells one product line to one industry with customers in many locations; here, the company would use a *territorial salesforce structure*. If the company sells many products to many types of customers, it might need a *product salesforce structure* or a *customer salesforce structure*. These three structures are discussed below.

### Territorial Salesforce Structure

In the **territorial salesforce structure**, each salesperson is given an exclusive territory in which to sell the company's full line. This salesforce structure is the simplest sales organization and has many advantages. It clearly defines the

**product salesforce structure** A salesforce organization under which salespeople specialize in selling only a portion of the company's products or lines.

**customer salesforce structure** A salesforce organization under which salespeople specialize in selling only to certain customers or industries.

**workload approach** An approach to setting salesforce size in which the company groups accounts into different size classes and then figures out how many salespeople are needed to call on them the desired number of times.

salesperson's job, and because only one salesperson works the territory, he or she gets all the credit or blame for territory sales. The territorial structure also increases the salesperson's desire to build local business ties that, in turn, improve the salesperson's selling effectiveness. Finally, because each salesperson travels within a small geographic area, travel expenses are relatively small.

Territorial sales organization is often supported by many levels of sales-management positions. For example, Campbell Soup recently changed from a product salesforce structure to a territorial one in which each salesperson is responsible for selling all Campbell Soup products. Starting at the bottom of the organization, *sales merchandisers* report to *sales representatives*, who report to *retail supervisors*, who report to *directors of retail sales operations*, who report to one of 22 *regional sales managers*. Regional sales managers are headed by one of four *general sales managers* (West, Central, South, and East), who report to a *vice-president and general sales manager*.[3]

### Product Salesforce Structure

Salespeople must know their products—especially when the products are numerous, unrelated, and complex. This need, together with the trend toward product management, has led many companies to the **product salesforce structure,** in which the salesforce sells along product lines. For example, the American Hospital Supply Corporation (AHS) has several product divisions, each with a separate salesforce. The product structure, however, can lead to problems if many of the company's products are bought by the same customers. Several AHS salespeople might, for example, end up calling on the same hospital on the same day. This means that they travel over the same routes and that each waits to see the same customer's purchasing agents. These extra costs must be compared with the benefits of better product knowledge and attention to individual products.

### Customer Salesforce Structure

Companies often use a **customer salesforce structure,** in which they organize the salesforce along customer lines. Separate salesforces may be set up for different industries, for serving current customers versus finding new ones, and for major versus regular accounts. Xerox, for example, classifies its customers into four major groups, each served by a different salesforce. The top group consists of large national accounts with multiple and scattered locations; these customers are handled by 250 to 300 *national account managers*. Next are major accounts that, although not national in scope, may have several locations within a region; these are handled by one of Xerox's 1,000 or so *major account managers*. The third customer group consists of standard commercial accounts with annual sales potential of $5,000 to $10,000; they are served by *account representatives*. All other customers are handled by *marketing representatives*.[4]

The major advantage of customer specialization is that each salesforce can know more about specific customer needs. The major disadvantage arises when customers are scattered across the country, resulting in a lot of travel by all the company's salesforces.

## Salesforce Size

Once the company has set its strategy and structure, it is ready to consider *salesforce size*. Salespeople constitute one of the company's most productive—and most expensive—assets. Therefore, increasing their number will increase both sales and costs.

Many companies use the **workload approach** to set salesforce size. Under this approach, a company groups accounts into different size classes and then figures out how many salespeople are needed to call on them the desired number of times. The company might think as follows: Suppose we have 1,000 Type-A accounts and 2,000 Type-B accounts. Type-A accounts require 36 calls a year and Type-B accounts 12 calls a year. In this case, the salesforce's *workload*—the number of calls it must make per year—is 60,000 calls [(1,000 × 36) + (2,000 × 12) = 36,000 + 24,000 = 60,000)]. Suppose our average salesperson can make 1,000 calls a year. The company thus needs 60 salespeople (60,000/1,000).

## Salesforce Compensation

To attract needed salespeople, a company must have an attractive compensation plan. These plans vary greatly, both by industry and by companies within the same industry. The level of compensation must be close to the "going rate" for the type of sales job and needed skills. For example, the average earnings of an experienced, middle-level salesperson in 1988 amounted to $38,900.[5] To pay less than the going rate would attract too few quality salespeople; to pay more would be unnecessary.

Compensation is made up of several elements—a fixed amount, a variable amount, expenses, and fringe benefits. The fixed amount, usually a salary, gives the salesperson some stable income. The variable amount, which might be commissions or bonuses based on sales performance, rewards the salesperson for greater effort. Expense allowances, which repay salespeople for job-related expenses, let salespeople undertake needed and desirable selling efforts. Fringe benefits, such as paid vacations, sickness or accident benefits, pensions, and life insurance, provide job security and satisfaction.

Management must decide what *mix* of these compensation elements makes the most sense for each sales job. Different combinations of fixed and variable compensation give rise to four basic types of compensation plans— straight salary, straight commission, salary plus bonus, and salary plus commissions. A recent study of salesforce compensation plans showed that about 14 percent paid straight salary, 19 percent paid straight commission, 37 percent paid salary plus commission, 26 percent paid salary plus bonus, and 10 percent paid salary plus commission plus bonus.[6]

# RECRUITING AND SELECTING SALESPEOPLE

Having set the strategy, structure, size, and compensation for the salesforce, the company now must set up systems for *recruiting and selecting, training, supervising,* and *evaluating* salespeople.

## Importance of Careful Selection

At the heart of successful salesforce operation is the selection of good salespeople. The performance levels of an average and a top salesperson can be quite different. In a typical salesforce, the top 30 percent of the salespeople might bring in 60 percent of the sales. Careful salesperson selection can thus greatly increase overall salesforce performance.

Beyond the differences in sales performance, poor selection results in costly turnover. One study found an average annual salesforce turnover rate for all industries of almost 20 percent. The costs of high turnover can be considerable. When a salesperson quits, the costs of finding and training a new salesperson—plus the costs of lost sales—can run as high as $50,000 to $75,000. And a salesforce with a lot of new people is less productive.[7]

## What Makes a Good Salesperson?

Selecting salespeople would not be a problem if the company knew what traits to look for. If it knew that good salespeople were outgoing, aggressive, and energetic, these characteristics could simply be checked among applicants. But many successful salespeople are also bashful, mild-mannered, and very relaxed. Successful salespeople include some men and women who are tall and short, some who speak well and some who speak poorly, some who dress well and some who dress shabbily.

Still, the search continues for the magic list of traits that spells sure-fire sales ability. Many such lists have been drawn up. One survey suggests that good salespeople have lots of enthusiasm, persistence, initiative, self-confidence, and job commitment. They are committed to sales as a way of life and have a strong customer orientation.[8] Charles Garfield found that good salespeople are goal-directed risk takers who identify strongly with their customers (see Marketing Highlight 17–2).

How can a company find out what traits salespeople in its industry should have? Job *duties* suggest some of the traits to look for. Is there a lot of

# Marketing Highlight 17–2

## What Makes a Supersalesperson?

Charles Garfield, clinical professor of psychology at the University of California, San Francisco School of Medicine, claims that his twenty-year analysis of more than 1,500 superachievers in every field of endeavor is the longest-running to date. *Peak Performance—Mental Training Techniques of the World's Greatest Athletes* is the first book Garfield wrote about his findings. Although he says it will be followed shortly by a book on business that will cover supersalespeople, many companies (such as IBM, which took 3,000) have ordered the current book for their salesforces. Garfield says that the complexity and speed of change in today's business world means that to be a peak performer in sales requires greater mastery of different fields than to be one in science, sports, or the arts. The following are the most common characteristics he has found in peak sales performance:

□ Supersalespeople are always taking risks and making innovations.

Unlike most people, they stay out of the "comfort zone" and try to surpass their previous levels of performance.

□ Supersalespeople have a powerful sense of mission and set the short-, intermediate-, and long-term goals necessary to fulfill that mission. Their personal goals are always higher than sales quotas set by their managers. Supersalespeople also work well with managers, especially if managers are also interested in peak performance.

□ Supersalespeople are more interested in solving problems than in placing blame or bluffing their way out of situations. Because they view themselves as professionals in training, they are always upgrading their skills.

□ Supersalespeople see themselves as partners with their customers and as team players rather than

adversaries. While peak performers believe their task is to communicate with people, mediocre salespeople psychologically change their customers into objects and talk about the number of calls and closes they made as if it had nothing to do with human beings.

□ Whereas supersalespeople take each rejection as information they can learn from, mediocre salespeople personalize rejection.

□ The most surprising finding is that, like peak performers in sports and the arts, supersalespeople use mental rehearsal. Before every sale, they review it in their mind's eye, from shaking the customer's hand when they walk in to discussing his problems and asking for the order.

*Source:* "What Makes a Supersalesperson?" *Sales & Marketing Management,* August 13, 1984, p. 86.

paperwork? Does the job call for much travel? Will the salesperson face a lot of rejections? The successful salesperson should be suited to these duties. The company should also look at the characteristics of its most successful salespeople for clues to needed traits.

## Recruiting Procedures

After management has decided on needed traits, it must *recruit*. The personnel department looks for applicants by getting names from current salespeople, using employment agencies, placing job ads, and contacting college students. Companies have sometimes found it hard to sell college students on selling. Many students think that selling is a job and not a profession, that salespeople must be deceitful to be effective, and that there is too much insecurity and travel in selling. In addition, some women believe that selling is a man's career. To counter such objections, recruiters talk about high starting salaries, income growth, and the fact that more than one-fourth of the presidents of large U.S. corporations started out in marketing and sales. They point out that more than 21 percent of the people selling manufactured products are women; in some industries, such as textiles and apparel and banking and financial services, the proportion of women in the salesforce is about 60 percent (see Marketing Highlight 17–3).[9]

## Selecting Salespeople

Recruiting will attract many applicants, and the company must then select the best ones. The selection procedure can vary from a single informal interview to lengthy testing and interviewing. Many companies give formal tests to sales applicants. Tests typically measure sales aptitude, analytical and organizational skills, personality traits, and other characteristics.[10] Test results are weighted heavily by such companies as IBM, Prudential, Procter & Gamble, and Gillette. Gillette claims that tests have reduced turnover by 42 percent and have correlated well with the later performance of new salespeople. But test scores provide only one piece of information in a set that includes personal characteristics, references, past employment history, and interviewer reactions.

# TRAINING SALESPEOPLE

Many companies used to send their new salespeople into the field almost immediately after hiring them. They would be given samples, order books, and general instructions to "sell west of the Mississippi." Training programs were luxuries. To many companies, a training program meant spending a lot of money for instructors, materials, and space, paying a person who was not yet selling, and losing sales opportunities because the person was not in the field.

Today's new salespeople, however, may spend from a few weeks to many months in training. The median training period is 17 weeks in industrial products companies and 20 in consumer products companies. IBM spends $1 billion a year educating its work force and customers. Initial sales training lasts 13 months, and new salespeople are not on their own for two years! Moreover, IBM expects its salespeople to spend 15 percent of their time each year in additional training.[11]

Training programs have several goals. Because salespeople need to know and identify with the company, most companies spend the first part of the training program describing the company's history and objectives, its organiza-

## ON THE JOB WITH A SUCCESSFUL XEROX SALESWOMAN

The word "salesman" is beginning to have an archaic ring. The entry of women into what was once a male bastion has been swift and dramatic. More than 21 percent of people selling manufactured products are women, vs. 7 percent a decade ago.

And women are making special strides selling high-tech equipment. At Xerox, for example, they are 39 percent of the salesforce.

Nancy Reck decided that sales offered the best opportunity when she and her

*Nancy Reck doing business despite the weather.*

husband, Miles, moved from Jacksonville, Florida, to Chapel Hill, North Carolina, 3½ years ago so he could work on a doctorate. They were holding down five jobs between them to make ends meet when Nancy, 30, found what she had been looking for: a single job that paid enough to support both of them. Sales, says the former schoolteacher, "is a field where compensation is related to performance. You write your own ticket."

Reck signed up with Xerox as a sales representative and quickly made her mark. In each of the last three years, she has qualified for the President's Club, which means she exceeded all of her sales goals, an honor won by only one of every five members of the sales force last year. Her income, which she won't discuss, is probably about $50,000 a year.

A native of tiny Seaboard, North Carolina, Reck earned her spurs on the "low volume" beat, selling Xerox copiers and electronic typewriters door to door to small businesses in 17 counties in her home state. Recently she was promoted to a new job that is a stepping stone to management.

Reck worried she would have to develop an artificial personality to succeed in sales. Instead she found she could just be herself: "I treat every customer as if he were my father, my brother, or my best friend."

*Source:* "On the Job with a Successful Xerox Saleswoman," *Fortune,* April 30, 1984, p. 102 © 1984 Time Inc. All rights reserved.

tion, its financial structure and facilities, and its chief products and markets. Because salespeople need to know the company's products, sales trainees are shown how products are produced and how they work in various uses. Because salespeople need to know customers' and competitors' characteristics. The training program teaches them about competitors' strategies and about different types of customers and their needs, buying motives, and buying habits. Salespeople need to know how to make effective presentations, so they get training in the principles of salesmanship, and the company outlines the major sales arguments for each product. Finally, salespeople need to understand field

*Companies spend hundreds of millions of dollars to train their salespeople in the art of selling.*

procedures and responsibilities. They learn how to divide time between active and potential accounts and how to use an expense account, prepare reports, and route communications effectively.

## Principles of Selling

One of the major objectives of training programs is to teach salespeople the "art" of selling. Companies spend hundreds of millions of dollars on seminars, books, cassettes, and other materials. Millions of copies of books on selling are purchased every year, with such tantalizing titles as *How to Sell Anything to Anybody, How I Raised Myself from Failure to Success in Selling, The Four-Minute Sell, The Best Seller, The Power of Enthusiastic Selling, Where Do You Go from No. 1?,* and *Winning through Intimidation.* One of the most enduring books on selling is Dale Carnegie's *How to Win Friends and Influence People.*

All the training approaches try to convert a salesperson from a passive *order taker* to an active *order getter.* Order takers assume that customers know their own needs, that they would resent any attempt at influence, and that they prefer salespeople who are polite and reserved. An example of an order taker is a salesperson who calls on a dozen customers each day, simply asking if the customer needs anything.

There are two approaches to training salespeople to be order *getters*—a sales-oriented approach and a customer-oriented approach. The *sales-oriented approach* trains the salesperson in high-pressure selling techniques, such as those used in selling encyclopedias or automobiles. This form of selling assumes that the customers will not buy except under pressure, that they are influenced by a slick presentation, and that they will not be sorry after signing the order (and that, if they are, it no longer matters).

The *customer-oriented approach*—the one most often used in today's professional selling—trains salespeople in customer problem solving. The salesperson learns how to identify customer needs and find solutions. This approach assumes that customer needs provide sales opportunities, that customers appreciate good suggestions, and that they will be loyal to salespeople

**selling process** The steps that the salesperson follows when selling, including prospecting and qualifying, preapproach, approach, presentation and demonstration, handling objections, closing, and follow-up.

**prospecting** The step in the selling process in which the salesperson identifies qualified potential customers.

**preapproach** The step in the selling process in which the salesperson learns as much as possible about a prospective customer before making a sales call.

who have their long-term interests at heart. In one survey, purchasing agents described the following qualities as the ones they *most disliked* in salespeople: pushy, arrogant, unreliable, too talkative, fails to ask about needs. The qualities they *valued most* included reliability and credibility, integrity, innovativeness in solving problems, and product knowledge.[12] The problem-solver salesperson fits better with the marketing concept than the hard seller or order taker.

## The Selling Process

Most training programs view the **selling process** as consisting of several steps that the salesperson must master. These steps are shown in Figure 17–2 and discussed below.[13]

### Prospecting and Qualifying

The first step in the selling process is **prospecting**—identifying qualified potential customers. The salesperson must approach many prospects to get a few sales. In the insurance industry, only one out of nine prospects becomes a customer. In the computer business, 125 phone calls result in 25 interviews leading to five demonstrations and one sale.[14] Although the company supplies some leads, salespeople need skill in finding their own. They can ask current customers for the names of prospects. They can build referral sources, such as suppliers, dealers, noncompeting salespeople, and bankers. They can join organizations to which prospects belong or can engage in speaking and writing activities that will draw attention. They can search for names in newspapers or directories and use the telephone and mail to track down leads. Or they can drop in unannounced on various offices (a practice known as "cold calling").

Salespeople need to know how to *qualify* leads—that is, how to identify the good ones and screen out the poor ones. Prospects can be qualified by looking at their financial ability, volume of business, special needs, location, and possibilities for growth.

### Preapproach

Before calling on a prospect, the salesperson should learn as much as possible about the organization (what it needs, who is involved in the buying) and its buyers (their characteristics and buying styles). This step is known as the **preapproach.** The salesperson can consult standard sources *(Moody's, Standard and Poor's, Dun and Bradstreet)*, acquaintances, and others to learn about the company. The salesperson should set *call objectives*, which may be either to qualify the prospect, to gather information, or to make an immediate sale. Another task is to decide on the best approach, which might be a personal visit, a phone call, or a letter. The best timing should be thought out because many prospects are busiest at certain times. Finally, the salesperson should give thought to an overall sales strategy for the account.

FIGURE 17–2  Major Steps in Effective Selling

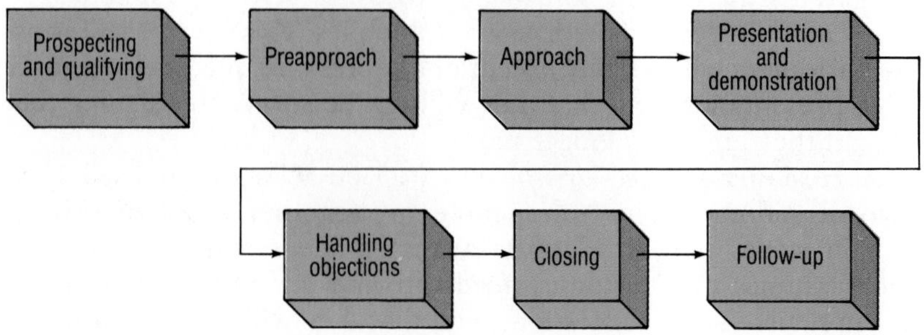

## Approach

During the **approach** step, the salesperson should know how to meet and greet the buyer and get the relationship off to a good start. This step involves the salesperson's appearance, opening lines, and follow-up remarks. Opening lines should be positive, such as "Mr. Johnson, I am Chris Anderson from the Alltech Company. My company and I appreciate your willingness to see me. I will do my best to make this visit profitable and worthwhile for you and your company." This opening might be followed by some key questions to learn more about the customer's needs or the showing of a display or sample to attract the buyer's attention and curiosity.

## Presentation and Demonstration

During the **presentation** step of the selling process, the salesperson tells the product "story" to the buyer, showing how the product will make or save money. The salesperson describes product features but concentrates on presenting customer benefits.

Companies use three styles of sales presentation. The oldest is the *canned approach*, which consists of a memorized or scripted talk covering the seller's main points. This approach has limited usefulness in industrial selling, but scripted presentations can be effective in some telephone-selling situations. A properly prepared and rehearsed script should sound natural and move the salesperson smoothly through the presentation. With electronic scripting, computers can lead a salesperson through a sequence of selling messages tailored on the spot to a prospect's responses.

Using the *formula approach*, the salesperson first identifies the buyer's needs, attitudes, and buying style. Then the salesperson moves into a formula presentation that shows how the product will satisfy that buyer's needs. Although not canned, the presentation follows a general plan.

The *need-satisfaction approach* starts with a search for the customer's needs by getting the customer to do most of the talking. This approach calls for good listening and problem-solving skills. One marketing director describes the approach this way:

> [High-performing salespeople] make it a point to understand customer needs and goals before they pull anything out of their product bag. . . . Such salespeople spend the time needed to get an in-depth knowledge of the customer's business, asking questions that will lead to solutions our systems can address.[15]

*In the sales presentation, the salesperson tells the product story to buyers.*

**approach** The step in the selling process in which the salesperson meets and greets the buyer to get the relationship off to a good start.

**presentation** The step in the selling process in which the salesperson tells the product "story" to the buyer, showing how the product will make or save money.

**handling objections** The step in the selling process in which the salesperson seeks out, clarifies, and overcomes customer objections to buying.

**closing** The step in the selling process in which the salesperson asks the customer for an order.

**follow-up** The step in the selling process in which the salesperson follows up after the sale to ensure customer satisfaction and repeat business.

Any style of sales presentation can be improved with demonstration aids such as booklets, flip charts, slides, videotapes or videodiscs, and product samples. If buyers can see or handle the product, they will better remember its features and benefits.

### Handling Objections

Customers almost always have objections during the presentation or when asked to place an order. The problem can be logical or psychological. And objections are often unspoken. In **handling objections,** the salesperson should use a positive approach, seek out hidden objections, ask the buyer to clarify any objections, take objections as opportunities to provide more information, and turn objections into reasons for buying. Every salesperson needs training in the skills of handling objections.

### Closing

The salesperson now tries to close the sale. Some salespeople do not get around to **closing** or do not handle it well. They may lack confidence, feel guilty about asking for the order, or not recognize the right moment to close the sale. Salespeople should know how to recognize closing signals from the buyer, including physical actions, comments, and questions. For example, the customer might sit forward and nod approvingly or ask about prices and credit terms. Salespeople can use one of several closing techniques. They can ask for the order, review points of agreement, offer to help write up the order, ask whether the buyer wants this model or that one, or note that the buyer will lose out if the order is not placed now. The salesperson may offer the buyer special reasons to close, such as a lower price or an extra quantity at no charge.

### Follow-Up

The last step in the selling process—**follow-up**—is necessary if the salesperson wants to ensure customer satisfaction and repeat business. Right after closing, the salesperson should complete any details on delivery time, purchase terms, and other matters. The salesperson should schedule a follow-up call when the initial order is received to make sure there is proper installation, instruction, and servicing. This visit would reveal any problems, assure the buyer of the salesperson's interest, and reduce any buyer concerns that might have arisen since the sale.

# SUPERVISING SALESPEOPLE

New salespeople need more than a territory, compensation, and training—they need *supervision*. Through supervision, the company *directs* and *motivates* the salesforce to do a better job.

## Directing Salespeople

Companies vary in how closely they supervise their salespeople. Salespeople who are paid mostly on commission and who are expected to hunt down their own prospects are generally left on their own. Those who are salaried and must cover assigned accounts are usually more closely supervised.

### Developing Customer Targets and Call Norms

Most companies classify customers into A, B, and C accounts, based on the account's sales volume, its profit potential, and its growth potential. They set the desired number of calls per period on each account class. Thus, A accounts may receive nine calls a year, B accounts six, and C accounts three. Such call norms depend on competitive call norms and profits expected from the account.

### Developing Prospect Targets and Call Norms

Companies often specify how much time their salesforces should spend prospecting for new accounts. For example, Spector Freight wants its salespeople to spend 25 percent of their time prospecting and to stop calling on a prospect after three unsuccessful calls. Companies set up prospecting standards for several reasons. If left alone, many salespeople will spend most of their time with current customers. Current customers are better-known quantities. Whereas a prospect may never deliver any business, salespeople can depend on current accounts for some business. Unless salespeople are rewarded for opening new accounts, they may avoid new-account development. Some companies thus rely on a special salesforce to open new accounts.

### Using Sales Time Efficiently

Salespeople need to know how to use their time efficiently. One tool is the *annual call schedule* showing which customers and prospects to call on in which months and which activities to carry out. Activities include taking part in trade shows, attending sales meetings, and carrying out marketing research. Another tool is *time-and-duty analysis*. In addition to time spent selling, a salesperson spends time traveling, waiting, eating, taking breaks, and doing administrative chores. On average, actual selling time accounts for only 25 percent of total working time![16] If selling time could be raised from 25 to 30 percent, there would be a 20 percent increase in the time spent selling. Companies are always looking for ways to save time—using phones instead of traveling, simplifying record-keeping forms, finding better call and routing plans, and supplying more and better customer information.

Advances in technological equipment—desktop and laptop computers, videocassette recorders, videodiscs, automatic dialers, teleconferencing—have allowed dramatic breakthroughs in improving salesforce productivity. Salespeople have truly gone "electronic." One expert predicts that by 1991, 28 percent of all salespeople will use personal computers on the job. Salespeople

*Many companies are computerizing their salesforces to make salespeople more efficient and effective.*

use computers to profile customers and prospects, analyze and forecast sales, schedule sales calls, enter orders, check inventories and order status, prepare sales and expense reports, process correspondence, and carry out many other activities. In a recent survey, salesforces using PCs reported an average 43 percent productivity gain.[17]

To reduce time demands on their *outside salesforces*, many companies have increased the size of their *inside salesforces*. Inside salespeople include three types. *Technical support people* provide technical information and answers to customers' questions. *Sales assistants* provide clerical backup for outside salespeople: They call ahead and confirm appointments, conduct credit checks, follow up on deliveries, and answer customers' questions when outside salespeople cannot be reached. *Telemarketers* use the phone to find new leads, qualify prospects, and sell to them (see Marketing Highlight 17–4). A telemarketer can call up to 50 customers a day, compared with the average four that an outside salesperson can see. The inside salesforce frees outside

# Marketing Highlight 17–4

## TELEMARKETING: A PHONE CAN BE BETTER THAN A FACE

Selling face-to-face is by far the best way to achieve personal rapport with a prospect, right? Wrong, says LeRoy Benham, president of Climax Portable Machine Tools. By combining telemarketing and computers, a small company can save money and lavish the kind of attention on buyers that will amaze them.

True, such a strategy depends on your market and your stake in it, but few managers would argue with Benham's track record. At a time when most U.S. machine tool manufacturers have been in a deep depression, Benham has carved out a niche for his portable cutting tools. This year, sales will rise 20 percent to $5 million. Company profits will climb more than 20 percent for the third year in a row since Climax began phasing out its distributor network and switched to telephone selling.

Under the old system, sales engineers spent one-third of their time on the road, training distributor salespeople and accompanying them on calls. "They'd make about four contacts a day," says Benham. "They found they actually got more information from the prospects when they were back here setting up travel appointments by phone." Now, each

of the five sales engineers on Benham's telemarketing team calls about 30 prospects a day, following up on leads generated by ads and direct mail. Since it takes about five calls to close a sale, sales engineers update a computer file on prospects each time they speak to them, noting their degree of commitment, requirements, next-call date, and personal comments.

"If someone mentions he's going on a fishing trip, our sales engineer enters that in the computer and uses it to personalize the next phone call," says Benham, noting that it is just one way to build good relations. Another: The first mailing to a

prospect includes the sales engineer's business card with his picture on it.

Of course, it takes more than friendliness to sell $15,000 machine tools (special orders may run $200,000) over the phone, but Benham has proof that personality pays. When customers were asked, "Do you see the sales engineer often enough?" the response was overwhelmingly positive. Obviously, many people didn't realize that the only contact they'd had with Climax had been on the phone.

*Source:* Adapted from "A Phone Is Better Than a Face," *Sales & Marketing Management*, October 1987, p. 29.

*Telemarketers use the phone to find new prospects and sell to them.*

salespeople to spend more time selling to major accounts and finding major new prospects.[18]

**sales quotas** Standards set for salespeople stating the amount they should sell and how sales should be divided among the company's products.

## Motivating Salespeople

Some salespeople will do their best without any special urging from management. To them, selling may be the most fascinating job in the world. But selling often involves frustration. Salespeople usually work alone, and they must sometimes travel away from home. They may face aggressive, competing salespeople and difficult customers. They sometimes lack the authority to do what is needed to win a sale and may thus lose large orders that they have worked hard to obtain. Thus, salespeople often need special encouragement to work at their best level. Management can boost salesforce morale and performance through its *organizational climate*, *sales quotas*, and *positive incentives*.

### Organizational Climate

Organizational climate describes the feeling that salespeople have about their opportunities, value, and rewards for a good performance within the company. Some companies treat salespeople as if they are not very important. Other companies treat their salespeople as their prime movers and allow virtually unlimited opportunity for income and promotion. Not surprisingly, a company's attitude toward its salespeople affects their behavior. If they are held in low esteem, there is high turnover and poor performance. If they are held in high esteem, there is less turnover and higher performance.

Treatment from the salesperson's immediate superior is especially important. A good sales manager keeps in touch with the salesforce through letters and phone calls, visits in the field, and evaluation sessions in the home office. At different times, the sales manager acts as the salesperson's boss, companion, coach, and confessor.

### Sales Quotas

Many companies set **sales quotas** for their salespeople—standards stating the amount they should sell and how sales should be divided among the company's products. Compensation is often related to how well salespeople meet their quotas.

Sales quotas are set when the annual marketing plan is developed. The company first decides on a sales forecast that is reasonably achievable. Based on this forecast, management plans production, work-force size, and financial needs. It then sets sales quotas for its regions and territories. Generally, sales quotas are set higher than sales forecasts to encourage managers and salespeople to their best effort. If they fail to make their quotas, the company may still make its sales forecast.

### Positive Incentives

Companies also use several incentives to increase salesforce effort. *Sales meetings* provide social occasions, breaks from routine, chances to meet and talk with "company brass," and opportunities to air feelings and identify with a larger group. Companies also sponsor *sales contests* to spur the salesforce to make a selling effort above what would normally be expected. Other incentives include honors, merchandise and cash awards, trips, and profit-sharing plans.

*Salesforce incentives: some companies award trips as incentives for outstanding sales performance.*

# EVALUATING SALESPEOPLE

We have described how management communicates what salespeople should be doing and motivates them to do it. But this process requires good *feedback*. And good feedback means getting regular information from salespeople to evaluate their performance.

## Sources of Information

Management gets information about its salespeople in several ways. The most important source is *sales reports*. Additional information comes from personal observation, customers' letters and complaints, customer surveys, and talks with other salespeople.

Sales reports are divided into plans for future activities and write-ups of completed activities. The best example of the first is the *work plan* that salespeople submit a week or month in advance. The plan describes intended calls and routing. This report leads the salesforce to plan and schedule activities, informs management of their whereabouts, and provides a basis for comparing plans and performance. Salespeople can then be evaluated on their ability to "plan their work and work their plan." Sometimes, managers contact individual salespeople to suggest improvements in work plans.

Companies are also beginning to require their salespeople to draft *annual territory marketing plans* in which they outline their plans for building new accounts and increasing sales from existing accounts. Formats vary greatly—

some ask for general ideas on territory development and others ask for detailed sales and profit estimates. Such reports cast salespeople as territory marketing managers. Sales managers study territory plans, make suggestions, and use them to develop sales quotas.

Salespeople write up their completed activities on *call reports*. Call reports keep sales management informed of the salesperson's activities, show what is happening with each customer's account, and provide information that might be useful in later calls. Salespeople also turn in *expense reports* for which they are partly or wholly repaid. Some companies also ask for reports on new business, reports on lost business, and reports on local business and economic conditions.

These reports supply the raw data from which sales management can evaluate salesforce performance. Are salespeople making too few calls per day? Are they spending too much time per call? Are they spending too much money on entertainment? Are they closing enough orders per hundred calls? Are they finding enough new customers and holding on to enough old customers?

## Formal Evaluation of Performance

Using salesforce reports and other information, sales management formally evaluates members of the salesforce. Formal evaluation produces three benefits. First, management must have and communicate clear standards for judging performance. Second, management must gather well-rounded information about each salesperson. Finally, salespeople know they will have to sit down one morning with the sales manager and explain their performance.

### Comparing Salespeople's Performance

One type of evaluation compares and ranks the sales performance of different salespeople. Such comparisons, however, can be misleading. Salespeople may perform differently because of differences in such factors as territory potential, workload, level of competition, and company promotion effort. Furthermore, sales are seldom the best indicator of achievement. Management should be more interested in how much each salesperson contributes to net profits—a concern that requires looking at each salesperson's sales mix and sales expenses.

### Comparing Current Sales with Past Sales

A second type of evaluation compares a salesperson's current and past performances. Such a comparison should directly indicate the person's *progress*. It can show trends in sales and profits over a period of years. It can also show the salesperson's record on making calls and building new accounts. It cannot, however, tell *why* the salesperson's performance is moving in one direction or another.

### Qualitative Evaluation of Salespeople

A *qualitative evaluation* usually looks at a salesperson's knowledge of the company, products, customers, competitors, territory, and tasks. Personal traits—general manner, appearance, speech, and temperament—can be rated. The sales manager can also review any problems in motivation or compliance. The sales manager should check to make sure that salespeople know the laws relating to personal selling (see Marketing Highlight 17–5). Each company must decide what would be most useful to know. It should communicate these criteria to salespeople so that they understand how their performance is evaluated and can make an effort to improve it.

## PERSONAL SELLING AND PUBLIC POLICY

Salespeople must follow the rules of "fair competition" in trying to obtain orders. Certain activities are illegal or heavily regulated. Salespeople are to refrain from offering bribes to buyers, purchasing agents, or other influence sources. It is illegal to procure the technical or trade secrets of competitors through espionage or bribery. They must not disparage competitors or their products by suggesting things that are not true. They must not sell used items as new or mislead the customer about buying advantages. They must inform customers of their rights, such as the 72-hour "cooling-off" period in which customers can return merchandise and receive their money back. They must not discriminate against buyers on the basis of race, sex, or creed.

*Source:* For more on the legal aspects of personal selling, see Louis W. Stern and Thomas L. Eovaldi, *Legal Aspects of Marketing Policy* (Englewood Cliffs, NJ: Prentice Hall, 1984), pp. 447–550.

## SUMMARY

Most companies use salespeople, and many companies assign them the key role in the marketing mix. The high cost of a salesforce calls for an effective *sales-management process* consisting of six steps: setting *salesforce objectives;* designing *salesforce strategy, structure, size,* and *compensation; recruiting and selecting; training; supervising;* and *evaluating.*

As an element of the marketing mix, the salesforce is very effective in achieving certain marketing objectives and carrying on such activities as prospecting, communicating, selling and servicing, and information gathering. A market-oriented salesforce needs skills in marketing analysis and planning in addition to traditional selling skills.

Once salesforce objectives have been set, strategy answers the questions of what type of selling will be most effective (solo selling, team selling), what type of salesforce structure will work best (territorial, product, or customer-structured),

how large the salesforce should be, and how the salesforce should be compensated in terms of salary, commissions, bonuses, expenses, and fringe benefits.

To hold down the high costs of hiring the wrong people, salespeople must be recruited and selected carefully. Training programs familiarize new salespeople not only with the "art" of selling but with the company's history, its products and policies, and the characteristics of its market and competitors. The art of selling involves a seven-step *selling process: prospecting and qualifying, preapproach, approach, presentation and demonstration, handling objections, closing,* and *follow-up.* All salespeople need supervision, and many need continuous encouragement because they must make many decisions and face many frustrations. Periodically, the company must evaluate their performance to help them do a better job.

## QUESTIONS FOR DISCUSSION

1. Media representatives sell advertising space or time for newspapers, radio stations, and other advertising media. How creative is this type of selling?

2. Describe the advantages to IBM of each of the three different salesforce structures. Which structure do you think would be most appropriate?

3. In general, how does a company's salesforce size relate to its spending on other forms of promotion?

4. Why do so many salesforce compensation plans combine salary with bonus or commission? What are the advantages and disadvantages of using bonuses instead of commissions as incentives?

5. What two personal characteristics do you think are most important to success in a sales career? What tests can be used to detect these characteristics in a salesforce applicant?

6. Many people feel they do not have the ability to be a successful salesperson. What role does training play in helping develop selling ability?

7. How would you apply the seven different steps in the selling process to a summer job selling encyclopedias door to door? Would these be the same steps when applied to selling copiers for Xerox?

8. What kinds of companies would benefit from an

inside salesforce? What major factors determine which companies benefit?

9. The surest way to become a salesforce manager is to be an outstanding salesperson. What are the advantages and disadvantages of promoting top salespeople to management positions? Why might an outstanding salesperson decline promotion?

10. Good salespeople are familiar with their competitors' products as well as their own. What would you do if your company expected you to sell a product you thought was inferior to the competition's?

## REFERENCES ▪

1. Adapted from Bill Kelley, "How to Sell Airplanes, Boeing-Style," *Sales & Marketing Management,* December 9, 1985, pp. 32–34. Also see Katherine M. Hafner, "Bright Smiles, Sweaty Palms," *Business Week,* February 1, 1988, pp. 22–23.

2. See Robert N. McMurry, "The Mystique of Super-Salesmanship," *Harvard Business Review,* March-April 1961, p. 114. For a comparison of several classifications, see William C. Moncrief III, "Selling Activity and Sales Position Taxonomies for Industrial Salesforces," *Journal of Marketing Research,* August 1986, pp. 261–70.

3. See Rayna Skolnik, "Campbell Stirs Up Its Salesforce," *Sales & Marketing Management,* April 1986, pp. 56–58.

4. See Thayer C. Taylor, "Xerox's Sales Force Learns a New Game," *Sales & Marketing Management,* July 1, 1986, pp. 48–51; and Taylor, "Xerox's Makeover," *Sales & Marketing Management,* June 1987, p. 68.

5. "1989 Survey of Selling Costs," *Sales & Marketing Management,* February 20, 1989, p. 16.

6. The percentages total to more than 100 percent because some companies use more than one type of plan. See "1989 Survey of Selling Costs," *Sales & Marketing Management,* February 20, 1989, p. 26.

7. George H. Lucas, Jr., A. Parasuraman, Robert A. Davis, and Ben M. Enis, "An Empirical Study of Salesforce Turnover," *Journal of Marketing,* July 1987, pp. 34–59.

8. Thayer C. Taylor, "Anatomy of a Star Salesperson," *Sales & Marketing Management,* May 1986, pp. 49–51.

9. See "'Pink Ghetto' in Sales for Women," *Sales & Marketing Management,* July 1988, p. 80; and

"Women Keep Coming On," *Sales & Marketing Management,* February 1989, p. 26.

10. See Richard Kern, "IQ Tests for Salesmen Make a Comeback," *Sales & Marketing Management,* April 1988, pp. 42–46.

11. See "Survey of Selling Costs: 1987," *Sales & Marketing Management,* February 16, 1987, p. 62; and Patricia Sellers, "How IBM Teaches Techies to Sell," *Fortune,* June 6, 1988, pp. 141-46.

12. "PAs Examine the People Who Sell to Them," *Sales & Marketing Management,* November 11, 1985, pp. 38–41.

13. Some of the following discussion is based on W.J.E. Crissy, William H. Cunningham, and Isabella C. M. Cunningham, *Selling: The Personal Force in Marketing* (New York: John Wiley, 1977), pp. 119–29.

14. Vincent L. Zirpoli, "You Can't 'Control' the Prospect, So Manage the Presale Activities to Increase Performance," *Marketing News,* March 16, 1984, p. 1.

15. Taylor, "Anatomy of a Star Salesperson," p. 50. Also see Harvey B. Mackay, "Humanize Your Selling Strategy," *Harvard Business Review,* March-April 1988, pp. 36–47.

16. "Are Salespeople Gaining More Selling Time?" *Sales & Marketing Management,* July 1986, p. 29.

17. Thayer C. Taylor, "Computers in Sales and Marketing: S&MM's Survey Results," *Sales & Marketing Management,* May 1987, pp. 50–53. Also see Jonathan B. Levine, "If Only Willy Loman Had Used a Laptop," *Business Week,* October 12, 1987, p. 137.

18. James A. Narus and James C. Anderson, "Industrial Distributor Selling: The Roles of Outside and Inside Sales," *Industrial Marketing Management,* 15 (1986), 55–62.

## MULTIFORM DESICCANTS: DESIGNING AN EFFECTIVE SALESFORCE

Steven Stepson, the new Director of Sales and Marketing at Multiform Desiccants, Inc. (MDI), knew when he accepted the job that he faced many hurdles in making MDI a top-notch sales and marketing organization. Sales were up—15 percent over last year. But company executives believed that a better-organized and better-managed salesforce could provide even greater sales growth. Stepson now faced the challenge of evaluating the current salesforce structure and recommending appropriate changes.

Most of us know desiccants as those little packets that you find in stereo equipment, cameras, and leather goods with the inscription "DO NOT EAT" on the wrapper. Desiccants absorb any moisture that could damage the product. More technically, however, desiccant applications are highly specialized and usually require a custom-blend of chemicals for each different use. MDI's safe, natural, nontoxic products eradicate moisture and odors in containers and packages, while dramatically reducing the destructive effects of oxygen. Desiccants come in many forms—from gels to capsules of all shapes and sizes. These innovative products can be found in a variety of goods ranging from vitamin bottles to automotive air conditioning units, from photographic film packages to seagoing shipping containers. A typical MDI account is a pharmaceutical company that must keep moisture from products during shipment and storage. Other uses range from anti-fogging pellets for optical sensors on missiles to packets that keep orange juice crystals dry. In all, MDI manufactures 774 products for 23 different markets.

MDI started in the late 1960s as a garage-shop operation founded by a young entrepreneur with a dream. As a chemist working for a large bulk-desiccant manufacturer, he saw the need for formulating and packaging desiccants in small, single-use packets. His employer had no desire to enter the packaging end of the business and so gave him permission to work on his ideas during non-working hours. And although most technical companies require their employees to sign an agreement giving the company all rights to any business-related inventions, this company allowed him to retain all patent rights.

Before MDI took on the task, companies had to buy desiccants in bulk and then package them for their own specialized uses. Packaging desiccants in a variety of bagging materials—and labeling them for the customers—thus met the needs of a previously neglected market. That was 25 years ago. Today, with annual sales topping $15 million, MDI is a leader in packaged desiccants.

Nevertheless, believing that sales could be much higher, MDI hired Stepson to boost sales volume. As in any sales-management position, Stepson was under immediate pressure to increase sales quickly. The area likely to make the greatest immediate impact on MDI's sales was its domestic salesforce. Thus, the new director first conducted a situation analysis to assess MDI's market position. This analysis included an external audit of competition and other market factors, a forecast of where market growth was likely to occur, and an internal audit of MDI's current salesforce.

Salesforce design presented several problems and a challenge to Stepson, who discovered that frequent salesforce turnover had plagued MDI in the past. MDI had only three salespeople to cover the entire United States; each was paid a direct salary. Together, they serviced over 3,850 accounts—although only 161 of these customers accounted for over 80 percent of MDI's business. Thus, it was important for the company to maintain this base while continuing to develop significant new accounts. Stepson found that three factors had influenced the structure of the current salesforce—the geographical location of customers, the technical skills needed to sell desiccants, and the long selling cycle dictated by the nature of the product.

Organizational markets tend to be geographically concentrated, and MDI's markets were typical in that regard. The majority of current and potential customers were located in large metropolitan areas east of the Mississippi River and along the West Coast, predominantly in California. MDI thus assigned sales representatives to geographically defined territories in order to take advantage of the clustering of its customers. Stepson realized that, unfortunately, geographical territory assignments created a situation in which sales representatives had to be knowledgeable in the assorted businesses of all their customers: One sales representative might call on customers in industries as diverse as automotives, pharmaceuticals, and aerospace.

Stepson also recognized a second problem. The complex nature of desiccants requires that salespeople have technical backgrounds. Sales representatives often had college degrees in engineering—either chemical or mechanical. Technical skills were thus essential to successful selling of the products. For example, to sell a desiccant product to a new customer, the sales representative had to analyze the customer's needs. How much moisture had to be absorbed? How fast must it be absorbed? In what environment (for example, temperature) will the desiccant be working? These are just some of the questions that sales representatives would need answered in order to solve the problem facing the customer. Naturally, the answers to these questions will be very technical. The customer-oriented approach thus demanded that, in addition to having knowledge about the technical qualities of the product, sales representatives had to be innovative in solving problems.

Finally, working with an important customer to find the MDI product to satisfy a particular need often took many sales calls, meetings, and telephone conversations. Because each new application undergoes rigorous testing before it is finally accepted as a routine purchase by the customer, the process of nurturing an important account takes at least 12 to 18 months. Since it took so long to land a new account, MDI felt that paying its salesforce on a salary basis would provide them with an even income flow. However, while the salary-only compensation system provided even income, it gave salespeople little incentive to strive for increased sales. Moreover, with 161 accounts representing over $15 million in annual revenue and the number of new accounts growing continuously, salespeople felt that they were not receiving their fair share of the revenues that they generated.

As Stepson discovered, travel and call planning were also problematic. Visits to various customers usually required air travel, car rental, and many overnight stays to service accounts properly. Travel accounted for at least three-quarters of a day per week. Salespeople usually spent two days per week in their offices to catch up on paper work and set up appointments for the following weeks. This schedule left only 2¼ days for customer visits. Thus, salespeople could on average make only five customer calls per week—an arrangement that did not provide the penetration necessary to meet projected sales. Moreover, salespeople kept busy serving existing accounts, allocating little time to prospect for new customers.

Stepson considered hiring additional salespeople, but the present salesforce balked at the idea. They felt that bringing in additional people at the same salary level would dilute their impact and diminish their importance and pay. The three current salespeople threatened to quit if such a policy were adopted.

Another problem was the background and training of the salesforce. Although the present salespeople had solid technical experience, Stepson felt that they lacked the sales skills required to sell MDI products effectively. For example, because there were a number of competitors selling substitutes, once a product was selected by the customer and purchased on a routine basis, the sales task turned from a technical issue to a pure price issue. Thus, making the initial sale and servicing the account in the future were very different kinds of selling activities requiring a variety of selling skills.

All in all, Stepson had his work cut out for him.

## Questions

1. How large should MDI's salesforce be and how should it be structured?

2. Should Stepson compensate MDI salespeople using salary only, commission only, or salary plus commission? How would each plan affect salespeople's motivation and performance?

3. What key qualities should Stepson look for in prospective new salespeople? What selection criteria should the company use? Briefly outline a training program that would properly round out the skills of the current salesforce.

*Source:* This case was written by Richard V. Resh, partner, DICRIS Company, Buffalo, New York.

# 18
# International Marketing

## CHAPTER OBJECTIVES

**After reading this chapter, you should be able to**

1. Explain how foreign trade, economic, political-legal, and cultural environments affect a company's international marketing decisions
2. Describe three key approaches to entering foreign markets
3. Explain how companies might adapt their marketing mixes for foreign markets
4. Identify the three major forms of international marketing organization

For more than 100 years, Eastman Kodak has been known for its easy-to-use cameras, high-quality film, and solid profits for investors. But during the past decade, Kodak's sales have flattened and its profits have declined. Perhaps complacent after its century of success, the company has been outpaced by more innovative competitors. In many cases, the competitors have been Japanese. Kodak dragged its feet in the 35-mm camera market and fell far behind Nikon, Canon, and Minolta. It lagged on video cameras and recorders and lost out to Sony, Matsushita, and Toshiba. And faster-moving Japanese competitors grabbed the market for self-contained, one-hour film-processing labs. So when another large Japanese competitor—Fuji Photo Film Company—moved in on Kodak's bread-and-butter color film business, Kodak took the challenge seriously.

Fuji entered the U.S. film market in the early 1970s. It offered high-quality color films at 10 percent lower prices and beat Kodak to the market with high-speed films. Fuji also pulled a major marketing coup by outbidding Kodak to become the official film of the 1984 Los Angeles Summer Olympic Games. Fuji's

share of the huge U.S. color film market grew from just 2 percent in 1972 to over 8 percent in 1984, and it announced a 15 percent market-share goal. Fuji's U.S. sales grew at a rate of 20 percent a year—much faster than the overall market-growth rate.

Kodak fought back fiercely to protect its whopping 85 percent share of the U.S. film market. It matched Fuji's new products and lower prices. It outspent Fuji by 20 to one on advertising and promotion and paid some $10 million to obtain sponsorship of the 1988 Summer Olympics in Seoul, South Korea. Most analysts agree that Kodak will defend its U.S. market position successfully. Fuji isn't likely to entice many consumers to abandon Kodak's familiar yellow-and-black film box to reach for Fuji green.

But Kodak is taking the battle a step further—it's attacking Japan, Fuji's home turf. Kodak is no stranger to international marketing: 45 percent of its $11 billion in sales come from 150 countries outside the United States. In fact, Kodak has been selling film in Japan since 1889. But until a few years ago, it didn't give the Japanese market much attention. Recently, however, Kodak has taken several aggressive steps to increase its Japanese presence and sales. It set up a separate subsidiary—Kodak Japan—and tripled its Japanese staff. It bought out a Japanese distributor and prepared to set up its own Japanese marketing and sales staff. It invested in a new technology center and a large Japanese research facility. Finally, Kodak has greatly increased its Japanese promotion and publicity. Kodak Japan now sponsors everything from television talk shows to sumo wrestling tournaments.

Despite these strong efforts, it may be as hard for Kodak in Japan as for Fuji in the United States. Fuji, with over $3 billion in annual sales, has the resources to blunt Kodak's attack. The Japanese giant is firmly entrenched with a 70-percent share of the Japanese market versus Kodak's 15 percent. Moreover, high tariffs on foreign film protect Fuji's interests. Still, Kodak will gain several benefits from its stepped-up attack on Japan. First, Japan offers big opportunities for increased sales and profits—its $1.5 billion film and photo paper market is second only to that of the United States. Second, much of today's new photographic technology comes out of Japan, so a greater presence in Japan will help Kodak keep up with the latest developments. Third, ownership and joint ventures in Japan will help Kodak to better understand Japanese manufacturing and to obtain new products for the U.S. and other world markets. Kodak already sells many Japanese-made products under its own name in the United States: Kodak video cameras are made by Matsushita, its video tape by TDK Electronics. Kodak owns 10 percent of Chinon Industries, which makes the company's 35-mm cameras. Kodak sells film-processing labs made by Japanese manufacturers, and its medium-volume copiers are made by Canon.

Kodak reaps one more important benefit from its attack on the Japanese market: If Fuji must devote heavy resources to defending its Japanese home turf against Kodak's attacks, it will have fewer resources to use against Kodak in the United States.[1]

---

In former times, American companies paid little attention to international trade. If they could pick up some extra sales through exporting, that was okay. But the big market was at home, teeming with opportunities. The home market was also much safer. Managers did not need to learn other languages, deal with strange and changing currencies, face political and legal uncertainties, or adapt their products to different customer needs and expectations.

Today, however, the situation is much different. The home market is no longer as rich in opportunity. Foreign firms are aggressively expanding into new international markets. What is even worse, these firms have also entered the U.S. market, often with higher-quality products offering more value. The American firm that stays at home to play it safe might not only lose its chance to enter other markets but also risk losing its home market.

Daily headlines tell us about Japanese victories in the consumer electronics market and about gains by Japanese, German, Swedish, and even Korean imports in the U.S. car market. They tell us about Bic's successful attacks on Gillette, Nestlé's gains in the coffee and candy markets, and the loss of textile and shoe markets to Third World imports. Such names as Sony, Toyota, Nestlé, Perrier, Norelco, Mercedes, and Panasonic have become household words. Other products that appear to be produced by American firms are really produced by foreign multinationals: Bantam Books, Baskin-Robbins Ice Cream, CBS Records, Firestone Tires, Kiwi Shoe Polish, Lipton Tea, and Saks Fifth Avenue. America is also attracting huge foreign investments in basic industries such as steel, petroleum, tires, and chemicals and in tourist and real estate ventures—for example, Japanese land purchases in Hawaii, Kuwait's resort development off the South Carolina coast, Arab purchases of Manhattan office buildings. Few American industries are now safe from foreign competition.

Although some companies would like to stem the tide of foreign imports through protectionism, this response would be only a temporary solution. In the long run, it would raise the cost of living and protect inefficient U.S. firms. The answer is that more American firms must learn to move abroad and increase their competitiveness. Several American companies have been successful at international marketing: General Motors, Coca-Cola, McDonald's, IBM, General Electric, Caterpillar, Du Pont, Ford, Kodak, Kellogg, Boeing, and dozens of other American firms have made the world their market. But there are too few

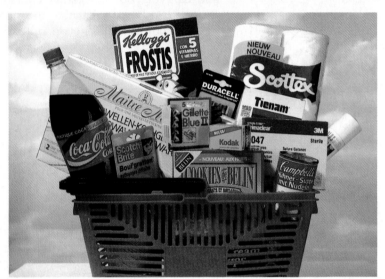

*Many American companies have made the world their market.*

like them. In fact, just five U.S. companies account for 12 percent of all exports; 1,000 manufacturers (out of 300,000) account for 60 percent.[2]

Ironically, while the need for companies to go abroad is greater, so are the risks. Several major problems confront companies that go global. First, high debt, inflation, and unemployment in several countries have resulted in highly unstable governments and currencies, limiting trade and exposing U.S. firms to many risks. Second, governments are placing more regulations on foreign firms, such as requiring joint ownership with domestic partners or the hiring of nationals and limiting profits that can be taken from the country. Finally, foreign governments often impose high tariffs or trade barriers in order to protect their own industries. Corruption is also an increasing problem— officials in several countries often award business not to the best bidder but to the highest briber.

We might thus tend to conclude that companies are doomed whether they stay at home or go abroad. But companies selling "global products" have no choice but to internationalize their operations. And they must do so before the window closes on them, since firms from other countries are already actively globalizing and achieving scale economies.

**Multinational company** A company that operates in many countries and has a major part of its operations outside its home country.

**Tariff** A tax, levied by a government against certain imported products, which is designed to raise revenue or protect domestic firms.

**Quota** A limit on the amount of goods that an importing country will accept in certain product categories.

**Embargo** A ban on the import of a certain product.

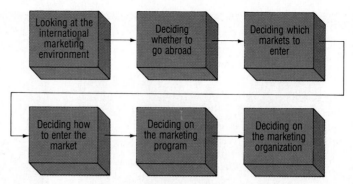

FIGURE 18–1   Major International Marketing Decisions

We might ask: Does international marketing involve any new marketing principles? In general, the answer is no—the principles of setting marketing objectives, choosing target markets, developing marketing positions and mixes, and carrying out marketing control still apply. But the differences among nations can be so great that the international marketer needs to understand foreign countries and how people in different countries respond to marketing efforts.

We will now look at the six decisions that a company faces in international marketing, as shown in Figure 18–1.

## LOOKING AT THE INTERNATIONAL MARKETING ENVIRONMENT

Before deciding whether to sell abroad, a company must thoroughly understand the international marketing environment. That environment has changed considerably in the last two decades, creating both new opportunities and new problems. World trade and investment have grown rapidly, with many attractive markets opening up in Western Europe, China, the USSR, and elsewhere. There has been a growth of global brands in automobiles, food, clothing, electronics, and many other product categories. The number of **multinational companies**—companies that operate in many countries and have a major part of their operations outside their home countries—has grown dramatically. Meanwhile, the United States' dominant position has declined. Other countries such as Japan and West Germany have increased their economic power in world markets (see Marketing Highlight 18–1). The international financial system has become more complex and fragile, and U.S. companies face increasing trade barriers designed to protect domestic markets against foreign competition.

### The International Trade System

The American company looking abroad must start by understanding the international *trade system.* When selling to another country, an American firm will face various trade restrictions. The most common is the **tariff**—a tax levied by a foreign government against certain imported products. The tariff may be designed either to raise revenue or to protect domestic firms. The exporter may also face a **quota,** which sets limits on the amount of goods that the importing country will accept in certain product categories. The purpose of the quota is to conserve on foreign exchange and protect local industry and employment. An **embargo** is the strongest form of quota, one under which some kinds of imports are totally banned.

American firms may face **exchange controls** that limit the amount of foreign exchange and the exchange rate against other currencies. The company may also face **nontariff barriers,** such as bias against American company bids or product standards that go against American product features:

> One of the cleverest ways the Japanese have found to keep foreign manufacturers out of their domestic market is to plead "uniqueness." Japanese skin is different, the government argues, so foreign cosmetics companies must test their products in Japan before selling there. The Japanese say their stomachs are small and have room for only the *mikan,* the local tangerine, so imports of U.S. oranges are limited. Now the Japanese have come up with what may be the flakiest argument yet: Their snow is different, so ski equipment should be too.[3]

**Exchange controls** Limits placed by a government on the amount of its foreign exchange with other countries and on its exchange rate against other currencies.

**Nontariff trade barrier** Nonmonetary barriers to foreign products such as biases against a foreign company's bids or product standards that go against a foreign company's product features.

# Marketing Highlight 18-1

## THE WORLD'S CHAMPION MARKETERS: THE JAPANESE?

Few dispute that the Japanese have performed an economic miracle since World War II. In a very short time, they have achieved global market leadership in many industries: automobiles, motorcycles, watches, cameras, optical instruments, steel, shipbuilding, computers, and consumer electronics. They are now making strong inroads into tires, chemicals, machine tools, and even designer clothes, cosmetics, and food. Some credit the global success of Japanese companies to their unique business and management practices. Others point to the help they get from Japan's government, powerful trading companies, and banks. Still others say Japan's success is based on low wage rates and unfair dumping policies.

In any case, one of the main keys to Japan's success is certainly its skillful use of marketing. The Japanese came to the United States to study marketing and went home understanding it better than many U.S. companies do. They know how to select a market, enter it in the right way, build market share, and protect that share against competitors.

*Selecting Markets.* The Japanese work hard to identify attractive global markets. First, they look for industries that require high skills and high labor intensity but few natural resources. These include consumer electronics, cameras, watches, motorcyles, and pharmaceuticals. Second,

they like markets in which consumers around the world would be willing to buy the same product designs. Finally, they look for industries in which market leaders are weak or complacent.

*Entering Markets.* Japanese study teams spend several months evaluating a target market, searching for market niches that are not being satisfied. Sometimes' they start with a low-priced, stripped-down version of a product, sometimes with a product that is as good as the competitions' but priced lower, sometimes with a product with higher quality or new features. The Japanese also line up good distribution channels in order to provide quick service. They also use effective advertising to bring products to the consumer's attention. Their basic entry strategy is to build market share rather than early profits: The Japanese are often willing to wait as long as a decade before realizing their profits.

*Building Market Share.* Once Japanese firms gain a market foothold, they begin to expand market share. They pour money into product improvements and new models so that they can offer more and better products than the competition. They spot new opportunities through market segmentation, develop markets in new countries, and work to build a network of world markets and production locations.

*Protecting Market Share.* Once the

Japanese achieve market leadership, they become defenders rather than attackers. Their defense strategy is continuous product development and refined market segmentation.

U.S. firms are now fighting back by adding new product lines, pricing more aggressively, streamlining production, buying or making components abroad, and forming strategic partnerships with foreign companies. Moreover, many U.S. companies are now operating successfully in Japan itself. American companies sell over 50,000 different products in Japan, and many hold leading market shares—Coke leads in soft drinks (60 percent share), Schick in razors (71 percent), Polaroid in instant cameras (66 percent), and McDonald's in fast food. Since the early 1980s, U.S. companies have increased their Japanese computer sales by 48 percent, pharmaceutical sales by 41 percent, and electronic parts sales by 63 percent.

*Sources:* See Philip Kotler, Liam Fahey, and Somkid Jatusripitak, *The New Competition* (Englewood Cliffs, NJ: Prentice Hall, 1985); Vernon R. Alden, "Who Says You Can't Crack Japanese Markets?" *Harvard Business Review,* January-February 1987, pp. 52-56; and Joel Dreyfuss, "How to Beat the Japanese at Home," *Fortune,* August 31, 1987, pp. 80-83.

**Economic community** A group of nations organized to work toward common goals in the regulation of international trade.

At the same time, certain forces *help* trade between nations—or at least between some nations. Certain countries have formed **economic communities**—a group of nations organized to work toward common goals in the regulation of international trade. The most important such community is the European Community (EC, also known as the Common Market). The EC's members are the major Western European nations, with a combined population of over 320 million people. It works to create a single European market by reducing physical, financial, and technical barriers to trade among member nations. It eliminates restrictions on its members while setting uniform tariffs and other restrictions on trade with nonmember nations. Founded in 1957, the European Community has yet to achieve the true "common market" originally envisioned. In 1985, however, member countries renewed their push to integrate economically. They jointly enacted the Single European Act, which commits each member nation to a target date of 1992 for completing the process of making Europe "an area without internal frontiers in which the free movement of goods, persons, services, and capital is ensured." Thus, the year 1992 has come to symbolize the complete transformation of the European economy. Since the EC's formation, other economic communities have been formed, such as the Latin American Integration Association (LAIA), the Central American Common Market (CACM), and the Council for Mutual Economic Assistance (CMEA) in Eastern Europe.[4]

Each nation has unique features that must be understood. A nation's readiness for different products and services and its attractiveness as a market to foreign firms depend on its economic, political-legal, and cultural environments.

## Economic Environment

In looking at foreign markets, the international marketer must study each country's economy. Two economic factors reflect the country's attractiveness as a market.

The first is the country's *industrial structure*. The country's industrial structure shapes its product and service needs, income levels, and employment levels. There are four types of industrial structures:

□ *Subsistence economies.* In a subsistence economy, the vast majority of people engage in simple agriculture. They consume most of their output and barter the rest for simple goods and services. They offer few market opportunities.

□ *Raw-material-exporting economies.* These economies are rich in one or more natural resources but poor in other ways. Much of their revenue comes from exporting these resources. Examples are Chile (tin and copper), Zaire (copper, cobalt, and coffee), and Saudi Arabia (oil). These countries are good markets for large equipment, tools and supplies, and trucks. If there are many foreign residents and a wealthy upper class, they are also a market for luxury goods.

□ *Industrializing economies.* In an industrializing economy, manufacturing accounts for between 10 and 20 percent of the country's economy. Examples include Egypt, the Philippines, India, and Brazil. As manufacturing increases, the country needs more imports of raw textile materials, steel, and heavy machinery, and fewer imports of finished textiles, paper products, and automobiles. Industrialization typically creates a new rich class and a small but growing middle class, both demanding new types of imported goods.

□ *Industrial economies.* Industrial economies are major exporters of manufactured goods and investment funds. They trade goods among themselves and also export them to other types of economies for raw materials and semifinished goods. The varied manufacturing activities of industrial nations and their large middle classes make them rich markets for all sorts of goods.

The second economic factor is the country's *income distribution.* The international marketer might find countries with five different income-distribution patterns: (1) very low family incomes, (2) mostly low family incomes, (3) very low/very high family incomes, (4) low/medium/high family incomes, and (5) mostly medium family incomes. Consider the market for Lamborghinis, an automobile costing $128,000. The market would be very small in countries with Type 1 or Type 2 income patterns. Most Lamborghinis are sold in large markets like the United States, Europe, and Japan, which have large segments of high-income consumers, or in small but wealthy countries like Saudi Arabia and Kuwait.

## Political-Legal Environment

Nations differ greatly in their political-legal environments. At least four political-legal factors should be considered in deciding whether to do business in a given country.

### Attitudes toward International Buying

Some nations are quite receptive to foreign firms; others are quite hostile. For example, Mexico has for many years been attracting foreign businesses by offering investment incentives and site-location services. On the other hand, India has bothered foreign businesses with import quotas, currency restrictions, and limits on the percentage of the management team that can be nonnationals. IBM and Coca-Cola left India because of all the "hassles." Pepsi,

*Income distribution: Expensive Lamborghinis sell well in small, wealthy countries like Saudi Arabia and Kuwait.*

**Countertrade** International trade involving the direct or indirect exchange of goods for other goods instead of cash.

on the other hand, took positive steps to persuade the Indian government to allow it to do business in that country on reasonable terms (see Marketing Highlight 18–2).

### Political Stability

Stability is another issue. Governments change hands, sometimes violently. Even without a change, a government may decide to respond to new popular feelings. The foreign company's property may be taken over, its currency holdings may be blocked, or import quotas or new duties may be set. International marketers may still find it profitable to do business in an unstable country, but the situation will affect how they handle business and financial matters.

### Monetary Regulations

Sellers want to take their profits in a currency of value to them. Ideally, the buyer can pay in the seller's currency or in other world currencies. Short of this, sellers might accept a blocked currency—one whose removal from the country is restricted by the buyer's government—if they can buy other goods in that country that they need or can sell elsewhere for a needed currency. Besides currency limits, a changing exchange rate also creates high risks for the seller.

Most international trade involves cash transactions. Yet many nations have too little hard currency to pay for their purchases from other countries. They want to pay with other items instead of cash. This situation has led to a growing practice called **countertrade**, which now accounts for about 25 percent of all world trade. Countertrade takes several forms. *Barter* involves the direct exchange of goods or services, as when the West Germans built a steel plant in Indonesia in exchange for oil. Another form is *compensation* (or *buyback*),

# Marketing Highlight 18–2

## BREAKING INTO AN UNRECEPTIVE MARKET

It is one thing to want to do business in a particular country, quite another to be allowed into the country on reasonable terms. The problem of entering an unreceptive or blocked country calls for *megamarketing*—using economic, psychological, political, and public relations skills to gain the cooperation of several parties in the country.

For example, Pepsi-Cola used megamarketing in its attempt to enter the huge India market. Pepsi worked with an Indian business group to seek government approval for its entry. Both domestic soft-drink companies and anti-multinational legislators objected to letting Pepsi in, so Pepsi had to make an offer that the Indian government would find hard to refuse. It thus offered to help

India export enough of its agricultural products to more than offset the outlay for importing soft-drink syrup. Pepsi also promised to focus a good deal of selling effort on rural areas to help in their economic development. The company further offered to give food-processing, packaging, and water-treatment technology to India.

Clearly, Pepsi's strategy was to bundle a set of benefits that would win the support of the various interest groups influencing the entry decision. Pepsi's marketing problem was not one of simply applying the four *P*'s in a new market, but rather one of just getting into the market in the first place. In trying to win over the government and public groups—and to maintain a reasonable relationship

once admitted—Pepsi had to add two more *P*'s: "politics" and "public opinion."

Many other large companies have learned that it pays to build good relations with host governments. Olivetti, for example, enters new markets by building housing for workers, supporting local arts and charities, and hiring and training local managers. IBM sponsors nutrition programs for Latin American children and gives agricultural advice to the Mexican government. Polaroid is helping Italy restore Leonardo da Vinci's *Last Supper*.

*Sources:* See Philip Kotler, "Megamarketing," *Harvard Business Review,* March-April 1986, pp. 117-24; Kenneth Labich, "America's International Winners," *Fortune,* April 14, 1986, p. 46; and Sheila Tefft, "The Mouse That Roared at Pepsi," *Business Week,* September 7, 1987, p. 42.

whereby the seller sells a plant, equipment, or technology to another country and agrees to take payment in the resulting products. Thus, Goodyear provided China with materials and training for a printing plant in exchange for finished labels. Another form is *counterpurchase*—the seller receives full payment in cash but agrees to spend some portion of the money in the other country within a stated time period. For example, Pepsi sells its cola syrup to the USSR for rubles and agrees to buy Soviet vodka for sale in the U.S.

Countertrade deals can be very complex. For example, Daimler-Benz recently agreed to sell 30 trucks to Romania in exchange for 150 Romanian jeeps, which it then sold to Ecuador for bananas, which were in turn sold to a West German supermarket chain for German currency. Through this round-about process, Daimler-Benz finally obtained payment in German money.[5]

### Government Bureaucracy

A fourth factor is the extent to which the host government runs an efficient system for helping foreign companies: efficient customs handling, good market information, and other factors that aid in doing business. A common shock to Americans is how quickly barriers to trade disappear if a suitable payment (a bribe) is made to some official.

## Cultural Environment

Each country has its own folkways, norms, and taboos. The way foreign consumers think about and use certain products must be examined by the seller before planning a marketing program. There are often surprises. For example, the average French man uses almost twice as many cosmetics and beauty aids as his wife does. The Germans and the French eat more packaged, branded spaghetti than do Italians. Italian children like to eat chocolate bars between slices of bread as a snack. And women in Tanzania will not give their children eggs for fear of making them bald or impotent.

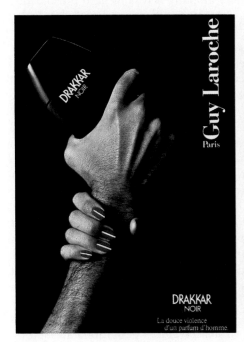

*Adapting to the cultural environment: compared with the European version of this ad (left), Guy Laroche tones down the sensuality in the Arab version (right): the man is clothed and the woman barely touches him.*

Business norms and behavior also vary from country to country. U.S. business executives need to be briefed on these factors before dealing in another country. Here are some examples of different foreign business behavior:

☐ South Americans like to sit or stand very close to each other when they talk business—in fact, almost nose-to-nose. The American business executive tends to keep backing away as the South American moves closer. Both may thus end up being offended.

☐ In face-to-face communications, Japanese business executives rarely say no to an American business executive. Americans tend to be frustrated and may not know where they stand. Americans come to the point quickly. Japanese business executives may find this behavior offensive.

☐ In France, wholesalers don't want to promote a product. They ask their retailers what they want and deliver it. If an American company builds its strategy around the French wholesaler's cooperation in promotions, it is likely to fail.

Thus, each country and region has cultural traditions, preferences, and behaviors that the marketer must study.

# DECIDING WHETHER TO GO ABROAD

Not all companies need to venture into foreign markets to survive. For example, many companies are local businesses that need to market well only in the local marketplace. Other companies, however, operate in global industries in which their strategic positions in major markets are strongly affected by their overall global positions. Thus, IBM must organize globally if it is to gain purchasing, manufacturing, financial, and marketing advantages. Firms in a global industry must compete on a worldwide basis if they are to succeed.

Companies get involved in international marketing in one of two ways. Someone—a domestic exporter, a foreign importer, a foreign government—asks the company to sell abroad. Or the company starts to think on its own about going abroad. For example, it might face overcapacity or see better marketing opportunities in other countries.

Before going abroad, a company should try to define its international marketing objectives and policies. First, it should decide what *volume* of foreign sales it wants. Most companies start small when they go abroad. Some plan to stay small, seeing foreign sales as a small part of their business. Other companies have bigger plans, seeing foreign business as equal to or even more important than domestic business.

Second, the company must choose *how many* countries it wants to market in. For example, the Bulova Watch Company decided to operate in many foreign markets and expanded into over 100 countries. However, it spread itself too thin, made profits in only two countries, and lost around $40 million. Generally, it makes better sense to operate in fewer countries with deeper penetration in each.

Third, the company must decide on the *types* of countries to enter. A country's attractiveness will depend on its product, geographical factors, income and population, political climate, and other factors. The seller may prefer certain country groups or parts of the world.

# DECIDING WHICH MARKETS TO ENTER

After listing possible international markets, the company will have to screen and rank them. Consider the following example:

Many mass marketers dream of selling to China's one billion people. Some think of the market less elegantly as two billion armpits. To PepsiCo, though, the market is mouths, and the People's Republic is especially enticing: it is the most populous country in the world, and Coca-Cola does not yet dominate it.[6]

PepsiCo's decision to enter the Chinese market seems fairly simple and straightforward. China is a huge market without established competition. In addition to selling Pepsi soft drinks, the company hopes to build many of its Pizza Hut restaurants there. Yet we can still question whether market size *alone* is reason enough for selecting China. PepsiCo must also consider other factors. Will the Chinese government be stable and supportive? Does China provide for the production and distribution technologies needed to produce and market Pepsi products profitably? Will Pepsi and pizza fit Chinese tastes, means, and life styles?

Possible foreign markets should thus be ranked on several factors, including market size, market growth, the cost of doing business, competitive advantage, and risk level. The goal is to figure out the potential of each market, using indicators such as those shown in Table 18–1. Then the marketer must decide which markets will offer the greatest long-run return on investment.

*Pepsi in China—a huge but risky market.*

**Exporting** Entering a foreign market by exporting products and selling them through international marketing middlemen (indirect exporting) or through the company's own department, branch, or sales representatives or agents (direct exporting).

TABLE 18-1   Indicators of Market Potential

| | |
|---|---|
| *Demographic Characteristics* | *Technological Factors* |
| Size of population | Level of technological skill |
| Rate of population growth | Existing production technology |
| Degree of urbanization | Existing consumption technology |
| Population density | Education levels |
| Age structure and composition of the population | *Sociocultural Factors* |
| *Geographic Characteristics* | Dominant values |
| Physical size of a country | Life-style patterns |
| Topographical characteristics | Ethnic groups |
| Climate conditions | Linguistic fragmentation |
| *Economic Factors* | *National Goals and Plans* |
| GNP per capita | Industry priorities |
| Income distribution | Infrastructure investment plans |
| Rate of growth of GNP | |
| Ratio of investment to GNP | |

*Source:* Susan P. Douglas, C. Samuel Craig, and Warren Keegan, "Approaches to Assessing International Marketing Opportunities for Small and Medium-Sized Business," *Columbia Journal of World Business,* Fall 1982, pp. 26–32.

# DECIDING HOW TO ENTER THE MARKET

Once a company has decided to sell in a foreign country, it must determine the best mode of entry. Its choices are *exporting, joint venturing,* and *direct investment.* These three market-entry strategies are shown in Figure 18–2, [fig(18–2)] along with the options under each. As the figure shows, each succeeding strategy involves more commitment and risk but also more control and potential profits.

## Exporting

The simplest way to enter a foreign market is through **exporting.** The company may passively export its surpluses from time to time, or it may make an active commitment to expand exports to a particular market. In either case, the company produces all its goods in its home country. It may or may not modify them for the export market. Exporting involves the least change in the company's product lines, organization, investments, or mission.

Companies typically start with *indirect exporting,* working through independent international marketing middlemen. Indirect exporting involves less

FIGURE 18–2   Market-Entry Strategies

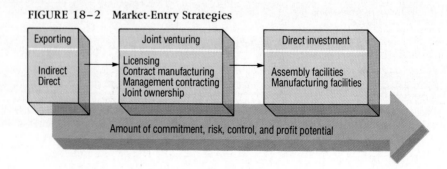

investment because the firm does not have to have an overseas salesforce or set of contacts. It also involves less risk. International marketing middlemen—domestic-based export merchants or agents, cooperative organizations, export-management companies—bring know-how and services to the relationship, and so the seller normally makes fewer mistakes.

Sellers may eventually move into *direct exporting,* handling their own exports. The investment and risk are somewhat greater, but so is the potential return. A company can carry on direct exporting in several ways. First, it can set up a domestic export department that carries out export activities. Or it can set up an overseas sales branch that handles sales, distribution, and perhaps promotion. The sales branch gives the seller more presence and program control in the foreign market, and it often serves as a display center and customer service center. Or the company can send home-based salespeople abroad at certain times in order to find business. Finally, the company can do its exporting either through foreign-based distributors who buy and own the goods or through foreign-based agents who sell goods on behalf of the company.

## Joint Venturing

A second method of entering a foreign market is **joint venturing**—joining with foreign companies to produce or market the products or services. Joint venturing differs from exporting in that the company joins with a partner to sell or market abroad. It differs from direct investment in that an association is formed with someone in the foreign country. There are four types of joint venture.

### Licensing

**Licensing** is a simple way for a manufacturer to enter international marketing. The company enters into an agreement with a licensee in the foreign market, offering the right to use a manufacturing process, trademark, patent, trade secret, or other item of value for a fee or royalty. The company thus gains entry into the market at little risk; the licensee gains production expertise or a well-known product or name without having to start from scratch. Coca-Cola markets internationally by licensing bottlers around the world and supplying them with the syrup needed to produce the product. In Japan, Budweiser beer flows from Suntory breweries, Lady Borden ice cream is churned out at Meiji Milk Products dairies, and Marlboro cigarettes roll off production lines at Japan Tobacco Inc.[7]

However, licensing has potential disadvantages. The firm has less control over the licensee than it would over its own production facilities. If the licensee is very successful, the firm has given up these profits, and if and when the contract ends, it may find it has created a competitor.

### Contract Manufacturing

Another option is **contract manufacturing**—contracting with manufacturers in the foreign market to produce its product or provide its service. Sears used this method in opening up department stores in Mexico and Spain. Sears found qualified local manufacturers to produce many of the products it sells. Contract manufacturing has the drawback of less control over the manufacturing process and the loss of potential profits on manufacturing. On the other hand, it offers the company a chance to start faster, with less risk, and with the later opportunity either to form a partnership with or to buy out the local manufacturer.

**Joint venturing** Entering foreign markets by joining with foreign companies to produce or market a product or service.

**Licensing** A method of entering a foreign market in which the company enters into an agreement with a licensee in the foreign market, offering the right to use a manufacturing process, trademark, patent, trade secret, or other item of value for a fee or royalty.

**Contract manufacturing** Joint venturing to enter a foreign market by contracting with manufacturers in the foreign market to produce a product.

**Management contracting** A joint venture in which the domestic firm supplies the management know-how to a foreign company that supplies the capital; the domestic firm exports management services rather than products.

**Joint ownership** Entering a foreign market by joining with foreign investors to create a local business in which the company shares joint ownership and control.

*Licensing: TOKYO DISNEYLAND is owned and operated by the Oriental Land Co., Ltd. (a Japanese development company) under license from Walt Disney Company.*

### Management Contracting

Under **management contracting,** the domestic firm supplies management know-how to a foreign company that supplies the capital. The domestic firm exports management services rather than products. Hilton uses this arrangement in managing hotels around the world.

Management contracting is a low-risk method of getting into a foreign market, and it yields income from the beginning. The arrangement is even more attractive if the contracting firm has an option to buy some share in the managed company later on. On the other hand, the arrangement is not sensible if the company can put its scarce management talent to better uses or if it can make greater profits by undertaking the whole venture. Management contracting also prevents the company from setting up its own operations for a period of time.

### Joint Ownership

**Joint-ownership** ventures consist of one company joining with foreign investors to create a local business in which they share joint ownership and control. A company may buy an interest in a local firm, or the two parties may form a new business venture. A jointly owned venture may be needed for economic or political reasons. The firm may lack the financial, physical, or managerial resources to undertake the venture alone. Or a foreign government may require joint ownership as a condition for entry.

Joint ownership has certain drawbacks. Partners may disagree over investment, marketing, or other policies. Whereas many American firms like to reinvest earnings for growth, local firms often like to take out these earnings. Whereas American firms give a large role to marketing, local investors may rely on selling.[8]

## Direct Investment

The biggest involvement in a foreign market comes through **direct investment**—developing foreign-based assembly or manufacturing facilities. If a company has gained experience in exporting, and if the foreign market is large enough, foreign production facilities offer many advantages. A firm may have lower costs in the form of cheaper labor or raw materials, foreign government investment incentives, and freight savings. It may improve its image in the host country because it creates jobs. Generally, a firm develops a deeper relationship with government, customers, local suppliers, and distributors, letting it better adapt its products to the local market. Finally, the firm keeps full control over the investment and can therefore develop manufacturing and marketing policies that serve its long-term international objectives.

The main disadvantage is that the firm faces many risks, such as restricted or devalued currencies, falling markets, or government takeovers. In some cases, a firm has no choice but to accept these risks if it wants to operate in the host country.

**Direct investment** Entering a foreign market by developing foreign-based assembly or manufacturing facilities.

**Standardized marketing mix** An international marketing strategy for using basically the same product, advertising, distribution channels, and other elements of the marketing mix in all the company's international markets.

# DECIDING ON THE MARKETING PROGRAM

Companies that operate in one or more foreign markets must decide how much, if at all, to adapt their marketing mixes to local conditions. At one extreme are companies that use a **standardized marketing mix** worldwide. Standardization of the product, advertising, distribution channels, and other elements of the marketing mix promises the lowest costs because no major changes have been

*Direct investment: General Motors owns production and marketing operations in many foreign countries.*

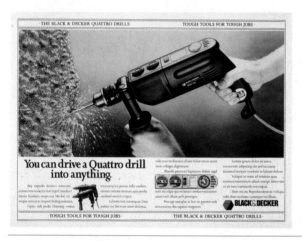

*Standardized advertising messages: Black & Decker uses about the same promotion approach in many different countries.*

**Customized marketing mix** An international marketing strategy for adjusting the marketing mix elements to each international target market, bearing more costs but hoping for a larger market share and return.

introduced. This thinking is behind the idea that Coca-Cola should taste the same around the world and that General Motors should produce a "world car" that suits the needs of most consumers in most countries.

At the other extreme is a **customized marketing mix.** The producer adjusts the marketing mix elements to each target market, bearing more costs but hoping for a larger market share and return. Nestlé, for example, varies its product line and its advertising in different countries. Many possibilities exist between the extremes of standardization and customization. For example, Coca-Cola sells the same beverage worldwide, and in most markets it uses television spots showing a thousand children singing the praises of Coke. For different local markets, however, it edits the commercials to include close-ups of children from those markets—at least 21 different versions of the spot are currently running. The question of whether it is best to customize or standardize the marketing mix has been much debated in recent years (see Marketing Highlight 18–3).

We will now look at possible changes in a company's product, promotion, price, and distribution as it goes abroad.

## Product

There are five strategies for adapting product and promotion to a foreign market (see Figure 18–3).[9] We will look at the three product strategies here and then at the two promotion strategies.

**Straight product extension** means marketing a product in a foreign market without any change. Top management tells its marketing people: "Take the product as is and find customers for it." The first step, however, should be to find out whether foreign consumers use the product and what form they prefer.

Straight extension has been successful in some cases but a disaster in others. Coca-Cola, Kellogg cereals, Heineken beer, McDonald's hamburgers—

**Straight product extension**
Marketing a product in the foreign market without any change.

# Marketing Highlight 18–3

## CUSTOMIZATION OR STANDARDIZATION?

Companies disagree on how much they should standardize products and marketing programs across world markets. However, most marketers believe that because consumers in different countries vary so much, marketing programs will be more effective if tailored to specific market needs. They point out that countries differ in economic, political, legal, and cultural respects. Consumers in different countries have varied geographic, demographic, economic, and cultural characteristics—a fact that results in different needs and wants, spending power, product preferences, and shopping patterns. Because most marketers believe that these differences are hard to change, they customize their products, prices, distribution channels, and promotion approaches to fit unique consumer desires in each country. They argue that too much standardization places a company at a disadvantage against competitors who produce the goods that consumers want.

Recently, however, many companies have moved toward global standardization. They have created so-called "world brands" that are manufactured and marketed in much the same way worldwide. These marketers believe that advances in communication, transportation, and travel are turning the world into a common marketplace. They

claim that people around the world want basically the same products and life styles. Everyone wants things that make life easier and increase both free time and buying power. Common needs and wants thus create global markets for standardized products.

Instead of focusing on differences between markets and customizing products to meet these differences, marketers who standardize globally sell more or less the same product the same way to all consumers. They agree that there *are* differences in consumer wants and buying behavior and that these differences cannot be entirely ignored. But they argue that wants are changeable. Despite what consumers *say* they want, all consumers want good products at lower prices.

> If the price is low enough, they will take highly standardized world products, even if these aren't exactly what mother said was suitable, what immemorial custom decreed was right, or what market research . . . asserted was preferred.

Thus, the global corporation customizes products and marketing programs only when local wants cannot be changed or avoided. Standardization results in lower production, distribution, marketing, and management costs, letting the company offer consumers high quality and more reliable products at lower prices.

So which approach is best —customization or standardization? Clearly, global standardization is not an all-or-nothing proposition, but rather a matter of degree. Companies are justified in looking for more standardization to help keep costs and prices down. But they must remember that although standardization saves money, competitors are always ready to offer more of what consumers in each country want and that they might pay dearly for replacing long-run marketing thinking with short-run financial thinking. One international marketer suggests that companies should "think globally but act locally to give the individual consumer more to say in what he or she wants." The corporate level gives strategic direction; local units focus on the individual consumer differences. Global marketing, yes; global standardization, no.

*Sources:* See John A. Quelch and Edward J. Hoff, "Customizing Global Marketing," *Harvard Business Review,* May-June 1986, pp. 59–68; "Modular Marketing Cracks International Markets," *Marketing News,* April 27, 1984, p. 10; Julie Skur Hill and Joseph H. Winski, "Goodbye Global Ads," *Advertising Age,* November 16, 1987, p. 22; and Theodore Levitt, "The Globalization of Markets," *Harvard Business Review,* May-June 1983, pp. 92–102. Excerpt reprinted by permission of the *Harvard Business Review.* Copyright 1983 by the President and Fellows of Harvard College; all rights reserved.

**Product adaptation** Adapting a product to meet local conditions or wants in foreign markets.

**Product invention** Creating new products or services for foreign markets.

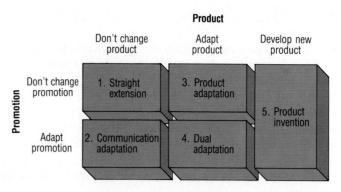

FIGURE 18–3   Five International Product and Promotion Strategies

all are sold in about the same form around the world. But General Foods introduced its standard powdered Jell-O in the British market only to find that British consumers prefer a solid-wafer or cake form. Likewise, Philips began to make a profit in Japan only after it reduced the size of its coffee makers to fit into smaller Japanese kitchens and its shavers to fit smaller Japanese hands. Straight extension is tempting because it involves no additional product-development costs, manufacturing changes, or new promotion. But it can be costly in the long run if products fail to satisfy foreign consumers.

**Product adaptation** involves changing the product to meet local conditions or wants. McDonald's serves beer in Germany and coconut, mango, and tropic mint shakes in Hong Kong. General Foods blends different coffees for the British (who drink their coffee with milk), the French (who drink their coffee black), and Latin Americans (who want a chicory taste). IBM adapts its worldwide product line to meet local needs. For example, IBM must make dozens of different keyboards to match different languages, 20 for Europe alone.[10]

**Product invention** consists of creating something new for the foreign market. This strategy can take two forms. It might mean reintroducing earlier product forms that happen to be well-adapted to the needs of a given country. For example, the National Cash Register Company reintroduced its crank-operated cash register at half the price of a modern cash register and sold large numbers in the Orient, Latin America, and Spain. On the other hand, a company might create a new product to meet a need in another country. There is, for example, an enormous need in less-developed countries for low-cost, high-protein foods. Companies such as Quaker Oats, Swift, and Monsanto are researching the nutrition needs of these countries, creating new foods, and developing advertising campaigns to gain product trial and acceptance. Product invention can be costly, but the payoffs can make it worthwhile.

## Promotion

Companies can adopt the same promotion strategy they used in the home market or change it for each local market.

Consider the message. Some multinational companies use a standardized advertising theme around the world. Exxon used "Put a tiger in your tank" and gained international recognition. Of course, the copy may be varied in minor ways to adjust for language differences. In Japan, where consumers have trouble pronouncing "snap, crackle, pop," the little Rice Crispies critters say "patchy, pitchy, putchy." Colors are sometimes changed to avoid taboos in other countries. Purple is associated with death in most of Latin America; white is a mourning color in Japan; and green is associated with jungle sickness in

Malaysia. Even names have to be changed. In Sweden, Helene Curtis changed the name of Every Night Shampoo to Every Day because Swedes usually wash their hair in the morning. Kellogg also had to rename Bran Buds cereal in Sweden, where the name roughly translates as "burned farmer."[11] (See Marketing Highlight 18-4 for more on language blunders in international marketing.)

Other companies ask their international divisions to fully adapt advertising messages to local markets. The Schwinn Bicycle Company might use a pleasure theme in the United States and a safety theme in Scandinavia. Kellogg ads in the United States promote the taste and nutrition of Kellogg's cereals versus competitors' brands. In France, where consumers drink little milk and eat little for breakfast, Kellogg's ads must convince consumers that cereals are a tasty and healthful breakfast.

Media also need to be adapted internationally because media availability varies from country to country. TV advertising time is very limited in Europe, ranging from four hours a day in France to none in Scandinavian countries. Advertisers must buy time months in advance, and they have little control over when their ads will be shown. Magazines also vary in effectiveness. For example, they are a major medium in Italy and a minor one in Austria. Newspapers are national in the United Kingdom but only local in Spain.

# Marketing Highlight 18—4

## WATCH YOUR LANGUAGE!

Many U.S. multinationals have had difficulty crossing the language barrier, with results ranging from mild embarrassment to outright failure. Seemingly innocuous brand names and advertising phrases can take on unintended or hidden meanings when translated into other languages. Careless translations can make a marketer look downright foolish to foreign consumers. We've all run across examples when buying products from foreign countries—here's one from a firm in Taiwan attempting to instruct children on how to install a ramp on a garage for toy cars:

Before you play with, please fix the waiting plate by yourself as per below diagram. But after you once fixed it, you can play with as is and no necessary to fix off again.

Many U.S. firms are guilty of similar atrocities when marketing abroad.

The classic language blunders involve standardized brand names that do not translate well. When Coca-Cola first marketed Coke in China in the 1920s, it developed a group of Chinese characters that, when pronounced, sounded like the product name. Unfortunately, the characters actually translated to mean "bite the wax tadpole." Today, the characters on Chinese Coke bottles translate as "happiness in the mouth."

Several car makers have had similar problems when their brand names crashed into the language barrier. Chevy's Nova translated into Spanish as *no va*—"It doesn't go." GM changed the name to Caribe and sales increased. Ford introduced its Fiera truck only to discover that the name means "ugly old woman" in Spanish. And it introduced its Comet car in Mexico as the Caliente—slang for "streetwalker." Rolls-Royce avoided the name Silver Mist in German markets, where "mist" means "manure." Sunbeam, however, entered the German market with its Mist-Stick hair curling iron. As should have been expected, the Germans had little use for a "manure wand."

One well-intentioned firm sold its shampoo in Brazil under the name Evitol. It soon realized it was claiming to sell a "dandruff contraceptive." An American company reportedly had trouble marketing Pet milk in French-speaking areas. It seems that the word "pet" in French means, among other things, "to break wind."

Such classic boo-boos are soon discovered and corrected, and they may result in little more than embarrassment for the marketer. But countless other more subtle blunders may go undetected and damage product performance in less obvious ways. The multinational company must carefully screen its brand names and advertising messages to guard against those that might damage sales, make it look silly, or offend consumers in specific international markets.

*Source:* Some of these and many other examples of language blunders are found in David A. Ricks, "Products That Crashed into the Language Barrier," *Business and Society Review,* Spring 1983, pp. 46–50.

**Whole-channel view** Designing international channels that take into account all the necessary links in distributing the seller's products to final buyers, including the seller's headquarters organization, channels between nations, and channels within nations.

## Price

Multinationals also face many problems in setting their international prices. For example, how might Coca-Cola set its prices globally? It could set a uniform price all around the world. But this amount would be too high in poor countries and not high enough in rich ones. Coca-Cola could charge what consumers in each country will bear. But this strategy ignores differences in the actual cost from country to country. Finally, the company could use a standard markup of its costs everywhere. But this approach might price Coca-Cola out of the market in countries where costs are high.

Regardless of how companies go about pricing their products, their foreign prices will probably be higher than their domestic prices. A Gucci handbag may sell for $60 in Italy and $240 in the U.S. Why? Gucci has to add the cost of transportation, tariffs, importer margin, wholesaler margin, and retailer margin to its factory price. Depending on these added costs, the product may have to sell for two to five times as much in another country to make the same profit. For example, a 1988 Chrysler automobile priced at $10,000 in the United States sold for more than $47,000 in South Korea.[12]

Another problem involves setting a price for goods that a company ships to its foreign subsidiaries. If the company charges a foreign subsidiary too much, it may end up paying higher tariff duties even while paying lower income taxes in that country. If the company charges its subsidiary too little, it can be charged with *dumping*. Dumping occurs when a company either charges less than its costs or less than it charges in its home market. Thus, Harley-Davidson accused Honda and Kawasaki of dumping motorcycles on the U.S. market. The U.S. International Trade Commission agreed and responded with a special five-year tariff on Japanese heavy motorcycles, starting at 45 percent in 1983 and gradually dropping to 10 percent by 1988.[13] The commission also recently ruled that Japan was dumping computer memory chips in the United States and laid stiff duties on future imports. Various governments are always watching for dumping abuses and often force companies to set the price charged by other competitors for the same or similar products.

## Distribution Channels

The international company must take a **whole-channel view** of the problem of distributing products to final consumers. Figure 18-4 [(fig(18-4)] shows the three major links between the seller and the final buyer. The first link, the *seller's headquarters organization*, supervises the channels and is part of the channel itself. The second link, *channels between nations*, gets the products to the borders of the foreign nations. The third link, *channels within nations*, gets the products from foreign entry points to final consumers. Some American manufacturers may think their job is done once the product leaves their hands, but they would do well to pay more attention to how it is handled within foreign countries.

Within-country channels of distribution vary greatly from nation to nation. First of all, there are large differences in the numbers and types of middlemen serving each foreign market. For example, a U.S. company marketing in China

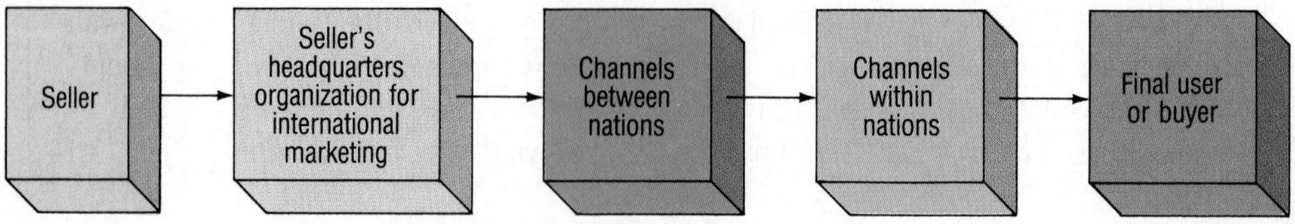

FIGURE 18-4  Whole-Channel Concept for International Marketing

must operate through a frustrating maze of state-controlled wholesalers and retailers. Chinese distributors often carry competitors' products and frequently refuse to share even basic sales and marketing information with their suppliers. Hustling for sales is an alien concept to Chinese distributors, who are used to selling all they can obtain. Working with or getting around this system sometimes requires substantial time and investment. When Coke and Pepsi first entered China, customers bicycled up to bottling plants to get their soft drinks. Now, both companies have set up direct-distribution channels, investing heavily in trucks and refrigeration units for retailers.[14]

Another difference lies in the size and character of retail units abroad. Whereas large-scale retail chains dominate the U.S. scene, most foreign retailing is done by many small independent retailers. In India, millions of retailers operate tiny shops or sell in open markets. Their markups are high, but the real price is brought down through price haggling. Supermarkets could offer lower prices, but they are difficult to start because of many economic and cultural barriers. People's incomes are low, and they prefer to shop daily for small amounts rather than weekly for large amounts. They also lack storage and refrigeration to keep food for several days. Packaging is not well developed because it would add too much to costs. These and other factors have kept large-scale retailing from spreading rapidly in developing countries.

# DECIDING ON THE MARKETING ORGANIZATION

Companies manage their international marketing activities in at least three different ways. Most companies first organize an *export department*, then create an *international division*, and finally become a *global organization*.

## Export Department

A firm normally gets into international marketing by simply shipping out its goods. If its international sales expand, it organizes an export department with a sales manager and a few assistants. As sales increase, the export department can then expand to include various marketing services so that it can go after business actively. If the firm moves into joint ventures or direct investment, the export department will no longer be adequate.

## International Division

Many companies get involved in several international markets and ventures. A company may export to one country, license to another, have a joint-ownership venture in a third, and own a subsidiary in a fourth. Sooner or later, it will create an international division or subsidiary to handle all its international activity.

International divisions are organized in a variety of ways. The international division's corporate staff consists of marketing, manufacturing, research, finance, planning, and personnel specialists. They plan for and provide services to various operating units. Operating units may be organized in one of three ways. They may be *geographical organizations*, with country managers who are responsible for salespeople, sales branches, distributors, and licensees in their respective countries. Or the operating units may be *world product groups*, each responsible for worldwide sales of different product groups. Finally, operating units may be *international subsidiaries*, each responsible for its own sales and profits.

## Global Organization

Several firms have passed beyond the international division stage and become truly multinational organizations. They stop thinking of themselves as national marketers who sell abroad and start thinking of themselves as global marketers. Top corporate management and staff plan worldwide manufacturing facilities, marketing policies, financial flows, and logistical systems. Global operating units report directly to the chief executive or the executive committee of the organization, not to the head of an international division. Executives are trained in worldwide operations, not just domestic *or* international. The company recruits from many countries, buys components and supplies where they cost the least, and invests where the expected returns are greatest.

Major companies must go more global in the 1990s if they hope to compete. As foreign companies successfully invade the domestic market, U.S. companies must move more aggressively into foreign markets. They will have to change from companies that treat their foreign operations as secondary to companies viewing the entire world as a single boarderless market.[15]

## ◼ SUMMARY

Companies today can no longer afford to pay attention only to their domestic market, no matter how large it is. Many industries are global industries, and those firms that operate globally achieve lower costs and higher brand awareness. At the same time, *global marketing* is risky because of variable exchange rates, unstable governments, protectionist tariffs and trade barriers, and several other factors. Given the potential gains and risks of international marketing, companies need a systematic way to make their international marketing decisions.

As a first step, a company must understand the *international marketing environment*, especially the international trade system. It must assess each foreign market's *economic, political-legal*, and *cultural characteristics*. Second, the company must consider what level of foreign sales it will seek, whether it will do business in a few or many countries, and what types of

countries it wants to market in. Third, the company must decide which specific markets to enter. This decision calls for weighing the probable rate of return on investment against the level of risk. Fourth, the company has to decide how to enter each chosen market—whether through *exporting, joint venturing*, or *direct investment*. Many companies start as exporters, move to joint venturing, and finally make a direct investment in foreign markets. Companies must next decide how much their products, promotion, price, and channels should be adapted for each foreign market. Finally, the company must develop an effective organization for international marketing. Most firms start with an *export department* and graduate to an *international division*. A few become *global organizations*, with worldwide marketing planned and managed by the top officers of the company.

## ◼ QUESTIONS FOR DISCUSSION

1. With all the problems facing companies that "go global," why are so many companies choosing to expand internationally? What are the major advantages of expanding beyond the domestic market?

2. When exporting goods to a foreign country, a marketer may be faced with various trade restrictions. Discuss the possible effects of the following on an exporter's marketing mix: (a) tariffs, (b) quotas, (c) embargoes.

3. Which of these will have the greatest impact on a soft drink manufacturer's appraisal of a foreign nation as an attractive market—the economic environment, the political-legal environment, or the cultural environment?

4. Why do you think so many companies in the United States and around the world are so eager to enter

markets in the Soviet Union? In answering this question, consider the factors listed in Table 18–1.

5. Discuss the steps an advertising agency could take in entering a foreign market. What types of joint venture would be worth considering?

6. Which combination of product and promotion strategies would you recommend to Campbell Soup in marketing canned soups in Brazil? Why?

7. Although the price of an exported product is often higher in foreign markets than in the domestic market, there are occasions when foreign prices are lower than domestic prices. Under what conditions can these situations develop?

8. "Dumping" leads to price savings to the consumer. Why, then, do many governments make dumping

illegal? What are the *disadvantages* to consumers of dumping by foreign firms?

9. Which type of international marketing organization would you suggest for the following companies: (a)

Schwinn Bicycles, selling three models in the Far East; (b) a small U.S. manufacturer of toys, marketing its products in Europe; (c) Dodge, planning to sell its full line of cars and trucks in Kuwait?

# REFERENCES

1. See James B. Treece, Barbara Buell, and Jane Sasseen, "How Kodak is Trying to Move Mount Fuji," *Business Week,* December 2, 1985, pp. 62–64; Joel Dryfuss, "How to Beat the Japanese at Home," *Fortune,* August 31, 1987, pp. 82–83; and Leslie Helm, "Has Kodak Set Itself Up for a Fall?" *Business Week,* February 22, 1988, pp. 134–38.

2. See Edward C. Baig, "50 Leading U.S. Exporters," *Fortune,* July 18, 1988, pp. 70–71.

3. "The Unique Japanese," *Fortune,* November 24, 1986, p. 8. Also see Rahul Jacob, "Export Barriers the U.S. Hates Most," *Fortune,* February 27, 1989, pp. 88–89.

4. For more on the European Community, see Frank J. Comes and Jonathon Kapstein, "Reshaping Europe: 1992 and Beyond," *Business Week,* December 12, 1988, pp. 49–51; and John F. Magee, "1992: Moves Americans Must Make," *Harvard Business Review,* May-June 1989, pp. 78–84.

5. For further reading, see John W. Dizard, "The Explosion of International Barter," *Fortune,* February 7, 1983; Leo G. B. Welt, *Trade without Money: Barter and Countertrade* (New York: Harcourt Brace Jovanovich, 1984); and Demos Vardiabasis, "Countertrade: New Ways of Doing Business," *Business to Business,* December 1985, pp. 67–71.

6. Louis Kraar, "Pepsi's Pitch to Quench Chinese Thirsts," *Fortune,* March 17, 1986, p. 58. Also see Maria Shao, "Laying the Foundation for the Great

Mall of China," *Business Week,* January 25, 1988, pp. 68–69.

7. Larry Armstrong, "A Cheaper Dollar Doesn't Always Mean Cheaper American Goods," *Business Week,* May 5, 1986, p. 43.

8. For more on joint ventures, see Gary Hamel, Yves L. Doz, and C. K. Prahalad, "Collaborate with your Competitors and Win," *Harvard Business Review,* January-February 1989, pp. 133–39; and Kenichi Ohmae, "The Global Logic of Strategic Alliances," *Harvard Business Review,* March-April 1989, pp. 143–54.

9. See Warren J. Keegan, *Multinational Marketing Management,* 3rd ed. (Englewood Cliffs, NJ: Prentice Hall, 1984), pp. 317–24.

10. For other examples, see Andrew Kupfer, "How to Be a Global Manager," *Fortune,* March 14, 1988, pp. 52–58.

11. See Kenneth Labich, "America's International Winners," *Fortune,* April 14, 1986, p. 44.

12. Dori Jones Yang, "Can Asia's Four Tigers Be Tamed?" *Business Week,* February 15, 1988, p. 47.

13. See Michael Oneal, "Harley-Davidson: Ready to Hit the Road Again," *Business Week,* July 21, 1986, p. 70.

14. See Shao, "Laying the Foundation for the Great Mall of China," p. 69.

15. See Kenichi Ohmae, "Managing in a Borderless World," *Harvard Business Review,* May-June 1989, pp. 152–61.

# Case 18

## SENECA COLD-DRAWN STEEL, INC.: DOING BUSINESS IN THE PEOPLE'S REPUBLIC OF CHINA

Jim Hoffmann, President of Seneca Cold-Drawn Steel, Inc., is considering possible ways to overcome the severe difficulty that his company has encountered in its domestic market. Seneca is a small cold-drawn precision-steel factory located in western New York. The company was founded in 1974 when a nearby large steel mill closed down its production line as part of a strategic contraction plan resulting from the oil crisis. Hoffmann seized the opportunity and set up Seneca three miles away from the larger mill.

In its first five years, Seneca's business involved buying hot-rolled steel bars from the large steel mill and "cold-drawing" them according to customers' required specifications, such as round, square, flat, or hexagonal bars. The cold-drawing process begins with the receipt of the "hot-rolled steel" in the form of bars or coils. The material is then shot-blasted to remove dirt, scale, and rust. Next, it is coated with a lime solution to prevent future rust and improve lubrication when it is drawn through the dies used for cutting and shaping. The steel is then drawn through the dies, which size it to customer specifications. The steel bar is then straightened and cut to desired length. Whereas hot-rolled steel is usually dirty, rusty, and inconsistent in size, cold-drawn steel is sized within precise tolerances, stronger, and finished to a clean, semi-polished surface. Finished cold-drawn products are then supplied to industrial users, mainly in the automobile and machinery industries.

Seneca operated profitably in its first five years, primarily because of its ability to meet customers' fluctuating delivery and specification requirements. And because of its small scale, local market demand was sufficient to keep Seneca operating at full capacity. After 1980, however, increasing competition from Japanese automobiles and machinery-products manufacturers in Pacific Rim countries (principally Japan, Korea, and Taiwan) drove many of Seneca's customers out of business. Moreover, the supplier providing Seneca with raw steel was forced to reduce its production. In turn, this development forced Seneca to buy most of its raw steel from mills located more than 500 miles away, greatly increasing raw-material costs and reducing Seneca's ability to meet its customers' rapidly fluctuating requirements. Given these changing customer and supplier markets, Seneca faced an important turning point.

However, at the same time that Seneca encountered severe difficulties in its domestic market, many opportunities were developing in international markets. For example, China, a vast market and a land of great resources, was opening its long-closed doors and attempting to play a role in the global economy. Recently, China had greatly increased its international trade. Since 1979—the year China implemented a new Open Door policy that allowed Western companies to establish joint ventures with Chinese investors—the Chinese government has encouraged direct foreign participation in order to develop its economy. Since that time, the Chinese gross national product has grown at least 10 percent annually, and international trade has grown at an annual rate of 17 percent. By 1987, some 140 wholly foreign-owned enterprises were operating in China. There were also numerous other cooperative undertakings, including nearly 8,000 joint-venture companies—300 of them American. Today, American-owned enterprises or Chinese-American joint ventures include both large, well-known companies (Xerox, Union Carbide, IBM, Occidental Chemical) and smaller, lesser-known companies (such as Mundi Westport Corp., Rochester Instruments, Pretolite Electric, and Kamsky Associates).

The Chinese government encourages such enterprises in order to secure the technology, financial resources, and management systems needed in such strategically important industries as communication and transportation, machinery, iron and steel, biochemicals, food production and processing. As a member of an industry now being courted by the Chinese government, Seneca may face a great new opportunity. With a population of over one billion people and a geographic territory exceeding that of the United States, China is a potential market that few companies can ignore. To tap this market, however, Seneca must be willing and able to transfer its production technology to China in a way that will enhance the Chinese steel industry.

In July of 1988, Jim Hoffmann had received a letter from an international management consulting firm asking that Seneca host a delegation of Chinese steel entrepreneurs. The Chinese delegation, known as the "China Entrepreneurs of Medium-Small Steel Plants Training and Studying Mission to U.S.A.," consisted of plant managers or directors of 45 medium-to-small steel plants located in 26 major Chinese steel-industry cities. Hoffmann had decided to participate in the program.

During the delegation's visit in October of 1988, Seneca provided a tour of its plant and arranged visits to two large steel mills. In a series of open discussions with the Chinese plant managers and directors, Hoffmann identified several business opportunities:

1. A *compensation-trading* opportunity: Because of the availability of less labor-intensive equipment, some production lines used to make small-sized products at Seneca's plant are obsolete in the United States. Seneca could sell these production lines to interested Chinese firms. With easy access to suitable raw materials and lower labor costs, the Chinese may be in a better position to produce such small-sized products. Seneca could then buy back the finished products and resell them to its current customers.

2. A *processing-and-assembling trade* opportunity: Seneca could acquire raw materials from Pacific Rim countries, send them to Chinese partners for cold-drawing, and then resell the finished products to its own U.S. customers.

3. A *joint-venture* opportunity: Seneca could enter a joint venture, using a Chinese partner's existing facilities to supply hot-rolled bars for its own U.S. plant. In addition, the joint-venture steel factory could further process hot-rolled bars into cold-drawn bars to serve the Chinese market.

4. A *wholly foreign-owned-enterprise* opportunity: Seneca could set up a wholly-owned factory in China, taking advantage of the availability and lower price of Chinese raw materials and the huge potential market for cold-drawn bars in China.

After the Chinese delegation had left, Hoffmann faced an important decision regarding which opportunity, if any, to pursue. To help with the decision, he hired a consulting company that specialized in U.S.-China trade. The consultants suggested that Seneca consider several factors before making a decision:

1. *Foreign Exchange:* Foreign exchange is perhaps the most important factor in any China-development decision. Foreign exchange woes are common in developing countries that have not yet created an industrial base capable of producing exportable goods. This is particularly important in China, a regulated market and a country trying to balance its foreign exchange. Because Chinese currency, called "IMB," has no value on international currency markets, companies doing business in China insist on payment in a major international currency. The Chinese government, however, tightly controls the availability of foreign currency, ensuring that what little international currency it does possess is channeled to the payment of important strategic products. Such policies can result in great inefficiencies and hamper the growth of key enterprises. Thus, foreign companies must often develop counter-trade arrangements and negotiate guarantees for payment in their own currencies. These arrangements can be very complicated—the issue of foreign exchange should therefore be addressed early in contract negotiations.

2. *Labor Practices:* Although China has abundant labor resources, the government is still wary of the foreign use of domestic labor, mainly because of memories of colonial exploitation. Foreign firms doing business in China do not pay workers directly: The money is paid to local governments that, in turn, pay the members of a particular "work unit." Thus, the Chinese labor force is neither cheap nor efficient. Although there have been recent signs of change toward more flexibility in hiring and firing practices, firms like Seneca must negotiate contracts that provide as much control over labor issues as possible.

3. *Legal Considerations:* China has no history of an international-style legal system. Its laws are vague and arbitrary, and there is always the concept of *neibu*—bureaucrats are not sure if they should give information about laws to foreigners and so will not openly discuss many rules and regulations. Foreign firms must thus negotiate patiently and adhere to their own basic principles and goals. The Chinese political system also continues to be highly "personalistic" in nature—there is often no commonly agreed-upon legal system, and government officials seldom interpret rules consistently. Thus, it would be important for Seneca to develop key contacts and become active on the Chinese banquet circuit.

   However, with recent refinements in business law and the popularization of legal study among some of China's top leaders, the legal situation is slowly changing. Chinese leadership has traditionally been determined to maintain control over the political system, but this attitude has softened because of the remarkable recent turnover of leadership at all levels. Many younger, better-educated, professionally qualified leaders have reduced the bureaucracy that has for years been a major obstacle to foreign investment.

4. *Relationship with Chinese the Counter-Party:* The contractual relationship formed with a company's Chinese counter-party can be summarized as follows: Everything is negotiable. In general, the importance of *guaxi*—the building up of good favors—is perhaps the best strategy for negotiating. The negotiation process does not *end* with the signing of a contract—it simply *begins* there. In addition, it is important to consider carefully what *type* of Chinese counter-party is best for a given business: Firms should seek counter-parties with strong political affiliations—if indeed such affiliations can be determined.

5. *Selecting a Business Location:* Each area of China is unique. China is not homogeneous: Cities differ, provinces differ, and languages differ. Foreign firms are encouraged to locate in special economic zones where banking, transportation, and utility services are readily available. Some companies, for example, have made mistakes by trying to locate in areas where the cost of labor and materials were lower but the services necessary for doing business not sufficiently developed. A company entering China should carefully investigate the rules, regulations, and idiosyncrasies of different areas.

Armed with this advice from his consultants, Hoffmann planned a business trip to visit several potential counter-parties in China. On his return, he would make a decision about Seneca's first step into China.

### Questions

1. Describe the marketing environment facing foreign firms in the People's Republic of China.

2. What criteria should be used to decide whether or not to pursue a business opportunity in China?

3. Evaluate the advantages and disadvantages of each business opportunity under consideration. Which opportunity would you recommend to Hoffmann?

*Source:* This case was written by Mr. Ben Liu, Research Assistant at the China Trade Center, School of Management, State University of New York at Buffalo. Although the case is based on an actual business situation, all names have been disguised to protect the interests of the company.

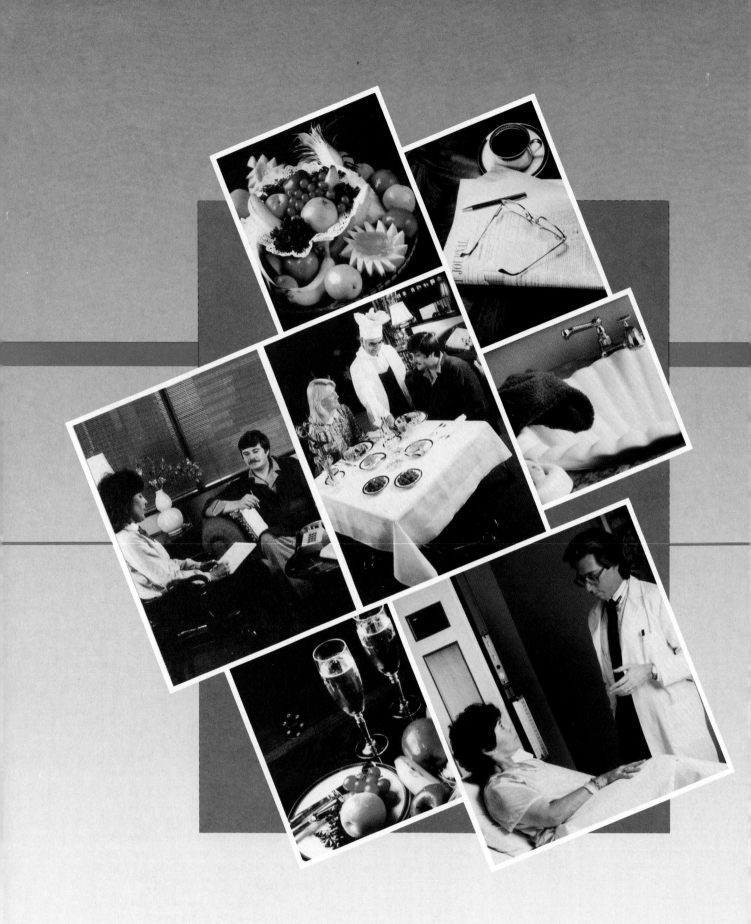

# 19
# Services Marketing and Nonprofit Marketing

## CHAPTER OBJECTIVES

After reading this chapter, you should be able to

1. Define *service* and describe four characteristics that affect the marketing of a service
2. Explain how organizations market themselves
3. Explain how persons and places are marketed
4. Define social marketing and explain how social ideas are marketed

Traditionally, hospitals have had the problem of too many patients. But over the past decade, they have begun to face falling admissions and low occupancy. In the scramble to pull in new patients, many hospitals turned to marketing. The more they looked at the problem, the more complex the marketing challenges appeared. Most hospitals realized that they couldn't be all things to all people. Some began to focus on offering certain specialties—heart, pediatrics, burn treatment, psychiatry. Others focused on serving the special needs of certain demographic segments.

Century City Hospital in Los Angeles provides a good example of modern hospital marketing. It recently unveiled its "Century Pavilion"—the hospital equivalent of a suite at the Ritz. The Pavilion consists of six luxury suites in which the area's affluent can get some of the finer things along with their basic health care. Since it opened, a steady stream of celebrities and other wealthy patients have lined up to pay the $1,000 per night required to stay in a classy Pavilion suite. From the moment they are whisked to their rooms by private elevator, Pavilion guests are pampered.

Century City did not stumble across the Pavilion idea by chance. The service is the result of a solid marketing program headed by the hospital's marketing director. A research study of the hospital's primary market area showed that almost 50 percent of the area residents were high-income, highly educated professionals. Thirty-seven percent of the area population lives in homes worth over $200,000; over 7 percent have household incomes above $75,000. And there are over 40,000 millionaires in the Los Angeles-Long Beach area. Century City set out to capture this segment of well-heeled residents who had come to expect the best in food, accommodations, and service.

While cost efficiency is the battle cry in most health-care corners, upscale patients want—and can afford—extras. Century City's research showed that this segment wanted privacy and exclusivity. So the hospital employed a noted interior design firm to create suites with understated luxury and an elegant but quiet atmosphere. In these posh rooms, gourmet food is served on imported china and specially selected silver flatware. And since four of the Pavilion's units come with guest suites (for family, friends, and bodyguards), each unit allows for gracious hospitality. The hospital has even catered parties in the suites. Finally, units come with many other extras, such as secretarial services to help patients to keep up with their business tasks.

Century City decided against flashy institutional ads to promote the Pavilion. Instead, direct-mail pieces were sent to about 10,000 households in Brentwood, Bel Aire, Beverly Hills, and wealthy areas of West Los Angeles. Direct mail was also used to reach 800 staff physicians, each of whom received a rose one day, a fancy notepad another, and a chocolate truffle in a third mailing—each alerting them that the service was available for their prominent patients.

Century City uses a low-key approach to marketing. Other hospitals have used flashier, mass-selling tactics to drum up business. Sunrise Hospital in Las Vegas ran a large ad showing a ship with the caption: "Introducing the Sunrise Cruise. Win a Once-in-a-Lifetime Cruise Simply by Entering Sunrise Hospital Any Friday or Saturday: Recuperative Cruise for Two." St. Luke's Hospital in Phoenix introduced nightly bingo games for all patients (except cardiac cases), producing immense patient interest and an annual profit of $60,000. A Philadelphia hospital served candlelight dinners with steak and champagne to parents of newborn children. Republic Health Corporation hospitals offer eleven branded "products," including Gift of Sight (cataract surgery), Miracle Moments (childbirth), and You're Becoming (cosmetic surgery).

Whatever the approach, most major hospitals now use some form of marketing; many have become quite good at it. Last year, American hospitals spent $1.6 billion on marketing. According to Century City's director: "The Century Pavilion represents one element of what is happening in hospital marketing. Hospitals are becoming very sophisticated in defining who their patients are, what their needs are, and they're creating the kinds of services—whether it be luxury suites or same-day surgery—to meet those needs. In short, hospitals are definitely consumer oriented—a very large factor in health care today."[1]

Marketing developed initially for selling physical products such as toothpaste, cars, steel, and equipment. But this traditional focus may cause people to overlook the many other types of things that are marketed. In this chapter, we will look at the special marketing requirements for *services, organizations, persons, places,* and *ideas.*

## SERVICES MARKETING

One of the major trends in American business has been the dramatic growth of services. Service jobs now account for 77 percent of total employment and 70 percent of the Gross National Product, and services will provide 90 percent of all new jobs in the next ten years.[2] Service jobs include not only people working in service industries—hotels, airlines, banks, and others—but also people providing services in product-based industries, such as corporate lawyers, medical staff, and sales trainers. As a result of rising affluence, more leisure time, and the growing complexity of products that require servicing, the United States has become the world's first *service economy.*

Service industries vary greatly. The government sector offers services through courts, employment services, hospitals, loan agencies, military services, police and fire departments, postal service, regulatory agencies, and schools. The private nonprofit sector offers services through museums, charities, churches, colleges, foundations, and hospitals. A good part of the business sector offers services through airlines, banks, hotels, insurance companies, consulting firms, medical and law practices, entertainment companies, real estate firms, advertising and research agencies, and retailers.

Not only are there traditional service industries but new types keep popping up all the time:

Want someone to fetch a meal from a local restaurant? In Austin, Texas, you can call EatOutIn. Plants need to be watered? In New York, you can call the Busy

*The convenience industry: services that save you time—for a price.*

Body's Helper. Too busy to wrap and mail your packages? Stop by any one of the 72 outlets of Tender Sender, headquartered in Portland, Oregon. "We'll find it, we'll do it, we'll wait for it," chirps Lois Barnett, the founder of Personalized Services in Chicago. She and her crew of six will walk the dog, shuttle the kids to Little League, or wait in line for your theater tickets. Meet the convenience peddlers. They want to save you time. For a price, they'll do just about anything that's legal.[3]

Some service businesses are very large, with total sales and assets in the trillions of dollars. Table 19–1 shows the five largest service companies in each of eight service categories. But there are also tens of thousands of smaller service providers. Selling services presents some special problems calling for special marketing solutions.[4] We will now look at the nature of services and their great variety, how the major characteristics of services affect their marketing, and how service firms can increase their differentiation, quality, and productivity.

**TABLE 19–1   The Largest U.S. Service Companies**

| | |
|---|---|
| *Commercial Banking* | *Diversified Financial* |
| Citicorp | American Express |
| Chase Manhattan | Federal National |
| Bank America | Mortgage Association |
| Chemical New York | Solomon |
| J.P. Morgan | Aetna Life & Casualty |
| | Merrill Lynch |
| *Life Insurance* | *Retailing* |
| Prudential | Sears |
| Metropolitan | K mart |
| Equitable | Safeway |
| Aetna | Kroger |
| Teacher's Insurance | Wal-Mart |
| and Annuity | |
| *Transportation* | *Utilities* |
| Allegis | GTE |
| United Parcel Service | BellSouth |
| Texas Air | NYNEX |
| CSX | Pacific Gas |
| AMR | and Electric |
| | Southwestern Bell |
| *Diversified Services* | *Savings Institutions* |
| Super Valu Stores | Financial Corporation |
| Fleming Companies | of America |
| McKesson | H.F. Almanson |
| Hospital Corporation | Great Western Financial |
| of America | Calfed |
| Ryder System | Meritor Financial Group |

*Source:* "The Service 500," *Fortune,* June 6, 1988, pp. D3-D38.

# Nature and Characteristics of a Service

We define a **service** as any activity or benefit that one party can offer to another that is essentially intangible and does not result in the ownership of anything; its production may or may not be tied to a physical product. Renting a hotel room, depositing money in a bank, traveling on an airplane, visiting a psychiatrist, getting a haircut, having a car repaired, watching a professional sport, seeing a movie, having clothes cleaned at a dry cleaner, getting advice from a lawyer—all of these activities involve buying a service.

A company must consider four service characteristics when designing marketing programs: *intangibility, inseparability, variability,* and *perishability*. We will look at each of these characteristics in the following sections.

## Intangibility

Services are **intangible**—they cannot be seen, tasted, felt, heard, or smelled before they are bought. People having cosmetic surgery cannot see the result before the purchase, and airline passengers have nothing but a ticket and the promise of safe delivery to their destinations.

To reduce uncertainty, buyers thus look for signs of service quality. They draw conclusions about quality from the place, people, equipment, communication material, and price that they can see. Therefore, the service provider's task is to make the service tangible in one or more ways. Whereas product marketers try to add intangibles to their tangible offers, service marketers try to add tangibles to their intangible offers.[5]

Consider a bank that wants to convey the idea that its service is quick and efficient. It must make this positioning strategy tangible in every aspect of customer contact. The bank's physical setting must suggest quick and efficient service: Its exterior and interior should have clean lines, internal traffic flow should be planned carefully, waiting lines should seem short, and background music should be light and upbeat. The bank's people should be busy and properly dressed. Its equipment—computers, copy machines, desks—should look modern. The bank's ads and other communications should suggest efficiency, with clean and simple designs and carefully chosen words and photos that communicate the bank's positioning. The bank should choose a name and symbol for its service that suggest speed and efficiency. Its pricing for various services should be kept simple and clear.

## Inseparability

Physical goods are produced, then stored, later sold, and still later consumed. But services are first sold, then produced and consumed at the same time. Thus, services are **inseparable** from their providers, whether the providers be people or machines. If a person provides the service, then that person is a part of the service. Because the client is also present when the service is produced, *provider-client interaction* is a special feature of services marketing. Both the provider and the client affect the service outcome.

In the case of entertainment and professional services, buyers care a great deal about *who* provides the service. It is not the same service at a Kenny Rogers concert if Rogers gets sick and is replaced by Billy Joel. A legal defense supplied by John Nobody differs from one supplied by F. Lee Bailey. When clients have strong provider preferences, price is used to ration the limited supply of the preferred provider's time. Thus, F. Lee Bailey charges more than do lesser-known lawyers, and only wealthy clients can afford his services.

Several strategies exist for getting around the problem of service-provider time limitations. First, the service provider can learn to work with larger groups. Some psychotherapists, for example, have moved from one-on-one therapy to small-group therapy to groups of over 300 people in larger hotel ballrooms. Second, the service provider can learn to work faster—the psychotherapist can spend 30 minutes with each patient instead of 50 minutes and thus see more patients. Finally, the service organization can train more service providers and build up client confidence, as H&R Block has done with its national network of trained tax consultants.

## Variability

Services are highly **variable**—their quality depends on who provides them and when, where, and how they are provided. For example, some hotels have reputations for providing better service than others. Within a given hotel, one registration desk employee may be cheerful and efficient while another standing just a few feet away may be unpleasant and slow. Even the quality of a single employee's service will vary with his or her energy and frame of mind at the time of each customer contact.

Service firms can take several steps toward quality control.[6] First, they can carefully select and train their personnel. Airlines, banks, and hotels spend large sums to train their employees to give good service. Consumers should find the same friendly and helpful personnel in every Marriott Hotel. Second, service firms can also provide employee incentives that emphasize quality, such as employee-of-the-month awards or bonuses based on customer feedback. Third, they can make service employees more visible and accountable to consumers— auto dealerships can let customers talk directly with the mechanics working on their cars. Finally, a firm can regularly check customer satisfaction through suggestion and complaint systems, customer surveys, and comparison shopping. When poor service is found, it can be corrected. How a firm handles problems resulting from service variability can dramatically affect customer perceptions of service quality. Here is a good example:

> A while back, we had a Federal Express package that, believe it or not, absolutely, positively didn't get there overnight. One phone call to Federal Express solved the problem. But that's not all. Pretty soon our phone rang, and one of Federal Express' senior executives was on the line. He wanted to know what happened and was very apologetic. Now that's service. With that one phone call, he assured himself of a customer for life.[7]

## Perishability

Services are **perishable**—they cannot be stored for later sale or use. Many doctors charge patients for missed appointments because the service value existed only at that point when the patient did not show up. The perishability of services is not a problem when demand is steady. When demand fluctuates, however, service firms often have difficult problems. For example, public transportation companies have to own much more equipment because of rush hour demand than they would if demand were uniform throughout the day.

Service firms can use several strategies for producing a better match between demand and supply.[8] On the demand side, charging different prices at different times will shift some demand from peak to off-peak periods. Examples include low early-evening movie prices and weekend discount prices for car rentals. Or nonpeak demand can be increased, as when McDonald's offered its Egg McMuffin breakfast and hotels developed mini-vacation weekends. Complementary services can be offered during peak time to provide alternatives to waiting customers, such as cocktail lounges to sit in while waiting for a restaurant table and automatic tellers in banks. Reservation systems can help to manage the demand level—airlines, hotels, and physicians use them regularly.

On the supply side, part-time employees can be hired to serve peak demand. Colleges add part-time teachers when enrollment goes up, and

**service variability** A major characteristic of services—their quality may vary greatly, depending on who provides them and when, where, and how they are provided.

**service perishability** A major characteristic of services—they cannot be stored for later sale or use.

**internal marketing** Marketing by a service firm to effectively train and motivate its customer-contact employees and all supporting service people to work as a team to provide customer satisfaction.

**interactive marketing** Marketing by a service firm which recognizes that perceived service quality depends heavily on the quality of buyer-seller interaction.

*Services are perishable: empty seats at slack times cannot be stored for later use during peak periods.*

restaurants call in part-time waiters and waitresses. Or peak-time demand can be handled more efficiently by having employees do only essential tasks during peak periods. Some tasks can be shifted to consumers, as when consumers fill out their own medical records or bag their own groceries. Providers can also share services, as when several hospitals share an expensive piece of medical equipment. Finally, a firm can plan ahead for expansion, as when an amusement park buys surrounding land for later development.

## Marketing Strategies for Service Firms

Service firms typically lag behind manufacturing firms in their use of marketing.[9] Many service businesses are small (shoe repair shops, barbershops) and often consider marketing too costly or unneeded. There are also service businesses (legal, medical, and accounting practices) that still believe that it is unprofessional to use marketing. Other service businesses (colleges, hospitals) once had so much demand that they did not need marketing until recently.

Furthermore, service businesses are more difficult to manage when they use only traditional marketing approaches. In a product business, products are fairly standardized and sit on shelves waiting for customers. In a service business, the customer interacts with a service provider whose service quality is less certain and more variable. The service outcome is affected not just by the service provider but by the whole supporting production process. Thus, service marketing requires more than just the traditional four *P*'s marketing. In addition, it requires both *internal marketing* and *interactive marketing*.[10]

**Internal marketing** means that the service firm must effectively train and motivate its customer-contact employees and all the supporting service people to work as a *team* to provide customer satisfaction. For the firm to deliver consistently high service quality, everyone must practice customer orientation. It is not enough to have a marketing department doing traditional marketing while the rest of the company goes its own way. Marketers must also get everyone else in the organization to practice marketing.[11]

**Interactive marketing** means that perceived service quality depends heavily on the quality of the buyer-seller interaction. In product marketing, product quality seldom depends on how the product is obtained. But in services marketing, service quality depends both on the service deliverer and on the quality of the delivery, especially in professional services. The customer judges service quality not just on *technical quality* (say, the success of the surgery) but also on its *functional quality* (whether the doctor showed concern and inspired confidence). Thus, professionals cannot assume that they will satisfy the client simply by providing good technical service. They must also master interactive marketing skills or functions.

Today, as competition increases, as costs rise, as productivity drops, and as service quality falls off, more service firms are taking an interest in marketing. Service companies face three major marketing tasks. They want to increase their *competitive differentiation, service quality,* and *productivity.*

## Managing Differentiation

In these days of intense price competition, service marketers often complain that it is hard to differentiate their services from those of competitors. To the extent that customers view the services of different providers as similar, they care less about the provider than the price.

The solution to price competition is to develop a differentiated offer and image. A service firm can add *innovative features* to set its offer apart. For example, airlines have introduced such innovations as in-flight movies, advanced seating, air-to-ground telephone service, and frequent-flyer programs to differentiate their offers. Singapore Airlines once even added a piano bar. Unfortunately, most service innovations are easily copied. Still, the service company that regularly finds desired service innovations will usually gain a succession of temporary advantages and may, by earning an innovative reputation, keep customers who want to go with the best.

Service companies can also work on differentiating their *images* through symbols and branding. The Harris Bank of Chicago adopted the lion as its symbol on its stationery, in its advertising, and even as stuffed animals offered to new depositors. The well-known "Harris Lion" confers an image of strength upon the bank. Humana, the nation's second-largest investor-owned system of hospitals and services, has developed a successful branding strategy. It has standardized the names of all of its 90 hospitals with the "Humana" prefix and then built tremendous awareness and a reputation for quality around that name.

## Managing Service Quality

One of the major ways to differentiate a service firm is for the firm to deliver consistently higher quality than its competitors. Many companies are finding that outstanding service quality can give them a potent competitive advantage leading to superior sales and profit performance. Some firms have become almost legendary for their high-quality service (see Marketing Highlight 19–1). The key is to meet or exceed customers' service-quality *expectations.* These expectations are based on past experiences, word of mouth, and service firm advertising. Customers often compare the *perceived service* of a given firm with their *expected service:* If the perceived service meets or exceeds expected service, customers are apt to use the provider again.

The service provider thus needs to identify the expectations of target customers concerning service quality. Unfortunately, service quality is harder to define and judge than product quality. It is harder to get agreement on the quality of a haircut than on the quality of a hair dryer. Moreover, although greater service quality means greater customer satisfaction, it also means higher costs. Thus, service firms cannot always meet consumers' service-quality desires—they face trade-offs between customer satisfaction and company profitability. Whatever the level of service provided, it is important that the service provider clearly define and communicate that level so that its employees know what they must deliver and customers know what they will get.

Studies of well-managed service companies show that they share a number

## COMPETITIVE ADVANTAGE THROUGH CUSTOMER SERVICE

Some companies go to extremes to coddle their customers with service. Consider the following examples:

□ An L. L. Bean customer says he lost all his fishing equipment—and nearly his life—when a raft he bought from the company leaked and forced him to swim to shore. He recovered the raft and sent it to the company along with a letter asking for a new raft and $700 to cover the fishing equipment he says he lost. He gets both.

□ A woman visits a Nordstrom department store to buy a gift for a friend. She's in a hurry and leaves the store immediately after making her purchase. The Nordstrom salesclerk gift-wraps the item at no charge and later drops it off at the customer's home.

□ At 11:00 p.m., a driver making a crucial delivery for Sigma Midwest is having electrical problems with his Ryder rental truck. He calls the company and within an hour the truck is fixed, yet the Ryder employee stays with the driver for the next five hours to help him make deliveries and remain on schedule.

□ An American Express cardholder fails to pay over $5,000 of his September bill. He explains that during the summer he'd purchased expensive rugs in Turkey. When he got home, appraisals showed that the rugs were worth half of what he'd paid. Rather than asking suspicious questions or demanding payment, the American Express representative notes the dispute, asks for a letter summarizing the appraisers' estimates, and offers to help solve the problem. Until the conflict is resolved, American Express doesn't ask for payment.

From a dollars-and-cents point of view, these examples sound like a crazy way to do business. How can you make money by giving away your products, providing free extra services, or letting customers get away without paying their bills on time? Yet studies show that good service, though costly, goes hand-in-hand with good financial performance. For example, despite its costly emphasis on service, or more likely *because* of it, American Express earns the *highest* profit margins of any credit card company. Similarly,

of common virtues regarding service quality. First, they have a history of *top management commitment to quality*. Management at companies such as Marriott, Disney, Delta, and McDonald's looks not only at financial performance but also at service performance. The best service providers *set high service-quality standards*. Swissair, for example, aims to have 96 percent or more of its passengers rate its service as good or superior; otherwise, it takes action. Top service firms also *watch service performance closely*—both their own and that of competitors. They use such methods as comparison shopping, customer surveys, and suggestion and complaint forms. General Electric sends out 700,000 response cards each year to households who rate their servicepeople's performance. Citibank takes regular measures of "ART"—accuracy, responsiveness, and timeliness—and sends out employees who act as customers to check on service quality. Finally, well-managed service companies *satisfy employees as well as customers*. They believe that good employee relations will result in good customer relations. Management creates an environment of employee support, gives rewards for good service performance, and monitors employee job satisfaction.[12]

### Managing Productivity

With their costs rising rapidly, service firms are under great pressure to increase productivity. There are several ways to improve service productivity. First, service providers can better train current employees or hire new ones who will work harder or more skillfully for the same pay. Or service providers can increase the quantity of their service by giving up some quality. Doctors working for health maintenance organizations (HMOs) have moved toward handling more patients and giving less time to each. Providers can "industria-

Nordstrom enjoys the highest sales per square foot of any department store, about *double* the industry average. And L. L. Bean has grown at almost *twice* the industry growth rate over the last five years. These and other companies know that good service is good for business. In today's highly competitive marketplace, companies that take the best care of their customers have a strong competitive advantage.

Good customer service involves more than simply opening a complaint department, smiling a lot, and being nice to customers. It requires hard-headed analysis and an intense commitment to helping customers. Outstanding service companies set high service standards and often make seemingly outlandish efforts to achieve them. They take great care to hire the right service people, train them well, and reward them for going out of their way to serve customers.

At these companies, exceptional service is more than a set of policies or actions—it's a company-wide attitude, an important part of the overall company culture. Concern for the consumer becomes a matter of pride for everyone in the company. American Express loves to tell stories about how its people have rescued customers from disasters ranging from civil wars to earthquakes, no matter what the cost. The company gives cash rewards of up to $1,000 to "Great Performers" such as Barbara Weber, who last year moved mountains of State Department and Treasury Department red tape to refund $980 in stolen traveler's checks to a customer stranded in Cuba. Similarly, Nordstrom thrives on stories about its service heroics—such as employees dropping off orders at customers' homes or warming up cars while customers spend a little more time shopping. There's even a story about a

customer who got a refund on a tire—Nordstrom doesn't carry tires, but it prides itself on a no-questions-asked return policy!

There's no simple formula for offering good service, but neither is it a mystery. According to the president of L. L. Bean, "A lot of people have fancy things to say about customer service . . . but it's just a day-in, day-out, on-going, never-ending, unremitting, persevering, compassionate type of activity." For the companies that do it well, it's also very rewarding.

*Sources:* Bill Kelley, "Five Companies That Do It Right—and Make It Pay," *Sales & Marketing Management,* April 1988, pp. 57–64; Bro Uttal, "Companies That Serve You Best," *Fortune,* December 7, 1987, pp. 98–116; and Joan O'C. Hamilton, "Why Rivals Are Quaking as Nordstrom Heads East," *Business Week,* June 15, 1987, pp. 89–90.

## Traditionally, in the world of business, those who perform best charge most. UPS proudly flies in the face of tradition.

When it comes to package delivery companies, UPS is a leader in the industry.

But unlike the competition, our high level of service is not reflected in our prices.

Because at UPS we work hard at being efficient. In fact, it's an obsession with us.

After all, it enables us to deliver packages for less. And, in turn, charge less.

We deliver Next Day Air to any address coast to coast for up to half what the competition charges.

And if you can afford to wait one more day, you can use UPS 2nd Day Air and save even more.

Our service and low prices extend to Japan and most of Western Europe.

So if you need a package delivery company you can depend on, call UPS.

Especially if being efficient is as much an obsession with you as it is with us.

We run the tightest ship in the shipping business.

**UPS**

*Service marketing strategies: UPS claims that greater efficiency and productivity allow it to offer high-quality service at a low price.*

**organization marketing** Activities undertaken to create, maintain, or change attitudes and behavior of target audiences toward an organization.

**organization image** The way an individual or a group sees an organization.

lize" services by adding equipment and standardizing production, as in McDonald's assembly-line approach to fast-food retailing. Commercial dishwashing, jumbo jets, multiple-unit movie theatres—all represent technological expansions of service.

Service providers can also increase productivity by designing more effective services. How-to-quit-smoking clinics and recommendations for jogging may reduce the need for expensive medical services later on. Hiring paralegal workers reduces the need for expensive legal professionals. Providers can also give customers incentives to substitute company labor with their own. For example, business firms that sort their own mail before delivering it to the post office pay lower postal rates.

However, companies must avoid pushing productivity so hard that it reduces perceived quality. Some productivity steps can help to standardize quality, increasing customer satisfaction. But other productivity steps lead to too much standardization and rob consumers of customized service. In some cases, the service provider accepts reduced productivity to create more differentiation.

# ORGANIZATION MARKETING

Organizations often carry out activities to "sell" the organization itself. **Organization marketing** consists of activities undertaken to create, maintain, or change the attitudes and behavior of target audiences toward an organization. Both profit and nonprofit organizations practice organization marketing. Business firms sponsor public relations or corporate advertising campaigns to polish their images. Nonprofit organizations such as churches, colleges, charities, museums, and performing arts groups market their organizations in order to raise funds and attract members or patrons. Organization marketing calls for assessing the organization's current image and developing a marketing plan to improve it.

## Image Assessment

The first step in image assessment is to research the organization's current image among key publics. The way an individual or a group sees an organization is called its **organization image.** Different people can have different images of the same organization. The organization might be pleased with its public image or might find that it has serious image problems.

For example, suppose a bank does some marketing research to measure its image in the community. Suppose it finds its image to be that shown by the red line in Figure 19–1. Thus, current and potential customers view the bank as

FIGURE 19–1  Image Assessment

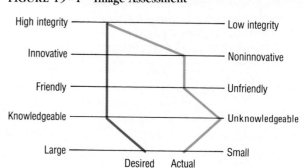

somewhat small, noninnovative, unfriendly, and unknowledgeable. The bank will want to change this image.

## Image Planning and Control

Next, the organization should decide what image it would like to have and can achieve. For example, our bank might decide that it would like the image shown by the blue line in Figure 19–1. It would like to be seen as a provider of more friendly and personal service and as being more innovative, knowledgeable, and larger.

The firm now develops a marketing plan to shift its actual image toward the desired one. Suppose the bank first wants to improve its image as giving friendly and personal service. The key step, of course, is to *actually provide* friendlier and more personal service. A bank can hire and train better tellers and others who deal with customers. It can change its décor to make the bank seem warmer. Once the bank is certain that it has improved performance on important image measures, it can then design a marketing program to communicate that new image to customers. Using public relations, the bank can sponsor community activities, send its executives to speak to local business and civic groups, offer public seminars on household finances, and issue press releases on newsworthy bank activities. In its advertising, the bank can position itself as "your friendly, personal neighborhood bank."

*Corporate image advertising* is a major tool that companies use to market themselves to various publics. Companies spend more than $785 million each year on image advertising.[13] They can use corporate advertising to build or maintain a favorable image over many years. Or they can use it to counter events

*Corporate image advertising: these ads attempt to reposition Hush Puppies as a modern, stylish brand.*

**person marketing** Activities undertaken to create, maintain, or change attitudes or behavior toward particular persons.

that might hurt an image. For example, Chrysler hired an image-consultant firm to tell it how to keep its positive image after Lee Iacocca moves on. Waste Management, the giant garbage disposal company, got into trouble a few years ago for dumping toxic wastes. So it countered with an advertising campaign emphasizing the company's work with various government agencies to help save a threatened species of butterfly.

Such organization marketing efforts can work only if the actual organization lives up to a projected image. No amount of advertising and public relations can fool the public for very long if the reality fails to match the image. Thus, Waste Management's image campaign worked only because the company had in fact worked to clean up toxic waste sites. Otherwise, even saving butterflies would not have helped its reputation.[14]

An organization must resurvey its publics occasionally to see whether its activities are improving its image. Images cannot be changed overnight: Campaign funds are usually limited and public images tend to stick. If a firm is making no progress, either its marketing offer or its organization marketing program will have to be changed.

# PERSON MARKETING

People are also marketed. **Person marketing** consists of activities undertaken to create, maintain, or change attitudes or behavior toward particular people. All kinds of people and organizations practice person marketing. Politicians market themselves to get votes and program support. Entertainers and sports figures use marketing to promote their careers and improve their incomes. Professionals such as doctors, lawyers, accountants, and architects market themselves in order to build reputations and increase business. Business leaders use person marketing as a strategic tool to develop their companies' fortunes as well as their own. Businesses, charities, sports teams, fine arts groups, religious groups, and other organizations also use person marketing. Creating, flaunting, or associating with well-known personalities often helps organizations to better achieve their goals.

Here are some examples of successful person marketing:

□ Lee Iacocca, the heavily marketed chairman of Chrysler Corporation, is highly visible. His direct, dramatic, and blunt style commands attention and respect. In Chrysler ads, Iacocca levels with consumers, conveying confidence and trust. In a typical press conference, he might attack the timid U.S. trade policy toward Japan, praise Chrysler cars and workers, speak out on the federal deficit, advise broadly on how to tackle tomorrow's business problems, and again deny that he will run for president. Iacocca's visibility helps Chrysler sell cars and gain the support of important consumer, financial, employee, government, media, and other publics. Iacocca's visibility is no accident; his transformation into a celebrity was as deliberate as the manufacture of his cars. Creating the image of the confident chairman in a sixty-second TV ad requires days of filming, weeks of editing, and months of planning and research. Iacocca's image as an old-style street fighter—tough, decisive, in control—is the result of extensive planning and practice by Iacocca and careful image crafting by a team of policy planners, media advisers, ghostwriters, and ad agencies.[15]

□ Michael Jordan, star of the Chicago Bulls, possesses remarkable basketball

*Person marketing: associating with well-known personalities can help organizations to better achieve their goals.*

skills—great court sense; quick, fluid moves; the ability to soar above the rim for dramatic dunks. And he has an appealing, unassuming personality to go along with his dazzling talents. All of this makes Jordan very marketable. After graduating from college, Jordan signed on with ProServ Inc., a well-known sports management agency. The agency quickly negotiated a lucrative five-year contract with the Bulls, paying Jordan some $4 million. But that was just the beginning. ProServ decided to market Jordan as the new Dr. J of basketball—a supertalented good guy and solid citizen. Paying careful attention to placement and staging, the agency booked Jordan into the talk-show circuit, accepted only the best products to endorse, insisted on only high-quality commercials, arranged appearances for charitable causes, and even had him appear as a fashion model. Jordan's market appeal soared, and so did his income. Person marketing has paid off handsomely for Jordan, for his team, and for the products he represents. Jordan recently signed a new eight-year, $25 million contract with the Bulls, and current endorsements for Nike, Wilson, Coca-Cola, Johnson Products, McDonald's, and other companies earn Jordan an additional $4 million per year. In its first full year with Jordan as its representative, Nike sold $110 million worth of "Air Jordan" basketball shoes and apparel. And last year the Bulls sold out all but one of their home games—more sellouts than they've totaled in their 22-year history.[16]

□ Ronald Reagan's presidential administration was unequaled in its use of marketing to sell the president and his policies to the American people.

Every move made by Reagan during his eight years as president was carefully managed to support the administration's positioning and marketing strategy. An army of specialists—marketing researchers, advertising experts, political advisers, speech writers, media planners, press secretaries, even make-up artists—worked tirelessly to define political market segments, identify key issues, and strongly position Reagan and his programs. The administration used extensive marketing research. It regularly polled voter segments to find out what was "hot" and what was not. Using focus groups, it pretested important speeches and platforms. "Theming it" was an important element of marketing strategy—the administration packaged key benefits into a few highly focused themes, then repeated these basic themes over and over and over. This focus on basic marketable themes, coupled with careful planning and delivery of messages and media exposures, helped control what was reported by the press. Reagan even made careful use of "regional marketing," tailoring timely speeches to the special needs of regional or local audiences.[17]

The objective of person marketing is to create a "celebrity"—a well-known person whose name generates attention, interest, and action. Celebrities differ in the *scope* of their visibility. Some are very well known, but only in limited geographic areas (a town mayor, a local businessperson, an area doctor) or specific segments (the president of the American Dental Association, a company vice-president, a jazz musician with a small group of fans). Still others have broad national or international visibility (major entertainers, sports superstars, world political and religious leaders).

Celebrities also differ in their *durability*. Figure 19–2A shows a standard

FIGURE 19–2   Celebrity Life Cycles

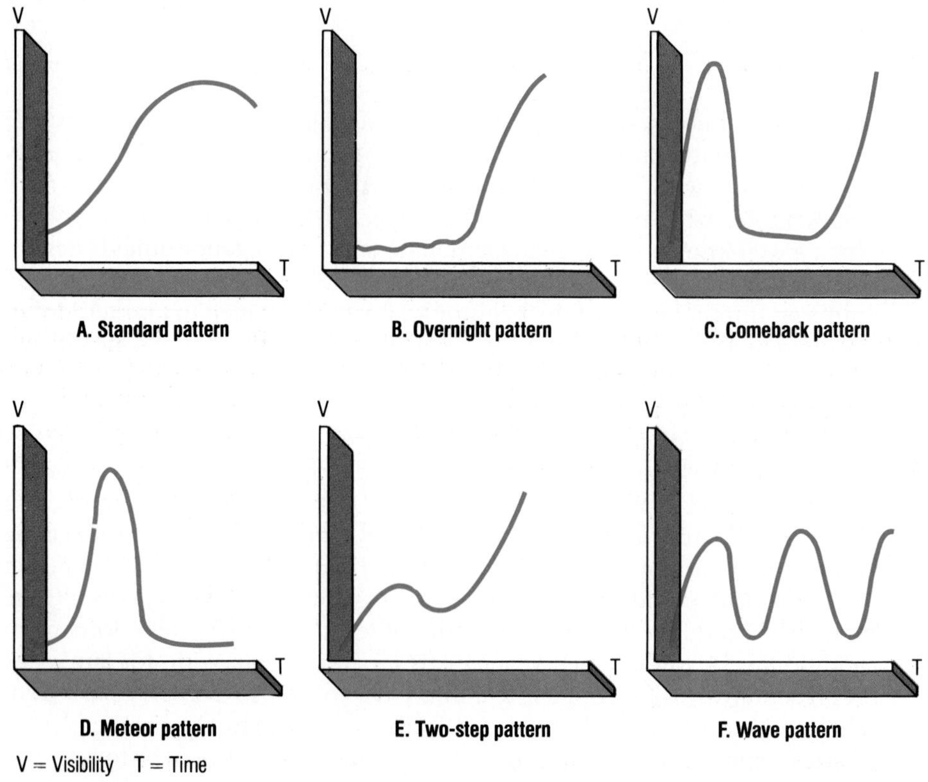

A. Standard pattern

B. Overnight pattern

C. Comeback pattern

D. Meteor pattern

E. Two-step pattern

F. Wave pattern

V = Visibility   T = Time

*Source:* Adapted from Irving Rein, Philip Kotler, and Martin Stoller. *High Visibility* (New York: Dodd, Mead & Company, 1987), pp. 109-10. Used with permission.

celebrity life-cycle pattern. The individual's visibility begins at a low level, gradually builds to a peak as the person matures and becomes well known, then declines as the celebrity fades from the limelight. But as the rest of Figure 19–2 shows, celebrity life-cycle patterns can vary greatly. For example, in the *overnight* pattern (19–2B), a person acquires quick and lasting visibility because of some major deed or event (Charles Lindbergh, Neil Armstrong). In the *comeback* pattern (Figure 19–2C), a celebrity achieves high visibility, loses it, then gets it back again (Tina Turner, George Burns). In the *meteor pattern* (19–2D), someone gains fame quickly and then loses it suddenly. For example, William "Refrigerator" Perry, the overweight Chicago defensive lineman, became an instant "hot property" after he was used as a running back on Monday Night Football, made millions of dollars from product endorsements, and then sank back into obscurity—all within about a year.

The person-marketing process is similar to the one used by product and service marketers. Person marketers begin with careful market research and analysis to discover consumer needs and market segments. Next comes product development—assessing the person's current qualities and image and transforming the person so as to better match market needs and expectations. Finally, the marketer develops programs to value, promote, and deliver the celebrity. Some people naturally possess the skills, appearances, and behaviors that target segments value. But for most, celebrity status in any field must be actively developed through sound person marketing.

**place marketing** Activities undertaken to create, maintain, or change attitudes or behavior toward particular places.

# PLACE MARKETING

**Place marketing** involves activities undertaken to create, maintain, or change attitudes or behavior toward particular places. Examples include business site marketing and vacation marketing.

## Business Site Marketing

*Business site marketing* involves developing, selling, or renting business sites for such uses as factories, stores, offices, warehouses, and conventions. Large developers research companies' land needs and respond with real estate solutions, such as industrial parks, shopping centers, and new office buildings. Most states operate industrial development offices that try to sell companies on the advantages of locating new plants in their states (see Marketing Highlight 19–2). They spend large sums on advertising and offer to fly prospects to the site at no cost. Some troubled cities, such as New York, Detroit, and Atlanta, have appointed task forces to improve their images and draw new businesses to their areas. They may build large centers to house important conventions and business meetings. Even nations, such as Canada, Ireland, Greece, Mexico, and Turkey, have marketed themselves as good locations for business investment.

## Vacation Marketing

*Vacation marketing* involves attracting vacationers to spas, resorts, cities, states, and even entire countries. The effort is carried on by travel agents, airlines, motor clubs, oil companies, hotels, motels, and governmental agencies.

## "THE GOODLIEST LAND": BUSINESS SITE MARKETING IN NORTH CAROLINA

In 1584, when two English explorers returned to their homeland with news of "The Goodliest Land Under the Cope of Heaven," they were describing what is now North Carolina. In recent years, numerous American and foreign companies have come to share this opinion of the Tar Heel state. In three successive *Business Week* surveys, North Carolina was named as first choice of the nation's top business executives for new-plant location. The state does offer a number of economic and cultural advantages, but much credit for the state's popularity goes to the North Carolina Department of Commerce's Business/Industry Development Division. The division employs a high-quality marketing program—including advertising, publicity, and personal selling—to convince targeted firms and industries to come to North Carolina.

The division's 24 industrial development representatives coordinate efforts with development professionals in more than 300 individual North Carolina communities. And the division provides extensive information to firms considering locating in the state—in-depth profiles of more than 325 communities, a computerized inventory of available industrial sites and buildings, estimates of state and local taxes for specific sites, analyses of labor costs and fringe benefits, details of convenient transportation to sites, and estimates of construction costs.

But the Business/Industry Development Division does more than simply provide information—it aggressively seeks out firms and persuades them to locate in North Carolina. It invites groups of business executives to tour the state and hear presentations, and it sets up booths at industry trade fairs. Its representatives (sometimes including the governor) travel to other states to carry the North Carolina story to executives in attractive businesses and industries. The division also communicates and persuades through informational and promotional brochures delivered by mail and through mass-media advertising. Ads and brochures such as that shown here tout North Carolina's benefits: a large and productive labor force, numerous educational and technical training institutions, low taxes, a good transportation network, low energy and construction costs, a good living environment, and plentiful government support and assistance.

The division's total budget runs only about $5 million a year, but the returns are great. From 1978 through 1989, new and expanding business announced investments of more than $25 billion in North Carolina, creating more than 341,000 new jobs.

*Source:* Based on information supplied by the North Carolina Department of Commerce, Business/Industry Development Division.

*North Carolina advertises to attract new business to the state.*

Today, almost every city, state, and country markets its tourist attractions. Miami Beach is considering legalizing gambling in order to attract more tourists. Texas advertises "Have a Big Time in Texas," and Michigan touts "YES M!CH!GAN." Philadelphia invites you to "Get to Know Us!" and Palm Beach, Florida, advertises "The Best of Everything" at low off-season prices. Some places, however, try to *demarket* themselves because they feel that the harm from tourism exceeds revenues. Thus, Oregon has actually publicized its own bad weather; Yosemite National Park may ban snowmobiling, conventions, and private cars; Finland discourages tourists from vacationing in certain areas.

**social marketing** The design, implementation, and control of programs seeking to increase the acceptability of a social idea, cause, or practice among a target group.

# IDEA MARKETING

Ideas can also be marketed. In one sense, all marketing is the marketing of an idea, whether it be the general idea of brushing your teeth or the specific idea that Crest is the most effective decay preventer. Here, however, we will discuss only the marketing of *social ideas*, such as public health campaigns to reduce smoking, alcoholism, drug abuse, and overeating; environmental campaigns to promote wilderness protection, clean air, and conservation; and other campaigns such as family planning, human rights, and racial equality. This area has been called *social marketing.*[18] **Social marketing** is the design, implementation, and control of programs seeking to increase the acceptability of a social idea, cause, or practice among a target group.

Social marketers can pursue different objectives. They might want to produce understanding (knowing the nutritional value of different foods) or trigger a one-time response (joining in a mass-immunization campaign). They might want to change behavior (discouraging drunk driving) or change a basic belief (convincing employers that handicapped people can make strong contributions in the work force).

The Advertising Council of America has carried out dozens of social advertising campaigns, including "Smokey the Bear," "Keep America Beautiful," "Join the Peace Corps," "Buy Bonds," and "Go to College." But social marketing is much broader than just advertising. Many public marketing campaigns fail because they assign advertising the primary role and fail to develop and use all the available marketing mix tools.

In designing effective social-change strategies, social marketers go through a normal marketing-planning process. First, they define the social-change objective—for example, "to reduce the percentage of teen-agers who drink and drive from 15 percent to 5 percent within 5 years." Next, they analyze the attitudes, beliefs, values, and behavior of teen-agers and the forces that encourage teen-age drinking. They consider communication and distribution approaches that might prevent teen-agers from driving while drinking, develop a marketing plan, and build a marketing organization to carry out the plan (see Marketing Highlight 19–3). Finally, they evaluate and, if necessary, adjust the program to make it more effective.

Social marketing is fairly new, and its effectiveness relative to other social-change strategies is hard to evaluate. It is hard to produce social change with any strategy, let alone one that relies on voluntary response. Social marketing has been applied mainly to family planning, environmental protection, energy conservation, improved health and nutrition, driver safety, and public transportation—and there have been some encouraging successes. But more applications are needed before we can fully assess social marketing's potential for producing social change.

## SOCIAL MARKETING OF SAFE AND SOBER DRIVING

The Reader's Digest Foundation, in partnership with the National Association of Secondary School Principals (NASSP), recently launched a two-year, $1 million social marketing campaign to deliver a sober message to teen-agers all across America. As part of the "Don't Drink and Drive Challenge," *Reader's Digest* magazine invited teams from leading advertising agencies to create posters for the campaign, with the winners receiving a Paris trip for two. In the first year of the campaign, more than 1,000 teams from top agencies competed. Shown here are some of the outstanding posters created for the program.

The foundation then distributed copies of the winning posters to 20,000 high schools. Students were challenged to compete for college scholarships by devising programs to promote sober driving. Over 700 schools submitted entries ranging from rock videos to puppet shows to anti-drunk-driving awareness weeks. Scholarships totaling $500,000 went to 115 winning schools. The program was held a second year, with advertising agencies and schools again taking part and another $500,000 in scholarships awarded. Reader's Digest Foundation continues to offer copies of its posters and summaries of winning student programs as a resource to educators, the media, and community organizations.

*Social marketing: marketing safe and sober driving.*

Marketing has been broadened in recent years to cover "marketable" entities other than products—namely, services, organizations, persons, places, and ideas.

As the United States moves increasingly toward a *service economy*, marketers need to know more about marketing services. *Services* are activities or benefits that one party can offer to another that are essentially intangible and do not result in the ownership of anything. Services are *intangible, inseparable, variable,* and *perishable*. Each characteristic poses problems and requires strategies. Marketers have to find ways to make services more tangible, to increase the productivity of providers who are inseparable from their products, to standardize quality in the face of variability, and to improve demand movements and supply capacities in the face of service perishability.

Service industries have typically lagged behind manufacturing firms in adopting and using marketing concepts, but this situation is now changing. Marketing strategy for services calls not only for external marketing but also for *internal marketing* to motivate employees and *interactive marketing* to create service-delivery skills among service providers. To succeed, service marketers must create *competitive differentiation,* offer high service quality, and find ways to increase *service productivity*.

Organizations can also be marketed. *Organization market-ing* is undertaken to create, maintain, or change the attitudes or behavior of target audiences toward an organization. It calls for assessing the organization's current image and developing a marketing plan for bringing about an improved image.

*Person marketing* consists of activities undertaken to create, maintain, or change attitudes or behavior toward particular persons.

*Place marketing* involves activities to create, maintain, or change attitudes or behavior toward particular places. Examples include business site marketing and vacation marketing.

*Idea marketing* involves efforts to market ideas. In the case of social ideas, it is called *social marketing* and consists of the design, implementation, and control of programs seeking to increase the acceptability of a social idea, cause, or practice among a target group. Social marketing goes further than public advertising—it coordinates advertising with the other elements of the marketing mix. The social marketer defines the social-change objective, analyzes consumer attitudes and competitive forces, develops and tests alternative concepts, develops appropriate channels for the idea's communication and distribution, and checks the final results. Social marketing has been applied to family-planning, environmental-protection, antismoking campaigns, and to other public issues.

1. A "hot" concept in fast-food marketing is home delivery of everything from pizza to hamburgers to fried chicken. Why is this demand growing? How can marketers gain competitive advantages by satisfying the growing demand for increased services?

2. Many banks have begun hiring marketing executives with experience in consumer packaged-goods marketing. What benefits and problems might they experience as a result of this practice?

3. How can a theater deal with the intangibility, inseparability, variability, and perishability of its service? Give examples.

4. Retail stores sell tangible products rather than services. Is interactive marketing important to retailers? How can retailers use internal marketing to improve the quality of buyer-seller interactions?

5. Why do organizations want to "sell" themselves and not just their products? List several reasons for organization marketing and relate them to familiar promotional campaigns.

6. Many people feel that too much time and money are spent marketing political candidates. They also complain that modern political campaigns overemphasize image at the expense of issues. What is your opinion of political candidate marketing? Would some other approach to campaigning help citizen-consumers make better voting decisions?

7. Reports of questionable, high-pressure tactics in the sale of vacation homes are common. For example, the "food processor" that one marketer used to attract prospects turned out to be a fork! Why do unethical practices appear to be so frequent in place marketing?

8. Social marketing is one approach to social change. What other methods are available? Compared with these other approaches, what advantages and disadvantages might social marketing have, for example, in attempting to reduce the amount of litter on the highways?

1. Portions adapted from Kevin T. Higgins, "Hospital Puttin' on the Ritz to Target High-End Market," *Marketing News,"* January 17, 1986, p. 14. Also see Robert B. Kimmel, "Should Hospitals Advertise?" *Advertising Age,* June 13, 1988, p. 20.

2. See Norman Jonas, "The Hollow Corporation,"

*Business Week,* March 3, 1986, pp. 57–59; and Edward Prewitt and Sarah E. Morgenthau, "Flush Times for the Money Men," *Fortune,* June 8, 1987, pp. 192-94.

3. "Presto! The Convenience Industry: Making Life a Little Simpler," *Business Week,* April 27, 1987, p. 86.

4. See Leonard L. Berry, "Services Marketing Is Different," *Business,* May-June 1980, pp. 24–30; and Karl Albrecht and Ron Zemke, *Service America! Doing Business in the New Economy* (Homewood, IL: Dow-Jones-Irwin, 1985).

5. See Theodore Levitt, "Marketing Intangible Products and Product Intangibles," *Harvard Business Review,* May-June 1981, pp. 94–102.

6. For more discussion, see James L. Heskett, "Lessons in the Service Sector," *Harvard Business Review,* March-April 1987, pp. 122–24.

7. See Ray Lewis, "Whose Job Is Service Marketing?" *Advertising Age,* August 3, 1987, pp. 14, 20.

8. See W. Earl Sasser, "Match Supply and Demand in Service Industries," *Harvard Business Review,* November-December 1976, pp. 133–40.

9. See A. Parasuraman, Leonard L. Berry, and Valarie A. Zeithaml, "Service Firms Need More Marketing," *Business Horizons,* November-December 1983, pp. 28–31.

10. See Christian Gronroos, "A Service Quality Model and Its Marketing Implications," *European Journal of Marketing,* Vol. 18, No. 4 (1984), 36–44.

11. See Leonard L. Berry, "Big Ideas in Services Market-ing," *Journal of Consumer Marketing,* Spring 1986, pp. 47–51.

12. For more on service quality, see A. Parasuraman, Valarie A. Zeithaml, and Leonard L. Berry, "A Conceptual Model of Service Quality and Its Implications for Future Research," *Journal of Marketing,* Fall 1985, pp. 41–50; Valarie A. Zeithaml, Leonard L. Berry, and A. Parasuraman, "Communication and Control Processes in the Delivery of Service Quality," *Journal of Marketing,* April 1988, pp. 35–48; and Patricia Sellers, "Getting Customers to Love You," *Fortune,* March 13, 1989, pp. 38–49.

13. Lori Kessler, "Corporate Image Advertising," *Advertising Age,* October 15, 1987, p. S1.

14. See Anne B. Fisher, "Spiffing Up the Corporate Image," *Fortune,* July 21, 1986, p. 69.

15. See Irving Rein, Philip Kotler, and Martin Stoller, *High Visibility* (New York: Dodd, Mead, 1987), pp. 1–2.

16. See Michael Oneal, "'Air' Jordan Has the Bulls Walking on a Cloud," *Business Week,* December 12, 1988, p. 124.

17. See Steven Colford, "Hail to the Image—Reagan Legacy: Marketing Tactics Change Politics," *Advertising Age,* June 27, 1988, pp. 3, 32; and Jack J. Honomichl, "How Reagan Took America's Pulse," *Advertising Age,* January 23, 1989, pp. 1, 25.

18. See Philip Kotler and Gerald Zaltman, "Social Marketing: An Approach to Planned Social Change," *Journal of Marketing,* July 1971, pp. 3-12.

# Case 19

## LIFELINE MAGAZINE: MARKET TARGETING ON THE NONPROFIT FRONT

Sometimes, target groups do not want to be reached. In that case, the only option is to communicate with those who can influence the target group. That's what the National Foundation for Alcoholism Communications, located in Seattle, plans to do with its new magazine, *Alcoholism-Codependency-Addiction Lifeline*.

The publication hit Waldenbooks' shelves in March of 1988. It is being billed as "America's answer book about alcoholism and addiction," focusing on prevention, treatment, and recovery. "People and families in trouble with drugs and alcohol have many personal and pressing questions that are not being answered by public service announcements and government-sponsored campaigns," said Jerauld D. Miller, publisher and executive director of the foundation.

"Hundreds of thousands of Americans need help and answers and resources, not just political platitudes," he added. "They need a publication with names and numbers and case histories from people who have successfully kicked their habits, and we intend to make this information available to every American who needs to know."

The magazine's difficulties rest in trying to reach some of these people—namely, the addicts or alcoholics themselves. Most people who have these dependencies either do not realize they have a problem or refuse to admit it exists, according to Bill Wipple, director of marketing and sales. "Our first marketing goal is to reach the addict," Wipple said. "But you can't reach the addict until he's reached the point of remorse."

This fact makes it almost impossible to reach most alcoholics or addicts when they need help the most. The foundation has thus decided to target *codependents* (those who live with addicts and alcoholics) and those recovering from the diseases. The principle is similar to the one adopted by Al-Anon in its relationship to Alcoholics Anonymous (AA), Wipple said. Once codependents know the facts about the diseases and how to deal with the people suffering from them, they can set the dependents on the road to recovery.

But the magazine has an edge on Al-Anon, he said. Many codependents will not attend the group's meetings for fear that the addict will find out where they are going. A magazine is something they can use in the privacy of offices or cars or when the dependent is not around. Besides providing education for codependents, it is hoped that addicts will find the magazines and get the clue that at least somebody thinks all is not well, Wipple said.

However, codependents are not *Lifetime*'s only direct target audience. The publication is also designed with recovering alcoholics and addicts in mind, partly because these people can spot others suffering from the diseases. For those going through the recovery process, the magazine features "articles of hope" about people who have pulled themselves out of the drinking or drug-use cycle.

Wipple believes the magazine will sell, largely because of the way it looks. It's kind of like *People*, with the first issue displaying a picture of Elizabeth Taylor on the cover and her tales of addiction inside. It is hoped that once people are attracted to the celebrity cover, they will take note of the other articles within, including "10 Tips for Tempted Teens" and "Warning Signs of Relapse."

In addition to trying to sell the magazine to consumers, the foundation wants to sell it to ad agencies. To do so, the foundation is emphasizing that recovering addicts and alcoholics are a strong target market, especially for health-oriented products. "These people have a new lease on life and usually become interested in other, more healthy habits after they've given up their addictions," Wipple explained.

More than 10 million books on alcoholism and other addictions were sold last year. Millions of phone calls are logged each year by hotlines, treatment programs, and self-help organizations. According to one Gallup survey, one out of every four American families has a member with a drug or drinking problem. Moreover, a survey conducted in 1987 by GMA Research Corp. indicated that among a sample of 100 recovering alcoholics and other dependents, more than 80 percent would buy *Lifeline*.

### Questions

1. What are the target markets for *Lifeline* magazine? Are there other appropriate markets not mentioned in the case?

2. What are the objectives of the magazine? What are the objectives of the National Foundation for Alcoholism Communications?

3. If you were Bill Wipple, how would you approach advertising agencies and consumer-products companies to sell advertising space in *Lifeline?*

4. In what ways are *Lifeline*'s marketing challenges different from those faced by a profit-seeking firm in the private sector?

*Source:* Reprinted from Diane Schneidman, "New Magazine Targets A Segment That May Not Want to Be Reached," *Marketing News,* Vol. 21 Dec. 4, 1987 pp. 1, 24, published by the American Marketing Association.

# 20
# Marketing and Society

After reading this chapter, you should be able to

1. List and respond to the social criticisms of marketing
2. Define *consumerism* and *environmentalism* and explain how they affect marketing strategies
3. Describe the principles of socially responsible marketing
4. Explain the role of ethics in marketing

Generations of parents have trusted the health and well-being of their babies to Gerber baby foods. Gerber sells over 1.3 billion jars of baby food each year, holding almost 70 percent of the market. But in early 1986, the company's reputation was threatened when over 250 customers in 30 states complained about finding glass fragments in Gerber baby food.

The company believed that these complaints were unfounded. Gerber plants are clean and modern, with machinery using many filters that would prevent such problems. There were no confirmed injuries from Gerber products. Moreover, the Food and Drug Administration had examined more than 40,000 jars of Gerber baby food without finding a single major problem. Gerber suspected that the glass was planted by the people making the complaints and seeking publicity or damages. Yet the complaints received widespread media coverage, and many retailers pulled Gerber products from their shelves. The state of Maryland forbid the sales of some Gerber baby foods, and other states considered similar bans.

The considerable attention given to the complaints may have resulted from the "Tylenol scares," in which Tylenol capsules laced with cyanide had caused consumer deaths. At the time, product tampering was a major public issue and consumer concern.

Gerber wanted to act responsibly, but social responsibility issues are rarely clear-cut. Some analysts believed that, to ensure consumer safety, Gerber should quickly recall all its baby food products from store shelves until the problem was resolved. That was how the makers of such products as Tylenol, Contac, and Gatorade had reacted to tampering scares for their products. But Gerber executives did not think that a recall was best either for consumers or for the company. After a similar scare in 1984, the company had recalled some 700,000 jars of baby food and had advertised heavily to reassure consumers. The isolated incident turned out to be the result of normal breakage during shipment. The recall cost Gerber millions of dollars in expenses and lost profits; the advertising caused unnecessary alarm and inconvenience to consumers. The company concluded that it had overreacted in its desire to be socially responsible.

The second time, therefore, Gerber decided to do

nothing, at least in the short run. It refused to recall any products—in fact, it filed a $150 million suit against Maryland to stop the ban on sales of Gerber products. It suspended its advertising, monitored sales and consumer confidence, reassured nervous retailers, and waited to see what would happen. This wait-and-see strategy could have been risky. If the complaints turned out to be well-founded and Gerber's failure to act quickly were to cause death or injury, Gerber's reputation would be seriously damaged.

Finally, when research showed that consumer concern was spreading, Gerber aired a few television ads noting its concern about "rumors you may have heard" and assuring buyers that Gerber products "meet the highest standards." The company also mailed letters to about two million new mothers, assuring them of Gerber's quality. In the end, the scare passed with little damage to Gerber's reputation or sales and with little consumer alarm or inconvenience.

Should Gerber have immediately recalled its products to prevent even the remote chance of consumer injury? Perhaps. But in many matters of social responsibility, the best course of action is unclear.[1]

Responsible marketers find out what consumers want and respond with the right products, priced to give good value to buyers and return profit to the producer. The *marketing concept* is a philosophy of service and mutual gain. Its practice leads the economy by an invisible hand to satisfy the many and changing needs of millions of consumers.

Not all marketers, however, follow the marketing concept. In fact, some companies use questionable marketing practices. And some marketing actions that seem innocent in themselves strongly affect the larger society. Consider the sale of cigarettes. Ordinarily, companies should be free to sell cigarettes and smokers should be free to buy them. But this transaction affects the public interest. First, the smoker may be shortening his or her own life. Second, smoking places a burden on the smoker's family and on society at large. Third, other people around the smoker may have to inhale the smoke and may suffer discomfort and harm. This is not to say that cigarettes should be banned. Rather, it shows that *private* transactions may involve larger questions of *public* policy.

This chapter will look at the social effects of private marketing practices. We will look at several questions: What are the most frequent social criticisms of marketing? What steps have private citizens taken to curb marketing ills? What steps have legislators and government agencies taken to curb marketing ills? What steps have enlightened companies taken to carry out socially responsible marketing? Let's examine the effects of marketing on each of these.

# SOCIAL CRITICISMS OF MARKETING

Some social critics claim that marketing hurts individual consumers, society as a whole, and other business firms.

## *Marketing's Impact on Individual Consumers*

Consumers have many concerns about how well the American marketing system serves their interests. Surveys usually show that consumers hold slightly unfavorable attitudes toward marketing practices.[2] A consumer survey conducted for Atlantic Richfield Company found that consumers are worried about high prices, poor-quality and dangerous products, misleading advertising claims, and several other marketing-related problems (see Figure 20–1). Consumer advocates, government agencies, and other critics have accused marketing of harming consumers through high prices, deceptive practices, high-pressure

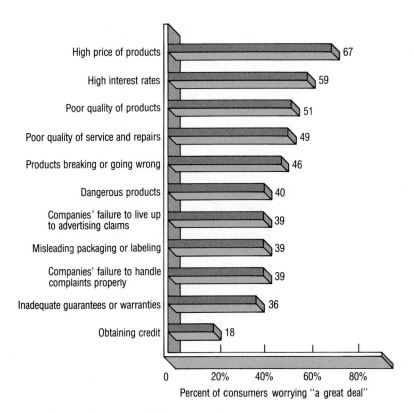

High price of products ▏67
High interest rates ▏59
Poor quality of products ▏51
Poor quality of service and repairs ▏49
Products breaking or going wrong ▏46
Dangerous products ▏40
Companies' failure to live up to advertising claims ▏39
Misleading packaging or labeling ▏39
Companies' failure to handle complaints properly ▏39
Inadequate guarantees or warranties ▏36
Obtaining credit ▏18

0    20%    40%    60%    80%

Percent of consumers worrying "a great deal"

FIGURE 20–1    Survey of Consumer Concerns
*Source:* Consumerism in the Eighties, poll of 1,252 adults October 15–26, 1982, conducted by Louis Harris and Associates for ARCO. See Myrlie Evers, "Consumerism in the Eighties," reprinted with permission from the August 1983 issue of *Public Relations Journal,* copyright 1983, pp. 24–26.

selling, shoddy or unsafe products, planned obsolescence, and poor service to disadvantaged consumers.

## High Prices

Many critics charge that the American marketing system causes prices to be higher than they would be under more "sensible" systems. They point to three factors—*high costs of distribution, high advertising and promotion costs,* and *excessive markups.*

*High Costs of Distribution* ▪ A longstanding charge is that greedy middlemen mark up prices beyond the value of their services. Critics charge either that there are too many middlemen or that middlemen are inefficient and poorly run, provide unnecessary or duplicate services, and practice poor management and planning. As a result, distribution costs too much and consumers pay for excessive costs in the form of higher prices.

How do retailers answer these charges? They argue as follows: First, middlemen do work that would otherwise have to be done by manufacturers or consumers. Second, the rising markup reflects improved services that consumers themselves want—more convenience, larger stores and assortment, longer store hours, return privileges, and others. Third, the costs of operating stores keep rising and force retailers to raise their prices. Fourth, retail competition is so intense that margins are actually quite low. For example, after taxes, supermarket chains are typically left with barely one percent profit on their sales.

***High Advertising and Promotion Costs*** ▪ Modern marketing is also accused of pushing up prices because of heavy advertising and sales promotion. For example, a dozen tablets of a heavily promoted brand of aspirin sell for the same price as 100 tablets of less-promoted brands. Differentiated products—cosmetics, detergents, toiletries—include promotion and packaging costs that can amount to 40 percent or more of the manufacturer's price to the retailer. Critics charge that much of the packaging and promotion adds only psychological rather than functional value to the product. Retailers use additional promotion—advertising, displays, and sweepstakes—that add several cents more to retail prices.

Marketers answer these charges in several ways. First, consumers *want* more than the merely functional qualities of products. They also want psychological benefits such as feeling wealthy, beautiful, or special. Consumers can usually buy functional versions of products at lower prices but are often willing to pay more for products that also provide desired psychological benefits. Second, branding gives buyers confidence. A brand name implies a certain quality, and consumers are willing to pay for well-known brands even if they cost a little more. Third, heavy advertising is needed to inform millions of potential buyers of the merits of a brand. If consumers want to know what is available on the market, they must expect manufacturers to spend large sums of money on advertising. Fourth, heavy advertising and promotion are necessary for a firm when its competitors are doing it. A business would lose "share of mind" if it did not match competitive spending. At the same time, companies are cost-conscious about promotion and try to spend their money wisely. Finally, heavy sales promotion is needed from time to time because goods are produced ahead of demand in a mass-production economy. Special incentives have to be offered in order to sell inventories.

***Excessive Markups*** ▪ Critics also charge that some companies mark up goods excessively. They point to the drug industry, in which a pill costing 5 cents to make may cost the consumer 40 cents. They point to the pricing tactics of funeral homes that prey on the emotions of bereaved relatives. They point to the high charges of television-repair and auto-repair people.

Marketers respond that most businesses try to deal fairly with consumers because they want repeat business. Most consumer abuses are unintentional. When shady marketers do take advantage of consumers, they should be reported to Better Business Bureaus and other consumer-protection groups. Marketers also respond that consumers often do not understand the reason for high markups. For example, pharmaceutical markups must cover the costs of purchasing, promoting, and distributing existing medicines plus the high research-and-development costs of finding new medicines.

### Deceptive Practices

Marketers are sometimes accused of deceptive practices that lead consumers to believe they will get more value than they actually do. Deceptive practices fall into three groups. *Deceptive pricing* includes such practices as falsely advertising "factory" or "wholesale" prices or advertising a large price reduction from a phony high list price. *Deceptive promotion* includes such practices as overstating the product's features or performance, luring the customer to the store for a bargain that is out of stock, and running rigged contests. *Deceptive packaging* includes exaggerating package contents through subtle design, not filling the package to the top, using misleading labeling, and describing size in misleading terms.

Deceptive practices have led to legislation and other consumer-protection actions. In 1938, the Wheeler-Lea Act gave the FTC power to regulate "unfair or deceptive acts or practices." The FTC has published several guidelines listing

*Some retailers use high markups, but the higher prices cover services that consumers want—assortment, convenience, personal service, and return privileges.*

deceptive practices. The toughest problem is defining what is "deceptive." Shell Oil advertised that Super Shell with platformate gave more mileage than the same gasoline without platformate. Now, this was true, but what Shell did not say is that almost *all* gasoline includes platformate. Its defense was that it had never claimed that platformate was found only in Shell gasoline. But even though the message was literally true, the FTC felt that the ad's *intent* was to deceive.

Marketers reply that most companies avoid deceptive practices because they harm their business in the long run. If consumers do not get what they expect, they will switch to more reliable products. In addition, consumers usually protect themselves from deception. Most consumers recognize a marketer's selling intent and are careful when they buy, sometimes to the point of not believing completely true product claims. Theodore Levitt claims not only that some advertising "puffery" is bound to occur, but that it may even be desirable:

> There is hardly a company that would not go down in ruin if it refused to provide fluff, because nobody will buy pure functionality. . . . Worse, it denies . . . man's honest needs and values. . . . Without distortion, embellishment, and elaboration, life would be drab, dull, anguished, and at its existential worst.. . . [3]

### High-Pressure Selling

Salespeople are sometimes accused of high-pressure selling that persuades people to buy goods they had no thought of buying. It is often said that encyclopedias, insurance, real estate, and jewelry are *sold*, not *bought*. Salespeople are trained to deliver smooth canned talks to entice purchase. They sell hard because sales contests promise big prizes to those who sell the most.

Marketers know that buyers can often be talked into buying unwanted or unneeded products. Laws require door-to-door salespeople to announce that they are in fact selling products. Buyers also have a "three-day cooling-off

**planned obsolescence** A strategy of causing products to become obsolete before they actually need replacement.

period" in which they can cancel a contract after rethinking it. In addition, consumers can complain to Better Business Bureaus or state consumer-protection agencies when they feel that undue selling pressure has been applied.

## Shoddy or Unsafe Products

Another criticism is that products lack the quality they should have. One complaint is that products are not made well. Automobiles bear the brunt of many such complaints—it seems that every new car has something wrong with it. Consumers grumble about rattles and pings, misalignments, dents, leaking, and creaking. Complaints have also been lodged against home- and auto-repair services, appliances, and clothing.

A second complaint is that some products deliver little benefit. Consumers got a shock on hearing that dry breakfast cereal may have little nutritional value. One nutrition expert told a Senate subcommittee: "In short, [cereals] fatten but do little to prevent malnutrition. . . . The average cereal . . . fails as a complete meal even with milk added."[4] The expert added that consumers could often get more nutrition by eating the cereal package than the contents.

A third complaint concerns product safety. For years, Consumers Union—the organization that publishes *Consumer Reports*—has reported various hazards in tested products: electrical dangers in appliances, carbon monoxide poisoning from room heaters, injury risks from lawn mowers, faulty automobile design.[5] The organization's testing and other activities have helped consumers to make better buying decisions and businesses to eliminate product flaws (see Marketing Highlight 20–1). Product quality has been a problem for several reasons, including manufacturer indifference, increased production complexity, poorly trained labor, and poor quality control.

On the other hand, most manufacturers *want* to produce quality goods. Consumers who are unhappy with one of a firm's products may avoid others and talk other consumers into doing the same. The way a company deals with product-quality and safety problems can damage or help its reputation. Companies selling poor-quality or unsafe products risk damaging conflicts with consumer groups. Moreover, unsafe products can result in product-liability suits and large awards for damages.[6]

## Planned Obsolescence

Critics have also charged that some producers follow a program of **planned obsolescence,** causing their products to become obsolete before they should actually need replacement. In many cases, producers have been accused of continually changing consumer concepts of acceptable styles in order to encourage more and earlier buying. An obvious example is constantly changing clothing fashions. Producers have also been accused of holding back attractive functional features, then introducing them later to make older models obsolete. Critics claim that this practice is found in the consumer electronics industry. Finally, producers have been accused of using materials and components that will break, wear, rot, or rust sooner than they should. For example, many drapery manufacturers are using a higher percentage of rayon in their drapes. They argue that rayon reduces the price of the drapes and has better holding power. Critics claim that using more rayon causes the drapes to fall apart sooner.

Marketers respond that consumers *like* style changes. They get tired of old goods and want a new look in fashion or a new design in cars. Moreover, no one has to buy a new look, and if too few people like it, it will simply fail. Companies frequently do withhold new features when they are not fully tested, when they add more cost to the product than consumers are willing to pay, and for other good reasons. But they do so at the risk of having a competitor introduce the

## WHEN *CONSUMER REPORTS* TALKS, BUYERS LISTEN—AND SO DO COMPANIES

Whether they're buying automobiles or life insurance, drain cleaner or refrigerators—or practically anything else—millions of shoppers won't plunk down their money until they consult *Consumer Reports.* For 51 years, the publication of Consumers Union has been a fiercely independent arbiter of quality goods and an ardent advocate of consumer rights. It has published CU's ratings of thousands of products and services without ever losing a libel suit. And today, its monthly circulation is at an all-time high of 3.8 million.

A 90-member technical team puts products through their paces at CU's headquarters in Mount Vernon, NY. When they can, they use the same tests industry uses. They check the laundering power of washing machines, for example, by washing presoiled fabric swatches and measuring their brightness with optical instruments. If no standard tests exist, *Consumer Reports* invents them. To rate facial tissues, CU's technical team built a "sneeze machine" that squirts a controlled spray of water and air through a tissue mounted on embroidery hoops.

CU describes its tests in detail when it rates products. But those explanations don't always placate the manufacturer whose product comes in last. If a company isn't happy with its rating, CU responds with an invitation to visit its labs.

Many companies have made changes in their products after getting a bad rating from CU. Although Whirlpool chafed at criticism that its washing-machine design made repair too difficult, on its new

models the cabinet pops off to allow access to key parts.

In its April, 1973, issue, *Consumer Reports* rejected an entire category of products—microwave ovens—because doors on all 14 models tested were leaking radiation. Since then, ovenmakers have changed their designs. Today, "there's very little leakage around those doors," says CU technical director R. David Pittle.

While *Consumer Reports* remains CU's major endeavor, the organization is branching out. In the last two years, it has launched a travel newsletter, produced six home videocassettes, spruced up its *Penny Power* children's magazine, and formed a book-publishing company. Since January, CU has been selling dealer's-cost listings for most auto models and options. Its media push also includes a thrice-weekly syndicated newspaper column, plus radio and television spots.

All this has helped CU's bottom line. Last year it earned $3.4 million.

Prosperity has not diluted CU's activism. Founded by labor unionists in the 1930s, it was among the first organizations to urge consumers to boycott goods made in Nazi Germany. Now *Consumer Reports* is alarmed that many Americans are slipping into poverty. So it is kicking off a three-part series on the working poor. But will the outspoken judge of what's good comment on how well U.S. manufacturers stack up against the Japanese? No way, says Pittle. "Our purpose is to provide an objective evaluation of a product—regardless of who made it."

*Source:* Mimi Bluestone, "When *Consumer Reports* Talks, Buyers Listen—and So Do Companies," *Business Week,* June 8, 1987, p. 135. Reprinted by permission.

*Consumers Union's ninety-member technical team puts products through their paces.*

new feature and steal the market. Moreover, companies often include new materials to lower costs and prices. They do not design products to break down earlier, because they do not want to lose their customers to other brands. Thus, much of so-called "planned obsolescence" is the working of the competitive and technological forces in a free society—forces that lead to ever-improving goods and services.

### Poor Service to Disadvantaged Consumers

Finally, the American marketing system has been accused of poorly serving disadvantaged consumers. Critics claim that the urban poor often have to shop in smaller stores that carry inferior goods and charge higher prices. The former chairman of the Federal Trade Commission (FTC), Paul Rand Dixon, summarized a Washington, D.C., study as follows:

> The poor pay more—nearly twice as much—for appliances and furniture sold in Washington's low-income area stores . . . Goods purchased for $100 at wholesale sold for $225 in the low-income stores compared with $159 in the general market stores. . . . Installment credit is a major marketing factor in selling to the poor . . . some low-income market retailers imposed effective annual finance charges as high as 33 percent. . . .[7]

Yet the merchants' profits were not too high:

> Low-income market retailers have markedly higher costs, partly because of bad debt expenses, but to a greater extent because of higher selling, wage, and commission costs. These expenses reflect in part greater use of home demonstration selling and expenses associated with the collection and processing of installment contracts. Thus, although their markups are often two or three times higher than general market retailers, on the average low-income market retailers do not make particularly high profits.[8]

Clearly, better marketing systems must be built in low-income areas—one hope is to get large retailers to open outlets in low-income areas. Moreover, low-income people obviously need consumer protection. The FTC has taken action against merchants who advertise false values, sell old merchandise as new, or charge too much for credit. It is also trying to make it harder for merchants to win court judgments against low-income people who were wheedled into buying something.

## Marketing's Impact on Society as a Whole

The American marketing system has been accused of adding to several "evils" in American society at large. Advertising has been a special target—so much so that the American Association of Advertising Agencies recently launched a campaign to defend advertising against what it felt to be common but undue criticisms (see Marketing Highlight 20–2). Here, we will examine claims that marketing creates false wants and too much materialism, too few social goods, cultural pollution, and too much political power.

### False Wants and Too Much Materialism

Critics have charged that the marketing system urges too much interest in material possessions. People are judged by what they *own* rather than by what they *are*. To be considered successful, people must own a suburban home, two cars, and the latest clothes and appliances. And indeed, this drive for wealth and possessions appears to have increased in recent years:

> Money, money, money is the incantation of today. Bewitched by an epidemic of money enchantment, Americans in the eighties wriggle in a St. Vitus's dance of materialism unseen since the Gilded Age of the Roaring Twenties. Under the blazing sun of money, all other values shine palely. . . . The evidence is everywhere. Open the scarlet covers of the Saks Fifth Avenue Christmas catalog, for starters, and look at what Santa Claus offers today's young family, from Dad's $1,650 ostrich-skin briefcase and Mom's $39,500 fur coat to Junior's $4,000, 15-mph miniature Mercedes.[9]

In a recent survey of teen-age girls, 93 percent listed shopping as their favorite pastime, far ahead of dating, which placed sixth. In another poll, 80 percent of college freshmen stated that it was very important for them to be quite well-off financially, against only 40 percent who said that developing a meaningful philosophy of life was an important objective.[10]

Critics do not view this interest in things as a natural state of mind but rather as a matter of false wants created by marketing. Business hires Madison Avenue to stimulate people's desires for goods, and Madison Avenue uses the mass media to create materialistic models of the good life. People work harder to earn the necessary money. Their purchases increase the output of American industry, and industry in turn uses Madison Avenue to stimulate *more* desire for

## Marketing Highlight 20–2

### ADVERTISING: ANOTHER WORD FOR FREEDOM OF CHOICE

During the past few years, the American Association of Advertising Agencies has run a campaign featuring ads such as these to counter common criticisms of advertising. The association is concerned about research findings of negative public attitudes toward advertising. Two-thirds of the public recognizes that advertising provides helpful buying information, but a significant portion feels that advertising is exaggerated or misleading. The association believes that its ad campaign will increase general advertising credibility and make advertisers' messages more effective. Several media have agreed to run the ads as a public service.

The American Association of Advertising Agencies runs ads to counter common advertising criticisms.

industrial output. Thus, marketing is seen as creating false wants that benefit industry more than they benefit consumers.

These criticisms, however, overstate the power of business to create wants. People have strong defenses against advertising and other marketing tools. Marketers are most effective when they appeal to existing needs rather than when they attempt to create new ones. Furthermore, people seek information when making important purchases and do not normally rely on single sources. Even minor purchases, which may be affected by advertising messages, lead to repeat purchases only if the product performs as promised. Finally, the high failure rate of new products shows that companies are not able to control demand.

On a deeper level, our wants and values are influenced not only by marketers but also by family, peer groups, religion, ethnic background, and education. If Americans are highly materialistic, these values arose out of basic socialization processes that go much deeper than business and mass media could foster alone.

### Too Few Social Goods

Business has been accused of overselling private goods at the expense of public goods. As private goods increase, they require more public services that are usually not forthcoming. For example, an increase in automobile ownership (a private good) requires more highways, traffic control, parking spaces, and police services (public goods). The overselling of private goods thus results in "social costs." For cars, the social costs include excessive traffic congestion, air pollution, and deaths and injuries from accidents.

A way must therefore be found to restore a balance between private and public goods. One argument is that producers should bear the full social costs of their operations. For example, the government could require automobile manufacturers to build cars with additional safety features and better pollution-control systems. Automakers would then raise their prices to cover extra costs. However, if buyers found the price of certain cars too high, the producers of those cars would disappear, and demand would move to those producers who could support the sum of the private and social costs.

### Cultural Pollution

Critics also charge the marketing system with creating *cultural pollution*. Our senses are constantly being assaulted by advertising. Commercials interrupt serious programs; pages of ads obscure printed matter; billboards mar beautiful scenery. These interruptions continuously pollute people's minds with messages promoting materialism, sex, power, or status. Although most people do not find advertising overly annoying (some even think it is the best part of television programming), some critics call for sweeping changes.

Marketers answer the charges of "commercial noise" with these arguments: First, they hope that their ads reach primarily the target audience. But because of mass-communication channels, some ads are bound to reach people who have no interest in a product and are therefore bored or annoyed. People who buy magazines addressed to their interests—such as *Vogue* or *Fortune*—rarely complain about the ads because the magazines advertise products of interest. Second, ads make television and radio free media and therefore keep down the costs of magazines and newspapers. Most people think commercials are a small price to pay.

### Too Much Political Power

Another criticism is that business wields too much political power. There are "oil," "tobacco," and "auto" legislators who support an industry's interests

*Cultural pollution: people's senses are sometimes assaulted by commercial messages.*

against the public interest. Advertisers are accused of holding too much power over the mass media, limiting their freedom to report independently and objectively. One critic has asked: "How can *Life* . . . and *Reader's Digest* afford to tell the truth about the scandalously low nutritional value of most packaged foods . . . when these magazines are being subsidized by such advertisers as General Foods, Kellogg's, Nabisco, and General Mills? . . . The answer is *they cannot and do not.*"[11]

Naturally, American industries do promote and protect their own interests. They have a right to representation in Congress and the mass media, although their influence can become too great. Fortunately, however, many powerful business interests once thought to be untouchable have been tamed in the public interest. Standard Oil was broken up in 1911, and the meatpacking industry was disciplined in the early 1900s after exposures by Upton Sinclair. Ralph Nader caused legislation making the automobile industry build more safety into its cars, and the Surgeon General's Report resulted in cigarette companies putting health warnings on packages. Moreover, because the media receive advertising revenues from many different advertisers, it is easier to resist the influence of one or a few of them. Too much business power tends to result in counterforces that check and offset powerful interests.

## Marketing's Impact on Other Businesses

Finally, critics charge that a company's marketing practices can harm other companies and reduce competition. Three problems are involved: acquisitions of competitors, marketing practices that create barriers to entry, and unfair competitive marketing practices.

Critics claim that firms are harmed and competition reduced when companies expand by acquiring competitors rather than by developing their own new products. In the food industry alone during the last few years, R. J. Reynolds acquired Nabisco Brands and was in turn purchased by Kohlberg Kravis Roberts, Philip Morris bought General Foods and Kraft, Procter & Gamble gobbled up Richardson-Vick, Beatrice joined Esmark, Nestlé absorbed Carnation, and Quaker Oats bought Stokely-Van Camp.[12] These and large acquisitions in other industries have caused concern that vigorous young competitors will eventually be absorbed and that competition will be reduced.

Acquisition is a complex subject. Acquisitions can sometimes be good for society. The acquiring company may gain economies of scale that lead to lower costs and lower prices. A well-managed company may take over a poorly managed company and improve its efficiency. An industry that was not very competitive might become more competitive after the acquisition. But acquisitions can also be harmful and are therefore closely regulated by the government.

Critics have also charged that marketing practices add barriers to the entry of new companies into an industry. Large marketing companies can use heavy promotion spending, patents, and tie-ups of suppliers or dealers to keep out or drive out competitors. People concerned with antitrust regulation recognize that some barriers are the natural result of the economic advantages of doing business on a large scale. Other barriers could be challenged by existing and new laws. For example, some critics have proposed a progressive tax on advertising spending to reduce the role of selling costs as a major barrier to entry.

Finally, some firms have in fact used unfair competitive marketing practices with the intention of hurting or destroying other firms. They may set their prices below costs, threaten to cut off business with suppliers, or discourage the buying of a competitor's products. Various laws work to prevent such predatory competition. It is difficult, however, to prove that the intent or action was really predatory. In the classic A&P case, this large retailer was able to charge lower prices than small "mom and pop" grocery stores. The question is whether this was unfair competition or the healthy competition of a more efficient retailer against less efficient retailers.

# CITIZEN AND PUBLIC ACTIONS TO REGULATE MARKETING

Because some people have viewed business as the cause of many economic and social ills, grass-roots movements have arisen from time to time to keep business in line. The two major movements have been *consumerism* and *environmentalism*.

## Consumerism

American business firms have been the target of organized consumer movements on three occasions. The first consumer movement took place in the early 1900s. It was fueled by rising prices, Upton Sinclair's writings on conditions in the meat industry, and scandals in the drug industry. The second consumer movement, in the mid-1930s, was sparked by an upturn in consumer prices during the Depression and another drug industry scandal.

The third movement began in the 1960s. Consumers had become better educated, products had become more complex and hazardous, and people were unhappy with American institutions in general. Ralph Nader appeared on the scene to force many issues, and other well-known writers accused big business of wasteful and unethical practices. President John F. Kennedy declared that consumers have a right to safety, to be informed, to choose, and to be heard. Congress investigated certain industries and proposed consumer-protection legislation. Since then, many consumer groups have been organized and several consumer laws have been passed. The consumer movement has spread internationally and has become very strong in Scandinavia and the Low Countries.[13]

But what is the consumer movement? **Consumerism** is an organized movement of citizens and government to improve the rights and power of buyers in relation to sellers. Traditional sellers' rights include the following:

□ The right to introduce any product in any size and style, provided it is not hazardous to personal health or safety; or, if it is, to include proper warnings and controls

□ The right to charge any price for the product, provided there is no discrimination among similar classes of buyers

□ The right to spend any amount to promote the product, provided the promotion is not defined as unfair competition

□ The right to use any product message, provided it is not misleading or dishonest in content or execution

□ The right to use any buying incentive schemes, provided they are not unfair or misleading

Traditional buyers' rights include the following:

□ The right not to buy a product that is offered for sale

□ The right to expect the product to be safe

□ The right to expect the product to perform as claimed

Comparing these rights, many analysts believe that the balance of power lies on the sellers' side. True, the buyer can refuse to buy. But many critics feel that the buyer has too little information, education, and protection to make wise decisions when facing sophisticated sellers. Consumer advocates call for the following additional consumer rights:

□ The right to be well-informed about important aspects of the product

□ The right to be protected against questionable products and marketing practices

□ The right to influence products and marketing practices in ways that will improve the "quality of life"

Each proposed right has led to more specific proposals by consumerists. The right to be informed includes the right to know the true interest on a loan (truth in lending), the true cost per unit of a brand (unit pricing), the ingredients in a product (ingredient labeling), the nutrition in foods (nutritional labeling), product freshness (open dating), and the true benefits of a product (truth in advertising). Proposals related to consumer protection include strengthening consumer rights in cases of business fraud, requiring greater product safety, and giving more power to government agencies. Proposals relating to quality of life include controlling the ingredients that go into certain products (detergents) and packaging (soft-drink containers), reducing the level of advertising "noise," and putting consumer representatives on company boards to protect consumer interests.

Consumers have not only the *right* but also the *responsibility* to protect themselves instead of leaving this function to someone else. Consumers who feel they got a bad deal have several remedies available, including writing to the company president or to the media; contacting federal, state, or local agencies; and going to small-claims courts.

**consumerism** An organized movement of citizens and government to strengthen the rights and power of buyers in relation to sellers.

*Consumer desire for more information led to putting ingredients, nutrition, and dating information on product labels.*

**environmentalism** An organized movement of concerned citizens and government to protect and improve people's living environment and quality of life.

## Environmentalism

While consumerists look at whether the marketing system is efficiently serving consumer wants, environmentalists look at how marketing affects the environment and at the costs of serving consumer needs and wants. During the past 30 years, several key books have promoted the cause of environmentalism by pointing out environmental dangers. In 1962, Rachel Carson's *Silent Spring* told us about pesticide pollution in our environment: It was no longer simply a matter of wasted resources, but one of human survival. In 1970, the Ehrlichs coined the term "eco-catastrophe" to point out the harmful impact of certain American business practices on the environment. And in 1972, the Meadowses published *The Limits to Growth,* which warned people that the quality of life would decline in the face of unchecked population growth, increased pollution, and the uncontrolled use of natural resources.[14]

These concerns are the basis for **environmentalism**—an organized movement of concerned citizens and government to protect and improve people's living environment. Environmentalists are concerned with strip mining, forest depletion, acid rain, loss of the ozone layer in the atmosphere, toxic wastes, billboards, and litter; with the loss of recreational areas; and with the increase in health problems caused by polluted air and water and chemically treated food.

Environmentalists are not against marketing and consumption—they simply want people and organizations to operate with more care for the environment. The marketing system's goal should not be to maximize consumption, consumer choice, or consumer satisfaction. Its goal should be to maximize life quality. And "life quality" means not only the quantity and quality of consumer goods and services but also the quality of the environment. Environmentalists want environmental costs included in producer and consumer decision making.

*Canon shows societal concern by discussing the role of photography in creating long-run environmental benefits.*

Environmentalism has hit some industries hard. Steel companies and public utilities have had to invest billions of dollars in pollution-control equipment and costlier fuels. The auto industry has had to introduce expensive emission controls in cars. The packaging industry has had to find ways to reduce litter. The gasoline industry has had to create new low-lead and no-lead gasolines. These industries resent environmental regulations, especially when imposed too rapidly to allow companies to make proper adjustments. Companies have had to absorb large costs and pass them on to buyers.

Thus, marketers' lives have become more complicated. Marketers must examine the ecological properties of their products and packaging. They must raise prices to cover environmental costs, knowing that the product will be harder to sell. Yet environmental issues have become so important in our society that there is no turning back to the time when few managers worried about the effects of product and marketing decisions on environmental quality.

## Public Actions to Regulate Marketing

Citizen concerns about marketing practices will usually lead to public attention and legislative proposals. New bills will be debated—many will be defeated, others will be modified, and a few will become workable laws.

We listed many of the laws affecting marketing in Chapter 5. The task is to translate laws into language that marketing executives understand as they make decisions about competitive relations, products, price, promotion, and channels

**enlightened marketing** A marketing philosophy holding that a company's marketing should support the best long-run performance of the marketing system.

**consumer-oriented marketing** A principle of enlightened marketing holding that a company should view and organize its marketing activities from consumers' point of view.

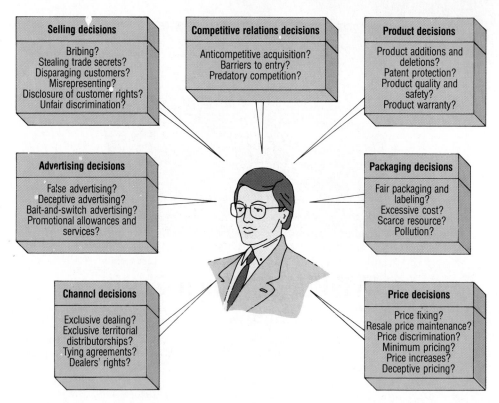

**Selling decisions**
Bribing?
Stealing trade secrets?
Disparaging customers?
Misrepresenting?
Disclosure of customer rights?
Unfair discrimination?

**Competitive relations decisions**
Anticompetitive acquisition?
Barriers to entry?
Predatory competition?

**Product decisions**
Product additions and deletions?
Patent protection?
Product quality and safety?
Product warranty?

**Advertising decisions**
False advertising?
Deceptive advertising?
Bait-and-switch advertising?
Promotional allowances and services?

**Packaging decisions**
Fair packaging and labeling?
Excessive cost?
Scarce resource?
Pollution?

**Channel decisions**
Exclusive dealing?
Exclusive territorial distributorships?
Tying agreements?
Dealers' rights?

**Price decisions**
Price fixing?
Resale price maintenance?
Price discrimination?
Minimum pricing?
Price increases?
Deceptive pricing?

FIGURE 20–2  Major Marketing Decision Areas that May Be Called into Question under the Law

of distribution. Figure 20–2 shows the major legal issues facing marketing management when making such decisions.

# BUSINESS ACTIONS TOWARD SOCIALLY RESPONSIBLE MARKETING

At first, many companies opposed consumerism and environmentalism. They thought criticisms were either unfair or unimportant. But by now, most companies have grown to accept consumer rights in principle. They might oppose some pieces of legislation as inappropriate ways to solve certain consumer problems, but they recognize the consumer's right to information and protection. Many companies have responded positively to consumerism and environmentalism in order to better serve consumer needs. Here, we will look at appropriate business responses to the changing marketing environment. We first outline a concept of *enlightened marketing* and then consider *marketing ethics*.

## A Concept of Enlightened Marketing

The concept of **enlightened marketing** holds that a company's marketing should support the best long-run performance of the marketing system. Enlightened marketing consists of five principles: *consumer-oriented marketing, innovative marketing, value marketing, sense-of-mission marketing,* and *societal marketing.*

### Consumer-Oriented Marketing

**Consumer-oriented marketing** means that the company should view and organize its marketing activities from the consumers' point of view. It should work hard to sense, serve, and satisfy the needs of a defined group of customers. Consider the following example:

> Barat College, a women's college in Lake Forest, Illinois, published a college catalog that openly spelled out Barat College's strong and weak points. Among the weak points it shared with applicants were the following: "An exceptionally talented student musician or mathematician . . . might be advised to look further for a college with top faculty and facilities in that field. . . . The full range of advanced specialized courses offered in a university will be absent. . . . The library collection is average for a small college, but low in comparison with other high-quality institutions."

The effect of "telling it like it is" is to build confidence so that applicants really know what they will find at Barat College and to emphasize that Barat College will strive to improve its consumer value as rapidly as time and funds permit.

### Innovative Marketing

The principle of **innovative marketing** requires that the company seek real product and marketing improvements. The company that overlooks new and better ways to do things will eventually lose out to a company that has found a better way. One of the best examples of an innovative marketer is Procter & Gamble (see Marketing Highlight 20–3).

### Value Marketing

According to the principle of **value marketing,** a company should put most of its resources into value-building marketing investments. Many things marketers do—one-shot sales promotions, minor packaging changes, advertising puffery—may raise sales in the short run but add less *value* than would actual improvements in the product's quality, features, or convenience. Enlightened marketing calls for building long-run consumer loyalty by continually improving the value consumers receive from the firm's marketing offer.

### Sense-of-Mission Marketing

**Sense-of-mission marketing** means that a company should define its mission in broad *social* terms rather than narrow *product* terms. When a company defines a social mission, its employees feel better about their work and have a clearer sense of direction. For example, defined in narrow product terms, International Minerals and Chemical Corporation's mission might be "to sell fertilizer." But the company states its mission more broadly:

> We're not merely in the business of selling our brand of fertilizer. We have a sense of purpose, a sense of where we are going. The first function of corporate planning is to decide what kind of business the company is in. Our business is *agricultural productivity*. We are interested in anything that affects plant growth, now and in the future.[15]

Reshaping the basic task of selling fertilizer into the larger mission of improving agricultural productivity in order to feed the world's hungry gives a new sense of purpose to employees.

### Societal Marketing

Following the principle of **societal marketing,** an enlightened company makes marketing decisions by considering consumers' wants, the company's requirements, consumers' long-run interests, and society's long-run interests. The

**innovative marketing** A principle of enlightened marketing that requires a company to seek real product and marketing improvements.

**value marketing** A principle of enlightened marketing holding that a company should put most of its resources into value-building marketing investments.

**sense-of-mission marketing** A principle of enlightened marketing holding that a company should define its mission in broad social terms rather than narrow product terms.

**societal marketing** A principle of enlightened marketing holding that a company should make marketing decisions by considering consumers' wants, the company's requirements, consumers' long-run interests, and society's long-run interests.

## PROCTER & GAMBLE LEADS WITH INNOVATION

P&G has always invested heavily to find innovative products that solve consumer problems. This constant innovation has made P&G the leader in the American consumer package-goods industry. For example, P&G spent years developing a toothpaste that would effectively reduce tooth decay. When introduced, Crest soon outsold less effective brands, and with constant improvement, it remained the leading toothpaste for over 30 years. In the same way, P&G looked at the shampoo market and found that no brand provided the dandruff control that consumers wanted. Years of research produced Head and Shoulders—an instant market leader. Then P&G looked at the paper-products business. It found that new parents wanted relief from handling and washing diapers. Again, P&G found an innovative solution: It introduced Pampers, an affordable disposable paper diaper that immediately won market leadership. Thus, innovative marketing took P&G to the top in consumer products.

Yet in the early 1980s, P&G appeared to lessen some of its pressure to innovate. More innovative competitors quickly challenged P&G's leadership in several product areas, especially toothpaste and disposable diapers.

Crest was hard hit. In 1983, Minnetonka innovated with Check-Up, the first plaque-fighting toothpaste packaged in a pump container. And Lever Brothers and Beecham introduced gels—clear and better-tasting forms of toothpaste that appeal strongly to children. While P&G lagged behind on these innovations, its major competitor, Colgate, surged ahead. Colgate poured money into research and development and beat P&G to the market by many months with the pump, gels, and a plaque-fighting formula. Colgate soon grabbed 50 percent of the pump segment and boosted its overall share of the $1 billion toothpaste market from 18 percent in 1979 to 28 percent by the end of 1984. During the last six months of 1984, Crest's share plunged from 36 percent to 30 percent.

Procter & Gamble took a similar beating in the disposable diaper market. Pampers had created the disposables category, and for years P&G's Pampers and Luvs brands dominated with a combined share exceeding 75 percent. But in 1984, while P&G coasted, Kimberly-Clark came out with Huggies—an innovative brand with greater absorbency, a contour shape, and refastenable tapes. By mid-1985, P&G found itself following rather than leading this market. Its overall share fell to 46 percent, and Pampers slid to second place behind Huggies. In 1985, P&G suffered its first income decline in 33 years.

P&G was down but far from out. It struck back hard with innovations in both product areas. In late 1985, P&G introduced a superior pump and extended its line to include gels. In addition, it did the challengers one better by introducing Crest Tartar Control Formula paste and gel in both pumps and tubes. P&G also spent over $500 million to create a new generation of Pampers and an improved Luvs. Competitors were left scrambling to match P&G's new Ultra Pampers, a super-thin, super-absorbent disposable diaper.

Procter & Gamble's surge of fresh innovation produced amazing results. In less than six months, Crest's share of the toothpaste market jumped to 38 percent while Colgate's fell to 22 percent. P&G's share of the disposable diaper market climbed quickly to 60 percent, and Pampers regained a comfortable market-share lead.

Thus, the weapon P&G used to reach the top originally was used by its competitors to threaten P&G's leadership—and used again by P&G to regain lost ground. The weapon was innovation. The message is a simple one—to stay ahead, P&G must continue to lead.

*Sources:* See Nancy Giges and Laurie Freeman, "Wounded Tiger? Trail of Mistakes Mars P&G Record," *Advertising Age*, July 29, 1985, pp. 1, 50–51; Faye Rice, "The King of Suds Reigns Again," *Fortune*, August 4, 1986, pp. 130–34; and Kenneth Labich, "The Innovators," *Fortune*, June 6, 1988, pp. 51–64.

**desirable products** Products that give both high immediate satisfaction and high long-run benefits.

**pleasing products** Products that give high immediate satisfaction but may hurt consumers in the long run.

**salutary products** Products that have low appeal but benefit consumers in the long run.

company is aware that neglecting the last two factors is a disservice to consumers and society. Alert companies view societal problems as opportunities.

A societally oriented marketer wants to design products that are not only pleasing but also beneficial. The difference is shown in Figure 20–3. Products can be classified according to their degree of immediate consumer satisfaction and long-run consumer benefit. **Desirable products** give both high immediate satisfaction and high long-run benefits. A desirable product with immediate satisfaction and long-run benefit would be a tasty, nutritious breakfast food. **Pleasing products** give high immediate satisfaction but may hurt consumers in the long run. An example is cigarettes. **Salutary products** have low appeal but benefit consumers in the long run. Seat belts are salutary products. Finally,

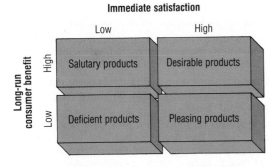

Immediate satisfaction

FIGURE 20–3    Societal Classification of Products

**deficient products,** such as bad-tasting yet ineffective medicine, have neither immediate appeal nor long-run benefits.

The challenge posed by pleasing products is that they sell very well but may end up hurting the consumer. The product opportunity, therefore, is to add long-run benefits without reducing the product's pleasing qualities. For example, Sears developed a phosphate-free laundry detergent that was also very effective. The challenge posed by salutary products is to add some pleasing qualities so that they will become more desirable in the consumers' minds. For example, synthetic fats and fat substitutes, such as Procter & Gamble's Olestra and NutraSweet's Simplesse, promise to improve the appeal of more healthful low-fat and low-calorie foods.

## Marketing Ethics

Conscientious marketers face many moral dilemmas. The best thing to do is often unclear. Because not all managers have refined moral sensitivity, companies need to develop *corporate marketing ethics policies*—broad guidelines that everyone in the organization must follow. These policies should cover distributor relations, advertising standards, customer service, pricing, product development, and general ethical standards.

The finest guidelines cannot resolve all the difficult ethical situations the marketer faces. Table 20–1 lists some difficult ethical situations marketers may face during their careers. If marketers choose immediate sales-producing actions in *all* these cases, their marketing behavior might well be described as immoral or amoral. If they refuse to go along with *any* of the actions, they might be ineffective as marketing managers and unhappy because of the constant moral tension. Managers need a set of principles that will help them analyze the moral importance of each situation and how far they can go in good conscience.

But *what* principle should guide companies and marketing managers on issues of ethics and social responsibility? One philosophy is that such issues are decided by the free market and the legal system. Under this principle, companies and their managers are not responsible for making moral judgments. Companies can in good conscience do whatever the system allows.

A second philosophy places responsibility not in the system, but in the hands of individual companies and managers. This more enlightened philosophy suggests that a company should have a "social conscience." Companies and managers should apply high standards of ethics and morality when making corporate decisions, regardless of "what the system allows." History provides an endless list of examples of company actions that were legal but highly irresponsible. Consider the following example:

Prior to the Pure Food and Drug Act, the advertising for a diet pill promised that a person taking this pill could eat virtually anything at any time and still lose weight. Too good to be true? Actually the claim was quite true; the product lived up to its billing with frightening efficiency. It seems that the primary active ingredient in

**TABLE 20–1  Some Morally Difficult Situations in Marketing**

1. You work for a cigarette company and up to now have not been convinced that cigarettes cause cancer. A report comes across your desk that clearly shows the link between smoking and cancer. What would you do?

2. Your R&D department has changed one of your products slightly. It is not really "new and improved," but you know that putting this statement on the package and in advertising will increase sales. What would you do?

3. You have been asked to add a stripped-down model to your line that could be advertised to pull customers into the store. The product won't be very good, but salespeople will be able to switch buyers up to higher-priced units. You are asked to give the green light for this stripped-down version. What would you do?

4. You are thinking of hiring a product manager who just left a competitor's company. She would be more than happy to tell you all the competitor's plans for the coming year. What would you do?

5. One of your top dealers in an important territory has had recent family troubles and his sales have slipped. It looks like it will take him a while to straighten out his family trouble. Meanwhile you are losing many sales. Legally, you can terminate the dealer's franchise and replace him. What would you do?

6. You have a chance to win a big account that will mean a lot to you and your company. The purchasing agent hints that a "gift" would influence the decision. Your assistant recommends sending a fine color television set to the buyer's home. What would you do?

7. You have heard that a competitor has a new product feature that will make a big difference in sales. The competitor will demonstrate the feature in a private dealer meeting at the annual trade show. You can easily send a snooper to this meeting to learn about the new feature. What would you do?

8. You have to choose between three ad campaigns outlined by your agency. The first (A) is a soft-sell, honest information campaign. The second (B) uses sex-loaded emotional appeals and exaggerates the product's benefits. The third (C) involves a noisy, irritating commercial that is sure to gain audience attention. Pretests show that the campaigns are effective in the following order: C, B, and A. What would you do?

9. You are interviewing a capable woman applicant for a job as salesperson. She is better qualified than the men just interviewed. At the same time, you know that some of your important customers prefer dealing with men, and you will lose some sales if you hire her. What would you do?

10. You are a sales manager in an encyclopedia company. Your competitor's salespeople are getting into homes by pretending to take a research survey. After they finish the survey, they switch to their sales pitch. This technique seems to be very effective. What would you do?

this "diet supplement" was tapeworm larvae. These larvae would develop in the intestinal tract and, of course, be well fed; the pill taker would in time, quite literally, starve to death.[16]

Each company and marketing manager must work out a philosophy of socially responsible and ethical behavior. Under the societal marketing concept, each manager must look beyond what is legal and allowed and develop standards based on personal integrity, corporate conscience, and long-run consumer welfare. A clear and responsible philosophy will help the marketing manager deal with the many knotty questions posed by marketing and other human activities. Many industrial and professional associations have suggested codes of ethics, and many companies are now adopting their own codes and developing programs to teach managers about important ethics issues and help them find the proper responses (see Marketing Highlight 20-4).[17]

Marketing executives of the 1990s will face even more challenges. They will have abundant marketing opportunities because of technological advances in solar energy, home computers and robots, cable television, modern medicine, and new forms of transportation, recreation, and communication. At the same time, however, forces in the socioeconomic environment will increase the limits under which marketing can be carried out. Those companies capable of creating new values and practicing societally responsible marketing will have a world to conquer.

## THE GENERAL DYNAMICS ETHICS PROGRAM

The General Dynamics ethics program is considered the most comprehensive in the industry. And little wonder—it was put together as generals from the Pentagon looked on. The program came about after charges that the company had deliberately overbilled the government on defense contracts.

Now at General Dynamics, a committee of board members reviews its ethics policies, and a corporate ethics director and steering group execute the program. The company has set up hot lines that let any employee get instant advice on job-related ethical issues and has given each employee a wallet card listing a toll-free number he or she can call to report suspected wrongdoing. Nearly all employees have attended workshops; those for salespeople cover such topics as expense accounts and supplier relations.

The company also has a 20-page code of ethics that tells employees in detail how to conduct themselves. Here are some examples of rules for salespeople:

☐ If it becomes clear that the company must engage in unethical or illegal activity to win a contract, it will not pursue that business further.

☐ To prevent hidden interpretations or understandings, all information provided relative to products and services should be clear and concise.

☐ Receiving or soliciting gifts, entertainment, or anything else of value is prohibited.

☐ In countries where common practices indicate acceptance of conduct lower than that to which General Dynamics

aspires, salespeople will follow the company's standards.

☐ Under no circumstances may an employee offer or give anything to customers or their representatives in an effort to influence them.

*Source:* Adapted from "This Industry Leader Means Business," *Sales & Marketing Management,* May 1987, p. 44; and Stewart Toy, "The Defense Scandal," *Business Week,* July 1, 1988, pp. 28–30.

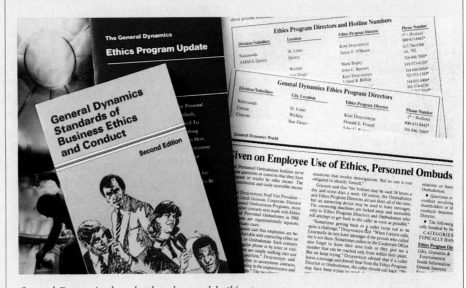

*General Dynamics has developed a model ethics program.*

# SUMMARY

A marketing system should sense, serve, and satisfy consumer needs and improve the quality of consumers' lives. In working to meet consumer needs, marketers may take some actions that are not to everyone's liking or benefit. Marketing managers should be aware of the main *criticisms of marketing.*

Marketing's *impact on individual consumer welfare* has been criticized for high prices, deceptive practices, high-pressure selling, shoddy or unsafe products, planned obsolescence, and poor service to disadvantaged consumers. Marketing's *impact on society* has been criticized for creating false wants and too much materialism, too few social goods, cultural pollution, and too much political power. Critics have also criticized marketing's *impact on other businesses* for harming competitors and reducing competition through ac-

quisitions, for practices that create barriers to entry, and for unfair competitive marketing practices.

Concerns about the marketing system have led to *citizen-action movements*—especially consumerism and environmentalism. *Consumerism* is an organized social movement to strengthen the rights and power of consumers relative to sellers. Alert marketers view it as an opportunity to serve consumers better by providing more consumer information, education, and protection. *Environmentalism* is an organized social movement seeking to minimize the harm done by marketing practices to the environment and quality of life. It calls for curbing consumer wants when their satisfaction would create too much environmental cost. Citizen action has led to the passage of many laws to protect consumers in the area of product safety, truth in packaging, truth in lending, and truth in advertising.

Many companies originally opposed these social movements and laws, but most of them now recognize the need for positive consumer information, education, and protection. Some companies have followed a policy of *enlightened market-ing* based on the principles of *consumer orientation, innovation, value creation, social mission,* and *societal orientation.* Increasingly, companies are responding to the need to provide company policies and guidelines to help managers deal with questions of *marketing ethics.*

## QUESTIONS FOR DISCUSSION

1. Was Gerber right in not recalling its baby food after customers complained about finding glass fragments in bottles? Disregarding what you know about the actual outcome, analyze the situation facing Gerber in 1986 and explain what action you would have recommended *at the time.*

2. If regulators limited the allowable number of levels in a distribution channel or set a cap on the maximum markup that middlemen could add to the prices of products, would the cost of distribution increase or decrease? What impact would these regulations have on consumers?

3. Does advertising add an excessive amount to the price of products?

4. Does marketing *create* barriers to entry or *reduce* them? How, for example, could a small manufacturer of household cleaning products use advertising to compete with Procter & Gamble?

5. If you were a marketing manager at Dow Chemical Company, which would you prefer—government regulations on acceptable levels of air and water pollution or a voluntary industry code for target levels of emissions?

6. Does Procter & Gamble practice the principles of enlightened marketing? Does your school?

7. Compare the marketing concept with the principle of societal marketing. Should marketers adopt the societal marketing concept?

8. Choose three of the situations described in Table 20–1 and explain what you would do in each case. Would you make the same decision if your company were having severe financial troubles? What if it had no stated policy supporting high ethical standards?

9. If you had the power to change our marketing system in any feasible way, what improvements *would* you make? What improvements *can* you make, either as a consumer or as an entry-level marketing practitioner?

## REFERENCES

1. See Patricia Strnad, "Gerber Ignores Tylenol Textbook," *Advertising Age,* March 10, 1986, p. 3; Strnad, "Gerber Shifts Stance in 'Reassurance' Spots," *Advertising Age,* March 17, 1986, p. 8; and Felix Kessler, "Tremors from the Tylenol Scare Hit Food Companies," *Fortune,* March 31, 1986, pp. 59–62.

2. See John F. Gaski and Michael Etzel, "The Index of Consumer Sentiment toward Marketing," *Journal of Marketing,* July 1986, pp. 71–81.

3. Excerpts from Theodore Levitt, "The Morality (?) of Advertising," *Harvard Business Review,* July-August 1970, pp. 84–92.

4. "The Breakfast of Fatties?" *Chicago Today,* July 24, 1970.

5. See Jim Treece, "If It Has Wheels and Carries People, Shouldn't It Be Safe?" *Business Week,* June 20, 1988, p. 48.

6. For more on product safety, see "Unsafe Products: The Great Debate over Blame and Punishment," *Business Week,* April 30, 1984, pp. 96-104; Michael Brody, "When Products Turn," *Fortune,* March 3, 1986, pp. 20–24; and Marisa Manley, "Product Liability: You're More Exposed Than You Think," *Harvard Business Review,* September-October 1987, pp. 28–40.

7. A speech delivered at Vanderbilt University Law School, reported in *Marketing News,* August 1, 1968, pp. 11, 15.

8. Ibid.

9. Myron Magnet, "The Money Society," *Fortune,* July 6, 1987, p. 26.

10. Ibid., p. 26. However, some social scientists predict a return to more basic values and social commitment. See Bill Barol, "The Eighties Are Over," *Newsweek,* January 4, 1988, pp. 40–48; and *"Busi-*

*ness Week*'s 1988 Hip Parade: Goodbye Greed, Hello Heartland,'' *Business Week,* January 18, 1988, p. 31.

11. From an advertisement for *Fact* magazine, which does not carry advertisements.

12. See Paul B. Brown, Zachary Schiller, Christine Dugas, and Scott Scredon, ''New? Improved? The Brand-Name Mergers,'' *Business Week,* October 21, 1985, pp. 108–10; and Kenneth Dreyfack, ''The Big Brands Are Back in Style,'' *Business Week,* January 12, 1987, p. 74.

13. For more details, see Paul N. Bloom and Stephen A. Greyser, ''The Maturing of Consumerism,'' *Harvard Business Review,* November-December 1981, pp. 130–39; Robert J. Samualson, ''The Aging of Ralph Nader,'' *Newsweek,* December 16, 1985, p. 57; and Douglas A. Harbrecht, ''The Second Coming of Ralph Nadar,'' *Business Week,* March 6, 1989, p. 28.

14. See Rachel Carson, *Silent Spring* (Boston: Houghton Mifflin, 1962); Paul R. Ehrlich and Ann H. Ehrlich, *Population, Resources, Environment: Issues in Human Ecology* (San Francisco: W. H. Freeman, 1970); and Donnella H. Meadows, Dennis L. Meadows, Jorgen Randers, and William W. Behrens III, *The Limits to Growth* (New York: Universe Books, 1972).

15. Gordon O. Pehrson, quoted in ''Flavored Algae from the Sea?'' *Chicago Sun-Times,* February 3, 1965, p. 54.

16. Dan R. Dalton and Richard A. Cosier, ''The Four Faces of Social Responsibility,'' *Business Horizons,* May-June 1982, pp. 19–27.

17. For examples, see the American Marketing Association's code of ethics, discussed in ''AMA Adopts New Code of Ethics,'' *Marketing News,* September 11, 1987, p. 1; and John A. Byrne, ''Businesses Are Signing Up for Ethics 101,'' *Business Week,* February 15, 1988, pp. 56–57.

# Case 20

## NESTLÉ: UNDER FIRE AGAIN

Questionable marketing techniques by a unit of Nestlé are raising the concerns of consumer products activists. And this is not the first time that Nestlé has been scrutinized by the public eye.

Nestlé S.A., headquartered in Vevey, Switzerland, is the world's largest food company, with annual worldwide sales of more than $25 billion. The company's products are produced in 383 factories operating in 50 countries. Many Nestlé products are quite familiar to you—Nestlé's chocolates, Nescafé, Taster's Choice, and Hills coffees, Libby and Contadina foods, Beech-Nut baby products, Stouffer foods, and Friskies, Fancy Feast, and Mighty Dog pet foods. In 1985, the company acquired Carnation Company, makers of Evaporated Milk, Hot Cocoa Mix, Instant Breakfast Mix, Coffee-Mate, and other familiar brands.

In the late 1970's and early 1980's, Nestlé came under heavy fire from health professionals who charged the company with encouraging Third-World mothers to give up breast feeding and use company-prepared formula. Critics accused Nestlé of using sophisticated promotional techniques to persuade hundreds of thousands of poverty-stricken, poorly educated mothers that formula feeding was better for their children. Unfortunately, formula feeding is not usually a wise practice in such countries. Because of poor living conditions and habits, people cannot or do not clean bottles properly and often mix formula with impure water. Furthermore, income level does not permit many families to purchase sufficient quantities of formula.

In 1977, two American social-interest groups spearheaded a worldwide boycott against Nestlé. The boycott ended in 1984, when the company complied with infant formula marketing codes adopted by the World Health Organization (WHO). The code adopted by the WHO eliminates all promotional efforts, requiring

companies to serve primarily as passive ''order takers.'' It prohibits advertising, samples, and direct contact with consumers. Contacts with professionals (such as doctors) are allowed only if professionals seek such contact. Manufacturers can package products with some form of visual corporate identity, but they cannot picture babies. In effect, then, the WHO code allows almost no marketing. However, the code contains only *recommended* guidelines. They become *mandatory* only if individual governments adopt national codes through their own regulatory mechanisms.

In addition to the formula controversy, Nestlé has had other public-relations difficulties in recent years. In contrast to the Third-World baby formula debacle, the next incident involved top-management ethics at a Nestlé subsidiary. Beech-Nut Nutrition Corp., one of Nestlé's U.S. baby-products units, found itself in hot water in 1987, when it was forced to admit to selling adulterated and mislabeled apple juice intended for babies. The product contained little if any apple juice and was made from beet sugar, cane sugar syrup, corn syrup, and other ingredients. After pleading guilty to federal charges, Beech-Nut agreed to pay a $2 million fine and $140,000 for Food & Drug Administration investigative costs. Two company executives were fined and imprisoned.

Nestlé may once again be in the limelight with a recent new-product entry in the U.S. infant formula market. To maintain its growth and profitability, Nestlé is planning to enter the U.S. baby formula market, a market that it dominates in Europe. In the $1.6 billion U.S. market, however, it faces several large, well-established competitors—Abbott Laboratories (with Similac and Isomil brands) has a 53-percent market share, followed by Bristol-Myers (Enfamil and ProSobee brands) with 36 percent, and American Home Products (SMA brand) with 11 percent. Despite the competition, formula sales are predicted to grow at 8 or 9 percent annually. Although there has been a trend toward breast feeding in recent years, this trend has been partially offset by the number of working mothers who have less time to breast-feed.

Nestlé's new infant formula, named Good Start, will be introduced by its Carnation unit—a company with a pure and sparkling reputation in the baby business. Nestlé claims that its product offers important benefits over current infant formulas. The new formula is a whey-based product designed for infants allergic to standard milk-based and soy-based formulas. The company estimates that 15 to 20 percent of all infants are allergic to the protein in standard formulas. By contrast, the Pediatric Academy's Committee on Nutrition says that the number is closer to 1 to 2 percent. Nevertheless, Carnation has declared the product a medical breakthrough. Good Start is "hypoallergenic"—a claim made in bold type on the can. The company claims that the product can prevent or reduce fussiness, sleeplessness, colic, rash, and other problems. Pediatricians, however, caution that although the formula is easier to digest than common milk-based formulas, it should be used only under recommendation from the child's physician.

Although the U.S. has not adopted the WHO marketing code for infant formula, most U.S. manufacturers abide, at least in part, by the code. The U.S. infant formula business is governed largely by relationships between marketers and health professionals. Except for hospital giveaway programs, Abbott and Bristol-Myers market their infant formula products mainly to physicians. Neither company promotes directly to consumers. Consequently, there is little consumer brand loyalty in the infant formula market. In addition, because pediatricians tell mothers what to buy, infant formula products are largely price-insensitive.

Observers expect Carnation to break from industry tradition by promoting Good Start directly to new mothers by using mass-media advertising. Carnation is certain to take advantage of its long association with such milk products as Evaporated Milk. The company is expected to spend from $50 to $100 million with its first entry in the infant formula market.

Some leading pediatricians, however, suggest that Nestlé's marketing is misleading—Good Start may not be mild enough for the small number of babies severely allergic to cow's milk. The danger, pediatricians argue, is that direct marketing to consumers may attract mothers of these high milk-allergic babies. These mothers would thus unknowingly expose their babies to a dangerous formula without physician supervision. Consumer groups, meanwhile, watch the situation carefully. A new citizen-action movement may renew criticisms of Nestlé's marketing practices.

## Questions

1. Think through the traditional buyers' and sellers' rights listed in Chapter 20. Which rights were violated in the Third-World infant formula situation? Which rights were violated in the Beech-Nut apple juice situation? Does Carnation have the right to promote Good Start infant formula in whatever way it wants?

2. Will Nestlé be practicing socially responsible marketing with its Good Start product?

3. What marketing plan would you recommend for Good Start?

# Case 21

## CLUB MED: PUTTING TOGETHER THE TOTAL MARKETING STRATEGY

Choosing the site of a new Club Med village is often as simple as going with what feels right. Jacques Giraud, president of New York-based Club Med, Inc., remembers how the company picked Huatulco as a village site. In 1985, he was walking along a stretch of Mexican beach 300 miles south of Acapulco with a group that included Vice-Chairman Serge Trigano, the founder's son. Recalls Giraud: "Suddenly Serge stopped, took off his shoes, rolled up his pants, went into the water, and said, "I want it here.'"

The instincts of Club Med officials have usually served them well. But a couple of slip-ups and some events beyond their control made 1987 a difficult year for the company that offers "the antidote for civilization." Club Med, Inc., 72-percent owned by France's Club Méditerranée, was spun off as a separate public company in 1984 to operate the villages in North America and Asia, the two fastest-growing markets in the worldwide system. By mid-December, 1987, the U.S. company was running 27 resorts, including its first in Japan, on Hokkaido Island. But after two solidly profitable years, net income for the year ending October 31, 1987, declined 5 percent on revenues of $363 million. Even before the market crashed, its stock had fallen below the 52-week high of 29¼.

The trouble stemmed partly from consumer resistance to a 13-percent price hike in the winter of 1986. Currency exchange losses also hurt the bottom line. And political unrest and labor strife caused the temporary closing of resorts in Haiti and in the Turks and Caicos Islands—just when the popular Paradise Island village was shut down for renovations. By 1987, these events limited the company's offerings, driving some customers to take vacations elsewhere.

Those troubles were good news for Club Med's competitors—which are springing up all over. While resorts are the fastest-growing sector of the lodging industry, the business "has been somewhat besieged with an oversupply," says Gary B. Hedges, a resort specialist in the Phoenix office of Laventhol & Horwath, a leisure-time consulting firm. Hedges says 17 percent of the 23,900 lodging properties in the United States were classified as resorts as of 1987, up from 13 percent in 1985.

Some of those competitors are mimicking Club Med. In recent years, a string of imitators—with such names as Hedonism II and Club Paradise—have appeared on Caribbean islands. And some of the hotel industry's biggest names are getting into the business. Resorts International, Inc., for example, built Club Paradise as a separate, all-inclusive resort adjacent to its hotel on Paradise Island.

These operators try to duplicate the Club Med formula, which combines an idyllic setting, a friendly, well-organized staff, and a single price that covers a wide range of activities. "There's no question that the people who are filling up these resorts are the right demographics to go to Club Med," says Thomas J. Garzilli, vice president of Fly Fare Vacations, a New York travel wholesaler.

The increasing popularity of the $4 billion cruise industry is also cutting into Club Med's market. These days, cruise vacations are being designed to appeal to a younger, more active clientele. "Cruising was once the domain of the rich, and now the average has decreased. Cruising is open to everyone," says Robert H. Dickinson, senior vice president for sales and marketing at Carnival Cruise Lines, Inc.

But Club Med executives insist that their villages are still in a class by themselves. Typical guests—*gentils membres,* or GMs, in the company vernacular—are baby boomers earning a median income of $60,000. Contrary to Club Med's reputation for catering to sybaritic singles, half the guests are married. And half are repeat visitors. Observes Ernest Levenstein, leisure-time analyst for Tucker, Anthony & R. L. Day, Inc., "Their objective is to get people to try the club. Once they do, they come back."

In 1988, the company hoped to win more converts with new commercials created by Ammirati & Puris, Inc., the New York ad agency that had in 1982 dubbed Club Med "the antidote for civilization." One memorable commercial showed an overstressed businessman evolving into a relaxed human being in a week's time. Despite the success of that campaign, Club Med switched agencies and ad strategies in 1985.

The new agency, N. W. Ayer, Inc., used more of a direct-sell campaign, emphasizing the value of the one-price-for-everything Club Med vacation. It didn't work. "We can't advertise on price because we're more expensive than other resorts," says Giraud. "The Ayer ads had nice atmosphere, nice couples, but they didn't stand out as something different." So after much thought, Giraud went back to the agency he felt best understood the spirit of Club Med. A new Ammirati & Puris spot reports the world news, Club Med-style. Oil spills along the coast, for example, translate into a woman applying suntan lotion.

Club Med is taking other steps to shore up marketing. It introduced a proprietary credit card with an interest rate tied to the prime, and it is giving better financial incentives to the most productive travel agents. More villages are offering family amenities such as "baby clubs," which provide child care for infants as young as six months. And for the 1989 Christmas season, the company went head-to-head with the cruise lines by launching a

218-cabin sailing vessel to operate primarily in the Caribbean.

Club Med is also making greater efforts to fill its facilities during off-peak times. "We're satisfied with the winter and not with the summer," says Gilbert Trigano, chairman and founder of 33-year-old Club Méditerranée, which derives 25 percent of its revenues and profits from the U.S. company. With the weak U.S. dollar, Club Med successfully marketed its new Sandpiper village in Port St. Lucie, Fla., to French visitors in the summer—not a big season for American tourists to visit Florida. While most Club Med resorts require a week's stay, Sandpiper permits bookings by the day, attracting vacationers who have little time off. And the seven-year-old corporate program, which allows companies to rent a village during the off-season, has boomed, with 1986 sales of $1.2 million swelling to $7.2 million in 1987.

In the meantime, Club Med is expanding steadily. Now that Sandpiper is up and running, the company will put United States developments in high gear, especially on the West Coast. Plans call for the opening of two new villages a year in the United States and Asia, with more deluxe accommodations than in the past. So it looks as if Club Med officials will be rolling up their trousers and wading through the surf on a lot more virgin beaches.

## Questions

1. How do you define Club Med's product?

2. Describe the competitive environment facing Club Med.

3. Assess the target-market options available to Club Med.

4. Develop a marketing strategy for the new "baby clubs" program. Be sure to discuss the target market, product positioning, and elements of the marketing mix.

*Source:* Adapted from "Now Club Med Wants an Antidote for Competition." Reprinted from November 2, 1987, issue of *Business Week* by special permission, copyright © 1987 by McGraw-Hill, Inc.

# *Appendix*
# **A**

# Marketing Arithmetic

One aspect of marketing not discussed within the text is marketing arithmetic. The calculation of sales, costs, and certain ratios is important for many marketing decisions. The purpose of this appendix is to describe three major areas of marketing arithmetic: the *operating statement, analytic ratios,* and *markups and markdowns.*

## OPERATING STATEMENT

The operating statement and the balance sheet are the two main financial statements used by companies. The **balance sheet** shows the assets, liabilities, and net worth of a company at a given time. The **operating statement** (also called **profit-and-loss statement** or **income statement**) is the more important of the two for marketing information. It shows company sales, cost of goods sold, and expenses during the time period. By comparing the operating statement from one time period to the next, a firm can spot favorable or unfavorable trends and take the appropriate action.

Table A1–1 shows the 1989 operating statement for Dale Parsons Men's Wear, a specialty store in the Midwest. This statement is for a retailer; the operating statement for a manufacturer would be somewhat different. Specifically, the section on purchases within the "cost of goods sold" area would be replaced by "cost of goods manufactured."

The outline of the operating statement follows a logical series of steps to arrive at the firm's $25,000 net profit figure:

| | |
|---|---|
| Net sales | $300,000 |
| Cost of goods sold | −175,000 |
| Gross margin | $125,000 |
| Expenses | −100,000 |
| Net profit | $ 25,000 |

We will not look at major parts of the operating statement separately.

The first part details the amount that Parsons received for the goods the firm sold during the year. The sales figures consist of three items: *gross sales, returns and allowances,* and *net sales.* **Gross sales** is the total amount charged to customers during the year for merchandise purchased in Parsons's store. As

**balance sheet** A financial statement that shows the assets, liabilities, and net worth of a company at a given time.

**operating statement** (also called **profit-and-loss statement** or **income statement**) A financial statement that shows company sales, cost of goods sold, and expenses during a given time period.

**gross sales** The total amount that a company charges customers during a given time period for merchandise purchased.

**cost of goods sold** The net cost to the company of all goods sold during a given time period.

TABLE A1–1   Operating Statement for Dale Parsons Men's Wear for the Year Ending December 31, 1989

| | | | |
|---|---:|---:|---:|
| Gross sales | | | $325,000 |
| Less: Sales returns and allowances | | | 25,000 |
| Net sales | | | $300,000 |
| Cost of goods sold | | | |
| Beginning inventory, January 1, at cost | | $ 60,000 | |
| Gross purchases | $165,000 | | |
| Less: Purchase discounts | 15,000 | | |
| Net purchases | $150,000 | | |
| Plus: Freight-in | 10,000 | | |
| Net cost of delivered purchases | | $160,000 | |
| Cost of goods available for sale | | $220,000 | |
| Less: Ending inventory, December 31, at cost | | $ 45,000 | |
| Cost of goods sold | | | $175,000 |
| Gross margin | | | $125,000 |
| Expenses | | | |
| Selling expenses | | | |
| Sales, salaries, and commissions | $ 40,000 | | |
| Advertising | 5,000 | | |
| Delivery | 5,000 | | |
| Total selling expenses | | $ 50,000 | |
| Administrative expenses | | | |
| Office salaries | $ 20,000 | | |
| Office supplies | 5,000 | | |
| Miscellaneous (outside consultant) | 5,000 | | |
| Total administrative expenses | | $ 30,000 | |
| General expenses | | | |
| Rent | $ 10,000 | | |
| Heat, light, telephone | 5,000 | | |
| Miscellaneous (insurance, depreciation) | 5,000 | | |
| Total general expenses | | $ 20,000 | |
| Total expenses | | | $100,000 |
| Net profit | | | $ 25,000 |

expected, some customers returned merchandise because of damage or a change of mind. If the customer gets a full refund or full credit on another purchase, we call this a *return*. Or the customer may decide to keep the item if Parsons will reduce the price; this is called an *allowance*. By subtracting returns and allowances from gross sales, we arrive at net sales—what Parsons earned in revenue from a year of selling merchandise:

| | |
|---|---:|
| Gross sales | $325,000 |
| Returns and allowances | −25,000 |
| Net sales | $300,000 |

The second major part of the operating statement calculates the amount of sales revenue Dale Parsons has left after paying the costs of the merchandise. We start with the inventory in the store at the beginning of the year. During the year, Parsons bought $165,000 worth of suits, slacks, shirts, ties, jeans, and other goods. Suppliers gave the store discounts totaling $15,000, so that net purchases were $150,000. Because the store is located away from regular shipping routes, Parsons had to pay an additional $10,000 to get the products delivered, giving the firm a net cost of $160,000. Adding the beginning inventory, the cost of goods available for sale amounted to $220,000. The $45,000 ending inventory of clothes in the store on December 31 is then subtracted to come up with the $175,000 **cost of goods sold.** Here again we have followed a logical series of steps to figure out the cost of goods sold:

| Amount Parsons started with (beginning inventory) | $ 60,000 |
|---|---|
| Net amount purchased | +150,000 |
| Any added costs to obtain these purchases | + 10,000 |
| Total cost of goods Parsons had available for sale during year | $220,000 |
| Amount Parsons had left over (ending inventory) | − 45,000 |
| Cost of goods actually sold | $175,000 |

The difference between what Parsons paid for the merchandise ($175,000) and what he sold it for ($300,000) is called the **gross margin** ($125,000).

In order to show the profit Parsons "cleared" at the end of the year, we must subtract from the gross margin the *expenses* incurred while doing business. *Selling expenses* included two sales employees, local newspaper and radio advertising, and the cost of delivering merchandise to customers after alterations. Selling expenses added up to $50,000 for the year. *Administrative expenses* included the salary for an office manager, office supplies such as stationery and business cards, and miscellaneous expenses including an administrative audit conducted by an outside consultant. Administrative expenses totaled $30,000 in 1989. Finally, the general expenses of rent, utilities, insurance, and depreciation came to $20,000. Total expenses were therefore $100,000 for the year. By subtracting expenses ($100,000) from the gross margin ($125,000), we arrive at the net profit of $25,000 for Dale Parsons Men's Wear during 1989.

**gross margin** The difference between net sales and the cost of goods sold.

**operating ratios** Ratios of selected operating statement items to net sales that allow marketers to compare the firm's performance in one year with that in previous years (or with industry standards and competitors in the same year).

# ANALYTIC RATIOS

The operating statement provides the figures needed to compute some key ratios. Typically these ratios are called **operating ratios**—the ratio of selected operating statement items to net sales. They let marketers compare the firm's performance in one year with that in previous years (or with industry standards and competitors in the same year). The most commonly used operating ratios are the *gross margin percentage,* the *net profit percentage,* the *operating expense percentage,* and the *returns and allowances percentage.*

Another useful ratio is the *stockturn rate* (also called *inventory-turnover rate*). The stockturn rate is the number of times an inventory turns over or is sold

| Ratio | | Formula | Computation From TABLE A1–1 | |
|---|---|---|---|---|
| Gross margin percentage | = | $\dfrac{\text{gross margin}}{\text{net sales}}$ | $= \dfrac{\$125,000}{\$300,000} =$ | 42% |
| Net profit percentage | = | $\dfrac{\text{net profit}}{\text{net sales}}$ | $= \dfrac{\$25,000}{\$300,000} =$ | 8% |
| Operating expense percentage | = | $\dfrac{\text{total expenses}}{\text{net sales}}$ | $= \dfrac{\$100,000}{\$300,000} =$ | 33% |
| Returns and allowances percentages | = | $\dfrac{\text{returns and allowances}}{\text{net sales}}$ | $= \dfrac{\$25,000}{\$300,000} =$ | 8% |

during a specified time period (often one year). It may be computed on a cost, selling, or unit price basis. Thus, the formula can be:

$$\text{Stockturn rate} = \frac{\text{cost of goods sold}}{\text{average inventory at cost}}$$

or

$$\text{Stockturn rate} = \frac{\text{selling price of goods sold}}{\text{average selling price of inventory}}$$

or

$$\text{Stockturn rate} = \frac{\text{sales in units}}{\text{average inventory in units}}$$

We will use the first formula to calculate the stockturn rate for Dale Parsons Men's Wear:

$$\frac{\$175,000}{\dfrac{\$60,000 + \$45,000}{2}} = \frac{\$175,000}{\$52,500} = 3.3$$

That is, Parson's inventory turned over 3.3 times in 1989. Normally, the higher the stockturn rate, the higher the management efficiency and company profitability.

**Return on investment (ROI)** is frequently used to measure managerial effectiveness. It uses figures from the firm's operating statement and balance sheet. A commonly used formula for computing ROI is:

$$\text{ROI} = \frac{\text{net profit}}{\text{sales}} \times \frac{\text{sales}}{\text{investment}}$$

You may have two questions about this formula: Why use a two-step process when ROI could be computed simply as net profit divided by investment? And what exactly is "investment"?

To answer these questions, let's look at how each component of the formula can affect the ROI. Suppose Dale Parsons Men's Wear has total investment of $150,000. Then we can compute ROI as follows:

$$\text{ROI} = \frac{\$25,000 \text{ (net profit)}}{\$300,000 \text{ (sales)}} \times \frac{\$300,000 \text{ (sales)}}{\$150,000 \text{ (investment)}}$$

$$8.3\% \qquad \times \qquad 2 \qquad = 16.6\%$$

Now suppose that Parsons had worked to increase its share of the market. The firm could have had the same ROI if sales doubled while dollar profit and investment stayed the same (accepting a lower profit ratio to get a higher turnover and market share):

$$\text{ROI} = \frac{\$25,000 \text{ (net profit)}}{\$600,000 \text{ (sales)}} \times \frac{\$600,000 \text{ (sales)}}{\$150,000 \text{ (investment)}}$$

$$4.16\% \qquad \times \qquad 4 \qquad = 16.6\%$$

Parsons might have increased its ROI by increasing net profit through more cost cutting and more efficient marketing:

$$\text{ROI} = \frac{\$50,000 \text{ (net profit)}}{\$300,000 \text{ (sales)}} \times \frac{\$300,000 \text{ (sales)}}{\$150,000 \text{ (investment)}}$$

$$16.6\% \qquad \times \qquad 2 \qquad = 33.2\%$$

Another way to increase ROI is to find some way to get the same levels of sales and profits while decreasing investment (perhaps by cutting the size of Parsons's average inventory):

$$\text{ROI} = \frac{\$25,000 \text{ (net profit)}}{\$300,000 \text{ (sales)}} \times \frac{\$300,000 \text{ (sales)}}{\$75,000 \text{ (investment)}}$$

$$8.3\% \quad \times \quad 4 \quad = 33.2\%$$

> **markup** The percentage of the cost or price of a product added to the cost in order to arrive at a selling price.

What is "investment" in the ROI formula? *Investment* is often defined as the total assets of the firm. But many analysts now use other measures of return to assess performance. These measures include *return on net assets (RONA)*, *return on stockholders' equity (ROE)*, or *return on assets managed (ROAM)*. Since investment is measured at a point in time, we usually compute ROI as the average investment between two time periods (Say, January 1 and December 31 of the same year). We can also compute ROI as an "internal rate of return" by using discounted cash flow analysis (see any finance textbook for more on this technique). The objective in using any of these measures is to figure out how well the company has been using its resources. As inflation, competitive pressures, and cost of capital increase, such measures become increasingly important indicators of marketing and company performance.

# MARKUPS AND MARKDOWNS

Retailers and wholesalers must understand the concepts of **markups** and *markdowns*. They must make a profit to stay in business, and the markup percentage affects profits. Markups and markdowns are expressed as percentages.

There are two different ways to compute markups—on *cost* or on *selling price:*

$$\text{Markup percentage on cost} = \frac{\text{dollar markup}}{\text{cost}}$$

$$\text{Markup percentage on selling price} = \frac{\text{dollar markup}}{\text{selling price}}$$

Dale Parsons must decide which formula to use. If Parsons bought shirts for $15 and wanted to mark them up $10, the markup percentage on cost would be $10/$15 = 66.7%. If Parsons based markup on selling price, the percentage would be $10/$25 = 40%. In figuring markup percentage, most retailers use the selling price rather than the cost.

Suppose Parsons knew the cost ($12) and desired markup on price (25%) for a man's tie and wanted to compute the selling price. The formula is:

$$\text{Selling price} = \text{cost} \div (1 - \text{markup})$$
$$\text{Selling price} = \$12 \div .75 = \$16$$

As a product moves through the channel of distribution, each channel member adds a markup before selling the product to the next member. This "markup chain" is shown for a suit purchased by a Parsons customer for $200:

|  |  | *$ Amount* | *% of Selling Price* |
|---|---|---|---|
| Manufacturer | Cost | $108 | 90% |
|  | Markup | 12 | 10% |
|  | Selling price | $120 | 100% |
| Wholesaler | Cost | $120 | 80% |
|  | Markup | 30 | 20% |
|  | Selling price | $150 | 100% |
| Retailer | Cost | $150 | 75% |
|  | Markup | 50 | 25% |
|  | Selling price | $200 | 100% |

The retailer whose markup is 25 percent does not necessarily enjoy more profit than a manufacturer whose markup is 10 percent. Profit also depends on how many items with that profit margin can be sold (stockturn rate) and on operating efficiency (expenses).

Sometimes a retailer wants to convert markups based on selling price to markups based on cost, and vice versa. The formulas are:

$$\text{Markup percentage on selling price} = \frac{\text{markup percentage on cost}}{100\% + \text{markup percentage on cost}}$$

$$\text{Markup percentage on cost} = \frac{\text{markup percentage on selling price}}{100\% - \text{markup percentage on selling price}}$$

Suppose that Dale Parsons found that a competitor was using a markup of 30 percent based on cost and wanted to know what this would be as a percentage of selling price. The calculation would be:

$$\frac{30\%}{100\% + 30\%} = \frac{30\%}{130\%} = 23\%$$

Since Parsons was using a 25 percent markup on the selling price for suits, he felt that the markup was suitable compared with that of the competitor.

Near the end of the summer Parsons still had an inventory of summer slacks in stock. Thus, he decided to use a *markdown,* a reduction from the original selling price. Before the summer he had purchased 20 pairs at $10 each and had since sold 10 pairs at $20 each. Parsons marked down the other pairs to $15 and sold 5 pairs. We compute the *markdown ratio* as follows:

$$\text{Markdown percentage} = \frac{\text{dollar markdown}}{\text{total net sales in dollars}}$$

The dollar markdown is $25 (5 pairs at $5 each) and total net sales are $275 (10 pairs at $20 + 5 pairs at $15). The ratio, then, is $25/$275 = 9%.

Larger retailers usually compute markdown ratios for each department rather than for individual items. The ratios provide a measure of relative marketing performance for each department and can be calculated and compared over time. Markdown ratios can also be used to compare the performance of different buyers and salespeople in a store's various departments.

# *Appendix*
# *B*

# Careers in Marketing

Now that you have completed your first course in marketing, you have a good idea of what the field entails. You may have decided that you want to pursue a marketing career because it offers constant challenge, stimulating problems, the opportunity to work with people, and excellent advancement opportunities. Marketing is a very broad field with a wide variety of tasks involving the analysis, planning, implementation, and control of marketing programs. You will find marketing positions in all types and sizes of institutions. This appendix will acquaint you with entry-level and higher-level marketing opportunities and list steps that you might take to select a career path and better market yourself.

## DESCRIPTION OF MARKETING JOBS

Almost a third of all Americans are employed in marketing-related positions. Thus, the number of possible marketing careers is enormous. Because of the knowledge of products and consumers gained in these jobs, marketing positions provide excellent training for the highest levels in an organization. A recent study by one executive recruiting firm found that more top executives have come out of marketing than any other field—31 percent of the *Fortune* 1000 chief executives spent the bulk of their careers in marketing.[1]

Marketing salaries vary by company and position. Starting marketing salaries usually rank only slightly below those for engineering and chemistry but equal or exceed those for economics, finance, accounting, general business, and the liberal arts. If you succeed in an entry-level marketing position, you will quickly be promoted to higher levels of responsibility and salary.

Marketing has become an attractive career for some people who have not traditionally considered the field. One trend is the growing number of women entering the marketing field. Women have historically been employed in the retailing and advertising areas of marketing. But they have now moved into all types of sales and marketing positions. Women now pursue successful sales careers in pharmaceutical companies, publishing companies, banks, consumer products companies, and an increasing number of industrial selling jobs. Their ranks are also growing in product and brand manager positions.

---

[1] See E. S. Ely, "Room at the Top: American Companies Turn to Marketers to Lead Them through the Eighties," *Madison Avenue*, September 1984, p. 57.

Another trend is the growing acceptance of marketing by nonprofit organizations. Colleges, arts organizations, libraries, and hospitals are increasingly applying marketing to their problems. They are beginning to hire marketing directors and marketing vice-presidents to manage their varied marketing activities.

Here are brief descriptions of some important marketing jobs.

## Advertising

Advertising is an important business activity that requires skill in planning, fact gathering, and creativity. Although compensation for starting advertising people tends to be lower than that in other marketing fields, opportunities for advancement are usually greater because of less emphasis on age or length of employment. Typical jobs in advertising agencies are described below.[2]

*Copywriters* help find the concepts behind the written words and visual images of advertisements. They dig for facts, read avidly, and borrow ideas. They talk to customers, suppliers, and *anybody* who might give them clues about how to attract the target audience's attention and interest.

*Art directors* constitute the other part of the creative team. They translate copywriters' ideas into dramatic visuals called "layouts." Agency artists develop print layouts, package designs, television layouts (called "storyboards"), corporate logotypes, trademarks, and symbols. They specify the style and size of typography, paste the type in place, and arrange all the details of the ad so that it can be reproduced by engravers and printers. A superior art director or copy chief becomes the agency's creative director and oversees all its advertising. The creative director is high in the ad agency's structure.

*Account executives* are liaisons between clients and agencies. They must know a lot about marketing and its various components. They explain client plans and objectives to agency creative teams and supervise the development of the total advertising plan. Their main task is to keep the client happy with the agency! Because "account work" involves many personal relationships, account executives are usually personable, diplomatic, and sincere.

*Media buyers* select the best media for clients. Media representatives come to buyers' offices armed with statistics to prove that *their* numbers are better, *their* costs per thousand are less, and *their* medium delivers more ripe audiences than competitive media. Media buyers also have to evaluate these claims. In addition, they must bargain with the broadcast media for best rates and make deals with the print media for good ad positions.

Large ad agencies have active marketing research departments that provide the information needed to develop new ad campaigns and assess current campaigns. People interested in marketing research should consider jobs with ad agencies.

## Brand and Product Management

Brand and product managers plan, direct, and control business and marketing efforts for their products. They are concerned with research and development, packaging, manufacturing, sales and distribution, advertising, promotion, market research, and business analysis and forecasting. In consumer goods companies, the newcomer—who usually needs a Master of Business Administration (MBA) degree—joins a brand team and learns the ropes by doing numerical analyses and watching senior brand people. This person eventually heads a team and later moves on to manage a larger brand. Many industrial goods companies

---

[2]This description of advertising positions is based on Jack Engel, *Advertising: The Process and Practice* (New York: McGraw-Hill, 1980), pp.429–34.

also have product managers. Product management is one of the best training grounds for future corporate officers.

## Customer Affairs

Some large consumer goods companies have customer affairs people who act as liaisons between customers and firms. They handle complaints, suggestions, and problems concerning the company's products, determine what actions to take, and coordinate the activities required to solve problems. The position requires an empathetic, diplomatic, and capable person who can work with a wide range of people both inside and outside a firm.

## Industrial Marketing

People interested in industrial marketing careers can go into sales, service, product design, marketing research, or one of several other positions. They sometimes need a technical background. Most people start in sales and spend time in training and making calls with senior salespeople. If they stay in sales, they may advance to district, regional, and higher sales positions. Or they may go into product management and work closely with customers, suppliers, manufacturing, and sales engineering.

## International Marketing

As U.S. firms increase their international business, they need people who are familiar with foreign languages and cultures and who are willing to travel to or relocate in foreign cities. For such assignments, most companies seek experienced people who have proved themselves in domestic operations. An MBA often helps but is not always required.

## Marketing Management Science and Systems Analysis

People who have been trained in management science, quantitative methods, and systems analysis can act as consultants to managers facing such difficult marketing problems as demand measurement and forecasting, market structure analysis, and new-product evaluation. Career opportunities exist mostly in larger marketing-oriented firms, management consulting firms, and public institutions concerned with health, education, or transportation. An MBA or a Master of Science (MS) degree is often required.

## Marketing Research

Marketing researchers interact with managers to define problems and identify the information needed to resolve them. They design research projects, prepare questionnaires and samples, analyze data, prepare reports, and present their findings and recommendations to management. They must understand statistics, consumer behavior, psychology, and sociology. A master's degree helps. Career opportunities exist with manufacturers, retailers, some wholesalers, trade and industry associations, marketing research firms, advertising agencies, and governmental and private nonprofit agencies.

## New-Product Planning

People interested in new-product planning can find opportunities in many types of organizations. They usually need a good background in marketing, marketing research, and sales forecasting; they need organizational skills to motivate and coordinate others, and they may need a technical background. Usually, these people work first in other marketing positions before joining the new-product department.

## Physical Distribution

Physical distribution is a large and dynamic field, with many career opportunities. Major transportation carriers, manufacturers, wholesalers, and retailers all employ physical-distribution specialists. Coursework in quantitative methods, finance, accounting, and marketing will provide students with the necessary skills for entering the field.

## Public Relations

Most organizations have a public relations person or staff to anticipate public problems, handle complaints, deal with media, and build the corporate image. People interested in public relations should be able to speak and write clearly and persuasively, and they should preferably have a background in journalism, communications, or the liberal arts. The challenges in this job are highly varied and very people-oriented.

## Purchasing

Purchasing agents are playing a growing role in firms' profitability during periods of rising costs, materials shortages, and increasing product complexity. In retail organizations, working as a "buyer" can be a good route to the top. Purchasing agents in industrial companies play a key role in holding down costs. A technical background is useful in some purchasing positions, along with a knowledge of credit, finance, and physical distribution.

## Retailing Management

Retailing provides people with an early opportunity to take on marketing responsibilities. Although retail starting salaries and job assignments have typically been lower than those in manufacturing or advertising, the gap is narrowing. The major routes to top management in retailing are merchandise management and store management. In merchandise management, a person moves from buyer trainee to assistant buyer to buyer to merchandise division manager. In store management, an individual moves from management trainee to assistant department (sales) manager to department manager to store (branch) manager. Buyers are primarily concerned with merchandise selection and promotion; department managers are concerned with salesforce management and display. Large-scale retailing lets new recruits move in only a few years into the management of a branch or part of a store doing as much as $5 million in sales.

## Sales and Sales Management

Sales and sales-management opportunities exist in a wide range of profit and nonprofit organizations and in product and service organizations, including financial, insurance, consulting, and government. Individuals must carefully match their backgrounds, interests, technical skills, and academic training with available sales jobs. Training programs vary greatly in form and length, ranging from a few weeks to two years. Career paths lead from salesperson to district, regional, and higher levels of sales management and, in many cases, the top management of a firm.

## Other Marketing Careers

There are many other marketing-related jobs in areas such as sales promotion, wholesaling, packaging, pricing, and credit management. Information on these positions can be gathered from sources like those listed below.

# CHOOSING AND GETTING A JOB

To choose and obtain a job, you must apply marketing skills, particularly marketing analysis and planning. Here are eight steps for choosing a career and finding that first job.

## Make a Self-Assessment

Self-assessment is the most important part of a job search. It involves honestly evaluating your interests, strengths, and weaknesses. What are your career objectives? What kind of organization do you want to work for? What do you do well or not so well? What sets you apart from other job seekers? Do the answers to these questions suggest which careers you should seek or avoid? For help in self-assessment, you might look at the following books, each of which raises many questions you should consider:

1. *What Color Is Your Parachute?*, by Richard Bolles
2. *Three Boxes in Life and How to Get Out of Them*, by Richard Bolles
3. *Guerrilla Tactics in the Job Market*, by Tom Jackson

Also consult the career counseling, testing, and placement services at your school.

## Examine Job Descriptions

Now look at various job descriptions to see what positions best match your interests, desires, and abilities. Descriptions can be found in the *Occupation Outlook Handbook* and the *Dictionary of Occupational Titles* published by the U.S. Department of Labor. These volumes describe what people in various occupations do, the specific training and education needed, the availability of jobs in each field, possibilities for advancement, and probable earnings.

## Develop Job-Search Objectives

Your initial career shopping list should be broad and flexible. Look broadly for ways to achieve your objectives. For example, if you want a career in marketing research, consider the public as well as the private sector and regional as well as national firms. Only after exploring many options should you begin to focus on specific industries and initial jobs. You need to set down a list of basic goals. Your list might say: "a job in a small company, in a large city, in the Sunbelt, doing marketing research, with a consumer products firm."

## Examine the Job Market and Assess Opportunities

You must now look at the market to see what positions are available. For an up-to-date listing of marketing-related job openings, refer to the latest edition of the *College Placement Annual* available at school placement offices. This publication lists current job openings for hundreds of companies seeking college graduates for entry-level positions. It also lists companies seeking experienced or advanced-degree people. At this stage, use the services of your placement office to the fullest extent in order to find openings and set up interviews. Take the time to analyze the industries and companies in which you are interested. Consult business magazines, annual reports, business reference books, faculty members, school career counselors, and fellow students. Try to analyze the future growth and profit potential of the company and industry, chances for advancement, salary levels, entry positions, amount of travel, and other important factors.

## Develop Search Strategies

How will you contact companies in which you are interested? There are several possible ways. One of the best ways is through on-campus interviews. But not all the companies that interest you will visit your school. Another good way is to phone or write the company directly. Finally, you can ask marketing professors or school alumni for contacts and references.

## Develop Résumé and Cover Letter

Your résumé should persuasively present your abilities, education, background, training, work experience, and personal qualifications—but it should also be brief, usually one page. The goal is to gain a positive response from potential employers.

The cover letter is, in some ways, more difficult to write than the résumé. It must be persuasive, professional, concise, and interesting. Ideally, it should set you apart from other candidates for the position. Each letter should look and sound original—that is, it should be individually typed and tailored to the specific organization being contacted. It should describe the position you are applying for, arouse interest, describe your qualifications, and tell how you can be contacted. Cover letters should be addressed to an individual rather than a title. You should follow up the letter with a telephone call.

## Obtain Interviews

Here is some advice to follow before, during, and after your interviews.

### Before the Interview

1. Interviewers have extremely diverse styles—the "chit chat," let's-get-to-know-each-other style; the interrogation style of question after question; the tough-probing why, why, why style; and many others. Be ready for anything.
2. Practice being interviewed with a friend and ask for a critique.
3. Prepare to ask at least five good questions that are not readily answered in the company literature.

4. Anticipate possible interview questions and prepare good answers ahead of time.

5. Avoid back-to-back interviews—they can be exhausting.

6. Dress conservatively and tastefully for the interview. Be neat and clean.

7. Arrive about ten minutes early to collect your thoughts before the interview. Check your name on the interview schedule, noting the name of the interviewer and the room number.

8. Review the major points you intend to cover.

## During the Interview

1. Give a firm handshake in greeting the interviewer. Introduce yourself using the same form the interviewer uses. Make a good initial impression.

2. Retain your poise. Relax. Smile occasionally. Be enthusiastic throughout the interview.

3. Good eye contact, good posture, and distinct speech are musts. Don't clasp your hands or fiddle with jewelry, hair, or clothing. Sit comfortably in your chair. Do not smoke, even if asked.

4. Have extra copies of your résumé with you.

5. Have your story down pat. Present your selling points. Answer questions directly. Avoid one-word answers but don't be wordy.

6. Most times, let the interviewer take the initiative, but don't be passive. Find good opportunities to direct the conversation to things you want the interviewer to hear.

7. To end on a high note, the latter part of the interview is the best time to make your most important point or to ask pertinent questions.

8. Don't be afraid to "close." You might say, "I'm very interested in the position and I have enjoyed this interview."

## After the Interview

1. After leaving the interview, record the key points that arose. Be sure to record who is to follow up on the interview and when a decision can be expected.

2. Objectively analyze the interview with regard to questions asked, answers given, your overall interview presentation, and the interviewer's response to specific points.

3. Send a thank-you letter mentioning any additional items pertinent to your application and your willingness to supply further information.

4. If you do not hear within the time specified, write or call the interviewer to determine your status.

## *Follow-Up*

If you are successful, you will be invited to visit the organization. The in-company interview will run from a few hours to a whole day. The company will examine your interest, maturity, enthusiasm, assertiveness, logic, and company and functional knowledge. You should ask questions about things that are important to you. Find out about the environment, job role, responsibilities, opportunity, current industrial issues, and the firm's personality. The company wants to know if you are the right person for the job; just as importantly, you want to know if this is the right job for you.

# Glossary

**Accessibility** The degree to which a market segment can be reached and served.

**Actionability** The degree to which effective programs can be designed for attracting and serving a given market segment.

**Action program** A detailed program that shows what must be done, who will do it, and how decisions and actions will be coordinated to implement marketing plans and strategy.

**Actual product** A product's parts, styling, features, brand name, packaging, and other attributes that combine to deliver core product benefits.

**Administered VMS** A vertical marketing system that coordinates successive stages of production and distribution, not through common ownership or contractual ties but through the size and power of one of the parties.

**Adoption** The decision by an individual to become a regular user of a product.

**Adoption process** The mental process through which an individual passes from first hearing about an innovation to final adoption.

**Advertising** Any paid form of nonpersonal presentation and promotion of ideas, goods, or services by an identified sponsor.

**Advertising objective** A specific communication *task* to be accomplished with a specific *target* audience during a specific period of *time*.

**Affordable method** Setting the promotion budget at what management thinks the company can afford.

**Age and life-cycle segmentation** Dividing a market into different age and life-cycle groups.

**Agent** A wholesaler who represents buyers or sellers on a relatively permanent basis, performs only a few functions, and does not take title to goods.

**Allowance** Promotional money paid by manufacturers to retailers in return for an agreement to feature the manufacturer's products in some way.

**Annual plan** A short-range marketing plan that describes company objectives, the current marketing situation, the marketing strategy for the year, the action program, budgets, and controls.

**Annual plan control** Evaluation and corrective action to ensure that the company achieves the sales, profits, and other goals set out in its annual plan.

**Approach** The step in the selling process in which the salesperson meets and greets the buyer to get the relationship off to a good start.

**Aspirational group** A group to which the individual wishes to belong.

**Atmospheres** Designed environments that create or reinforce the buyer's leanings toward consumption of a product.

**Attitude** A person's consistently favorable or unfavorable evaluations, feelings, and tendencies toward an object or idea.

**Augmented product** Additional consumer services and benefits built around the core and actual products.

**Automatic vending** Selling through vending machines.

**Baby boom** The major increase in the annual birthrate following World War II and lasting until the early 1960s.

**Balance sheet** A financial statement that shows the assets, liabilities, and net worth of a company at a given time.

**Barter transaction** A marketing transaction in which goods or services are traded for other goods or services.

**Basing-point pricing** A geographic pricing strategy in which the seller designates a given city as a basing point and charges all customers the freight cost from that city to the customer location, regardless of the city from which the goods are actually shipped.

**Behavior segmentation** Dividing a market into groups based on their knowledge, attitudes, uses, or responses to a product.

**Belief** A descriptive thought that a person has about something.

**Benefit segmentation** Dividing the market into groups according to the different benefits that consumers seek from the product.

**Brand** A name, term, sign, symbol, or design—or a combination of these—intended to identify the goods or services of one seller or group of sellers and to differentiate them from those of competitors.

**Brand-extension strategy** A strategy under which a new or modified product is launched under an already successful brand name.

**Brand image** The set of beliefs consumers hold about a particular brand.

**Brand mark** That part of a brand that can be recognized but is not utterable, such as a symbol, design, or distinctive coloring or lettering; examples are the Pillsbury doughboy, the Metro-Goldwyn-Mayer lion, and the red K on the Kodak film box.

**Brand name** That part of a brand that can be vocalized—the utterable, such as Avon, Chevrolet, Tide, Disneyland, American Express, and UCLA.

**Breakeven pricing** Setting price to break even on the costs of making and marketing a product.

**Broker** A wholesaler who does not take title to goods and whose function is to bring buyers and sellers together and assist in negotiation.

**Business analysis** A review of the sales, costs, and profit projections for a new product to find out whether these factors satisfy the company's objectives.

**Business portfolio** The collection of businesses and products that make up the company.

**Buyer-readiness states** The stages consumers normally pass through on their way to purchase, including awareness, knowledge, liking, preference, conviction, and purchase.

**Buying center** All the individuals and units that participate in the organizational buying-decision process.

**By-product pricing** Setting a price for by-products in order to make the main product's price more competitive.

**Capital items** Industrial goods that enter the finished product partly, including installations and accessory equipment.

**Captive-product pricing** The pricing of products that must be used along with a main product, such as blades for razors and film for cameras.

**Cash cows** Low-growth, high-share businesses or products—established and successful units which generate cash that the company uses to pay its bills and which support other business units that need investment.

**Cash discount** A price reduction to buyers who pay their bills promptly.

**Cash refund offers (or rebates)** Offers to refund part of the purchase price of a product after the purchase to consumers who send a "proof of purchase" to the manufacturer.

**Catalog marketing** Selling through catalogs mailed to a select list of customers or made available in stores.

**Catalog showroom** A retail operation that sells a wide selection of high-markup, fast-moving, brand-name goods at discount prices.

**Causal research** Marketing research to test hypotheses about cause-and-effect relationships.

**Chain stores** Two or more outlets that are commonly owned and controlled, have central buying and merchandising, and sell similar lines of merchandise.

**Channel conflict** Disagreement among marketing channel members on goals and roles—on who should do what and for what rewards.

**Channel level** A layer of middlemen who perform some work in bringing the product and its ownership closer to the final buyer.

**Closing** The step in the selling process in which the salesperson asks the customer for an order.

**Cognitive dissonance** Postpurchase consumer discomfort caused by after-purchase conflict; consumers feel uneasy about acquiring the drawbacks of the purchased brand and about losing the benefits of the brands not purchased.

**Combination stores** Combined food and drug stores.

**Commercialization** Introducing a new product into the market.

**Company culture** A system of values and beliefs shared by people in an organization—the company's collective identity and meaning.

**Company marketing opportunity** An attractive arena for marketing action in which the company would enjoy a competitive advantage.

**Comparison advertising** Advertising that compares one brand directly or indirectly with one or more other brands.

**Competitive advantage** An advantage over competitors gained by offering consumers lower prices than competitors or by providing more benefits that justify higher prices.

**Competitive-parity method** Setting the promotion budget to match competitors' outlays.

**Concentrated marketing** A market-coverage strategy in which a firm goes after a large share of one or a few submarkets.

**Concept testing** Testing new-product concepts with a group of target consumers to find out if the concepts have strong consumer appeal.

**Consumer buying behavior** The buying behavior of final consumers—individuals and households who buy goods and services for personal consumption.

**Consumer cooperative** A retail firm that is owned by its customers.

**Consumer franchise-building promotions** Sales promotions that promote the product's positioning and include a selling message along with the deal.

**Consumer goods** Those bought by final consumers for personal consumption.

**Consumerism** An organized movement of citizens and government to strengthen the rights and power of buyers in relation to sellers.

**Consumer market** The set of all final consumers—individuals and households who buy goods and services for personal consumption.

**Consumer-oriented marketing** A principle of enlightened marketing holding that a company should view and organize its marketing activities from the consumers' point of view.

**Consumer promotion** Sales promotion designed to stimulate consumer purchasing, including samples, coupons, rebates, prices-off, premiums, patronage rewards, displays, and contests and sweepstakes.

**Containerization** Putting the goods in boxes or trailers that are easy to transfer between two transportation modes; they are used in "multimode" systems commonly referred to as piggyback, fishyback, trainship, and airtruck.

**Contests, sweepstakes,** and **games** Promotional events that give consumers the chance to win something—such as cash, trips, or goods —by luck or through extra effort.

**Continuity** Scheduling ads evenly within a given period.

**Contract manufacturing** Joint venturing to enter a foreign market by a contracting with manufacturers in the foreign market to produce a product.

**Contractual VMS** A vertical marketing system in which independent firms at different levels of production and distribution join together through contracts to obtain more economies or sales impact than they could achieve alone.

**Convenience goods** Consumer goods that a customer usually buys frequently, immediately, and with a minimum of comparison and buying effort.

**Convenience store** A small store located near a residential area, open long hours seven days a week, and carrying a limited line of high-turnover convenience goods.

**Conventional distribution channel** A channel consisting of one or more independent producers, wholesalers, and retailers, each a separate business seeking to maximize its own profits even at the expense of profits for the system as a whole.

**Copyright** The exclusive legal right to reproduce, publish, and sell the matter and form of a literary, musical, or artistic work.

**Copy testing** Measuring the communication effect of an advertisement before or after it is printed or broadcast.

**Core product** The problem-solving services or core benefits that consumers are really buying when they obtain a product.

**Corporate VMS** A vertical marketing system that combines successive stages of production and distribution under single ownership; channel leadership is established through common ownership.

**Cost of goods sold** The net cost to the company of all goods sold during a given time period.

**Cost-plus pricing** Adding a standard markup to the cost of the product.

**Countertrade** International trade involving the direct or indirect exchange of goods for other goods instead of cash; forms include barter, compensation (buyback), and counterpurchase.

**Coupons** Certificates that give buyers savings when they purchase specified products.

**Cultural environment** Institutions and other forces that affect society's basic values, perceptions, preferences, and behaviors.

**Culture** The set of basic values, perceptions, wants, and behaviors learned by members of society from family and other important institutions.

**Current marketing situation** The section of a marketing plan that describes the target market and the company's position in it.

**Customer-attitude tracking** Tracking the attitudes of customers, dealers, and other marketing system participants and their effects on sales.

**Customer salesforce structure** A salesforce organization under which salespeople specialize in selling only to certain customers or industries.

**Customized marketing mix** An international marketing strategy for adjusting the marketing mix elements to each international target market, bearing more costs but hoping for a larger market share and return.

**Decision and reward systems** Formal and informal operating procedures that guide such activities as planning, information gathering, budgeting, recruiting and training, control, and personnel and rewards.

**Decline stage** The product life-cycle stage at which a product's sales decline.

**Deficient products** Products that have neither immediate appeal nor long-run benefits.

**Demand curve** A curve showing the number of units the market will buy in a given time period at different prices that might be charged.

**Demands** Human wants that are backed by buying power.

**Demarketing** Marketing in which the task is to reduce demand either temporarily or permanently.

**Demographic segmentation** Dividing the market into groups based on demographic variables such as age, sex, family size, family life cycle, income, occupation, education, religion, race, and nationality.

**Demography** The study of human populations in terms of size, density, location, age, sex, race, occupation, and other statistics.

**Department store** A retail organization that carries a wide variety of product lines—typically, clothing, home furnishings, and household goods; each line is operated as a separate department managed by specialist buyers or merchandisers.

**Derived demand** Organizational demand that ultimately comes from (derives from) the demand for consumer goods.

**Descriptive research** Marketing research to better describe marketing problems, situations, or markets—such as the market potential for a product or the demographics and attitudes of consumers.

**Desirable products** Products that give both high immediate satisfaction and high long-run benefits.

**Differentiated marketing** A market-coverage strategy in which a firm decides to target several market segments and designs separate offers for each.

**Direct investment** Entering a foreign market by developing foreign-based assembly or manufacturing facilities.

**Direct-mail marketing** Direct marketing through single mailings that include letters, ads, samples, foldouts, and other "salespeople on wings" sent to prospects on mailing lists.

**Direct marketing** Marketing through various advertising media that interact directly with consumers, generally calling for the consumer to make a direct response.

**Direct-marketing channel** A marketing channel that has no intermediary levels.

**Discount** A straight reduction in price on purchases during a stated period of time.

**Discount store** A retail institution that sells standard merchandise at lower prices by accepting lower margins and selling at higher volume.

**Discriminatory pricing** Selling a product or service at two or more prices even though the difference in prices is not based on differences in costs.

**Distribution center** A large and highly automated warehouse designed to receive goods from various plants and suppliers, take orders, fill them efficiently, and deliver goods to customers as quickly as possible.

**Distribution channel (marketing channel)** The set of firms and individuals that take title, or assist in transferring title, to a good or service as it moves from the producer to the consumer or industrial user.

**Distribution programming** Building a planned, professionally managed vertical marketing system that meets the needs of both the manufacturer and the distributors.

**Diversification** A strategy for company growth by starting up or acquiring businesses outside the company's current products and markets.

**Dogs** Low-growth, low-share businesses and products that may generate enough cash to maintain themselves but do not promise to be a large source of cash.

**Door-to-door retailing** Selling door-to-door, office-to-office, or at home-sales parties.

**Durable goods** Tangible goods that normally survive many uses.

**Economic community** A group of nations organized to work toward common goals in the regulation of international trade.

**Economic environment** Factors that affect consumer buying power and spending patterns.

**Embargo** A ban on the import of a certain product.

**Emotional appeals** Message appeals that attempt to stir up negative or positive emotions that will motivate purchase; examples include fear, guilt, shame, love, humor, pride, and joy appeals.

**Engel's laws** Differences noted over a century ago by Ernst Engel in how people shift their spending across food, housing, transportation, health care, and other goods and services categories as family income rises.

**Enlightened marketing** A marketing philosophy holding that a company's marketing should support the best long-run performance of the marketing system; its five principles include consumer-oriented marketing, innovative marketing, value marketing, sense-of-mission marketing, and societal marketing.

**Environmentalism** An organized movement of concerned citizens and government to protect and improve people's living environment and quality of life.

**Environmental management perspective** A management perspective in which the firm takes aggressive actions to affect the publics and forces in its marketing environment rather than simply watching and reacting to it.

**Events** Occurrences staged to communicate messages to target audiences, such as news conferences and grand openings.

**Exchange** The act of obtaining a desired object from someone by offering something in return.

**Exchange controls** Limits placed by a government on the amount of its foreign exchange with other countries and on its exchange rate against other currencies.

**Exclusive distribution** Giving a limited number of dealers the exclusive right to distribute a company's products in their territories.

**Executive summary** The opening section of the marketing plan, presenting a short summary of the main goals and recommendations to be presented in the plan.

**Expense-to-sales analysis** Analyzing the ratio of marketing expenses to sales in order to keep marketing expenses in line.

**Experimental research** The gathering of primary data by selecting matched groups of subjects, giving them different treatments, controlling related factors, and checking for differences in group responses.

**Exploratory research** Marketing research to gather preliminary information that will help to better define problems and suggest hypotheses.

**Exporting** Entering a foreign market by exporting products and selling them through international marketing middlemen (indirect exporting) or through the company's own department, branch, or sales representatives or agents (direct exporting).

**Factory outlets** Off-price retailing operations that are owned and operated by manufacturers and normally carry the manufacturer's surplus, discontinued, or irregular goods.

**Fads** Fashions that enter quickly, are adopted with great zeal, peak early, and decline very fast.

**Family life cycle** The stages through which families might pass as they mature over time.

**Fashion** A currently accepted or popular style in a given field.

**Financial intermediaries** Banks, credit companies, insurance companies, and other businesses that help finance transactions or insure against the risks associated with the buying and selling of goods.

**Fixed costs (overhead)** Costs that do not vary with production or sales level.

**FOB-origin pricing** A geographic pricing strategy in which goods are placed free on board (FOB) a carrier and the customer pays the freight from the factory to the destination.

**Focus-group interviewing** Personal interviewing that consists of inviting six to ten people to gather for a few hours with a trained interviewer to talk about a product, service, or organization; the interviewer "focuses" the group discussion on important issues.

**Follow-up** The step in the selling process in which the salesperson follows up after the sale to ensure customer satisfaction and repeat business.

**Forecasting** Predicting what consumers will do under a given set of circumstances.

**Franchise** A contractual association between a manufacturer, wholesaler, or service organization (a franchiser) and independent businesspeople (franchisees) who buy the right to own and operate one or more units in the franchise system.

**Franchise organization** A contractual vertical marketing system in which a channel member called a franchiser links several stages in the production-distribution process.

**Freight-absorption pricing** A geographic pricing strategy in which the company absorbs all or part of the actual freight charges in order to get desired business.

**Frequency** The number of times the average person in the target market is exposed to an advertising message during a given period.

**Full-service retailers** Retailers that assist customers in every phase of the shopping process and provide a wide variety of additional services.

**Full-service wholesalers** Wholesalers that provide a full set of services such as carrying stock, using a salesforce, offering credit, making deliveries, and providing management assistance.

**Functional discount** (or **trade discount**) A price reduction offered by the seller to trade channel members who perform certain functions such as selling, storing, and record keeping.

**Functional organization** An organization structure in which marketing specialists are in charge of different marketing activities or functions such as advertising, marketing research, and sales management.

**General need description** The stage in the industrial buying process in which the company describes the general characteristics and quantity of a needed item.

**Geographic organization** An organization structure in which a company's national salesforce (and perhaps other functions) specializes by geographic area.

**Geographic segmentation** Dividing a market into different geographical units such as nations, states, regions, counties, cities, or neighborhoods.

**Going-rate pricing** Setting price based largely on competitors' prices rather than on company costs or demand.

**Government market** Governmental units—federal, state, and local—that purchase or rent goods and services for carrying out the main functions of government.

**Gross margin** The difference between net sales and the cost of goods sold.

**Gross sales** The total amount that a company charges customers for merchandise purchased during a given time period.

**Growth-share matrix** A tool used in strategic planning to classify a company's strategic business units according to market-growth rate and market share.

**Growth stage** The product life-cycle stage at which a product's sales start climbing quickly.

**Handling objections** The step in the selling process in which the salesperson seeks out, clarifies, and overcomes customer objections to buying.

**Horizontal marketing systems** A channel arrangement in which two or more companies at one level join together to follow a new marketing opportunity.

**Human need** A state of felt deprivation.

**Human resources** The people with needed skills, motivation, and personal characteristics who fill out the organization structure.

**Human want** The form taken by a human need as it is shaped by culture and individual personality.

**Hypermarkets** Huge stores that combine supermarket, discount, and warehouse retailing; in addition to food, they carry furniture, appliances, clothing, and many other items.

**Idea generation** The systematic search for new-product ideas.

**Idea screening** Screening new-product ideas in order to spot good ideas and drop poor ones as soon as possible.

**Income segmentation** Dividing a market into different income groups.

**Industrial goods** Goods bought by individuals and organizations for further processing or for use in conducting a business.

**Industrial market** All the individuals and organizations acquiring goods and services that enter into the production of other products and services that are sold, rented, or supplied to others.

**Inelastic demand** Total demand for a product that is not much affected by price changes, especially in the short run.

**Informative advertising** Advertising used to inform consumers about a new product or feature and to build primary demand.

**Innovative marketing** A principle of enlightened marketing that requires a company to seek real product and marketing improvements.

**Intensive distribution** Stocking a product in as many outlets as possible.

**Interactive marketing** Marketing by a service firm which recognizes that perceived service quality depends heavily on the quality of buyer-seller interaction.

**Internal marketing** Marketing by a service firm to effectively train and motivate its customer-contact employees and all supporting service people to work as a team to provide customer satisfaction.

**Internal records information** Information gathered from sources within the company to evaluate marketing performance and to detect marketing problems and opportunities.

**Introduction stage** The product life-cycle stage when the new product is first distributed and made available for purchase.

**Joint ownership** Entering a foreign market by joining with foreign investors to create a local business in which the company shares joint ownership and control.

**Joint venturing** Entering foreign markets by joining with foreign companies to produce or market a product or service.

**Learning** Changes in an individual's behavior arising from experience.

**Licensing** A method of entering a foreign market in which the company enters into an agreement with a licensee in the foreign market, offering the right to use a manufacturing process, trademark, patent, trade secret, or other item of value for a fee or royalty.

**Life style** A person's pattern of living as expressed in his or her activities, interests, and opinions.

**Limited-service retailers** Retailers that provide limited sales assistance and additional services such as credit and merchandise return.

**Limited-service wholesalers** Wholesalers that offer only limited services to their suppliers and customers.

**Long-range plan** A marketing plan that describes the major factors and forces affecting the organization over the next several years. It includes long-term objectives, major marketing strategies, and resources required.

**Macroenvironment** The larger societal forces that affect the whole microenvironment—demographic, economic, natural, technological, political, and cultural forces.

**Management contracting** A joint venture in which the domestic firm supplies the management know-how to a foreign company that supplies the capital; the domestic firm exports management services rather than products.

**Managerial climate** The company climate resulting from the way managers work with others in the company.

**Manufacturer's brand** (or **national brand**) A brand created and owned by the producer of a product or service.

**Manufacturers' sales branches and offices** Wholesaling by sellers or buyers themselves rather than through independent wholesalers.

**Market** The set of all actual and potential buyers of a product.

**Market development** A strategy for company growth by identifying and developing new market segments for current company products.

**Marketing** A social and managerial process by which individuals and groups obtain what they need and want through creating and exchanging products and value with others.

**Marketing audit** A comprehensive, systematic, independent, and periodic examination of a company's environment, objectives, strategies, and activities to determine problem areas and opportunities and to recommend a plan of action to improve the company's marketing performance.

**Marketing budget** A section of the marketing plan that shows projected revenues, costs, and profits.

**Marketing concept** The marketing management philosophy that holds that achieving organizational goals depends on determining the needs and wants of target markets and delivering the desired satisfactions more effectively and efficiently than competitors.

**Marketing control** The process of measuring and evaluating the results of marketing strategies and plans, and taking corrective action to ensure that marketing objectives are attained.

**Marketing environment** The actors and forces outside marketing that affect marketing management's ability to develop and maintain successful transactions with its target customers.

**Marketing implementation** The process that turns marketing strategies and plans into marketing actions in order to accomplish strategic marketing objectives.

**Marketing information system (MIS)** People, equipment, and procedures to gather, sort, analyze, evaluate, and distribute needed, timely, and accurate information to marketing decision makers.

**Marketing intelligence** Everyday information about developments in the marketing environment that helps managers prepare and adjust marketing plans.

**Marketing intermediaries** Firms that help the company to promote, sell, and distribute its goods to final buyers; they include middlemen, physical distribution firms, marketing services agencies, and financial intermediaries.

**Marketing management** The analysis, planning, implementation, and control of programs designed to create, build, and maintain beneficial exchanges with target buyers for the purpose of achieving organizational objectives.

**Marketing mix** The set of controllable marketing variables that the firm blends to produce the response it wants in the target market.

**Marketing research** The function that links the consumer, customer, and public to the marketer through information—information used to identify and define marketing opportunities and problems; to generate, refine, and evalute marketing actions; to monitor marketing performance; and to improve understanding of the marketing process.

**Marketing services agencies** Marketing research firms, advertising agencies, media firms, marketing consulting firms, and other service providers that help a company to target and promote its products to the right markets.

**Marketing strategy** The marketing logic by which the business unit hopes to achieve its marketing objectives; marketing strategy consists of specific strategies for target markets, marketing mix, and marketing expenditure level.

**Marketing strategy development** Designing an initial marketing strategy for a new product based on the product concept.

**Marketing strategy statement** A statement of the planned strategy for a new product that outlines the intended target market, the planned product positioning, and the sales, market share, and profit goals for the first few years.

**Market management organization** An organization structure in which market managers are responsible for developing plans for sales and profits in their specific markets.

**Market penetration** A strategy for company growth by increasing sales of current products to current market segments without changing the product in any way.

**Market-penetration pricing** Setting a low price for a new product in order to attract a large number of buyers and a large market share.

**Market positioning** Arranging for a product to occupy a clear, distinctive, and desirable place relative to competing products in the minds of target consumers; formulating competitive positioning for a product and a detailed marketing mix.

**Market segment** A group of consumers who respond in a similar way to a given set of marketing stimuli.

**Market segmentation** The process of classifying customers into groups with different needs, characteristics, or behaviors; dividing a market into distinct groups of buyers who might require separate products or marketing mixes.

**Market-share analysis** Analysis and tracking of the company's market share.

**Market-skimming pricing** Setting a high price for a new product to skim maximum revenue from the segments willing to pay the high price; the company makes fewer but more profitable sales.

**Market targeting** The process of evaluating each market segment's attractiveness and selecting one or more segments to enter.

**Markup** The percentage of the cost or price of a product added to the cost in order to arrive at a selling price.

**Mass and selective media** Print media (newspapers, magazines, direct mail), broadcast media (radio, television), and display media (billboards, signs, posters) aimed at large, unsegmented audiences (mass media) or at selected audiences (selective media).

**Materials and parts** Industrial goods that enter the manufacturer's product completely, including raw materials and manufactured materials and parts.

**Maturity stage** The stage in the product life cycle at which sales growth slows or levels off.

**Measurability** The degree to which the size and purchasing power of a market segment can be measured.

**Media impact** The qualitative value of an exposure through a given medium.

**Media vehicles** Specific media within each general media type, such as specific magazines, television shows, or radio programs.

**Membership groups** Groups that have a direct influence on a person's behavior and to which a person belongs.

**Merchandising conglomerates** Corporations that combine several different retailing forms under central ownership and share some distribution and management functions.

**Merchant wholesaler** An independently owned business that takes title to the merchandise it handles.

**Microenvironment** The forces close to the company that affect its ability to serve its customers—the company, market channel firms, customer markets, competitors, and publics.

**Middlemen** Distribution channel firms that help the company find customers or make sales to them.

**Mission statement** A statement of the organization's purpose—of what it wants to accomplish in the larger environment.

**Modified rebuy** An industrial buying situation in which the buyer wants to modify product specifications, prices, terms, or suppliers.

**Monetary transaction** A marketing transaction in which goods or services are exchanged for money.

**Monopolistic competition** A market in which many buyers and sellers trade over a range of prices rather than a single market price.

**Moral appeals** Message appeals that are directed to the audience's sense of what is right and proper.

**Motive (or drive)** A need that is sufficiently pressing to direct the person to seek satisfaction of the need.

**Multibrand strategy** A strategy under which a seller develops two or more brands in the same product category.

**Multimarketing** Multichannel distribution, as when a single firm sets up two or more marketing channels to reach one or more customer segments.

**Multinational company** A company that operates in many countries and has a major part of its operations outside its home country.

**Natural environment** Natural resources that are needed as inputs by marketers or are affected by marketing activities.

**New product** A good, service, or idea that is perceived by some potential customers as new.

**New-product development** The development of original products, product improvements, product modifications, and new brands through the firm's own R&D efforts.

**New task** An industrial buying situation in which the buyer purchases a product or service for the first time.

**Nondurable goods** Tangible goods normally consumed in one or a few uses.

**Nonpersonal communication channels** Media that carry messages without personal contact or feedback, including mass and selective media, atmospheres, and events.

**Nontariff trade barriers** Nonmonetary barriers to foreign products such as biases against a foreign company's bids or product standards that go against a foreign company's product features.

**Objective-and-task method** Developing the promotion budget by defining specific objectives, determining the tasks that must be performed to achieve these objectives, and estimating the costs of performing these tasks; the sum of these costs is the proposed promotion budget.

**Observational research** The gathering of primary data by observing relevant people, actions, and situations.

**Occasion segmentation** Dividing the market into groups according to occasions when buyers get the idea, make a purchase, or use a product.

**Off-price retailers** Retailers who buy at less than regular wholesale prices and sell at less than retail, usually carrying a changing and unstable collection of higher-quality merchandise, often leftover goods, overruns, and irregulars obtained from manufacturers at reduced prices; they include factory outlets, independents, and warehouse clubs.

**Oligopolistic competition** A market in which there are a few sellers highly sensitive to each other's pricing and marketing strategies.

**Operating ratios** Ratios of selected operating statement items to net sales that allow marketers to com-

pare the firm's performance in one year with that in previous years (or with industry standards and competitors in the same year).

**Operating statement** (also called **profit-and-loss statement** or **income statement**) A financial statement showing company sales, cost of goods sold, and expenses during a given time period.

**Optional-product pricing** The pricing of optional or accessory products along with a main product.

**Order routine specification** The stage of the industrial buying process in which the buyer writes the final order with the chosen supplier or suppliers, listing the technical specifications, quantity needed, expected time of delivery, return policies, warranties, and so on.

**Organizational buying** The decision-making process by which formal organizations establish the need for purchased products and services, identifying, evaluating, and choosing among alternative brands and suppliers.

**Organization image** The way an individual or a group sees an organization.

**Organization marketing** Activities undertaken to create, maintain, or change the attitudes and behavior of target audiences toward an organization.

**Organization structure** A structure that breaks up the company's work into specialized jobs, assigns these jobs to people and departments, and then coordinates the jobs by defining formal ties between people and departments and by setting lines of authority and communication.

**Packaging** The activities of designing and producing the container or wrapper for a product.

**Packaging concept** What the package should *be* or *do* for the product.

**Parallel product development** An approach to developing new products in which various company departments work closely together, overlapping the steps in the product-development process to save time and increase effectiveness.

**Patronage rewards** Cash or other awards for the regular use of a certain company's products or services.

**Perceived-value pricing** Setting price based on the buyer's perceptions of value rather than on the seller's cost.

**Percentage-of-sales method** Setting the promotion budget at a certain percentage of current or forecasted sales or as a percentage of the sales price.

**Perception** The process by which people select, organize, and interpret information to form a meaningful picture of the world.

**Performance review** The stage of the industrial buying process in which the buyer rates its satisfaction with suppliers, deciding whether to continue, modify, or drop them.

**Personal communication channels** Channels through which two or more people communicate directly with each other, including face-to-face, person-to-audience, over the telephone, or through the mail.

**Personal influence** The effect of statements made by one person on another's attitude or probability of purchase.

**Personality** The unique psychological characteristics that lead to relatively consistent and lasting individual responses to one's own environment.

**Personal selling** Oral presentation in a conversation with one or more prospective purchasers for the purpose of making sales.

**Person marketing** Activities undertaken to create, maintain, or change attitudes or behavior toward particular persons.

**Persuasive advertising** Advertising used to build selective demand for a brand by persuading consumers that it offers the best quality for their money.

**Physical distribution** The tasks involved in planning, implementing, and controlling the physical flow of materials and final goods from points of origin to points of use in order to meet the needs of customers at a profit.

**Physical distribution firms** Warehouse, transportation, and other firms that help a company to stock and move goods from their points of origin to their destinations.

**Place marketing** Activities undertaken to create, maintain, or change attitudes or behavior toward particular places.

**Planned obsolescence** A strategy of causing products to become obsolete before they actually need replacement.

**Pleasing products** Products that give high immediate satisfaction but may hurt consumers in the long run.

**Point-of-purchase (POP) promotions** Displays and demonstrations that take place at the point of purchase or sale.

**Political environment** Laws, government agencies, and pressure groups that influence and limit various organizations and individuals in a given society.

**Portfolio analysis** A tool by which management identifies and evaluates the various businesses that make up the company.

**Preapproach** The step in the selling process in which the salesperson learns as much as possible about a prospective customer before making a sales call.

**Premiums** Goods offered either free or at low cost as an incentive to buy a product.

**Presentation** The step in the selling process when the salesperson tells the product "story" to the buyer, showing how the product will make or save money.

**Price** The amount of money charged for a product or service or the sum of the values consumers exchange for the benefits of having or using the product or service.

**Price elasticity** A measure of the responsiveness of demand to changes in price.

**Price packs (or cents-off deals)** Reduced prices that are marked by the producer directly on a label or package.

**Primary data** Information collected for the specific purpose at hand.

**Primary groups** Groups with whom a person interacts informally and regularly, such as family, friends, neighbors, and co-workers.

**Private brand (or middleman, distributor, or dealer brand).** A brand created and owned by a reseller of a product or service.

**Problem recognition** The stage of the industrial buying process in which someone in the company recognizes a problem or need that can be met by acquiring a good or a service.

**Product** Anything that can be offered to a market for attention, acquisition, use, or consumption and might satisfy a need or want; it includes physical objects, services, persons, places, organizations, and ideas.

**Product adaptation** Adapting a product to meet local conditions or wants in foreign markets.

**Product-bundle pricing** Combining several products and offering the bundle at a reduced price.

**Product concept** The idea that consumers will favor products that offer the most quality, performance, and features and that the organization should therefore devote its energy to making continuous product improvements; a detailed version of the new-product idea stated in meaningful consumer terms.

**Product design** The process of designing a product's style and function and creating a product that is attractive; easy, safe, and inexpensive to use and service; and simple and economical to produce and distribute.

**Product development** A strategy for company growth by offering modified or new products to current market segments; developing the product concept into a physical product in order to ensure that the product idea can be turned into a workable product.

**Product idea** An idea for a possible product that the company can see itself offering to the market.

**Product image** The way consumers perceive an actual or potential product.

**Product invention** Creating new products or services for foreign markets.

**Production concept** The philosophy that consumers will favor products that are available and highly affordable and that management should therefore focus on improving production and distribution efficiency.

**Product life cycle (PLC)** The course of a product's sales and profits over its lifetime; it involves five distinct stages—product development, introduction, growth, maturity, and decline.

**Product line** A group of products that are closely related either because they function in a similar manner, are sold to the same customer groups, are marketed through the same types of outlets, or fall within given price ranges.

**Product line featuring** Selecting one or a few items in a product line to feature.

**Product line filling** Increasing the product line by adding more items within the present range of the line.

**Product line pricing** Setting the price steps between various products in a product line based on cost differences between the products, customer evaluations of different features, and competitors' prices.

**Product line stretching** Increasing the product line by lengthening it beyond its current range.

**Product management organization** An organization structure in which product managers are responsible for developing and implementing marketing strategies and plans for a specific product or brand.

**Product mix** The set of all product lines and items that a particular seller offers for sale to buyers.

**Product position** The way the product is defined by consumers on important attributes—the place the product occupies in consumers' minds relative to competing products.

**Product quality** The ability of a product to perform its functions; it includes the product's overall durability, reliability, precision, ease of operation and repair, and other valued attributes.

**Product salesforce structure** A salesforce organization under which salespeople specialize in selling only a portion of the company's products or lines.

**Product specification** The stage of the industrial buying process in which the buying organization decides on and specifies the best technical product characteristics for a needed item.

**Product-support services** Services that augment actual products.

**Profitability control** Evaluation and corrective action to ensure the profitability of various products, territories, customer groups, trade channels, and order sizes.

**Promotional allowance** A payment or price reduction to reward dealers for participating in advertising and sales-support programs.

**Promotional pricing** Temporarily pricing products below the list price—

and sometimes even below cost—to increase short-run sales.

**Promotion mix** The specific mix of advertising, personal selling, sales promotion, and public relations that a company uses to pursue its advertising and marketing objectives.

**Proposal solicitation** The stage of the industrial buying process in which the buyer invites qualified suppliers to submit proposals.

**Prospecting** The step in the selling process in which the salesperson identifies qualified potential customers.

**Psychographics** The technique of measuring life styles and developing lifestyle classifications; it involves measuring the major AIO dimensions (activities, interests, opinions).

**Psychographic segmentation** Dividing a market into different groups based on social class, life style, or personality characteristics.

**Psychological pricing** A pricing approach that considers the psychology of prices and not simply the economics—the price is used to say something about the product.

**Public** Any group that has an actual or potential interest in or impact on an organization's ability to achieve its objectives.

**Publicity** Activities to promote a company or its products by planting news about it in media not paid for by the sponsor.

**Public relations** Building good relations with the company's various publics by obtaining favorable publicity, building a good "corporate image," and handling or heading off unfavorable rumors, stories, and events; major PR tools include press relations, product publicity, corporate communications, lobbying, and counseling.

**Pull strategy** A promotion strategy that calls for spending a lot of money on advertising and consumer promotion to build up consumer demand; if successful, consumers will ask their retailers for the product, the retailers will ask the wholesalers, and the wholesalers will ask the producers.

**Pulsing** Scheduling ads unevenly in bursts over a time period.

**Pure competition** A market in which many buyers and sellers trade in a uniform commodity—no single buy-

er or seller has much effect on the going market price.

**Pure monopoly** A market in which there is a single seller—it may be a government monopoly, a private regulated monopoly, or a private nonregulated monopoly.

**Push strategy** A promotion strategy that calls for using the salesforce and trade promotion to push the product through channels; producers promote the product to wholesalers, wholesalers promote to retailers, and retailers promote to consumers.

**Quantity discount** A price reduction to buyers who buy large volumes.

**Question marks** Low-share business units in high-growth markets which require a lot of cash to hold their share or build into stars.

**Quota** A limit on the amount of goods that an importing country will accept in certain product categories; it is designed to conserve on foreign exchange and protect local industry and employment.

**Rational appeals** Message appeals that relate to the audience's self-interest and show that the product will produce the claimed benefits; examples include appeals of product quality, economy, value, or performance.

**Reach** The percentage of people in the target market exposed to an ad campaign during a given period.

**Reference groups** Groups that serve as direct (face-to-face) or indirect points of comparison or reference in the forming of a person's attitudes or behavior.

**Reference prices** Prices that buyers carry in their minds and refer to when they look at a given product; they are usually formed by noting current prices, remembering past prices, or assessing the buying situation.

**Reminder advertising** Advertising used to keep consumers thinking about a product.

**Reseller market** All the individuals and organizations that acquire goods for the purpose of reselling or renting them to others at a profit.

**Retailer cooperatives** Contractual vertical marketing systems in which retailers organize a new, jointly owned business to carry on wholesaling and possibly production.

**Retailers** Businesses whose sales come *primarily* from retailing.

**Retailing** All the activities involved in selling goods or services directly to final consumers for their personal, nonbusiness use.

**Return on investment (ROI)** A common measure of managerial effectiveness—the ratio of net profit to investment.

**Role** The activities people are expected to perform according to the persons around them.

**Sales analysis** Measuring and evaluating actual sales in relation to sales goals.

**Salesforce management** The analysis, planning, implementation, and control of salesforce activities, including setting salesforce objectives; designing salesforce strategy; and recruiting, selecting, training, supervising, and evaluating the firm's salespeople.

**Salesforce promotion** Sales promotion designed to motivate the salesforce and make salesforce selling efforts more effective, including bonuses, contests, and sales rallies.

**Salesperson** An individual acting for a company by performing one or more of the following activities: prospecting, communicating, servicing, and information gathering.

**Sales promotion** Short-term incentives to encourage purchase or sales of a product or service.

**Sales quotas** Standards set for salespeople stating the amount they should sell and how sales should be divided among the company's products.

**Salutary products** Products that have low appeal but benefit consumers in the long run.

**Sample** A segment of the population selected for marketing research to represent the population as a whole.

**Samples** Offers of a trial amount of a product to consumers.

**Sealed-bid pricing** Setting price based on how the firm thinks competitors will price rather than on its own costs or demand—used when a company bids for jobs.

**Seasonal discount** A price reduction to buyers who buy merchandise or services out of season.

**Secondary data** Information that already exists somewhere, having been collected for another purpose.

**Secondary groups** Groups with whom a person interacts more formally and less regularly, such as religious groups, professional associations, and trade unions.

**Selective distortion** The tendency of people to adapt information to personal meanings.

**Selective distribution** The use of more than one but less than all the middlemen who are willing to carry a company's products.

**Selective exposure** The tendency of people to screen out most of the information to which they are exposed.

**Selective retention** The tendency of people to retain only part of the information to which they are exposed, usually information that supports their attitudes and beliefs.

**Self-concept** Self-image, or the complex mental picture people have of themselves.

**Self-service retailers** Retailers that provide very few services; customers perform their own locate-compare-select process to save money.

**Selling concept** The idea that consumers will not buy enough of the organization's products unless the organization undertakes a large-scale selling and promotion effort.

**Selling process** The steps that the salesperson follows when selling, including prospecting and qualifying, pre-approach, approach, presentation and demonstration, handling objections, closing, and follow-up.

**Sense-of-mission marketing** A principle of enlightened marketing holding that a company should define its mission in broad social terms rather than narrow product terms.

**Sequential product development** A new-product development approach in which one company department works individually to complete its stage of the process before passing the new product along to the next department and stage.

**Service inseparability** A major characteristic of services—they are produced and consumed at the same time and cannot be separated from their providers, whether the providers are people or machines.

**Service intangibility** A major characteristic of services—they cannot be seen, tasted, felt, heard, or smelled before they are bought.

**Service perishability** A major characteristic of services—they cannot be stored for later sale or use.

**Services** Activities, benefits, or satisfactions that are offered for sale; any activity or benefit that one party can offer to another that is essentially intangible and does not result in the ownership of anything.

**Service variability** A major characteristic of services—their quality may vary greatly, depending on who provides them and when, where, and how they are provided.

**Sex segmentation** Dividing a market into different groups based on gender.

**Shopping center** A group of retail businesses planned, developed, owned, and managed as a unit.

**Shopping goods** Consumer goods that the customer, in the process of selection and purchase, characteristically compares on such bases as suitability, quality, price, and style.

**Social classes** Relatively permanent and ordered divisions in a society whose members share similar values, interests, and behaviors.

**Social marketing** The design, implementation, and control of programs seeking to increase the acceptability of a social idea, cause, or practice among a target group.

**Societal marketing** A principle of enlightened marketing holding that a company should make marketing decisions by considering consumers' wants, the company's requirements, consumers' long-run interests, and society's long-run interests.

**Societal marketing concept** The idea that the organization should determine the needs, wants, and interests of target markets and deliver the desired satisfactions more effectively and efficiently than competitors in a way that maintains or improves the consumer's and society's well-being.

**Specialty goods** Consumer goods with unique characteristics or brand identification for which a significant group of buyers is willing to make a special purchase effort.

**Specialty store** A retail store that carries a narrow product line with a deep assortment within that line.

**Standardized marketing mix** An international marketing strategy for using basically the same product, advertising, distribution channels, and other elements of the marketing mix in all the company's international markets.

**Stars** High-growth, high-share businesses or products; they often require heavy investment to finance their rapid growth.

**Status** The general esteem given to a role by society.

**Straight product extension** Marketing a product in the foreign market without any change.

**Straight rebuy** An industrial buying situation in which the buyer routinely reorders something without any modifications.

**Strategic business unit (SBU)** A unit of the company that has a separate mission and objectives and can be planned independently of other company businesses; an SBU can be a company division, a product line within a division, or sometimes a single product or brand.

**Strategic control** A critical review of the company's overall marketing effectiveness.

**Strategic planning** The process of developing and maintaining a strategic fit between the organization's goals and capabilities and its changing marketing opportunities; it relies on developing a clear company mission, supporting objectives, a sound business portfolio, and coordinated functional strategies.

**Style** A basic and distinctive mode of expression.

**Subculture** A group of people with shared value systems based on common life experiences and situations.

**Substantiality** The degree to which a market segment is large or profitable enough.

**Supermarkets** Large, low-cost, low-margin, high-volume, self-service stores that carry a wide variety of food, laundry, and household products.

**Superstore** A store almost twice the size of a regular supermarket carrying a large assortment of routinely purchased food and nonfood items, and offering such services as laundry, dry cleaning, shoe repair, check cashing, bill paying, and bargain lunch counters.

**Suppliers** Firms and individuals that provide the resources needed by the company and its competitors to produce goods and services.

**Supplier search** The stage of the industrial buying process in which the buyer tries to find the best vendors.

**Supplier selection** The stage of the industrial buying process in which the buyer reviews proposals and selects a supplier or suppliers.

**Supplies and services** Industrial goods that do not enter the finished product at all.

**Survey research** The gathering of primary data by asking people questions about their knowledge, attitudes, preferences, and buying behavior.

**Systems buying** Buying a packaged solution to a problem without making all the separate decisions involved.

**Target profit pricing** Setting price to cover the costs of making and marketing a product plus a target profit.

**Tariff** A tax, levied by a government against certain imported products, which is designed to raise revenue or protect domestic firms.

**Technological environment** Forces that create new technologies, creating new product and market opportunities.

**Telemarketing** Using the telephone to sell directly to consumers.

**Television marketing** Using television to market goods to consumers through direct-response advertising or home shopping channels.

**Territorial salesforce structure** A salesforce organization that assigns each salesperson to an exclusive geographic territory in which that salesperson carries the company's full line.

**Test marketing** The stage of new-product development at which the product and marketing program are tested in more realistic market settings.

**Total costs** The sum of the fixed and variable costs for any given level of production.

**Trade-in allowance** A price reduction given for turning in an old item when buying a new one.

**Trademark** A brand or part of a brand that is given legal protection; it protects the seller's exclusive rights to use the brand name or brand mark.

**Trade promotion** Sales promotion designed to gain reseller support and to improve reseller selling efforts, including discounts, allowances, free goods, cooperative advertising, push money, and conventions and trade shows.

**Transaction** A trade between two parties that involves at least two things of value, agreed-upon conditions, a time of agreement, and a place of agreement.

**Two-part pricing** A strategy for pricing services in which price is broken into a fixed fee plus a variable usage rate.

**Undifferentiated marketing** A market-coverage strategy in which a firm decides to ignore market segment differences and go after the whole market with one market offer.

**Uniform delivered pricing** A geographic pricing strategy in which the company charges the same price plus freight to all customers regardless of location.

**Unsought goods** Consumer goods that the consumer does not know about or knows about but does not normally think of buying.

**Value analysis** An approach to cost reduction in which components are carefully studied to determine if they can be redesigned, standardized, or made by cheaper methods of production.

**Value marketing** A principle of enlightened marketing holding that a company should put most of its resources into value-building marketing investments.

**Variable costs** Costs that vary directly with the level of production.

**Vertical marketing system (VMS)** A distribution channel structure in which producers, wholesalers, and retailers act as a unified system—either one channel member owns the others, has contracts with them, or has so much power that they all cooperate.

**Warehouse clubs** (or **wholesale clubs**) Off-price retailers that sell a limited selection of brand-name grocery items, appliances, clothing, and a hodgepodge of other goods at deep discounts to members who pay annual membership fees.

**Wheel of retailing concept** A concept of retailing that states that new types of retailers usually begin as low-margin, low-price, low-status operations but later evolve into higher-priced, higher-service operations, eventually becoming like the conventional retailers they replaced.

**Whole-channel view** Designing international channels that take into account all the necessary links in distributing the seller's products to final buyers, including the seller's headquarters organization, channels be-

tween nations, and channels within nations.

**Wholesalers** Firms engaged *primarily* in wholesaling activity.

**Wholesaler-sponsored voluntary chain** Contractual vertical marketing systems in which wholesalers organize voluntary chains of independent retailers to help them compete with large corporate chain organizations.

**Wholesaling** All the activities involved in selling goods and services to those buying for resale or business use.

**Word-of-mouth influence** Personal communication about a product be-

tween target buyers and neighbors, friends, family members, and associates.

**Workload approach** An approach to setting salesforce size in which the company groups accounts into different size classes and then figures out how many salespeople are needed to call on them the desired number of times.

**Zone pricing** A geographic pricing strategy in which the company sets up two or more zones—all customers within a zone pay the same total price, which is higher in the more distant zones.

## MARKETING

# Porsche Succeeds in Revving Up U.S. Sales By Throttling Down Prices of Some Cars

By Thomas F. O'Boyle
*Staff Reporter of* The Wall Street Journal

STUTTGART, West Germany — When directors of sports-car maker **Porsche** AG decided two months ago to cut the prices of several U.S. models, some may well have feared they were cutting the company's throat.

After all, price reductions are a rarity anywhere in the auto business. But they are particularly dreaded in the luxury-car segment, where image counts as much as engine performance. "There's definitely an unwritten rule that says it makes no sense to lower prices," says Porsche chief executive Heinz Branitzki, "but I felt strongly that this time the rule needed to be broken."

In the end, he persuaded the board to trim the list prices for several U.S. models by 6% to 9%. The result: Porsche has sold as many cars in the two months since the

### End of a Slide?

Porsche's annual car production for the years ended July 31
(In thousands)

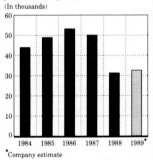

\* Company estimate

price decrease as it did in the three months prior to it. Although the company's U.S. sales still trail those of a year ago — and will probably never again reach the lofty levels of the mid-1980s — Porsche is showing signs of improvement.

### Strong Balance Sheet

True, the company isn't fully back on track. But its balance sheet, which has no bank debt, remains strong. That — plus the controlling shareholdings held by the Porsche and Piech families — has damped once-persistent speculation that Porsche was about to be gobbled up by a bigger mass-production rival. Mr. Branitzki predicts that earnings for the year ending July 31 will be about 50 million West German marks ($25.5 million), twice what Porsche earned in fiscal 1988.

But whether future earnings will ultimately prove sufficient to guarantee Porsche's independence remains to be

seen. The company is increasingly confronted by tough new rivals, including the Japanese, who are pushing sporty luxury cars. Meanwhile, overall sales of luxury cars peaked in 1986 and have been steadily shrinking since. And Porsche's small size allows little room for error. Its average development cost of one billion West German marks for each new model is supported by just three billion marks in annual sales.

For now, however, Mr. Branitzki is being lauded for re-routing a company that only a year and a half ago seemed to be running on empty. "He inherited a very difficult situation, and he has addressed the problems in a very direct and pragmatic manner," says auto analyst Stephen Reitman at UBS Phillips & Drew in London.

### Return to Tradition

His turnaround strategy has at its core a return to tradition and the basics that Mr. Branitzki clearly feels were ignored during the go-go years of his flamboyant predecessor, Peter Schutz, who was sacked in December 1987.

An accountant who formerly served as chief financial officer, Mr. Branitzki upon replacing Mr. Schutz immediately set to work lowering costs and reassessing Porsche's model and marketing policy. Since then he has trimmed the white-collar staff by 10% as part of a cost-cutting program that has cut down on frills (including the entertainment at a private casino that Porsche used to offer its customers the night before they picked up their cars). The program is expected to save the company about $100 million this year, savings that, along with the stronger dollar, gave it the latitude to lower U.S. prices.

At the same time, Porsche has discontinued the least expensive of its four model lines and revamped the remaining three in an effort to rebuild its exclusive image. Although the new models are just now coming to the U.S. market, they have been well received in Europe, where customers must wait more than a year for delivery.

That in itself is a change from the excess inventories that crowded dealers' showrooms just a few years ago. Under the direction of Mr. Schutz, Porsche increased its sales goal to 60,000 cars a year mainly by targeting customers in the U.S. for its lower-priced four-cylinder models. Profit zoomed along for a few years. But the company had an earnings blowout when the double shocks of a falling dollar and a crashing stock market jolted U.S. sales.

Now the company aims to sell no more than 40,000 cars a year — about the same as in 1982 — and to concentrate on the high end of the market, where it gets most of its earnings. "We're not after volume any-

more," says Brian Bowler, the new president of Porsche's U.S. sales unit. "We're going back to our roots, building exclusive, high-priced, high-performance cars."

The building of those cars begins in the Stuttgart suburb of Zuffenhausen, in a factory adjacent to Mr. Branitzki's office. Porsche turns out just 95 cars a day, and the assembly line, when it moves at all, creeps along at a barely discernible pace.

Elsewhere in the factory, workers fashion seat coverings out of the elephant-hide shot by one customer; and they paint a car in the same red shade as the lipstick worn by another customer's wife. "We're a fancy company that sometimes makes crazy things," Mr. Branitzki says.

Too fancy at times for his taste, however. Mr. Schutz, the former chief executive, was an engineer and would often request small modifications that tended to add greatly to costs, company insiders say. One example: At his wife's request, he once asked designers to move the vanity mirror from the passenger's to the driver's side. Although the engineers relented then, they are more cost-conscious now.

"It makes no sense to change a car 100 times a year for small things," says the new chief executive.

The changeover in the executive suite was a U-turn for Porsche. While Mr. Schutz loved publicity and cars, Mr. Branitzki has a personality that reflects his no-frills management style (though he, too, drives a Porsche). He is the first non-engineer to serve as chief executive in the company's 58-year history. And in contrast to the flashy looks of the cars themselves, the 60-year-old executive, who spends his leisure time playing chess, reading history books and hiking in the mountains, has a soft-spoken, unassuming manner.

### 'A Little Quieter'

"I am a little quieter than my predecessor," he admits, "but our name should be handled discreetly." Instead of boasting, he believes that Porsche should observe noblesse oblige and "not talk too loudly."

Meanwhile, Mr. Branitzki has been trying to steer Porsche back to its engineering roots. Hence, two new models introduced this year, the Speedster and the Carrera 4, are both updated versions of its classic 911 model.

Coming up with new classics will be Porsche's biggest challenge in the future. But the executive appears unfazed. "Can we make it without having a big partner?" Mr. Branitzki asks rhetorically. "Surely we can."

## ADVERTISING / By Joanne Lipman

# Procter & Gamble Promotions May Be Demoted in Favor of Ads

**Procter & Gamble** is taking steps to reduce its heavy reliance on promotions and "produce a greater balance toward advertising," said John G. Smale, chairman and chief executive officer.

Mr. Smale's comments come as the trend toward pouring money into promotions—coupons, contests, and discounts to retailers—instead of brand advertising seems finally to be slowing. In recent months, several major consumer companies, including Kraft General Foods, a **Philip Morris** unit, have embarked on aggressive initiatives to strengthen traditional brand advertising. The number of coupons issued has been leveling off. Healthy ad-spending forecasts have been attributed in part to a resurgence in brand advertising by fast-food companies and others.

Mr. Smale was careful to note he isn't "trying to predict that there won't be promotions or allowances in the future." But he did say Procter has taken some cost-cutting steps in the packaging and distribution of its brands, and that promotions will become a smaller part of the marketing mix as a result.

"Our relationship with our customers [retailers] is changing as we develop the capacity to understand costs—their costs as well as ours. We're beginning to work much more cooperatively to reduce those costs. Along with that brings some diminution of the amount of focus brought to promotions, payments and allowances and that sort of thing," he said.

He added: "That will affect the total balance of advertising and promotional support. I think there's an opportunity, not just for Procter alone, for some rebalancing to take place."

Mr. Smale didn't quantify how much the balance would shift away from promotions, and the actual figure is probably relatively small. But any movement at all by Procter, perhaps the company most closely watched by the advertising industry, is significant. No figures are available on promotion spending, but most consumer companies spend more on promotion than they do on advertising.

Procter poured some $1.39 billion into advertising last year, according to Advertising Age, for a stable of brands running the gamut from Crest toothpaste and Ivory soap to Folgers coffee and Citrus Hill orange juice. Although Philip Morris is the country's biggest advertiser following its acquisition of Kraft, Procter still dominates television advertising.

Mr. Smale detailed two Procter efforts to cut promotion spending. First, he said, Procter is "experimenting" with doing away with "price packs"—packages marked with a special price, rebate offer, or other promotion. Not only is the packaging itself expensive to produce, but if Procter makes more product than it can sell to retailers during a given time period, it is left with "remnants" which it must sell at a marked-down price.

If it did away with price packs, Procter would still offer retailers occasional discounts. But by not producing special packaging, it could go back to full pricing after a promotion, instead of unloading specially marked products at a lower price.

Procter is also working on streamlining its distribution of products, in a way that entails cutting back on promotions. Currently, when Procter offers its occasional discounts to retailers, the retailers stock up on the product, then don't buy more for a while. But Procter is working on "continuous supply," in which it would ship the product to retailers on a continuous basis, in a smaller but steady stream.

The new distribution system is less expensive for Procter because it eliminates peaks and valleys of demand; it should save money for retailers, since they won't need to tie up money and warehouse space.

Moreover, the process could reduce promotions in a number of ways. Marketing executives say Procter could cut the number of discount promotions it offers to keep retailers' demand fairly steady. Or, instead of offering occasional discounts, it could offer smaller discounts for a longer period of time to keep demand steady. When it does offer discounts, retailers theoretically would only receive as much as they need, no longer hoarding the product.

Mr. Smale revisited the subject of ad-agency mergers. He was an early and outspoken critic of the huge mergers reshaping the ad business, and Procter pulled business from some agencies following mergers. But the bulk of its business remains at huge agencies, particularly the ultimate symbol of megamergers, Saatchi & Saatchi. Asked if the mergers have affected the quality of the advertising work Procter received in recent years, Mr. Smale said, "It's impossible to say. Would you have gotten more world-class campaigns? I don't know."

## ADVERTISING / By THOMAS R. KING

# American Express Ads for Money Transfers Are High on Anxiety

**American Express,** perhaps the marketing world's prime purveyor of fear and anxiety, knows well the power of well-placed panic. You've seen the ads: Stolen wallets, stranded automobiles and ruined vacations abound. They warn of disaster if Susie is sent off to college without her own charge card.

This month, American Express turns up the heat even more to sell another of its businesses—money transfer—with a set of dramatic television advertisements that portray desperate consumers stuck in bleak situations without cash.

The financial-services giant is trying hard to make a strong impression with the new campaign, and it had better succeed: While American Express is a huge presence in the credit-card and traveler's-checks markets, it's a tiny and relatively new player in the money-transfer business, which is dominated by **Western Union.** The pioneer of money transfers, Western Union, based in Upper Saddle River, N.J., has more than 130 years of experience and boasts a well-established network of more than 13,000 agents.

American Express, meanwhile, is building up its tiny business from scratch. It introduced its money-wiring service, called MoneyGram, in January 1988, but hardly anyone knows yet that it exists. American Express declines to disclose the revenue generated by MoneyGram, but analysts term Western Union's lock on the business a "monopoly." No one else comes close.

Analysts say that American Express, with its strong financial and marketing track record, does have a good chance of making MoneyGram a profitable venture. But the way won't be easy or cheap. Others have failed before. **Citicorp,** for example, introduced Express Money in March 1987, but folded it 14 months later, admitting the road was too difficult. "We couldn't see long-term business propositions," a spokesman says.

Others have failed mostly because start-up costs are prohibitive. Today, only Western Union, American Express and a number of very small competitors are in the business.

But if American Express succeeds with MoneyGram, there is tremendous money to be made. Fees vary based on the amount of money transferred, but American Express charges $11 for every $100 wired, while Western Union charges $14 for each $100. Industry executives say there are currently about 10 million transfers a year totaling some $3 billion; industrywide revenue is estimated at $250 million to $300 million annually.

With stepped-up marketing efforts and cheaper prices, American Express is signaling it plans to become a major player. Since MoneyGram's introduction, the New York-based firm has launched a direct marketing blitz to its cardholders and has been aggressively recruiting its own network of agents, which its says now totals about 6,000. And it claims to have a significant edge in delivering money internationally: Western Union promises money in two to three days; American Express says it'll have it there in less than 10 minutes.

Meanwhile, with a new $7 million ad campaign created by **WPP Group**'s Ogilvy & Mather unit, American Express is playing on everybody's money nightmares—or their guilt. One ad shows a man in his 60s sitting in a modest living room looking somberly at a bill he doesn't have the cash to cover. His wife places a hand on his shoulder. They exchange a saddened, embarrassed look. "Far away, someone you love needs money," the announcer says. "Now you can wire it there in minutes with the American Express MoneyGram."

In another ad, an American teen-ager in Europe is shown stranded on the steps of a church on a cold, stormy night. Lightning flashes as the kid looks nervously up at the sky. "Across the ocean, someone you love needs money," the announcer says.

"We very clearly are taking a serious businesslike tone in these ads," says Rob Ayers, senior vice president at American Express. "We are being careful not to make light of a person's plight."

Western Union, on the other hand, has long been making lighthearted commercials, like the one featuring a doo-wop singing group pulled over by a state trooper. Now, it is girding to take on American Express with a bigger ad budget and a new humorous campaign. Its new commercials, showing mothers whining about their children's spending habits, promotes the company's new toll-free telephone number that can be used to send money by phone.

"We're concerned about the entry of any competitor and what the implications will be to us," says Edward Fuhrman, president of Western Union's consumer services. "But we remain confident that we provide a superior service."

**ADVERTISING** / By JOANNE LIPMAN

# Colgate Tests Putting Its Name On Over-the-Counter Drug Line

Colgate may be a fine name for toothpaste, but do people really want to take Colgate aspirin or Colgate antacid? Would people use Colgate laxative or wash their hair with Colgate dandruff shampoo?

**Colgate-Palmolive** is about to find out. The massive packaged-goods company has gone to Peoria, Ill., to quietly test market a line of 10 over-the-counter medicines and a shampoo, all using the Colgate name. There's Colgate aspirin-free, to compete with Tylenol, and Colgate ibupro-fen, to compete with Advil. There's Colgate cold tablets (like Contac), Colgate nighttime cold medicine (like Nyquil), Colgate calcium antacid tablets (like Rolaids), Colgate natural fiber laxative (like Metamucil), as well as Colgate dandruff shampoo (like Head & Shoulders).

Colgate won't talk about its new line, but Peoria drugstore operators say the company began test-marketing the products last fall. Since then, it has blanketed the town with coupons and ads. A few months ago, it gave away a free tube of toothpaste with any Colgate purchase; it has offered coupons worth virtually the full price of the products and has sent Colgate representatives to local stores to hand out coupons at the door. "They're spending some major money out here," reports Ron Rude, assistant manager of the Super-X drug store on Knoxville Avenue.

If all that weren't enough, the Colgate line is priced well below competing brands, perhaps 20% below, says David Wasson, manager of a local Walgreens. He says sales are strong: "With all the promotion they've done, they should be. They're cheaper, and they've got Colgate's name on them."

Yet even if Colgate's test is a resounding success, marketing consultants say expanding the new line could prove dangerous—and ultimately more expensive than Colgate can imagine. "If you put the Colgate brand name on a bunch of different products, if you do it willy-nilly at the lowest end, you're going to dilute what it stands for—and if you stand for nothing, you're worthless," says Clive Chajet, chairman of Lippincott & Margulies, a corporate identity firm.

Mr. Chajet says that Colgate also might end up alienating customers by slapping its name on so many products. If a consumer "is dissatisfied with one product, they might be dissatisfied with everything across the board. I wouldn't risk it," he says. What would have happened to Johnson & Johnson during the Tylenol poison scare, he asks, if the Tylenol name were plastered across everything from baby shampoo to birth control pills?

Colgate's test is one of the bolder forays into line extensions by consumer products companies. Companies saddled with "mature" brands—brands that can't grow much more—often try to use those brands' solid-gold names to make a new fortune, generally with a related product. Thus, Procter & Gamble's Ivory Soap came up with a shampoo and conditioner. Coca-Cola concocted Diet Coke. Arm & Hammer baking soda expanded into carpet deodorizers.

But unlike those products, Colgate is traveling far afield from its familiar turf. And while its new line is selling well, sales might not stay so strong without the budget prices and barrage of advertising and promotion. "People are looking at it right now as a generic-style product," says Mr. Rude. "People are really price conscious, and as long as the price is cheaper, along with a name that you can trust, people are going to buy that over others."

If Colgate were to raise its prices equal to name-brand prices, "they would have to do more advertising than they're doing," Mr. Rude adds. "They would have to compete more directly with Tylenol" and the other big brands.

Al Ries, chairman of Trout & Ries, a Greenwich, Conn., marketing consultant, questions whether any line extensions make sense—not just for Colgate, but for other strong brand names. He says the reason Colgate has been able to break into the over-the-counter drug market in the first place is because other drugs have expanded and lost their niche; Tylenol and Alka-Seltzer both now make cold medicines, for example, and "that allows an opportunity for the outsiders, the Colgates, to come in and say there's no perception that anybody is any different. The consumer will look for any acceptable brand name."

Mr. Ries says Colgate, and the traditional over-the-counter medicine companies, are basically turning their products into generic drugs instead of brands. They're losing "the power of a narrow focus," he says, adding, "It reflects stupidity on the part of the traditional over-the-counter marketers. . . .if the traditional medicines maintained their narrow focus, they wouldn't leave room for an outsider such as Colgate."

If Colgate is too successful, meanwhile, it also risks cannibalizing its flagship product. Consultants note that almost all successful line extensions, and a lot of not-so-successful ones, hurt the product from which they took their name. They cite Miller High Life, whose share of the beer market has dwindled since the introduction of Miller Lite. "If Colgate made themselves to mean over-the-counter medicine, nobody would want to buy Colgate toothpaste," contends Mr. Ries.

Mr. Chajet agrees. Colgate could "save tens of millions of dollars by not having to introduce a new brand name" for its new products, he says. But in doing so, it might also "kill the goose that laid the golden egg."

## ADVERTISING / By Joanne Lipman

# Nielsen to Track Hispanic TV Ratings

A.C. Nielsen Co. is close to an agreement to track Hispanic television ratings, a move the nation's two major Hispanic networks hope will help them attract more national advertisers.

The Spanish-language networks, **Telemundo Group** Inc. and **Univision** Inc., said that their boards approved a tentative three-way agreement with Nielsen to set up a Nielsen Hispanic ratings service. John Dimling, executive vice president of Nielsen's media-research unit, said Friday that he wasn't aware that the two boards had already approved the contract, but said that a deal was "very close." He said the agreement should be announced formally within the next few weeks.

For Telemundo and Univision, Nielsen ratings could be the ticket to broader acceptance by the ad community. Henry R. Silverman, Telemundo's president, estimates that the two Hispanic networks combined attract about 5% of the total television audience during prime time—but pull in less than 1% of TV advertising dollars. "We need to be able to prove to the advertisers and their agencies that we really do have 5% of the viewers," he says.

Several research companies follow Hispanic television, but their ratings estimates aren't exactly comparable to Nielsen ratings, which are the industry standard. Nielsen doesn't break out the ratings for the Hispanic networks, but lumps them in its "other" category.

"We want to be able to compete with ABC by showing the same Nielsen results that they do," says Mr. Silverman.

According to the tentative agreement, Nielsen, a unit of **Dun & Bradstreet**, would test-market its Hispanic ratings system in Los Angeles, where it plans to wire 200 Hispanic homes with people meters later this year. After the test is completed next fall, Nielsen would analyze the system and ultimately roll it out nationwide, monitoring 800 Hispanic homes.

If the Nielsen results confirm the Hispanic networks' audience estimates, the networks hope advertisers will give them a second look. Currently Univision, the larger and older of the two, has attracted the nation's 25 largest advertisers, but remains weak in a number of advertiser categories. Insurance companies, corporate accounts, and automobiles are all a hard sell, says Joaquin Blaya, president.

Founded 27 years ago, Univision reaches about 85% of the nation's six million Hispanic households.

Telemundo, founded just three years ago, reaches about 75% of the U.S. Hispanic population.

Mr. Silverman estimates that "of the 500 largest advertisers on English-language television, about 100 advertise on Spanish-language television, which means 400 don't. I'd like to get the 80% of advertisers on network TV that don't advertise with us."

Even if Nielsen ratings indicate a large audience, many advertisers may still be put off because the median household income for Hispanic homes is about 80% of that of all U.S. homes. But the Hispanic networks point out that the average Hispanic household is also larger, giving advertisers more viewers per home. And they note that the Hispanic population is growing faster than the general population, making it too important a segment to ignore.

In any case, Telemundo's Mr. Silverman insists most advertisers needn't worry about Hispanics' lower median income. "Perhaps Tiffany won't be a charter advertiser on Telemundo, but 98% of the advertisers on [the big three networks] should be advertising with us," he says. "Consumers are consumers. Their money is green."

## Caterpillar Net Fell 2.8% in 2nd Quarter; Higher Costs Cited

*By a* WALL STREET JOURNAL *Staff Reporter*

PEORIA, Ill.—**Caterpillar** Inc. said its second-quarter earnings fell 2.8%, reflecting higher costs resulting from five additional calendar days, material price increases, and wage and benefit increases for all payrolls.

The maker of construction equipment earned $141 million, or $1.39 a share. In the year-earlier quarter, it earned $145 million, or $1.44 a share. Sales rose 17% to $3.04 billion from $2.6 billion.

Caterpillar also cited higher start-up costs, particularly for factory modernization and product introductions.

Most of the sales increase in the quarter reflected higher physical sales volume and stronger demand outside the U.S., Caterpillar said. The company now is reporting financial results based on calendar quarters rather than internally developed cutoff schedules.

The company said that price increases implemented since the first quarter are helping offset inflationary cost increases. Caterpillar said price increases, however, were partially offset by the effects of a stronger dollar.

Caterpillar said sales in the U.S. rose 6%, although dealer machine sales declined as the tight monetary policy of the Federal Reserve Board resulted in reduced construction activity, particularly housing. Sales outside the U.S. continued to post strong gains, rising 28% mostly on physical sales volume.

In the first six months, the company earned $282 million, or $2.78 a share, compared with $263 million, or $2.60 a share, a year earlier. Sales rose 15% to $5.72 billion from $4.98 billion.

ADVERTISING / By JOANNE LIPMAN

# From '60s Uniform to '90s Niche: Wrangler Targets the Family Man

Back when you weren't supposed to trust anybody over 30, when boys looked like girls and everybody wore denim, selling blue jeans was as easy as burning a draft card.

Ah, the good old days. Marketers of blue jeans advertised to "the broad market. . . . Jeans were the uniform," says Mary Tetlow, an account supervisor at **Martin Agency** of Richmond, Va. "But times have changed, and people's behavior has changed, and now niche strategies are making more sense."

At least, that's the thinking behind Martin Agency's new campaign for Wrangler jeans. The $10 million effort, breaking today, unabashedly chases a very specific "niche" market: blue-collar family men who wear jeans daily, who are over 30, who love the outdoors, and who, for the most part, live in small towns.

These ads are a very far cry from the ads for trendier blue jeans, like Levi, Lee and Guess, which go after the hip, young, urban crowd. Guess ads revel in ripe young women whose clothes are generally falling off; Levi's 501 jeans ads are shot with a jumpy camera amidst stark, crumbling cityscapes. Few of the actors and models in these ads seem to be over 20, much less listing toward middle age.

The new campaign for Wrangler, a unit of **VF** Corp., by contrast, doesn't even attempt to woo the chic young set. Instead, it embraces the folksy, patriotic America tinged in rose and bathed in warm light that most people see only in commercials, especially in commercials by Hal Riney, the master of Americana whose dulcet voice narrates his own ads for Alamo rental cars, Blue Cross/Blue Shield, and the old Gallo wine campaign.

The Wrangler ads, like the Riney commercials they echo, seek to bring a little tear to the eye with their heartwarming depiction of family men—in this case, beefy family men in blue jeans. In one of the commercials, an unseen wife narrates as her man gets up at the crack of dawn and slips on a pair of "those old jeans" to go fishing. As the camera lovingly pans over the man and his dog sitting in a rowboat by the dawn light, a deep voice intones, "Here's to old dogs, Saturday mornings, and comfortable blue jeans."

In another ad, a father teaches his son to drive an old pickup truck on a dusty country road, and the boy smashes into a mailbox. Instead of getting mad, blue-jeans-clad dad—who bears a passing resemblance to "Roseanne" husband John Goodman—cracks a smile. This one ends with our folksy announcer murmuring, "Here's to fathers and sons, first-time driving lessons, and comfortable blue jeans."

"Our audience lives in blue jeans; they wear them to work, then change into another pair to go out at night," says Mike Hughes, Martin Agency's vice chairman and creative director. "We wanted to talk to people in a different way than Levi's and Lee are talking to people. We want people to know that Wranglers are good-looking jeans, but we also want it to be more real. Our people don't live in the mean streets of New York."

Industry executives say Wrangler's strategy of concentrating on the blue-collar market makes sense. Wrangler is the fourth-largest blue-jeans brand, with about 7% of the market compared with **Levi Strauss**'s 20% of the market. (Lee and Rustler, also units of VF Corp., rank second and third). Slightly cheaper than Levi jeans, with a much smaller ad budget, and distributed through inexpensive mass merchandisers, Wrangler jeans can't exactly compete effectively for the yuppie crowd.

Besides, Levi itself has been making a concerted effort to woo the more upscale thirtysomething man. Its commercials feature images such as a father teaching his young son to fish. Levi's ads are "a little more contemporary, more the yuppie kind of guy" than the Wrangler dad, says Dan Chew, Levi marketing manager.

The Wrangler commercials, and print and radio ads with similar themes, are actually introducing a new Wrangler jean that is cut a bit fuller for—let's be euphemistic now—the "mature" man. But the new jeans' distinguishing features, such as a roomier crotch, aren't alluded to at all in the TV commercials because the ads are supposed to stand "for Wrangler jeans in general," Mr. Hughes says.

Mr. Hughes is convinced that other blue-jeans makers will have to follow in Wrangler's folksy wake. "There's a movement in the country generally for things that are more real," he says. "A lot of the other jeans, especially the ones we think of as hip fashion jeans, are going to be moving towards more real things, too."

# Unit of Nestle Settles Dispute On Infant Ads

By ALIX M. FREEDMAN
*Staff Reporter of* THE WALL STREET JOURNAL

State attorneys general in nine states reached a settlement with **Nestle** S.A.'s Carnation Co. unit over what they claimed was "misleading, deceptive and unfair" marketing and advertising of its Good Start H.A. infant formula.

Under terms of the agreement, Carnation must refrain from using the word "hypoallergenic" to advertise Good Start or any other formula, so consumers won't get the impression that the product can't cause an allergic reaction. Hypoallergenic doesn't mean nonallergenic, but having a reduced potential for allergenic reactions.

Among other stipulations, Carnation is prohibited from asserting that any expert endorses an infant formula without also disclosing whether the individual is affiliated with or has been paid by the company. It also can't falsely represent that its product claims are supported by scientific evidence.

Carnation, which is based in Los Angeles, also agreed to pay $90,000 to cover the costs of the investigation that was launched in March, initially by the states of New York, Texas and California.

"The essence of this settlement is that Carnation simply can't misrepresent that its product is incapable of causing an allergic reaction," said Robert Roth, an assistant attorney general in New York. Mr. Roth added: "This product was being marketed in such a way as to appeal to precisely the parents of those infants who were most at risk."

In a prepared statement, Timm F. Crull, Carnation's chief executive officer, said: "We are convinced the characterizations made by the attorneys general in the settlement agreement are not supported by the facts. However, solely to avoid the time and expense that contesting these characterizations would require, Carnation has entered into this agreement."

State officials acknowleged that the settlement is essentially moot since Carnation—a scant two weeks after the states began to look into its ad claims—hastily made the changes that the states' agreement now stipulates. These included dropping the key claim, hypoallergenic, which appeared in bold type on the front of Good Start cans.

The probe by state officials grew out of Nestle's bid to crack the $1.6 billion U.S. infant formula market in late 1988. Good Start claimed to prevent or reduce sleeplessness, colic, rashes and other ailments in infants because it was hypoallergenic.

But the product quickly came under sharp criticism from some doctors. In February, the Food and Drug Administration began investigating Nestle's aggressive claims for Good Startm as well as six cases of severe reactions in infants for whom the formula wasn't hypoallergenic enough.

# For Many, Road to the Right PC Is Paved With Glitches

## But Help Is Growing for Entrepreneurs Searching for Computer Systems

By Jeffrey A. Tannenbaum
*Staff Reporter of* The Wall Street Journal

On his first attempt to computerize his business two years ago, dry cleaner David Berliner wasted $10,000. The Caldwell, N.J., business owner needed all kinds of instantly accessible information, such as the whereabouts of every fur coat entrusted to his shop. But his computer system could do little except write cleaning tickets.

Last year, Mr. Berliner leased an entirely different system. But because of a software glitch, the four terminals couldn't communicate with each other as promised. "I'm still fighting to get my name off the lease," says Mr. Berliner, who had the system yanked out after only two months.

In his third try, Mr. Berliner this year leased yet another system and finally struck pay dirt. Though his business at last is happily computerized, getting there was no fun. "It has been very frustrating and expensive," he says. "If I were starting the process again, I would talk to a lot more people. When I started with this, I wasn't really aware of computers."

He isn't alone. Most small-business owners find buying the right computer system a daunting experience filled with perils. But help is more plentiful than many business owners realize, and it is proliferating.

As computer vendors increasingly subdivide the market into small niches with highly specialized products, more businesses are able to get exactly what they need. But they must know how to find it.

More than 15,000 software packages are being marketed just for International Business Machines Corp. computers and their compatibles, let alone other brands. One package allows video stores to keep track of films. Others help farmers to adjust chicken-feed blends if egg production falters and sausage makers to switch their recipes frequently to capitalize on fluctuations in ingredient costs. Moreover, computers keep getting cheaper and better.

Yet "computer phobia" is still common. "There are business people who know they must have a computer but are terrified by it," says Arlene Borden, owner of **Doc's**

---

## Small Businesses Computerize

More than half of U.S. small businesses have at least begun to computerize, usually using personal computers. BIF CAP International, a Norwell, Mass., research and consulting firm, studied the rise in PC ownership over a single year:

| NUMBER OF EMPLOYEES | PCT. WITH AT LEAST ONE PC | |
|---|---|---|
| | END OF 1987 | END OF 1988 |
| Under 5 | 41.5% | 44.2% |
| 5 to 9 | 48.4 | 58.5 |
| 10 to 19 | 57.5 | 67.6 |
| 20 to 49 | 59.7 | 76.0 |
| 50 to 99 | 67.9 | 76.0 |

---

**Computer Center** Inc., Ardmore, Pa. Even calm shoppers face a dizzying proliferation of choices of software, or programming.

Business owners say a smart approach can minimize the risks—and give companies a big edge over competitors that shun computer systems or buy them foolishly. From the start, companies must be "absolutely unrelenting" with suppliers, ordering only when the equipment and software fully meet their needs, warns Jim Warnat, financial vice president of **Gordon Aluminum & Vinyl** Inc., Peabody, Mass.

The custom-window maker was awash in paper and losing control of its growing operation when it spent about $40,000 for its first computer system in 1986. "It was a disaster—worse than useless because it made some of our operating personnel a slave to the system," says Mr. Warnat. He adds that the system, paradoxically, was good only at generating more paper.

With a further $60,000 and help from **Grant Thornton**, a New York accounting and consulting firm, Gordon in 1987 got new software and computerized successfully. The computer now speeds order-taking, factory work flow, deliveries, invoicing and accounting; the company has slashed its typical turnaround time on orders to less than two weeks from six. Sales have surged. And customers say they have noticed the better service.

---

While demanding precisely the right systems, companies must focus on software, the packages of instructions that enable computers to carry out specific tasks, experts say. Software can be costlier than hardware and is crucial in any case. "It's the software that is going to make you or break you," says Amy Wohl, a Bala Cynwyd, Pa., computer consultant.

William M. Zeitler, an IBM marketer in White Plains, N.Y., suggests asking suppliers four fundamental questions related to software: Exactly what applications programs are available? How easy are they to use? What kind of support, such as house calls if trouble arises, does the supplier include in the price? And is the system affordable in the first place?

Though thousands of pre-packaged programs are on the market, they are never in one place. To find what's available, many business owners read trade magazines, visit computer vendors' displays at trade shows and call trade associations. But far more information is handily available than ever before.

In choosing the software, many business owners recommend emphasizing ease of use. For small businesses with many low-skilled workers, this can be crucial. Help teaching the program also counts. Some vendors will enter into long-term service and training contracts.

If computerization poses problems, at least it's getting cheaper. While $15,000 and $25,000 systems are common, very small businesses nowadays can often get by with $3,000 in hardware and less than $200 in software, Ms. Borden says. Even $15,000 systems can be leased for as low as $360 a month over five years, IBM says.

Even companies that have had trouble with computers say the right choice can pay handsomely. In Norwalk, Conn., **Sanitary Cleaners** Inc.'s first computer crashed frequently, plunging the business into chaos for hours at a time. But a new system made the company far more efficient. "I can't believe anyone could run a business without a computer," co-owner Gail Epstein now says. "I don't know how we did it."

## Cashing In on Credit Cards, 1950

CREDIT CARDS HAVE BEEN AROUND since 1915, when Western Union and a handful of railroads, hotels and department stores began issuing them to preferred customers, but their real impetus came in 1950 when a New York lawyer found himself short of cash in a Manhattan restaurant. That embarrassing moment prompted Frank X. McNamara to found the Diners Club, which let card-carriers charge their tabs at 27 swank New York eating places. The idea caught on from the start. A year later the club was billing more than $1 million and by 1981, when Citicorp acquired it, it counted more than four million members.

Serious competition came in October 1958, when American Express Co. moved in. In three months that year, American Express signed up 253,000 members. By 1988, it had issued 30 million green, gold and platinum cards, and more than 2.3 million service establishments were accepting them.

Bank cards were another story. After McNamara's cards caught on, more than 100 banks tried them, but their localized programs limited their markets and half soon dropped out. Then, Bank of America, with all of California as its bailiwick, issued its BankAmerica card, which proved so successful the bank was soon franchising it to others. Bank cards exploded when individual institutions worked out interchange arrangements. Four big Chicago banks started MasterCard in 1965; four in California began MasterCharge in 1967.

The BankAmericard eventually evolved into Visa International, a free-standing service company with more than 21,000 financial institutions as members and 187 million cards outstanding. Last year, Visa had world-wide volume of almost $210 billion. MasterCard, its main competitor, claims 29,000 member institutions and 145 million cards.

The "cashless society" was one long step closer.

## Pizza Garners a Slice of the Pie, 1949

BY 1949, AMERICA'S VERSION OF ITALIAN PIZZA was starting to become as popular as mom's apple pie.

GIs brought their craving for the cheesy, tomato pies back from Europe after World War II and within five years pizza's soaring sales path was clear. Customers waited in lines outside Pizzeria Uno in Chicago to savor its new deep-dish concoction; Salvatore Marra's in Philadelphia was jammed.

Pizzas had been around since about the year 1000 in the Naples area. They got some zip when Peruvian tomatoes were added in the 1550s and emerged in modern form with mozzarella cheese in 1889 when Raffaele Esposito, a pizzaiolo (pizza cook), made it for Queen Margherita.

Gennaro Lombardi, an Italian immigrant, probably had the first U.S. pizzeria—in New York in 1905. But the round dish stayed mostly in urban Italian neighborhoods until all those ex-GIs' appetites hit the U.S.

Special ovens were built for pizza; Bakers Pride Oven offered a new one in 1946 and Blodgett Co., making bakery ovens since 1848, introduced a special model for the pizza trade early in 1953. Conveyor-belt ovens arrived six years ago.

Pizza parlors swept across the U.S. with such new chains as Pizza Hut, formed in 1958. "By the sixties, pizza was mass-produced, but pizza had arrived," wrote Evelyne Slomon in her "The Pizza Book—Everything There Is To Know About The World's Greatest Pie." She added: "It was one of America's most popular foods—up there with hot dogs."

Pizzerias passed hamburger eateries in 1984 and have kept their lead. In 1988, people in the U.S. chomped a record $20 billion of pizzas, according to the National Association of Pizza Operators.

## No Longer a Black-and-White Issue, 1950

COLOR TELEVISION IS THE STORY of how Columbia Broadcasting won all the battles but National Broadcasting won the war.

Peter Goldmark, the legendary head of CBS research, had a color TV system as early as 1940. It was shelved when he went to war to develop radar-jamming devices. It was revived on his return, and CBS was demonstrating baseball games in color by the late 1940s. A major drawback was that the CBS system, which involved a Rube Goldberg arrangement of whirling disks, could not be received on black-and-white receivers—and there were 10 million of these by 1950.

CBS's major rival, Gen. David Sarnoff of RCA and NBC, meanwhile was working on compatible color. This, in effect, sent a color signal over the channel carrying the black-and-white picture. Nonetheless, when the Federal Communications Commission held a showdown session between CBS and NBC, the Goldmark system won the nod. RCA sued all the way to the Supreme Court—and lost. In June 1951, the FCC okayed CBS to start color broadcasts. That November, however, the U.S. banned manufacture of color TV sets because of Korean War shortages, and CBS apparently gave up.

Sarnoff stayed the route, using 100 engineers and $130 million to perfect his compatible system. When the government took another look at color TV in 1953, the National Television Standards Committee gave Sarnoff the victory. RCA and its NBC network would have color TV practically to themselves for 10 years.

Thus Sarnoff had his revenge for the defeat Goldmark had handed him with the long-playing record in 1948, a product RCA eventually had to adopt. But it wasn't a total loss. RCA paid royalties to the CBS engineer for a masking device it used in its sets. And when the Apollo astronauts needed a color-TV system to send back pictures from the moon voyages, they picked Goldmark's.

# Acknowledgment of Illustrations

## Chapter 1

**2** Clockwise: Apple Computer, Inc.; Michal Heron/ Woodfin Camp & Associates; George Haling/Photo Researchers; Jon Feingersh/TSW-Glick/Chicago Ltd. **5** Kaiser Sand & Gravel Company, a subsidiary of Koppers Company, Inc. **7** Fotheringham & Associates **11** American Gas Association **13** General Electric Company **15** McDonald's; Glenn Kulbako/The Picture Cube **19** U. S. Postal Service.

## Chapter 2

**24** Greyhound Corporation **29** Visa International **34** Church & Dwight Co., Inc.; Jockey International, Inc. **38** Holiday Corporation **40-41** Oshkosh Truck Corporation **42** Embassy Suites, Inc.; Westin Hotels and Resorts **45** The Greyhound Corporation.

## Chapter 3

**50** International Business Machines Corporation **54** State of Florida, Division of Economic Development **57** Ken Lax **62** Hewlett-Packard **67** © Mark Seliger **70** Carol Lee/West Stock.

## Chapter 4

**78** Clockwise: Rob Nelson/ Picture Group; Rich Frishman/Picture Group; Roger Ressmeyer **82** Steve Weber/Stock, Boston **84** Elliot Schwartz **91** Information Resources, Inc. **95** Research Triangle Institute, Research Triangle Park, NC **97** Ken Kerbs **102** Datapoint Corp.

## Chapter 5

**106** Seth Resnick **111** Ross Sturdevant **114** NCR Corporation **116** Pete Saloutos/TSW-Click/Chicago Ltd. **118** Thomas J. Lipton, Inc. **121** Arthur Tress **123** Weyerhaeuser Company **124** General Motors Corporation **125** Clockwise: Fasterty/Liaison Agency; Texas Instruments; NASA; Tony Frank/Sygma **131** David Stroecklein/West Stock **132** Plymouth Division, Chrysler Motors Corporation.

## Chapter 6

**140** Clockwise: Adamsmith Productions/West Light; Vic Huber/West Light; Rob Nelson/Picture Group **143** DuPont Company **146** Lawrence Migdale/Stock, Boston; Jeffry Myers/Southern Stock; Julie O'Neil/The Picture Cube **150** Gabe Palmer/The Stock Market **153** Bank of America **156** Laima Druskis **159** Jack Fields/ Photo Researchers **161** Brownie Harris/The Stock Market **153** Bank of America **156** Laima Druskis **159** Jack Fields/Photo Researchers **161** Brownie Harris/ The Stock Market **164** Minolta Corporation **166** Teri Stratford **169** International Business Machines Corporation.

## Chapter 7

**174** Clockwise: Gulfstream Aerospace Corp.; Tom Tracy/The Stock Shop; Gulfstream Aerospace Corp.; Gulfstream Aerospace Corp. **178** The Nutrasweet Company **180** Honeywell Inc. **184** Esselte Pendaflex Corporation **185** Peterbilt Motors Co. **191** L'Eggs Products, Inc. Winston-Salem, NC/Maged & Behar, NYC **193** Mark Seliger.

## Chapter 8

**200** Procter & Gamble **205** © 1988 Colgate-Palmolive Co. **206** The Quaker Oats Company **209** Greyhound Lines, Inc. **217** Teri Stratford **219** American Express, Wilt Chamberlain, and William Shoemaker, Inc. **212** Steelcase, Inc.

## Chapter 9

**224** Revlon, Inc. **227** Sony Corporation of America **229** Clockwise: Chris Jones/The Stock Market; Gabe

Palmer/The Stock Market; Jeffry W. Myers/Stock, Boston **231** Texas Instruments, Inc. **232** Ford Motor Co. **234** Black & Decker Corp. **236** Ted Kappler **237** Painting by James Gurney, © National Geographic Society **241** The Arrow Company **242** Westvaco Envelope Division **244** Ken Lax **247** Furnished by GE Appliances, Louisville, Kentucky **248** Olympus Corporation

## Chapter 10

**256** Clockwise: 3M Corporation; 3M Corporation; 3M Corporation; Michael L. Abramson **262** The Pillsbury Company **263** Donald Dietz/Stock, Boston **267** Teri Stratford **268** Ford Motor Co. **271** Kikkoman International, Inc. **273** Sony Corporation of America

## Chapter 11

**280** Clockwise: Sears, Roebuck and Co.; Sears, Roebuck and Co.; Sears Roebuck and Co.; Marc PoKempner **285** Sub-Zero Freezer Co., Inc. **286** Ford Motor Co.; Jaguar Cars, Inc. **289** Stanley Hardware Division of The Stanley Works, New Britain, CT 06052 **291** Fuddruckers, Inc. **298** Waterford Wedgwood

## Chapter 12

**302** Caterpillar Inc. **305** Polaroid Corporation **307** Snapper Power Equipment **308** Hyatt Hotels Grand Cypress **312** Page Poore; Laima Druskis **316** Bausch & Lomb Professional Products Division **317** Jean Patou, Inc.

## Chapter 13

**322** Craig Aurness/West Light; Associated Pix Service **326** Clockwise: The Coca-Cola Company; Michael S. Yamashita/West Light; John Zoiner/International Stock Photo; Smith/Garner/The Stock Market **333** Toys 'R' Us **334** McDonald's and Sears, Roebuck and Co. **336** Michael Rizza/Stock, Boston; Lee Lockwood/Black Star **337** Dario Perla/International Stock Photo; Christina Mufson/Comstock **343** Tom Carroll/International Stock Photo **345** Clockwise: CSX Creative Services; CSX Creative Services; American Airlines; Conrail

## Chapter 14

**350** IKEA, Inc. **356** Bigg's, Cincinnati **358** 47th Street Photo **361** Minneapolis Convention and Visitors Bureau **363** Teri Stratford **368** Ted Hardin **372** Fleming Companies, Inc., Oklahoma City OK **375** Foremost-McKesson

## Chapter 15

**380** The Quaker Oats Company **386** Vistakon™, a Johnson & Johnson Company **387** Procter & Gamble **390** PepsiCo, Inc. **395** John Lei/Stock, Boston **397** McGraw-Hill, Inc.

## Chapter 16

**404** California Raisin Advisory Board **410** Kraft General Foods **413** Cunard Line; Heinz Pet Products **414** Kraft General Foods **418-19** John M. Roberts; Ted Kappler; Parking Meter Advertising **422** Jayne Conte **424** PepsiCo, Inc. **428** Coleco **429** Teri Stratford

## Chapter 17

**436** Boeing **440** Linda Bohm/Leo de Wys; Gabe Palmer/The Stock Market **446** © Rebecca Chao, used with permission **447** Wilson Learning Corporation **449** Lawrence Migdale/Photo Researchers **451** Hewlett-Packard **452** Comstock **454** Princess Cruises

## Chapter 18

**460** Clockwise: David H. Durland; Steven E. Sutton; David H. Durland; Eastman Kodak Company; Steven E. Sutton; Eastman Kodak Company **463** International Business Machines Corporation; Caroline Parsons; McDonald's Corporation; Ted Morrison **467** Thomas Zimmermann/FPG International **469** Prestige & Collections **471** Pepsi-Cola International **474** © 1986 The Walt Disney Company **475** General Motors Corporation **476** Black & Decker Corp.

## Chapter 19

**486** Century City Hospital **489** Robert Holmgren; John C. Hillery **492** Reuben E. Lee/The Stock Shop **495** United Parcel Service of America, Inc. **497** Hush Puppies Division of Wolverine World Wide Inc. **499** Coca-Cola and Coca-Cola Classic are registered trademarks of The Coca-Cola Company. Permission for their use is granted by the Company; ProServ Incorporated; Nike, Inc. **502** North Carolina Department of Commerce **504** *Readers Digest*

## Chapter 20

**508** © Marty Katz **513** Paolo Koch/Photo Researchers **515** Rob Kinmonth **517** American Association of Advertising Agencies **519** Tom McHugh/Photo Researchers **522** Campbell Soup Company **523** Canon, Inc. **529** Ken Lax

# Author Index

# Company/Product Index

# Subject Index

North Carolina, business site marketing in, 502
Nutritional labeling, 246, 521, 522

## O

Objections, handling, 450
Objective-and-task method of promotion budgeting, 394
Objectives and goals:
    advertising, 408–10
    company, 29–30, 55
    job search, 545
    long-term and short-term, trade-offs between, 58–59
    in marketing plan, 55
    of marketing research, 88
    pricing decisions and, 283–84
    public relations, 429–30
    sales management, 440–41
    sales promotion, 421
    strategic planning and, 29–30
Observational research, 91–92
Obsolescence, planned, 514–15
Occasion market segmentation, 209
Occupation, consumer buying behavior and, 152
*Occupation Outlook Handbook*, 545
Office of Consumer Affairs, 130
Off-price retailers, 357
Oil, 123–24
Oligopolistic competition, 289
Open-bid buying, 195
Open dating, 245, 246, 521, 522
Open-end questions, 96
Operating expense percentage, 537
Operating ratios, 537–39
Operating statement, 535–37
Opinion leaders, 389, 390
Opportunities, marketing, 54–55
    *See also* Environment, marketing; Marketing information system (MIS); Marketing research
Optional-product pricing, 307
Order processing, 342
Order routine specification, 189
Organization:
    channel, 329–34
    image, 496–98
    of international marketing, 481–82
    of marketing department, 64–68
    physical distribution and, 346–47
    structure, 60–62
Organizational buyer behavior, 175–99
    defined, 176
    government, 192–95
    industrial. *See* Industrial buyer behavior
    model of, 181
    reseller, 190–92
Organizational climate, 453

Organizational factors in industrial buyer behavior, 186
Organizational markets:
    characteristics of, 177–81
    types of, 177
Organization audit, 72
Organization marketing, 496–98
Outdoor advertising, 415, 416, 418–19
Outlets, control of, 353, 359–40, 359–60
Outside salesforces, 452
Overhead costs, 287
Ownership, joint, 474–75

## P

Packaging, 242–45
    deceptive, 512
Parallel product development, 268–69
Patent protection, 252
Patriotism, 132, 133
Patronage rewards, 423
People meters, 91, 97
Perceived product performance, 165
Perceived service, 493
Perceived-value pricing, 294, 297–98
Percentage labeling, 245
Percentage-of-sales method of program budgeting, 393
Perception, 156
    subliminal, 158–59
Performance review, supplier, 189–90
Periodicals, secondary data in, 89–90
Perishability of services, 491–92
Personal communication channels, 389
Personal factors, consumer buying behavior and, 145, 151–54
Personal influence, new product adoption and, 168
Personal interviewing, 91, 94–95
Personality:
    consumer buying behavior and, 153–54
    market segmentation and, 208–9
Personal selling:
    as promotion tool, 382–83, 395, 399
    public policy and, 456
    retailing and, 368
    wholesaling and, 374
    *See also* Sales management
Person marketing, 498–501
Persuasive advertising, 409–10
Physical distribution, 340–46
    careers in, 544
    firms, 110
Physical needs, 5
Physiological needs, 155
Piggyback, 346
Pipelines, 345, 346
Place:
    in marketing mix, 43–44

Place: *(cont.)*
    retail, 368
    wholesale, 375
    *See also* Distribution channels
Place marketing, 501–3
Planned obsolescence, 514–15
Planning:
    benefits of, 27
    isolated, 58
    kinds of, 27
    marketing, 44, 52, 53–57
    strategic. *See* Strategic planning
Pleasing products, 526, 527
Point-of-purchase (POP) promotions, 423
Political environment, 128–30
Political-legal environment, 467–69
Political power, 518–19
Political stability, 468
Pollution, 245, 522–23
    increased levels of, 124
Population, 115–20
Portfolio design, 30–34
Position, product, 42–43, 218–20, 223
Positive incentives, 453–54
Postal Service, 18, 290
Postpurchase behavior, 165–66
Preapproach step of selling process, 448
Preference for product, 385–86
Premiums, 423
Presentation step of selling process, 449–50
Prestige goods, 337
Pretesting, 425
Preticketing, 192
Price, 281–301
    buyer-based, 294, 297–98
    competition-based, 294, 298
    consumer perception of, 290, 291
    cost-based, 294, 295–97
    cuts, 315
    deceptive, 512
    defined, 282
    demand and, 288–93
    discrimination, 310
    elasticity, 293
    external factors affecting, 288–94
    general approaches to, 294–98
    of generics, 236–37
    growth stage of product and, 273, 275
    internal factors affecting, 283–88
    in international marketing, 480
    location and, 313–14
    in marketing mix, 43
    markups, 295–96
    objectives of decisions on, 283–84
    packs, 422–23
    product quality and, 311
    psychological, 311–12
    public policy and, 295